# Lecture Notes in Computer Science     10851

*Commenced Publication in 1973*
Founding and Former Series Editors:
Gerhard Goos, Juris Hartmanis, and Jan van Leeuwen

More information about this series at http://www.springer.com/series/7412

Lucio Tommaso De Paolis · Patrick Bourdot (Eds.)

# Augmented Reality, Virtual Reality, and Computer Graphics

5th International Conference, AVR 2018
Otranto, Italy, June 24–27, 2018
Proceedings, Part II

 Springer

*Editors*
Lucio Tommaso De Paolis (ID)
University of Salento
Lecce
Italy

Patrick Bourdot
University of Paris-Sud
Orsay
France

ISSN 0302-9743           ISSN 1611-3349   (electronic)
Lecture Notes in Computer Science
ISBN 978-3-319-95281-9           ISBN 978-3-319-95282-6   (eBook)
https://doi.org/10.1007/978-3-319-95282-6

Library of Congress Control Number: 2018947461

LNCS Sublibrary: SL6 – Image Processing, Computer Vision, Pattern Recognition, and Graphics

This Springer imprint is published by the registered company Springer Nature Switzerland AG
The registered company address is: Gewerbestrasse 11, 6330 Cham, Switzerland

# Preface

Virtual Reality (VR) aims to develop computer systems that give humans the ability to perceive and interact in realistic multisensory motor ways, with 3D digital data or virtual worlds that are more or less realistic depending on the applications. Computer graphics is used to create a realistic visual scene, while physical-based rendering makes, for instance, 3D audio perception and haptic interactions possible. All this is meant to provide a feeling of immersion to the users (i.e., the sensation of being in a 3D world in a perceptive way), and even a feeling of presence (i.e., the sensation of being somewhere: apart from the immersive perception, this sensation targets cognitive factors, such as affordance of virtual objects and implication/involvement of users in their virtual activity).

Augmented Reality (AR) technology allows the real-time fusion of computer-generated digital content with the real world. Adding virtual content to reality makes it possible to understand information or knowledge of the real world that is not directly accessible, and/or may provide assistance to users during the execution of their tasks. Regarding the perception of immersion and feeling of presence, designing such 3D user interfaces remains challenging, but the result may greatly improve the accuracy of users' interaction in the real world, and the efficiency or even security of their activity.

Human–Computer Interaction (HCI) technology is a research area concerned with the design, implementation, and evaluation of interactive systems that make more simple and intuitive the interaction between user and computer.

This book contains the contributions to the 5th International Conference on Augmented Reality, Virtual Reality, and Computer Graphics (SALENTO AVR 2018) that has held in Otranto (Italy) during June 24–27, 2018. We cordially invite you to visit the SALENTO AVR website (http://www.salentoavr.it) where you can find all relevant information about this event.

SALENTO AVR 2018 intended to bring together researchers, scientists, and practitioners to discuss key issues, approaches, ideas, open problems, innovative applications, and trends in virtual and augmented reality, 3D visualization, and computer graphics in the areas of medicine, cultural heritage, arts, education, entertainment, as well as industrial and military sectors.

We are very grateful to the Program Committee and local Organizing Committee members for their support and for the time spent to review and discuss the submitted papers and for doing so in a timely and professional manner. We would like to sincerely thank the keynote and tutorial speakers who willingly accepted our invitation and shared their expertise through illuminating talks, helping us to fully meet the conference objectives.

In this edition of SALENTO AVR, we were honored to have the following invited speakers:

- Marco Sacco – ITIA-CNR, Italy
- Arcadio Reyes-Lecuona – Universidad de Malaga, Spain
- Roberto Pierdicca – Università Politecnica della Marche, Italy
- Marcello Carrozzino – Scuola Superiore Sant'Anna, Italy
- Donato Maniello – Studio Glowarp, Italy

We extend our thanks to the University of Salento for the enthusiastic acceptance to sponsor the conference and to provide support in the organization of the event.

We would also like to thank the EuroVR Association, which has supported the conference since its first issue, by contributing each year to the creation of the international Program Committee, proposing invited keynote speakers, and spreading internationally the announcements of the event.

SALENTO AVR attracted high-quality paper submissions from many countries. We would like to thank the authors of all accepted papers for submitting and presenting their work at the conference and all the conference attendees for making SALENTO AVR an excellent forum on virtual and augmented reality, facilitating the exchange of ideas, fostering new collaborations, and shaping the future of this exciting research field.

For greater readability, the papers are organized in two volumes and are classified into seven main parts:

- Virtual Reality
- Augmented and Mixed Reality
- Computer Graphics
- Human–Computer Interaction
- Applications of VR/AR in Medicine
- Applications of VR/AR in Cultural Heritage
- Applications of VR/AR in Industry

We hope the readers will find in these pages interesting material and fruitful ideas for their future work.

June 2018                                                    Lucio Tommaso De Paolis
                                                                    Patrick Bourdot

# Organization

## Conference Chair

Lucio Tommaso De Paolis    University of Salento, Italy

## Conference Co-chairs

Patrick Bourdot          CNRS/LIMSI, University of Paris-Sud, France
Marco Sacco             ITIA-CNR, Italy
Paolo Proietti          MIMOS, Italy

## Honorary Chair

Giovanni Aloisio         University of Salento, Italy

## Scientific Program Committee

Andrea Abate             University of Salerno, Italy
Giuseppe Anastasi        University of Pisa, Italy
Selim Balcisoy           Sabancı University, Turkey
Vitoantonio Bevilacqua   Polytechnic of Bari, Italy
Monica Bordegoni         Politecnico di Milano, Italy
Davide Borra             NoReal.it, Turin, Italy
Andrea Bottino           Politecnico di Torino, Italy
Pierre Boulanger         University of Alberta, Canada
Andres Bustillo          University of Burgos, Spain
Massimo Cafaro           University of Salento, Italy
Sergio Casciaro          IFC-CNR, Italy
Marcello Carrozzino      Scuola Superiore Sant'Anna, Italy
Mario Ciampi             ICAR/CNR, Italy
Pietro Cipresso          IRCCS Istituto Auxologico Italiano, Italy
Arnis Cirulis            Vidzeme University of Applied Sciences, Latvia
Lucio Colizzi            CETMA, Italy
Mario Covarrubias        Politecnico di Milano, Italy
Rita Cucchiara           University of Modena, Italy
Yuri Dekhtyar            Riga Technical University, Latvia
Matteo Dellepiane        National Research Council (CNR), Italy
Giorgio De Nunzio        University of Salento, Italy
Francisco José Domínguez  University of Seville, Spain
    Mayo
Aldo Franco Dragoni      Università Politecnica delle Marche, Italy
Italo Epicoco            University of Salento, Italy

| Robert Stone | University of Birmingham, UK |
| João Manuel R. S. Tavares | Universidade do Porto, Portugal |
| Daniel Thalmann | Nanyang Technological University, Singapore |
| Nadia Magnenat-Thalmann | University of Geneva, Switzerland |
| Franco Tecchia | Scuola Superiore Sant'Anna, Italy |
| Carlos M. Travieso-González | Universidad de Las Palmas de Gran Canaria, Spain |
| Manolis Tsiknaki | Technological Educational Institute of Crete (TEI), Greece |
| Antonio Emmanuele Uva | Polytechnic of Bari, Italy |
| Volker Paelke | Bremen University of Applied Sciences, Germany |
| Aleksei Tepljakov | Tallinn University of Technology, Estonia |
| Kristina Vassiljeva | Tallinn University of Technology, Estonia |
| Krzysztof Walczak | Poznań University of Economics and Business, Poland |
| Anthony Whitehead | Carleton University, Canada |

## Local Organizing Committee

| Ilenia Paladini | University of Salento, Italy |
| Silke Miss | Virtech, Italy |
| Valerio De Luca | University of Salento, Italy |
| Cristina Barba | University of Salento, Italy |
| Giovanni D'Errico | University of Salento, Italy |

# Spatial Augmented Reality: A Way to Increase Content in Cultural Heritage Context (Tutorial)

Donato Maniello

Studio Glowarp, Italy

The technique called Spatial Augmented Reality – better known as video mapping – is constantly growing. Several fields of application have tested the potential and particularity of use. This contribution aims to discuss the well-known potential of this medium in the urban redevelopment through forms of "augmented architecture" and enhancement in the museum in the case of "augmented archaeology" and to expose some of the techniques used to map generic surfaces in relation to their complexity and size. This allows the construction of a workflow that transforms this raw data into useful contents to enhance the asset itself through multimedia installation and digital storytelling, taking care not to replace the asset itself.

In this way the user is not placed in front of the object in a detached manner, but is catapulted and projected into it, as if he were in a parallel reality. In this case video mapping becomes a medium through which the museum experience is integrated and completed, without going beyond the real world but simply making discernment easier and emphatic.

# Keynote Speakers

# Augmented and Virtual Reality Enabler for the "Factory 4.0"

Marco Sacco

ITIA-CNR, Italy

Manufacturing sector transformation (the so call Factory 4.0) requires the introduction of advanced tools for both the knowledge representation and simulation. For over 10 years, Virtual Reality and Augmented Reality have generated benefits in several sectors thanks to the potentialities offered by these visualisation technologies able to provide an added value to the contents and data enrichment.

Manufacturing companies, thanks to the reduction of cost and a widespread of devices, could now take advantage integrating AR/VR to simulation and emerging AI.

The result is a Virtual Factory, a full digital twin of the real plant, that could be used for several purposes, from design to monitoring and logistics, from reconfiguration to training. Some industrial applications will be presented.

# 3D Audio for VR Applications: Fundamentals and Practicalities

Arcadio Reyes-Lecuona

Universidad de Malaga, Spain

Immersive Virtual Reality has been experimenting a constant development and has become more and more popular in the last times. This development has been mainly focused in the visual modality. However, auditory stimuli can also be very powerful in creating immersive perceptions. In this context, three-dimensional localization of sound sources plays an important role in these systems.

3D audio techniques allow to produce the perception in the listener that a sound source is virtually located anywhere in the 3D space, including behind or above the listener. They are not new, but, with the advancements in computational power, it is now possible to perform the required processing in real time using affordable equipment. Therefore, the interest for 3D sound has been increasing.

Additionally, the environment modifies sound and this is especially relevant when simulating spatial sound. The perception of sound includes a combination of the original sound emitted by the source, modifications due to the environment and modifications produced by the listener's head. All those modifications can be characterized and applied in a simulation in order to virtually locate a source in a specific place within a given environment.

In this talk, the fundamentals of several techniques of 3D audio will be presented, with special attention to those more suitable for affordable Virtual Reality systems. More specifically, the potential of binaural audio and virtual Ambisonics will be presented. In addition to this, the role of the environment and how it can be considered will also be discussed. Finally, using 3D audio in a Virtual Reality system requires to know some basic concepts of real time audio, which will be addressed as well. Moreover, the main decisions and trade-off to be taken when implementing a 3D sound renderer will be discussed, presenting the practical implications of each of them.

# Sensing Cultural Heritage: User-Centered Approaches Towards Senseable Spaces

Roberto Pierdicca

Università Politecnica della Marche, Italy

Cultural Heritage domain (both tangible and intangible) has witnessed, in the last decade, to a tremendous improvement on the way in which the users can be in contact with cultural goods. The reasons are many, but one can summarize all of them: ICT are everywhere, pervasive like never in the past, and at the same time more and more cheaper and available in the market. Following this wave, 3D reconstructions, new advanced interfaces, wireless connections and interactions are becoming the backbone for AR/VR experiences, which can be definitively defined as the mainstream for communicating and valorizing the priceless values of cultural goods in a more efficient way. State of art solutions for the development of such experiences are mature enough to allow an effective storytelling and are designed to be exploited by heterogeneous users.

However, several limitations still prevent the adoption of a real and efficient digital agenda for the management of Cultural Heritage. One of them, and probably the most urgent, is that digital experiences are developed by experts or insiders, without taking into account the real needs of the users. There is thus the necessity of adopting strategies to understand the users' behaviours by analysing and studying their habits, preferences and knowledge. Nowadays this process is made possible by the increasing miniaturization of new technologies, which allows providing contextual information to the users and, at the same time, to infer information from the digital footprints they leave (the so-called Users' Generated Data).

The talk, besides providing a complete overview of the latest achievements in the field of DCH, will provide prospective visions about a new paradigm of spaces (both indoor and outdoor) where a bidirectional exchange of information from the space to the user and vice versa is possible. These Spaces can be defined Senseable Spaces, which can be both indoor and outdoor scenario where the service to the users are designed following their behaviours and need, in a seamless way. To show the feasibility of such approach, some research projects (developed by a multi-disciplinary group) will be broadly discussed.

# Opportunities of the Use of Embodied Agents in Virtual Reality for Cultural Heritage

Marcello Carrozzino

Scuola Superiore Sant'Anna, Italy

Virtual Reality is becoming an increasingly important tool for the research, the communication and the popularization of cultural heritage. However most of the available 3D interactive reconstructions of artefacts, monuments and sites often miss an important factor: human presence. Thanks to the advancements in the technology, in latest years Virtual Humans have started being used in a variety of cultural-related VR applications. From simple 2D characters to complex 3D avatars, technology continues to evolve and so is the adoption of virtual assistants in digital heritage. The acceptance of such tools deserves a greater attention from the scientific community.

This talk will explore the state-of-the-art on this subject, underlining the technological challenges and also analysing the effects of avatar interaction on user engagement, sense of immersion and learning effectiveness.

# Contents – Part II

**Applications of VR/AR in Cultural Heritage**

## Applications of VR/AR in Industry

**Human-Computer Interaction**

# Contents – Part I

**Computer Graphics**

# Applications of VR/AR in Medicine

# Web-Based Vascular Flow Simulation Visualization with Lossy Data Compression for Fast Transmission

Rok Oblak, Ciril Bohak$^{(\boxtimes)}$, and Matija Marolt

Faculty of Computer and Information Science, University of Ljubljana,
Večna pot 113, 1000 Ljubljana, Slovenia
2448.rok@gmail.com, {ciril.bohak,matija.marolt}@fri.uni-lj.si

**Abstract.** In this paper, we present a web-based system for visualization of flow simulation results in the vascular system for use with consumer-level hardware. The presented tool allows users to design, execute and visualize a flow simulation with a simple workflow on a desktop computer or a mobile device. The web interface allows users to select a vascular model, define the flow simulation parameters, execute the simulation, and interactively visualize the simulation results in real time using multiple visualization techniques. The server-side prepares the model for simulation and performs the simulation using SimVascular. To provide a more efficient transfer of the large amounts of simulation results to the web client, as well as reduce storage requirements on the server, we introduce a novel hybrid lossy compression method. The method uses an octree data subdivision approach combined with an iterative approach that regresses the data points to a B-Spline volume. The evaluation results show that our method achieves compression ratios of up to 5.7 for the tested examples at a given error rate, comparable to other approaches while specifically intended for visualization purposes.

**Keywords:** Visualization Toolkit · Blood flow simulation
Data visualization

## 1 Introduction

Cardiovascular diseases are the primary cause of deaths in modern developed world and consist of conditions with any kind of cardiovascular system malfunction caused by the heart or the vascular system itself [1]. Many of these can be predicted, explained or identified in an early stage by examining the blood flow dynamics causing various loads and stresses to the cardiovascular system [2].

There were many attempts to describe the cardiovascular system using mathematical models, but in recent years the most efficient ones directly simulate the blood flow in the veins and arteries. They include the generation of patient-specific cardiovascular structures models [3], construction of hypothetical vascular structures to test their flow dynamics, and the combination of both to

© Springer International Publishing AG, part of Springer Nature 2018
L. T. De Paolis and P. Bourdot (Eds.): AVR 2018, LNCS 10851, pp. 3–17, 2018.
https://doi.org/10.1007/978-3-319-95282-6_1

examine the implications of surgeries changing the patient's vasculature. Such example applications are a stent placement or a bypass surgery, procedures that change the blood vessel geometry and pose significant risks because of various unknowns in hemodynamics. The simulation results can be analyzed to provide insights that could not otherwise be obtained. These simulations are non-invasive and do not require the presence of a patient. They can be performed many times with many different parameters and thus provide more detailed data about flow dynamics. Their applications have been expanded in recent years as modern advances in imaging technologies enabled scans of live patients to be used for patient-specific model generation and medical result analysis.

The goal of the presented work was to develop a web application focused on accessibility, ease of use and fast workflow iterations where the user can quickly and effortlessly advance from a basic input model to the final visualization of simulation results. Nevertheless, the practical use-cases of the application cover the most frequent cases and offer the same quality of results as other proprietary systems without the need of installing any additional user-side tools. The application integrates the most common simulation result visualization options, relieving the user from need of exporting the results and importing them into a third-party tool, thus shortening the workflow. The simulation result files are compressed in an efficient manner with visualization purposes in mind, enabling large simulation results to be saved on the server without taking up too much of disk space and speeding up the data transmission to the user. The advantages of using the presented client-server approach to simulation are: (1) accessibility of simulation and visualization on low-end devices (such as ultra books, tablets and/or mobile phones), (2) the accessibility of the system from any location with fast enough Internet connection and (3) a possibility of queuing multiple simulation calculations on the server and their overview after they are finished at later time.

## 2   Related Work

The complete process from taking patient observations to analyzing the simulated blood flow results typically involves four major stages: (1) data acquisition where patient-specific data is gathered, (2) model generation where meshes are created from the gathered data and prepared for simulation, (3) the simulation itself and lastly, (4) results gathering and post-processing [2]. Our application workflow follows the same steps, excluding the step (1) of data acquisition.

Stanford Virtual Vascular Laboratory (SVVL) was one of the first attempts to model blood flow in blood vessels by developing a software framework integrating model construction, mesh generation, flow simulation and visualization [4]. It introduced a knowledge-based engineering approach to build a more complex vascular model from a hierarchy of simpler primitives defined parametrically. The results were collected at pre-defined nodal points and visualized in different ways, including flow vector fields and streamlines. [5] was one of the first attempts to reduce the time needed for patient-specific model generation by performing automatic level-set segmentation of 2D slices to create a model and a simulation-suitable mesh. In recent years, various more sophisticated approaches have been developed for user-guided modeling and meshing from medical image data, such as the Vascular Modeling Toolkit [6], Vascular Editor [7], sweep surfaces based approach presented [8] or SimVascular [9], frameworks which provide powerful functionality for vascular modeling and mesh generation. SimVascular was used for meshing the vascular models in our application.

The simulation itself is a task of solving Navier-Stokes equations describing the flow. The solution to these equations is a flow velocity field, which serves as a basis for calculating other physical quantities such as pressures or temperatures. Software CFD solvers have initially simulated blood flow in two dimensions and later in three as technological progress enabled more detailed and faster simulations. Today, flow simulations of the entire vasculature can be performed, as demonstrated by [10]. Many CFD solvers are also available as open source packages, such as: Palabos [11], HemeLB [12] and MUPHY [13]. Among them is also the solver in SimVascular, which was used to perform the simulation in our case. Also relevant is a recent survey on cardiac 4D PC-MRI data processing is presented in [14].

Visual representation of flow simulation results is an important aspect of post-simulation analysis. Scalar values such as pressures or velocity magnitudes are usually displayed by sprite points or 3D spheres colored and scaled proportionally to their values. Volumetric rendering is common for displaying medical images from Magnetic Resonance Imaging [15] or Computed Tomography scans. Velocity field can also be visualized with streamlines and derived methods [16] which display flow movement through space (streamlines) or time (streampaths).

Commercial visualization software is usually limited to use of unconventional file formats and often requires additional preprocessing for visualization purposes. Visualization Toolkit (VTK) [17] is a very general visualization toolkit supported by many popular simulation (e.g. Palabos [11]) and visualization software packages (e.g. ParaView and ParaViewWeb [18]). The VTK file format is also used internally in our application but we also use our own file format for storing and transferring the results due to our use of a custom compression method.

Flow simulations produce results in form of scalar or vector values for different quantities (e.g. velocity, pressure, wall shear stress etc.). The results can consist of millions of values depending of the number of measured quantities and number of time steps in the simulation yielding gigabytes of data for a single simulation run. To optimize the storage and shorten the transfer times it is meaningful to use data compression.

A general approach to floating point data compression is presented in works [19,20]. To address medical domain, researchers have proposed lossless compression methods, such as lossless stationary wavelet transform on 2D slices of 4D medical images (volumetric data through time) [21]. Wavelets have also been used for flow simulation data, such as [22] where a discrete wavelet transform was used on an octree subdivision of airflow simulation data. Other types of regressions have also been described, such as using polynomials [23] on rectangular blocks of 2D medical images and encoding the polynomial coefficients with Huffman coding, and also encoding the residual error with run-length encoding to achieve lossless compression. Another approach for rapid high-quality compression of volumetric data is presented in [24].

While the above methods are suitable for storing the original simulation data for further analysis, we can exploit the fact that the data will be used for visualization purposes only. In this case, the required precision is substantially lower than the IEEE 754 double-precision binary floating-point format [25].

For purposes of real-time rendering of time-varying volumetric data researchers have extended and adapted an MPEG compression method for isosurface and volumetric data [26]. Another approach [27] aims for high-accuracy compression by linearizing the data points, sorting them and fitting them to a precise one-dimensional B-Spline. In [28], authors present a lossy compression method for structured and unstructured grid simulation data modeled as a graph decomposition problem, where sets of vertices are replaced with a constant value bounded by a user defined error. Because the above presented approaches are targeted to specific domains, mostly for non-porous media and higher compression accuracy, they could not be directly applied to our case.

Our approach combines the meshing, simulation and visualization steps in a single application able to process crude 3D models without the need of additional manual annotations. No additional software is thus needed in the workflow and since the application is web-based, no installation is required. Ease of use is also of note, as the intuitive user interface doesn't need additional documentation and can be used by anybody not previously acquainted with CFD software.

In the following section we present the developed application and the novel compression methods used for compressing the simulation results data. In Sect. 4 we present the qualitative application evaluation and quantitative evaluation of compression method. In Sect. 5 we present the conclusions and give the guidelines for possible future work.

## 3   Methods

In this section we present the application workflow, how the system functionality is split between front-end and back-end part, and a novel lossy compression method for flow simulation data compression used in our system for optimizing the storage space and for faster transmission of simulation data from back-end to front-end part of the system for visualization purposes displayed in the diagram in Fig. 1.

### 3.1   Application Workflow

The application consists of two parts. The back-end is a Node.js server application and performs the meshing operations and executes the flow simulation. The front-end is a web application developed using the Angular.js JavaScript

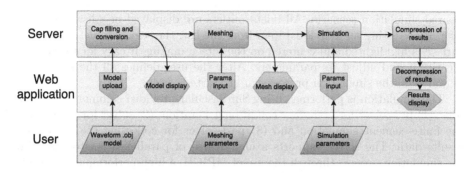

**Fig. 1.** The pipeline of the proposed system which also presents the user work-flow.

framework intended for flow simulation results visualization using Three.js, a WebGL graphics library, used for interactive display of the simulation models and simulation results.

**Preprocessing.** The first step in the workflow is to upload a 3D model of a vascular system in Wavefront .obj file format. The uploaded model must have holes for inlets/outlets (inflow and outflow caps) and is converted into VTK polydata format for further processing. All the faces of the model are annotated as either blood vessel walls or input/output cap surfaces. This preprocessing is done with a custom back-end Python script, which centers the mesh geometry, identifies the cap holes, constructs the appropriate cap surfaces and annotates the individual faces. The script also estimates each cap radius from its surface area to provide the user with a suggested initial edge length value in the following tetrahedral meshing step. The resulting model, along with cap surface annotations, is displayed in the front-end application for user inspection.

**Meshing.** After the user confirms the preprocessing step results the second step is executed on the back-end – a tetrahedral mesh generation. The generated mesh is suitable for use with numerical simulation methods such as the subsequent flow simulation. The user has to provide the desired tetrahedron edge length value for defining the simulation resolution. While the user is already given a suggested edge length from the previous step, he can define a different value in the dialog window before starting the meshing process. In our system, TetGen is used for mesh generation, exposed through the SimVascular TCL (Tool Command Language) shell.

**Simulation.** The most processing-intensive back-end step of the system workflow is the simulation step. To start a simulation, the user has to define set of simulation parameters containing the inlet/outlet configuration, inlet flow rates, and outlet flow resistances. The user is already provided with the default parameter values for an individual inlet/outlet but should adjust them according to the desired simulation scenario. All inlets/outlets are displayed in a list (see Fig. 2 left). By selecting an individual item from the list, the selected inlet/outlet cap surface is highlighted and centered on the screen making it easy for the user to identify it and adjust its parameters. After the user defines all the simulation parameters, the simulation process can be started.

The simulation is performed using SimVascular-provided command-line utilities: (1) pre-solver for boundary condition generation, (2) solver for performing the finite-element simulation and (3) post-solver for collecting the simulation results data. The solver supports a high-degree of parallelization to speed up the simulation process through the use of MPICH, a high-performance portable implementation of the Message Passing Interface standard.

**Compression.** In the following step, the obtained simulation results in VTK format are parsed and compressed by the compression module using the compression method presented in Sect. 3.2, before they are stored to the disk or sent to the front-end for visualization. They contain time step data for flow velocities, flow pressures, in-plane tractions, wall shear stresses and time-derivatives of flow velocities.

**Visualization.** In the final workflow step, the flow simulation data is transmitted to the front-end application where it is visualized. The visualization is implemented using the Three.js library and allows the user to move and rotate the view as well as change the zoom. The visualization parameters can be set in the side panel of the web application. The user can also move between the individual time steps of simulation using time slider at the bottom and see what values are represented by individual colors in the legend on the right.

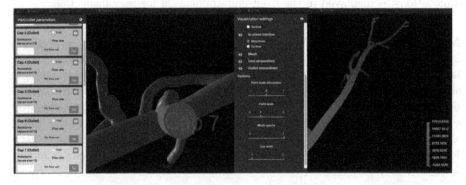

**Fig. 2.** Left: the application interface when previewing cap faces and setting inlet/outlet parameters. Right: the interface when visualizing the simulation results.

The visualization component supports different visualization types:

**Mesh display** with adjustable mesh opacity, enabling quantities inside the mesh to be visible while the overall structure of the vascular system is displayed.

**Scalar point display** shows individual simulation values as 2D sprites colored and scaled relative to their values, with adjustable scale and attenuation factors (Fig. 3a).

**Vector display** shows individual lines, scaled and colored relative to the vector data (Fig. 3b).

**Surface display** shows a mesh texture of the vascular system generated by interpolating between vertex values, intended for quantities along the vessel surfaces such as wall shear stresses (Fig. 3c).

**Streamlines** generated by sampling starting points at mesh inlets or outlets and following the flow in a forward or backward direction (Fig. 3d).

(a) Flow velocity displayed as scalar points.

(b) Flow velocity displayed as a vector field.

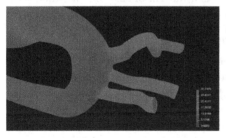

(c) Wall shear stresses displayed on the mesh's surface.

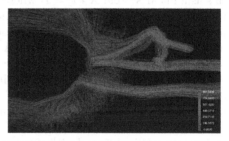

(d) Streamlines and resulting vortices of four inlets and two outlets.

**Fig. 3.** The four implemented visualization methods.

## 3.2 Compression of Flow Simulation Data

Simulations on meshes with hundreds of thousands to millions of data points can produce large result files measuring several gigabytes in size if no compression is used and the data is stored at its original (usually 64-bit) precision. This presents challenges when transferring these files over the network or storing them on a medium.

Our problem domain is specific enough to justify the development of a new compression method. Specifically, (1) the points are not distributed evenly and only take values on sparse positions of blood vessels, requiring the use of a space-decomposition method, (2) the targeted accuracy is lower than is usual for others since the data is intended for visualization purposes only - for example, [27] targets a higher compression accuracy but requires an index to be stored for each value, requiring an additional amount of bits per each point.

In our approach we use an octree to subdivide the data points into blocks ($N$), where each block is treated independently, to take advantage of local data coherence. The subdivision level depends on the point density so that the majority of blocks contain a predefined number of points $n$ (in our experiments, $n = 1000$ turned out to be the most suitable for most meshes).

The process of compressing each block consists of a iterative approach that attempts to fit the data points to a B-Spline volume $S$:

$$S(u, v, w) = \sum_{g=0}^{n} \sum_{h=0}^{n} \sum_{i=0}^{n} N_{g,k}(u) \, N_{h,k}(v) \, N_{i,k}(w) \, p_{g,h,i},$$

where $u$, $v$ and $w$ are our point coordinates and $p_{g,h,i}$ are B-Spline control points in a cubic formation. We can rearrange the basis function outer products in a single three-dimensional matrix:

$$x = [N_{0,k}(u), \ldots N_{n,k}(u)] \otimes [N_{0,k}(v), \ldots N_{n,k}(v)] \otimes [N_{0,k}(w), \ldots N_{n,k}(w)],$$

where $\otimes$ is the outer product of two vectors. Having M values we can express this as a linear system $X * P = B$ where $X$ is a matrix of size $M \times n^3$ filled with rows of matrices $x$ flattened into vectors of size $1 \times n^3$, $P$ is a vector of control points of size $1 \times n^3$ and $B$ is a vector of quantity values of size $1 \times M$. We can find a best fit solution $P = (X^T X)^{-1} X^T B$ using linear least squares approach to minimize the sum of squared differences.

The method attempts to perform iterative B-Spline fitting to encode the data by going through a list of "presets" defining the number of B-Spline control points $N_c$ in one dimension, starting with 2 (total 8 points) and going through to 9 (total 729 points). After every iteration, the average error level is measured and the process is repeated with the next control point preset until the measured error level is sufficiently low; this way a suitable B-Spline solution is found. The control points are converted to IEEE 754 half-precision format (16 bits) [25] in order to save additional space. The process for a single octree block is described in Algorithm 1.

The iteration stops when the number of bits required to encode the control points ($16N_c^3$) is larger than the number of bits required to do local quantization ($bn$ where $b$ is the number of bits per point and $n$ is the number of points in the block), or if the error level was not sufficiently low. If the local value range $|V_{max} - V_{min}|$ is smaller than the desired error level, the values are encoded as a constant, implicitly set to be the midpoint between the minimum and the maximum values ($\frac{V_{min}+V_{max}}{2}$).

**Algorithm 1.** Iteration process for an octree block

```
1:  errThr ← getErrorThreshold(blockVals)
2:  bitsPerPoint ← getBitsPerPoint(blockVals)
3:  solution ← null
4:  for numCtrlPts ∈ {2, ..., 9} do
5:      if 16 · numCtrlPts³ ≥ bitsPerPoint · len(blockVals) then
6:          break
7:      end if
8:      avgErr, encData ← encode(blockVals, numCtrlPts)
9:      if avgErr ≤ errThr then
10:         solution ← encdData
11:         break
12:     end if
13: end for
14: if solution ≡ null then
15:     solution ← quantize(blockVals)
16: end if
```

**Table 1.** The binary file format of a single octree block, depending on the type of encoding used for this block (B-Spline regression, quantization or constant encoding).

| Bit block num | 1 | 2 | 3 | 4 | 5 | 6 | ... |
|---|---|---|---|---|---|---|---|
| B-Spline | type (2) | $V_{min}$ (32) | $V_{max}$ (32) | $N_c$ (5) | $c_1$ (16) | $c_2$ (16) | ... |
| Quantization | type (2) | $V_{min}$ (32) | $V_{max}$ (32) | $b$ (4) | $v_1$ ($b$) | $v_2$ ($b$) | ... |
| Const. enc | type (2) | $V_{min}$ (32) | $V_{max}$ (32) | – | – | – | – |

Each region is encoded in a binary format with the following information: compression type used for this region, minimum local value $V_{min}$, maximum local value $V_{max}$, followed by data depending on the type of compression used, as displayed in Table 1. The constant encoding does not need any further data, while the other two types need the number of control points along one dimension $N_c$ and the control points $c_i$ for B-Spline compression, or the number of bits per point $b$ and quantized values $v_i$ for quantization.

Decompression is performed on the front-end to decode the data. Since point positions are sent separately, the octree can be reconstructed implicitly.

## 4    Results

The application was deployed on a Ubuntu server with an 8-core, 16-thread Intel Xeon CPU enabling fast simulations (the tested scenarios all completed within a few minutes). To evaluate our application, we tested the simulations on seven blood-vessel models, most of which were modeled after real volumetric scans in SimVascular or other modeling and segmentation tools. We needed to validate the proper input parameter parsing - the inlet-outlet mappings, flow rates and resistances - as well as how the visualized results (after a lossy compression) compared with an external tool, ParaView (Fig. 4). The main differences between left (our system) and right (ParaView) image in Fig. 4 is the used color map and the orientation of the vascular model. One can clearly see that the emerging parts of the vessel tree are same in both cases.

Another thing we tested was rendering performance since real-time 3D interaction is crucial for informative visualizations. While the web interface was intended for larger displays, the visualizations were rendered with smooth framerates even on mobile phones, including the largest of scenarios tested in Table 2, which is an important advantage of our web-based approach with server-side computational offloading. Table 2 contains the properties of simulation models used during system testing. While the smallest model has approx. 43 thousand mesh points and 685 thousand total simulation data points in the 16-step simulation scenario the most complex model consists of more than 200 thousand mesh points and over 3.4 million total simulation data points in 16-step simulation scenario.

**Table 2.** Model set used along with the number of caps, mesh points and total data points for 6 and 16 simulation steps.

|  | DoubleCylinder | ForkFlat | AortaSmall | ForkSmall | Coronary | AortaBig | ForkBig |
|---|---|---|---|---|---|---|---|
| Caps | 3 | 3 | 6 | 3 | 11 | 18 | 20 |
| Mesh pts. | 42864 | 50674 | 185447 | 107652 | 212519 | 132049 | 181411 |
| 6 st. pts. | 257184 | 304044 | 1112682 | 645912 | 1275114 | 792294 | 1088466 |
| 16 st. pts. | 685824 | 810784 | 2967152 | 1722432 | 3400304 | 2112784 | 2902576 |

The streamlines present the largest rendering bottleneck because of the high number of individual line segments they consist of. A mobile phone (Samsung Galaxy S6) could render a combined display of 26,695 scalar points and 752,949 streamline line segments with an average framerate of 18 frames per second. A larger model with 181,411 points rendered at 27 frames per second in case of scalar points and 34 frames per second in case of velocity vectors. A larger number of streamline segments becomes unpractical for the mobile phone, but can still be rendered on a laptop computer. A scenario with 4,356,391 streamline segments renders at 48 frames per second, on average on a 2015 MacBook Pro.

The first part of our evaluation was ensuring the input parameters affect the simulation as intended. For this task, we tested several models using different inlet-outlet mappings and different flow rates and outlet resistances, and visually evaluated the simulation results. An example of two quantities being displayed in a model of aorta can be seen on Fig. 5.

### 4.1   Compression Results

The developed compression method was compared with (1) the baseline method where 6 or 8 bits of precision is used to quantize the values (yielding an average

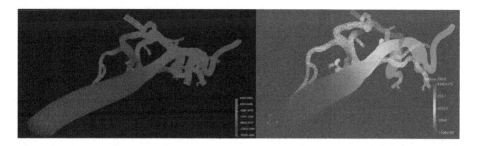

**Fig. 4.** Comparison of pressure visualizations in our application (left) and ParaView (right).

target error rate of 0.09% and 0.39%, respectively), (2) a method where the values are quantized in a time dimension over consecutive time steps, and (3) the hybrid method without using B-Spline regression (instead quantizing all blocks). We evaluated the performance on the set of models presented in Table 2 for two main quantities – pressures and velocities – over four scenarios, dividing them in terms of precision (6-bit or 8-bit error target or 0.09%/0.39% maximum average error rate, respectively) and simulation parameters. The simulation was performed over 16 consecutive time steps with varying sinusoid-shaped pulse flow.

The charts displayed in Fig. 6 present the comparison of the four compression methods in terms of the average number of bits needed to encode a single data point (each 1D component in case of 3D velocity vectors).

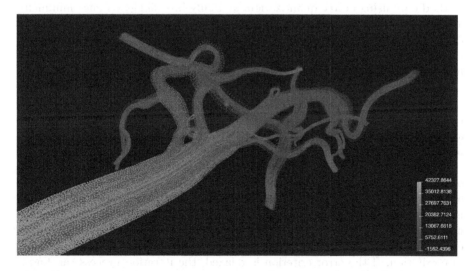

**Fig. 5.** Simulation results in a model of aorta, with pressures displayed as scalar points alongside streamlines.

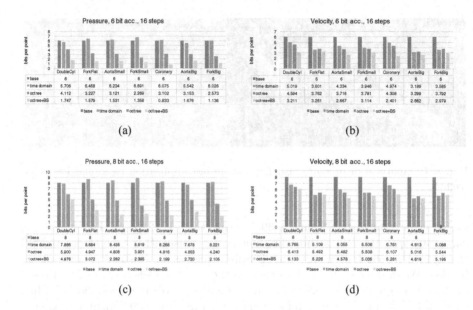

**Fig. 6.** Comparison ratios of compression methods at 6 bit accuracy target (max. avg. error of 0.39%) (a) and (b) and comparison ratios at 8 bit accuracy target (max. avg. error of 0.09%) (c) and (d).

The results show that our hybrid method using a mix of B-Spline regression and quantization in octree subdivisions is always more effective than the method only using octree quantization, and only in a single instance minimally less efficient than time-domain quantization. The amount of improvement over the method using just octree quantization is larger in case of pressure values than it is in case of velocity vectors, ranging from 40% to 55% and 6% to 25% fewer bits per point on average for pressures and velocity vectors, respectively, translating to compression ratios of up to 5.7 over the baseline in case of pressures encoded with 6-bit accuracy target, on average. The method is very sensitive to the initial error rate target, being much more efficient on larger maximum average error rates (e.g. 6 bit target or maximum average error of 0.39%), especially in case of velocity vectors.

Velocity vectors encoded under a stricter accuracy constraint (8 bit target or maximum average error of 0.09%) are the least efficient scenario, providing 6% to 9% fewer bits per point compared to just using octree quantization. This is due to larger numbers of "outliers" skewing the smoothness of the values and making it harder for a regressed B-Spline volume to fit the data, making the error rate unsuitable and thus requiring more control points to meet the error rate criterion. If the error criterion is relaxed, the iteration process can find a suitable B-Spline model in a significantly larger portion of regions and thus the method's effectiveness is larger. This is also the reason why this method is more efficient when encoding pressure values, as these values usually have a much lower number of outliers and values' transitions are much "softer".

The average number of bits per point for compressed data is thus sufficiently low to enable network transfers and convenient disk storage. For example, in case of pressures in a *Coronary* model simulation with 6 time steps, the original data size of 10.2 MB with 64-bit accuracy was compressed to 0.083 MB with 6-bit accuracy, a compression ratio of 122.9. In case of velocities and 16 time steps, the original data size of 81.6 MB at 64-bit accuracy MB was compressed to 3.06 MB with 6-bit accuracy, a compression ratio of 26.6.

## 5   Conclusions

Simulation of cardiovascular systems and informative display of results is an interesting field with great past record and even greater future promises in providing alternative means for cardiovascular disease study and surgery planning. In this work we developed an application for accepting cardiovascular models, simulating the blood flow inside them and visualizing the results in different ways. We exposed the functionality through a web application with a simple and intuitive GUI to enable fast workflow iterations and the ability to load previously saved results and models. We connected the web application to a back-end application performing the computationally intensive parts of the process. We implemented different ways of visualizing the results through an interactive 3D canvas. We also implemented a method for result data compression to minimize the amount of storage needed and maximize network file transfer speeds.

Our evaluations showed successful simulations and visualizations in line with provided parameters and expectations. The model conversion, meshing and simulation processes performed as expected and the simulation results mirrored the desired changes to the input parameters. The visualizations displayed interesting features formed by blood flow and were each able to provide an informative and complete display of data. Their performance was good enough to enable smooth real-time interaction even on mobile devices. The developed compression method was able to achieve good results, producing relatively small file sizes and retaining the accuracy needed for the visualization without the accuracy loss being noticeable to the user, even though the improvement of the hybrid method compared to the others was not always as big in the best performing cases.

This work could serve as a base for several further improvements. The user interface could accept more parameters for more advanced usage and more advanced users wanting more fine-tuning in their simulations. More visualization options could be developed, such as volumetric rendering which requires the development of an efficient method to enable real-time rendering, and other 3D structures derived from streamlines, such as streamribbons.

The hybrid compression method could also see improvements in tweaking the B-Spline parameters and regression to enable a larger ratio of optimal B-Spline regressions in octree blocks since its performance is limited by the number of blocks suitable for efficient B-Spline regression. Different volume subdivision methods could also be attempted to achieve better data distribution in individual subdivisions and limit the number of subdivisions unfit for B-Spline regression. Finally, the compression algorithm could be rewritten in a more efficient language and executed on a GPU to improve its execution speed.

# References

1. Mendis, S., Puska, P., Norrving, B., et al.: Global Atlas on Cardiovascular Disease Prevention and Control. World Health Organization (2011)
2. Doost, S.N., Ghista, D., Su, B., Zhong, L., Morsi, Y.S.: Heart blood flow simulation: a perspective review. Biomed. Eng. Online **15**(1), 101 (2016)
3. Arts, T., et al.: Patient-specific modeling of cardiovascular dynamics with a major role for adaptation. In: Kerckhoffs, R. (ed.) Patient-Specific Modeling of the Cardiovascular System, pp. 21–41. Springer, New York (2010). https://doi.org/10.1007/978-1-4419-6691-9_2
4. Taylor, C.A., Hughes, T.J., Zarins, C.K.: Finite element modeling of blood flow in arteries. Comput. Methods Appl. Mech. Eng. **158**(1–2), 155–196 (1998)
5. Wilson, N., Wang, K., Dutton, R.W., Taylor, C.: A software framework for creating patient specific geometric models from medical imaging data for simulation based medical planning of vascular surgery. In: Niessen, W.J., Viergever, M.A. (eds.) MICCAI 2001. LNCS, vol. 2208, pp. 449–456. Springer, Heidelberg (2001). https://doi.org/10.1007/3-540-45468-3_54
6. Antiga, L., Piccinelli, M., Botti, L., Ene-Iordache, B., Remuzzi, A., Steinman, D.A.: An image-based modeling framework for patient-specific computational hemodynamics. Med. Biol. Eng. Comput. **46**(11), 1097 (2008)
7. Marchenko, Y., Volkau, I., Nowinski, W.L.: Vascular editor: from angiographic images to 3D vascular models. J. Digit. Imaging **23**(4), 386–398 (2010)
8. Kretschmer, J., Godenschwager, C., Preim, B., Stamminger, M.: Interactive patient-specific vascular modeling with sweep surfaces. IEEE Trans. Vis. Comput. Graph. **19**(12), 2828–2837 (2013)
9. Updegrove, A., Wilson, N.M., Merkow, J., Lan, H., Marsden, A.L., Shadden, S.C.: Simvascular: an open source pipeline for cardiovascular simulation. Ann. Biomed. Eng. **45**(3), 525–541 (2017)
10. Zhou, M., Sahni, O., Kim, H.J., Figueroa, C.A., Taylor, C.A., Shephard, M.S., Jansen, K.E.: Cardiovascular flow simulation at extreme scale. Comput. Mech. **46**(1), 71–82 (2010)
11. Meier, S., Hennemuth, A., Tchipev, N., Harloff, A., Markl, M., Preusser, T.: Towards patient-individual blood flow simulations based on PC-MRI measurements. Inform. J. **41**, 4–7 (2011)
12. Mazzeo, M., Coveney, P.: HemeLB: a high performance parallel lattice-Boltzmann code for large scale fluid flow in complex geometries. Comput. Phys. Commun. **178**(12), 894–914 (2008)
13. Bernaschi, M., Melchionna, S., Succi, S., Fyta, M., Kaxiras, E., Sircar, J.: MUPHY: a parallel multi physics/scale code for high performance bio-fluidic simulations. Comput. Phys. Commun. **180**(9), 1495–1502 (2009)
14. Köhler, B., Born, S., van Pelt, R.F.P., Hennemuth, A., Preim, U., Preim, B.: A survey of cardiac 4D PC-MRI data processing. Comput. Graph. Forum **36**(6), 5–35 (2017)

15. Anastasi, G., Bramanti, P., Di Bella, P., Favaloro, A., Trimarchi, F., Magaudda, L., Gaeta, M., Scribano, E., Bruschetta, D., Milardi, D.: Volume rendering based on magnetic resonance imaging: advances in understanding the three-dimensional anatomy of the human knee. J. Anat. **211**(3), 399–406 (2007)
16. Ueng, S.K., Sikorski, K., Ma, K.L.: Fast algorithms for visualizing fluid motion in steady flow on unstructured grids. In: Proceedings of the IEEE Conference on Visualization, pp. 313–320 (1995)
17. Schroeder, W., Martin, K., Lorensen, B.: The Visualization Toolkit, 4th edn. Kitware, New York (2006)
18. Jourdain, S., Ayachit, U., Geveci, B.: ParaViewWeb: a web framework for 3D visualization and data processing. Int. J. Comput. Inf. Syst. Ind. Manag. Appl. **3**, 870–877 (2011)
19. Lindstrom, P., Isenburg, M.: Fast and efficient compression of floating-point data. IEEE Trans. Vis. Comput. Graph. **12**(5), 1245–1250 (2006)
20. Lindstrom, P.: Fixed-rate compressed floating-point arrays. IEEE Trans. Vis. Comput. Graph. **20**(12), 2674–2683 (2014)
21. Belhadef, L., Maaza, Z.M.: Lossless 4D medical images compression with motion compensation and lifting wavelet transform. Int. J. Signal Process. Syst. **4**(2), 168–171 (2016)
22. Sakai, R., Sasaki, D., Obayashi, S., Nakahashi, K.: Wavelet-based data compression for flow simulation on block-structured Cartesian mesh. Int. J. Numer. Methods Fluids **73**(5), 462–476 (2013)
23. Al-Khafaji, G., George, L.E.: Fast lossless compression of medical images based on polynomial. Int. J. Comput. Appl. **70**(15), 28–32 (2013)
24. Nguyen, K.G., Saupe, D.: Rapid high quality compression of volume data for visualization. Comput. Graph. Forum **20**(3), 49–57 (2001)
25. 754-2008: IEEE standard for floating-point arithmetic. Standard. IEEE, August 2008
26. Sohn, B.S., Bajaj, C., Siddavanahalli, V.: Feature based volumetric video compression for interactive playback. In: Proceedings of the 2002 IEEE Symposium on Volume Visualization and Graphics, VVS 2002, Piscataway, pp. 89–96. IEEE Press (2002)
27. Lehmann, H., Werzner, E., Mendes, M.A.A., Trimis, D., Jung, B., Ray, S.: In situ data compression algorithm for detailed numerical simulation of liquid metal filtration through regularly structured porous media. Adv. Eng. Mater. **15**(12), 1260–1269 (2013)
28. Iverson, J., Kamath, C., Karypis, G.: Fast and effective lossy compression algorithms for scientific datasets. In: Kaklamanis, C., Papatheodorou, T., Spirakis, P.G. (eds.) Euro-Par 2012. LNCS, vol. 7484, pp. 843–856. Springer, Heidelberg (2012). https://doi.org/10.1007/978-3-642-32820-6_83

# Interactive System Using Myoelectric Muscle Sensors for the Strengthening Upper Limbs in Children

Victoria M. López[(✉)], Pablo A. Zambrano[(✉)], Marco Pilatasig[(✉)],
and Franklin M. Silva[(✉)]

Universidad de las Fuerzas Armadas ESPE, Sangolquí, Ecuador
{vmlopez2,pazambrano,mapilatagsig,
fmsilva}@espe.edu.ec

**Abstract.** This work presents a system for strengthening upper limbs in children through an interactive videogame system and the use of myoelectric muscle sensors. The system allows the acquisition of myoelectric signals taken by electrodes placed in the muscles of interest so they are sent to the computer to be visualized in the virtual interface. Several virtual interfaces were developed in the Unity 3D graphical engine in which the degree of difficulty of the videogame can be selected as well as the muscle affectation and the duration of the repetitions of each exercise. User personal data is stored in a data sheet. The data transmission is carried out using Bluetooth wireless technology in charge of establishing a reliable and real-time communication. Tests were performed on 5 users (3 boys and 2 girls) with ages between 6 to 12 years, and the SUS usability test was applied with results (84.5 ± 0.62), which allows to determine that the system has a good acceptance to be used in muscle strengthening.

**Keywords:** Muscle strengthening · Interactive system
Myoelectric muscle sensor · Unity 3D

## 1 Introduction

Disability in children leads to problems in health, education, social relation and economy as indicated by the World Health Organization (WHO) [1]. In childhood, muscle strengthening and the development of motor skills are decisive to carry out activities in their daily lives. Through this process the child can learn about their environment so, as a consequence, every motor skill plays a fundamental role in the intelligence development [2]. With the growth, every child is reaching achievements in their development, reflected in skills which are done according to their age [3]. The increase in muscular strength and motor skills depend on the physical and psychological properties of the child. Additionally, factors such as tasks difficulty, the possibilities and opportunities of the environment are involved [4].

Studies on physical rehabilitation include people with muscle diseases (myopathy), balance problems, cerebrovascular accidents (CVA), cerebral palsy (CP), spasticity and others [5–7]. In this type of research, several devices have been included that improve the user interaction with a virtual system. One of the main areas of incursion of these kind of devices is medicine as an assistance system of rehabilitation and strengthening oriented to different parts of the body, in which movement is its fundamental basis of development [8, 9]. Validity has been demonstrated using haptic devices and feedback of forces together with virtual environments to improve motor skills [10, 11].

Innovation in rehabilitation and strengthening systems includes methods composed of sensory devices and virtual systems to support virtual rehabilitation processes. These types of elements are integrated into different systems for manipulating them by analyzing the electrical impulses generated during muscle activities [12, 13]. They also participate in studies for the development of effective tools for the treatment of upper and lower extremities. [14–16] In addition, these devices have participated along with virtual systems in the control and effective simulation of prostheses [17].

The inclusion of sensors that measure muscle electrical activity allows the generation of different prototypes and applications associated with the strengthening of upper limbs to analyze problems of mobility, coordination, rigidity and muscle weakness [18]. The fusion with virtual environments forms therapy exercises in friendly, entertaining and immersive environments, turning a repetitive therapy into an interactive training program thus promoting sustained attention and increasing motivation [19].

Interactive systems that use virtual interfaces represents a great support in the treatment of users with motor problems. Virtual environments provide a motivational system for the user to continue treatment consecutively so, it becomes a distraction for the discomfort caused by disabilities [20–22]. Therefore, these virtual environments provide rehabilitation systems of high relevance and degree of satisfaction that under medical experience demonstrate that the evaluation of the strength and mobility of the isolated muscles of the upper limbs can be useful and collaterally the child can recover from an injury, and thus achieve greater autonomy [10].

Due to different factors, users who suffer from problems in their upper limbs have less ability to explore different environments, social interact and a lower life quality. It means that these disorders cause them to be considered less able than other social groups, preventing them from demonstrating their abilities [23]. Thus to help them, users need to follow a treatment, but in most cases it requires the presence of a professional expert in physical therapy, which means a high-cost and long-term investment [24]. A lot of virtual systems have an increased cost because they use virtual reality headsets along with unnecessary wiring for the integration of other devices and computers [26]. Therefore, this work proposes the development of a low cost interactive system using application boards and economic sensors where the communication is performed wirelessly by using the Bluetooth protocol for the strengthening of upper extremities in children through the use of interactive and controlled videogames through the electrical impulses of the muscles coming from 4 myoelectric muscle sensors placed in the arm and forearm.

This work is divided in 5 sections where the introduction is included. Section 2 presents the system methodology, the way of use of the system is presented in Sect. 3. Section 4 presents evaluations and results, and finally, conclusions and future works are detailed in Sect. 5.

## 2  System Methodology

This section explains the proposal system stages. Figure 1 shows the block diagram of the whole system.

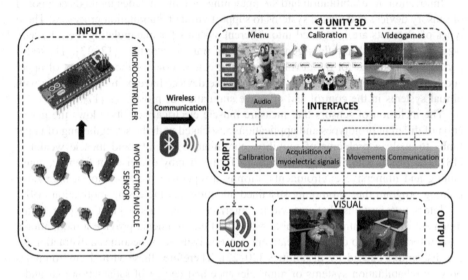

**Fig. 1.**  Block diagram of the strengthening system.

### 2.1  Signal Acquisition

The contraction and relaxation movements of the arm and forearm muscles from the right and left upper extremities are acquired by myoelectric sensors, these signals contain the information of the muscular activity with the electrical potential generated by the cells of the fiber muscle at a certain time; they are received and conditioned in a micro Arduino board that sends data wirelessly to the computer.

To place the sensors on the skin, disposable surface electrodes are used, which are connected to the sensor through clips facilitating their placement, two of these electrodes are for acquisition of the signals and the third is used as a reference. The position and orientation of the sensors and electrodes have a great effect on the strength and quality of the signal, these must be placed in the center of the muscle and aligned with the orientation of the muscle fibers as seen in Figs. 2(a) and 2(b). Placing the sensor in other positions means reducing the strength and quality of the myoelectric signal.

Myoelectric signals provided by sensors are stored in a string data and separated by commas in the Arduino software, these data are sent to the computer through Bluetooth communication. Every string data is separated in the graphic engine Unity 3D through arrays and comparison algorithms programed in the Virtual Studio software so they are can be used for give movement to the virtual interface objects.

This communication type sends real-time data, delete the cables use and provide an ergonomic system for the user.

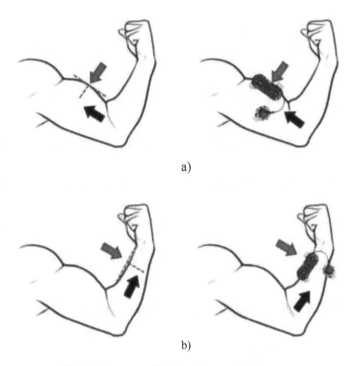

a)

b)

**Fig. 2.** Sensor positioning: (a) arm, (b) forearm.

## 2.2  Scripts Development

In this section, the Visual Studio software organizes and interprets the received information and through the different scripts the interaction between the virtual objects is done to fulfill the activities proposed in each videogame, these scripts are programmed to respond immediately according to the movements of the objects and the user. In Fig. 3, a flow chart of the management of the received information is shown.

## 2.3  Design of Interactive Interface

The virtual interfaces have been developed with the Unity 3D graphics engine to improve and give more reliability to the system, these interfaces give the user interaction between the real world and the virtual world with great visual and auditory appeal because of the combination of hardware and software. These interfaces include interactive videogames to dodge obstacles, collect coins and generate jumps on platforms, where the user first observes and then generates the movements recommended by the therapist based on their injury.

The application contains an interface where you can calibrate each of the sensors, it has images that indicate the movement to be made as seen in Fig. 4. This allows each user to obtain and save a range of minimum and maximum values depending on the strength and physical conditions they have to facilitate their movements.

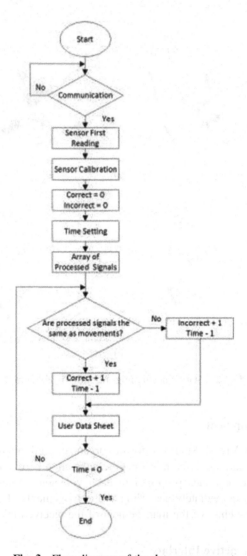

**Fig. 3.** Flow diagram of the data management.

This application also has a menu that allows the user to record data such as name, age and execution time for each videogame, from 30 to 180 s and, select the level of difficulty that can be easy, medium or hard, as shown in Fig. 5.

The easy level (first videogame) presents a virtual city, where the user must avoid balloons. The interface provides the time and the number of successes and mistakes made during the game (as shown in Fig. 6a). In addition, these errors are indicated by a collision audio.

The medium level (second videogame) is an underwater environment where the shark must collect coins. The interface specifies the time and the number of collected

**Fig. 4.** Sensor calibration interface.

a)                                      b)

**Fig. 5.** (a) Menu, (b) User data.

coins, in this level an audio is displayed each time a coin has been collected (see Fig. 6b).

The hard level (last videogame) has a character that must jump between mobile platforms and platforms that fall. The interface provides information about the execution time (see Fig. 6c). The system delivers important data at the end of each videogame for further analysis.

## 3   Interactive System Way of Use

To use the interactive system, users must place the vest and sensors in the foreseen zones. For the correct placement of the stuff mentioned above it is suggested to: (i) clean the skin in the area where the sensors will be located to eliminate impurities, and (ii) fit the electrodes in the sensor connectors and place them in the desired muscle. To place the sensor, it must be taken into account that two of the connected electrodes are in the center of the muscle and the other is located in the posterior part of the

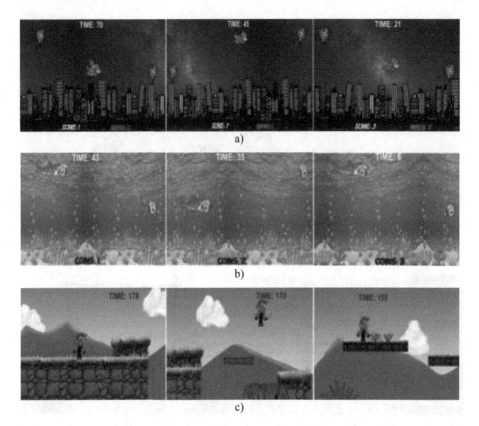

**Fig. 6.** (a) Easy level, (b) Medium level, (c) Hard level.

muscle. Then the back of the electrodes should be peeled off to expose the adhesive and apply it to the skin, the reference electrode should not be placed near the target muscle.

In the developed interface, each sensor must be calibrated to obtain the initial movement values of each upper extremity of the user. In the main screen you select the level of the videogame you want to play.

For the first videogame, slight movements of the left and right arms are required alternately and repetitively. For the second videogame, several series of opening and closing of the hands must be performed, while the third videogame will be a combination of precise and coordinated exercises of contraction and relaxation of the arms and hands muscles.

In the proposed system, the therapist is the one in charge of adjusting the time of each videogame to perform the indicated exercises. The system delivers a data sheet indicating the number of successes and errors, with these data the therapist can perform a controlled follow-up to the user and, in addition, there is an auditory and visual feedback that allows a better cognitive development.

Is important to remember that the first strengthening session is the one and only which has to be supervised by the therapist, the other ones could be performed from the user home without any face-to-face assistance and with a more flexible schedule for him. Travel costs will also be considerable reduced because there is no need to move continuously to a rehabilitation center to take every session and pay for it but, instead users can do the rehabilitation with close relatives making it more confidence for the patient when strengthening his upper limbs.

After many home sessions, it is necessary to visit the therapist in order to check the user progress where he can go forward to a more intensive treatment or gradually reduce the intense of every session because of a good response of his limbs.

## 4 Tests and Results

### 4.1 Test

The system was tested by 5 users (3 boys and 2 girls) with ages between 6 and 12 years. Users receive information on the functionality of the system through a brief explanation, then they use the interactive system according to the procedure detailed in Sect. 3. The following inclusion criterion was used: children over 5 years and under 13 years of age and having some muscular disease (myopathy). The exclusion criterion was: to have visual and auditive deficiency. In Fig. 7 the tests carried out by the users in the interactive system are presented.

### 4.2 Results

At the end of each videogame, the results are displayed in a text file that is automatically generated with the user's name as shown in Fig. 8.

In addition, the SUS evaluation test, also known as the System Usability Scale created by John Brooke in 1986 [25], was applied to users. It is a reliable, simple and precise tool that allows determining the user's acceptance. Information has a great importance to determine safety, sensation and discomfort when using an interactive system. The questions posed to users about the interactive system and the results of the usability test are presented in Table 1.

The result of the SUS test carried out by five users after using the interactive system is: (84.5 ± 0.62). If the result obtained is greater than 68%, the system responds to an acceptable usability for muscle strengthening.

The present work is focused in developing videogames with the use of the Unity 3D Software, also we measure its usability in children who have different pathology which doesn't allow them to perform normal movements of the upper limbs; hence, there are no experimental results which show the force increasing of the affected limb.

## 5 Conclusions and Future Work

An interactive system for strengthening upper extremities using myoelectric sensors and Bluetooth wireless communication was developed, the virtual interfaces are designed in the Unity 3D graphics engine and are made up of three interactive

a)

b)

c)

**Fig. 7.** Tests made in the interactive system.

videogames that allow the generation of movements such as arms contraction and relaxation and the opening and closing of hands. In addition, the system has visual and auditory feedback which provides the user a better cognitive development.

This is an innovative and alternative system to the classic strengthening techniques and causes great interest in users when developing motor skills to achieve greater

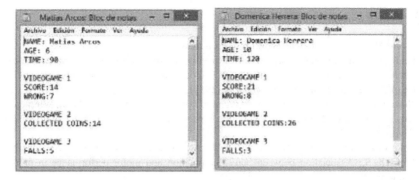

**Fig. 8.** Users text file.

**Table 1.** SUS results

| Question | Result (N = 5) | |
|---|---|---|
| | Mean | SD |
| 1. I think I would like to use this Virtual Reality system frequently | 4.2 | 0.75 |
| 2. I found the Virtual Reality system to be unnecessarily complex | 2 | 0.63 |
| 3. I thought that the Virtual Reality system was easy to use | 4.4 | 0.8 |
| 4. I think I would need the support of a technical person to be able to use this Virtual Reality system | 2.6 | 0.49 |
| 5. I found that the various functions in this Virtual Reality system were well integrated | 4.4 | 0.8 |
| 6. I thought there was too much inconsistency in this Virtual Reality system | 1.6 | 0.49 |
| 7. I would imagine that most people would learn to use this Virtual Reality system very quickly | 4.6 | 0.49 |
| 8. I found the Virtual Reality system to be very cumbersome to use | 1.6 | 0.49 |
| 9. I felt very confident using the Virtual Reality system | 4.6 | 0.49 |
| 10. I needed to learn a lot of things before I could get going with this Virtual Reality system | 2.2 | 0.75 |
| GLOBAL SCORE(Total) | 84.5 | 0.62 |

autonomy. The results obtained in the SUS questionnaire indicate that the system has an acceptance to be used in the strengthening of upper limbs.

As future work, the aim is to design a control system capable of acquiring and processing the myoelectric signals produced by the forearm of a child with the purpose of controlling a hand-held myoelectric prosthesis.

**Acknowledgements.** We thank the "Universidad de las Fuerzas Armadas ESPE" for financing the investigation project number 2016-PIC-0017.

# References

1. World Health Organization: World report on disability (2011)
2. Feldman, H.M., Chaves-Gnecco, D., Hofkosh, D.: Developmental-behavioral pediatrics. In: Zitelli, B.J., McIntire, S.C., Norwalk, A.J. (eds.) Atlas of Pediatric Diagnosis, 6th edn, Chap. 3. Elsevier Saunders, Philadelphia (2012)
3. Newell, K.: Constraints on the development of coordination. In: Wade, M.G., Whiting, H.T. (eds.) Motor Development in Children: Aspects of Coordination and Control. Nijhoff, Dordrecht (1986)
4. Kakebeeke, T.H., Lanzi, S., Zysset, A.E., Arhab, A., Messerli-Bürgy, N., Stuelb, K., Munsch, S.: Association between body composition and motor performance in preschool children. Obes. Facts **10**(5), 420–431 (2017)
5. Albiol-Pérez, S., Gómez, J.-A.G., Olmo, E., Soler, A.M.: A virtual fine rehabilitation system for children with cerebral palsy: assesment of the usability of a low-cost system. In: Rocha, Á., Correia, A.M., Adeli, H., Reis, L.P., Costanzo, S. (eds.) WorldCIST 2017. AISC, vol. 570, pp. 619–627. Springer, Cham (2017). https://doi.org/10.1007/978-3-319-56538-5_63
6. Booth, V., Masud, T., Connell, L., Bath-Hextall, F.: The effectiveness of virtual reality interventions in improving balance in adults with impaired balance compared with standard or no treatment: a systematic review and meta-analysis. Clin. Rehabil. **28**, 419–431 (2014)
7. Bonnechère, B.: Serious Games in Physical Rehabilitation: From Theory to Practice. Springer, Brussels (2017). https://doi.org/10.1007/978-3-319-66122-3
8. Atashzar, S.F., Shahbazi, M., Samotus, O., Tavakoli, M., Jog, M.S., Patel, R.V.: Characterization of upper-limb pathological tremors: application to design of an augmented haptic rehabilitation system. IEEE J. Sel. Top. Sign. Proces. **10**(5), 888–903 (2016)
9. Jiang, T.T., Qian, Z.Q., Lin, Y., Bi, Z.M., Liu, Y.F., Zhang, W.J.: Analysis of virtual environment haptic robotic systems for a rehabilitation of post-stroke patients. In: 2017 IEEE International Conference on Industrial Technology (ICIT), pp. 738–742. IEEE, Toronto (2017)
10. Andaluz, V.H., et al.: Virtual reality integration with force feedback in upper limb rehabilitation. In: Bebis, G., Boyle, R. (eds.) ISVC 2016. LNCS, vol. 10073, pp. 259–268. Springer, Cham (2016). https://doi.org/10.1007/978-3-319-50832-0_25
11. Andaluz, V.H., et al.: Virtual environments for motor fine skills rehabilitation with force feedback. In: De Paolis, L.T., Bourdot, P., Mongelli, A. (eds.) AVR 2017. LNCS, vol. 10324, pp. 94–105. Springer, Cham (2017). https://doi.org/10.1007/978-3-319-60922-5_7
12. Kim, W.-S.: Development and Validation of Assessment Tools Using Robotic and Virtual Reality Technologies in Stroke Rehabilitation, Seoul, August 2016
13. Berger, D.J., d'Avella, A.: Towards a myoelectrically controlled virtual reality interface for synergy-based stroke rehabilitation. In: Ibáñez, J., González-Vargas, J., Azorín, J., Akay, M., Pons, J. (eds.) Converging Clinical and Engineering Research on Neurorehabilitation II. BIOSYSROB, vol. 15, pp. 965–969. Springer, Cham (2017). https://doi.org/10.1007/978-3-319-46669-9_156
14. Bolgla, L.A., Cruz, M.F., Roberts, L.H., Buice, A.M., Pou, T.S.: Relative electromyographic activity in trunk, hip, and knee muscles during unilateral weight bearing exercises: implications for rehabilitation. Physiother. Theor. Pract. **32**, 130–138 (2016)
15. Dorsch, S., Ada, L., Canning, C.G.: EMG-triggered electrical stimulation is a feasible intervention to apply to multiple arm muscles in people early after stroke, but does not improve strength and activity more than usual therapy: a randomized feasibility trial. Clin. Rehabil. **28**, 482–490 (2014)

16. Calabrò, R.S., Naro, A., Russo, M., Leo, A., Luca, R.D.: The role of virtual reality in improving motor performance as revealed by EEG: a randomized clinical trial. J. NeuroEng. Rehabil. **14**, 53 (2017)
17. Blana, D., Kyriacou, T., Lambrecht, J.M., Chadwick, E.K.: Feasibility of using combined EMG and kinematic signals for prosthesis control: a simulation study using a virtual reality environment. J. Electromyogr. Kinesiol. **29**, 21–27 (2016)
18. Hoda, M., Hafidh, B., El Saddik, A.: Haptic glove for finger rehabilitation. In: 2015 IEEE International Conference on Multimedia and Expo Workshops (ICMEW), Turin, pp. 1–6 (2015)
19. Connelly, L., Jia, Y., Toro, M.L., Stoykov, M.E., Kenyon, R.V., Kamper, D.G.: A pneumatic glove and immersive virtual reality environment for hand rehabilitative training after stroke. IEEE Trans. Neural Syst. Rehabil. Eng. **18**(5), 551–559 (2010)
20. Gunel, M.K., Kara, O.K., Ozal, C., Turker, D.: Virtual Reality in Rehabilitation of Children with cerebral palsy. INTECH, Ankara (2014)
21. Won, A.S., Bailey, J., Bailenson, J., Tataru, C., Yoon, I.A.: Immersive Virtual Reality for Pediatric Pain, Children (2017)
22. Garner, T.: Applications of virtual reality. In: Echoes of Other Worlds: Sound in Virtual Reality, pp. 299–361 (2018)
23. Lemmens, R.J.M., Seelen, H.A.M., Timmermans, A.A.A., Schnackers, M.L.A.P., Eerden, A., Smeets, R.J.E.M., Janssen-Potten, Y.J.M.: To what extent can arm–hand skill performance—of both healthy adults and children—be recorded reliably using multiple bodily worn sensor devices? IEEE Trans. Neural Syst. Rehabil. Eng. **23**(4), 581–590 (2015)
24. Wen, X., Duan, F., Yu, Y., Tan, J.T.C., Cheng, X.: Design of a multi-functional system based on virtual reality for stroke rehabilitation. In: 11th World Congress on Intelligent Control and Automation, pp. 2412–2417. IEEE, Shenyang (2014)
25. Sharfina, Z., Santoso, H.B.: An Indonesian adaptation of the System Usability Scale (SUS). In: 2016 International Conference on Advanced Computer Science and Information Systems (ICACSIS), pp. 145–148. IEEE, Malang (2016)
26. Jannink, M.J., Van Der Wilden, G.J., Navis, D.W., Visser, G., Gussinklo, J., Ijzerman, M.: A low-cost video game applied for training of upper extremity function in children with cerebral palsy: a pilot study. Cyberpsychol. Behav. **11**(1), 27–32 (2008)

# Immersive Virtual System Based on Games for Children's Fine Motor Rehabilitation

Edwin Pruna[✉], Jenny Tigse, Alexandra Chuquitarco, Ivón Escobar,
Marco Pilatásig, and Eddie Daniel Galarza

Universidad de las Fuerzas Armadas ESPE, Sangolqui, Ecuador
{eppruna, jptigse, eachuquitarco, ipescobar,
mapilatagsig, gqeddie}@espe.edu.ec

**Abstract.** We present a 3D virtual system for children's fine motor rehabilitation, it is created three environments with the software Unity. These environments generate playful and entertaining backgrounds; several tests for the system operation are performed which include working with children with ages of 5 to 14 years. The results allow to determine the fine motor movements, in addition it is determined that the trajectories made by children's fingers when performing the games are suitable for fine motor rehabilitation. Finally, the usability test SEQ is also performed, which give us results of (56.4 ± 0.37), this shows the user's acceptance of the system.

**Keywords:** Virtual reality · Rehabilitation · Motor · LeapMotion
Oculus rift

## 1 Introduction

As children grow they achieve goals in their development, these goals are tasks or abilities they perform according to their age. Considering the perspective for the dynamic motor system, the development of motor abilities is based on the interaction between the task, the organism and the environment [1].

The evolution of motor abilities in any particular case depends of the task's difficulty, the possibilities and opportunities of the environment and the psychological and physic properties of the child [2]. Is important to consider the specific limitations of: the tasks, the children and the environment around them to study the motor development; for example, it is not the same to create n stimulation environment for children with cerebral palsy or mental retardation as creating it for children with hearing or visual impairment, the last one receive less stimulation and, hence, the motor abilities development will be affected [3, 4].

The development of fine psychomotor abilities is decisive for a child. The children's achievements in this field will open a door for experimentation and learning of his environment and, as consequence, the fine psychomotor plays an important role in intelligence development [5].

The control of fine motor is coordination between muscles, bones and nerves to produce small and precise movements, it requires a precise eye hand coordination in order to grab or manipulate objects [6]. Fine motor involves an elevated level of

© Springer International Publishing AG, part of Springer Nature 2018
L. T. De Paolis and P. Bourdot (Eds.): AVR 2018, LNCS 10851, pp. 30–42, 2018.
https://doi.org/10.1007/978-3-319-95282-6_3

maturity and long learning to really acquire each of its aspects, since there are different difficulty and precision levels. Taking into account this definition, emphasis has been placed on tasks related to dexterity and less in speed, this is because speed tasks have shown weaker links with language and cognitive abilities of superior order [7, 8].

Studies have shown difficulties in graphomotor tend to group in learning, the attention [9] and weakness of processing speed, these indicators show a high grade of exactitude in the prediction of presence or absence of learning disability in reading, mathematics and written expression [10]. It was analyzed that fine motor writing abilities are an important factor linked with academic success that a child could achieve in the future [11, 12], this is the importance of developing fine motor abilities in children.

Physical therapy in children with slight motor deterioration of hemiplegic type is one of the elements from a child development program, in this program the therapists have to incorporate authentic efforts to achieve a varied, with quality and stimulating environment, considering that a child needs new experiences and interaction with the world in order to learn [13, 14]. The traditional therapies are based in repetitive practices or movements that could bore children because of the limitations in exercises [15].

Therapy based on virtual reality is an interactive recognized tool used for patients' immersion and motivation within a virtual environment [16–18], studies have demonstrated an improvement on manual functions and in cortical organization specially in children with cerebral palsy after therapies based on Virtual Reality (VR) [19, 20]. The utilization of VR games in motor rehabilitation process of upper limbs has been increased [21–24], in a VR environment there are several backgrounds very close to reality which brings visual, audible and concentration feedback, these factors could be manipulated in a precise and systematic mood, also they allow individual formation and motor learning [25].

As mentioned before, in this work it is presented a virtual system through games to improve fine motor in children, it is made three flashy and friendly environments, which are: (i) Virtual environment for object's throwing, (ii) Virtual environment for object's classification by color and (iii) Virtual environment for object's classification by shape.

The present work is divided in three different sections: Introduction, System Development, Tests and Results, Conclusions.

## 2 System Development

In this section, it is explained the system's implementation, the considered stages are: Signal acquisition from input peripherals, Script development and 3D Environment design. In Fig. 1 it is presented the block diagram for the implemented system.

### 2.1 Data Acquisition from Input Peripherals

The input peripherals for the system are Oculus Rift, leap motion and the camera. Through leap motion it is acquired data from hands and finger movements in real time, the infrared lights and sensors act like a camera to obtain the best precision of all the

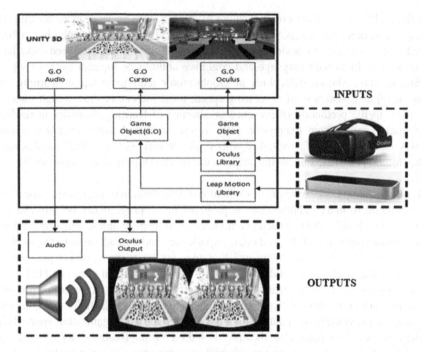

**Fig. 1.** System's block diagram.

movements. With the HMD (Head-Mounted Display) the user's head movement is captured, this movement travels to the camera control which observes the virtual reality environment. The movement's capture is done through the infrared camera located on top of the computer and in front of the device mounted on the user's head.

The obtained movements from the hands and fingers are sent to the controller which uses an internal hand model (Brush Hand) and compares the data sent by sensors, later they are called through different libraries for its programming in C which help to interpret all their information. The programming performed in Visual Studio allow to receive, analyze and interpret frame by frame the data for a specific function in each of the proposed applications.

## 2.2   Script Development

For the script development it was considered fine movements used in traditional rehabilitation; by using the leap motion and the compatible libraries with unity, data will be sent from the leap motion microcontroller to the computer, then the data will be visualized with Unity. In order to identify the movements and the grip between the hand and a virtual object it is used functions for collision between objects, this allow to determine the interaction and depending on the action, the virtual object can be moved around the environment to be directed to the objective.

In this section, it is explained the script development for the created applications.

**Virtual Environment for Object Throwing.** For the application's making it is used scripts that allow the verification of collision with virtual objects and then perform counting of successful objects through the interaction with a throwing object, these objects must have gravity and rigidity too. In Fig. 2 it is presented the flow diagram for the Object Throwing Application.

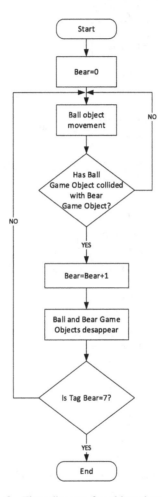

**Fig. 2.** Flow diagram for object throwing

**Virtual Environment for Object Classification by Colors.** For the two applications which involve classification by color or shape, it is used a script which verifies if the objects were placed correctly, if it is not the case, there will be a virtual object which warns that there is an error executed and then the placement and interaction with the object must be performed again.

Figure 3 presents the flow diagram with the classification by color or shape application.

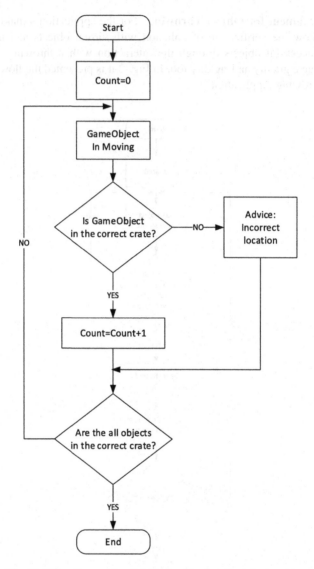

**Fig. 3.** Flow diagram for object classification by color or shape.

## 2.3    3D Environments Design

The design of the three virtual environments is based on the creation of objects trough 3D design programs like: Blender, this program allows to save objects with the .fbx or .obj extensions, the objects then are imported to Unity 3D for the application's visual design. The objects will need to be colored and be given different textures in order to highlight the real immersion to the environment.

**Virtual Environment for Object Throwing.** It is made a room that catches the child's attention, to do this it is added many elements, for example a bed, pillows, night stands, frames, a desk, a chair, all this elements help the environment to be realistic, in the same mood the walls will be colored and presented with flashy pictures for children. To perform the ball catching and throwing, it was added 7 bears to the background and a basket which contains very small balls. Figure 4 presents the background for the designed virtual environment.

**Fig. 4.** A top and front view of the virtual environment for object throwing. (Color figure online)

**Virtual Environment for Object Classification by Colors.** When making this environment it is added two sofas with a realistic and flashy color, it is also included 3 baskets with green, red and yellow colors. It is developed three kinds of objects:

1. Cubes, designed with different color textures marked with letters A, B and C.
2. Stars, including color materials.
3. Bowling pins, they have textures designed based on animal shapes like parrot, giraffe and frog with their own label. Figure 5 presents the designed virtual environment.

**Fig. 5.** Top and front view of the virtual environment for object classification by colors. (Color figure online)

**Virtual Environment for Object Classification by Shape.** It is made three textures with different pictures which includes stars, cubes and bowling pins, for shape design it was added in parts the basket's base, each basket has a main picture of the object, the other elements of the virtual environment are the same from environment 2, but considering changing the material color. In Fig. 6 the designed virtual environment is presented.

**Fig. 6.** Top and front view of the virtual environment for object classification by shapes. (Color figure online)

Each element that is going to interact with the user's hand in the virtual environment will have a script which will be called "Interaction Behavior", this script reacts to the hand movement, also, it is included special dynamics for each game through some components like the collision mesh, rigidity, animations and audio. When there is physic interaction between the hand and the virtual object, this object will change to a green mesh which verifies if the object's grip is correct and if it could be moved around the virtual environment. While there is not the correct grip, the mesh will keep being blue and this will prevent the objects to move.

## 3   Tests and Results

### 3.1   Test

It is performed tests for the implemented system with 5 children with ages between 5 and 14 years, the procedure for the system's utilization is detailed below:

The user places himself in front of the oculus rift's camera to determine his position inside the virtual environment, then he must show the hands in front of the oculus rift DK2 helmet so the leap motion could detect them. The application has an interactive start menu, which allows the user to select one of the three application he would like to perform.

In the first application, there is an environment with stuffed bears and many balls, the user will the pick up the balls with his hands and then throw them to the bears, if he hits the bears they will disappear, the playing time will end when there are no more stuffed bears. Below it is shown some sequences performed by users (Fig. 7).

**Fig. 7.** System gameplay, it is presented the interaction between the user and the virtual environment for object's throwing.

In the second application, the objects will be classified by color, the user pick up every object and then he will put it into a basket depending on the object's color, if the object falls into a wrong color basket, it will show an error through an appearing virtual object and also it will sound so the user can make a correction and finish it adequately. In Fig. 8 it is presented the sequences performed by users.

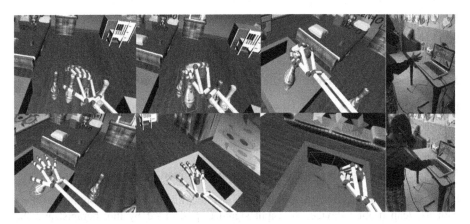

**Fig. 8.** System gameplay, it is presented interaction between the user and the virtual environment for object's classification by color. (Color figure online)

The third application consists of classifying objects depending on the shape, the user visualizes every object and also observes what image is inside the basket, and depending on the shape inside the basket the user must select the basket to throw the object. The sequence is presented in Fig. 9.

**Fig. 9.** System gameplay, it is presented the interaction between the user and the virtual environment for object's classification by the shape.

To evaluate the usability of virtual systems in most scientific work, authors validate the virtual tools for rehabilitation through the usability test [20–23], this test allows to determine the user acceptation, this information is of great importance to determine the easiness, security, sensation, inconveniences, etc., in virtual systems utilization; the performed test for usability of this system is SEQ developed by Gil-Gómez et al. [26], it has 14 clear questions, which 13 have a score from 1 to 5 points. Once the game is finished, the users perform a SEQ poll to determine the acceptation of the system.

### 3.2  Results

This section shows the following results:

### 3.3  Movements Performed by the User When Executing the Tasks

It was identified two kinds of movements: pin's grip and hook's grip, they help to improve fine motor, in Fig. 10 it is shown the movements performed by user inside the virtual environment.

### 3.4  Generated Signals from the System in a Defined Reference

It was performed a movement comparison in the 5 fingers when grabbing an object with the leap motion device, the input signal is performed by the therapist and the output signal is performed by the user. In Fig. 11 it is presented the obtained signals in the performed tasks when doing a clamp grip.

### 3.5  System Usability Results

It is presented the result for system usability, the SEQ poll was completed by 5 children with ages between 5 and 14 years, the results are (56,4 ± 0,37) shown in Table 1; according to [26], if the result obtained in SEQ is in the range of 40–65, the application will be considered valid for rehabilitation.

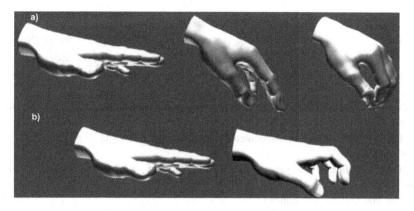

**Fig. 10.** (a) Pin's grip and (b) Hook's grip.

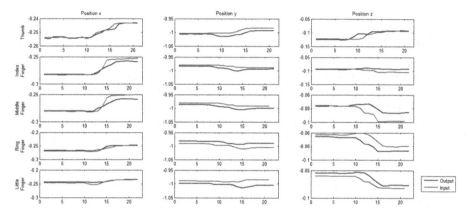

**Fig. 11.** Defined trajectory (red line) vs user movements (blue line). (Color figure online)

**Table 1.** SEQ test with children.

| Questions | Result (N = 5) | |
| --- | --- | --- |
| | Mean | SD |
| Q1. How much did you enjoy your experience with the system? | 4.8 | 0.4 |
| Q2. How much did you sense to be in the environment of the system? | 4.4 | 0.8 |
| Q3. How successful were you in the system? | 3.8 | 0.75 |
| Q4. To what extent were you able to control the system? | 4 | 0.89 |
| Q5. How real is the virtual environment of the system? | 4.6 | 0.8 |
| Q6. Is the information provided by the system clear? | 4.8 | 0.4 |
| Q7. Did you feel discomfort during your experience with the system? | 1.2 | 0.4 |

(*continued*)

**Table 1.** (*continued*)

| Questions | Result (N = 5) | |
|---|---|---|
| | Mean | SD |
| Q8. Did you experience dizziness or nausea during your practice with the system? | 1.6 | 0.8 |
| Q9. Did you experience eye discomfort during your practice with the system? | 1.4 | 0.48 |
| Q10. Did you feel confused or disoriented during your experience with the system? | 2.2 | 0.4 |
| Q11. Do you think that this system will be helpful for your rehabilitation? | 4.4 | 0.49 |
| Q12. Did you find the task difficult? | 2.2 | 0.74 |
| Q13. Did you find the devices of the system difficult to use? | 1.8 | 0.97 |
| GLOBAL SCORE (Total) | 56.4 | 0.37 |

## 4   Conclusions

It was implemented a virtual 3D system, based on 3 interactive games, which provide a realistic and attractive environment to children, the system awakens the interest of children to perform the games; the movements to accomplish the challenges of each game are pin's grip and hook's grip, this movements help the rehabilitation of fine motor. Finally, the usability test SEQ performed by users give results of (56,4 ± 0,37), this shows the system is easy to use, is safe, participants don't have any inconvenience when using it and they are motivated to use it.

As future work, it will be developed an immersive system which will provide force feedback.

**Acknowledgements.** We thank the "Universidad de las Fuerzas Armadas ESPE" for financing the investigation project number 2016-PIC-0017.

## References

1. Newell, K.: Constraints on the development of coordination. In: Wade, M., Whiting, H.T. (eds.) Motor Development in Children: Aspects of Coordination and Control, pp. 341–360. Martinus Nijhoff, Dordrecht (1986)
2. Kakebeeke, T.H., Lanzi, S., Zysset, A.E., Arhab, A., Messerli-Bürgy, N., Stuelb, K., Munsch, S.: Association between body composition and motor performance in preschool children. Obes. Facts **10**(5), 420–431 (2017)
3. Levtzion-Korach, O., Tennenbaum, A., Schnitzer, R., Ornoy, A.: Early motor development of blind children. J. Paediatr. Child Health **36**, 226–229 (2000)
4. Gheysen, F., Loots, G., Van Waelvelde, H.: Motor development of deaf children with and without cochlear implants. J. Deaf Stud. Deaf Educ. **13**, 215–224 (2008)

5. Feldman, H.M., Chaves-Gnecco, D., Hofkosh, D.: Developmental-behavioral pediatrics. In: Zitelli, B.J., McIntire, S.C., Norwalk, A.J. (eds.) Atlas of Pediatric Diagnosis, 6th edn, Chap. 3, Elsevier Saunders, Philadelphia (2012)

6. Luo, Z., Jose, P.E., Huntsinger, C.S., Pigott, T.D.: Fine motor skills and mathematics achievement in East Asian American and European American kindergartners and first graders. Br. J. Dev. Psychol. **25**, 595–614 (2007). https://doi.org/10.1348/026151007X185329

7. Brookman, A., McDonald, S., McDonald, D., Bishop, D.V.: Fine motor deficits in reading disability and language impairment: same or different? PeerJ **1**(3), e217 (2013). https://doi.org/10.7717/peerj.217

8. Martzog, P.: Feinmotorische Fertigkeiten und kognitive Fähigkeiten bei Kindern im Vorschulalter [Fine motor skills and cognitive development in preschool children], 1st edn. Tectum, Marburg (2015)

9. Fenollar-Cortés, J., Gallego-Martínez, A., Fuentes, L.J.: The role of inattention and hyperactivity/impulsivity in the fine motor coordination in children with ADHD. Res. Dev. Disabil. **69**, 77–84 (2017)

10. Mayes, S.D., Calhoun, S.L., Learning, A.: Writing, and processing speed in typical children and children with ADHD, autism, anxiety, depression, and oppositional-defiant disorder. Child Neuropsychol. **13**(6), 469–493 (2007)

11. Dinehart, L.H.: Handwriting in early childhood education: current research and future implications. J. Early Childhood Lit. **15**(1), 97–118 (2015). https://doi.org/10.1177/1468798414522825

12. Grissmer, D., Grimm, K., Aiyer, S.: Fine motor skills and early comprehension of the world: two new school readiness indicators. Dev. Psychol. **46**(5), 1008–1017 (2010). https://doi.org/10.1037/a0020104

13. De Campos, A.C., da Costa, C.S., Rocha, N.A.: Measuring changes in functional mobility in children with mild cerebral palsy. Devel. Neurorehabil. **14**, 140–144 (2011)

14. Prosser, L.A., Lee, S.C., Barbe, M.F., VanSant, A.F., Lauer, R.T.: Trunk and hip muscle activity in early walkers with and without cerebral palsy – a frequency analysis. J. Electromyogr. Kinesiol. **20**, 851–859 (2010)

15. Galil, A., Carmel, S., Lubetzky, H., Heiman, N.: Compliance with home rehabilitation therapy by parents of children with disabilities in Jews and Bedouin in Israel. Dev. Med. Child Neurol. **43**(4), 261–268 (2001)

16. Mitchell, L., Ziviani, J., Oftedal, S., Boyd, R.: The effect of virtual reality interventions on physical activity in children and adolescents with early brain injuries including cerebral palsy. Dev. Med. Child Neurol. **54**, 667–671 (2012)

17. Snider, L., Majnemer, A., Darsaklis, V.: Virtual reality as a therapeutic modality for children with cerebral palsy. Dev. Neurorehabil. **13**, 120–128 (2010)

18. Levac, D.E., Galvin, J.: When is virtual reality "therapy"? Arch. Phys. Med. Rehabil. **94**(795), 8 (2013)

19. Golomb, M.R., McDonald, B.C., Warden, S.J., Yonkman, J., Saykin, A.J., Shirley, B., et al.: In-home virtual reality videogame telerehabilitation in adolescents with hemiplegic cerebral palsy. Arch. Phys. Med. Rehabil. **91**, 1–8 (2010)

20. Shin, J., Song, G., Hwangbo, G.: Effects of conventional neurological treatment and a virtual reality training program on eye-hand coordination in children with cerebral palsy. J. Phys. Ther. Sci. **27**(7), 2151–2154 (2015). https://doi.org/10.1589/jpts.27.2151

21. Pruna, E., Acurio, A., Tigse, J., Escobar, I., Pilatásig, M., Pilatásig, P.: Virtual system for upper limbs rehabilitation in children. In: De Paolis, L.T., Bourdot, P., Mongelli, A. (eds.) AVR 2017. LNCS, vol. 10325, pp. 107–118. Springer, Cham (2017). https://doi.org/10.1007/978-3-319-60928-7_9

22. Pruna, E., Acurio, A., Escobar, I., Pérez, S.A., Zumbana, P., Meythaler, A., Álvarez, F.A.: 3D virtual system using a haptic device for fine motor rehabilitation. In: Rocha, Á., Correia, A.M., Adeli, H., Reis, L.P., Costanzo, S. (eds.) WorldCIST 2017. AISC, vol. 570, pp. 648–656. Springer, Cham (2017). https://doi.org/10.1007/978-3-319-56538-5_66
23. Albiol-Pérez, S., Mena-Cajas, J., Escobar-Anchaguano, I.P., Pruna-Panchi, E.P., Zumbana, P.: Virtual fine rehabilitation in patients with carpal tunnel syndrome using low-cost devices. In Proceedings of the 4th Workshop on ICTs for improving Patients Rehabilitation Research Techniques, pp. 61–64. ACM (2017)
24. Tatla, S.K., Shirzad, N., Lohse, K.R., Virji-Babul, N., Hoens, A.M., Holsti, L., et al.: Therapists' perceptions of social media and video game technologies in upper limb rehabilitation. JMIR Serious Games. 3(1), e2 (2015). https://doi.org/10.2196/games.3401
25. Chen, Y.P., Kang, L.J., Chuang, T.Y., Doong, J.L., Lee, S.J., Tsai, M.W., Jeng, S.F., Sung, W.H.: Use of virtual reality to improve upper-extremity control in children with cerebral palsy: a single-subject design. Phys. Ther. 87(11), 1441–1457 (2007). https://doi.org/10.2522/ptj.20060062
26. Gil-Gómez, J.A., Gil-Gómez, H., Lozano-Quilis, J.A., Manzano-Hernández, P., Albiol-Pérez, S., Aula-Valero, C.: SEQ: suitability evaluation questionnaire for virtual rehabilitation systems. Application in a virtual rehabilitation system for balance rehabilitation. In: 2013 7th International Conference on Pervasive Computing Technologies for Healthcare and Workshops, Venice, pp. 335–338 (2013)

# Virtual Reality Serious Game for Musculoskeletal Disorder Prevention

Maria Sisto[1(✉)], Mohsen Zare[2], Nabil Ouerhani[3], Christophe Bolinhas[1],
Margaux Divernois[3], Bernard Mignot[2], Jean-Claude Sagot[2],
and Stéphane Gobron[1]

[1] Image Processing and Computer Graphics Group,
HE-Arc, HES-SO, Neuchâtel, Switzerland
{maria.sisto,stephane.gobron}@he-arc.ch
[2] ERCOS Group (pole), Laboratory of ELLIAD-EA4661,
UTBM-University of Bourgogne Franche-Comt, Belfort, France
[3] Interaction Technology Group, HE-Arc, HES-SO, Neuchâtel, Switzerland

**Abstract.** Musculo Skeletal Disorders (MSDs) is the most common disease in the workplaces causing disabilities and excessive costs to industries, particularly in EU countries. Most of MSDs prevention programs have focused on a combination of interventions including training to change individual behaviors (such as awkward postures). However, little evidence proves that current training approach on awkward postures is efficient and can significantly reduce MSDs symptoms. Therefore, dealing with awkward postures and repetitive tasks is the real challenge for practitioners and manufacturers, knowing that the amount of risk exposure varies increasingly among workers depending on their attitude and expertise as well as on their strategy to perform the task. The progress in MSDs prevention might come through developing new tools that inform workers more efficiently on their gestures and postures. This paper proposes a potential Serious Game that immerses industrial workers using Virtual Reality and helps them recognize their strategy while performing tasks and trains them to find the most efficient and least risky tactics.

**Keywords:** Serious game · Musculoskeletal Disorder
Health application · Virtual reality · Virtual environment
Head-mounted display

## 1 Introduction

Musculoskeletal Disorders (MSDs) are the most common work-related injuries in Western countries, reaching up to 2% of the gross domestic product (GPD) in European countries. In France, for example, MSDs represent more than 87% of all the occupational diseases in 2016 [1]. In Europe, millions of people suffer from MSD-associated diseases [2,3], which impact the workers' life quality and have a substantial economic and social burden on companies and communities [2]. Absenteeism, permanent disability, compensation and medical expenses are the

© Springer International Publishing AG, part of Springer Nature 2018
L. T. De Paolis and P. Bourdot (Eds.): AVR 2018, LNCS 10851, pp. 43–59, 2018.
https://doi.org/10.1007/978-3-319-95282-6_4

**Fig. 1.** Concept image of a user playing the game. A feedback is then given on its posture (upper right).

main, tangible consequences while intangible costs of MSDs (such as a family income shortage, mental damage in the workplace, and loss of skillful workforces) are less considered and might have more social and economic effects [4,5]. Recent etiological MSDs risk models have well established the role of physical, organizational and psychosocial risk factors in the MSDs development [6,7]. Although all those factors interact with each other, the physical risk factor - particularly awkward and static postures - remains the most hazardous element of industrial tasks [8].

Many ergonomic intervention studies have focused on reducing hazardous tasks by job redesigning, training workers and participation of stakeholders (especially workers). Ergonomic interventions are mostly implemented through the use of new equipment (like lifting tools), staff training and organizational changes [9–11]. Most of these studies report workers' participation and training as a key element for the intervention success [12–15]. However, several recent studies questioned the effectiveness of ergonomic interventions and showed that classic physical and organizational ergonomic interventions have low efficiency [16–18].

Classic training programs (such as lectures, on-site training, posters and brochures) are insufficient to change workers behaviors and improve their postures [11,19,20]. Although some studies have found classic ergonomic training to be significantly effective in the short term, sustainability of posture and behavior changes was reported in very few cases [15,21,22], the post-intervention effects of training often reducing rapidly after several months. Therefore, manufacturing industries need new methods, which not only involve active workers training to improve postures and behaviors [12,13,20] but also provide a sustainable approach in the prevention of MSDs. With this study we want to know whether modern technologies such as Virtual Reality (VR) could contribute to a sustainable MSD prevention. A Serious Game (SG) is introduced as a potential option to provide a sustainable training and behavior changes, particularly in MSD care. Although these technologies are a novelty in MSD prevention, serious games as a pedagogic tool for health and safety purposes have already been used in previous studies [23–25]. We also want to know whether a fully immersive environment, which provides feedback on the users MSD risk exposure, contributes to MSD prevention in manufacturing industries (see Fig. 1).

More specifically, this paper wants to propose a SG that combines VR and Motion Capture (MoCap) to prevent work-related MSDs. We hypothesize that an attractive SG increases the workers' knowledge of MSD risk factors and helps them develop new strategies to reduce risk exposure. That's why we proposed an innovative tool as a possible alternative to replace the classic training approach.

## 2  State of the Art

### 2.1  MSDs Prevention

Ergonomic interventions focusing on MSDs risk factors such as static and awkward postures, frequent bending and twisting, and repetitive work could reduce the risk of MSDs. However, the various components of these interventions are difficult to implement [26]. Recent studies propose a combination of ergonomic interventions to reduce MSDs symptoms: job redesign, technical modifications, ergonomic training, postural advice and organizational changes as the most common interventions used to reduce MSDs symptoms [10,12,16]. As industrial workers are directly involved in work and influenced by MSD risk factors, ergonomic worker-targeted interventions (for example, physical exercise program, training, ergonomic advice and instruction on working methods) are mostly integrated into the ergonomic intervention studies [15,16,21]. Health promotion actions at the workplace are similarly used to inform workers of good practices and promote preventive interventions at work (e.g., stretching program) or at home (e.g. diet or exercise programs) [27]. However, recent high-quality studies did not confirm the effectiveness of interventions (particularly training and postural advice) in behavior changes [11,19,22,28]: McDermott et al. (2012) investigated the practical implementation of manual material handling training within 150 industry sectors in the UK and concluded that training is more efficient when adapted to a specific task or job. Although the majority of industries currently propose regular training based on legislation, the training efficiency remains unknown. Systematic reviews showed inconsistent and insufficient evidence to conclude that current training approach is effective to reduce awkward postures and MSDs [19,29]. Changing workers behaviors (such as awkward postures and non-adapted strategies in performing a task) based on current training approach (general lectures and classroom-based activities) is a challenge for MSDs prevention. The novelty in MSDs prevention through training would be to develop a new tool that could suppress the deficiencies of current training approaches. An sector-adapted training approach that implies training a worker in a familiar task might improve training efficiency and achieve successful behavior changes. VR and game technologies are new tools that might change workers behaviors in a playful setting and we believe that they can increase the intervention success and reduce awkward postures by providing an efficient training.

## 2.2   Serious Games for MSD Prevention

Many SGs for the rehabilitation of those already suffering from MSDs exist [30–33], but few SGs focus on MSD prevention. A French company (*daesign* [34]) conceived a MSD prevention SG that is meant as a one-time use. It contains a little of gamification by means of quizzes, an interactive desk and a "find the mistakes" game. The other SGs focus on encouraging stretching exercises as a specific MSD prevention technique. Motion tracking is used to validate the user's action. Rodrigues et al. have developed a SG joining the stretching and game phase where the user must correct the posture of some virtual workers [35,36]. Freitas et al. did a series of mini-games that focused on the hands and used stretching exercises as an input for the game [37]. All those games target office workers and we need a SG that targets the occupational risk factors in factories.

## 2.3   Prevention, Training and Virtual Reality

Even if there are few SGs on MSDs, SGs have largely been used in the rehabilitation and health fields [38] often paired with motion tracking or haptic devices and have proven to be efficient [38]. Moreover, it has been proven that Virtual Reality (VR) helps teach assembly tasks/procedure sequences [39] and is often used as a support for immersive SGs [40]. SGs have even been used with VR and Motion Capture in a prevention game [41], but not for MSD prevention.

## 2.4   Our Approach

This study proposes a new approach to MSDs prevention, with a SG focusing on real-life movements and applied to industrial workers. We used the different workers' strategies to develop a SG that combines VR and Motion capture and provides real-time feedback on the user's awkward postures. This SG is decontextualized in virtual reality to get rid of the effects of the environmental components that play a role in MSDs.

# 3    Data Collection in Real Industrial Settings

## 3.1    Data Acquisition

To develop a game close to real work settings, we first created a database of the postures and movements (biomechanical data) of industrial tasks selected from different workstations in the automotive and watchmaking industries. We chose four sectors of the automobile industry (namely injection press, painting, change parts and bumper assembly) and four operations in watchmaking (placing watch dial, setting watch hands, casing movement and visiting). The principal tasks from the automobile industry were packing the bumper and its small parts, preparing, painting and assembling different types of car bumpers. The watchmaker first puts manually the dial on the movement and then fits the hands to the right height and correct position. The operator cases the movement after cleaning the glass and closes the case back. We decided to include these tasks in our study after several visits to the workstations and discussions with industrial stakeholders. These tasks seemed to be more appropriate to develop game scenarios. Twenty automobile assembly operators (8 women and 12 men) and twelve women watchmakers accepted to participate in this experiment. They had a good physical condition without health problems or distress. Most of the participants were polyvalent and could work on several workstations allowing us to measure their postures and movements in different situations. We used nine light T-motion sensors (32 g, 60 × 35 × 19 mm) to continuously measure the upper limb joint angles at a 64 Hz frequency. Each sensor includes a triaxial gyroscope (it measures angular velocity in degrees/sec), a triaxial accelerometer (it measures linear acceleration in m/s2), and a triaxial magnetometer (it measures magnetic field strength in uT). The T-motion sensors were set by adjustable straps on the head, thorax (fixed on the back), pelvis (located on the hip bone), arms and wrists according to the previous literature [42] and the instructions of the manufacturer (TEA, Nancy, France). The participant was equipped in a separate room near the workstation, then T-motion sensors were set at zero in a reference position. The anatomical reference position is described as the human body upright, feet close together, arms to the side and palms facing inward [43]. These reference positions and the relaxed position of the operator were registered at the start and the end of each experiment. Two cameras filmed simultaneously both sides of the worker. We registered ten cycle times of the subjects' activity after they got accustomed to the devices placed on their body and the camera installed near them (5 min).

## 3.2    Activity Analysis and Data Treatment

An experienced researcher in ergonomics and job analysis manually coded the videotaping-recorded activity in CAPTIV software. The subtasks were identified, as far as possible, thanks to the job descriptions provided by the companies. On the basis of the biomechanical model developed by the motion capture system developer (TEA, Nancy, France), we calculated the head, upper arms, forearms, wrists and lower back joint angles in 20° of freedom. The data were synchronized with the subtasks identified in the videos. Each subtask finally had a precise measurement of the upper limbs and trunk joint angles. A global risk score was calculated for each subtask based on the algorithm of the Rapid Upper Limb Assessment (RULA) method [44]. This algorithm generates a single score for each subtask which represents the MSDs risk level (score 1–2: negligible risk, score 3–4: medium risk, score 5–7: high risk).

## 4 User Posture and Gesture Acquisition

### 4.1 Upper Body Tracking for Coarse Posture Acquisition

In this project context, the main goal of posture and gesture acquisition is to provide an objective and systematic assessment of the trainee posture in regards to widely-used ergonomic standards. The objective assessment feeds into the Serious Game in the form of a score that gives feedback to the user on his posture and gestures ergonomics. To do so, a system combining coarse and fine gesture acquisition was set up, tested and tuned. An posture and gesture assessment tool based on the Rapid Upper Limb Assessment (RULA) methodology was then developed.

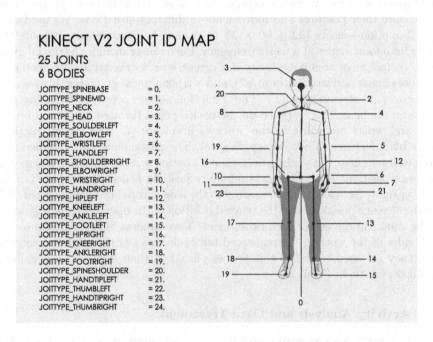

**Fig. 2.** Human body joints captured by Kinect.

Furthermore, the acquired 3D fine and coarse body motions were used to animate the avatar in the Serious Game presented in the next Chapter.

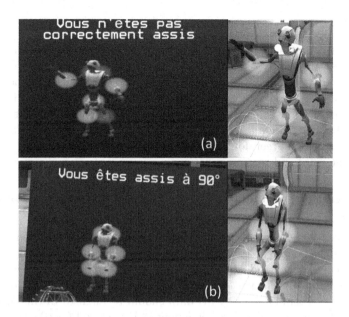

**Fig. 3.** Human posture assessment using RULA. (a) You are not correctly seated, (b) You are seated at 90°.

In many industry and work situations, operators suffer from upper body (shoulder, neck, arms, etc.) MSDs due inadequate postures and motions while executing repetitive tasks. That's why the posture and gestures assessment at the upper-body level is crucial.

The system that has been developed for the acquisition of upper-body gestures and motion is based on Microsoft Kinect 2. Kinect provides the 25 joint angles of the human body as shown in Fig. 2. Most of these angles have been used as provided by the Kinect SDK for posture assessment. Specific rule-based post-processing algorithm for shoulder joints has been implemented to resolve shoulder joint orientation ambiguity [45].

Spatio-temporal smoothing filters have been applied to the extracted silhouette in order to avoid the flickering effect [46].

## 4.2 Hand and Fingers Tracking

Fine hand and finger movements are of high interest to assess operators' gesture and posture in high-precision manipulation like in watchmaking industry. The LeapMotion device is used to acquire relevant information about hand posture and gestures: parameters like hand rotation angle, finger flexion and extension angles, computed from the LeapMotion phalanx data (Bones), are extracted.

### 4.3  Gesture Assessment with RULA

In this project, RULA [47] is used for data analysis of on-site capture data (see Subsect. 3.2), but also to assess the user's movement during the game. To do so, we developed a tool that automates RULA based on the acquired 3D posture and gesture of human bodies. For each acquired joint we implemented an assessment rule regarding the joint angle and orientation. The different assessment rules have been provided by ergonomic experts. The Fig. 3 illustrates a posture assessment based on two colors: green for safe posture and red for risky posture according to ergonomic rules and recommendations.

### 4.4  Integration of Fine and Coarse Motions for Avatar Animation

The Serious Game described in the next Chapter includes an avatar that mimics the user gestures and movements. On the one hand, the Kinect is used to capture and forward the coarse body gestures and movements to the avatar animation module. On the other hand, the LeapMotion is used to capture and forward the fine gestures and movements. To have consistencies of both types of gestures and motions, the hand and body 3D data should be aligned. In this project, we implemented a simple, yet robust alignment of Kinect and LeapMotion 3D data using geometric transformations. The Fig. 4 illustrates, through a test avatar arm, the result of this alignment.

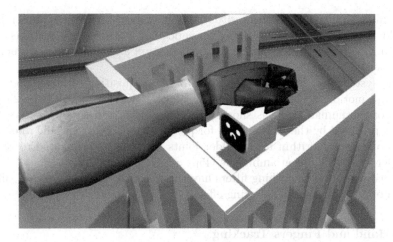

**Fig. 4.** Illustration of the hand-arm integration by combining Kinect and LeapMotion data.

## 5  Serious Game Design and Scenario

### 5.1  Scenario

To define a game concept and scenario, we had to study the output of the measures taken in the industry workshops. To stay as close as possible to real work situations, the game must replicate real life posture and gesture configuration. We had to avoid the pitfall of losing the game part by making an application which is more a gamified simulation than a game [48]. This means that the game should not represent the objects used in the workplace and that the environment has to be decontextualized. Furthermore, one of the significant challenges is the fact that the game should be scalable in order to adapt to industries handling big pieces (as in the automotive industry) and small ones (as in the watchmaking industry). It should also include the option to be standing vertically or lay horizontally on a flat surface. To sum up, these are the constraints:

- The game must induce movements close to the ones performed in the workplace;
- The game must propose an environment and activity that differ from the real work ones;
- The task must be scalable in size to fit different industries;
- The task must allow horizontal or vertical layout.

To meet these requirements, we imagined a puzzle-like game (see Figs. 1 and 5), using gears that have to be correctly aligned to adapt to different industries (gears can easily be reduced or enlarged). The user has a board with some gears already placed and empty gear spaces. He must complete the puzzle by placing gears in the right place on the board. At the end of the level, a score is displayed, informing the user of the body parts that are most at risk with MSD according to the actions he took during the session.

## 5.2   Environment

In a preliminary study on this project [49], it was found that the environment impact is important and that the environment can be changed without disturbing the user in his tasks. To allow future inclusion of these transitions in our scenario, the user was put in a spaceship (see Fig. 6). This leaves a lot of freedom with the game physics or objects apparition and disappearing. More specifically, in the environment transition, it is possible to put the user in a "holographic room" and change the holographic environment at each new level. These transitions have not been implemented yet, but the environment has already been chosen to ease future work.

## 5.3   Level Design

*Levels.* One important thing in building the levels is to balance the cognitive load with the game difficulty. If the cognitive load is too high, the user will not be able to learn the movements, as he will be too taken by the game. But if the cognitive load is too low, the user will be bored and lose motivation and engagement in the game. As it is a Serious Game, we do not want to forget the primary aim, which is MDS prevention. We give feedback to the user at each level validation to incorporate MSD into the game. He gets a global MSD score and a detailed score on the problem he encountered. If the MSD score is too low, the user has to do the puzzle again.

**Fig. 5.** Figure illustrating the application including the hardware and the game. (a) Oculus Rift Headset and sensors, (b) Leap Motion controller (head mounted), (c) Kinect V2, (d) Virtual game.

**Fig. 6.** Spaceship environment.

*Time.* The time is a classical game-play element and a normal constraint in companies, so it is natural to include it in our game. However, it must be used with caution. In fact, introducing time constraints too early in the game will only stress the user. Our primary aim is to teach him to do the things right without rushing or making harmful movements. As it is not the main objective of the game, time will impact the score in the first levels but will not prevent the user from going to the next level.

## 6   Results

### 6.1   Gear-Based Serious Game

As described in the previous chapter, the chosen game is a gear puzzle game. To avoid too high cognitive load, the different gears are color-coded. Each missing gear has its colored axle already on the board and each level contains exactly the right number of gears to complete the puzzle. The user must pick the right gear and put it on its axle. If the gear is released close enough to its intended place, it will automatically set correctly. The gear at this point cannot be picked up. Once all the gears are in place, the system begins to rotate and the user can proceed to the next level. Figure 7 describes the different phases of solving the puzzle, as done by the user in Fig. 8.

**Fig. 7.** One level of the game. (a) Starting point, (b) One gear has been placed, (c) Two gears have been placed, (d) All gears have been placed, the level is finished.

**Fig. 8.** Upper part: user in action on the left with the avatar animated on the right. Lower part: User in action with the first-person view in the corner.

## 6.2 First Users in Action

The Kinect and Leap Motion are used to animate the users' avatar and allow the wanted interactions with the environment elements (see the setup in Fig. 5). The body is tracked, represented in the game and aligned with the camera. To grab the gears, the user can use his own hands.

## 6.3 Scoring

The scoring in a serious game is important. The main scoring component is the MSD score, computed by analyzing the user's movements and postures. If the MSD score is too low, the user has to repeat the level. Time is the other score component, which allows the user to have bonus points if the levels are

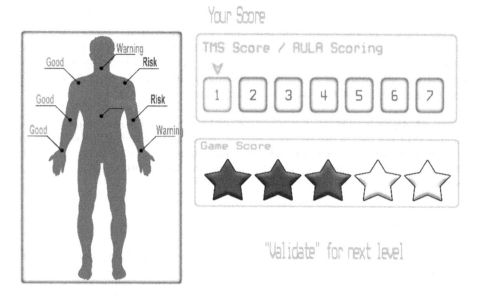

**Fig. 9.** Scoring board. On the left, the body is represented with a risk evaluation for each joint. The RULA Score is displayed on the top right and the game score, solely based on the time, on the top middle.

completed within a defined time frame. At the end of every level the user gets feedback, letting him know which articulation has been at risk during his past actions. The global RULA score is also displayed on a scale from one to seven (see Fig. 9).

## 7 Discussion

### 7.1 Conclusion

This paper has investigated how the game technologies (SG and VR) as innovative tools can provide an alternative for MSDs prevention. We hypothesize that SGs have a significant potential to increase workers' awareness in MSDs risks prevention. A data acquisition campaign was first conducted in several factories, highlighting the most problematic situations in regards to ergonomic risks. Based on these results, a SG was developed, capturing the user's real postures, analyzing them and producing feedback in the form of a MSD score. To enforce good practices, the user must have a passing score to access the next game level.

### 7.2 Perspectives

The first results of this project are promising, as the problematic movements for the target industries have been identified and the positions in-game by scenario and object placement. The next step will be to provide seated levels simulating all the positions requiring a real table and chair. So, after letting the user adjust the table and chair as he wants, we will provide him with a feedback. Transitional environments are one of the main features we are currently including in our application [49], allowing a smooth transition from a virtual, learning-adapted and calm environment to a realistic work environment.

**Acknowledgment.** This project was supported by the EU Interreg program, grant number 1812 as a part of the *Serious Game for Health at Work towards Musculoskeleta Disorders* (SG4H@W>MSD) project. The authors would like to thank Sebastien Chevriau, Maxime Larique, et Gerard Touvenot for their contribution in data collection.

# References

1. CNAMTS: Cour des comptes, Rapport public thmatique: La gestion du risque accidents du travail et risques professionnels. annuel, caisse nationale d assurance maladie des travailleurs salaris, Paris (2016)
2. Bevan, S.: Economic impact of musculoskeletal disorders (MSDs) on work in Europe. Best Pract. Res. Clin. Rheumatol. **29**(3), 356–373 (2015). https://doi.org/10.1016/j.berh.2015.08.002
3. Perruccio, A.V., Yip, C., Badley, E.M., Power, J.D.: Musculoskeletal disorders: a neglected group at public health and epidemiology meetings? Am. J. Public Health **107**(10), 1584–1585 (2017). https://doi.org/10.2105/AJPH.2017.303990
4. Rezagholi, M., Bantekas, A.: Making economic social decisions for improving occupational health a predictive cost-benefit analysis. Occup. Med. Health Aff. **03**(06) (2015). https://doi.org/10.4172/2329-6879.1000225
5. Rezagholi, M.: Differential socio-economic effects of work environmental risk factors. J. Health Med. Econ. **2**(2), 1–8 (2016)
6. Widanarko, B.: Interaction between physical and psychosocial work risk factors for low back symptoms. Ph.D. thesis (2013)
7. Karsh, B.T.: Theories of work-related musculoskeletal disorders: implications for ergonomic interventions. Theor. Issues Ergon. Sci. **7**(1), 71–88 (2006). https://doi.org/10.1080/14639220512331335160
8. Takala, E.P., Pehkonen, I., Forsman, M., Hansson, G.A., Mathiassen, S.E., Neumann, W.P., Sjøgaard, G., Veiersted, K.B., Westgaard, R.H., Winkel, J.: Systematic evaluation of observational methods assessing biomechanical exposures at work. Scand. J. Work Environ. Health **36**(1), 3–24 (2010)
9. Daniels, K., Gedikli, C., Watson, D., Semkina, A., Vaughn, O.: Job design, employment practices and well-being: a systematic review of intervention studies. Ergonomics **60**(9), 1177–1196 (2017). https://doi.org/10.1080/00140139.2017.1303085
10. Sultan-Taïeb, H., Parent-Lamarche, A., Gaillard, A., Stock, S., Nicolakakis, N., Hong, Q.N., Vezina, M., Coulibaly, Y., Vézina, N., Berthelette, D.: Economic evaluations of ergonomic interventions preventing work-related musculoskeletal disorders: a systematic review of organizational-level interventions. BMC Public Health **17**(1), 935 (2017). https://doi.org/10.1186/s12889-017-4935-y

11. Hoe, V.C., Urquhart, D.M., Kelsall, H.L., Sim, M.R.: Ergonomic design and training for preventing work-related musculoskeletal disorders of the upper limb and neck in adults. Cochrane Database Syst. Rev. (2012). https://doi.org/10.1002/14651858.CD008570.pub2

12. Rivilis, I., Van Eerd, D., Cullen, K., Cole, D.C., Irvin, E., Tyson, J., Mahood, Q.: Effectiveness of participatory ergonomic interventions on health outcomes: a systematic review. Appl. Ergon. **39**(3), 342–358 (2008). https://doi.org/10.1016/j.apergo.2007.08.006

13. van Eerd, D., Cole, D., Irvin, E., Mahood, Q., Keown, K., Theberge, N., Village, J., St. Vincent, M., Cullen, K.: Process and implementation of participatory ergonomic interventions: a systematic review. Ergonomics **53**(10), 1153–1166 (2010). https://doi.org/10.1080/00140139.2010.513452

14. Nastasia, I., Coutu, M.F., Tcaciuc, R.: Topics and trends in research on non-clinical interventions aimed at preventing prolonged work disability in workers compensated for work-related musculoskeletal disorders (WRMSDs): a systematic, comprehensive literature review. Disabil. Rehabil. **36**(22), 1841–1856 (2014). https://doi.org/10.3109/09638288.2014.882418

15. Aghilinejad, M., Kabir-Mokamelkhah, E., Labbafinejad, Y., Bahrami-Ahmadi, A., Hosseini, H.R.: The role of ergonomic training interventions on decreasing neck and shoulders pain among workers of an Iranian automobile factory: a randomized trial study. Med. J. Islamic Repub. Iran **29**, 190 (2015)

16. Driessen, M.T., Proper, K.I., van Tulder, M.W., Anema, J.R., Bongers, P.M., van der Beek, A.J.: The effectiveness of physical and organisational ergonomic interventions on low back pain and neck pain: a systematic review. Occup. Environ. Med. **67**(4), 277–285 (2010). https://doi.org/10.1136/oem.2009.047548

17. Gupta, N., Wåhlin-Jacobsen, C.D., Abildgaard, J.S., Henriksen, L.N., Nielsen, K., Holtermann, A.: Effectiveness of a participatory physical and psychosocial intervention to balance the demands and resources of industrial workers. Scand. J. Work Environ. Health **44**(1), 58–68 (2018). https://doi.org/10.5271/sjweh.3689

18. Driessen, M.T., Proper, K.I., Anema, J.R., Knol, D.L., Bongers, P.M., van der Beek, A.J.: Participatory ergonomics to reduce exposure to psychosocial and physical risk factors for low back pain and neck pain: results of a cluster randomised controlled trial. Occup. Environ. Med. **68**(9), 674–681 (2011). https://doi.org/10.1136/oem.2010.056739

19. Hogan, D.A.M., Greiner, B.A., O'Sullivan, L.: The effect of manual handling training on achieving training transfer, employee's behaviour change and subsequent reduction of work-related musculoskeletal disorders: a systematic review. Ergonomics **57**(1), 93–107 (2014). https://doi.org/10.1080/00140139.2013.862307

20. Yu, W., Yu, I.T.S., Wang, X., Li, Z., Wan, S., Qiu, H., Lin, H., Xie, S., Sun, T.: Effectiveness of participatory training for prevention of musculoskeletal disorders: a randomized controlled trial. Int. Arch. Occup. Environ. Health **86**(4), 431–440 (2013). https://doi.org/10.1007/s00420-012-0775-3

21. Mehrparvar, A.H., Heydari, M., Mirmohammadi, S.J., Mostaghaci, M., Davari, M.H., Taheri, M.: Ergonomic intervention, workplace exercises and musculoskeletal complaints: a comparative study. Med. J. Islamic Repub. Iran **28**, 69 (2014)

22. Shuai, J., Yue, P., Li, L., Liu, F., Wang, S.: Assessing the effects of an educational program for the prevention of work-related musculoskeletal disorders among school teachers. BMC Public Health **14**, 1211 (2014). https://doi.org/10.1186/1471-2458-14-1211

23. Pront, L., Mller, A., Koschade, A., Hutton, A.: Gaming in nursing education: a literature review. Nurs. Educ. Perspect. **39**(1), 23 (2018). https://doi.org/10.1097/01.NEP.0000000000000251

24. Lu, A.S., Kharrazi, H.: A state-of-the-art systematic content analysis of games for health. Games Health J. **7**(1), 1–15 (2018). https://doi.org/10.1089/g4h.2017.0095

25. Li, X., Yi, W., Chi, H.L., Wang, X., Chan, A.P.C.: A critical review of virtual and augmented reality (VR/AR) applications in construction safety. Autom. Constr. **86**, 150–162 (2018). https://doi.org/10.1016/j.autcon.2017.11.003

26. Campbell, M., Fitzpatrick, R., Haines, A., Kinmonth, A.L., Sandercock, P., Spiegelhalter, D., Tyrer, P.: Framework for design and evaluation of complex interventions to improve health. BMJ Br. Med. J. **321**(7262), 694–696 (2000)

27. Petit, A., Ha, C., Bodin, J., Rigouin, P., Descatha, A., Brunet, R., Goldberg, M., Roquelaure, Y.: Risk factors for carpal tunnel syndrome related to the work organization: a prospective surveillance study in a large working population. Appl. Ergon. **47**, 1–10 (2015)

28. McDermott, H., Haslam, C., Clemes, S., Williams, C., Haslam, R.: Investigation of manual handling training practices in organisations and beliefs regarding effectiveness. Int. J. Ind. Ergon. **42**(2), 206–211 (2012). https://doi.org/10.1016/j.ergon.2012.01.003

29. Clemes, S.A., Haslam, C.O., Haslam, R.A.: What constitutes effective manual handling training? Syst. Rev. Occup. Med. **60**(2), 101–107 (2010). https://doi.org/10.1093/occmed/kqp127

30. Collado-Mateo, D., Merellano-Navarro, E., Olivares, P.R., García-Rubio, J., Gusi, N.: Effect of exergames on musculoskeletal pain: a systematic review and meta-analysis. Scand. J. Med. Sci. Sports, 1–12 (2017). https://doi.org/10.1111/sms.12899

31. Idriss, M., Tannous, H., Istrate, D., Perrochon, A., Salle, J.Y., Ho Ba Tho, M.C., Dao, T.T.: Rehabilitation-oriented serious game development and evaluation guidelines for musculoskeletal disorders. JMIR Serious Games **5**(3), e14 (2017). https://doi.org/10.2196/games.7284

32. Jansen-Kosterink, S.M., Huis in't Veld, R.M., Schönauer, C., Kaufmann, H., Hermens, H.J., Vollenbroek-Hutten, M.M.: A serious exergame for patients suffering from chronic musculoskeletal back and neck pain: a pilot study. Games Health J. **2**(5), 299–307 (2013). https://doi.org/10.1089/g4h.2013.0043

33. Deutsch, J.E.: Virtual reality and gaming systems to improve walking and mobility for people with musculoskeletal and neuromuscular conditions. Stud. Health Technol. Inform. **145**(2009), 84–93 (2009). https://doi.org/10.3233/978-1-60750-018-6-84

34. Daesign: Serious Game Daesign: "Halte aux TMS" (FR) (2013). https://www.youtube.com/watch?v=oLlgg18MycM, https://www.daesign.com/

35. Rodrigues, M.A.F., Macedo, D.V., Pontes, H.P., Serpa, Y.R., Serpa, Y.R.: A serious game to improve posture and spinal health while having fun. In: 2016 IEEE International Conference on Serious Games and Applications for Health (SeGAH), pp. 1–8. IEEE, May 2016. https://doi.org/10.1109/SeGAH.2016.7586260

36. Rodrigues, M.A.F., Serpa, Y.R., Macedo, D.V., Sousa, E.S.: A serious game to practice stretches and exercises for a correct and healthy posture. Entertain. Comput. (2017). https://doi.org/10.1016/j.entcom.2017.11.002

37. Freitas, Hélder, Soares, Filomena, Carvalho, Vítor, Matos, Demetrio: Serious games development as a tool to prevent repetitive strain injuries in hands: first steps. In: Auer, Michael E., Guralnick, David, Simonics, Istvan (eds.) ICL 2017. AISC, vol. 715, pp. 954–964. Springer, Cham (2018). https://doi.org/10.1007/978-3-319-73210-7_108

38. Bartolome, N.A., Zorrilla, A.M., Zapirain, B.G.: Can game-based therapies be trusted? Is game-based education effective? A systematic review of the Serious Games for health and education. In: 2011 16th International Conference on Computer Games (CGAMES), pp. 275–282. IEEE, July 2011. https://doi.org/10.1109/CGAMES.2011.6000353

39. Sportillo, D., Avveduto, G., Tecchia, F., Carrozzino, M.: Training in VR: a preliminary study on learning assembly/disassembly sequences. In: De Paolis, L.T., Mongelli, A. (eds.) AVR 2015. LNCS, vol. 9254, pp. 332–343. Springer, Cham (2015). https://doi.org/10.1007/978-3-319-22888-4_24

40. Gobron, S.C., Zannini, N., Wenk, N., Schmitt, C., Charrotton, Y., Fauquex, A., Lauria, M., Degache, F., Frischknecht, R.: Serious games for rehabilitation using head-mounted display and haptic devices. In: De Paolis, L.T., Mongelli, A. (eds.) AVR 2015. LNCS, vol. 9254, pp. 199–219. Springer, Cham (2015). https://doi.org/10.1007/978-3-319-22888-4_15

41. Saenz-de Urturi, Z., Garcia-Zapirain Soto, B.: Kinect-based virtual game for the elderly that detects incorrect body postures in real time. Sensors 16(5), 704 (2016). https://doi.org/10.3390/s16050704

42. Vignais, N., Bernard, F., Touvenot, G., Sagot, J.C.: Physical risk factors identification based on body sensor network combined to videotaping. Appl. Ergon. 65, 410–417 (2017). https://doi.org/10.1016/j.apergo.2017.05.003

43. Zare, M., Malinge-Oudenot, A., Hglund, R., Biau, S., Roquelaure, Y.: Evaluation of ergonomic physical risk factors in a truck manufacturing plant: case study in SCANIA Production Angers. Ind. Health 54(2), 163–176 (2016)

44. McAtamney, L., Nigel Corlett, E.: RULA: a survey method for the investigation of work-related upper limb disorders. Appl. Ergon. 24(2), 91–99 (1993). https://doi.org/10.1016/0003-6870(93)90080-S

45. Cicirelli, G., Attolico, C., Guaragnella, C., D'Orazio, T.: A kinect-based gesture recognition approach for a natural human robot interface. Int. J. Adv. Robot. Syst. 12(3), 22 (2015). https://doi.org/10.5772/59974

46. Pirovano, M., Ren, C.Y., Frosio, I., Lanzi, P.L., Prisacariu, V., Murray, D.W., Borghese, N.A.: Robust silhouette extraction from kinect data. In: Petrosino, A. (ed.) ICIAP 2013. LNCS, vol. 8156, pp. 642–651. Springer, Heidelberg (2013). https://doi.org/10.1007/978-3-642-41181-6_65

47. Ansari, N.A., Sheikh, M.J.: Evaluation of work posture by RULA and REBA: a case study. IOSR J. Mech. Civ. Eng. (IOSR-JMCE) 11, 18–23 (2014)

48. Wenk, N., Gobron, S.: Reinforcing the difference between simulation, gamification, and serious game. In: Proceedings of the Gamification & Serious Game Symposium 2017 (GSGS 2017), pp. 1–3. HE-Arc / HES-SO Press, Neuchatel, 1 July 2017

49. Sisto, M., Wenk, N., Ouerhani, N., Gobron, S.: A Study of Transitional Virtual Environments. In: De Paolis, L.T., Bourdot, P., Mongelli, A. (eds.) AVR 2017. LNCS, vol. 10324, pp. 35–49. Springer, Cham (2017). https://doi.org/10.1007/978-3-319-60922-5_3

# Proposal for Muscle Rehabilitation of Lower Limbs Using an Interactive Virtual System Controlled Through Gestures

Edwin Pruna[✉], Gabriel Corrales, Catherine Gálvez, Ivón Escobar,
and Luis Mena

Universidad de las Fuerzas Armadas ESPE, Sangolquí, Ecuador
{eppruna,lgcorrales,clgalvez,ipescobar,
lemena}@espe.edu.ec

**Abstract.** This work presents the development of an interactive virtual rehabilitation system as an assistant tool to help in the rehabilitation process of lower
limbs muscles, specifically focused on children from seven years and older who
suffer sicknesses that limit the normal movement of the body. The system is
mainly based in algorithms that recognize gestures of the user captured through
the Microsoft Kinect 2.0. Furthermore, the experimental results are presented
and discussed since the point of view of the usability and the advantages that the
proposed system achieves.

**Keywords:** Virtual interface · Kinect 2.0 · Gestual control · Unity 3D

## 1 Introduction

The considerable number of cases of patients with brain injuries that lead to problems
of the musculoskeletal system shows that rehabilitation fulfills a necessary and
important function, since the lack of movement induces a high risk of contracting
metabolic syndromes and chronic diseases that decline the quality of life [1–6].
A neurorehabilitation entails exploiting motor learning by involving the patient in an
intervention that generates favorable conditions to stimulate the modification of the
residual neural networks of the brain [3, 7, 8]; therapeutic exercise techniques have
been shown to correct deterioration and improve the functions of the musculoskeletal
system in a variety of disease states. Some exercises performed during a rehabilitation
process are based on natural movements of joints that are intended to strengthen or
maintain the existing strength of specific muscles; this may delay the progression of
weakness or proactively prevent painful musculoskeletal syndromes associated with
lack of mobility and atrophy due to disuse [2, 6, 9, 10].

Studies indicate that traditional physical therapy processes, which include
strengthening exercises, have been successful in cases of brain damage, however,
fundamental problems have been identified that may prevent achieving the goal of
rehabilitation. The most notorious ones are related to the fact that they do not consider
the individual differences in motor and cognitive capacity that can influence differently
the reaction of each patient, as well as being a complex and long-term process with

L. T. De Paolis and P. Bourdot (Eds.): AVR 2018, LNCS 10851, pp. 60–77, 2018.
https://doi.org/10.1007/978-3-319-95282-6_5

repetitive exercises [6–9, 11, 12]. As a consequence, psychological problems may arise in the patient that diminish his motivation and interest in performing the exercises, this becomes even more problematic when dealing with children, who generally lack enthusiasm in participating in the tedious process of rehabilitation. Because of this inconvenience, it becomes necessary to implement alternative solutions that motivate patients to actively perform the exercises [8, 12–15].

In recent years there has been a growth in research and development of technological systems that aim to help the patient in the rehabilitation process; these include complex and expensive systems such as the implementation of robotic systems, as well as low-cost systems such as the development of motion-based games through motion sensor technology that stimulate the patient to participate in the exercises intentionally caused by the games. Systems with virtual environments can be used to optimize motor learning because it is possible to explicitly involve motivation and learning mechanisms based on sensory feedback [4, 7, 8, 10, 11, 13, 14, 16–18]. Added to this is the way in which users interact with the game with the integration of non-invasive and low-cost devices such as the Microsoft Kinect, which captures skeletal movement without compromising the freedom of limb movement [3, 5, 6, 15, 19–21]. Several applications are presented using this device, *e.g.*, related to evaluation and postural control, identification of injuries, improving mobility, etc. Many of these applications are complemented by methods of classification and recognition of gestures or body postures for the fulfillment of their purposes, achieving satisfactory results [1, 3, 12, 14, 17, 21, 22].

In this context, this paper presents the development of a virtual assistance system in the rehabilitation process focused on the strengthening of lower extremities, which is not intended to replace the work and supervision of the expert professional. This low-cost system uses the Microsoft Kinect 2.0 as a unique and main input device, which digitally captures in real time the movements of the user while he exercises the muscles of his lower limbs with an exercise machine approved by the expert. The digital data of the movements of the body of the user are processed by the algorithms implemented so that the virtual interface recognizes the exercises and executes graphic animation subroutines. In the implementation of the virtual interface are considered the computer-aided design, CAD, and graphics engines as a complement of Unity software that allow to obtain graphics and animations of high quality in 3D virtual games. Each of the 3D virtual games developed have three levels of complexity. These characteristics make the use of the application attractive and intuitive, so the user will perceive that he performs an activity that emulates a real situation, which requires and demands the concentration of his mind and the movement of his extremities to be completed successfully. Additionally, the system is complemented with subroutines for recording relevant data in a local server, which allow the rehabilitator to analyze the progress of the therapies. Figure 1 indicates the components and functionality of the proposed system.

The work is organized in IV Sections including the Introduction. Section 2 presents the development of the system based on the use of Unity and the Microsoft Kinect 2.0 SDK to create the intuitive virtual interface and the algorithms, respectively. The experimental results and discussion that validate the implementation, functionality and the achieves of the proposal system are presented in Sect. 3. Finally, the conclusions are found in Sect. 4.

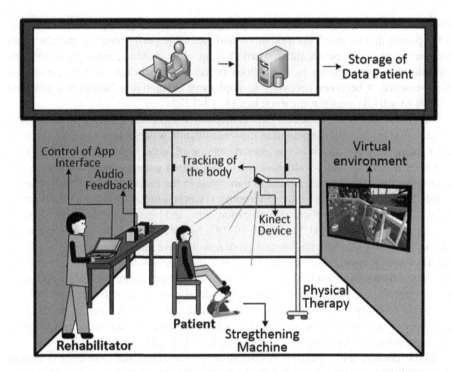

**Fig. 1.** General scheme of the proposed virtual system that uses the Microsoft Kinect device.

## 2 Development of the Virtual Rehabilitation System

### 2.1 Virtual System Operation

The system is designed to be used by one user at a time. The Kinect 2.0 captures the movements of the user while exercising using an exercise machine. The digital data corresponding to the movements of the user are used in an algorithm that recognizes when an exercise has been properly performed. The recognition of exercises is used to execute movement animations of 3D graphics in a virtual interface developed and programmed in the Unity software. In this way, virtual applications are created that monitor and stimulate the patient to properly perform rehabilitation activities, while capturing their attention with game objectives and positive reinforcement.

In Fig. 2, the flow diagram of the general operation of the implemented application is indicated. The system is structured mainly in the functions of the routines programmed in C# language in the Unity software, where a virtual interface is developed, which is the stage of the system that users perceive and interact with. The rehabilitation user intervenes, who defines the parameters that govern the difficulty and the objectives of the virtual game, and the patient user, who performs his rehabilitation session through the challenges required by the virtual game.

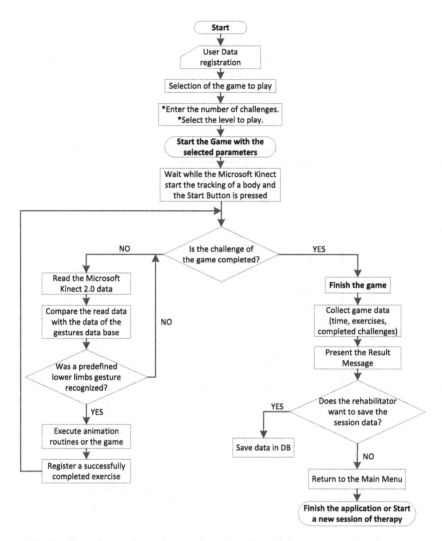

**Fig. 2.** General operation scheme of the algorithm of the proposed virtual system.

The operation of the system is fundamentally based on the subroutine of recognition of movements of the body of the user. The Microsoft Kinect 2.0 device, which acts as a single input device, acquires the data of the 25 points of the body that it is able to identify, these data are processed as quaternions values that define the rotation of each point in a three-dimensional space. The position and position variations of these quaternions are compared with data from a predefined pattern gesture, which are found in a created gesture database that is accessed through the Microsoft Kinect 2.0 SDK. The rest of the subroutines correspond to animations, data logging, game administration, menus, 3D object collision detectors, among others.

In Unity, a programming based on classes and objects is handled, which is why the so-called Game Objects are created, which are associated with scripts in C# that control and define the operation of the application. Several Game Objects depend on the data and the operation of others, which resembles a parallel execution. In a Unity project you will also find software packages necessary for the compilation of the application. A more specific outline of the elements that operate in Unity is shown in Fig. 3.

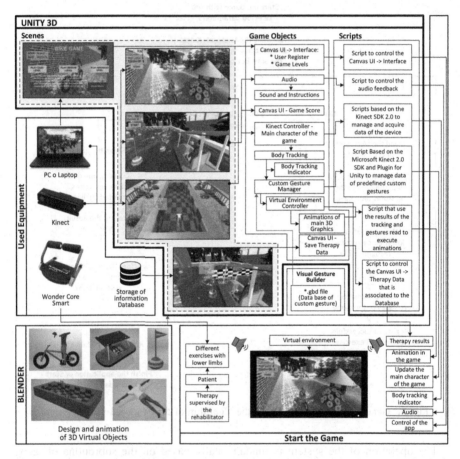

**Fig. 3.** Specific diagram of the hardware and software operation in the virtual system developed in Unity.

The acquisition of data from the Microsoft Kinect input device occurs through the Body Tracking object, this object is associated with Unity-specific Kinect Plugins that allow the management of the functions associated with the official Microsoft Kinect SDK. In addition, the Body Tracking object is directly related to the animations control scripts of the 3D characters that operate according to the captured movements of the user.

The main object, Custom Gesture Manager, is responsible for accessing the database of gestures, processing the comparison and providing the results of whether a predefined gesture has been identified (built in the Visual Gesture Builder software) to the other objects that depend on that result to execute their routines. The database of gestures corresponds to a *.gbd file that must be stored in the Unity project, specifically in a folder called *StreamingAssets*. It is also necessary to add the Kinect *VisualGestureBuilder* Plugin of Unity in the project for the compilation of the codes.

The objects that contain their respective scripts that control the animations have been modeled with the Blender software, these 3D objects, like the avatars, are characterized mainly by having a structure or skeleton that allows the individual rotation of their joints. According to the gesture recognition phase, actions such as the rotation and translation of 3D objects in three-dimensional space, the appearance of sounds, or executions of animation frames configured in the Blender software are produced.

The interaction between the application and the user is also produced by the objects of type Canvas that write on the screen data and information messages and motivation, as well as read instructions and input data and instructions through buttons and text boxes.

By last, an object is oriented only to the execution of scripts that manage the insertion of data, generated in the game, creating a communication channel with a script *.php, which runs on a local server (managed and created by XAMPP software) and directly controls a MySQL database from the same local server. The fields of the database and the scores in the games have been implemented based on the analysis of which data are useful for recording the progress of the patient in each rehabilitation session. These correspond to the number of correct exercises accounted for, the times in which the challenges have been completed, the number of correct and incorrect decisions as appropriate, date and time of the session; as well as patient data, name and surname, identity card, age and pathology presented.

## 2.2   Gestural Recognition Through Microsoft Kinect 2.0

Each implemented virtual game is based on a specific exercise, so that the application interprets these exercises as Boolean commands in a software subroutine, it is necessary to decompose the exercise into different movements that will be interpreted as a set of gestures reproduced in an orderly and periodic way. In this work, machine learning has been implemented through the use of Microsoft Visual Gesture Builder software, VGB, where it is necessary to load pre-recorded files of the gestures to be recognized.

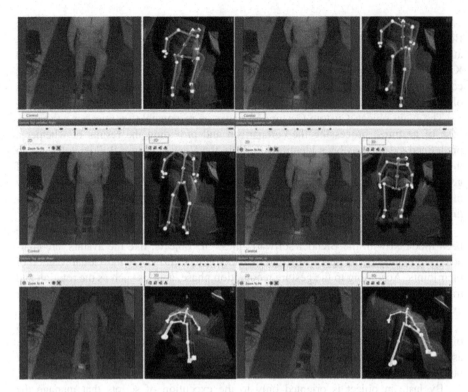

**Fig. 4.** Utilization of the Microsoft VGB software to build the gestures to be acknowledged by the games.

The Fig. 4 indicates a sequence of images of the learning process in the VGB software of the three exercises considered in this work: movement of the legs alternately as a pedaling while sitting (left pedaling and right pedaling), in a similar position but pedaling with the legs together (gestures legs up and legs together below) and in a lying position on the back performing an alternate movement of the legs similar to pedaling (left leg down and right leg down).

Next, a portion of the code that is executed in an object in the application made in Unity is indicated to access the database (*.gbd), where the information of each gesture is stored. When accessing the database of gestures, a frame captured by Kinect 2.0 is entered, which contains data on the skeletal movement of the user, so that the comparison with the data of each pre-established gesture is executed.

```
----------------------------------------------------------------
if (!_kinect.IsOpen){
  _kinect.Open();
}
_gestureFrameSource=VisualGestureBuilderFrameSource.Cre-
ate(_kinect, 0);
_gestureFrameReader=_gestureFrameSource.OpenReader();
if (_gestureFrameReader != null){
  _gestureFrameReader.IsPaused=true;

  _gestureFrameReader.FrameArrived += _ges-
  tureFrameReader_FrameArrived;
}
string path= Path.Combine(Application.streamingAs-
setsPath,"bote_pedal.gbd");
_gestureDatabase=VisualGestureBuilderDatabase.Cre-
ate(path);
IList<Gesture>gesturesList= _gestureDatabase.Availa-
bleGestures;
for (int g=0; g < gesturesList.Count; g++){
  Gesture gesture=gesturesList[g];
  _gestureFrameSource.AddGesture(gesture);
}
----------------------------------------------------------------
```

The next portion of the code that is presented corresponds to the access to the result of the comparison that has occurred. The result is presented with a floating confidence value between 0 and 1. It is necessary to extract the confidence value of each one of the gestures that form an exercise, in this way it can be identified which of them has happened or has not happened to later execute the corresponding animations and other subroutines of the application.

```
----------------------------------------------------------------
IDictionary<Gesture,DiscreteGestureResult>discreteResults
=frame.DiscreteGestureResults;
if (discreteResults != null){
  foreach (Gesture in _gestureFrameSource.Gestures){
    DiscreteGestureResult result=null;
    discreteResults.TryGetValue(gesture, out result);
    if (gesture.Name == "pedal_down"){
      conf_pedalear_down=result.Confidence;
    }
    if (gesture.Name == "pedal_up"){
      conf_pedalear_up=result.Confidence;
    }
  }
}
----------------------------------------------------------------
```

## 2.3  Virtual Interface Functionalities

The virtual environments have been designed with children's content, *i.e.*, with colorful, eye-catching and animated 3D graphics, so that the games promote concentration in the virtual activity that the three-dimensional characters are performing, trying to make the experience of performing the exercises entertaining. Each virtual game has different objectives; challenges; animations; indicators of scores, errors and time; informative and stimulating messages; sounds controlled by the corresponding algorithms of the application.

The application also has intuitive user menus, where you can define parameters such as the desired level of the game and/or change the number of repetitions of exercises as appropriate; so too with Canvas that contain buttons that command the data record of the game session in the database that operates with the XAMPP software.

In the Fig. 5 the corresponding environment is indicated for the game that is designed for the user to relate his presence to that of an avatar that goes on a bicycle, as the avatar pedals an advance of the bicycle towards the front takes place. Animation scripts validate if the exercise has been completed and is being done correctly, *i.e.*, if it is pedaled alternately, so that if the exercises are done improperly the bicycle does not advance and even slows down when a new correct exercise reading has not been recorded.

**Fig. 5.** Virtual environment of the game 1 (bike).

In the second virtual game, indicated in Fig. 6, we have included objects, textures and animations that give the effect of water movement in an artificial lagoon on which a pedal boat sails. The animations that cause the avatar to push and contract the pedals are related to those produced by the advance of the boat towards the front and the effect of the navigation movement. In the same way the exercises are validated through the reading of gestures, so that the braking animations of the boat are produced when the correct execution of the exercise is not identified.

**Fig. 6.** Virtual environment of the game 2 (pedal boat).

Finally, the swimmer's game consists of an avatar that is in a pool which reproduces animations of movement of his limbs imitating the action of swimming on his back. The effects of movement and animation are based on the method applied in the two games described above. The environment developed in Unity of the virtual game of the swimmer is indicated in Fig. 7.

**Fig. 7.** Virtual environment of the game 2 (swimmer).

In all the games, the main objects (bicycle-avatar, boat-avatar, swimmer avatar) are moved by defined routes within the virtual environment. The control of movement from one point to another is done through the identification of collisions of the main characters with invisible objects that are placed at strategic points of the three-dimensional environment.

## 3 Results and Discussion

The first results of the project presented in this section are divided in three aspects, the first one is related to the experimentation of the proposed virtual system, *i.e.*, it is shown the software routines functioning of the virtual application. Secondly, the results of a test applied to the users who participated in the test of the proposed system are presented and analyzed. Finally, it is realized an analysis of the exercises that the proposed system motivates to the user to do, and the benefits that these exercises represent in a rehabilitation process.

### 3.1 Experimentation of the Virtual Rehabilitation System

For the execution of the proposed system is used a computer with the following features: Intel core i7-7500 2.9 GHz of seventh generation, 16 GB of RAM, a Graphic Card Intel HD 620, Windows 10 Home operative system of 64 bits. The implemented algorithms and animations of the application run satisfactorily, however, the response of the execution can be improved with a computer with advanced features, specially related to the graphic card.

The user is located in front of the Microsoft Kinect 2.0 positioning to perform an exercise with the Woder Core Smart machine. At the beginning it may be necessary to wait a while until the Kinect device recognizes the body shape of the user and tracking occurs, an indicator of this action will appear on the screen, and at that time the game can be executed by pressing a start button. The rehabilitator will be guiding the patient at all times, and he will define the repetitions, times, challenges and/or levels of play using the interactive and intuitive menu that is part of the application. The menu also allows you to select one of the three virtual games and their corresponding levels that are presented in this experiment.

The first virtual game contains an environment of a park with a cycling track, an avatar is on a bicycle, as the user performs the exercise of pedaling (alternating left and right legs) the animations and the progress of the bicycle until a defined route is fulfilled; the application measures time and counts the exercises performed by each lower limb. The sequences of images of the operation of virtual game 1 are presented in Fig. 8.

The second virtual game consists of driving a pedal boat. There is a virtual environment of an artificial lagoon in a park; the move of the boat occurs when the user performs the exercise of stretching and contracting both legs at the same time using the exercise machine, as shown in Fig. 9. The application identifies and records the number of exercises performed correctly and the time it takes for a complete tour.

**Fig. 8.** Images sequence of the game 1 functioning.

The third virtual game contains an avatar that must swim backwards and meet a certain number of laps in the pool. The virtual environment is designed so that the user perceives in a visual and sound way a pool surrounded by nature. The exercises that the user performs with the exercise machine resemble the movements performed by the legs during swimming. When performing the exercise correctly, alternating the two legs, the animation that allows you to advance to the virtual avatar is produced, as shown by the sequences of images in Fig. 10. The application identifies and records the number of exercises performed by each leg in a way correct, the number of objectives achieved (laps in the pool) and the time in which this objective is completed.

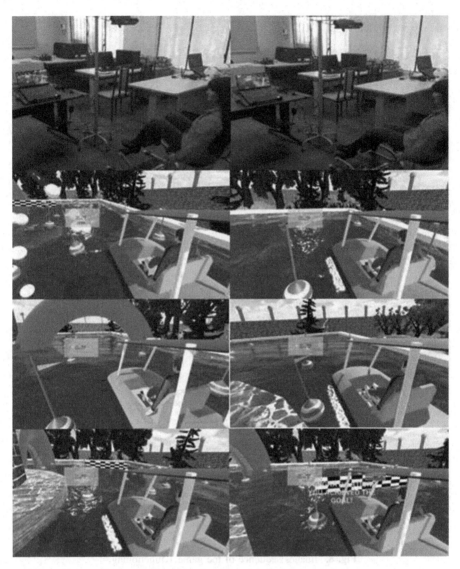

**Fig. 9.** Images sequence of the game 2 functioning.

## 3.2   Usability of the Virtual Rehabilitation System

The weighting of the usability of the system has been obtained from a survey of users, which correspond to five children aged between seven and eleven years (the results of each question are presented in Table 1). The questions have been formulated according to a child's level of comprehension, *i.e.*, simple, concrete and easy to understand questions that only have the option to choose one of the five answers (bad, regular, acceptable, good, excellent). Specifically, the orientation of the survey is centered on three relevant aspects: *(i)* The characteristics and operation of the application, which

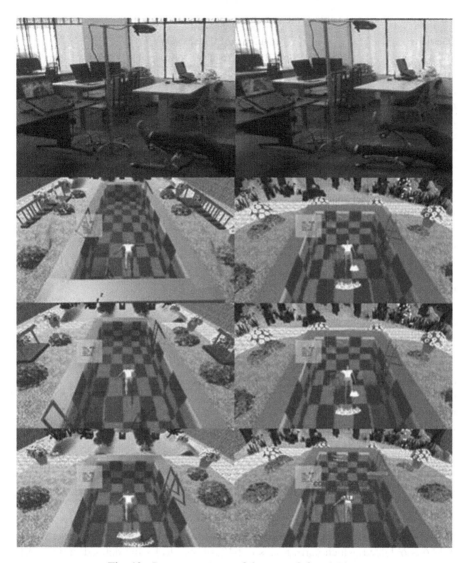

**Fig. 10.** Images sequence of the game 3 functioning.

refers to whether environments, animations, 3D graphics, sounds, menus and indicator messages were considered intuitive, pleasant and did not generate annoyance. *(ii)* The level of concentration and attention that the application captures, *i.e.*, if the challenges and environments generate some level of immersion that focuses the great part of the attention of the user on the video game while exercising. *(iii)* The opinion of the user regarding the utility and the benefits that the proposed system can provide.

Each question has a maximum score of 4 points (excellent) and a minimum of 0 points (bad), so that the maximum weight of the survey is given over 40 points. With

**Table 1.** Result of the applied usability test.

| Questions | Number of the answers | | | | |
|---|---|---|---|---|---|
| | Bad | Regular | Acceptable | Good | Excellent |
| Q1. Did you understand the objective of the games easily? | – | – | 1 | 1 | 3 |
| Q2. Were the message of the interface clear to understand for you? | – | – | – | 1 | 4 |
| Q3. Did you like the 3D graphics and the environments of the interfaces? | – | – | – | 1 | 4 |
| Q4. How did you feel your view with the colors of the interface? | – | – | – | 1 | 4 |
| Q5. Did you think the games capture your attention? | – | – | – | – | 5 |
| Q6. Did you think the interface makes feel you like you were inside the game? | – | – | 2 | 2 | 1 |
| Q7. Do you think the application motivates you to do the exercises correctly? | – | – | – | – | 5 |
| Q8. Did you think that you were only playing a video game and not doing therapy exercises? | – | – | – | – | 5 |
| Q9. Do you think this method of rehabilitation is more attractive and fun than the traditional methods that you have experimented? | – | – | – | – | 5 |
| Q10. Do you think the application will help you in the rehabilitation process? | – | – | – | – | 5 |

the five surveys carried out, as a result of the usability of the system, an average weight of 37.6 is obtained, which corresponds to 94% of the ideal score defined in this work.

The score reflects the acceptance of the usability of the system by the users who participated in the experiment; in addition, the results of the survey indicate that the participants agree that the methods of rehabilitation, presented in this work, can positively stimulate the correct performance of rehabilitation activities by promoting entertainment and eliminating the monotony of traditional methods. In contrast, minimum indices have been obtained that the aspect to be improved corresponds to increasing the level of immersion of the user in the virtual environment, provided that the objective is to obtain a higher level of capture of the concentration of the user in the game, which it does not allow the patient to think that he is doing a therapy session.

### 3.3    Discussion of the Rehabilitation Benefits Achieved

The most important aspect to highlight corresponds to the impact of the positive reinforcement generated by the proposed system in the patient, since it is evident, through the results of the survey, that rehabilitation therapies can be perceived as a video game that avoids monotony and the consequences of tiredness that conventional methodologies can generate, which could lead to psychological problems. In addition, in the experiment performed that tests the operation of the proposed system, users were consulted about the areas of their extremities where they felt the physical effort. Based on this evaluation, the muscles involved in the movements of the limbs that stimulate the virtual games implemented were analyzed.

In the game of the bicycle (Fig. 8) the muscles of the thigh are exercised in the zones corresponding to the sartorius, long adductor, rectus femur, and the greatest effort is concentrated in the femoral quadriceps; while the involved muscles of the leg are biceps femoris, external twin, internal twin, sinew of the twins, peroneus longus, and the ligament of the patella is included. In the pedal boat game (Fig. 9) the same muscles described above are involved, however, the effort is intensified by exercising both legs at the same time. Finally, in the swimmer's game (Fig. 10) the thigh muscles corresponding to the femur square, adductor minimums, adductor magnus are exercised, and the greatest intensity is felt in the femoral biceps.

In addition to the muscles that benefit from the exercises that the proposed system induces in the experimentation, it is important to consider that there is no probability of generating repercussions in the joints involved in the movement of the exercise, because they do not suffer impact and must not support excessive weights.

## 4    Conclusions

This work presents the implementation of a non-invasive system based on a virtual application, which is programmed to assist and stimulate the patient in rehabilitation therapies that contemplate the muscular strengthening of upper and lower extremities. In the experimentation the correct accomplishment of the exercises that stimulate the effort of groups of muscles of thighs and legs has been promoted. The virtual application, developed in the Unity software, contains games with environments and intuitive, high-quality three-dimensional graphics that are animated to emulate a real activity with challenging objectives, this allows capturing the patient's attention and motivating them to correctly carry out rehabilitation activities, according to the affirmation of the result of the usability test applied to 5 users, which reached an acceptability of 94%. The use of the Microsoft Kinect device to digitally capture the movement of the body of the user, and the algorithms implemented based on machine learning, which is enhanced by Microsoft Visual Gesture Builder software, has the advantage of immediately implementing different exercises, decomposing them as different gestures of the body to be recognized in the corresponding subroutines. As future work, adding animations, subroutines and devices that increase the level of immersion of the application that the user perceives is proposed.

**Acknowledgements.** We thank the "Universidad de las Fuerzas Armadas ESPE" for financing the investigation project number 2016-PIC-0017.

# References

1. Hoang, T.C., Dang, H.T., Nguyen, V.D.: Kinect-based virtual training system for rehabilitation. In: Proceedings of the International Conference on IEEE System Science and Engineering (ICSSE), pp. 53–56 (2017)
2. Abresch, R.T., Carter, G.T., Han, J.J., McDonald, C.M.: Exercise in neuromuscular diseases. Phys. Med. Rehabil. Clin. **23**(03), 653–673 (2012)
3. Liao, W.W., McCombe Waller, S., Whitall, J.: Kinect-based individualized upper extremity rehabilitation is effective and feasible for individuals with stroke using a transition from clinic to home protocol. Cogent Med. 1428038 (2018) (just-accepted)
4. Bai, J., Song, A., Xu, B., Nie, J., Li, H.: A novel human-robot cooperative method for upper extremity rehabilitation. Int. J. Soc. Robot. **9**(2), 265–275 (2017)
5. Simonsen, D., Popovic, M.B., Spaich, E.G., Andersen, O.K.: Design and test of a Microsoft Kinect-based system for delivering adaptive visual feedback to stroke patients during training of upper limb movement. Med. Biol. Eng. Comput. **55**(11), 1927–1935 (2017)
6. Albiol-Pérez, S., Gómez, J.A.G., Olmo, E., Soler, A.M.: A virtual fine rehabilitation system for children with cerebral palsy: assesment of the usability of a low-cost system. In: Rocha, Á., Correia, A.M., Adeli, H., Reis, L.P., Costanzo, S. (eds.) WorldCIST 2017. AISC, vol. 570, pp. 619–627. Springer, Cham (2017). https://doi.org/10.1007/978-3-319-56538-5_63
7. Bejarano, N.C., Maggioni, S., De Rijcke, L., Cifuentes, C.A., Reinkensmeyer, D.J.: Robot-assisted rehabilitation therapy: recovery mechanisms and their implications for machine design. In: Pons, J., Raya, R., González, J. (eds.) Emerging Therapies in Neurorehabilitation II. Biosystems and Biorobotics, vol. 10, pp. 197–223. Springer, Cham (2016). https://doi.org/10.1007/978-3-319-24901-8_8
8. Levin, M.F., Weiss, P.L., Keshner, E.A.: Emergence of virtual reality as a tool for upper limb rehabilitation: incorporation of motor control and motor learning principles. Phys. Ther. **95**(03), 415–425 (2015)
9. Valdebenito, V.R., Ruiz, R.D.: Relevant aspects in the rehabilitation of children with neuromuscular diseases. Revista Médica Clínica Las Condes **25**(02), 295–305 (2014)
10. Zhu, M.H., Yang, C.J., Yang, W., Bi, Q.: A kinect-based motion capture method for assessment of lower extremity exoskeleton. In: Yang, C., Virk, G., Yang, H. (eds.) Wearable Sensors and Robots. LNEE, vol. 399, pp. 481–494. Springer, Singapore (2017). https://doi.org/10.1007/978-981-10-2404-7_37
11. Tannous, H., Istrate, D., Tho, M.H.B., Dao, T.T.: Serious game and functional rehabilitation for the lower limbs. Eur. Res. Telemed./La Recherche Européenne en Télémédecine **5**(02), 65–69 (2016)
12. Zhao, L., Lu, X., Tao, X., Chen, X.: A Kinect-based virtual rehabilitation system through gesture recognition. In: Proceedings of the International Conference on IEEE Virtual Reality and Visualization (ICVRV), pp. 380–384 (2016)
13. Chang, Y.J., Chen, S.F., Huang, J.D.: A Kinect-based system for physical rehabilitation: a pilot Study for young adults with motor disabilities. Res. Dev. Disabil. **32**(06), 2566–2570 (2011)

14. Adinolfi, F., et al.: SmartCARE—an ICT platform in the domain of stroke pathology to manage rehabilitation treatment and telemonitoring at home. In: Pietro, G., Gallo, L., Howlett, R., Jain, L. (eds.) Intelligent Interactive Multimedia Systems and Services 2016. Smart Innovation, Systems and Technologies, vol. 55, pp. 39–49. Springer, Cham (2016). https://doi.org/10.1007/978-3-319-39345-2_4
15. Abreu, J., Barroso, João, et al.: Assessment of microsoft kinect in the monitoring and rehabilitation of stroke patients. In: Rocha, Á., Correia, A.M., Adeli, H., Reis, L.P., Costanzo, S. (eds.) WorldCIST 2017. AISC, vol. 570, pp. 167–174. Springer, Cham (2017). https://doi.org/10.1007/978-3-319-56538-5_18
16. Han, S.H., Kim, H.G., Choi, H.J.: Rehabilitation posture correction using deep neural network. In: Proceedings of the International Conference on IEEE Big Data and Smart Computing (BigComp), pp. 400–402 (2017)
17. Caggianese, G., et al.: A rehabilitation system for post-operative heart surgery. In: De Pietro, G., Gallo, L., Howlett, R.J., Jain, L.C. (eds.) KES-IIMSS 2017. SIST, vol. 76, pp. 554–564. Springer, Cham (2018). https://doi.org/10.1007/978-3-319-59480-4_55
18. Hoda, M., Hoda, Y., Hafidh, B., El Saddik, A.: Predicting muscle forces measurements from kinematics data using kinect in stroke rehabilitation. Multimed. Tools Appl. **77**(2), 1885–1903 (2018)
19. Beaulieu-Boire, L., et al.: Balance rehabilitation using Xbox Kinect among an elderly population: a pilot study. J. Nov. Physiother. **5**(02), 261 (2015)
20. Mousavi Hondori, H., Khademi, M.: A review on technical and clinical impact of microsoft kinect on physical therapy and rehabilitation. J. Med. Eng. **2014** (2014)
21. Baldominos, A., Saez, Y., del Pozo, C.G.: An approach to physical rehabilitation using state-of-the-art virtual reality and motion tracking technologies. Procedia Comput. Sci. **64**, 10–16 (2015)
22. Ge, Z., Fan, L.: Social development for children with autism using kinect gesture games: a case study in Suzhou Industrial Park Renai School. In: Cai, Y., Goei, S., Trooster, W. (eds.) Simulation and Serious Games for Education. Gaming Media and Social Effects, pp. 113–123. Springer, Singapore (2017). https://doi.org/10.1007/978-981-10-0861-0_8

# Virtual Rehabilitation System for Fine Motor Skills Using a Functional Hand Orthosis

Manuel A. León[1(✉)], Paul A. Romero[1(✉)],
Washington X. Quevedo[1(✉)], Oscar B. Arteaga[1(✉)],
Cochise Terán[1(✉)], Marco E. Benalcázar[2(✉)],
and Víctor H. Andaluz[1(✉)]

[1] Universidad de Las Fuerzas Armadas ESPE, Sangolquí, Ecuador
{maleon14, promero6, wjquevedo, obarteaga, hcteran,
vhandaluz1}@espe.edu.ec
[2] Escuela Politécnica Nacional EPN, Quito, Ecuador
marco.benalcazar@epn.edu.ec

**Abstract.** This article describes a virtual rehabilitation system with work and entertainment environments to treat fine motor injuries through an active orthosis. The system was developed in the Unity 3D graphic engine, which allows the patient greater immersion in the rehabilitation process through proposed activities; to identify the movement performed, the Myo armband is used, a device capable of receiving and sending the signals obtained to a mathematical algorithm which will classify these signals and activate the physical hand orthosis completing the desired movement. The benefits of the system is the optimization of resources, infrastructure and personnel, since the therapy will be assisted by the same virtual environment, in addition it allows selecting the virtual environment and the activity to be carried out according to the disability present in the patient. The results show the correct functioning of the system performed.

**Keywords:** Virtual reality · Rehabilitation · Unity 3D · Orthosis
Disability

## 1 Introduction

In the labor sphere, certain tasks are performed repeatedly which entails to that a large number of workers suffering from injuries, increasing the number of people with disabilities and access early retirement [1, 2]. A similar study shows that unnatural postures, irregular or violent movements, body contractions and the repetition of movements produce negative consequences for health [3]. According to global statistics over the course of a year there is a high percentage of fatal work accidents and daily there is much influence of injuries due to occupational accidents [4]. Ergonomic factors within a work environment must govern by rules in order to provide the worker with the necessary comfort to perform their tasks. If these factors are not optimal, they can cause injuries, affecting both the health of the personnel and the productivity of the companies; that is because measures are taken for the recovery of the staff through rehabilitation therapies allowing patients to recover the lost functionalities.

© Springer International Publishing AG, part of Springer Nature 2018
L. T. De Paolis and P. Bourdot (Eds.): AVR 2018, LNCS 10851, pp. 78–94, 2018.
https://doi.org/10.1007/978-3-319-95282-6_6

Physical rehabilitation has a positive impact on the quality of life of people, helping them to recover the mobility of their joints and avoiding muscle atrophy [5]. Depending on the technological progress in the field of rehabilitation. Currently there are different therapies such as conventional rehabilitation in which the collaboration of a physiotherapist is needed to supervise the patient's movements throughout the rehabilitation session; and on the other hand the inclusion of technological devices, *e.g.* robots or virtual systems, among which several studies can be highlighted, such as a robot that assists in the rehabilitation of stroke patients and a manual assistance robot with multiple degrees of freedom for rehabilitation therapies [6, 7]. Certain service robots contribute to the rehabilitation through compensating the movement, allowing reaching assisted movements and with more repetitions. Others are responsible for providing specific training for the patient to perform the movements correctly, such as virtual systems [7].

The use of virtual environments in rehabilitation therapies often empowers the patient to perform movements that the clinical environment does not allow, helping the patient to feel more interested in their treatment and immersing it in their daily environment [8, 9]. Virtual reality (VR) is an immersion of an individual in a new world created based on real environments, allowing him to interact through the use of virtual devices, *e.g.* glasses, audio helmets, gloves, movement traction sensors etc. [9, 10]. Some projects that have been proposed in VR work in open loop, *i.e.*, that do not have a feedback system, as a result the rehabilitation phase will depend a lot on the endeavor that the patient is willing to put in order to perform the correct movements [1, 9, 11]. For rehabilitation tasks, it is necessary that the system is fed back in order to confirm that the correct movements are made and the number of repetitions necessary, as can be seen in the diagram of Fig. 1. By implementing a feedback system, the error is reduced by completing the rehabilitation movements of the patient and allowing their recovery to be faster. One of the ways to close the loop is the implementation of sensors that acquire electromyographic signals (EMG) to obtain muscle signals and recognize that the indicated movement was execute.

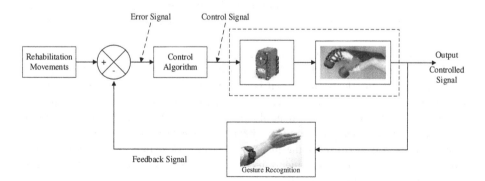

**Fig. 1.** Closed loop system

As described earlier in this article, the development of a VR system that allows the patients to immerse themselves in a daily or work environment to perform rehabilitation tasks and prevent recovery from being a monotonous activity is proposed. For this a hand functional orthosis will be used, designed in a software CAD (Computer Aided Design) and printed in 3D with flexible materials that allow the comfort that the patient requires [12]. For the feedback system it is proposed to use EMG signals from the Myo Armband sensor which contains eight myoelectric sensors that are sent to a computer via Bluetooth, these EMG signals are processed in real time and each of the gestures are labeled and that are performed with the aim of having a closed loop system and checking that the movements are correct at the time of rehabilitation [13].

This document is divide into five Sections, including the Introduction. The second section presents a general description of the problem and proposed solution. In the third section, it is explained how the project is conformed to the use of a multilayer scheme. The results of the tests after the implementation in the system analyzed in the fourth section, and finally in the fifth section, all the conclusions of the project are presented.

## 2    Problem Formulation

Upper extremity traumatisms are complex injuries, many of these injuries are due to monotonous tasks and prolonged efforts. Between the diseases by repetitive efforts in the hand exist the CTS (Carpal Tunnel Syndrome), tenosynovitis, trigger finger, among others; At present, this type of lesion is common, which originates in some work environments [14–16].

CTS is one of the most common entrapment neuropathies in the upper extremity [17]. Among the symptoms that can be had is severe pain, tingling, numbness and loss of motor control, reducing the ability to grip [18]. The high-pressure damages the blood flow in the median nerve, this pressure increase occurs in the carpal tunnel region shown in Fig. 2a. The treatments of this pathology are complex, which is why many experts agree to perform the following methods: orthoses, corticoids or surgical treatment. Each one exposed according to the severity of the disease [19]. From the presented solutions, it will be necessary to know the movements and postures to achieve the rehabilitation of the hand, either through an active functional orthosis or according to postoperative movements. Several of these movements must be repeated for periods indicated by the physiotherapist. The movements are observed in Fig. 2b.

As for Quervain's tenosynovitis, it is defined as one of the main skeletal muscle diseases linked to overload [20]. Described as an acute inflammation in the tendons that occupy the first extensor compartment of the hand, long abductor and short extensor of the thumb. The diagnosis is based on the Finkelstein test shown in Fig. 3a; when closing the fist and performing the maneuver of ulnar deviation, intense pain is perceived [15]. Some of the movements recommended for the recovery of Quervain's tenosynovitis are shown in Fig. 3b.

The trigger finger or flexor tenositis is a disease that acts on the flexor tendons of the fingers, producing pain and limiting the movement of the finger when flexing or extending the finger as shown in Fig. 4a. This pathology is attributed to factors such as diseases and excessive effort of the hand; however, the causes of appearance of the trigger finger are also due to advanced age and occur more frequently in women than in men [19, 21]. Among the movements that help in the rehabilitation of this trauma, it is important to focus mainly on the affected finger, see Fig. 4b.

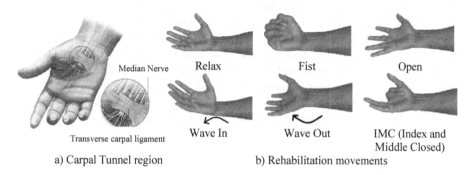

Median Nerve     Relax          Fist          Open

Transverse carpal ligament    Wave In      Wave Out      IMC (Index and
                                                          Middle Closed)
a) Carpal Tunnel region        b) Rehabilitation movements

**Fig. 2.** Carpal tunnel syndrome

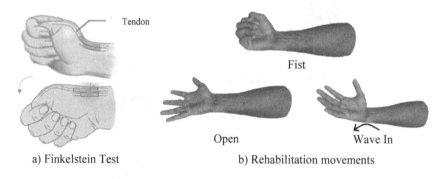

Tendon

Fist

Open          Wave In

a) Finkelstein Test        b) Rehabilitation movements

**Fig. 3.** De Quervain's tenosynovitis

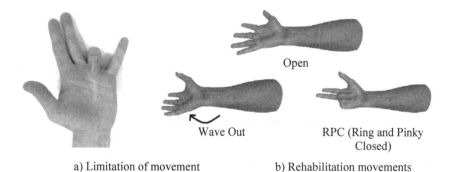

Open

Wave Out          RPC (Ring and Pinky
                  Closed)

a) Limitation of movement        b) Rehabilitation movements

**Fig. 4.** Trigger finger

For instance, this work has been previously described the development of an application in VR oriented to fine motor rehabilitation is proposed. The application considers two virtual environments: (i) *Industrial process*, which has activities related to different areas of work, *e.g.* engineering, medicine, industry, etc.; and (ii) *Rehabilitation game*, this environment will have entertainment activities that will help at the same time in the rehabilitation of hand. Each developed environment will allow the patient to execute guided actions through visual instructions, which according to the type of injury present will be informed the movement to be emulated. To achieve the movement, a functional hand orthosis is used, manipulated according to signals obtained from a mathematical algorithm that will classify the signals of the Myo armband. The link of these control processes, which will allow responding to operations of several processes attached to the virtual devices in the Unity environment, see Fig. 5.

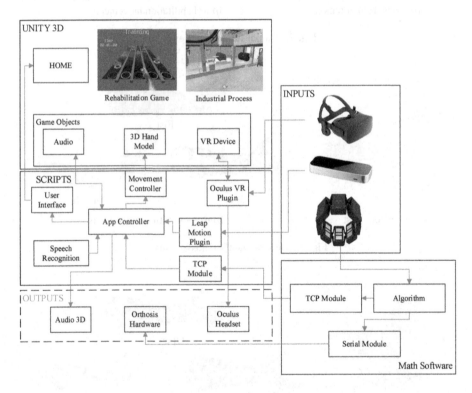

**Fig. 5.** Component interrelation diagram

The scene simulation module contains the VR programming, where the 3D model of the hand links the motion controller; this module also presents the necessary configuration of the physical properties, which simulate the rehabilitation movements according to the selected environment.

In the *Input Module* is consider the Oculus Rift device, which allows observing the virtual environment, in addition to hand tracking devices that allow interaction with the environment such as Leap Motion and Myo Armband. When making use of different input units it is required that the structure of the code is general, being compatible with several platforms, avoiding the reconstruction of the project, managing to detect automatically all the devices.

The *SCRIPTS Module* is responsible for managing communication with all control blocks, input devices and output devices through the application controller, providing the virtual reality environment with the necessary functionality. In addition, it has the user interface, which allows selecting the rehabilitation environment according to the necessary characteristics of the injury; on the other hand, the motion controller and the Leap Motion Plugin serve as a link to the simulation module. For the interaction of the virtual environment and the patient, there are the voice recognition modules and Oculus VR Plugin. While the TCP module transfers data from the mathematical software.

The *Mathematical Software Module* is implemented the algorithm of classification of movements that receives the signals of the Myo Armband sensors, processes them and determines the movement made by the patient sending signals through the serial module to a controller that will activate the motors of the orthosis hand.

Finally, in the *Output Module*, the feedback is produced by means of the orthosis that moves according to the predicted rehabilitation exercise. It also provides audio and visual feedback to the patient to monitor movements within the VR environment.

## 3    Virtual Interaction and Immersion

CAD software is a design tool that allows users to create virtual mechanisms through an apprehensible graphical environment. An example is SolidWorks, which is a package of mechanical tools that allows the modeling of objects in 2D and 3D; it also has CAE (Computer Aided Engineering) tools, which allow to perform analyzes and simulations of the model designed with real parameters [22].

Within the present document, a multi-layered scheme proposes for the development of the application in a virtual environment with the purpose of providing greater immersion and interaction to patients in rehabilitation tasks for hand injuries caused by repetitive activities see Fig. 6.

*Layer 2* establishes the relationship between the 3D model and the Unity3D graphics engine 3DS Max software is used. The interaction process establishes that hierarchies of the model must be obtained according to the elements, positions and restrictions of the designed object, it is also necessary to determine reference points (pivot) that will serve as location and orientation of the model. The model visualized in the virtual environment is that of a hand, the model of the orthosis is not used so that the patient has greater sensitivity when observing a real hand. Finally, the process performed in the link software will have an .fbx output file, which is compatible with the Unity3D software, allowing applications to be developed for the VR environment. One of the applications is an industrial environment, specifically a tannery, in which the patient can develop work activities while rehabilitating his hand; another application has to do with motor games designed.

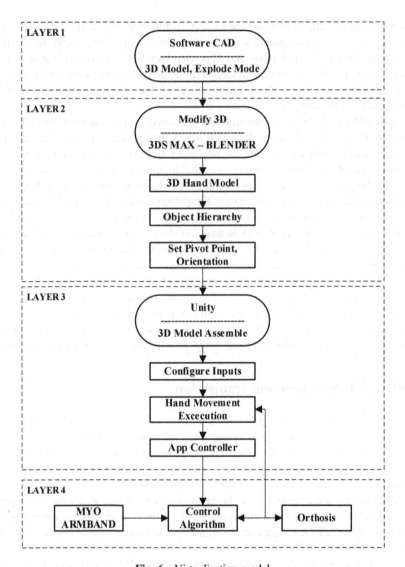

**Fig. 6.** Virtualization model

On the other hand, *Layer 3* performs the configuration of inputs for the interaction of the moving parts that make up the 3D model and the user interface using the Oculus Rift device for the generation of the virtual environment, while the *Leap motion* device tracks the position of the hand at the moment of making movements by the patient and transfers them to the virtual environment obtaining a visual feedback on the rehabilitation movements already established, see Fig. 7. To the *Hand Movement Execution* block comes the signal coming from the mathematical algorithm in order to that in the virtual environment the movements made are visualized; the *App Controller* block ensures that the mathematical algorithm classifies the signals in order to complete the desired movement, this block also contains the instructions for the movements to be made, for which the user accesses by means of the voice command *"Help"* and a panel is show in which is indicated the movement that the patient must make step by step. Once the instructions are understood, the voice command *"Close"* is used, the instruction window is hidden, and rehabilitation begins.

**Fig. 7.** System device

In *Layer 4* the communication of the Myo Armband is developed, whose function is to obtain signals from the sensors and send them to the computer, where the algorithm predicts the movement executed according to the training and programming carried out in the mathematical software. These signals are sent to the motors of the orthosis in order to assist in the different movements to be performed by the patient. Layer 4 can be subdivided into 3 stages, in the first stage the Myo Armband is described, which is a non-invasive surface sensor that records the electrical signals of the muscles through its 8 sensors, see Fig. 8. These signals are sampled at a speed of 200 Hz and with a resolution of 8 bits for each sensor; these signals are taken from the muscles of the forearm because these are responsible for the movements of the different parts of the hand. The Myo Armband has an inertial measurement unit with 9 degrees of freedom (accelerometer, gyroscope and orientation, in the three axes X, Y and Z); all registered data is sent via Bluetooth to the computer. Both amplitude and spectrum of the signals coming from the armband vary according to the thickness of the skin, its temperature, the blood flow and the percentage of body fat of the person, it will also depend on the location of the sensors. Fatigue, neuromuscular diseases and aging affect the quality of electromyographic signals.

Regarding the second stage, the mathematical algorithm of classification of movements was developed that was carried out through five phases: *1. Acquisition of*

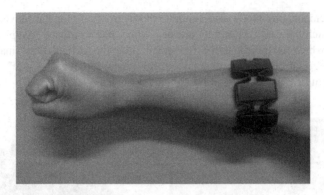

**Fig. 8.** Surface sensor: Myo Armband.

*signals,* made by the Myo armband; *2. Preprocessing,* in this phase the signal obtained is rectified to avoid that in the average sum of each channel of the signal is zero, in addition a low pass filter is applied to reduce the noise and soften the channels; *3. Characteristics extraction,* here we define a characteristics matrix that contains the 200 samples of each channel, these samples are obtained after observing the EMG signals through a 1 s window with a sampling frequency of 200 Hz; *4. Classification,* for this phase the rule of the nearest k-neighbors is used, which is a supervised classification method together with the algorithm of dynamic temporal alignment that measures similarities between sequences that vary in time; *5. Post Processing,* in this last phase the model allows to classify the superimposed windows of the same gesture by delivering different labels [13]. For its training, the rehabilitation movements of Figs. 2b, 3b and 4b were used, with this a matrix is established according to the environment, disability and movement to be performed, presented in Table 1.

**Table 1.** Rehabilitation movements according to the disability and environment present.

| Environment | Disability | Movement |
|---|---|---|
| Industrial Process (Tannery) | CTS | Fist, Open, Wave In, Wave Out |
| | Tenosynovitis | Fist, Open |
| | Trigger Finger | Open, Wave Out |
| Rehabilitation Game | CTS | Fist, open, Wave In, Wave Out, IMC |
| | Tenosynovitis | Fist, Open, Wave In |
| | Trigger Finger | Open, Wave Out, RPC |

Finally, in the last stage, a functional orthosis is used which is designed in CAD software, based on anthropometric measurements of the hand to provide the necessary ergonomics to the patient; It is considered that the measurements of the fingers vary from one person to another and proceeds to make a design that allows an easy exchange of the fingers of the orthosis in order to have a correct fit on the patient's fingers, see Fig. 9. The orthosis was printed in 3D for which it is considered a preliminary study on the characterization of flexible materials printed in 3D, within which standardized test pieces were used based on ASTM D638, these test pieces were printed from a thermoplastic elastomer (NinjaFlex) and the testing it was carried out by means of a Universal Testing Machine MT-50, being able to reach the conclusion that the best printing direction to withstand greater efforts and forces is in the XZ plane [12].

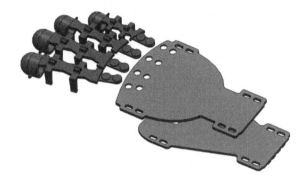

**Fig. 9.** Modelo CAD de la Órtesis

# 4 Results and Discussion

In this section, the results obtained from the project are presented, for which first the *Classification of Movements* is exposed, where the interface of the mathematical algorithm that allows classifying the signals coming from the Myo Armband is shown, in addition, the *Virtual Application* is shown, which contains two virtual environments, which offers the patient a more interactive rehabilitation session motivating the patient with their treatment and recovery.

## 4.1 Classification of Movements

The classifier of movements has a graphical interface, which has three modules: Initialization, Control and Display. The *Initialization Module* allows entering user information *e.g.* name, age, gender, measurement of the perimeter of the arm, distance from the ulna to the elbow and distance of the Myo Armband to the elbow. This information will be used to create a database, used in the training of the classifier.

The *Control Module* has four buttons: Start, it initialize the program and store the user's data in the database; Restart, it allows access to the database and continue with the collection of signals from a previously entered user; Record, it capture the signals from the Myo Armband with a sampling frequency of 200 Hz; Repeat, it erase the signals of the last captured movement.

To observe the captured signals, the interface has the *Display Module*, it consisting of 8 windows that indicate the signal of each sensor, see Fig. 10.

In the training, 50 people are considered to execute 4 gestures: Fist, Open, IMC and RPC. The parameters for the training are in the Initialization Module, having 50

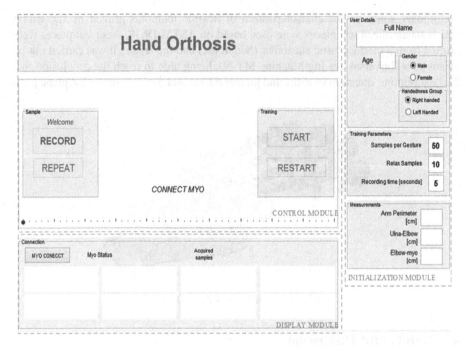

**Fig. 10.** Graphical interface for training

samples by default for each gesture with a recording time of 5 s, plus 10 samples of the movement called Relax, that consists of not realize any action, necessary for training the classification algorithm since it allows to distinguish when each movement begins.

The windows of the signals recorded according to each movement are shown in Fig. 11. Wave In and Wave Out movements are not trained as they are controlled in open loop.

## 4.2 Virtual Application

Displays the virtual environment that offers the patient two different applications, the one an industrial process for which it was considered a tannery of hides and the other a game of rehabilitation that allow to perform tasks and exercises for rehabilitation of hand injured because of repetitive exercises, Fig. 12a shows the application start up screen. The onscreen Game and Industrial Process accessing an information panel which gives to know which activities can make the patient within the selected scenario, see Fig. 12b.

### 4.2.1 Rehabilitation Game

This application allows entertainment, also a better rehabilitation for the patient for the reason that it is not restricted movements focused on activities of an industrial process, the rehabilitation game includes movements such as IMC, and RPC to treat injuries of CTS and Trigger Finger, see Fig. 13.

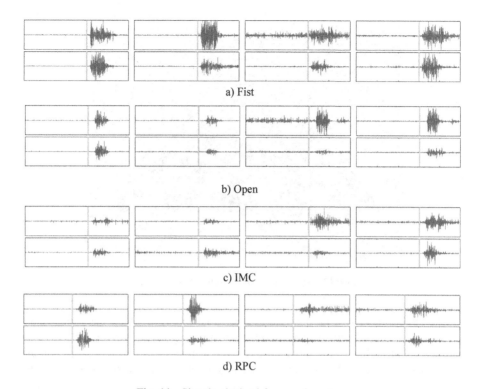

**Fig. 11.** Signals obtained from each gesture

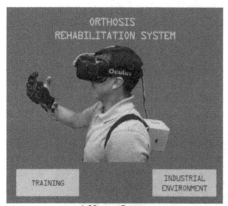

a) Home Screen

b) Information of activities to do in the
virtual environment

**Fig. 12.** Virtual Application

**Fig. 13.** Start screen of the rehabilitation game

The environment is a musical video game application in which the patient must perform the specified movement the exact moment the signal is shown on the screen, so that the patient performs, the movement is given a time of 5 to 10 s in order that the movement is completed correctly and can continue to the next movement. The

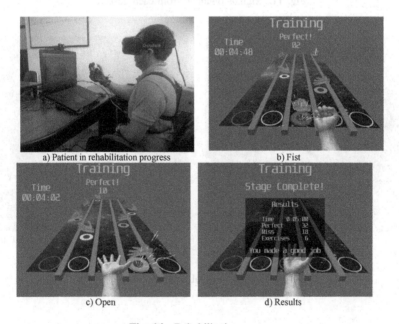

**Fig. 14.** Rehabilitation game

application begins to accumulate points in the case of a correct movement with the aim of presenting at the end of the exercise a table where the progress of the patient is observed, see Fig. 14.

### 4.2.2   Industrial Process: Tannery

Once entered into the industrial process, as in the game, the panel with the activities of the applications that the patient can perform is shown first, see Fig. 15a. The following screen shows the industrial environment: a tannery where the process of transformation

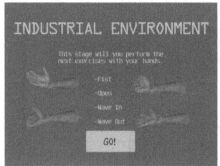

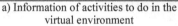

| a) Information of activities to do in the virtual environment | b) Start screen of the Industrial Environment |

**Fig. 15.**  Virtual application

of animal skins to leather is simulated, in Fig. 15b the operations carried out in the tannery where it includes the Leather Squeeze Machine, drums and actuators are shown for each process [23]. The environment also has the respective instructions to comply with the activity.

The activity proposed in this environment has to do with the activation of the Leather Squeeze machine responsible for the process of eliminating excess fat in the leather, this activity consists of four actions in which rehabilitation movements are

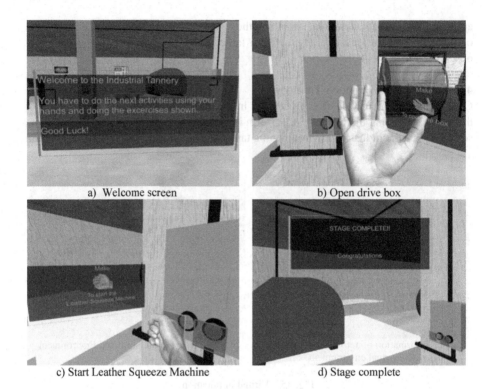

a) Welcome screen                                  b) Open drive box

c) Start Leather Squeeze Machine                     d) Stage complete

**Fig. 16.** Industrial environment

developed. The actions are: open the process drive box, press the start button, press the stop button to finish the tanning process and close the drive box. Figure 16 shows the activity described.

## 5   Conclusions

The interaction of the patient with an environment different from the conventional one produces motivation to carry out the rehabilitation sessions, since they are entertaining activities that help the patient in their progress. That is why it was necessary to create the mathematical algorithm of classification of movements, having to perform gestures such as RPC and IMC that are not recognized by the Myo Armband software; the algorithm has a high gesture recognition accuracy, but it can be improved by training it with a greater number of users. In addition, the virtual rehabilitation environment demonstrates a good alternative for rehabilitation sessions, since it allows the user to correct their fine motor skills and reduce the progress of injuries inherent to the patient.

**Acknowledgements.** The authors would like to thanks to the Corporación Ecuatoriana para el Desarrollo de la Investigación y Academia–CEDIA for the financing given to research, development, and innovation, through the CEPRA projects, especially the project CEPRA-XI-2017-

06; *Control Coordinado Multi-operador aplicado a un robot Manipulador Aéreo*; also to Universidad de las Fuerzas Armadas ESPE, Universidad Técnica de Ambato, Escuela Superior Politécnica de Chimborazo, and Universidad Nacional de Chimborazo, and Grupo de Investigación en Automatización, Robótica y Sistemas Inteligentes, GIARSI, for the support to develop this paper.

# References

1. Sanchez, J.S., et al.: Virtual Rehabilitation System for Carpal Tunnel Syndrome Through Spherical Robots. Accepted 2014
2. Naiker, A.: Repetitive Strain Injuries (RSI) - an ayurvedic approach. J. Ayurveda Integr. Med. Sci. **2**(2), 170–173 (2017). ISSN 2456-3110
3. Rosales, R.S., Martin-Hidalgo, Y., Reboso-Morales, L., Atroshi, I.: Reliability and construct validity of the Spanish version of the 6-item CTS symptoms scale for outcomes assessment in carpal tunnel syndrome. BMC Musculoskelet. Disord. **17**, 115 (2016)
4. Uehli, K., et al.: Sleep problems and work injuries: a systematic review and meta-analysis. Sleep Med. Rev. **18**(1), 61–73 (2014)
5. Patti, F., et al.: The impact of outpatient rehabilitation on quality of life in multiple sclerosis. J. Neurol. **249**(8), 1027–1033 (2002)
6. Ueki, S., et al.: Development of a hand-assist robot with multi-degrees-of-freedom for rehabilitation therapy. IEEEASME Trans. Mechatron. **17**(1), 136–146 (2012)
7. Chang, W.H., Kim, Y.-H.: Robot-assisted therapy in stroke rehabilitation. J. Stroke **15**(3), 174–181 (2013)
8. Laver, K., George, S., Thomas, S., Deutsch, J.E., Crotty, M.: Virtual reality for stroke rehabilitation. Stroke **43**(2), e20–e21 (2012)
9. Lohse, K.R., Hilderman, C.G.E., Cheung, K.L., Tatla, S., der Loos, H.F.M.V.: Virtual reality therapy for adults post-stroke: a systematic review and meta-analysis exploring virtual environments and commercial games in therapy. PLoS ONE **9**(3), e93318 (2014)
10. North, M.M., North, S.M., Coble, J.R.: Virtual reality therapy: an effective treatment for the fear of public speaking. Int. J. Virtual Real. IJVR **03**(3), 1–6 (2015)
11. Turolla, A., et al.: Virtual reality for the rehabilitation of the upper limb motor function after stroke: a prospective controlled trial. J. Neuroeng. Rehabil. **10**, 85 (2013)
12. Romero, P., León, A., Arteaga, O., Andaluz, V.H., Cruz, M.: Composite materials for the construction of functional orthoses. Accepted 2017
13. Benalcázar, M.E., Jaramillo, A.G., Jonathan, A., Zea, A., Páez, V.H.: Andaluz: hand gesture recognition using machine learning and the Myo armband. In: 2017 25th European Signal Processing Conference (EUSIPCO), pp. 1040–1044 (2017)
14. Maroukis, B.L., Chung, K.C., MacEachern, M., Mahmoudi, E.: Hand trauma care in the united states: a literature review. Plast. Reconstr. Surg. **137**(1), 100e–111e (2016)
15. Feron, L.O., Boniatti, C.M., Arruda, F.Z., Butze, J., Conde, A.: lesões por esforço repetitivo em cirurgiões-dentistas: uma revisão da literatura. Rev. Ciênc. Saúde **16**(2), 79–86 (2014)
16. Putz-Anderson, V.: Cumulative Trauma Disorders. CRC Press, Boca Raton (2017)
17. Oktayoglu, P., Nas, K., Kilinç, F., Tasdemir, N., Bozkurt, M., Yildiz, I.: Assessment of the presence of carpal tunnel syndrome in patients with diabetes mellitus, hypothyroidism and acromegaly. J. Clin. Diagn. Res. JCDR **9**(6), OC14–OC18 (2015)
18. Villafañe, J., Cleland, J., Fernánde-de-las-Peñas, C.: the effectiveness of a manual therapy and exercise protocol in patients with thumb carpometacarpal osteoarthritis: a randomized controlled trial. J. Orthop. Sports Phys. Ther. **43**(4), 204–213 (2013)

19. Langer, D., Maeir, A., Michailevich, M., Applebaum, Y., Luria, S.: Using the international classification of functioning to examine the impact of trigger finger. Disabil. Rehabil. **38**(26), 2530–2537 (2016)
20. da Silva Dulci Medeiros, M., Santana, D.V.G., de Souza, G.D., Souza, L.R.Q.: Tenossinovite de Quervain: aspectos diagnósticos. Rev. Med. E Saúde Brasília **5**(2), 307–312 (2016)
21. Werthel, J.-D., Cortez, M., Elhassan, B.T.: Modified percutaneous trigger finger release. Hand Surg. Rehabil. **35**(3), 179–182 (2016)
22. Chang, K.-H.: Motion Simulation and Mechanism Design with SOLIDWORKS Motion 2016. SDC Publications (2016)
23. Andaluz, V.H., Pazmiño, A.M., Pérez, J.A., Carvajal, C.P., Lozada, F., Lascano, J., Carvajal, J.: Training of tannery processes through virtual reality. In: De Paolis, L.T., Bourdot, P., Mongelli, A. (eds.) AVR 2017. LNCS, vol. 10324, pp. 75–93. Springer, Cham (2017). https://doi.org/10.1007/978-3-319-60922-5_6

# Proof of Concept: Wearable Augmented Reality Video See-Through Display for Neuro-Endoscopy

Marina Carbone[1,2]([⊠]), Sara Condino[1]([⊠]), Fabrizio Cutolo[1,2],
Rosanna Maria Viglialoro[1], Oliver Kaschke[3], Ulrich W. Thomale[4],
and Vincenzo Ferrari[1,2]

[1] EndoCAS Center, Department of Translational Research
and New Technologies in Medicine and Surgery, University of Pisa, Pisa, Italy
marina.carbone@endocas.org,
sara.condino@endocas.unipi.it
[2] Information Engineering Department, University of Pisa, Pisa, Italy
[3] Ear-Nose-Throat Department,
Sankt Gertrauden-Krankenhaus GmbH, Berlin, Germany
[4] Department of Neurosurgery with Pediatric Neurosurgery,
Charité Universitätsmedizin, Berlin, Germany

**Abstract.** In mini-invasive surgery and in endoscopic procedures, the surgeon operates without a direct visualization of the patient's anatomy. In image-guided surgery, solutions based on wearable augmented reality (AR) represent the most promising ones. The authors describe the characteristics that an ideal Head Mounted Display (HMD) must have to guarantee safety and accuracy in AR-guided neurosurgical interventions and design the ideal virtual content for guiding crucial task in neuro endoscopic surgery. The selected sequence of AR content to obtain an effective guidance during surgery is tested in a Microsoft Hololens based app.

**Keywords:** Minimally invasive surgery · Augmented reality and visualization
Computer assisted intervention · Neuroendoscopy

## 1 Introduction

During the last 15 years, neuronavigation has become an essential neurosurgical tool for pursuing minimal invasiveness and maximal safety [1]. Unfortunately, ergonomics of such devices are still not optimal [2]. The neurosurgeon has to look away from the surgical field at a dedicated workstation screen. Then, the operator is required to mentally transfer the information from the "virtual" environment of the navigation system to the real surgical field. The virtual environment includes virtual surgical instruments and patient-specific virtual anatomy details (generally obtained from pre-operative 3D images).

Intraventricular endoscopy is a routine technique for the therapy of cerebral-spinal-fluid (CSF) dynamic disorders such as hydrocephalus in which membranes are fenestrated in order to restore physiological CSF flow for the patient. Endoscopic

L. T. De Paolis and P. Bourdot (Eds.): AVR 2018, LNCS 10851, pp. 95–104, 2018.
https://doi.org/10.1007/978-3-319-95282-6_7

interventions are also the mainstay for the treatment of paraventricular cysts that may cause relevant mass effect: in this case an endoscopic fenestration may be required in order to re-establish regular CSF spaces or when paraventricular tumors need biopsy, which might also be accompanied by hydrocephalus treatment [3]. In this context, it is important to mention that endoscopy will be applied through one borehole as entry point. The determination of this entry point will impact the safety and efficacy of the procedure. Thus, endoscopic procedures have frequently been used together with navigation systems in order to apply these goals. Neurosurgical navigation enables, through the registration of the patient's anatomy. the identification of instruments, endoscopes and microscopes in spatial relation to the patient's anatomy [1, 2, 4–11].

In commercial neuronavigation systems the navigation information, also in the form of augmented views of external or endoscopic cameras, is normally presented on a stand-up monitor. This means that the practicing surgeon must turn away from the operation field for perceiving surgical navigation information [10, 12–14].

In order to allow an uninterrupted concentration on the area of intervention, wearable AR devices are starting to be tested to enter the surgical room [11, 15].

The purpose of this paper is twofold: to lay down the technical specifications that an ideal Head Mounted Display (HMD) should have to guarantee safety and accuracy in AR-guided neurosurgical interventions, and to design the most suitable AR visualization modality for the guidance of a crucial task in such surgery.

## 2    Materials and Methods

### 2.1    Design of the HMD

The design of the HMD started from a deep analysis of currently available HMD technologies.

Existing wearable augmented reality displays can deploy Optical see-through (OST) or Video see-through (VST) approaches. Typically, in OST visors, the user's direct view of the real world is augmented through the projection of the virtual content on a beam combiner and then into the user's line of sight. The user sees the virtual information displayed on a semi-transparent surface of projection (SSP). Differently, in VST visors the virtual content is merged with camera images captured by two external cameras rigidly fixed on the visor [16].

Both approaches have benefits and drawbacks depending on the task they are designed for. In the context of image-guided surgery, the AR content offered may be simply informative (e.g., textual or numerical values relevant to what is under observation as patient data from the anesthesia monitor) or it may consist of three-dimensional virtual objects inserted within the real environment in spatially defined positions. In the latter case, the virtual content seeks to provide a patient-specific virtual representation of the hidden anatomy (obtained from diagnostic images as CT, MRI, 3DUS...) so as to guide the surgeon's hand during precision tasks as tissue incisions or vessels isolation. Generally, the VST paradigm yields an accurate and robust alignment between virtual and real content at the expenses of a less realistic and authentic perception of the "real world", being this affected by the intrinsic features of the camera and display; with OST there is an inevitable lag between real and virtual information and at the same time an accurate alignment between real scene and virtual content cannot be achieved without a specific, and often error-prone, eye-to-display calibration routine. Nonetheless, the main benefit of OST visors is to maintain an unobstructed view of the real world. This is why, depending on the surgical task to be aided, a system that provided both the see-through mechanisms together with a switching mechanism allowing a transition between the two modalities could represent a disruptive asset in the context of AR-based neuronavigators.

An AR HMD that addresses human factors issues towards the achievement of optimal ergonomics and perfect usability in surgery means to target at least the following:

- To develop a new hybrid video-optical see through AR HMD that allows both the see-through modalities.
- To develop a mechanism that manages the transition between occluded and non-occluded view. The occluded view is used for the video see-through (VST) modality, whereas the non-occluded view is necessary for implementing the optical see-through (OST) modality.
- Integrate a real-time eye pose estimation routine (i.e. OST-to-eye calibration) whose goal is to achieve a geometrically consistent augmentation of the reality.
- Design and develop a software framework capable of managing several video or optical see through-based surgical navigation applications. The application will have to be user-friendly, ergonomic and highly configurable so as to make it suitable for many typologies of potential applications.

This hardware developing phase is currently ongoing in an European project (H2020) coordinated by the authors whose aim is to design, develop and validate a wearable augmented reality (AR) microdisplay-based system to be used in the operating theatre [17, 18].

The VOSTARS project aims to design, develop and validate an immersive and ground-breaking wearable augmented reality (AR) microdisplay-based system to act as surgical navigator. The new AR-based head mounted display (HMD) is bound to massively revolutionize the paradigms through which wearable AR HMD systems are commonly implemented.

## 2.2   Design of the Virtual Content, Presentation and Interaction Modality

The definition of the virtual content that is intended to augment the surgical experience starts from the decomposition of the addressed intervention into surgical tasks [19].

A major issue in the designing of AR-based surgical navigation system is related to the need of providing consistent visual cues for correct perception of depth and spatial relations in the augmented scene [20, 21]. In fact, as showed by previous studies [11, 22–26], the visualization of virtual content in AR applications are effective in aiding the surgeon executing a specific medical procedure only if they are strongly related to the task. For example, sometimes the superimposition of a semi-transparent virtual anatomy, albeit visually appealing, can be rather confusing for the surgeon. This is due to the surgeon's limited perception of the relative distances between real and virtual elements within the AR scene and it may be affected by the presence of unnatural occlusions between real and virtual structures. Further, the presentation of a too detailed and complex virtual content, may confound the surgeon instead of being of assistance.

Starting from the previous work [11], in this work the AR content was conceived together with a surgical team to aid the surgeon in planning the optimal trajectory for accessing the surgical target. The tasks selected for guidance in the OST modality are: craniotomies, targeting of the entry point of the endoscope, trajectory alignment.

The defined virtual content are represented by:

- A viewfinder to clearly show the ideal entry point on the patient's skull. This entry point would also allow the definition of a proper area for craniotomy.
- The trajectory to be followed by the endoscope.
- The virtual frustum of the endoscope; this would help the surgeon in assessing the field of view covered by the endoscope in a specific position.
- The targeted lesion and some anatomical landmarks (ventricles) (Fig. 1).

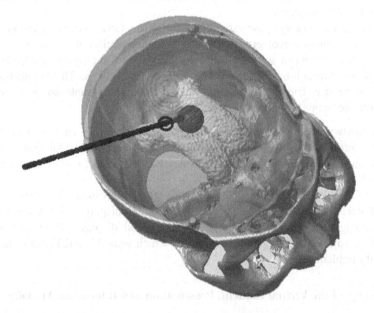

**Fig. 1.** Virtual planning of the intervention. The trajectory and the viewfinder are showed together with the patient anatomy.

Considering that in the surgical room the surgeon could never violate the sterility of the surgical field, manual gesture interaction will be used to allow the user to interact with the AR application without the need for any sort of physical interface; moreover considering the need to keep hands within the surgical field, voice commands will be added to provide a hands-free interaction modality with the AR application.

## 2.3    Evaluation Study

To bring forward the assessment of the most effective AR visualization modality pending the development of a fully functional hybrid OST/VST HMD, we developed a Microsoft HoloLens based app. Microsoft Hololens was chosen as testing tool for assessing the ergonomics of the AR visualization modality.

The HoloLens is a stand-alone OST HMD that provides unique features such as a high-resolution display, ability to spatially map objects, handle gesture interface, easy interaction through straight gaze-to-target cursor management and voice recognition control mechanism [27]; it has no physical tethering constrains which can limit the movements/gestures of the user during the simulation of the surgical tasks. MixedRealityToolkit, a freely available collection of scripts and components, allows an easy and fast development of AR applications.

Tests also required the fabrication of a physical simulator (i.e., patient specifichead mannequin) similar to that used in [11]; based on the 3D model of this mannequin,an expert surgeon planned the best entry point on the skull cap and the optimal endoscope trajectory for the simulated surgical case.

**Physical Simulator Development**

The phantom was built starting from an high resolution magnetic resonance imaging study (MRI) suitable for neuronavigation. The image sequence data set was used for volumetric reconstruction combined with thin sliced axial T2-weighted images. The ITK-Snap 5.1 with a custom modified plugin was used to segment ventricles and skull [28]. A simplified lesion model was added close to the ventricular area to simulate the target for endoscopy. The skull model, with the simulated lesion, were 3D printed using acrylonitrile butadiene styrene (ABS) (with a Dimension Elite 3D Printer). A silicone mixtures was used for the manufacturing of the scalp to improve the simulation realism.

A physical support for a registration target (a Vuforia [29] Image Target, as described in the following section), was rigidly anchored to the bone synthetic replica to allow the registration of the virtual content to the real scene.

**AR App Development**

Unity3D (5.6.1f) was used to create the application. The MixedRealityToolkit (2017.1.2) script collection was used to interact with the virtual content by means of cursor management through gaze-to-target interaction, gesture ("air-tap"), and voice. As already said, the virtual environment include: the targeted lesion and ventricle models, and the preoperative plan (viewfinder and trajectory). A virtual cursor was added to the virtual scene to indicate the straight gaze direction, estimated from the position and orientation of the user's head in the Microsoft HoloLens based app (the final hybrid OST/VST HMD will allow eye-tracking, thus the virtual cursor position will be fully controllable with eye movement).

The detection and tracking functionalities offered by the Vuforia SDK were used for registration purposes. In particular, two Vuforia Image Targets were used to track in real-time the physical simulator and the endoscope.

## 3   Results

Several tests were conducted to evaluate the most ergonomic AR visualization sequence in function of the task to be accomplished. In this phase, experienced and young surgeons were asked to perform the percutaneous task wearing the Hololens with the AR app running (Fig. 2).

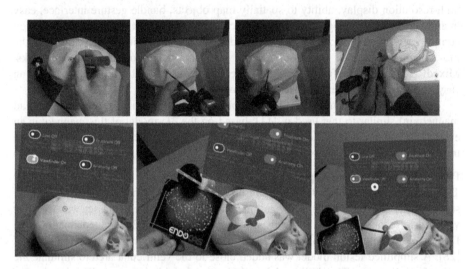

**Fig. 2.**   AR functionalities in neurosurgery - first row: concept; second row: early (Microsoft Hololens based) demo implementation to define surgical needs and study feasibility. (a) viewfinder visualization (b) endoscope trajectory and frustum towards anatomy, (c) frustum and anatomy visualization

During the test they were requested to execute the craniotomy and reach the target with the endoscope maintaining the ideal trajectory. The testing phase was essential to define the exact sequence to be used to visualize the AR content.

The users were able to interact with the application via voice commands or hand gestures so to tailor the augmented experience to the user's own needs.

The testing phase confirmed that the visualized virtual elements are useful to accomplish the surgical target. It underlined that a correct sequencing is of outmost importance for a fruitful augmented experience:

- Firstly, the surgeon can choose to visualize the target anatomy just for a rehearsal.
- Only the viewfinder will be visualized to guide the craniotomy.
- Once the surgical access is prepared the ideal trajectory is showed and the surgeon pivoting on the access point can align the endoscope to the trajectory.
- While entering the anatomy also the endoscope virtual frustum and the target anatomy are added to improve surgeon spatial awareness during the surgical task.

# 4 Conclusion

Clinical navigation systems are nowadays routinely used in a variety of surgical disciplines to assist surgeons with minimally invasive and open interventions for supporting spatial orientation and targeting [30–36]. In surgical navigators, AR-based techniques are often used for identifying the precise location of target lesions or body regions to improve the safety and accuracy of the interventions [15, 37–40].

There is a growing interest on the use of AR systems as new surgical navigation systems. The introduction of AR in neurosurgery, both for training purposes [13, 41–44] and as surgical navigators, can lead to positive and encouraging results in terms of increased accuracy and reduced trauma to the patient.

Wearable AR systems based on HMDs allows the surgeon to have an ergonomic viewpoint of the surgical field and of the patient's anatomy and reduce the problems related to eye-hand coordination [23].

When conceiving innovative navigation paradigm in terms of hardware and software the way virtual content is provided to the user is highly impacting on the usability of the wearable device in terms of ergonomics, effectiveness of the navigation experience, and confidence in the device.

**Acknowledgments.** Funded BY THE HORIZON2020 Project VOSTARS, Project ID: 731974. Call: ICT-29-2016 - Photonics KET 2016.

# References

1. Inoue, D., Cho, B., Mori, M., Kikkawa, Y., Amano, T., Nakamizo, A., Yoshimoto, K., Mizoguchi, M., Tomikawa, M., Hong, J., Hashizume, M., Sasaki, T.: Preliminary study on the clinical application of augmented reality neuronavigation. J. Neurol. Surg. A Cent. Eur. Neurosurg. **74**, 71–76 (2013)
2. Kockro, R.A., Tsai, Y.T., Ng, I., Hwang, P., Zhu, C., Agusanto, K., Hong, L.X., Serra, L.: Dex-ray: augmented reality neurosurgical navigation with a handheld video probe. Neurosurgery **65**, 795–807 (2009). discussion 807-798
3. Schulz, M., Bohner, G., Knaus, H., Haberl, H., Thomale, U.-W.: Navigated endoscopic surgery for multiloculated hydrocephalus in children. J. Neurosurg. Pediatr. **5**, 434–442 (2010)
4. King, A.P., Edwards, P.J., Maurer Jr., C.R., de Cunha, D.A., Hawkes, D.J., Hill, D.L., Gaston, R.P., Fenlon, M.R., Strong, A.J., Chandler, C.L., Richards, A., Gleeson, M.J.: A system for microscope-assisted guided interventions. Stereotact. Funct. Neurosurg. **72**, 107–111 (1999)
5. Edwards, P.J., King, A.P., Maurer Jr., C.R., de Cunha, D.A., Hawkes, D.J., Hill, D.L., Gaston, R.P., Fenlon, M.R., Jusczyzck, A., Strong, A.J., Chandler, C.L., Gleeson, M.J.: Design and evaluation of a system for microscope-assisted guided interventions (MAGI). IEEE Trans. Med. Imaging **19**, 1082–1093 (2000)
6. Stadie, A.T., Reisch, R., Kockro, R.A., Fischer, G., Schwandt, E., Boor, S., Stoeter, P.: Minimally invasive cerebral cavernoma surgery using keyhole approaches - solutions for technique-related limitations. Minim. Invasive Neurosurg. **52**, 9–16 (2009)

7. Cabrilo, I., Bijlenga, P., Schaller, K.: Augmented reality in the surgery of cerebral arteriovenous malformations: technique assessment and considerations. Acta Neurochir. (Wien) **156**, 1769–1774 (2014)
8. Deng, W.W., Li, F., Wang, M.N., Song, Z.J.: Easy-to-Use augmented reality neuronavigation using a wireless tablet PC. Stereot. Funct. Neuros. **92**, 17–24 (2014)
9. Besharati Tabrizi, L., Mahvash, M.: Augmented reality-guided neurosurgery: accuracy and intraoperative application of an image projection technique. J. Neurosurg. **123**, 206–211 (2015)
10. Citardi, M.J., Agbetoba, A., Bigcas, J.L., Luong, A.: Augmented reality for endoscopic sinus surgery with surgical navigation: a cadaver study. Int. Forum Allergy Rhinol. **6**, 523–528 (2016)
11. Cutolo, F., Meola, A., Carbone, M., Sinceri, S., Cagnazzo, F., Denaro, E., Esposito, N., Ferrari, M., Ferrari, V.: A new head-mounted display-based augmented reality system in neurosurgical oncology: a study on phantom. Comput. Assist. Surg. **22**, 39–53 (2017)
12. Kawamata, T., Iseki, H., Shibasaki, T., Hori, T.: Endoscopic augmented reality navigation system for endonasal transsphenoidal surgery to treat pituitary tumors: technical note. Neurosurgery **50**, 1393–1397 (2002)
13. Meola, A., Cutolo, F., Carbone, M., Cagnazzo, F., Ferrari, M., Ferrari, V.: Augmented reality in neurosurgery: a systematic review. Neurosurg. Rev. **40**, 537–548 (2017)
14. Finger, T., Schaumann, A., Schulz, M., Thomale, U.W.: Augmented reality in intraventricular neuroendoscopy. Acta Neurochir. (Wien) **159**, 1033–1041 (2017)
15. Cutolo, F.: Augmented Reality in Image-Guided Surgery. In: Lee, N. (ed.) Encyclopedia of computer graphics and games, pp. 1–11. Springer, Cham (2017)
16. Rolland, J.P., Fuchs, H.: Optical versus video see-through head-mounted displays in medical visualization. Presence Teleoper. Virtual Environ. **9**, 287–309 (2000)
17. Cutolo, F., Fontana, U., Carbone, M., D'Amato, R., Ferrari, V.: Hybrid video/optical see-through HMD. Adjunct. In: Proceedings of the 2017 IEEE International Symposium on Mixed and Augmented Reality (Ismar-Adjunct), pp. 52–57 (2017)
18. www.vostars.eu
19. Kersten-Oertel, M., Jannin, P., Collins, D.L.: The state of the art of visualization in mixed reality image guided surgery. Comput. Med. Imag. Grap. **37**, 98–112 (2013)
20. Bichlmeier, C., Wimme, F., Heining, S.M., Navab, N.: Contextual anatomic mimesis hybrid in-situ visualization method for improving multi-sensory depth perception in medical augmented reality. In: 6th IEEE and ACM International Symposium on Mixed and Augmented Reality, 2007, ISMAR 2007, pp. 129–138 (2007)
21. Kersten-Oertel, M., Chen, S.J.S., Collins, D.L.: An evaluation of depth enhancing perceptual cues for vascular volume visualization in neurosurgery. IEEE Trans. Vis. Comput. Graph. **20**, 391–403 (2014)
22. Badiali, G., Ferrari, V., Cutolo, F., Freschi, C., Caramella, D., Bianchi, A., Marchetti, C.: Augmented reality as an aid in maxillofacial surgery: Validation of a wearable system allowing maxillary repositioning. J. Cranio. Maxill. Surg. **42**, 1970–1976 (2014)
23. Cutolo, F., Parchi, P.D., Ferrari, V.: Video see through AR head-mounted display for medical procedures. In: IEEE International Symposium on Mixed and Augmented Reality (ISMAR), 2014, pp. 393–396. IEEE (2014)
24. Parrini, S., Cutolo, F., Freschi, C., Ferrari, M., Ferrari, V.: Augmented reality system for freehand guide of magnetic endovascular devices. In: 36th Annual International Conference of the IEEE Engineering in Medicine and Biology Society (EMBC), pp. 490–493. IEEE (2014)

25. Ferrari, V., Viglialoro, R.M., Nicoli, P., Cutolo, F., Condino, S., Carbone, M., Siesto, M., Ferrari, M.: Augmented reality visualization of deformable tubular structures for surgical simulation. Int. J. Med. Robot. Comput. Assist. Surg. **12**(2), 231–240 (2015)

26. Cutolo, F., Badiali, G., Ferrari, V.: Human-PnP: ergonomic AR interaction paradigm for manual placement of rigid bodies. In: Linte, Cristian A., Yaniv, Z., Fallavollita, P. (eds.) AE-CAI 2015. LNCS, vol. 9365, pp. 50–60. Springer, Cham (2015). https://doi.org/10.1007/978-3-319-24601-7_6

27. Evans, G., Miller, J., Pena, M.I., MacAllister, A., Winer, E.: Evaluating the Microsoft HoloLens through an augmented reality assembly application. Degrad. Environ. Sens. Process. Display **2017**, 10197 (2017)

28. Ferrari, V., Carbone, M., Cappelli, C., Boni, L., Melfi, F., Ferrari, M., Mosca, F., Pietrabissa, A.: Value of multidetector computed tomography image segmentation for preoperative planning in general surgery. Surg. Endosc. **26**, 616–626 (2012)

29. https://www.vuforia.com/

30. Badiali, G., Roncari, A., Bianchi, A., Taddei, F., Marchetti, C., Schileo, E.: Navigation in orthognathic surgery: 3D accuracy. Facial Plast. Surg. FPS **31**, 463–473 (2015)

31. Volonte, F., Pugin, F., Bucher, P., Sugimoto, M., Ratib, O., Morel, P.: Augmented reality and image overlay navigation with OsiriX in laparoscopic and robotic surgery: not only a matter of fashion. J Hepatobiliary Pancreat. Sci. **18**, 506–509 (2011)

32. Zheng, G., Nolte, L.P.: Computer-assisted orthopedic surgery: current state and future perspective. Front. Surg. **2**, 66 (2015)

33. Luebbers, H.T., Messmer, P., Obwegeser, J.A., Zwahlen, R.A., Kikinis, R., Graetz, K.W., Matthews, F.: Comparison of different registration methods for surgical navigation in cranio-maxillofacial surgery. J. Cranio-Maxillo-Facial Surg. **36**, 109–116 (2008). Official publication of the European Association for Cranio-Maxillo-Facial Surgery

34. Condino, S., Calabro, E.M., Alberti, A., Parrini, S., Cioni, R., Berchiolli, R.N., Gesi, M., Ferrari, V., Ferrari, M.: Simultaneous tracking of catheters and guidewires: comparison to standard fluoroscopic guidance for arterial cannulation. Eur. J. Vasc. Endovasc. Surg. **47**, 53–60 (2014). The official journal of the European Society for Vascular Surgery

35. Parrini, S., Zhang, L., Condino, S., Ferrari, V., Caramella, D., Ferrari, M.: Automatic carotid centerline extraction from three-dimensional ultrasound Doppler images. In: 36th Annual International Conference of the IEEE Engineering in Medicine and Biology Society, EMBC 2014, pp. 5089–5092 (2014)

36. Condino, S., Ferrari, V., Freschi, C., Alberti, A., Berchiolli, R., Mosca, F., Ferrari, M.: Electromagnetic navigation platform for endovascular surgery: how to develop sensorized catheters and guidewires. Int. J. Med. Robot. + Comput. Assist. Surg. MRCAS **8**, 300–310 (2012)

37. Ukimura, O., Gill, I.S.: Image-fusion, augmented reality, and predictive surgical navigation. Urol. Clin. North Am. **36**, 115–123, vii (2009)

38. Lamata, P., Ali, W., Cano, A., Cornella, J., Declerck, J., Elle, O.J., Freudenthal, A., Furtado, H., Kalkofen, D., Naerum, E., Samset, E., Sánchez-Gonzalez, P., Sánchez-Margallo, F.M., Schmalstieg, D., Sette, M., Stüdeli, T., Sloten, J.V., Gómez, E.J.: Augmented Reality for Minimally Invasive Surgery: Overview and Some Recent Advances (2010)

39. Nicolau, S., Soler, L., Mutter, D., Marescaux, J.: Augmented reality in laparoscopic surgical oncology. Surg. Oncol. **20**, 189–201 (2011)

40. Rankin, T.M., Slepian, M.J., Armstrong, D.G.: Augmented reality in surgery. In: Latifi, R., Rhee, P., Gruessner, W.G.R. (eds.) Technological Advances in Surgery, Trauma and Critical Care, pp. 59–71. Springer, New York (2015)

41. Ferrari, V., Viglialoro, R.M., Nicoli, P., Cutolo, F., Condino, S., Carbone, M., Siesto, M., Ferrari, M.: Augmented reality visualization of deformable tubular structures for surgical simulation. Int. J. Med. Rob. + Comput. Assist. Surg. MRCAS **12**, 231–240 (2016)
42. Viglialoro, R., Ferrari, V., Carbone, M.C.M., Condino, S., Porcelli, F., Puccio, F.D., Ferrari, M., Mosca, F.: A physical patient specific simulator for cholecystectomy training. In: CARS Proceedings of the 25th International Congress and Exhibition, Pisa, Italy, June 27–30 (2012)
43. Francesconi, M., Freschi, C., Sinceri, S., Carbone, M., Cappelli, C., Morelli, L., Ferrari, V., Ferrari, M.: New training methods based on mixed reality for interventional ultrasound: design and validation. In: Engineering in Medicine and Biology Society (EMBC), 2015, 37th Annual International Conference of the IEEE, pp. 5098–5101. IEEE (2015)
44. Freschi, C., Parrini, S., Dinelli, N., Ferrari, M., Ferrari, V.: Hybrid simulation using mixed reality for interventional ultrasound imaging training. Int. J. Comput. Assist. Radiol. Surg. **10**(7), 1109–1115 (2014)

# Virtual Reality-Based System for Hand Rehabilitation Using an Exoskeletal Orthosis

Patricio D. Cartagena[1] , Jose E. Naranjo[1] , Carlos A. Garcia[2] ,
Carmen Beltran[1], Maritza Castro[1], and Marcelo V. Garcia[1,3(✉)]

[1] Universidad Tecnica de Ambato, UTA, Ambato, Ecuador
{pcartagena6205, jnaranjo0463, cdlm. beltran,
me. castro, mv. garcia}@uta. edu. ec
[2] Universidad de las Fuerzas Armadas, ESPE, Latacunga, Ecuador
cagarcia15@espe. edu. ec
[3] University of the Basque Country, UPV/EHU, Bilbao, Spain
mgarcia294@ehu. eus

**Abstract.** This research shows an alternative device in the field of fine motor rehabilitation. This device is a flexible orthosis that helps the flexion and contraction of the hand fingers using a virtual interface environment. In addition, it has been designed with the ability to perform different assistive and resistive tasks, allowing its adaptation to the recovery status of the patient. The mechatronic prototype is controlled by algorithms based on fuzzy logic that compares data from the Unity3D graphics engine and flex sensors from the device. For the correct execution of the rehabilitation tasks the proposed fuzzy algorithms have been implemented using a Raspberry Pi. The proposed system is aimed to users with deficits in fine motor skills because of tendon injuries, achieving excellent control results for an efficient execution of tasks.

**Keywords:** Virtual reality · Virtual rehabilitation · Assistive task
Fuzzy logic · Orthosis

## 1 Introduction

The upper extremities are the essential axis to perform daily activities, however, when there is some type of injury in this area, the autonomy of the person is limited making physical rehabilitation the main choice when it comes to recover mobility of damaged limbs. Traditional rehabilitation has advanced on issues that prioritize the recovery of upper extremities functionality, despite this, the application of virtual systems, prosthetics, orthosis and control systems, are rarely taken into account either by economic or technical aspects.

That is why technological advances point to the development of rehabilitation systems focused on upper extremities, specifically on hands since these are the means to acquire data from the environment that surrounds us [1, 2]. In countries such as USA, Germany, Japan, have focused on the recovery of patients who have suffered sports injuries, traffic accidents and multiple sclerosis [3, 4].

© Springer International Publishing AG, part of Springer Nature 2018
L. T. De Paolis and P. Bourdot (Eds.): AVR 2018, LNCS 10851, pp. 105–117, 2018.
https://doi.org/10.1007/978-3-319-95282-6_8

In order to obtain significant support in the rehabilitation self-management, the introduction of the term virtual reality which allows to represent scenes, objects and actions that exist in the real world in controlled digital environments is essential [5]. The main feature that enhances the use of virtual reality in physical rehabilitation systems is the use of HMD (Head-Mounted Display) devices that provide a total immersion in a three-dimensional space. The relationship that exists between virtual reality and physical rehabilitation has technical and scientific foundations that are based on motor learning since any capacity of the human being can be improved by experience and practice. On the other hand, for virtual reality to be efficient, it is necessary to implement an orthosis or prosthesis according to the patient needs; this with the purpose of employing a control system that allows to develop movements approximations to produce exact results in the rehabilitation of the patient.

Because of all these reasons, through the development of activities and exercises in digitalized environments, it is possible to optimize the functioning of physical abilities as well as perception, attention, reasoning, abstraction, memory and orientation. The results obtained with virtual rehabilitation in relation to the conventional are justified, since the tasks generated are easier, less risky, with a high degree of personalization and entertainment. Nowadays, in the market there is a great diversity of robotic devices that assist the rehabilitation therapy of the hand, however, it is important to offer systems that enable a more complete rehabilitation, i.e., not only muscle strengthening or basic movement acquisition, but an increase of his cognitive abilities of oculo-motor coordination. In addition, this seeks to make patients feel included and able to perform normal activities of their daily life, as well as motivate them to develop their therapy with greater effectiveness [6, 7].

As described above, this article proposes the development of a control system based on fuzzy logic that allows fine motor rehabilitation of the hand. For a better control of patients' progress, an active orthosis is presented as movement support, this generates a force feedback while allowing the patient to interact with environments RGS (Rehabilitation Gaming System). The orthosis makes use of servo motors as force actuators, flexibility sensors and the Leap Motion optoelectronic device that virtualize the human hand in the programmed 3D environment.

This article is divided into 8 sections including the Introduction. The Sect. 2 shows some Related Articles. In Sect. 3, the State of the Technology is presented. The Case Study is presented in Sect. 4. The Implementation Proposal of the system is explained in Sect. 5, while the Virtual Environment is detailed in Sect. 6. In Sect. 7 the obtained Results are presented. Finally, the Conclusions and Future research are developed in Sect. 8.

## 2   Related Articles

This section presents the methodology with which different authors have developed studies of control systems applied to the rehabilitation of upper limbs. Holmes [5], presents a study that is based on the generation of virtual reality interfaces for arm and hand rehabilitation, in which the use of optoelectronic sensors (Leap Motion, Microsoft Kinect V2, the bracelets Myo and Oculus Rift DK1) is necessary. These, allow to capture the movements of the user and translate them into digital environments which motivate the user to participate in entertaining rehabilitation sessions. It is settled that, when using these systems of virtual reality, the user needs frequent training. Gutiérrez [8], focuses on designing an exoskeleton prosthesis for the arm, which allows three degrees of freedom and is controlled by a diffuse system. The input data of this system are position errors that are turn into qualitative terms in which each of them corresponds to a numerical range. In addition, it obtains a Pulse Width Modulation (PWM) signal as the output of the system, which is responsible for triggering the actuator elements. He affirms that the control by diffuse logic requires several technical tests to effectively meet the robustness and adaptability requirements that the user requires.

*Enríquez, y Narváez* [9], on the other hand, disclose the design and structure of an exoskeletal prosthesis for rehabilitation of the hand, in which an anatomical study is carried out, showing angles of flexion, extension and the laterality that the different sections of the hand have. The study comes to the conclusion that it is required that the structure fulfill its function of rehabilitating, and that the prototype must be sketched in order to analyze degrees of freedom and consider economic-flexible materials.

Finally, Andaluz [10], seeks to perform exercises to improve fine motor skills and visualize them in digital environments at the same time that signals are sent to an On-Off controller. This study provides great information in virtual rehabilitation due to the force feedback; however, the control is not intuitive and hardly adapts to the progressive movements of rehabilitation.

Once the papers presented in this section have been analyzed, it is feasible to carry out the proposed study since there is no precedent for a diffuse control system applied to the virtual rehabilitation of the hand.

## 3   State of Technology

### 3.1   Virtual Rehabilitation

Virtual reality is defined as a set of techniques and methodologies that have the purpose of recovering a lost or reduced function through advanced interfaces that allow users to interact with computer-generated three-dimensional environments in real time. In addition, virtual rehabilitation offers standardization of training protocols, and undoubtedly presents a great functional, useful and motivating profile.

The process of developing virtual environments for rehabilitation is carried out through the execution of the following aspects:

- Select the rehabilitation protocol to be executed and analyze the motion kinematics that the patient must perform.
- Collect information on mechanisms that meet the protocol's objectives.
- Construct geometric figures based on numerical descriptions that allow the mechanism to be shaped.
- Place objects in 3D space and define focus cameras.
- Convert the mathematical information of the figures and their characteristics into screen pixels.

## 3.2   Physical Rehabilitation Focused on the Mobilization of the Hand

It contains aspects of balance and movement stabilization recovery. It consists in the acquisition of minor movements by light flexions of the joints of the hand and the stabilization that involves muscle strengthening through activation exercises. In a general case of rehabilitation, the exercise that the patient must execute is the stretching and contraction of the fingers as shown in Fig. 1 [11, 12].

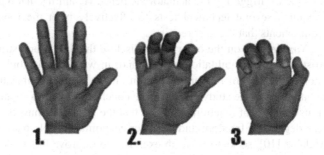

**Fig. 1.** Stretching and contraction of the fingers

It is important that the flexion angles in this type of exercise change gradually, for example; initially the angles of the metacarpophalangeal joint (MCF) must be between 0° to 30°, later they should reach 50° and finally there must be a difference greater than 50° so that it could reach the appropriate mobility value of 90° [13].

## 3.3   Fuzzy Control System

Expressed better as a control by means of words that are interpreted with common logic and sentences, however, the processes are measured numerically. Due to this, the variables must be adapted before entering to the controller. This process of adaptation is called fuzzification and consists in giving a degree of membership within possible expressions, consequently each value of the variables will have a higher level of belonging in one expression than in the rest of expressions. After the fuzzification, variables of a linguistic form are created. In these variables the logical relationships (IF-THEN) are applied. Therefore, once the controller interprets relationships, these are translated from linguistic to numerical expressions [14].

## 3.4   Hand Orthosis

It is a therapeutic device that collaborates in the fulfillment of rehabilitation objectives, allowing a control of possible medical complications. The essential objectives are stabilization, limitation of amplitude, and suppression of pain. It is important that the orthosis covers most of the limb to be treated, however, when it comes to the hand, it is necessary that both the palmar areas of the fingers and the hand remain completely free.

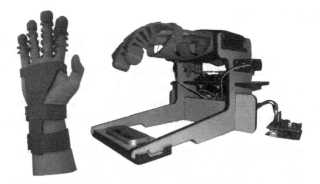

**Fig. 2.** Flexible material orthosis and armrest

Regarding its constitution, it is recommended the use of flexible thermoplastic materials that provide comfort and ease of movement [15]. The Fig. 2 shows the orthosis made with flexible thermoplastic materials and an armrest.

## 4 Case Study

Within the field of medicine, virtual rehabilitation has taken up a large space in the last five years. Therefore, the use of technological tools with greater flexibility has been necessary, introducing devices with a high degree of immersion for their users. In the traditional rehabilitation, the patient makes use of his senses to have a feedback of the tasks he performs, so the virtual world must emulate these situations.

In fact, if a comparison is made between conventional physical rehabilitation and rehabilitation with the use of virtual reality, it can be seen that the second one not only emulates the progress that physical rehabilitation offers but surpasses it. This new therapy has been used to optimize learning processes or relearning movement patterns in people with cerebral stroke, perceptive-motor deformation, acquired brain injury, Parkinson's disease, orthopedic rehabilitation, balance training and tele-rehabilitation. In Ecuador, there are 202,216 people who have some type of physical disability. 4,616 people [16] from this total are located in Tungurahua. The purpose of the case study is to use a flexible hand orthosis as a means of fine motor rehabilitation for people with musculoskeletal disorders in Tungurahua.

The Leap Motion sensor is used for detection and virtualization of hand movements, allowing the patient to interact with the virtual environment. The purpose of this control system is to integrate, through the use of fuzzy logic, personalized virtual systems with external devices that modify the functional-structural aspects of the neuro-musculoskeletal system.

## 4.1    Rehabilitation Protocol

The proposed activities to improve fine motor skills encompass a variety of options due to the different factors involved in rehabilitation. These can be classified by the type of injury or severity: (i) Individual fingers rehabilitation, the patient must execute alternating movements of the fingers at a certain angle depending on the size of the objects programmed in the virtual environment. Once the exercise is completed (5 min), it is important to have a rest period (2 min) in order to repeat 3 times, the rehabilitation process.

It is important that the patient begins his therapy with levels of difficulty in which virtual objects demand a reduced flexion of fingers, advancing progressively with levels in which the contact with the virtual environment requires a greater angle of flexion; (ii) Collective finger rehabilitation, the patient performs opening and closing exercises of the hand simulating the grip of existing objects in a person's daily routine. By means of the orthosis, the patient performs the exercises in sessions (6 min) with breaks of (2 min), this type of routine presents objects with variable sizes, with which the orthosis tries to reactivate the nervous memories gradually returning the flexibility and movements of the injured hand.

# 5    Implementation Proposal

## 5.1    Proposed Architecture

The system allows feedback of hand strength in patients with no or little mobility in their upper extremities. This system allows a safe, adaptable and relatively economical rehabilitation.

The system is related to the user through a bilateral communication; (i) Initially, in the graphic interface designed using the UNITY framework, the patient is informed about the objectives of the rehabilitation exercise, as well as the position and angle reference of his injured limb ($h_{ref}$, $\Theta_{ref}$). (ii) The patient generates an initial movement in the fulfillment of the preset exercise, in this step the position of the hand is measured ($h_d$) as well as its angle ($\Theta_d$). (iii) Due to the poor motility of the user fingers, it is possible that in a certain instance he will be unable to complete the rehabilitation objective, in this step the flexion of the fingers is measured using a flexion sensor, in this way the angular position and flex error ($F_e$, $\Theta_e$) of the finger are calculated. These calculated values together with the size of the virtual object, allow the fuzzy controller to govern the orthosis to progressively fulfill the proposed exercise.

The orthosis plays an important role in the system, since the forces emitted by the servomotors must be controlled in magnitude and direction to contribute to the direct rehabilitation without any collateral damage. In Fig. 3. the interaction between the patient and the proposed system is described.

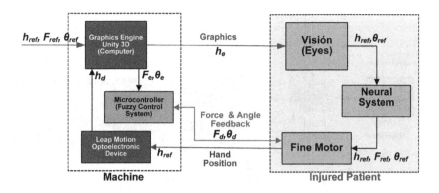

**Fig. 3.** Block diagram of the rehabilitation system

## 5.2    Proposed Hardware Platform

This research presents the ergonomic design of an orthosis prototype printed on flexible material mainly aimed to exercise upper limbs. The structure is controlled by four actuators responsible for the generation of traction force in each finger, allowing a high degree of efficiency in a semi-assisted rehabilitation. Furthermore, in order to have a better performance of the system, an armrest has been developed that together with the orthosis provides support for the actuators. Both the orthosis and the actuators share fluorocarbon filaments, invisible and resistant, useful in the transmission of force.

The proposed hardware is subdivided into five stages. (i) Virtual Interface, essentially consists of a computer that allows the user to visualize the exercises generated in the powerful graphics engine Unity3D; (ii) Control System: it is composed of the Raspberry Pi 3 microcontroller, which is responsible for processing the information sent by Unity3D and the flex sensors. This in order to perform the comparison process with the fuzzy sets and thus send the appropriate control signal to the servomotors; (iii) Leap Motion: captures the movement of the hand in inertial reference to three coordinate axes X, Y, Z. It is an optoelectronic device that captures the reflection of light generated by infrared sensors by means of two integrated cameras, storing in matrices data of the digitized image; (iv) Actuators consist of a group of servomotors HS-311 that support a current of 180 mA and can generate a torque of up to 3.0 kg/cm, it also incorporates drivers that allow to manipulate the actuators without voltage drops that could compromise the controller; (v) Power Supply consists of an external source that converts 110[v] of alternate current (AC) to 5[v] direct current (DC) with the purpose to supply the necessary voltage and current for the control system.

For a better understanding of what was expressed previously, Fig. 4 shows the diagram that constitutes the hardware of the system.

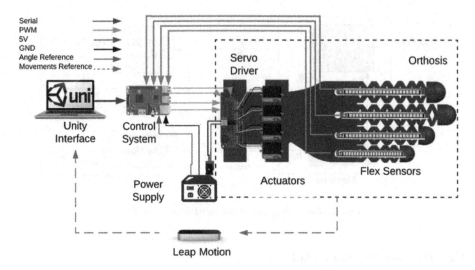

**Fig. 4.** System hardware diagram

### 5.3 Fuzzy Control

In this section the methodology to obtain the fuzzy control design which will be implemented and programmed in the RPI card is presented. The system control starts from obtaining the transfer function of the actuators. A unipolar rectangular signal is applied to the servomotor and recorded by means of a transducer. The information obtained by the acquisition system is interpreted by the Matlab software (Control System Toolbox) in order to publicize the third-degree transfer model (1).

$$F_{ref}(s) = \frac{\theta(s)}{V_\alpha(s)} = \frac{19630}{S^3 + 198s^2 + 6280s} \tag{1}$$

Once the transfer function has been obtained (1), a Fuzzy Logic Controller (FLC) is designed for a higher order system. Prior to this, the Fuzzy Inference System (FIS) is built by means of Matlab's Logic Fuzzy Design software in which readings of the response stability of the system are performed. The basic structure of an FLC consists of three stages: merger, fuzzy inference and defuzzification. Figure 5, shows the graph generated by the angular behavior present in the servomotor before the application of a rectangular stimulus.

The fuzzification stage consists of assigning data with a certain degree of membership to fuzzy sets, for this it is essential to know the system's membership functions: (i) Entry membership function "size", generated by emitted values due to the interaction among virtual objects, it is activated when the digital image of the hand comes into contact with the programmed environment; (ii) Entry membership function "angle", it is generated by the resultant values of the analog-digital conversion of the flex transducer which sets the angular position of the fingers; (iii) Output function "degrees" conformed by the values included in the operating range of the servomotor from 0 to 200°.

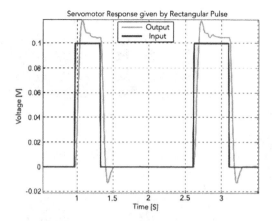

**Fig. 5.** Actuator response to a rectangular impulse

The final stage occurs in the defuzzification or decision making of the system, these decisions are obtained by the centroid method that is simplified by solving the Eq. (2).

$$Cog = \frac{\int_a^b F(x)xdx}{\int_a^b F(x)x} \qquad (2)$$

By means of the Center of gravity (Cog) of the figures formed by the fuzzy sets, the system begins to make decisions in compliance with the control rules.

## 6  Virtual Environment

It is the work space where environments composed of collision regions in a real environment are operated. It is ideal for rehabilitation due to its innovation, interaction with the patient, as well as its flexibility and personalization. In the Unity3D environment, the movements obtained by the Leap Motion Sensor are displayed in real time. In the virtual context the system consists of three stages as shown in Fig. 6.

The proposed phases are: *(i) Input Peripherals:* allow control of the closed loop between the patient and the virtual environment, using the Leap Motion device to sense the vectorized position of the hand. In addition, the option of using HMD, Oculus Rift is proposed, this device will allow a total immersion of the patient; *(ii) Interface module* develops different and novel virtual environments in order that the patient can interact efficiently with their rehabilitation protocol, and *(iii) Output Peripherals:* require communication ports and advanced programming to generate a software link between the actuators of the orthosis and the virtual environment, as well as the graphic response obtained with the application of an HMD. The interaction with the virtual environment is carried out with the Leap Motion device which allows the digitization of strategic points of the hand. With the use of the orthosis the behavior of these points

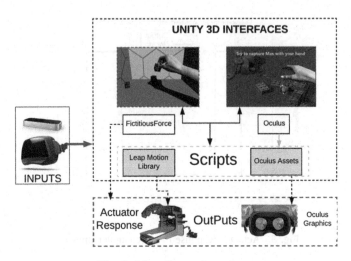

**Fig. 6.** Virtual operation scheme

is verified when performing activities of opening-closing and individual movements of the fingers. Figure 7 shows the capture of the strategic points of the hand by the Leap Motion sensor in full execution of rehabilitation tasks.

**Opening-closing movement**              **Individual movement**

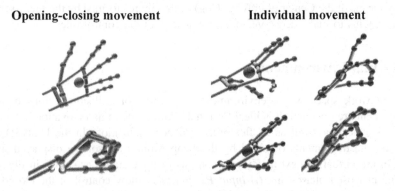

**Fig. 7.** Virtual rehabilitation exercises.

Through virtual environments RGS, personalized virtual training programs and rehabilitation protocols have been designed aiming the individual and collective recovery of the fingers. Figure 8 shows examples of the proposed RGS environments in this system.

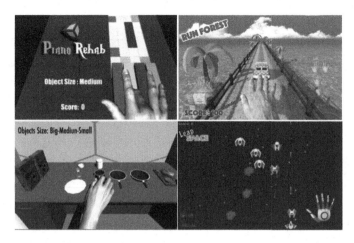

**Fig. 8.** RGS environments for individual and collective rehabilitation of the fingers.

# 7  Experimental Results

In patients with fine motor lesions, the prototype served as a significant support for the recovery of muscle memory. To verify the functioning of the system, the orthosis was applied without the help of the control system, this in order to visualize the mobility of a patient with slight injuries of the hand. In the graphic engine, when a small object is visualized, the patient needs to execute a 90° movement to complete the exercise, however, due to his low mobility, the task will not be completed, generating an error between the desired position and the ideal goal of rehabilitation as shown in Fig. 9.

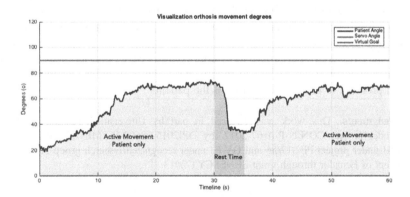

**Fig. 9.** Rehabilitation protocol without intervention of the control system.

Subsequently, the patient performs the same rehabilitation exercise, but this time supported by the control system. As depicted in Fig. 10, there is a point at which the patient fulfills his goal through the actuators implemented in the orthosis, i.e., the control

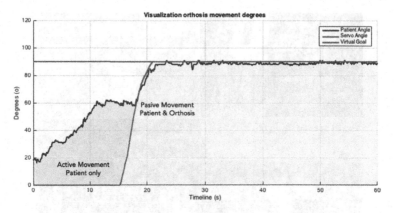

**Fig. 10.** Rehabilitation protocol with intervention of the control system

system detects when the user is unable to move forward with the exercise, activating the actuators with the necessary force feedback to complete the established protocol.

# 8 Conclusions and Future Work

The proposed system presents an efficient alternative for the rehabilitation of the hand through an orthosis that allows to execute a series of exercises that support the increase of performance in the active mobility of the hand. The flexible structural design of the orthosis was adapted to different patients in terms of the size of its limb. Fuzzy logic adapts excellently to systems with several inputs and several outputs, showing robustness and adaptability to the variation of parameters such as the angles of the fingers and the size of virtual objects. The use of virtual environments for rehabilitation with force feedback, introduces an innovative way to improve motivation, concentration and physical efficiency.

For future research, it is proposed to improve the visual interface with augmented reality implementation, as well as to modify the orthosis in order to apply the rehabilitation protocol to the wrist and arm of the patient.

**Acknowledgments.** This work was financed in part by Universidad Tecnica de Ambato (UTA) under project CONIN-P-0167-2017, by DPI2015-68602-R (MINECO/FEDER, UE), UPV/EHU under project PPG17/56 and GV/EJ under recognized research group IT914-16 and Government of Ecuador through grant SENESCYT-2013.

# References

1. Arteaga, J.M., Reyes, H.C., Escalante, F.A.: Hand rehabilitation patterns for designing interactive environments, vol. 14, no. 2, pp. 922–929 (2016)
2. Herraiz, I., Peña, A., Garcia, L., Martinez, G., Aguilar, F.: Arthroplasty of the wrist and hand. Rev. la Soc. Española Rehabil. y Med. Física, **41**, 266–272 (2007)

3. Atemoztli de la Cruz Sánchez, B., Arias Montiel, M., Lugo González, E.: Design of an Exoskeleton Prototype for Hand Rehabilitation. Pistas. Educativas Nº 125, Mexico (2017)
4. Mendoza, J., Márquez, A., Moxo, S., Servín, J.: Validation coordinating movements in upper limbs for virtual rehabilitation using slopes. Rev. Cuba. Informática Médica **8**, 12–29 (2016)
5. Holmes, D.E., Charles, D.K., Morrow, P.J., McClean, S., McDonough, S.M.: Leap motion controller and oculus rift virtual reality headset for upper arm stroke rehabilitation. In: Virtual Reality: Recent Advances in Virtual Rehabilitation System Design, vol 1, pp. 83–102. Nova Science Publishers Inc., USA (2017)
6. Byl, N., et al.: Effectiveness of sensory and motor rehabilitation of the upper limb following the principles of neuroplasticity: patients stable poststroke. Neurorehabil. Neural Repair **17**(3), 176–191 (2003)
7. Diez, J., Badesa, F.J., Sabater, J.M.: Robotic system of exoskeleton type for rehabilitation of the hand. Actas las XXXV Jornadas Automática, pp. 3–5 (2014)
8. Gutiérrez, R., Duque, J.: Design and Control of an Exoskeleton for Motor Rehabilitation in Superior Member, May 2015
9. Vivas, O.A., Enriquez, S.C.: Rehabilitacion De Mano Mediante Funda Termoretractil, pp. 3–5 (2014)
10. Andaluz, V.H., Patricio, C., José, N.: Augmented Reality, Virtual Reality, and Computer Graphics, vol. 10325, pp. 94–105 (2017)
11. Morales, G.: Introduction to fuzzy logic. Cent. Investig. y Estud. Av. IPN (2002)
12. Guzmán, E., Londoño, J.: Upper limb rehabilitation with virtual environments: a review. Rev. Mex. Ing. Biomédica **37**, 271–285 (2016)
13. Florez, C.A.C., Montanez, J.A.M., Moreno, R.J.: Design and construction of a prototype rehabilitation machine to hand and wrist. In: 2013 II International Congress Engineering Mechatronics Automation, pp. 1–6, October 2013
14. Kouro, S., Rodrigo, R.: Control with Fuzzy Logic, pp. 1–7
15. Paysant, J., et al.: Orthosis of the hand. EMC - Kinesiterapia - Med. Física **28**(2), 1–15 (2007)
16. M. de S. Publica/(CONADIS): Población Ecuatoriana, Quito, (2018)

# Virtual Reality System for Assistance in Treating Respiratory Disorders

César A. Naranjo[✉], Paola M. Velasco[✉],
Washington X. Quevedo[✉], Grace R. Naranjo[✉],
David Rivas-Lalaleo[✉], Franklin M. Silva[✉],
and Víctor H. Andaluz[✉]

Universidad de las Fuerzas Armadas ESPE, Sangolqui, Ecuador
{canaranjo,pmvelascol,wjquevedo,drrivas,fmsilva,
vhandaluz1}@espe.edu.ec, gracenaranjo14@gmail.com

**Abstract.** This paper presents a virtual reality app for pulmonary diseases treatment in children through VR game, which consists of visual and auditory stimulation thus the therapy won't be annoying to the patient. The procedure consists of a previous stage of respiratory training which the patient is asked for a deep inhalation followed by an exhalation, both within a period of 3 to 6 s and requested 3 times. The app will offer the patient different activities in a virtual environment depending on the inhalation and exhalation exercise required by the stages of their therapy, using HTC VIVE virtual reality glasses. Recognition of inhalation and exhalation exercises is performed using a DTW classifier running in real time in MATLAB and with a direct, two-way connection to Unity. Therefore, the app encourages the patient to perform the exercises therapy in an accurate and fun way and as a result respiratory signal graphs are shown for evaluation by the therapist.

**Keywords:** Virtual reality · Virtual learning environments · Spirometry
Pulmonary rehabilitation

## 1 Introduction

Respiratory function is sometimes affected by hereditary genetic diseases or problems, but today, gas emissions and chemicals generated by industrial development and urban growth produce harmful agents that affect people's health. These factors cause allergic manifestations that cause damage to the organs of the respiratory system *i.e.* nasal cavity, pharynx, larynx, trachea, bronchi and lungs, so there are a greater number of people with respiratory affections *e.g.* asthma, rhinitis, pulmonary hypertension, sinusitis and others [1–3]. The treatment of patients is through medication *e.g.* antibiotics, corticosteroids, anti-inflammatory drugs, or surgical procedures, the same ones that are performed in specialized medical centers by a team of professionals such as pulmonologists, nutritionists, physiotherapists, among other experts whose aim is to improve people's quality of life [4].

Respiratory rehabilitation is an alternative that complements medical treatment for patients of all ages and includes a range of techniques and instruments applied to

© Springer International Publishing AG, part of Springer Nature 2018
L. T. De Paolis and P. Bourdot (Eds.): AVR 2018, LNCS 10851, pp. 118–135, 2018.
https://doi.org/10.1007/978-3-319-95282-6_9

reduce the symptoms of respiratory disease [5], including the following: *(i) FR respiratory physiotherapy,* is a set of techniques that are applied so that the patient can eliminate secretions from the respiratory tract, as well as control breathing to improve pulmonary ventilation; *(ii) mechanical instruments* as well as physiotherapy are applied to eliminate secretions and clear the respiratory tract, generally applied in cases where the patient has more difficulty to perform the activity on his or her own and requires assistance through these instruments *e.g.* flutter, cornet, intrapulmonary ventilator; and *(iii) exercise* as part of any treatment, physical activity is a constant recommendation by physicians, in this case it favors the functioning of the cardiovascular and respiratory systems, and should always be supervised by the treating physician [6, 7].

The application of the different types of respiratory therapies depends on the respiratory physiopathology, age and psychoemotional state of the patient. In the case of young children and infants, the application of mechanical instruments is the most commonly used alternative [8]. FR is a technique that involves the patient, family members and the physiotherapist, who work together to correctly execute the exercise sequences, providing the patient with comfort and avoiding muscle fatigue and breathing difficulty. However, because FR requires prolonged sessions during treatment, it can be observed that children have difficulty maintaining concentration in their activity. For this reason, it is necessary to propose an attractive and entertaining way to assist the children in each FR session and to facilitate the physiotherapist in the execution of the therapy [9, 10]. One of these forms is through games, which are currently an alternative in several areas where children work with *e.g.*, health, education, psychology among others.

The insertion of new technological trends in different areas of medicine makes it possible to propose alternatives to traditional medical treatments, an example of which is the application of virtual reality VR in various areas of health such as: *(i) traumatology* where VR and haptic devices are applied to recreate similar scenarios to the real ones for the execution of rehabilitation sessions of the upper and lower extremities in patients with motor problems due to injuries or degenerative diseases [11–13]; *(ii) paediatrics* with the development of VR applications based on games for the therapy of children with cerebral palsy [14, 15]. In [16] a virtual reality program is presented to analyze the emotional consequences caused by the treatment of catastrophic illnesses in hospitalized children and adolescents; *(iii) psychology* has been one of the most developed areas for the treatment of different illnesses *e.g.* application of virtual environments to conduct studies on eating disorders [17]. For the treatment of phobias, where the patient is immersed in a real environment according to the type and degree of phobia and where it is possible to record the levels of biometric signals to be evaluated by the specialist during therapy [18, 19]. VR applications to reduce the level of anxiety in cancer patients prior to receiving chemotherapy sessions [20].

For this reason, this work proposes an application in a 3D virtual environment in the field of pneumology to perform FR as part of conventional clinical treatment in children with respiratory diseases and/or pathologies. For this purpose, games will be developed in virtual environments where the patient performs different exercises that, depending on the inhalation and exhalation time, allow him to complete the activity and move on to the next exercise until the therapy session is completed. These exercises will be supervised by the specialist, who will guarantee the functioning of the developed application.

This paper is divided into the following sections: Sect. 2 describes the methodology used for the development of this application for FR; Sect. 3 presents how the FR system is structured; Sect. 4 indicates the results obtained using the application developed and Sect. 5 indicates the conclusions of the work developed.

## 2 Methodology

The work consists in the development of an application for mobile devices or virtual reality devices, which will support the performance of three types of breathing exercises, using a non-invasive data acquisition system and a virtual reality graphic environment to motivate the patient to perform the therapy correctly.

The exercises selected for therapy consist of: (a) one nasal and one oral aspiration and one oral exhalation, (b) two nasal and one oral exhalation and (c) three nasal and one oral inhalation and one oral exhalation; when these exercises are performed, a displacement of air into and out of the body is caused, thus generating a sound. In this case, this is the signal to be picked up by means of a microphone, constituting the patient's data signal that will be used to carry out the comparison with the standard signals, Fig. 1 shows the signal acquired in each of the exercises.

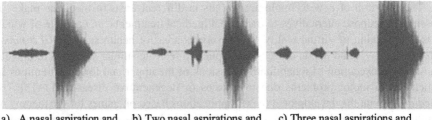

a) A nasal aspiration and     b) Two nasal aspirations and     c) Three nasal aspirations and
   an oral exhalation              one oral exhalation                 one oral exhalation

**Fig. 1.** Signals acquired by the microphone

These signals show the presence of certain patterns such as the presence of peaks in aspiration and exhalation, and the lack of synchronization of each of them. The treatment of the information will be carried out through a process involving the criteria of amplitude and time. The technique used is the Dynamic Temporal Alignment, DTW; in addition, this lack of alignment in the acquired signals does not obey a fixed law, that is, a constant delay, but it occurs in a heterogeneous way, producing localised variations that increase or decrease the duration of the analysis section. The associated problem refers to the added difficulty in the process of measuring the distance between standards, since sections that may correspond to different units will be compared. It will therefore be necessary to temporarily align the sweeper to proceed to a distance measurement between patterns whose new time axis has homogenized the initial variations. Therefore, this process will allow the comparison of each exercise with its respective pattern which was obtained by processing 100 samples of each of the exercises, calculating the DTW of the formed matrix and obtaining the average value of the matrix whose value is the DTW distance to be taken as a reference for this application using a threshold of 80% of maximum coincidence of tolerance to validate that the exercise of the therapy is correctly performed. Figure 2 shows the signals taken for each of the exercises and their respective patterns for comparison and validation.

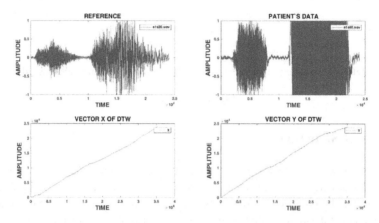

(a)  Reference or pattern signals and patient data for one inhalation and one exhalation

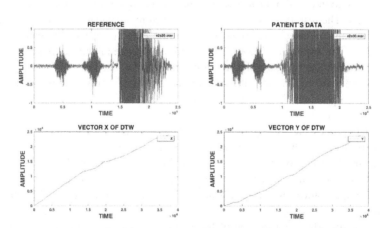

(b)  Reference or pattern signals and patient data for two inhalations and one exhalation

**Fig. 2.** Representation of input signals and patterns, with vectors X and Y of the DTW calculation between both signals

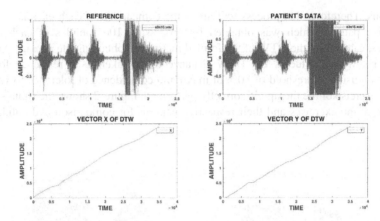

(c)   Reference or pattern signals and patient data for three inhalations and one exhalation

**Fig. 2.**   (*continued*)

## 3   System Structure

The system proposed in this work considers that the user enters the virtual environment where the instructions are indicated and the exercise to be performed is modeled, the user performs the proposed exercise when acquiring the signal the system compares it if it has a coincidence level greater than 80% it is given as a satisfactorily completed exercise which allows him to continue with the remaining two exercises of the therapy will allow a maximum of 3 erroneous repetitions per exercise to avoid hyperventilation in the patient. The results of the exercises are stored in a database in order to generate a report with the exercises performed, the time the exercise lasted, the date, time and patient data. The application developed for this experimentation consists of 5 stages: Inputs, processing, scripts, graphic platform and output, see Fig. 3.

The input stage synthesizes the data to be acquired from the environment. In this case, the microphone is the sensor to be used to capture the information which will be recorded and entered by the device's audio card.

The data processing is carried out in several steps. The data acquired by the sensor is stored in a vector, this vector is compared with the previously trained pattern, the technique used for the comparison is the DTW implemented using the Matlab software, the result of this comparison is transmitted to the script developed in Unity for the control of the graphical interface, this data is communicated through a TCP/IP port in real time.

The scripting stage is made up of the following modules: *(i) APP Controller* unit responsible for processing, managing and storing the input and output data of the system. This driver is associated with the modules; *(ii) Audio Effects* which commands the sound effects of the virtual environment; *(iii) Operations Control* manages the commands registered within the system for interaction with the user defining the activities to be performed; *(iv) Report Creator* records the data generated by the user in its interaction with the system; *(v) Data Structure* manages the data structure that

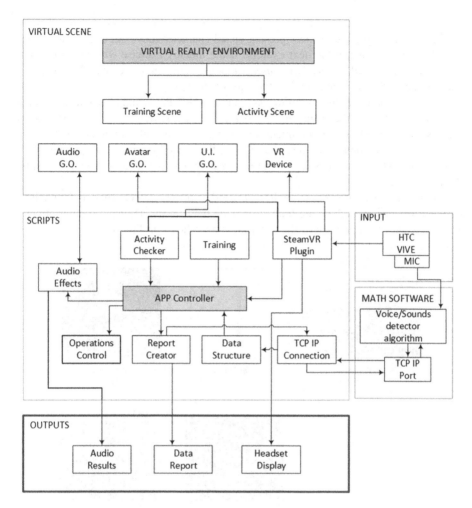

**Fig. 3.** System diagram

comes from the I/O communication ports; *(vi) Steam VR Plugin* manages the data entered by the controls or commands into the VR environment and communicates with the APP Controller; *(vii) Training* is the module that manages the training instructions. This module is trained with the conditions required to carry out the exercises; *(viii) Activity Checker* allows you to compare the proposed exercise by classifying the exercises according to the previously established parameters.

The graphic stage, which contains the environments in which the exercise will take place, consists of several Game Objects: *Audio G.O.* which is an audio source that generates sounds for the environments where the activity takes place; *Avatar G.O.* which highlights the avatar that represents the user; *U.I.G.O.* allows you to navigate within the application and select the training scene or exercise activity; *VR Device* represents the virtual reality glasses within the environment; the *Training Scene* and

*Activity Scene* modules are the training events prior to the execution of the therapy exercise to develop the sequences present visual characteristics both in time and space and allow to continue to the next exercise if the therapy exercise was correctly completed and the *Virtual Reality Environment* module is the Home screen where you can choose one of the two scenarios for the start of therapy.

In stage 5 there are: the *Audio Results* output where the sound is originated, which gives more realism to the virtual environment, the *Headset Display* module that allows the visualization of the environment in response to the inhalation and exhalation activity on the microphone at the beginning for the execution of the therapy and in the *Data Report* where the recording of the informative data of the activity carried out by the user is recorded.

In the virtualization process, replica 3D models of real models such as luminaires, bridges, benches and others are built to include them in the application environment. The sequence for the design of the environment is shown in Fig. 4.

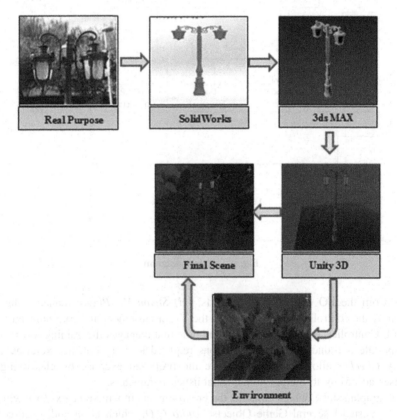

**Fig. 4.** 3D object construction diagram

The design of the virtual environments uses the 3D models replica of the real models for which CAD software is used, in this case SolidWorks was used. Once the 3D objects are obtained, their properties related to the axes, orientation and hierarchy of elements are modified through 3ds MAX, which provides agility in the manipulation and location of the objects in the virtual environment. The generated file is imported to the 3D Unity in.fbx format where the texturization and programming for the use of each object within the virtual environment is carried out. As a final product, a virtual representation of the real object in functionality and aesthetics is obtained.

The entire game environment has been developed with the unity tools because it offers a good tool to make realistic scenarios for the app. The principal environment features (see Fig. 5) used to develop the app are the next: *(i) Ambient Lightning* place light points in strategic places to feel sense of a road to follow, *(ii) Heightmap* using raise/lower terrain modeling tool and a brush style from the options panel it's possible to make some mountains and small valleys in the environment, *(iii) Forest Texture* using the

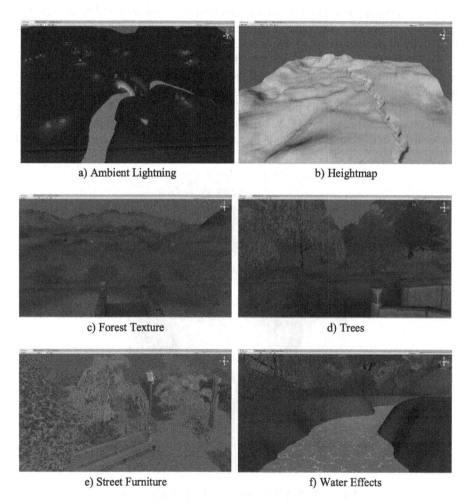

a) Ambient Lightning          b) Heightmap

c) Forest Texture          d) Trees

e) Street Furniture          f) Water Effects

**Fig. 5.** Game environment develop

resources of Environment package it's possible to assign textures and grass, soil, rocks and so on, *(iv) Trees* there are many types of trees inside the environment package that will be placed manual or randomly in a specific area, *(v) Street Furniture* its necessary place bridges, light posts, park benches and others from a CAD-CAM (SolidWorks) or 3D modelling software (3dsMAX, blender), *(vi) Water effects* to bring the effect of a small river through the park, there are a prefab inside the Environment package.

## 4  Analysis and Results

This section presents the execution of the preliminary tests using the developed app, and also shows the results obtained after the use of the application. The system developed allows the evaluation of respiratory physiotherapy (RP) techniques aimed at children with lung disorders, in order to strengthen the performance of the therapy in an entertaining and motivating way for the patient. The special characteristics of respiratory physiotherapy in children suffering from lung problems are based on the activity-disposition relationship, due to the complexity of maintaining the child's readiness with the activity of the therapy to be performed.

The application shows an open world environment in which the patient must perform FR micro-tasks to interact with the environment and unlock new sequential missions in the game. The HTC VIVE headset connected to a VR Ready computer (see Fig. 6) with Core i7-6700HQ processor, GTX1070 video card and 16 GB RAM are used for testing. The headset HTC VIVE was elected because their workspace of 12 m$^2$ that enables free movement in any direction by: walking, running, bending and

**Fig. 6.**  HTC VIVE Glasses and VR Ready laptop

jumping in virtual reality. These features bring immersive experience to the patient that make exercises without think in make exercises of therapy. The software of HTC VIVE has a plugin to connect directly to unity and execute the program while is in development to check details in VR without build all project in an executable file.

When the application is opened, the Home screen is displayed, showing the name of the application and its opening to the other screens as shown in Fig. 7. The application has constant visual and auditory support that allows the user to interact intuitively with the application without the need for a third person to constantly guide the user. On the Training screen the user receives a tutorial to perform the 3 exercises that will be asked of the user, see Fig. 8.

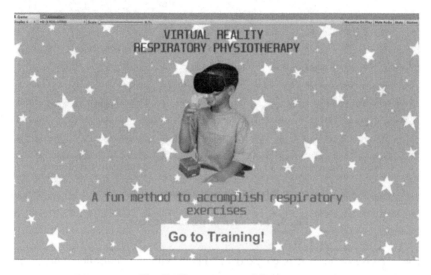

**Fig. 7.** Home screen of the app

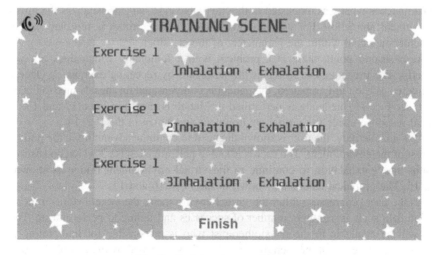

**Fig. 8.** Training screen of the app

In the next level the user appears at the starting point of the forest where he can follow the visual and auditory instructions that guide the user to the next point where he will have to perform a task to complete the passage through that place. As a first point, exercise N°1 is performed (see Fig. 9). If the execution is successful, the user is allowed to advance to the next point; if the execution fails, the user is encouraged to perform a second time; if he or she fails the test, the system will enter a process loop until the user succeeds in performing the task.

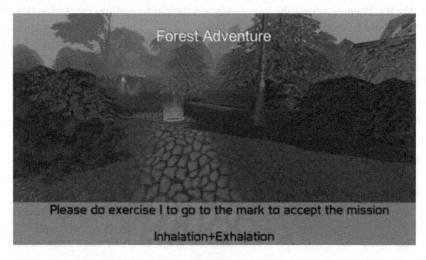

**Fig. 9.** Execution of the first exercise

The exercise performed is checked in Matlab with the controller running at the same time as the application. If the Euclidean distance and the result of the DTW algorithm are within the training values see Fig. 10, it is resolved that the exercise signal matches what was requested in this favorable case, which visualizes the mission achievement animation. For an unfavorable case, the algorithm is repeated until the user enters a signal within the parameters of the classifier.

As a second point, there is a problem with a luminaire, which does not work properly. The user's task is to repair the luminaire by repeating exercise 2. Once the luminaire has been fully repaired, the patient is compensated for the advance to the next point, see Fig. 11, the analysis performed in Matlab is shown in Figs. 12 and 13. The optical response inside the virtual environment are shown in the Fig. 14.

As a next activity, the user is shown the need to continue advancing in the points of interest of the environment. The user is asked to perform exercise 3 which consists of 3 breaths and 1 exhalation to continue to the virtual environment bridge as shown in Fig. 15. The graphical results are shown in the Figs. 16 and 17.

As the user progresses within the virtual environment, the system stores important session data such as: runtime, number of successes and failure to perform tests. These data will be available to the physiotherapist who is responsible for interpreting and verifying the progress of the therapy. The activity is validated by the completion of the

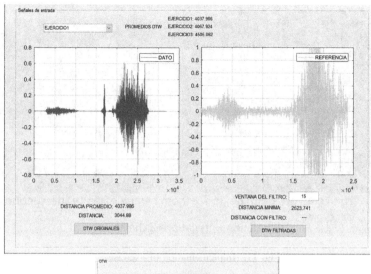

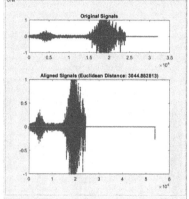

**Fig. 10.** Resulting data in Matlab for exercice N° 1

task according to the development in the execution of the exercise performed by children with lung disease in the execution of the RF according to the activity indicated in each of the exercises, and the level of user satisfaction in the use of the application developed is also established.

## 4.1 Task Fulfillment

The techniques and strategies used are based on the therapist defining the objective of the therapy and independently activating the stage according to the established inhalation and exhalation times and at the end of the three stages of established exercises, the therapy will be evaluated verifying the degree of compliance with the activity performed by the children.

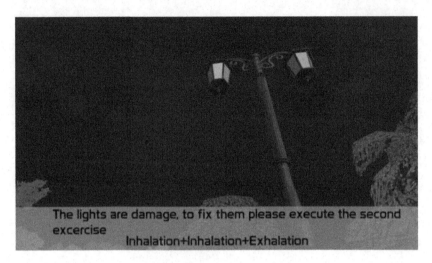

**Fig. 11.** Implementation of exercise 2

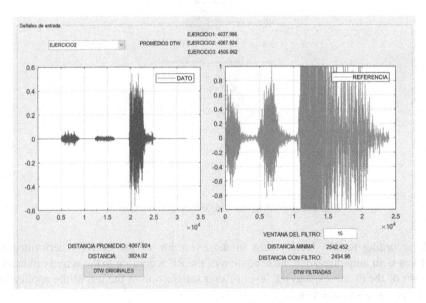

**Fig. 12.** Comparing two respiratory signals in Matlab

For the evaluation process, the group consisted of 10 children with lung disease problems between the ages of 6 and 10 years old who have the same level of disease. The indicator to be validated is the fulfilment of the activities defined by the therapist, which are indicated in Table 1.

According to the data, it is observed that the evaluated group registers a greater compliance with the parameters, which indicates that the work carried out in the virtual environment of the therapy is interactive and the attention of the child is constant due to

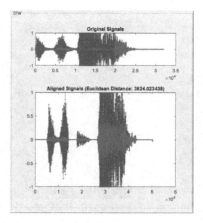

**Fig. 13.** DTW results of the exercise 2 in Matlab

**Fig. 14.** Graphical response made after the successful completion of exercise 2

the presence of virtual scenarios, whose purpose is to guide the child in the process of compliance with the therapy in a correct way, see Fig. 18.

As the application is fun, it can be observed that it has a great acceptance by the user since it allows him/her to interact in virtual environments different from the traditional ones, such as the medical offices, maintaining the concentration and mental stimulation during the process. Therefore, applications of this type developed in virtual environments encourage the realization of the therapy, improving the recovery of the patients.

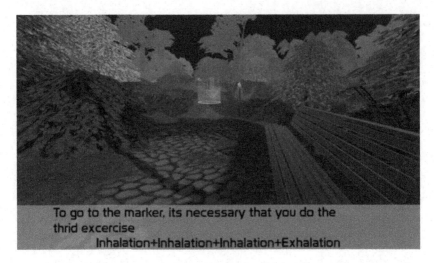

**Fig. 15.** Hearing of the request for implementation for the exercise 3

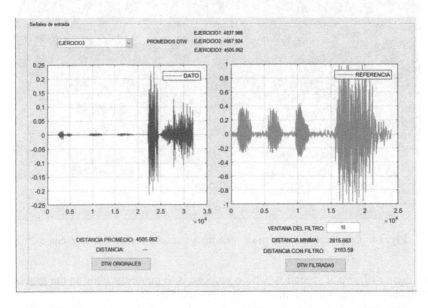

**Fig. 16.** Comparing of respiratory user signs with the reference sign in Matlab

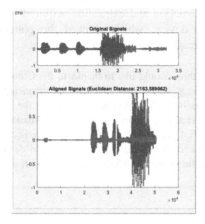

**Fig. 17.** DTW results of the implementation of the third exercise in Matlab

**Table 1.** Parameters to evaluate.

| Questions |
| --- |
| Q1. Children with lung problems completed the defined task |
| Q2. Maintain an appreciated concentration for the realization of therapy in the virtual environment |
| Q3. Children are attracted to virtual devices when doing FR |
| Q4. The children performed the therapy levels without any problems |
| Q5. Virtual reality can be applied to other types of exercises for FR |

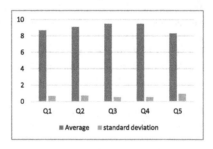

**Fig. 18.** Results of task accomplishment.

## 5  Conclusions

The results obtained from the implementation of the virtual reality system for the assistance in the treatment of respiratory disorders in child patients prove to be efficient for the rehabilitation treatment under the supervision of the therapist, since it allowed the patient to maintain concentration and perform the therapy in a very entertaining and productive way. The system developed considers three stages as virtual games that adjust to the degree of inhalation and exhalation acquired in real time from patients through the HTC VIVE device, which allowed the patient to interact with the respective exercise for therapy in the virtual environment.

**Acknowledgement.** The authors would like to thanks to the Corporación Ecuatoriana para el Desarrollo de la Investigación y Academia–CEDIA for the financing given to research, development, and innovation, through the CEPRA projects, especially the project CEPRA-XI-2017-06; Control Coordinado Multi-operador aplicado a un Robot Manipulador Aéreo; also to Universidad de las Fuerzas Armadas ESPE, Universidad Técnica de Ambato, Escuela Superior Politécnica de Chimborazo, Universidad Nacional de Chimborazo, and Grupo de Investigación en Automatización, Robótica y Sistemas Inteligentes, GIARSI, for the support to develop this paper.

# References

1. Goldizen, F.C., Sly, P.D., Knibbs, L.D.: Respiratory effects of air pollution on children. Pediatr. Pulmonol. **51**(1), 94–108 (2016)
2. Tao, Y., Mi, S., Zhou, S., Wang, S., Xie, X.: Air pollution and hospital admissions for respiratory diseases in Lanzhou, China. Environ. Pollut. **185**, 196–201 (2014)
3. Schachter, E.N., Moshier, E., Habre, R., Rohr, A., Godbold, J., Nath, A., Kat-tan, M.: Outdoor air pollution and health effects in urban children with moderate to severe asthma. Air Qual. Atmos. Health **9**(3), 251–263 (2016)
4. Torres-Castro, R., Zenteno, D., Rodriguez-Núñez, I., Villarroel, G., Alvarez, C., Gatica, D., Soto, R.: Guías de rehabilitación respiratoria en niños con enfermedades respiratorias crónicas: actualización 2016. Neumol. pediátr. (En línea) **11**(3), 114–131 (2016)
5. Laurino, R.A., Barnabe, V., Saraiva-Romanholo, B.M., Stelmach, R., Cukier, A., Nunes, M.D.P.T.: Respiratory rehabilitation: a physiotherapy approach to the control of asthma symptoms and anxiety. Clinics **67**(11), 1291–1297 (2012)
6. Vega, N.A., Torres, F.D.G., González, I.V., Veranes, I.B.D., González, Y.F.: Utilidad de la fisioterapia respiratoria en pacientes con enfermedad pulmonar obstructiva crónica. Revista de Información Científica **96**(4), 675–684 (2017)
7. Rous, M.R.G., Lobato, S.D., Trigo, G.R., Vélez, F.M., San Miguel, M., Cejudo, P., Servera, E.: Rehabilitación respiratoria. Archivos de Bronconeumología **50**(8), 332–344 (2014)
8. Chacon, P.F.S., Schon, C.F., Furtado, V.H.L.A., Signoretti, G.L.A.M., Oliveira, J.P.P., Ribeiro, A.G., Soares, H.B.: Support and rehabilitation of patients with pulmonary expansion deficit by using game therapy. In: 2016 IEEE 38th Annual International Conference of the Engineering in Medicine and Biology Society (EMBC), pp. 5632–5635. IEEE, August 2016
9. Moss, M., Nordon-Craft, A., Malone, D., Van Pelt, D., Frankel, S.K., Warner, M.L., Schenkman, M.: A randomized trial of an intensive physical therapy program for patients with acute respiratory failure. Am. J. Respir. Crit. Care Med. **193**(10), 1101–1110 (2016)
10. Puppo, K.H., Torres-Castro, K.R., Rosales-Fuentes, K.J.: Rehabilitación respiratoria en niños. Revista Médica Clínica Las Condes **28**(1), 131–142 (2017)
11. Quevedo, W.X., et al.: Assistance system for rehabilitation and valuation of motor skills. In: De Paolis, L.T., Bourdot, P., Mongelli, A. (eds.) AVR 2017. LNCS, vol. 10325, pp. 166–174. Springer, Cham (2017). https://doi.org/10.1007/978-3-319-60928-7_14
12. Menezes, R.C., Batista, P.K.A., Ramos, A.Q., Medeiros, A.F.C.: Development of a complete game based system for physical therapy with kinect. In: Serious Games and Applications for Health (SeGAH), pp. 1–6 (2014)

13. Pruna, E., et al.: VRAndroid system based on cognitive therapeutic exercises for stroke patients. In: Rocha, Á., Correia, A.M., Adeli, H., Reis, L.P., Costanzo, S. (eds.) WorldCIST 2017. AISC, vol. 570, pp. 657–663. Springer, Cham (2017). https://doi.org/10.1007/978-3-319-56538-5_67

14. Cho, C., Hwang, W., Hwang, S., Chung, Y.: Treadmill training with virtual reality improves gait, balance, and muscle strength in children with cerebral palsy. Tohoku J. Exp. Med. **238**(3), 213–218 (2016)

15. Albiol-Pérez, S., et al.: A neurocognitive virtual rehabilitation system for children with cerebral palsy: a preliminary usability study. In: Rocha, Á., Correia, A., Adeli, H., Reis, L., Mendonça Teixeira, M. (eds.) New Advances in Information Systems and Technologies. AISC, vol. 444, pp. 1057–1063. Springer, Cham (2016). https://doi.org/10.1007/978-3-319-31232-3_100

16. Flujas-Contreras, J.M., Ruiz-Castañeda, D., Botella, C., Gómez, I.: Un programa de bienestar emocional basado en Realidad Virtual y Terapia Online para enfermedades crónicas en infancia y adolescencia: La Academia Espacial. Revista de Psicología Clínica con Niños y Adolescentes **4**(3), 17–25 (2017)

17. Agliaro-López, M., Ferrer-Garcia, M., Pla-Sanjuanelo, J., Gutiérrez-Maldonado, J.: Inducción de craving por comida mediante realidad virtual no inmersiva. Revista de psicopatología y psicología clínica **19**(3), 243–251 (2014)

18. Ortiz, J.S., et al.: Realism in audiovisual stimuli for phobias treatments through virtual environments. In: De Paolis, L.T., Bourdot, P., Mongelli, A. (eds.) AVR 2017. LNCS, vol. 10325, pp. 188–201. Springer, Cham (2017). https://doi.org/10.1007/978-3-319-60928-7_16

19. Naranjo, C.A., et al.: Teaching process for children with Autism in virtual reality environments. In: International Conference on Education Technology and Computers, pp. 41–45. ACM (2017)

20. Espinoza, M., Baños, R.M., García-Palacios, A., Botella, C.: La realidad virtual en las intervenciones psicológicas con pacientes oncológicos. Psicooncología **10**(2/3), 247–261 (2013)

# Virtual System Using Haptic Device for Real-Time Tele-Rehabilitation of Upper Limbs

Ivón Escobar, Catherine Gálvez, Gabriel Corrales, Edwin Pruna[(✉)],
Marco Pilatasig, and Javier Montaluisa

Universidad de las Fuerzas Armadas ESPE, Sangolquí, Ecuador
{ipescobar, clgalvez, lgcorrales, eppruna, mapilatagsig,
fjmontaluisa}@espe.edu.ec

**Abstract.** This paper proposes a tool to support the rehabilitation of upper limbs assisted remotely, which makes it possible for the physiotherapist to be able to assist and supervise the therapy to patients who can not go to rehabilitation centers. This virtual system for real-time tele-rehabilitation is non-invasive and focuses on involving the patient with mild or moderate mobility alterations within a dynamic therapy based on virtual games; Haptics Devices are used to reeducate and stimulate the movement of the upper extremities, at the same time that both motor skills and Visual-Motor Integration skills are developed. The system contains a virtual interface that emulates real-world environments and activities. The functionality of the Novint Falcon device is exploited to send a feedback response that corrects and stimulates the patient to perform the therapy session correctly. In addition, the therapy session can vary in intensity through the levels presented by the application, and the amount of time, successes and mistakes made by the patient are registered in a database. The first results show the acceptance of the virtual system designed for real-time tele-rehabilitation.

**Keywords:** Tele-rehabilitation · 3D virtual environment · Haptic device
Motor skills

## 1 Introduction

Cerebral Palsy (CP) is a set of neuromotor disorders, which cause limitation of activity, which are attributed to a non-progressive aggression on a developing brain [1]. Infantile cerebral palsy has been considered as one of the most frequent causes of motor disability in children [2]. Approximately half of the children who suffer PC present difficulty in the upper extremities in activities such as grasping, reaching and manipulating objects [3]. The development of fine motor skills is decisive for a child. His achievements in this field open the door to experimentation and learning about his environment and consequently, it allows the development of intelligence [4].

Therapeutic interventions for the control of the upper extremities in children with CP suggest the repeated practice of functional activities in several contexts and that have feedback [5–7]. However, participating in repeated practices or movements can

© Springer International Publishing AG, part of Springer Nature 2018
L. T. De Paolis and P. Bourdot (Eds.): AVR 2018, LNCS 10851, pp. 136–152, 2018.
https://doi.org/10.1007/978-3-319-95282-6_10

cause boredom in children due to limitations in the exercises [8]. For the physical therapy of children with mild motor impairment, therapists develop programs with the aim of achieving a stimulating, varied and quality environment, since the child with cerebral palsy, like any child, needs new experiences and interaction with the child. outside world to be able to learn [9, 10].

Interactive technologies based on movement such as Virtual Reality (VR) have helped improve motor functionality in children [11]. Virtual reality-based therapies are increasingly recognized tools because they generate positive feedback and provide long-term motivation [12–14]. Studies show an improvement in manual function and in cortical organization, especially in children with cerebral palsy after therapies based on Virtual Reality (VR) [15, 16].

The environments created with VR present environments very close to reality that provide auditory and tactile visual feedback, factors that can be manipulated in a precise and systematic way and allow individualized training in motor learning [17, 18]. Interaction with haptic devices generate tactile feedback and achieve greater immersion of patients in the virtual environment [19–21]. This feedback improves the participation and commitment of patients during motor exercises, activating the multisensory system [22]. The haptic systems generate force feedback which can be useful in motor recovery of the upper limbs either due to trauma or injury [23]. These rehabilitation systems can help a patient complete a rehabilitation task [24]. Studies have shown that after training with haptic devices patients are more likely to improve their activities of daily living and improve arm function [25].

In this context, the present work presents the development of a virtual system focused on tele rehabilitation using the Novint Falcon haptic device as an assistant that bases its operation on the repetition of forces generated by the rehabilitation movements carried out by a rehabilitator located in distant place to the patient. The application of the servomotors forces of the Novint Falcon, which generate the reading and repetition of movements, are produced in real time due to the implementation of bidirectional wireless communication algorithms based on the UDP protocol. The proposed tele-rehabilitation is complemented with the processing of the data generated in the haptic device in graphic animation subroutines in a 3D virtual interface developed in Unity software, which builds virtual games with different levels of complexity. The implementation of the virtual interface is enhanced using computer-aided design, CAD, and graphics engines as a complement to Unity for high-quality graphics and animations in 3D virtual games of child content that aim to capture the attention of the user. These characteristics make the use of the application attractive and intuitive, so they guide the applicability of this work to non-monotonous rehabilitation, mainly of infants of seven years and older, and intends to avoid transfer to a rehabilitation center that, on occasion It can be a problem for the patient due to certain circumstances. Additionally, it has been considered the integration of a data recording system in a local server that allows the rehabilitator to monitor and analyze the progress of the therapies in a versatile way. Figure 1 presents the general scheme of the tele-rehabilitation system proposed in this work.

The work is organized in VI Sections, including the Introduction. Section 2 presents the system methodology based on the use of Unity software to create the intuitive virtual interface. In Sect. 3, the algorithm implemented in the virtual application is

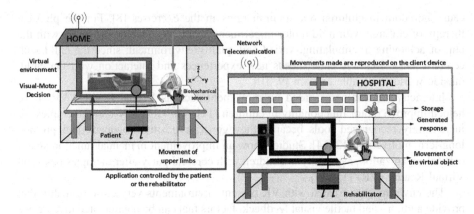

**Fig. 1.** General diagram of tele-rehabilitation system of uppers limbs.

detailed. The experimental results and discussion that validate the implementation and functionality of the proposal system are presented in Sect. 4. Finally, the conclusions are found in Sect. 5.

## 2 Methodology for Tele-Rehabilitation System Development

The proposed system includes the development of a multi-user virtual application with two games, each with three levels of complexity, with the aim of assisting the patient in their reeducation, stimulation and development of motor skills and visual-motor integration skills. The proposed system is designed and implemented in the Unity software, in which a programming based on classes and objects is handled. Each object is associated with scripts (written in C# language) that control different operations of the application, which are related to the acquisition of data from the Novint Falcon haptic device, animations of 3D graphics, transmission and reception of data, etc. The Fig. 2 shows a block diagram that summarizes the objects and functions programmed in Unity that apparently run in parallel, because one subroutine is related and/or depends on the data of another.

The virtual system is associated with the Novint Falcon haptic device, which digitizes and produces a three-dimensional movement of its axis (sphere where the hand of the user is positioned) by reading the position of its three servomotors and the application of forces respectively. The operation of the Novint Falcon is controlled from a Unity object through a library that accesses the functions of the official SDK of the device. This access is managed through a software package or wrapper that must be placed in the Unity project in a folder called Plugins.

The focus of this system is centered on tele-rehabilitation, for this fact the communication subroutines are also programmed in Unity, which allow the transfer and reception of data between two terminals that are in different places, *i.e.*, a computer that executes the application for both the rehabilitation user and the patient user, in addition,

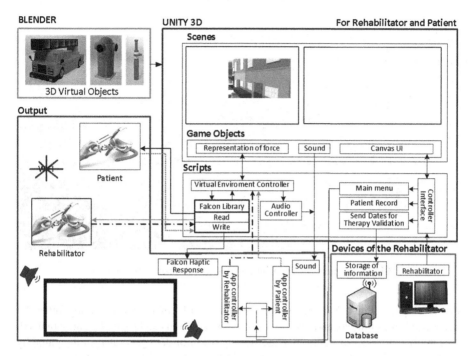

**Fig. 2.** Blocks diagram of the proposed tele-rehabilitation system for development the motor skills.

each user uses a Novint Falcon device. The communication algorithms are based on the UDP protocol, at the transport level of the TCP/IP model, so the communication implemented is server-client type and occurs in real time. The data exchanged between the client and the server correspond to the values of the three-dimensional position vector of the axis of each Novint Falcon. The server is responsible for managing the communication, *i.e.*, admit and manage the connection with the client, as well as fully govern the operation of the virtual application in the two terminals.

The data of the position vector of the axis of the Novint Falcon are processed by the animations scripts, this phase produce the movements of translation and rotation of the main 3D graphic that intervene in the virtual game (fire truck). In addition, the animation scripts are responsible for the control of the interface, collisions between 3D objects, reproduction of sounds, appearance of messages, among other effects provided to other objects in the virtual environment. The 3D graphics have been modeled in the Blender software, as *.fbx* files, which together with the Unity graphic engine functions make up the virtual environment. The virtual environment has been designed with child content and resembles a city, as indicated in Fig. 3.

The application is also composed of Canvas UI objects whose function is to indicate and receive information from the user, *i.e.*, execute the operations of interaction between the user and the system through the on-screen printing of data and information and/or motivation messages. In addition, based on the functions of objects

**Fig. 3.** Virtual environment composed with many 3D graphics.

are developed menus that manage the execution of game levels, among other UI elements such as buttons and text boxes where instructions and input data are obtained.

Finally, an object in Unity manages the insertion of data generated in the game by creating a communication channel with a *.php script, which is executed on a local server (managed and created by the XAMPP software only on the server terminal that is used by the rehabilitator) and directly controls a MySQL database. The fields of the database have been defined based on the analysis of which data are useful for recording and analyzing the progress of the patient in each rehabilitation session. These correspond to the times in which the challenges have been completed, the number of hits and misses, date and time of the session; as well as patient information such as name and surname, identity card, age and pathology presented.

## 3  Functioning of the Tele-Rehabilitation System

The tele-rehabilitation system is centered on a dynamic virtual application with games of child guidance. The games are related to the activities of the firefighter profession, specifically the objective is to drive a fire truck to get to extinguish a fire that is occurring in a building in the city. The route to the fire is marked by hydrants that must be collected to obtain prizes. The user must avoid colliding the fire truck to avoid losing points of life. If the truck totally loses the points of life the game will end, otherwise, if it reaches the fire, the next stage of the game will continue, which corresponds to extinguishing the fire by moving a 3D hose that throws water. The complexity of the game depends on the length of the routes and the necessary time that must be used to achieve the objectives of the game. To fulfill these design criteria of the virtual application, the programming of the subroutines in Unity is carried out following a general operating algorithm indicated in Fig. 4.

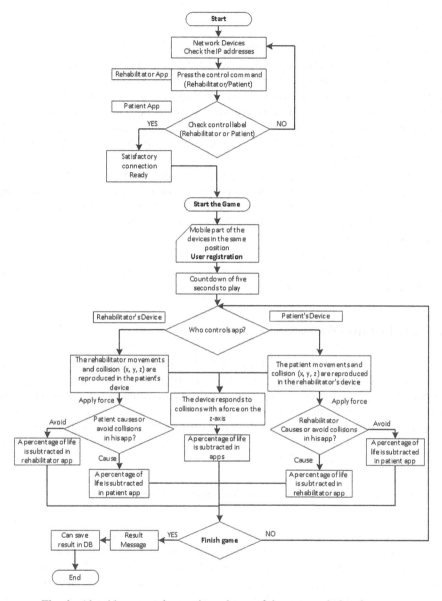

**Fig. 4.** Algorithm general operation scheme of the proposed virtual system.

The mode of operation of the algorithm starts with the verification of the functioning of the system by the rehabilitator, who has the functions of starting the game, selecting the control command and registering the patient. At the start of the game, the countdown is activated that alerts the patient and the rehabilitator to perform the game activities successfully. The control of the game is assigned to the patient or to the rehabilitator (action defined by the rehabilitator), the movements $x$, $y$, $z$ made with the

Novint Falcon device are reproduced at the same time in the other device that does not have control of the virtual game.

If the application of a force in the Novint Falcon device causes a virtual three-dimensional object to collide, it generates a decrease in the percentage of life indicated in the corresponding interface. In addition, if there is a collision there is a feedback response from the Novint Falcon device, *i.e.*, the application of a force on the $z$ axis that gives the sensation of rebound in the collision. With the purpose that the rehabilitator has the possibility of evaluating the patient, the application admits that the control of the movements of the fire truck, through the handling of the Novint Falcon, exchanges at any moment of the game.

At the end of the game, different messages are shown to indicate if the mission ended successfully or did not reach the percentage of life to meet the objective. In addition, the rehabilitator has the power to define or validate the therapy session, so it may or may not save the game data (time, percentage of life, etc.) in the database that is managed independently.

The algorithm is the same for the different levels of game that the application presents, with the difference that the different routes are defined, among other variables that increase the complexity of the game.

## 4    Results and Discussion

The first results of the project presented in this section are divided in three aspects, the first one is related to the experimentation of the proposed virtual system, *i.e.*, it is shown the software routines functioning of the virtual application. Secondly, it is realized an analysis of the tele rehabilitation propose trough the analysis of the communication response between the server (rehabilitator) and the client (patient). Finally, the results of a test applied to the users who participated in the test of the proposed system are presented and analyzed.

### 4.1    Experimentation of the Virtual Tele-Rehabilitation System

For the execution of the proposed system is used two different computers with the following features: Intel core i7-7500 2.9 GHz of seventh generation, 16 GB of RAM, a Graphic Card Intel HD 620, Windows 10 Home operative system of 64 bits (server) - Intel core i7-3610QM 2.30 GHz, 8 GB of RAM, a Graphic Card NVIDIA Geforce GT 650 M 2 GB, Windows 10 Home operative system of 64 bits (client). The algorithms, animations and sounds of the application are executed satisfactorily in the two computers, however, it is recommended to use computers of the same or advanced features in such a way that the speed of execution is the same. Regarding the equipment of the system are distributed as shown in Fig. 5 to demonstrate its use, as well as the real-time operation of the virtual interface.

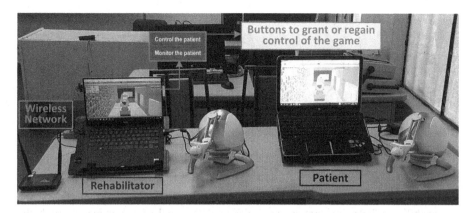

**Fig. 5.** Components of the tele-rehabilitation system.

The experimentation begins with the verification of the functioning of the Novint Falcon devices in the axes $(x, y, z)$ as shown in Fig. 6, in this way the position of the two devices is synchronized.

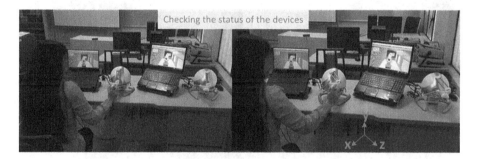

**Fig. 6.** Verification of the functioning of Novint Falcon devices.

Figures 7 and 8 show how the patient and the rehabilitator take the control of the virtual game in the two screens, the same scene is observed, which demonstrates that remote assisted rehabilitation will allow the patient to feel that the rehabilitator is supervising him during the therapy.

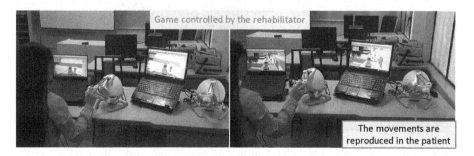

**Fig. 7.** Device controlled by the rehabilitator.

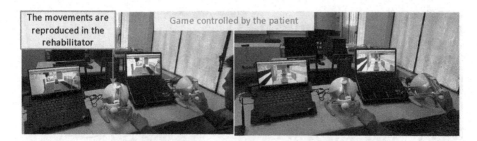

**Fig. 8.** Device controlled by the patient.

The Fig. 9 and 10 show the displacements that occur in the virtual interface when the rehabilitator helps the patient to understand the goal of the game, through the indications about how to get the message of congratulation for a successful session. If a negative message appears, the application prompts the user to try again, in this way the patient develops his visual motor integration skills. On the other hand, when the patient

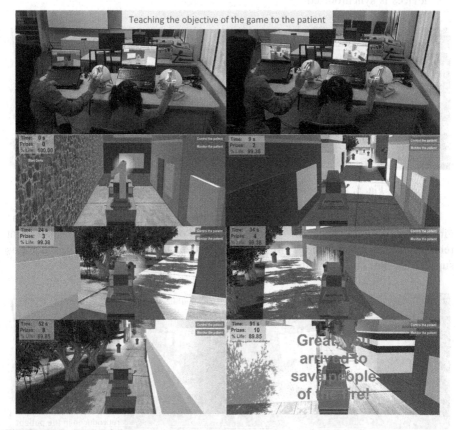

**Fig. 9.** Movements of the virtual object so that the patient understands the objective of the game.

**Fig. 10.** Game supervised by the rehabilitator when the patient manipulates the device.

performs the movements the rehabilitator supervises each one of these displacements; this means that if is detected problems in the patient to fulfill the activity, the rehabilitator can help and indicate the procedure again.

All the levels of the game are executed in the equivalent way with the correspondent differences of complexity. The Fig. 11 shows the three levels of the second phase of game that requires greater concentration and speed to complete it, the operating principle is the same as the previous one.

## 4.2 Captured Signals of the Novint Falcon Devices

The application is executed independently in two computers with different characteristics, however, the displacement of the virtual object in each of the applications operate in equal times, *i.e.*, the movements that are made with the control device are reproduced in real-time in the controlled device. The figures presented below show the signals of the interaction movements between the patient and the rehabilitator; this data have been stored in the computer of the rehabilitator with a rate of five samples per second during the path following of the virtual object through the scenario that represents forty-eight seconds.

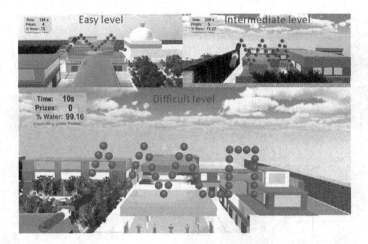

**Fig. 11.** Scenarios of the game with high complexity and its three levels of difficulty.

The signals in the Fig. 12 indicate the movements performed by the rehabilitator on the $x$ and $y$ axis, and the reproduction of these movements on the device of the patient. This result was obtained with a patient who was familiar with the application and has improved the visual-motor integration skills. The movements in the $x$ axis move the virtual object to the left or right and the movements in the $y$ axis move it forward or backward. It can be seen that the two signals have the same movement tendency, although the amplitudes do not coincide in various parts of the graph, which is due to the fact that the patient has a slight resistance to the movement performed by the rehabilitator, *i.e.*, in the virtual environments the three-dimensional objects follow similar routes at the same time, and the slight difference in amplitude does not influence in the route because the difference of the displacement that exists between the two objects is not appreciable.

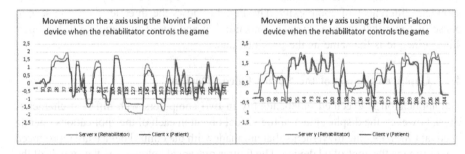

**Fig. 12.** Signs provided by Novint Falcon devices when controlling the rehabilitator

The signals of the Fig. 13 indicate the movements that the patient performs on the $x$ axis and $y$ axis, which are reproduced in the device of the rehabilitator, with a patient who has an average experience respect to the use of the application. It is observed that the two signals have the same movement tendency, although the amplitudes do not coincide in several parts of the graph because the rehabilitator corrects some movements made by the patient, *i.e.*, the rehabilitator is guided by the patient, but when the rehabilitator observes that exists repeated errors, corrects them and again lets the patient to take the control. In this way, the flaws presented by the patient in terms of mobility abilities of the upper extremity are evaluated, in addition, it avoids losing the path that the virtual object of the patient follows.

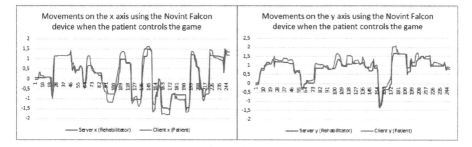

**Fig. 13.** Signs provided by Novint Falcon devices when controlling the patient

The signals of Fig. 14 show the movements that both the patient and the rehabilitator make when controlling the game in different time intervals, *i.e.*, the patient who has average experience with the handling of the game is the one who starts with control until the rehabilitator obtains the control to teach the correct movement, this exchange is highlighted in the graphs. Therefore, it is appreciated that the signals have the same tendency of movement and in relation to the amplitude. On the *x* axis, when the exchange occurs, there is no difference, *i.e.*, the patient can follow the movements performed by the rehabilitator on that axis, however, when the change of control occurs, a difference between the amplitudes of the signals is shown in the *y* axis; this is due to the fact that the patient presents a resistance to the movement made by the rehabilitator.

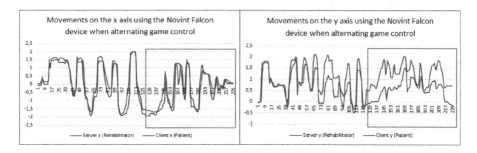

**Fig. 14.** Signals provided by Novint Falcon devices when the control is changed

The signals of Fig. 15 indicate the movement generated by the device in the $z$ axis as a stimulus to the patient and the rehabilitator, with the purpose of indicating that exists a collision within the game. It is appreciated that the responses of the devices have similar tendencies with different magnitudes; this fact indicates that the collisions were presented at the same time in the two applications, however, when the users feel a force perform different resistance to the movement that causes a difference in amplitude.

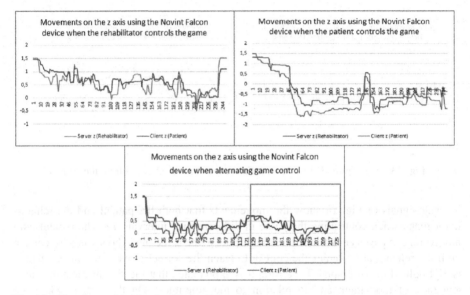

**Fig. 15.** Signals provided by the Novint Falcon devices in response to the events that occur in the game.

The objective of the proposed rehabilitation is to obtain similar graphs, which demonstrate that the patient has improved the skills of superior visual motor integration, *i.e.*, that is able to intuit and easily follow movements made by the rehabilitator, as well as to interact correctly with the application avoiding collisions.

### 4.3    Usability of the Virtual Rehabilitation System

The weighting of the usability of the system has been obtained from a survey carried out on users, which correspond to five children aged between seven and eleven years. The questions have been formulated according to the level of comprehension of a child, *i.e.*, simple, concrete and easy to understand questions that only have the option to choose one of the five answers (bad, regular, acceptable, good, excellent). The results of each question are presented in Table 1. Specifically, the orientation of the survey is centered on three relevant aspects: *(i)* The characteristics and operation of the application, related to whether environments, animations, graphics are considered 3D, sounds, menus and indicator messages were intuitive, attractive and did not generate discomfort. *(ii)* The level of entertainment, concentration and attention captured by the application, *i.e.*, if the challenges and environments generate interest in the video game and if there is a level of immersion that motivates and captures the attention of the user while performs the therapy. *(iii)* Opinion of the user regarding the utility and benefits that the proposed tele-rehabilitation system can provide.

**Table 1.** Result of the applied usability test.

| Questions | Number of the answers | | | | |
|---|---|---|---|---|---|
| | Bad | Regular | Acceptable | Good | Excellent |
| Q1. Did you easily understand the game instructions? | – | – | – | 1 | 4 |
| Q2. Do you think that the movements of the device, the sounds and messages helped you to understand the objective of the game? | – | – | – | 1 | 4 |
| Q3. Did you like the environment, colors and 3D graphics of the game? | – | – | – | – | 5 |
| Q4. How did your eyes feel when you finished playing? | – | – | – | – | 5 |
| Q5. Did you have fun playing and you wanted to play again? | – | – | – | – | 5 |
| Q6. Did you feel like you were driving the truck inside the city? | – | – | 3 | 1 | 1 |
| Q7. When playing several times did you feel that your visual motor skills improved? | – | – | – | – | 5 |
| Q8. Did you think that the haptic device helps you to perform the movements in a similar form as a rehabilitator help you? | – | – | – | 2 | 3 |
| Q9. Would you like to perform therapy from your home without the need to go to rehabilitation centers? | – | – | – | – | 5 |
| Q10. Do you like to perform a therapy based on games other than traditional therapies? | – | – | – | – | 5 |

Each question has a maximum score of 4 points (excellent) and a minimum of 0 points (bad), so that the maximum weight of the survey is given over 40 points. With the five surveys conducted, an average weight of 37.8 is obtained as a result of the usability of the system, which corresponds to 94.5% of the ideal qualification defined in this study.

In the survey, minimum indices have been obtained that the aspect to be improved corresponds to increasing the level of immersion of the user in the virtual environment, provided that the objective is to increase the level of capture of the concentration of the user in the game, however, the score indicates that there is acceptance of the usability of the system by the users who participated in the experiment. In addition, the results indicate that the participants agree that the method of tele rehabilitation presented in this work can positively stimulate the performance of therapy sessions promoting entertainment, eliminating the monotony of traditional methods and, above all, providing the benefit of avoiding the patient goes to rehabilitation centers in the pertinent cases.

## 5   Conclusions

This work presents the implementation of a non-invasive system based on a virtual application, which is programmed to assist and stimulate the patient in rehabilitation therapies of upper extremities without the need for the patient and the rehabilitator to be present in the same place. The virtual application, developed in Unity software, contains games with environments and intuitive, high-quality three-dimensional graphics that are animated based on the processed data of the Novint Falcon haptic device. Based on the results of the survey applied to five users, it is affirmed that exists acceptance of the proposed system because of the positive motivation generated by the animations of the virtual interface and the scope, possibilities and advantages that a rehabilitation carried out entails. distance, through a haptic device that captures and reproduces movements. The experimentation carried out in this work consists of a bidirectional communication in real-time from point to point, however, the communication algorithms have been developed to allow a communication server (rehabilitator) and multiple clients (patients). Finally, this proposal would complement and enhance, in a future work, increasing the level of immersion of the virtual interface, *i.e.*, coupling the animations of the environments and 3D graphics with subroutines that introduce the use of Head Mounted Displays (HMD), which will result in the implementation of a virtual reality application.

**Acknowledgements.** We thank the "Universidad de las Fuerzas Armadas ESPE" for financing the investigation project number 2016-PIC-0017.

## References

1. Ingram, T.T.S.: A historical review of the definition of cerebral palsy, the epidemiology of the cerebral palsies. In: Stanley, F.A.E. (ed.) The Epidemiology of the Cerebral Palsies, pp. 1–11. Lippincott, Philadelphia (1984)
2. Jones, M.W., Morgan, E., Shelton, J.E., Thorogood, C.: Cerebral palsy: introduction and diagnosis (part I). J. Pediatr. Health Care **21**(3), 146–152 (2007)
3. Aicardi, J.: Disease of the Nervous System in Childhood. MacKeith Press, London (1992)

4. Feldman, H.M., Chaves-Gnecco, D., Hofkosh, D.: Developmental-behavioral pediatrics. In: Zitelli, B.J., McIntire, S.C., Norwalk, A.J. (eds.) Atlas of Pediatric Diagnosis, Chap. 3, 6th edn. Elsevier Saunders, Philadelphia (2012)
5. Ketelaar, M., Vermeer, A., Hart, H., et al.: Effects of a functional therapy program on motor abilities of children with cerebral palsy. Phys. Ther. **81**, 1534–1545 (2001)
6. Taub, E., Ramey, S., DeLuca, S., Echols, K.: Efficacy of constraint-induced movement therapy for children with cerebral palsy with asymmetric motor impairment. Pediatrics **113**, 305–312 (2004)
7. Sakzewski, L., Ziviani, J., Boyd, R.N.: Efficacy of upper limb therapies for unilateral cerebral palsy: a meta-analysis. Pediatrics **133**(1), e175–e204 (2014)
8. Galil, A., Carmel, S., Lubetzky, H., Heiman, N.: Compliance with home rehabilitation therapy by parents of children with disabilities in Jews and Bedouin in Israel. Dev. Med. Child Neurol. **43**(4), 261–268 (2001)
9. De Campos, A.C., da Costa, C.S., Rocha, N.A.: Measuring changes in functional mobility in children with mild cerebral palsy. Dev. Neurorehabil. **14**, 140–144 (2011)
10. Prosser, L.A., Lee, S.C., Barbe, M.F., VanSant, A.F., Lauer, R.T.: Trunk and hip muscle activity in early walkers with and without cerebral palsy – a frequency analysis. J. Electromyogr. Kinesiol. **20**, 851–859 (2010)
11. Weiss, P.L.T., Tirosh, E., Fehlings, D.: Role of virtual reality for cerebral palsy management. J. Child Neurol. **29**(8), 1119–1124 (2014). 0883073814533007
12. Mitchell, L., Ziviani, J., Oftedal, S., Boyd, R.: The effect of virtual reality interventions on physical activity in children and adolescents with early brain injuries including cerebral palsy. Dev. Med. Child Neurol. **54**, 667–671 (2012)
13. Snider, L., Majnemer, A., Darsaklis, V.: Virtual reality as a therapeutic modality for children with cerebral palsy. Dev. Neurorehabil. **13**, 120–128 (2010)
14. Chen, Y.P., Lee, S.Y., Howard, A.M.: Effect of virtual reality on upper extremity function in children with cerebral palsy: a meta-analysis. Pediatric Phys. Therapy **26**(3), 289–300 (2014)
15. Golomb, M.R., McDonald, B.C., Warden, S.J., Yonkman, J., Saykin, A.J., Shirley, B., et al.: In-home virtual reality videogame telerehabilitation in adolescents with hemiplegic cerebral palsy. Arch. Phys. Med. Rehabil. **91**, 1–8 (2010)
16. Shin, J., Song, G., Hwangbo, G.: Effects of conventional neurological treatment and a virtual reality training program on eye-hand coordination in children with cerebral palsy. J. Phys. Therapy Sci. **27**(7), 2151–2154 (2015). https://doi.org/10.1589/jpts.27.2151
17. Chen, Y.P., Kang, L.J., Chuang, T.Y., Doong, J.L., Lee, S.J., Tsai, M.W., Sung, W.H.: Use of virtual reality to improve upper-extremity control in children with cerebral palsy: a single-subject design. Phys. Therapy **87**(11), 1441–1457 (2007)
18. Bortone, I., Leonardis, D., Solazzi, M., Procopio, C., Crecchi, A., Bonfiglio, L., Frisoli, A.: Integration of serious games and wearable haptic interfaces for Neuro Rehabilitation of children with movement disorders: a feasibility study. In: 2017 International Conference on Rehabilitation Robotics (ICORR), pp. 1094–1099. IEEE, July 2017
19. Gupta, A., O'Malley, M.K.: Design of a haptic arm exoskeleton for training and rehabilitation. IEEE/ASME Trans. Mechatron. **11**(3), 280–289 (2006)
20. Kozhaeva, T., Zhestkov, S., Bulakh, D., Houlden, N.: Programmable gesture manipulator for hand injuries rehabilitation. In: Internet Technologies and Applications (ITA), pp. 134–136. IEEE, September 2017
21. Pruna, E., et al.: 3D virtual system using a haptic device for fine motor rehabilitation. In: Rocha, Á., Correia, A.M., Adeli, H., Reis, L.P., Costanzo, S. (eds.) WorldCIST 2017. AISC, vol. 570, pp. 648–656. Springer, Cham (2017). https://doi.org/10.1007/978-3-319-56538-5_66

22. Bortone, I., Leonardis, D., Solazzi, M., Procopio, C., Crecchi, A., Briscese, L., Andre, P., Bonfiglio, L., Frisoli, A.: Serious game and wearable haptic devices for neuro motor rehabilitation of children with cerebral palsy. In: Converging Clinical and Engineering Research on Neurorehabilitation II, pp. 443–447. Springer, Cham (2017). https://doi.org/10.1007/978-3-319-46669-9_74

23. Khor, K.X., Chin, P.J.H., Hisyam, A.R., Yeong, C.F., Narayanan, A.L.T., Su, E.L.M.: Development of CR2-Haptic: a compact and portable rehabilitation robot for wrist and forearm training. In: IEEEIECBES International Conference on Biomedical Engineering and Sciences, pp. 424–429 (2014)

24. Maciejasz, P., Eschweiler, J., Gerlach-Hahn, K., Jansen-Troy, A., Leonhardt, S.: A survey on robotic devices for upper limb rehabilitation. J. Neuroeng. Rehabil. **11**, 3 (2014)

25. Lum, P.S., Burgar, C.G., Shor, P.C., Majmundar, M., Van der Loos, M.: Robot-assisted movement training compared with conventional therapy techniques for the rehabilitation of upper-limb motor function after stroke. Arch. Phys. Med. Rehabil. **83**, 952–959 (2002)

# Virtual Rehabilitation of Carpal Tunnel Syndrome Through Force Feedback

Mauricio Tamayo[2(✉)], Pablo J. Salazar[2(✉)],
D. Carlos Bustamante[1(✉)], S. Marcelo Silva[1(✉)],
V. Miguel Escudero[1(✉)], and Victor H. Andaluz[1(✉)]

[1] Universidad de las Fuerzas Armadas ESPE, Sangolquí, Ecuador
{cibustamante,mjsilval,mdescuderol,
vhandaluzl}@espe.edu.ec
[2] Universidad de Técnica de Ambato, Ambato, Ecuador
{fm.tamayo,pj.salazar}@uta.edu.ec

**Abstract.** The present paper proposes a system oriented to the rehabilitation of carpal tunnel syndrome by means of the use of haptic devices with force feedback. The system, based on entertainment, handles different applications, as well as movements in a 3D graphic environment, which is devised with daily tasks that allow to develop skills and abilities to reduce patient's affection. The system is designed with the integration of Unity3D, as well as Novint Falcon haptic device. In which, the patient interacts with the developed applications while receives force feedback. At the same time, the patient performs physiotherapeutic exercises that attack the affection in a proper manner to improve patient's health. Experimental results manifest the system's validity, which generates necessary and efficient exercises for the process of carpal tunnel rehabilitation. In addition, the system deploys a human – machine interaction oriented to the development of physic therapies.

**Keywords:** Carpal tunnel syndrome · CTS · Rehabilitation system
Force feedback · Unity3D

## 1 Introduction

Nowadays, the development of applications, as well as virtual environments, allows to generate rehabilitation systems for upper limb based on the entertainment and immersion of the patient with the environment [1]. The coalescence of technologic methods, such as: virtual reality and haptic devices to health systems, attracts the scrutiny of researchers and specialists in the development of novel alternatives to medicine, which generates potential benefits to the achievement of brand – new rehabilitation systems [2, 3]. Correspondingly, in [4], it is presented the implementation and association of different kinds of devices, such as: Leap Motion, Oculus Rift and Novint Falcon with the purpose of promoting a rehabilitation system based on entertainment and total immersion between the patient, as well as the interaction with virtual reality and augmented reality environments at the instant of performing the therapy.

© Springer International Publishing AG, part of Springer Nature 2018
L. T. De Paolis and P. Bourdot (Eds.): AVR 2018, LNCS 10851, pp. 153–164, 2018.
https://doi.org/10.1007/978-3-319-95282-6_11

Physic therapies need a validation point of its efficacy within the medicine, for that reason, presently, several rehabilitation techniques are questioned due to its abrupt mechanism, as well as its interaction technique; which, in most of the cases are vulnerable to the patient [5]. In this framework, the analysis and implementation of interfaces, which involve virtual environments, stimulate the patient in the achievement of objectives, as well as the performance of the therapy in its totality, which generates greater motor learning and less mind effort. In most of conventional rehabilitation methods, the patient does not conclude the rehabilitation cycle due to mental burden [6, 7].

Upper limbs present different kinds of affections inside its osseous composition, membranes or tissues due to its continuous movement, as well as its excessive contact with the environment. One of the most common affections in upper limbs is the Carpal Tunnel Syndrome (CTS).

Carpal Tunnel Syndrome is a disorder that is brought about the compression of the median nerve from the wrist to the hand. Its symptomatology is detected by means of a previous diagnostic. Its main causes are: diabetes, thyroid disorder, excess of alcohol, as well as arthritis. In the present day, the main cause of developing CTS is the excessive load in fine motor movement systems. Ergonomic designs, as well as the fabrication of wrist supports in technological systems play an important role at the prevention or treatment of CTS [8].

The affection, brought about CTS decreases productivity and life quality of a person at the time to perform functions in which a slight force or wrist extension is required [9]. The exercises for this type of affection are carried out by means of stretching postures and force compression in the wrist areas. In this way, the circulation within the tissues is improved; for this reason, non-surgical treatments are the first option at the time of detection of the CTS which is responsible for subjecting the patient to continuous rehabilitation sessions in which specific exercises are executed for the area of affection. Extreme cases of pain and evolution of the disease leads to surgical interventions, but these in turn promote much longer and expensive treatments [8, 10].

In this context, the work presents a system of entertainment and rehabilitation based on video games, which provides interaction capabilities based on the immersion and transparency of an ergonomic process to generate the comfort, as well as the required response by the movement of objects with different forces that generate rehabilitation exercises for carpal tunnel syndrome. Nowadays, simulation systems show complex and dynamic environments that focus on the development of a tool for transmitting forces with a virtual environment that results to be able to interact with the patient based on entertainment and rehabilitation as essential elements of the new systems of medicine and interactive rehabilitation [11].

## 2   System Structure

The system aims to provide a virtual reality interaction with the patient. The applications developed in Unity 3D software by means of a computer, integrated with the force feedback through the Novint Falcon device encourage the patient to accomplish a rehabilitation in a safe way in benefit to the performance of the patient's movements, as

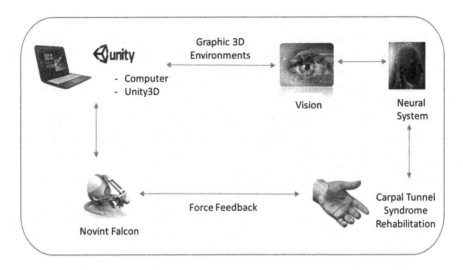

**Fig. 1.** Rehabilitation system's block diagram

well as to get an improve of the quality of life [12]. Figure 1 shows the block diagram of the system.

The proposed interaction relates movements that are focused on the rehabilitation of carpal tunnel syndrome, which are immersed in intuitive visualization applications for efficient control and performance of the patient. Figure 1 describes the interaction flow of the system, in which, the graphic environments that are observed by the patient are analyzed by the neural system to generate movements by force feedback driven by the haptic device. In such a way, there is direct contact with the patient's part of affection which allows to stimulate the nerves and muscles of the area of interest.

## 3  System Development

### 3.1  Graphic Environment

The medium performs a manipulation of the virtual objects in a real environment. In which, the target interacts with the entire environment of the interface with the determination to help to maintain healthy muscles, tendons and joints of the patient [8]. In the system, the main features of rehabilitation therapy for carpal tunnel syndrome are identified, to improve motor skills depending on the specific function of the environment and according to the specific movements to treat this injury in the patient [2, 5, 7].

Assisted therapies are selected from: (i) improving muscle strength (e.g., pulling or moving objects of different weight and size); (ii) improve eye-hand coordination (e.g., solving puzzles, mazes); (iii) increasing the range of motion (e.g., stretch rubber); and finally, (iv) increase sensitivity (e.g., touching objects with different textures) [2, 13]. Therefore, the graphic environments are able to interact with the patient, in order to evaluate the movements and the force in which the execution of the activities results in diminishing the disorders or afflictions of the fine upper limb.

## 3.2   Force Feedback

The virtual environments present an interface, adequate to generate force feedback in the affected area. Each of the impulses, made by the haptic device, create traction movements in the wrist joint area, which incite the exercises for the rehabilitation of carpal tunnel syndrome. Similarly, at the time of perform the mentioned movements, the patient interacts with the virtual environment. Thus, the patient plays while rehabilitates. The therapeutic exercises are repetitive and take different types of strength and position depending on the interaction of the environment and the task that is performed, which generates motivation and entertainment that eradicates the tedious mental burden of a conventional rehabilitation session in a clinical center.

Novint Falcon is a device, able to generate forces in the $X$ - $Y$ - $Z$ plane of the mobile reference system $<R>$ of magnitude between 0 to 2.5 [lbf]; its work area comprises a spherical region of 10 [cm] radius. The patient's hand is responsible for interacting directly with the operative end effector of the haptic device, from which, it directly receives forces $f_x$, $f_y$, as well as $f_z$, in addition to the positions $P_x$, $P_y$, as well as $P_z$, with respect to the reference system $<R>$ that composes rehabilitation exercises in the injury area. The device is moved adjacent to the involvement area to establish concentric forces. In this virtue, feedback of force plays an important role in the development of the present therapeutic method due to its generation of synchronous and specific movements for the condition.

The forces are specific in each level of the applications in order to directly contribute to the recovery of the condition without causing collateral damage to the limbs in movement. The forces, exerted on the $X$ - $Y$ - $Z$ axes impart on the affectation area basic exercises of flexion, extension and grip; the composition of these exercises originate the needed therapy to aim to treat carpal tunnel syndrome, Fig. 2 represents the interaction of the haptic device with the area of affection to generate the necessary therapeutic exercises for rehabilitation. The movements do not generate rotation because the degrees of freedom of the haptic device does not allow it.

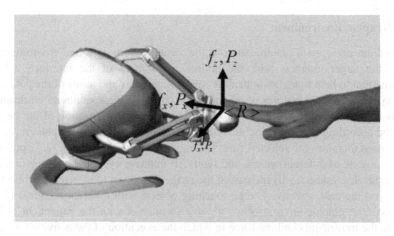

**Fig. 2.** Interaction of Novint Falcon with the affection zone

## 4   Rehabilitation Session

The development of exercises, oriented towards the recovery of the carpal tunnel syndrome, finds different types of training applied to patients in traditional rehabilitation sessions developed in medical centers. The complex physiological structure of the wrist requires exercises with a certain degree of inclination and strength, Fig. 3 details the basic exercises in which the rehabilitation of carpal tunnel syndrome is developed; (a) details the upper neutral position of the hand at a 90° inclination and (b) describes the horizontal neutral position of the hand; These exercises are performed repetitively in order to improve circulation in the tissues and areas of the wrist to eliminate significantly the symptoms of the carpal tunnel [9].

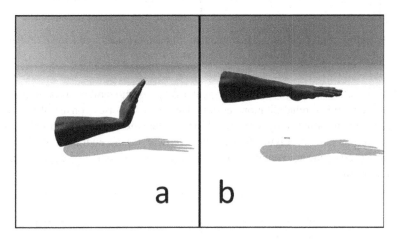

**Fig. 3.** Basic exercises for carpal tunnel rehabilitation

The interaction with the wrist or affection area is achieved through the proper position control in the translation and application of forces. These positions are composed of different movements at different strength and magnitude within the development of the application. The main objective of the exercises is to promote recovery and training of the Carpal nerve through the performance of the Carpal ligament [9]. The exercises and non-surgical methods are composed of different exercises that are capable to generate a total rehabilitation, in analysis of stretching exercises as well as the correct implementation of the rehabilitation instructions considerably reduce the musculoskeletal disorders of the hand and medium carpal [8].

The exercises for carpal tunnel syndrome rehabilitation are numerous. However, within them, there are effective methods and movements in the rehabilitation session, in Fig. 4 the main rehabilitation exercises used in conventional carpal tunnel methods are described in which it is represented: (a) palm extended to the left, (b) palm extended to the right, (c) flexion of fist and palm and (d) extension of arms, fingers and palm [8].

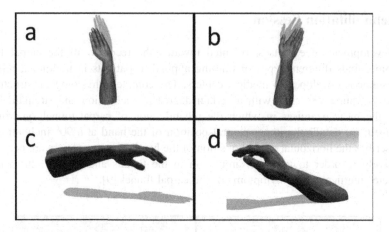

**Fig. 4.** Exercises of (a) palm extended to the left, (b) palm extended to the right, (c) flexion of the fist and palm and (d) extension of arms, fingers and palm

All these exercises allow to reach a greater range of movement, as well as manual sliding for a complete rehabilitation session. The main exercises consist of the flat and vertical movement of the wrist, where each one of them describes a better behavior and recovery of the patient. Figure 5 describes vertical (a) ascending movements and (b) vertical descending movements where there is a greater range of coverage in CTS rehabilitation [8].

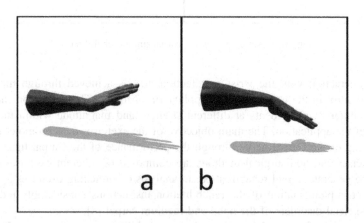

**Fig. 5.** Movements (a) vertical ascending and (b) vertical descending.

The movements and exercises, which are described, are originated in the video game, which provides a force feedback with different position and magnitude, as well as the quality of the action to encourage participation and concentration. Each game is designed to perform a parameter of hand movement in range, speed of movement, or strengthening of the affected areas [14]. The effectiveness of the therapy focuses on capturing the patient's attention through the inclusion of visual objects in the game combined with force feedback, exercises and movements that are aimed to improve the patient's abilities whose mechanisms determine the success of the therapy.

## 5 Virtual Interface

The virtual environments are implemented to generate rehabilitation exercises in an effective way, focused on daily tasks that create entertainment, immersion of the patient with the environment and eliminates mental loads. The interaction of the patient with 3D graphic environments generates the appropriate rehabilitation movements as specified in Figs. 6, 7 and 8 respectively, which creates improvement of strength and resistance gain in the muscles, tendons and joints of the patient. The virtual system includes two interfaces in charge of interacting with the patient based on precision games for achieving objectives in order to obtain the established exercises with a different strength and direction.

**Fig. 6.** First environment's virtual interface

The initial part of the rehabilitation session is aimed at carrying out the appropriate exercises for rehabilitation mentioned in Sect. 4 as a method of initialization, familiarization and warm-up of the muscles of the hand so that the patient has a favorable performance with the environment and the device, the first environment consists in the manipulation of objects of different weight towards a container where each of them is deposited consecutively and at random by the user. At the moment of performing this interaction, concentric forces of different magnitudes are applied to the patient's wrist, producing the appropriate rehabilitation exercises. Figure 6 presents the interface of the

**Fig. 7.** Handling of objects

first environment in which the methodology described above is developed, Fig. 7 shows the consecutive handling of the objects of different weight towards the container.

In the second instance, the patient interacts with a different virtual environment, in which, the purpose is to order each of the objects inside the room where each of them has different weights. In turn, with greater weights than those specified in the first interface, this application allows to reinforce the rehabilitation exercises carried out in the previous steps. In Fig. 8(a) the disorganized room is presented, Fig. 8(b) represents the movement of the object with the greatest weight, Fig. 8(c) indicates the displacement of the object with the least weight, finally, Fig. 8(d) presents the fulfillment of the final objective defined as the oganized room.

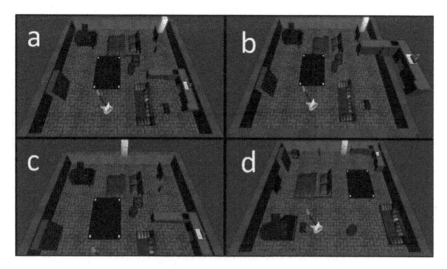

**Fig. 8.** Second environment's virtual interface

## 6  Experimental Results

According to the tests carried out, the feedback of forces allows specific movements of rehabilitation according to the medical parameters required for the treatment of Carpal Tunnel Syndrome (CTS). The position of the movements of the haptic device has been taken into account as well as the interaction of the patient with the applications developed to relate the movements that the patient performs with the force generated by the haptic device.

Figure 9 describes the movements performed on the x-axis between the patient and the haptic device, where at the beginning of the rehabilitation session the exercises described in Fig. 4(a), (b) are performed; the displacement of the patient's affliction site (blue) follows directly to the feedback of force exerted by the haptic device (red), therefore the instructions arranged to be performed on this axis are fulfilled.

Similarly, Fig. 10 describes the movements produced in the y-axis and where the detailed displacements are made in Fig. 5, which continues with the familiarization routine of the patient with the device; the displacement of the place of patient's affection (blue) is according to the movement generated by the device (red), in this way, the rehabilitation exercises proposed for this axis are fulfilled.

Correspondingly, Fig. 11, describes the movements made by the patient on the Z axis (blue) vs the feedback of forces delivered by the haptic device (red), the graph represents the fulfillment of the exercises described in Fig. 3; with which the main movements for the rehabilitation of carpal tunnel syndrome (CTS) are carried out.

Finally, when executing the application of daily tasks, Fig. 12, presents the displacement of the objects within which the different weights exerted by each manipulated body are demonstrated; in such virtue the execution of the movements described in Fig. 4(c) and (d) is demonstrated.

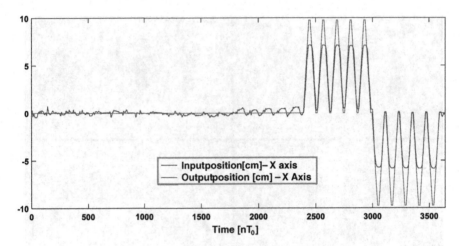

**Fig. 9.**  X – axis movements (Color figure online)

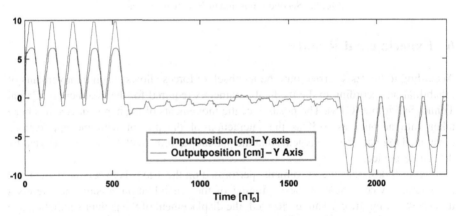

**Fig. 10.**  Y – axis movements (Color figure online)

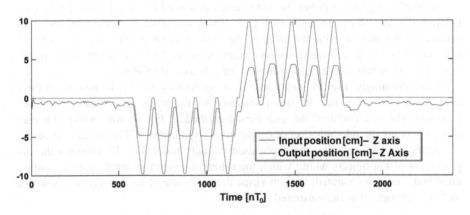

**Fig. 11.**  Z – axis movements (Color figure online)

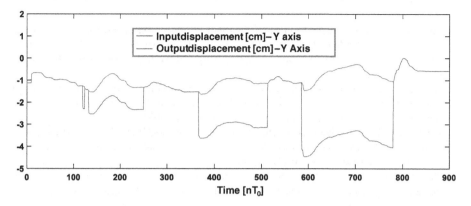

**Fig. 12.** Manipulation of objects with different weight

# 7 Conclusions

Force feedback promotes the necessary movements for the treatment of the condition, provides the number of repetitions of each exercise according to the rehabilitation session, in such a way that the present tool has the potential to serve as a complement to traditional rehabilitation. The obtained results provide a necessary tool for the specialist to perform a pertinent assessment of the patient's condition, as well as monitoring the progress of the rehabilitation of the patient.

As future work, the implementation of this tool is proposed in patients suffering from this type of condition, to obtain an assessment of the usability of the system.

**Acknowledgement.** The authors would like to thanks to the Corporación Ecuatoriana para el Desarrollo de la Investigación y Academia – CEDIA for the financing given to research, development, and innovation, through the CEPRA projects, especially the project CEPRA-XI-2017- 06; Control Coordinado Multi-operador aplicado a un robot Manipulador Aéreo; also to Universidad de las Fuerzas Armadas ESPE, Universidad Técnica de Ambato, Escuela Superior Politécnica de Chimborazo, and Universidad Nacional de Chimborazo, and Grupo de Investigación en Automatización, Robótica y Sistemas Inteligentes, GIARSI, for the support to develop this paper.

# References

1. Andaluz, V.H., Salazar, P.J., Silva, M., Escudero, M., Bustamante, C.: Rehabilitation of upper limb with force feedback. In: 2016 IEEE International Conference on Automatica (ICA-ACCA), Curicó, Chile, pp. 99–104 (2016)
2. Ramírez-Fernández, C., Morán, A.L., García-Canseco, E.: Haptic feedback in motor hand virtual therapy increases precision and generates less mental workload. In: 2015 9th International Conference on Pervasive Computing Technologies for Healthcare (PervasiveHealth), Istanbul, pp. 280–286 (2015)

3. Ramírez-Fernández, C., García-Canseco, E., Morán, A.L., Orihuela-Espina, F.: Design principles for hapto-virtual rehabilitation environments: effects on effectiveness of fine motor hand therapy. In: Fardoun, H.M., Penichet, V.M.R., Alghazzawi, D.M. (eds.) REHAB 2014. CCIS, vol. 515, pp. 270–284. Springer, Heidelberg (2015). https://doi.org/10.1007/978-3-662-48645-0_23

4. Andaluz, V.H., et al.: Virtual reality integration with force feedback in upper limb rehabilitation. In: Bebis, G., et al. (eds.) ISVC 2016. LNCS, vol. 10073, pp. 259–268. Springer, Cham (2016). https://doi.org/10.1007/978-3-319-50832-0_25

5. Zepeda-Ruelas, E., Gudiño-Lau, J., Durán-Fonseca, M., Charre-Ibarra, S., Alcalá-Rodríguez, J.: Control Háptico con Planificación de Trayectorias Aplicado a Novint Falcon. La Mecatrónica en México 3(2), 65–74 (2014)

6. Haarth, R., Ejarque, G.E., Distefano, M.: Interfaz HÁPTICO aplicada en la manipulación de objetos. In: Instituto de Automática y Electrónica Industrial, Facultad de Ingeniería Universidad Nacional de Cuyo (2010)

7. Hamza-Lup, F.G., Baird, W.H.: Feel the static and kinetic friction. In: Isokoski, P., Springare, J. (eds.) EuroHaptics 2012. LNCS, vol. 7282, pp. 181–192. Springer, Heidelberg (2012). https://doi.org/10.1007/978-3-642-31401-8_17

8. Uribe-Quevedo, A., Ortiz, S., Rojas, D., Kapralos, B.: Hand tracking as a tool to quantify carpal tunnel syndrome preventive exercises. In: 2016 7th International Conference on Information, Intelligence, Systems & Applications (IISA), Chalkidiki, Greece, pp. 1–5 (2016)

9. Silişteanu, C.S., Crăciun, D.M., David, M.: The importance of the sensor devices in the recovery of the patients with the carpal tunnel syndrome. In: 2016 International Conference and Exposition on Electrical and Power Engineering (EPE), Iasi, Romania, pp. 426–430, (2016)

10. Arita, S., Hashshizume, H., Honda, M.: A new approach to clarify the fuzziness of medical diagnosis by diagnostic layers — a diagnostic system for Carpal Tunnel Syndrome with two layers of diagnostic filters using clinical indicators. In: 2014 Joint 7th International Conference on Soft Computing and Intelligent Systems (SCIS) and 15th International Symposium on Advanced Intelligent Systems (ISIS), Kitakyushu, pp. 845–850, (2014)

11. Renon, P., Yang, C., Ma, H., Cui, R.: Haptic interaction between human and virtual iCub robot using Novint Falcon with CHAI3D and MATLAB. In: 32nd Chinese Control Conference (CCC), Xi'an, pp. 6045–6050 (2013)

12. Song, Z., Guo, S., Yazid, M.: Development of a potential system for upper limb rehabilitation training based on virtual reality. In: 2011 4th International Conference on Human System Interactions (HSI), Yokohama, pp. 352–356 (2011)

13. Gupta, A., OMalley, M.K.: Design of a haptic arm exoskeleton for training and rehabilitation. IEEE/ASME Trans. Mechatron. 11(3), 280–289 (2006)

14. Adamovich, S., et al.: A virtual reality–based exercise system for hand rehabilitation post-stroke. Teleoper. Virtual Environ. 14, 161–174 (2005)

# SLT-Game: Support System for Therapies of Children with Communication Disorders

Accel Guamán$^{(\boxtimes)}$, Marcelo Álvarez V.$^{(\boxtimes)}$, Jorge S. Sánchez$^{(\boxtimes)}$, and Víctor H. Andaluz$^{(\boxtimes)}$

Universidad de las Fuerzas Armadas ESPE, Sangolquí, Ecuador
{alguaman3, rmalvarez, jssanchez,
vhandaluz1}@espe.edu.ec

**Abstract.** This article proposes an application of assistance for speech and language therapies, aimed at children suffering from this pathology. The system was implemented in a virtual environment developed with the graphics engine Unity 3D, in order to provide an application that optimizes both the use of materials, infrastructure, time resources, among others. The developed system consists of five games based on Speech and Language Therapy, SLT, which encourage the child to perform the different exercises of the five areas of this disorder, hearing, structure and oral function, linguistic formulation, expressive language and Articulation, receptive language. The proposed tool allows the user to select both the work environment and the level of difficulty during the therapy process.

**Keywords:** Therapy · Speech · Language · Android · SLT · Unity 3D

## 1 Introduction

Communication disorders make it difficult for people to function normally in their daily activities, causing problems of adaptation at some point in their lives, whether in a social, family or educational environment; the majority of this type of difficulty can be overcome with the passage of time; However, some people do not manage to overcome this condition and require different types of therapies [1, 2]. Communication disorders include speech disorders and language disorders. A language disorder makes it difficult to find the right words and build clear sentences when speaking, as well as to understand what other people say [3]. While speech disorders refer to the limitation in pronouncing letters, words or sounds understandable and the difficulty of recognizing them [4].

Deficiencies in speech and language are characteristic of some common disorders in childhood such as: autistic spectrum disorder, learning difficulties, speech and language disorders, dysplasia, dysphonia, among others; that are present in more than 7% of monolingual children [5, 6], these disorders can be caused by: alterations in the normal development of the brain, premature birth, use of a pacifier and bottle until the preschool age, etc.; what can cause for example the difficulty of movement in the facial gold, delay in speech and language [7, 8].

© Springer International Publishing AG, part of Springer Nature 2018
L. T. De Paolis and P. Bourdot (Eds.): AVR 2018, LNCS 10851, pp. 165–175, 2018.
https://doi.org/10.1007/978-3-319-95282-6_12

There are three types of language disorders: (i) Difficulty of receptive language. - It implies inability to understand what others are saying; (ii) Difficulty of expressive language. - Involves inability to express thoughts and ideas; and (iii) Mixed disorder of receptive-expressive language. - Involves inability to understand and use spoken language [9].

While speech disorders are deficient with respect to: (a) Articulation. - Approximately at the age of 5 or 6 years, it is desirable that children leave out certain sounds (*nana* instead of *banana*), to replace sounds (*cado* instead of *carro*) or have problems making certain sounds (*pero* replacing to *perro*). If the persistence of these sounds is detected, it could be a sign of a joint problem [4, 7]; (b) Phonology. - People with phonological difficulties, can consistently substitute the sounds that are made in the throat, by the sounds that are made in the front of the mouth, p. ej. say *ugo* instead of *jugo* or *toche* instead of *coche*, etc. [4]; (c) Voice. - Difficulty with the voice when hoarse, nasal or choppy, could speak too loud or not loud enough for the situation [4, 6]; and (d) Fluency. - Refers to the action of stuttering, babbling or pausing in the "wrong" place when they speak [3, 4].

Therefore, the present project proposes the development of an application in virtual reality oriented to mobile devices; The purpose of the application is to encourage the execution of different types of exercises to treat speech and language pathology, SLT. The implemented therapy considers different types of didactic games oriented to the therapy of the five areas of this disorder, that is to say, Hearing, Structure and oral function, Linguistic Formulation, Expressive Language and Articulation, Receptive Language. In addition, the performance of the developed application is presented, which was evaluated in a children's center.

This work is divided into 6 Sections including the Introduction. Section 2 presents the Problem and justifies this paper, Sect. 3 details the structure of the Virtual System, the operation of the system, as well as the tools used in its construction are described in Sect. 4; after the corresponding analysis, the results obtained in Sect. 5 are considered; and finally, the conclusions are presented in Sect. 6.

## 2   Problem Formulation

Children showing problems in speech or language often have problems of adaptation and learning associated with this circumstance [9], This encourages the development of studies that favor access to therapies, however, a high percentage of people consider that services are deficient [10, 11].

Currently, speech and language therapy is divided into five main areas, each of which is associated with activities focused on specifically improving the condition of the disorder; In a traditional way, the person presenting this pathology must perform exercises supervised by therapists that indicate the necessary tasks for each area of the disorder [12], Table 1.

The *Hearing* area is reinforced with tasks of recognition of sounds, in a traditional way the speech therapist imitates certain sounds of nature that are easily identified by children, the patient must determine by means of illustrated cards which object represents that sound, additionally for children with evolutionary dyslalia, exercises are carried out to identify the correct pronunciation of phonemes in words.

The area of *Linguistic Formulation* is strengthened with exercises of whistling, clicking with the tongue, and blowing; to make this activity more entertaining the speech therapist uses elements such as sorbets, water, streamers and confetti; However, the distraction of children is a limitation in the development of these activities.

For the stimulation of the *Expressive Language and Articulation*, the speech therapist uses illustrations that represent activities, subjects, and adjectives. The objective of this procedure is that the child understands the grammatical structure, forming a sentence and playing with the order of the elements without losing logical.

The *Receptive Language* is strengthened with exercises that reinforce the logical reasoning, the speech therapist uses a technique in which the patient must sequentially order an activity; For example, downloading an apple from the tree consists of the following activities: 1.- Climbing the tree, 2.- Taking the apple, 3.- Getting off the tree, 4.- Eating the apple.

For the area of *Structure and Oral Function*, the speech therapist relies on songs, images and sweets that are placed around the mouth to perform the movements of the tongue. The most effective method is that of sweets.

**Table 1.** Activities for each area of the disorder

|   | Area | Therapy |
|---|------|---------|
| 1 | Hearing | Recognize different sounds e.g. Nature sounds |
|   |         | Detect presence or absence of sounds |
| 2 | Structure and oral function | Exercises with movements of the tongue |
|   |                             | Exercises with the lips |
| 3 | Linguistic formulation | Inhalation and exhalation exercises |
|   |                        | Breath exercises |
| 4 | Expressive Language and Articulation | Construction of sentences based on a word |
|   |                                      | Activities that reinforce the grammatical structure |
| 5 | Receptive language | Organization of figures forming sequences |
|   |                    | Logic reasoning |

In this area there are several technological applications developed during the last years; one of these describes a web-based tool that focuses on the field of speech therapy and learning disability [8], on the other hand, technological applications have been used in women diagnosed with bilateral nodules of vocal cords that received intensive voice treatment through a free video conferencing platform [13], in virtue of this, it is considered of great interest to continue applying technology in the search to support language rehabilitation and education [14].

The use of video games in children with language disorders, greatly improves the attention given to the therapies, since the Speech and Language Pathologies, SLP, are generally related to other disorders such as hyperactivity, it is difficult to keep a child concentrated in a task, for this reason, the implementation of an interactive game focused on providing speech and language therapy would allow improving the condition of patients suffering from this pathology [15, 16].

The present work shows the development of an application based on speech and language therapy, which allows improving communication skills in children, this proposal offers an alternative and low budget support for the speech therapist. The system consists of 5 games focused on each of the areas of disorder and a device with Android, Windows or iOS operating system is necessary; for its functionality.

## 3   Virtual System Structure

The present work is implemented in a virtual environment that offers children with language problems who perform exercises according to the area of disorder they wish to work. In addition, the proposed application allows users to use tools for the detection of people on a personal basis, while they are in an entertainment program.

Figure 1 describes the interaction of the user with the proposed system, establishing as input elements the microphone, speaker and screen as input devices to the system.

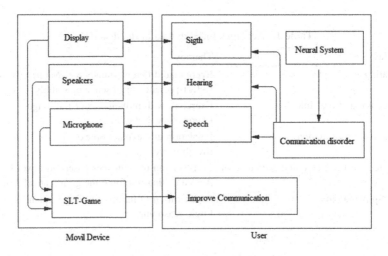

**Fig. 1.** Diagram of system components

The interaction between the patient and the system is established through bilateral communication, that is, first a graphical interface shows the environment of the game giving the possibility of choosing the area of disorder that will work; second, the user generates the necessary stimulus (blowing, moving the tongue, moving the lips, etc.), so that the selected game works. On the other hand, in the 2D environment the user also has the option of executing his therapy session, implementing the mirror effect in some sections, which through visual feedback will allow the user to correct the movements that he is executing to perform with success therapy activities.

The linguistic formulation module consists of an algorithm that distinguishes when the child is blowing and when it is not. The algorithmic structure analyzes the frequency spectrum of the audio captured in real time by the microphone, the average volume, and compares it with data previously taken from murmur sounds. Multiple design and animation utilities were used to develop the multimedia elements (images and sound), such as: Adobe Illustrator Cs6, for the vector design; Photoshop Cs6 in retouching images; Spriter-2D in the development of 2D animations; and Audacity for sound production.

It is important to emphasize that the images for children should be striking, especially if they are about animals and cartoons, for this reason the orientation of the system is towards an environment of this type.

The system is going to be used by children between 4 and 7 years old, being in the pre-school stage and not knowing how to read, they must follow instructions by means of representative figures, or sound instructions Fig. 2; the strategy used is to change the tone by 17% in the frequency, giving a child's voice feeling, which gives the user a sense of confidence.

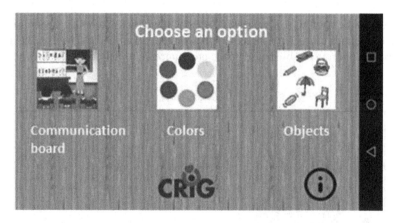

**Fig. 2.** Application related to textual instructions

Another strategy used is the design of animations, for this reason, the game SLT-Game consists of a large number of animated objects, such as clouds, plants, animals, buttons, etc.; Each animation was made with the Animator tool that is in the editor of Unity, this is because it seeks to draw the attention of the child and avoid distractions.

Once the application in Unity 3D is finished, it is necessary to have fixed the Android development environment before testing the game on the device. This involves downloading and installing the Android SDK that contains each of the different versions and Android platforms that will be worked on and adding your physical device to the system.

The recommended device to run the application is a touch device, with the following minimum features: 7-in. PLS LCD screen at $1024 \times 600$ resolution pixels, dual-core 1 GHz processor, 1 GB RAM, front VGA camera.

## 4   System Operation

The automation of the different therapies is described, implemented in a game, this consists of 5 scenes developed in Unity 3D, each of them focuses on the execution of the exercises, in each of the language and speech disorders; on the other hand, a "Main Menu" scene, which applies a type of main navigation, Fig. 3; whose implementation in the system is cyclical, providing the user with a better disposition in its manipulation.

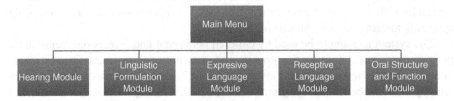

**Fig. 3.** System flow diagram

Based on the need to recognize the different sounds of nature, the hearing module reproduces sounds of animals, these must be correctly identified by the user, the person also has the option to establish a sentence pronounced correctly between two generated Fig. 4.

**Fig. 4.** Implementation of the hearing module

The application developed in the field of Linguistic Formulation is to blow the microphone, to raise a character within the game as a therapy, when it stops blowing it starts to fall; The objective is to keep the character flying as long as possible through the proposed scenario, generating that the child is always motivated in the realization of this activity contributing to their therapy Fig. 5.

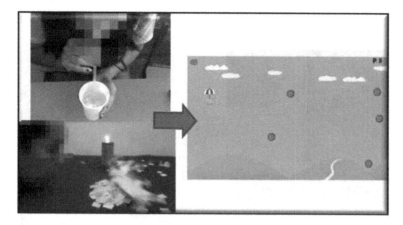

**Fig. 5.** Linguistic formulation module

The automated module in the area of Expressive Language and Articulation allows the user to choose a word and then 3 groups of cards (including the selected word) appear, the user can exchange the images in the groups, forming different sentences, respecting the grammatical structure of a sentence (subject, verb and predicate) Fig. 6.

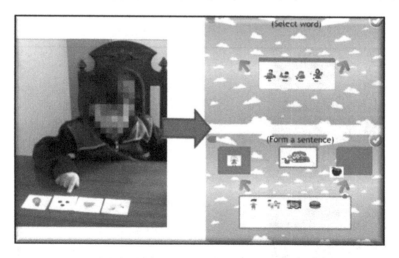

**Fig. 6.** Expressive Language and Articulation

The system for Receptive Language therapy, shows a set of images with activities performed on a daily basis, the user must place them in the corresponding order to form the correct sequence Fig. 7.

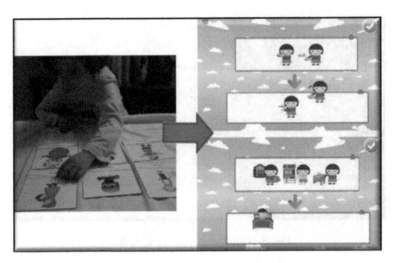

Fig. 7. Receptive language module

The module that allows to develop the therapy in the area of oral structure and function, visualizes a character performing exercises with the lips and tongue, the user aims to mimic these movements and execute the necessary exercises in both tongue and lips Fig. 8.

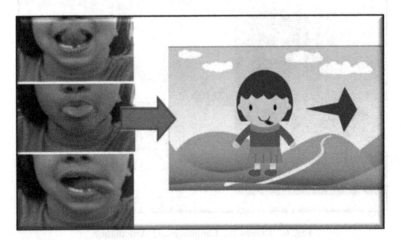

Fig. 8. Module structure and oral function

## 5  Analysis of Experimental Results

Videogames arise from the need of the human being to obtain a new mechanism to enjoy in leisure moments using an interactive system, that is to say that it depends on the actions of a user to perform a task. When a Traditional Interactive Software, TIS, is developed, it is created to perform tasks with the help of the computer and are considered tools that should be useful for the user within its design, taking advantage of these features an application has been made that was used by children with speech and language problems.

The usefulness of an interactive system has a functional component and another that indicates how users can use this functionality. This is where the concept of usability appears as a measure in which certain users can use a product to achieve specific objectives with effectiveness, efficiency and satisfaction in a context of specific use. It is for this reason that it is important to apply the System Usability Scale, SUS, which has a Likert style that generates a single number, representing a composite measure of the usability of the global system under study. It should be noted that independent scores are not significant by themselves. The realization of usable software produces reduction of costs of production, maintenance, use and improvements in the final quality of the product.

In this experiment the usability of the support system for speech and language therapies is evaluated, applying the SUS questionnaire, whose questions are detailed in Table 2; the 15 users who perform the tests with the therapy system are immediately subject to the test, these data are processed and analyzed.

**Table 2.** Questionnaire questions

| |
|---|
| 1. I would like to use this system frequently |
| 2. I find this system unnecessarily complex |
| 3. The system is easy to use |
| 4. Technical support is needed to make use of the system |
| 5. The various functions of the system are quite well integrated |
| 6. There is inconsistency in this system |
| 7. Most people would learn to use the system quickly |
| 8. I found the system quite uncomfortable to use |
| 9. I felt very safe using the system |
| 10. I need to learn many things before I can manage the system |

It is important to mention that the analyzed application must exceed 68% as a global average to determine its usability according to the SUS questionnaire standard, the result obtained exceeds 85%, which indicates that the speech and language treatment support system is highly Wearable, comfortable and without manipulation complexity.

## 6  Conclusions

SLT-Game is an application that would allow children with language disorders, to carry out a more entertaining therapy and to have an alternative to traditional activities such as the use of cards with illustrations.

When dealing with a technological proposal it is necessary that prior to its application in patients, a methodological proposal is prepared by a specialist in the area, to perform an adequate validation of the software product. Speech therapists have a technological tool that supports the application of language therapies in children suffering from this type of pathology.

The applications in two dimensions are considered suitable in this type of applications since, having an orientation of children users, the developed environment is easier to retain in the mind of the spectator.

**Acknowledgment.** The authors would like to thanks to the Corporación Ecuatoriana para el Desarrollo de la Investigación y Academia – CEDIA for the financing given to research, development, and innovation, through the CEPRA projects, especially the project CEPRA-XI-2017-06; *Control Coordinado Multi-operador aplicado a un robot Manipulador Aéreo*; also to Universidad de las Fuerzas Armadas ESPE, Universidad Técnica de Ambato, Escuela Superior Politécnica de Chimborazo, and Universidad Nacional de Chimborazo, and Grupo de Investigación en Automatización, Robótica y Sistemas Inteligentes, GI-ARSI, for the support to develop this paper.

# References

1. Rosselli, M., Matute, E., Ardila, A.: Neuropsicología del desarrollo infantil. Editorial El Manual Moderno (2010)
2. Quevedo, W.X., et al.: Assistance system for rehabilitation and valuation of motor skills. Presented at the International Conference on Augmented Reality, Virtual Reality and Computer Graphics, pp. 166–174 (2017)
3. Trauner, D.A., Nass, R.D.: Developmental language disorders. In: Swaiman's Pediatric Neurology, 6th edn., pp. 431–436. Elsevier (2018)
4. Arocena, J.G., Gallego, M.G., Gimenez, J.V., Guerrero, J.M.: Valoración de la deficiencia y la discapacidad en los trastornos del lenguaje, el habla y la voz. Ministerio de Trabajo y Asuntos Sociales (1997)
5. Enderby, P., Emerson, J.: Speech and language therapy: does it work? BMJ **312**(7047), 1655 (1996)
6. Tomblin, J.B., Records, N.L., Buckwalter, P., Zhang, X., Smith, E., O'Brien, M.: Prevalence of specific language impairment in kindergarten children. J. Speech Lang. Hear. Res. **40**(6), 1245–1260 (1997)
7. Vargha-Khadem, F., et al.: Neural basis of an inherited speech and language disorder. Proc. Natl. Acad. Sci. **95**(21), 12695–12700 (1998)
8. Mashima, P.A., Doarn, C.R.: Overview of telehealth activities in speech-language pathology. Telemed. E-Health **14**(10), 1101–1117 (2008)
9. Newbury, D.F., Monaco, A.P.: Genetic advances in the study of speech and language disorders. Neuron **68**(2), 309–320 (2010)
10. Ross, K., Heiny, E., Conner, S., Spener, P., Pineda, R.: Occupational therapy, physical therapy and speech-language pathology in the neonatal intensive care unit: patterns of therapy usage in a level IV NICU. Res. Dev. Disabil. **64**, 108–117 (2017)
11. James, D.M.: The applicability of normalisation process theory to speech and language therapy: a review of qualitative research on a speech and language intervention. Implement. Sci. **6**(1), 95 (2011)

12. Robles-Bykbaev, V.E., López-Nores, M., Pazos-Arias, J.J., Arévalo-Lucero, D.: SPELTA: an expert system to generate therapy plans for speech and language disorders. Expert Syst. Appl. **42**(21), 7641–7651 (2015)
13. Fischer, F., Kollar, I., Stegmann, K., Wecker, C.: Toward a script theory of guidance in computer-supported collaborative learning. Educ. Psychol. **48**(1), 56–66 (2013)
14. Naranjo, C.A., et al.: Teaching process for children with autism in virtual reality environments. Presented at the Proceedings of the 2017 9th International Conference on Education Technology and Computers, pp. 41–45 (2017)
15. Franceschini, S., Gori, S., Ruffino, M., Viola, S., Molteni, M., Facoetti, A.: Action video games make dyslexic children read better. Curr. Biol. **23**(6), 462–466 (2013)
16. Lüke, C.: Impact of speech-generating devices on the language development of a child with childhood apraxia of speech: a case study. Disabil. Rehabil. Assist. Technol. **11**(1), 80–88 (2016)

# Sales Maximization Based on Neuro-Marketing Techniques in Virtual Environments

Washington X. Quevedo[✉], Paulina F. Venegas[✉],
Viviana B. López[✉], Cristian M. Gallardo[✉], Aldrin G. Acosta[✉],
Julio C. Tapia[✉], and Víctor H. Andaluz[✉]

Universidad de las Fuerzas Armadas ESPE, Sangolqui, Ecuador
{wjquevedo,pfvenegas,vblpezv,agacosta,jctapia3,
vhandaluz1}@espe.edu.ec, cmgallardop@gmail.com

**Abstract.** This article describes an analysis of the merchandising techniques used in Neuromarketing through a virtual reality application to inquire the consumer behavior when purchasing mass consumption products. The results of the virtual test will affect the costs optimization, reduction of time, and logistics when studying the effectiveness of each technique. The application consists of a virtual environment replica of a real supermarket, which allows the user to interact with the products according to: the conscious and unconscious perception at a purchase and the influence of merchandising techniques (location of the products, assortment management and accessibility, and so on). The results of the experiment validate the merchandising techniques with product rotation processes and sales increase, without study them in a real supermarket.

**Keywords:** Virtual · Marketing · Neuromarketing · Merchandising
Consumer study

## 1 Introduction

The success capacity of the companies in general is in the development of learning reflected in the dynamics of the organization within the market, through a multidisciplinary marketing systematization in the context of a "buyer-seller association, network structures and arrangements, sales management, channel relationships, marketing services and alliances" [1, 2]. However, in recent years the marketing function has been significantly weakened in many companies, reducing the capacity of frequent performance about the experienced marketing [3].

Marketing is the act of perceive the behavior of consumers in order to provide efficient tools to implement in target markets, also consider strategies linked to improvement productivity and sales maximizing [4, 5]. Therefore, the marketing covers different strategies, through interaction techniques and efficient capacities [2, 5]. The interest of a specific market research has left aside the use of obsolete methods and taken modifications which provide perceptible benefits such as Neuromarketing [6].

© Springer International Publishing AG, part of Springer Nature 2018
L. T. De Paolis and P. Bourdot (Eds.): AVR 2018, LNCS 10851, pp. 176–191, 2018.
https://doi.org/10.1007/978-3-319-95282-6_13

Neuromarketing is the study of neuroscience measurement techniques to detect the pattern that consumers respond to marketing strategies in a conscious and unconscious way [6, 7]. In this context, the purpose of this method is shown in relation to the perception and action which detects the neurobiological components conducive to decision making. Therefore, neuromarketing is an important booster of the performance of a company that has generated interest in most companies seeking to position themselves in a target market [4, 6, 7]. In fact, the ability to predict the efficient results of this technique is the use of technologies in neuromarketing studies that promote sales through the use of virtual reality [8].

Virtual reality has become a tool that links innovative processes in the research of consumer behavior [9]. Nowadays, virtual reality has been transformed into technology from business innovation that offers a creative way to reach consumers [10]. Therefore, the Eye-Tracking Neuromarketing technique (based on monitoring the user's visual perception in real time) is used as I/O method in virtual reality headsets. This promotes the use of virtual environments where the user can immerse in different situations that the merchandising technique determines, within the field of neuroscience, economics, and psychology [10–15].

In this context, this article shows the analysis of the merchandising technique immersed in neuromarketing. Oriented to maximize sales through the use of a virtual reality application, the developed application considers as a case of study the recreation of a supermarket, where it is allowed the user (consumer) to interact with the products located in a strategic way achieving a visual sale and increase the value of the acquisition. The results of the test allows to verify the performance of the developed virtual application, validate processes which improve product turnover without implementing them in a real supermarket, minimize costs, and reduce time and logistics. In addition the application allows the implementation of different market strategies in order to influence the consumer to purchase sumptuary products.

This article is divided into 5 sections, including the Introduction. Section 2 presents the formulation of the problem about the location of the products for the maximization of sales; the structure of the system with developed virtual reality blocks is presented in Sect. 3; Sect. 4 illustrates the experimental results made with the application; and finally the conclusions of the work are presented in Sect. 5.

## 2 Problem Statement

The human being has a different behavior when making a purchase, it is influenced by brand, logos, location of products and subliminal images [16]; this behavior generates different scenarios to observe the same product, for this reason the placement of products in a supermarket should be focused to capture the attention and generate emotions in the consumer to achieve a visual sale [16, 17, 21]. For create different sales strategies focused on the needs and emotions of client is necessary understand the consumer like the essence of an organization [17]. It is always observed that the owners of stores and supermarkets perform marketing strategies to draw the attention of customers towards complementary products and in this way increase the product demand [18, 20].

In this way, owners of supermarkets are looking for strategies and methods to gather and capture all the suggestions of their clients, but this implies in costs at changing the location of products of the shelves several times and the time that involves; The solution is not to ask the client how he would like to, but to analyze his conscious and unconscious behavior, because currently emotional factors are important to make a purchase [19]. The analysis of the problem leads to determine factors that intervene in the purchase decision, the consumers acquire a product determining their primary necessity, i.e., there must be a requirement to achieve satisfaction. Another factor which visually attracts the customer is the strategic location of the products in the points of sale to stimulate and accelerate consumption.

In response to the problem described in the previous paragraphs, this paper proposes the implementation of a virtual reality app to analyze the reaction of customers to Neuromarketing and Merchandising techniques applied to the products offer within a virtual supermarket, Fig. 1 presents a block diagram of proposal app, focused to analyze internal and external factors that influence when making a purchase and the implementation of techniques to maximize sales.

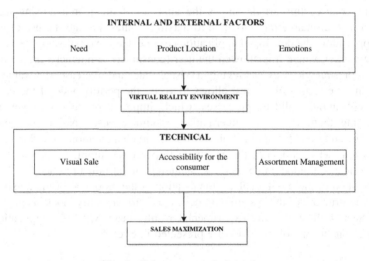

**Fig. 1.** Scheme to maximize sales.

## 3   System Structure

In this section, the description of the implemented system is presented, in which 4 modules interact. In the first one, there is the virtual SCENE where all graphic resources are organized through scenes; the second block corresponds to the SCRIPTS, where the control functions are developed in C# scripts; the INPUT block describe the devices that the app will run; and the last block is the OUTPUT where it shows the results of interaction inside the virtual reality world, see Fig. 2.

In the *Virtual Scenes block,* the stage of graphic development is shown in which two scenes are handled: Supermarket and Test Configuration. The two scenes have

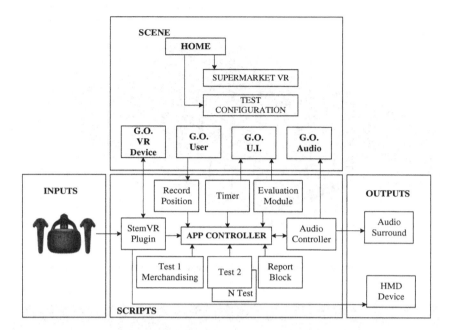

**Fig. 2.** Interrelation component diagram

general elements called game objects which are placed in the scenes according to the objective of each of them. Among the main Game Objects: *(i) VR Device* is the representation in the virtual environment of the virtual reality headset used by the consumer; *(ii) User* allows the control and data collection (position and interaction with objects) of the user within the virtual environment like an avatar; *(iii) User Interface* that allows the visualization of information and navigation through user options with emphasis on the execution of tasks; and *(iv) Audio Game Object* that provides the audio sources for indication from real world and effects to achieve the level of immersion of the app.

The 3D objects used for the development of the graphic scenes of supermarket and its furniture have been developed following the workflow established in [23]. For the creation of the models SolidWorks has been used according to the requirements of replicating real objects and structures in form and function see Fig. 3.

The axes, orientation, and hierarchy properties of single 3D models and mechanisms are edited in 3ds MAX, where it is necessary to manipulate objects through their geometric center and placement in the environment referenced to the pivot point, see Fig. 4. The texturing, generation of animations a stage has been developed in the UNITY with their own tools, see Fig. 5.

In the *Scripts block,* the behavior of the whole app is programmed through the use of specific modules for each function. The main one is the App Controller which manages the control actions among the other modules. The SteamVR module controls the entries of sensor data (position, acceleration, velocity) from the HTC VIVE device and transfers them to G.O. in Virtual Scene as a mirror of the movements made by the

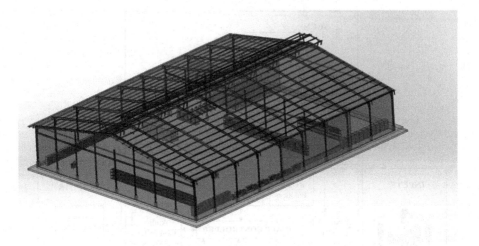

**Fig. 3.** Build of supermarket structure in SolidWorks

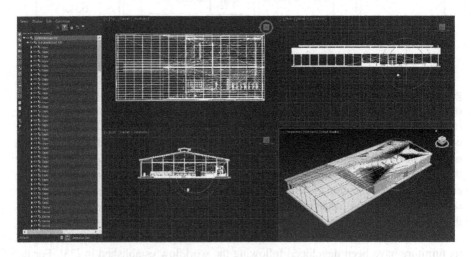

**Fig. 4.** 3ds MAX editing: hierarchy, axes and orientation.

user, and the App Controller to manage the actions and obtain and store coordinates of its position using the Record Position module. The Timer and Evaluation modules act simultaneously to register the acquired products and measure time intervals of activities and sub activities inside the test respectively. The Test modules establish the purchase objectives and the initial conditions of the supermarket to evaluate the behavior of the consumer in the face of said changes. The programming has been carried out in such a way that N additional modules of different tests can be added. The Report Block module collects data from the Record Position, Timer, Evaluation modules and groups them in text format as a result of the test performed. Finally, the Audio Controller allows hearing effects of audio and environmental music, and it will send the audio

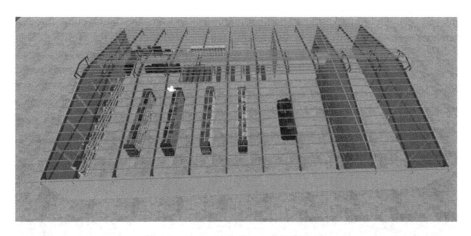

**Fig. 5.** Texturized 3D model in Unity

effects to each source established in the scenes and as a response of Audio Surround to the respective hardware in OUTPUTS block.

The INPUTS and OUTPUTS blocks represent the hardware devices as an I/O method to the user's stimuli. The entry device is the HTC VIVE glasses due to its 4 × 3 m working field and the efficient controllers tracking; these are useful features to move the user in real space and perform the tasks of taking an object in high or low positions in the virtual scenes. An output device is the surround audio headset, which plays effects with binaural audio properties that enables sense environmental and directional audio, and the Head Mounted Display (HMD) shows the changes of camera view in the virtual scene like a response to the movement in the real world of the client and is part of the HTC VIVE device.

## 4   Experimentation and Discussion

In this section, the results of the development and execution of the virtual application are shown. The technical equipment used to carry out the experiment consists of a VR-Ready PC with the specifications shown in Table 1. The virtual reality device used in the test is the HTC VIVE Headset, given the 4 × 3 m work area which allows the user a natural movement by taking virtual objects on high and low shelves.

**Table 1.** Technical specifications of the VR Ready PC

| Processor | Intel(R) Core(TM) i7-6700HQ CPU @ 2.60 GHz |
|---|---|
| RAM | 16 GB |
| Graphic Card | Nvidia GeForce GTX1070 8 GB |

Both experiments show a supermarket with products of mass consumption (dairy products, cereals, bakery, meats), cleaning, technology, and so forth (see Fig. 1), in order to apply neuromarketing techniques and test their influence on the client through purchase tests. The consumer is allowed to take a virtual tour with the ability to take any item and buy it through the payment stations. The data resulting from the experiment allows determining the influence of these techniques for the maximization of sales (Fig. 6).

**Fig. 6.** Supermarket and inside view

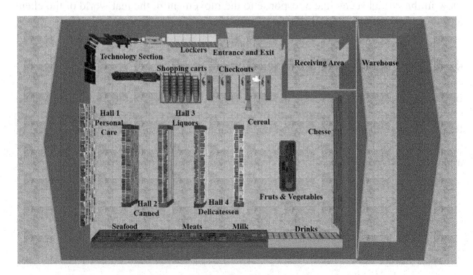

**Fig. 7.** Virtual supermarket design

In the construction of the supermarket it have been considered: the dimension of the corridors, shopping carts, number of shelves and cash registers, lockers, and location of products; using the technique of assortment of products known as Visual Merchandising, Fig. 7.

When the application begins, the user observes a data entry screen (see Fig. 3) and it is asked for their genre, marital status, and age. This information allows the system to identify the type of consumer and establish the primary purchase need reflected in the list of items to be purchased, the budget allocated and a purchase time limit of 20 min, see Fig. 4. In case of do not specify the acquisition in the suggested period of time; the

a)    User interface to enter data

b)    User walking in the supermarket

**Fig. 8.** UI to enter user data

purchase is made automatically without paying at the stations. (An extra budget is given according to the total value of the purchase and the income variables in the system) (Figs. 8 and 9).

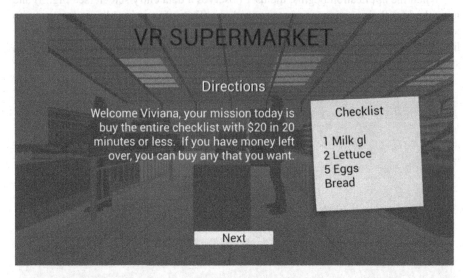

**Fig. 9.** Directions for the experiment and checklist in the user's HUD

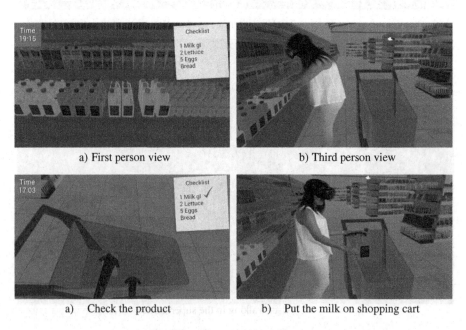

a) First person view                    b) Third person view

a)    Check the product            b)    Put the milk on shopping cart

**Fig. 10.** Client taking a milk case

**Experiment 1**

The test begins with a countdown timer running on the user's HUD. The user takes shopping cart and proceeds to move quickly through the virtual environment, using the teleportation system in search of the products in the list, see Fig. 10.

After making the purchase of the designated items, the user can have the balance of the budget granted to buy additional items according to their tastes and preferences, see Fig. 11.

| a)  Taking a beer | b)  Checking price of beer |
|---|---|

**Fig. 11.** Shop additional products

Finally, the user must approach the cashier to pay for all the products purchased according to the calculation of prices that the client has made when taking the products, see Fig. 12.

| a)   Pass products by register | b)   Verifying prices |
|---|---|

**Fig. 12.** Client paying for the products

As a result of these activities, the system produces a report in which the following variables are analysed: fulfilment of the assigned purchase, additional items purchased, price, budget balance, purchase time (Fig. 13). The output format is similar to a purchase receipt, while the scroll detail is displayed by an image, see Fig. 14.

**VR SUPERMARKET**

| | |
|---|---|
| Client: | Sharon Carter |
| Genre: | Female |
| Age: | 22 |
| Marital state: | Single |
| Date: | 30/03/2018 |
| Time: | 18:53 |

**Original Items**

- 1 Milk gl — $1.75
- 2 Lettuce — $0.89
- 5 eggs — $1.46
- Bread — $1.86

**Additional items**

- Beer six pack — $6.00
- Nail polish — $1.50
- Thin loin of meat — $5.30

**Total** — $18.76

**Fig. 13.** Experiment results detailed of Experiment N° 1

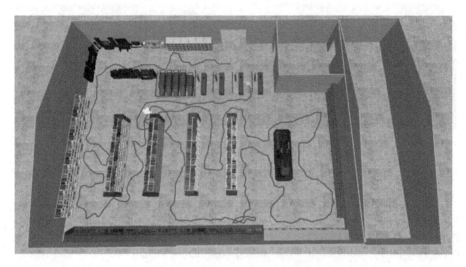

**Fig. 14.** User's movement tracking

## Experiment 2

The previous experiment is repeated with some changes of initial variables such as the change of location of the products see Fig. 15, and the following results are obtained in the purchase made by the user.

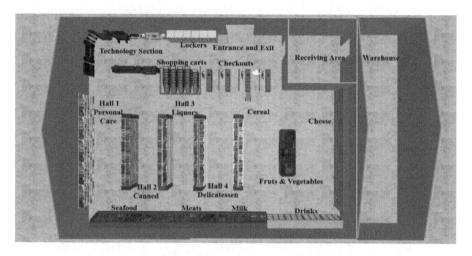

**Fig. 15.** Product place change detailed

| VR SUPERMARKET | |
|---|---|
| Client: | Peg Carter |
| Genre: | Female |
| Age: | 27 |
| Marital state: | Single |
| Date: | 30/03/2018 |
| Time: | 15:53 |
| **Original Items** | |
| • 1 Milk gl | $1.75 |
| • 2 Lettuce | $0.89 |
| • 5 eggs | $1.46 |
| • Bread | $1.86 |
| **Additional items** | |
| • Cereal | $2.00 |
| • Makeup | $2.50 |
| • ½ chicken | $4.70 |
| Total | $15.16 |

**Fig. 16.** Purchase detailed of Experiment N° 2

The results of both experiments suggest that the change in the location of luxury items (in which the buyer had no purchase goal) were the most purchased vs items that were not in privileged locations of the supermarket, see Figs. 16 and 17.

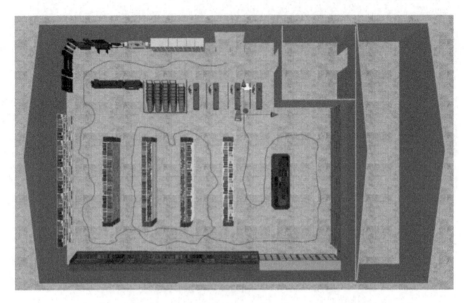

**Fig. 17.** User displacement record in second experiment

At the end of the experimentation stage, participants are asked to complete a satisfaction survey to check the level of acceptance of the application. The survey method to be used is the SUS summary evaluation method [23] and the Likert-scale

**Table 2.** Quiz results

| Questions | Score | Operation |
|---|---|---|
| 1. Do I think I would like to use this system frequently? | 4 | 4 − 1 = 3 |
| 2. Do I find this system unnecessarily complex? | 2 | 5 − 2 = 3 |
| 3. Do I think the system is easy to use? | 4 | 4 − 1 = 3 |
| 4. Do I think I would need technical support to make use of the system? | 1 | 5 − 1 = 4 |
| 5. Do I find the various functions of the system fairly well integrated? | 4 | 4 − 1 = 3 |
| 6. Is there too much inconsistency in this system? | 1 | 5 − 1 = 4 |
| 7. Do I think most people would learn to use the system quickly? | 4 | 4 − 1 = 3 |
| 8. I found the system quite uncomfortable to use? | 1 | 5 − 1 = 4 |
| 9. Have I found the system too cumbersome to use? | 4 | 4 − 1 = 3 |
| 10. Would I need to learn a lot of things before I could manage the system? | 2 | 5 − 2 = 3 |
| Total |  | 33 |

scale weighting [24]. The survey yields a unique numerical result, which describes the composite mean of the usability of the system subjected to preliminary tests. The 10 questions of the survey and the weighting for each question are presented in Table 2.

To find the SUS factor, the number resulting from the question weighting of the questionnaire must be multiplied by 2.5. In this case, the resulting value is 82.5, which falls on the improvement opportunity existing in question 2 and 10 to achieve a base of 90 in which the software can offer better usability to the user.

## 5   Conclusions

The paper shows a virtual reality application that contributes to the maximization of sales through the implementation of Neuromarketing and Merchandising techniques with elements such as: visual sale, accessibility to the consumer, assortment management, conscious and unconscious interaction with the products, and so on. The app provides benefits to companies that are dedicated to the sale of mass products, focusing on the effectiveness of Neuromarketing techniques that produce sales maximization and allows the optimization of resources, time and logistics by not testing them in a real supermarket. The technical variables obtained from the experiments and visualized in the purchase tickets demonstrate the effectiveness or inefficiency of the specific applied Neuromarketing technique and that together with the customer's consumption habits will allow making informed decisions for the real supermarket.

**Acknowledgement.** The authors would like to thanks to the Corporación Ecuatoriana para el Desarrollo de la Investigación y Academia – CEDIA for the financing given to research, development, and innovation, through the CEPRA projects, especially the project CEPRA-XI-2017-06; *Control Coordinado Multi-operador aplicado a un robot Manipulador Aéreo;* also to Universidad de las Fuerzas Armadas ESPE, Universidad Técnica de Ambato, Escuela Superior Politécnica de Chimborazo, and Universidad Nacional de Chimborazo, and Grupo de Investigación en Automatización, Robótica y Sistemas Inteligentes, GI-ARSI, for the support to develop this work.

## References

1. Sheth, J.N., Parvatiyar, A.: Relationship marketing in consumer markets: antecedents and consequences. J. Acad. Mark. Sci. **23**, 255–271 (1995)
2. Wilden, R., Gudergan, S.P.: The impact of dynamic capabilities on operational marketing and technological capabilities: investigating the role of environmental turbulence. J. Acad. Mark. Sci. **43**, 181–199 (2015)
3. Homburg, C., Vomberg, A., Enke, M., Grimm, P.H.: The loss of the marketing department's influence: is it really happening? And why worry? J. Acad. Mark. Sci. **43**, 1–13 (2015)
4. Ulman, Y.I., Cakar, T., Yildiz, G.: Ethical issues in neuromarketing: I consume, therefore I am! Sci. Eng. Ethics **21**, 1271–1284 (2015)
5. Agarwal, S., Dutta, T.: Neuromarketing and consumer neuroscience: current understanding and the way forward. Decision **42**, 457–462 (2015)

6. Trettel, A., Cherubino, P., Cartocci, G., Rossi, D., Modica, E., Maglione, A.G., di Flumeri, G., Babiloni, F.: Transparency and reliability in neuromarketing research. In: Thomas, A.R., Pop, N.A., Iorga, A.M., Ducu, C. (eds.) Ethics and Neuromarketing, pp. 101–111. Springer, Cham (2017). https://doi.org/10.1007/978-3-319-45609-6_6
7. Daugherty, T., Hoffman, E.: Neuromarketing: understanding the application of neuroscientific methods within marketing research. In: Thomas, A.R., Pop, N.A., Iorga, A.M., Ducu, Cristian (eds.) Ethics and Neuromarketing, pp. 5–30. Springer, Cham (2017). https://doi.org/10.1007/978-3-319-45609-6_2
8. Castro, J.C., Quisimalin, M., Córdova, V.H., Quevedo, W.X., Gallardo, C., Santana, J., Andaluz, V.H.: Virtual reality on e-Tourism. In: Kim, K.J., Kim, H., Baek, N. (eds.) ICITS 2017. LNEE, vol. 450, pp. 86–97. Springer, Singapore (2018). https://doi.org/10.1007/978-981-10-6454-8_13
9. Burke, R.R.: Virtual reality for marketing research. In: Moutinho, L., Sokele, M. (eds.) Innovative Research Methodologies in Management, pp. 63–82. Palgrave Macmillan, Cham (2018). https://doi.org/10.1007/978-3-319-64400-4_3
10. Quevedo, W.X., Sánchez, J.S., Arteaga, O., Álvarez, M., Zambrano, V.D., Sánchez, C.R., Andaluz, V.H.: Virtual reality system for training in automotive mechanics. In: International Conference on Augmented Reality, Virtual Reality and Computer Graphics, pp. 185–198, June 2017
11. Vecchiato, G., Jelic, A., Tieri, G., Maglione, A.G., De Matteis, F., Babiloni, F.: Neurophysiological correlates of embodiment and motivational factors during the perception of virtual architectural environments. Cogn. Process. 16, 425–429 (2015)
12. Marasco, A., Buonincontri, P., van Niekerk, M., Orlowski, M., Okumus, F.: Exploring the role of next-generation virtual technologies in destination marketing. J. Destin. Mark. Manag., 2–5 (2018)
13. Van Kerrebroeck, H., Brengman, M., Willems, K.: Escaping the crowd: an experimental study on the impact of a virtual reality experience in a shopping mall. Comput. Hum. Behav. 77, 437–450 (2017)
14. Dos Santos, R.D.O.J., de Oliveira, J.H.C., Rocha, J.B., Giraldi, J.D.M.E.: Eye tracking in neuromarketing: a research agenda for marketing studies. Int. J. Psychol. Stud. 71, 32 (2015)
15. Daugherty, T., Hoffman, E.: Neuromarketing: understanding the application of neuroscientific methods within marketing research. In: Ethics and Neuromarketing, pp. 5–30 (2017)
16. Ungureanu, F., Lupu, R.G., Cadar, A., Prodan, A.: Neuromarketing and visual attention study using eye tracking techniques. In: 21st International Conference on System Theory, Control and Computing (ICSTCC), Sinaia, pp. 553–557 (2017)
17. Jaramilllo, E., Gómez, V., Peña, A., Osuna, S., Lopera, L.: Automatic identification of emotional patterns in audiovisual adverstising by bioelectrical brian activity of an individual. In: 11th Iberian Conference on Information Systems and Technologies (CISTI), Gran Canaria, pp. 1–7 (2016)
18. Wang, C.H., Shih, Y.H., Lo, Y.C., Huang, C.Y.: Researching the adolescent visual color perception and brain wave in dynamic images. In: International Conference on Advanced Materials for Science and Engineering (ICAMSE), Tainan, pp. 162–164 (2016)
19. Bouzakraoui, M.S., Sadiq, A., Enneya, N.: Towards a framework for customer emotion detection. In: IEEE/ACS 13th International Conference of Computer Systems and Applications (AICCSA), Agadir, pp. 1–6 (2016)
20. Taqwa, T., Suhendra, A., Hermita, M., Darmayantie, A.: Implementation of Naïve Bayes method for product purchasing decision using neural impulse actuator in neuromarketing. In: International Conference on Information & Communication Technology and Systems (ICTS), Surabaya, pp. 113–118 (2015)

21. Pukach, P., Shakhovska, K.: The mathematical method development of decisions supporting concerning products placement based on analysis of market basket content. In: 14th International Conference The Experience of Designing and Application of CAD Systems in Microelectronics (CADSM), pp. 347–350 (2017)

22. Wu, J., Kim, A., Koo, J.: Co-design visual merchandising in 3D virtual stores: a facet theory approach. Int. J. Retail Distrib. Manag. **43**(6), 538–560 (2015)

23. Andaluz, V.H., Sánchez, J.S., Chamba, J.I., Romero, P.P., Chicaiza, F.A., Varela, J., Quevedo, W.X., Gallardo, C., Cepeda, L.F.: Unity3D virtual animation of robots with coupled and uncoupled mechanism. In: De Paolis, L.T., Mongelli, A. (eds.) AVR 2016, Part I. LNCS, vol. 9768, pp. 89–101. Springer, Cham (2016). https://doi.org/10.1007/978-3-319-40621-3_6

24. Sauro, J., Lewis, J.R.: When designing usability questionnaires, does it hurt to be positive? In: Proceedings of the SIGCHI Conference on Human Factors in Computing Systems, pp. 2215–2224. ACM, May 2011

# IMPACT

## Immersive Mirror for Pain Control and Treatment

Francesco Carrino[✉], Omar Abou Khaled, and Elena Mugellini

University of Applied Sciences and Arts Western Switzerland,
Fribourg, Switzerland
{francesco.carrino, omar.aboukhaled,
elena.mugellini}@hefr.ch

**Abstract.** We present an overview of IMPACT, a system that uses virtual and augmented reality to enhance the mirror therapy for the treatment of phantom limb pain and stroke rehabilitation. The system tracks users' movements and the head position using a combination of depth cameras and inertial sensors. This information is then fused together in a 3D full-body human model able to adapt to the patient's characteristics (e.g., skin color, limb size) and avoid unnatural movements due to possible bad tracking (e.g., a joint bended in an unnatural way). IMPACT includes three serious games that can be played in first-person point of view and that allow different levels of immersion according to the needs of the treatment.

**Keywords:** Augmented reality · Virtual reality · Mirror therapy
Phantom limb pain

## 1 Introduction

"Phantom limb" is a term that commonly describes the sensation of anomalous persistence of a limb after its amputation. People suffering from this phenomenon usually experience painful sensations in their amputated limb. This painful sensation is known as "phantom limb pain" (plp).

In order to appreciate the prominence of the phenomenon in statistical terms, 80% of people report experiencing the phantom limb syndrome after an amputation; uncomfortable or painful sensations accompany 85% of them and are recognized as major causes of distress, physical limitations and disability [1]. In about 70% of instances, phantom sensations remain painful even 25 years after the loss of the limb [2].

In conjunction or as alternative to the pharmacological treatment, the main approaches described in literature aim at recreating a correct cerebral representation of the missing limb. Among them, the mirror therapy has been used for several years to treat the plp as well as, in stroke rehabilitation, to treat the complex regional pain syndrome [3]. In 1995, V. S. Vilayanur Ramachandran invented the "mirror box" [4]. This tool allowed positioning a mirror between the two limbs creating the illusion of replacing the stump (hidden within the box) by a reflection of the healthy limb

L. T. De Paolis and P. Bourdot (Eds.): AVR 2018, LNCS 10851, pp. 192–200, 2018.
https://doi.org/10.1007/978-3-319-95282-6_14

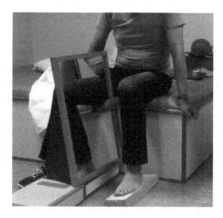

**Fig. 1.** A healthy user testing the mirror therapy on the lower limbs

(see Fig. 1). In this way, the patient is able to perform symmetric movements with both limbs, the healthy limb and its reflection.

Randomized controlled trials demonstrated good results of the mirror therapy for motor recovery after a stroke [5]. However, only small-scale studies showed encouraging results in the treatment of plp, especially when combined with other approaches, such as motor imagery, or when used regularly over an extended period of time [6].

This may be explained by the fact that the use of an optical mirror comes with three significant limitations: the mirror itself restricts the patient's mobility; the amount of possible exercises is limited to basic symmetric movements; the patient has to ignore the healthy limb in order to focus solely on the reflection [7]. These limitations make it harder for the patient to focus on the mirror reflection, perhaps limiting the effects of the treatment.

A possible way to overcome these problems could come from the use of new technologies and, in particular, Augmented Reality (AR) or Virtual Reality (VR). The general idea is that the patient is able to see a virtual limb in the place of the compromised one by simply looking in the general direction of the stump. This could: (*i*) facilitate and increase the immersion; (*ii*) allow new exercises that are simply not possible with an optical mirror; (*iii*) increase the engagement of the patient during the treatment using serious games or gamification; (*iv*) open the way to new evidence, allowing more extensive studies towards new treatments.

In this paper, we present IMPACT, a system based on VR and AR developed in collaboration with therapists to enhance mirror therapy for the treatment of plp. The system includes three serious games that propose different levels of immersion. Considering future development for homecare, in this project we considered only off-the-shelf and relatively low-cost technologies.

## 2    Related Works

Augmented and Virtual Reality can challenge our sense of what we recognize and believe to be real. In VR, the user is totally immersed in a virtual world while, in AR, virtual elements are added to the reality. Applied appropriately, these technologies represent new chances for understanding and treating a range of human functional impairments as well as studying the underlying psychological foundations of these phenomena [8]. Especially in recent years, many works explored the use of VR or AR to improve the mirror therapy for the treatment of plp. Usually, the goal was to provide a more immersive experience aiming at making the mirror therapy less tiring, more engaging and, hopefully, more effective.

Murray et al. investigated the use of a VR-based system as a treatment for plp with three patients [7]. The authors tracked the healthy hand using a data glove and then animated consequently a virtual model. They reported that all participants expressed a decrease in pain in at least one of the sessions with the VR system. Shen et al. compared a VR and AR systems for the hand movement rehabilitation [9]. Their study showed that the AR approach provided better results, especially in terms of realism of the simulation. Desmond et al. [10] proposed a mirror therapy approach based on AR using a data glove for the hand tracking. For the visual feedback, they used a screen. They tested their system with three patients comparing the results with the optical mirror therapy. In addition, they tested the effects on plp of inconsistent feedback (e.g., they presented a stationary image of the virtual limb while the participant was in fact trying to move the phantom fingers). The optical and the AR mirror provided similar results with the exception of a more intense sensation experienced by the patients when the AR system was used to display unexpected or abnormal movements.

A more recent work based on AR has been presented in [11]; the authors developed an AR system capable of overlapping a virtual arm on the stump using a fiducial marker (i.e., a tag similar to QRcodes). Hence, the virtual arm was animated taking into account the mark position and orientation and the myoelectric activity of the residual muscles on the stump. A screen in front of the user showed the AR. Between 2014 and 2015, they extended their research by testing the same approach with 14 patients with chronic plp considered as "intractable" (i.e., all the conventional treatments previously used with these patients failed) [12]. The authors report that patients showed statistically and clinically significant improvements in all metrics of plp. In average, after 12 sessions, they measured a decrease in plp by 47%. This work is the only one that we were able to find that clearly showed results statistically significant on a sample of a reasonable size. However, as in most of the other works, theirs focus was on the treatment of upper limbs despite the fact that the great majority of amputations concerns the lower extremities [13]. To the best of our knowledge, none of the existing work proposed an AR-based system able to deal with lower- and upper-limbs while offering *full immersion* with a first-person point of view.

IMPACT, the system that we present in this paper, has exactly this objective. In addition, we chose to use off-the-shelf technologies and relatively low-cost sensors in order to make it easier, in the future, to transfer this approach from the hospital to the patients' homes. This work represents an upgrade of the system presented in [14], which had limitations in terms of technologies (e.g., limited field of view and slow refresh rate) and precision of the tracking algorithm. In addition, IMPACT provides three serious games conceived to help the therapist to conduct the treatment and to increase the immersion and the engagement of the patient.

## 3   System Overview

### 3.1   Architecture

The IMPACT system has two types of users: the therapist and the patient (see Fig. 2). The therapist has the role of configuring the system to adapt the treatment to the specificity of the patient and to the planned therapy session. The patient has to wear a Head-Mounted Display (HMD) and to follow the instructions of the therapist and/or the system.

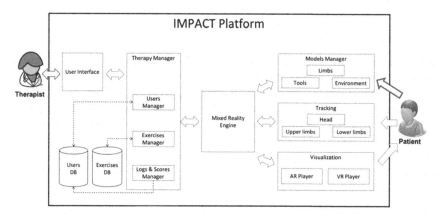

**Fig. 2.** The architecture of the IMPACT platform

The therapist access the system through the User Interface module. This interface has been conceived to be as simple as possible to be suitable for users not necessarily proficient in the use of computers. The interface provides access to the Therapy Manager module that allows the full setup of the following therapy session. To do that, the therapist inserts the patient data into the system (e.g., height, skin color, type of amputation, etc.) and selects the exercises to be performed. According to this information, the system loads all the 3D models required by the session (i.e., the virtual limb and the virtual objects that are used during the treatment). Furthermore, the therapist has the possibility to monitor and manage the session in real-time (restart, pause, stop, continue) as well as to monitor the patient evolution during the weeks of treatment recorded by the Logs & Scores Manager. Finally, the therapist has the possibility to add, edit and remove users. Information about patients and exercises scenarios are stored in databases and therefore reused in the following sessions.

In the next step, the information about the therapy is transferred to the Mixed Reality Engine module. This module represents the core of the system: it animates the 3D objects according to the current exercise and the movements of the patient tracked in real-time by the Tracking module.

The Tracking module provides information in real-time about the patient's body and head position and orientation. Different sub-modules manage the tracking of different body parts since they may depend on very different technologies and approaches and they may evolve in time.

The Models Manager module manages the 3D models present in the system and its behavior is strictly related to the chosen exercise. The top arrow from the patient to the module (stylized with a bolder line in Fig. 2) represents the step needed at the beginning of the first therapy session to gather information (possibly in an automatic way) about the patient's features.

Finally, the Mixed Reality Engine transmits the processed information to the Visualization module that manages the delivery of feedback to the patient (mainly, using AR or VR) in the optimal way.

### 3.2    Setup

Many of the previous works discussed in Sect. 2 are somehow limited by the technologies they used. In terms of visual feedback, most works used simple screens at the expense of the immersion possibilities. In order to provide the immersion required for such applications and to make it as natural as possible, we believe that HMD represents the suitable choice. In addition, some of the works used markers to track the stump. This solution could work well in specific scenarios but it could be quite a limitation in many others (e.g., the marker has to be constantly in the field of view of the camera).

After testing different solutions, we used the following setup:

**HMD:** Oculus Rift Consumer version (OLED display; resolution: 1080 × 1200 per eye; refresh rate: 90 Hz; diagonal field of view: 100–100°)

**AR:** OVRvision Pro (stereo camera; resolution: 1280 × 800 × 2; frame rate; 60 fps, horizontal: 115°; vertical field of view: 90°).

**Body tracking – lower limbs:** Kinect V2 (color camera resolution: 1920 × 1080; depth camera resolution: 512 × 424; frame rate: 30 fps).

**Body tracking – lower and upper limbs:** Perception Neurons (dynamic range: 360°; accelerometer range: ±16g; gyroscope range: ±2000 dps; frame rate: 120 fps).

**Head tracking:** Kinect V2 and Oculus Rift 6 degree of freedom head tracking (3-axis rotational tracking, 3-axis positional tracking).

**3D Engine:** Unity 3D.

As showed by this list, we fused the information coming from multiple sensors to improve the tracking accuracy. In the next section, we will discuss how we performed this fusion.

# 4    Tracking

In order to get a realistic, real-time body tracking, we combined two approaches: the first, based on computer vision (Kinect v2), and the second, based on inertial sensors (Perception Neuron). The main advantages of using a depth camera are that it allows to avoid sticking markers on the patient's body, it requires minimal or no calibration and can be used to get some information automatically such as the patient's limb size and skin color. However, the choice of using off-the-shelf solutions brings some additional challenges. Kinect is not precise enough to track movements of fingers and ankles. In addition, since it works at 30 fps, it introduces a perceivable delay into the system. On the other hand, the inertial sensors that we used go up to 120 fps, are very precise and can be used to track any joint. However, they are quite sensible to electromagnetic fields and a drift effect becomes noticeable after a couple of minutes of use. The consequent recalibration is time consuming and requires that the patient assumes some predefined postures. These problems lead to a noisy signal that translates in an incorrect, flickering animation of the virtual limbs or in joints of the model twisted into unnatural postures.

In order to take advantage of both approach and filter out or reduce the noise, we developed a retargeting system (see Fig. 3). It consists of mapping separately the data coming from the computer vision sensor and from the inertial sensors into two different avatars. Then we retarget and merge the two avatars into the final one. For this first implementation of the merge, we used a simple linear interpolation with an additional weight parameter for each joint. This parameter indicates which system we trust more for that given joint and adds more importance to its data (e.g., knowing that Kinect does not track reliably the flexion/extension of ankles, for this joint, we privileged data coming from the Perception Neuron).

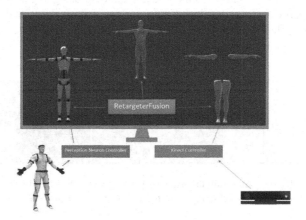

**Fig. 3.** A schema describing the retargeting system

In addition, before merging, it is possible to calibrate and filter separately the signal coming from the two modules. For instance, we used a spherical interpolation to smooth the signal coming from the Kinect and reduce the flickering and quivering of the avatar. After the merge, when the tracking data are used to animate the last 3D model (the only one visible to the users), we apply constraints to each joint to avoid that the virtual limb could assume unnatural postures.

Finally, we used the computer vision data to facilitate the "in-game" recalibration of the inertial sensors to limit the drift effect. We did this by readjusting the inertial data to the information coming from the cameras while the patient is in a simple static sitting position or in a T-pose (both of them fairly well tracked by Kinect).

## 5   Serious Games (Rehabilitation Exercise)

With the support of a team of occupational therapists, we developed a treatment scenario that described the exercises required in each session. The exercises are divided in four types of increasing difficulty (however, if the patient has a very limited mobility due to the plp, a session can be composed of only exercises of type one and two).

**Type one - familiarization with the virtual limb.** The therapist asks the patient to simply observe and focus on the virtual limb in order to become familiar with the technique.

**Type two - unilateral analytical movements.** The patient performs analytical movements (i.e., movements that focus on a single joint and/or target a specific muscle) with the unaffected limb.

**Type three - bilateral analytical movements.** The patient performs analytical exercises with both limbs simultaneously.

**Type four - bilateral manipulation of objects or therapeutic equipment.** The patient manipulates objects or therapeutic equipment using both the virtual and the healthy limb.

We used the previous classification as a guideline for designing and developing our exercises. In particular, we developed three serious games: the "Shadow game", the "Penalty game", the "Music" game. The three games can be played in VR or AR according to the preferences of the therapist and/or the patient.

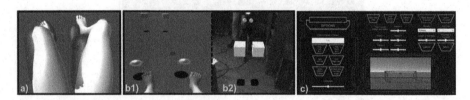

**Fig. 4.** (a) The Shadow game from the patient's point of view; (b) The Music game in VR (b1) and in AR (b2); (c) The Penalty game (from the therapist's point of view).

The **Shadow game** is the most basic of the three but is very flexible and it can be used for exercises from type one to type three. A 3D shadow surrounds the patient's body (see Fig. 4a). As a demonstration, the shadow shows a pre-recorded movement a first time. After a countdown, it changes its color and it repeats the movement. The patient has to perform the same movement at the same time. The more the patient's movement matches the movement of the shadow, the more points she/he gets. This game can be used to perform mirrored movements (i.e., similarly to the optical mirror), parallel movements (i.e., the left and right limbs move simultaneously in the same direction) or movements that involve just the healthy limb. The system easily allows recording new movements with the Perception Neuron and adding them to the Exercises database.

The **Music game** focuses on exercises of type three. It is inspired by the well-known game "Guitar Hero". During the game, couples of virtual objects move towards the patient at different height and distances (see Fig. 4b). The speed and numbers of these objects depend on the tempo of the music and the chosen level of difficulty while their shapes and colors indicate the limb or joint that the patient has to use to hit them (e.g., we used golden spheres for the feet and blue cubes for the knees). At the end of the session, the game gives a score to the user.

The **Penalty game** focuses on exercises of type four for patients with a lower-limb amputation. The patient needs to perform a symmetrical movement to push two buttons and summon a ball. Then, she/he has to shoot it in the football goal (see Fig. 4c). Advancing with the game, the football goal becomes smaller and smaller and changes position requiring an increasing accuracy to score points.

# 6  Conclusion

In this "work in progress" paper, we presented an overview of the IMPACT system, a platform developed to improve the mirror therapy for the treatment of plp using VR and AR. The system offers a first-person point of view to increase the immersion and includes three serious games that can be played in AR and VR. In order to facilitate future developments towards homecare, we used off-the-shelf and relatively low-cost technologies.

We pre-tested the system usability with 6 healthy subjects achieving a good score with System Usability Scale [15] (even though, not statistically significant given the reduced number of participants). However, these pre-tests showed that it was quite difficult for the participants to understand the size/distance of virtual objects in AR even though we added a virtual shadow to avoid this problem (see Fig. 4-b2) and we need to improve this aspect.

Finally, the main goal of this project was to develop a system ready for clinical trials that will take place in the next months. These tests will evaluate and compare the differences in efficacy for plp treatment between the use of an optical mirror, VR and AR. The possibility to use VR alongside AR will allow further studies also for stroke rehabilitation (in which AR is probably not the best option given the presence of the impaired limb).

**Acknowledgement.** This research project was supported by the Hasler Stiftung and by the University of Applied Sciences Western Switzerland. In addition, the authors would like to thank Elisa Nannini, Vincent Brodard, Quentin Seydoux, Luc Francey, and Charlotte Junod for their contribution to develop the system and games.

# References

1. Kooijman, C.M., Dijkstra, P.U., Geertzen, J.H.B., Elzinga, A., van der Schans, C.P.: Phantom pain and phantom sensations in upper limb amputees: an epidemiological study. Pain **87**, 33–41 (2000)
2. Tzionas, D., Vrenas, K., Eleftheriadis, S., Georgoulis, S., Petrantonakis, P., Hadjileontiadis, L.: Phantom limb pain management using facial expression analysis, biofeedback and augmented reality interfacing. In: Proceedings of the 3rd International Conference on Software Development for Enhancing Accessibility and Fighting Info-exclusion (DSAI 2010). UTAD & SAE Institute, Oxford, United Kingdom (2010)
3. McCabe, C.S., Haigh, R.C., Ring, E.F.J., Halligan, P.W., Wall, P.D., Blake, D.R.: A controlled pilot study of the utility of mirror visual feedback in the treatment of complex regional pain syndrome (type 1). Rheumatology **42**, 97–101 (2003)
4. Ramachandran, V.S., Rogers-Ramachandran, D.: Synaesthesia in phantom limbs induced with mirrors (1996)
5. Ezendam, D., Bongers, R.M., Jannink, M.J.: Systematic review of the effectiveness of mirror therapy in upper extremity function. Disabil. Rehabil. **31**, 2135–2149 (2009)
6. Moseley, G.L.: Graded motor imagery is effective for long-standing complex regional pain syndrome: a randomised controlled trial. Pain **108**, 192–198 (2004)
7. Murray, C.D., Pettifer, S., Howard, T., Patchick, E.L., Caillette, F., Kulkarni, J., Bamford, C.: The treatment of phantom limb pain using immersive virtual reality: three case studies. Disabil. Rehabil. **29**, 1465–1469 (2007)
8. Rizzo, A. "Skip", Kim, G.J.: A SWOT analysis of the field of virtual reality rehabilitation and therapy. Presence Teleoperators Virtual Environ. **14**, 119–146 (2005)
9. Shen, Y., Ong, S., Nee, A.: An augmented reality system for hand movement rehabilitation. In: Proceedings of the 2nd International Convention on Rehabilitation Engineering & Assistive Technology, pp. 189–192. Singapore Therapeutic, Assistive & Rehabilitative Technologies (START) Centre (2008)
10. Desmond, D.M., O'Neill, K., De Paor, A., McDarby, G., MacLachlan, M.: Augmenting the reality of phantom limbs: three case studies using an augmented mirror box procedure. JPO J. Prosthetics Orthot. **18**, 74 (2006)
11. Ortiz-Catalan, M., Sander, N., Kristoffersen, M.B., Håkansson, B., Brånemark, R.: Treatment of phantom limb pain (PLP) based on augmented reality and gaming controlled by myoelectric pattern recognition: A case study of a chronic PLP patient. Front. Neurosci. **8**, 1–7 (2014)
12. Ortiz-Catalan, M., Guðmundsdóttir, R.A., Kristoffersen, M.B., Zepeda-Echavarria, A., Caine-Winterberger, K., Kulbacka-Ortiz, K., Widehammar, C., Eriksson, K., Stockselius, A., Ragnö, C., Pihlar, Z., Burger, H., Hermansson, L.: Phantom motor execution facilitated by machine learning and augmented reality as treatment for phantom limb pain: a single group, clinical trial in patients with chronic intractable phantom limb pain. Lancet **388**, 2885–2894 (2016)
13. Gregory-Dean, A.: Amputations: statistics and trends. Ann. R. Coll. Surg. Engl. **73**, 137–142 (1991)
14. Carrino, F., Rizzotti, D., Gheorghe, C., Kabasu Bakajika, P., Francescotti-Paquier, F., Mugellini, E.: Augmented reality treatment for phantom limb pain. In: Shumaker, R., Lackey, S. (eds.) VAMR 2014, Part II. LNCS, vol. 8526, pp. 248–257. Springer, Cham (2014). https://doi.org/10.1007/978-3-319-07464-1_23
15. Lewis, J.R., Sauro, J.: The factor structure of the system usability scale. In: Kurosu, M. (ed.) HCD 2009. LNCS, vol. 5619, pp. 94–103. Springer, Heidelberg (2009). https://doi.org/10.1007/978-3-642-02806-9_12

# A Microsoft HoloLens Mixed Reality Surgical Simulator for Patient-Specific Hip Arthroplasty Training

Giuseppe Turini[1,2], Sara Condino[2,3(✉)], Paolo Domenico Parchi[2,4],
Rosanna Maria Viglialoro[2], Nicola Piolanti[4], Marco Gesi[5,6],
Mauro Ferrari[2], and Vincenzo Ferrari[2,3]

[1] Computer Science Department, Kettering University, Flint, MI, USA
gturini@kettering.edu
[2] EndoCAS Center, Department of Translational Research and of New Surgical
and Medical Technologies, University of Pisa, Pisa, Italy
{sara.condino,rosanna.viglialoro,
vincenzo.ferrari}@endocas.unipi.it,
mauro.ferrari@med.unipi.it
[3] Department of Information Engineering, University of Pisa, Pisa, Italy
[4] 1st Orthopaedic and Traumatology Division, Department of Translational
Research and of New Surgical and Medical Technologies,
University of Pisa, Pisa, Italy
paolo.parchi@unipi.it, nicpio@hotmail.it
[5] Department of Translational Research and of New Surgical and Medical
Technologies, University of Pisa, Pisa, Italy
marco.gesi@med.unipi.it
[6] Center for Rehabilitative Medicine "Sport and Anatomy",
University of Pisa, Pisa, Italy

**Abstract.** Surgical simulation can offer novice surgeons an opportunity to practice skills outside the operating theatre in a safe controlled environment. According to literature evidence, nowadays there are very few training simulators available for Hip Arthroplasty (HA).

In a previous study we have presented a physical simulator based on a lower torso phantom including a patient-specific *hemi-pelvis* replica embedded in a soft synthetic foam. This work explores the use of Microsoft HoloLens technology to enrich the physical patient-specific simulation with the implementation of wearable mixed reality functionalities. Our HA multimodal simulator based on mixed reality using the HoloLens is described by illustrating the overall system, and by summarizing the main phases of the design and development.

Finally, we present a preliminary qualitative study with seven subjects (5 medical students, and 2 orthopedic surgeons) showing encouraging results that suggest the suitability of the HoloLens for the proposed application. However, further studies need to be conducted to perform a quantitative test of the registration accuracy of the virtual content, and to confirm qualitative results in a larger cohort of subjects.

© Springer International Publishing AG, part of Springer Nature 2018
L. T. De Paolis and P. Bourdot (Eds.): AVR 2018, LNCS 10851, pp. 201–210, 2018.
https://doi.org/10.1007/978-3-319-95282-6_15

**Keywords:** Surgical simulation · Augmented reality · Microsoft HoloLens
Hip arthroplasty

# 1 Introduction

Hip arthroplasty (HA) is a surgical procedure which involves replacing a damaged hip joint with a prosthetic implant to reduce pain and improve mobility. HA is one of the most widely performed procedures in orthopedic practice and it is considered to be one of the most successful orthopedic interventions of the 20$^{th}$ century. However primary and revision total hip arthroplasty (THA) have been ranked third and fourth among the orthopedic interventions accounted for the greatest share of adverse events and excess hospital stay [1]. The risk of HA complications is strongly related to the surgeon's case volume. According to a research study [2], surgeons should perform at least 35 THA procedures annually to reduce the risk of complications. Another study [3] focalized on the anterior approach, shows that 50 or more procedures are required before reaching the performance (in terms of revision rate) of surgeons with an experience of 100 or more cases.

In this context, surgical simulation could play a pivotal role, offering novices an opportunity to practice skills outside the operating theatre, in a safe controlled environment. Several techniques of simulation are today available including: physical, virtual reality (VR), and hybrid simulation. This latter is based on the combination of computer simulation with synthetic models of the anatomy. The physical models can mimic the mechanical properties of human tissue [4–7] offering the learner the possibility to practice skills using real surgical instruments; whereas computer graphics enables the visualization and animation of virtual content, enhancing the surgical simulation. Thus, hybrid simulators can guarantee a realistic haptic feedback, overcoming the limitations of current VR technologies which are still unable to accurately model in real-time the instruments-anatomy interactions. At the same time, augmented reality (AR) features allow the guidance of the trainee during the execution of surgical tasks, and the visualization of hidden anatomical structures as virtual organs [8–13].

According to a recent review study [14], nowadays there are very few training simulators available for HA. Indeed, even if VR systems have been developed for planning purposes, there are not many simulators aimed at training.

In a previous work [15] we have presented the "HipSim", a physical simulator based on a *lower torso* phantom including a patient-specific *hemi-pelvis* replica embedded in a soft synthetic foam. The "HipSim" was validated by 13 orthopedic surgeons and considered a realistic and useful learning tool.

This work explores the use of Microsoft HoloLens technology to enrich the physical patient-specific simulation with the implementation of wearable mixed reality functionalities.

The Microsoft HoloLens, one of the most advanced head-mounted displays (HMDs) available today, can provide users hands-free access to complex data, and an unobstructed view of the real environment. Recent literature works have addressed the usage of the HoloLens in the operating room to improve decision-making and surgical workflow [16], remote supervision and annotation, 3D image viewing and manipulation, telepathology in a mixed-reality environment, and real-time pathology-radiology correlation [17].

In this paper we present the design and development of a HA multimodal simulator based on mixed reality using the Microsoft HoloLens: combining patient-specific synthetic replicas, AR features, and audio technology.

## 2    Material and Methods

The following paragraphs briefly describe the HoloLens Technology, and the main steps for the design of the proposed Mixed Reality Surgical Simulator.

### 2.1    Head-Mounted Display: Overview of the HoloLens Technology

The HoloLens, is an optical see-through (OST) HMD: it allows superposition of digital information onto the real-world view, while optically maintaining see-through view which assures that visual and proprioception information is synchronized. This HMD, was chosen for the development of our HA multimodal simulator since it provides significant benefits over other commercial HMDs from human factors and ergonomics standpoints [18] and integrates important functionalities for an immersive and interactive simulation experience.

The HoloLens technology is based on an undisclosed Intel 32-bit processor, with a custom-built Microsoft Holographic Processing Unit (HPU 1.0) which supports Universal Windows Platform (UWP) apps. It is equipped with 2 GB of RAM (1 GB for CPU, and 1 GB for HPU) and 64 GB of flash memory; it features network connectivity via Wi-Fi 802.11ac and Bluetooth 4.1 LE wireless technology. The HPU processes data from multiple sensors: 4 *"environment understanding cameras"*; 1 depth camera; and 1 world-facing photo/video camera (2 MP); 1 inertial measurement unit (IMU) to track head movements; 4 microphones; and 1 ambient light sensor.

Thanks to these technologies the HoloLens provides distinctive features such as: spatial mapping, interactions by means of head movements ("gaze" is estimated from head tracking), hand gesture, and voice commands. The speakers integrated into the headset enable binaural audio to simulate effects such as spatial sounds within the user's environment.

For all these reasons, HoloLens can be considered a perfect candidate for the implementation of mixed-reality surgical simulators. However, some technical issues have to be considered, such as: restricted overlay field of view (FOV) (only about 35°); vergence-accommodation conflict; mismatch between the focal distance of real and virtual objects (HoloLens features a fixed focal length of 2.0 m); difficulties in handling occlusions between the real and virtual contents. For a complete overview of these issues refer to [19]. Finally, the weight of 579 g can make it uncomfortable to wear for prolonged periods of time.

For all these reasons, tests should be performed to evaluate the usability of the proposed HDM for our specific scenario: orthopedic open surgery simulation.

## 2.2   Design of the Mixed Reality Surgical Simulator

**Virtual and Physical Contents.** The development of the simulator started from the extraction of the anatomical components from a real radiological computed tomography (CT) data set. CT images were processed using a semi-automatic tool, the EndoCAS Segmentation Pipeline, integrated in the open source software ITK-SNAP 1.5. Then mesh optimization stages (artifacts removal, holes filling, simplification, and filtering) were performed using the open source software MeshLab and Blender. Segmented anatomical models include: *pelvis*, hip bones, *sacrum*, *coccyx*, femoral heads, principal muscles around the hip joint (such as: *gluteal muscles*, *piriformis*, *inferior gemellus*, *superior gemellus*, *obturator internus*).

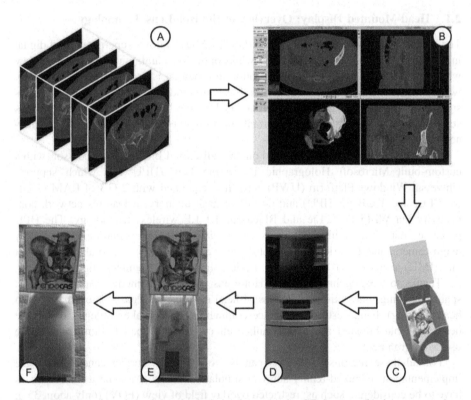

**Fig. 1.** The manufacturing of the physical simulator: (a) the CT data set, (b) the segmentation stage, (c) the CAD design, (d) and (e) the 3D printing for the rapid prototyping of the synthetic anatomy, and (f) the complete physical simulator including the support for a Vuforia Image Target used to register the virtual content with the mannequin.

Rapid prototyping (Dimension Elite 3D Printer) and casting techniques were used to fabricate synthetic replicas of anatomical parts for which it is important to guarantee the surgeon the possibility of physical interaction. These include: a soft replica of the *pelvis* with a skin-like covering which allows an accurate simulation of palpation and surgical incision; a model of the *acetabulum* in acrylonitrile butadiene styrene (ABS), a material commonly used for the manufacturing of bone replicas for surgical drilling simulation. The main stages of the manufacturing of the physical simulator are illustrated in Fig. 1.

Other segmented anatomical structures, important to increase the anatomical knowledge of the user trainee, are instead visualized as virtual organs (virtual content). This virtual anatomy is enriched with:

- a collection of radiological images, which present the surgical case to the learner at the beginning of the simulation (see Fig. 2, and the Medical Image Navigator module in Fig. 3);
- information from a simulated planning phase with the 3D Hip Plugin [15]: a pair of "viewfinders", and a virtual line showing the surgeon the optimal trajectory to insert the surgical reamer (see Figs. 3 and 4).

The detection and tracking functionalities offered by the Vuforia SDK were used for the real-time registration of the virtual content to the real scene. At this end, the physical environment includes the support for a Vuforia Image Target, which was rigidly anchored to the bone synthetic replica (see Fig. 1).

**Software Implementation.** Unity3D (5.6.1f) was used to implement the software application, using the MixedRealityToolkit (2017.1.2), a freely available collection of C# scripts which allows an easy and fast development of AR applications. The developed mixed reality app allows the user to interact with the virtual content by means of: head movements ("gaze" is estimated from the position and orientation of the user's head), HoloLens gestures (Air Tap and Bloom), and voice commands (detected by Microsoft Cortana speech recognition on the HoloLens). A virtual menu with toggle buttons has been implemented to allow the user to control the visualization of the virtual content (*pelvis*, bones, muscles, pre-operative plan).

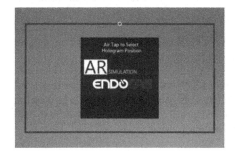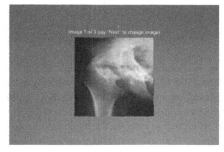

**Fig. 2.** Two "screenshots" of the Medical Image Navigator module: the opening screen to allow the user to anchor the mixed reality window using the Air Tap gesture (left), and the first medical image of a collection of 3 that the user can navigate using voice commands (right).

Operating room sounds effects (including voices and hospital machines sounds) are added to improve *immersion* and increase the realism of the simulation.

A Medical Image Navigator module (Fig. 2) was implemented for the visualization of radiological images. This navigator allows: the anchoring of the radiological images collection in a user-defined position (using the Air Tap gesture), and the switching to the next image in the collection (using the voice command "Next").

Figure 3 shows the system diagram of the "HipSim" mixed reality application illustrating all the interactions between the hardware and software modules and showing all the user-interactions involved.

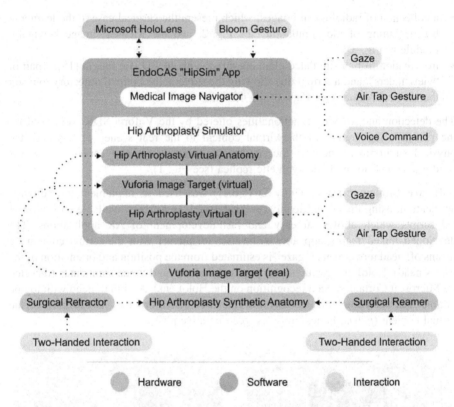

**Fig. 3.** Scheme of the "HipSim" mixed reality application for the Microsoft HoloLens, illustrating all the interactions between the hardware and software modules (dotted lines), the different types of interactions (voice, gestures etc.), as well as the "rigid" geometrical transformations (solid lines) between some physical and virtual modules. "Gaze" is the term used by Microsoft to indicate the interaction based on head movements.

## 3   Evaluation of the Mixed Reality Surgical Simulator

Seven (7) subjects, two (2) orthopedic surgeons and five (5) medical students of the University of Pisa, were recruited to participate in a preliminary qualitative study of our hip arthroplasty multimodal simulator. None of the participants had any previous experience with the Microsoft HoloLens. Table 1 summarizes the demographic characteristics of the participants. The experimental setup is depicted in Fig. 4.

**Table 1.** Demographic characteristics of the participants.

| | |
|---|---|
| Position held (medical students, orthopedic surgeons) | 5, 2 |
| Gender (male, female, non-binary) | 5, 2, 0 |
| Age (min, max, mean, STD) | 23, 39, 30, 6 |
| Vision (10/10 naked eyes, corrected to 10/10 with contact lenses) | 2, 5 |
| Experience with AR (none, limited, familiar, experienced) | 3, 3, 1, 0 |
| Experience with VR (none, limited, familiar, experienced) | 2, 4, 1, 0 |
| Experience with HoloLens (none, limited, familiar, experienced) | 7, 0, 0, 0 |
| Color Blindness (no, yes) | 20, 0 |

Each subject performed the calibration of the HoloLens using the Microsoft "Calibration" app, and then was asked to familiarize with gestural controls using the Microsoft "Learn Gestures" app. Finally, each candidate used our HA multimodal simulator for 30 min, inspecting the AR content and evaluating: positioning, stability, and visual quality of all the virtual content. More in particular they were instructed to use:

- the Head Tracking based interaction to move the Medical Image Navigator in the physical space, and to select toggle buttons of the Hip Arthroplasty Virtual UI;
- the voice command "Next" to scroll images of the Medical Image Navigator;
- the Air Tap gesture to anchor the Medical Image Navigator Module in the desired position, and to turn on/off the toggle buttons of the Hip Arthroplasty Virtual UI.

After each trial, the candidate was asked to complete a 5-points Likert survey (from 1 = strongly disagree, to 5 = strongly agree) (Table 2) grouped in 4 headings: AR Positioning and Time Response, Interaction and Guidance, FOV, and Spatial Sounds.

**Fig. 4.** Two "screenshots" of the Hip Arthroplasty Simulator, showing the virtual user interface the virtual anatomy in two different configurations: the visualization of the bones, pelvis, and preoperative planning (left), with the muscles hidden (deactivated); and the visualization of the complete virtual content (right).

## 4 Preliminary Results and Discussion

Table 2 summarizes the results of the preliminary study. The central tendencies of responses to a single Likert item are summarized by using median, with dispersion measured by interquartile range. A positive feedback was received about the AR Positioning and Time Response, and the suitability of the HoloLens FOV for the proposed application. Participants strongly agreed that Head Tracking based, Gesture, and Voice interactions are easy and intuitive; however, a neutral opinion was expressed about the ease of aligning the surgical instrument to the AR viewfinders. Finally, participants strongly agreed that spatial sounds make the experience more immersive.

**Table 2.** Likert questionnaire results

| Questionnaire items | | Median | IQR-Range |
|---|---|---|---|
| AR positioning and time response | The virtual content is correctly aligned to the real objects | 4.5 | 5–4 |
| | The positioning of virtual content is stable over the time | 4 | 5–4 |
| | It is easy to perceive the spatial relationships between real and virtual objects | 4.5 | 5–4 |
| | I did not notice latency (lag, delay) between virtual content and objects real | 4 | 5–4 |
| Interaction and guidance | Head Tracking based interaction is easy and intuitive | 5 | 5–4 |
| | Gesture interactions are easy and intuitive | 5 | 5–4 |
| | Voice interactions are easy and intuitive | 5 | 5–4 |
| | It is easy to align the surgical tool to the AR viewfinders | 3.5 | 4.25–2.75 |
| FOV | The Field of View (FOV) is adequate for the application | 4 | 3–4 |
| Spatial sounds | Spatial sounds make the experience more immersive | 5 | 5–4 |

Obtained results suggest the suitability of the HoloLens for the proposed application. However, further studies need to be conducted to perform a quantitative test of the registration accuracy of the virtual content, and to confirm qualitative results in a larger cohort of subjects.

**Acknowledgment.** The research leading to these results has been partially supported by the European Project VOSTARS (H2020 Call ICT-29-2016 G.A. 731974) and by the SThARS project, funded by the Italian Ministry of Health and Regione Toscana through the call "RicercaFinalizzata2011–2012".

# References

1. Wolf, B.R., Lu, X., Li, Y., Callaghan, J.J., Cram, P.: Adverse outcomes in hip arthroplasty: long-term trends. J. Bone Joint Surg. Am. **94**, e103 (2012)
2. Hasegawa, Y., Amano, T.: Surgical skills training for primary total hip arthroplasty. Nagoya J. Med. Sci. **77**, 51–57 (2015)
3. de Steiger, R.N., Lorimer, M., Solomon, M.: What is the learning curve for the anterior approach for total hip arthroplasty? Clin. Orthop. Relat. Res. **473**, 3860–3866 (2015)
4. Carbone, M., Condino, S., Mattei, L., Forte, P., Ferrari, V., Mosca, F.: Anthropomorphic ultrasound elastography phantoms - characterization of silicone materials to build breast elastography phantoms. In: Proceedings of the Annual International Conference of the IEEE Engineering in Medicine and Biology Society, pp. 492–494. IEEE Engineering in Medicine and Biology Society (2012)
5. Nysaether, J.B., Dorph, E., Rafoss, I., Steen, P.A.: Manikins with human-like chest properties–a new tool for chest compression research. IEEE Trans. Bio-Med. Eng. **55**, 2643–2650 (2008)
6. Sparks, J.L., Vavalle, N.A., Kasting, K.E., Long, B., Tanaka, M.L., Sanger, P.A., Schnell, K., Conner-Kerr, T.A.: Use of silicone materials to simulate tissue biomechanics as related to deep tissue injury. Adv. Skin Wound Care **28**, 59–68 (2015)
7. Botden, S.M., Jakimowicz, J.J.: What is going on in augmented reality simulation in laparoscopic surgery? Surg. Endosc. **23**, 1693–1700 (2009)
8. Carbone, M., Condino, S., Ferrari, V., Ferrari, M., Mosca, F.: Surgical simulators integrating virtual and physical anatomies. In: CEUR Workshop Proceedings, pp. 13–18 (2011)
9. Condino, S., Carbone, M., Ferrari, V., Faggioni, L., Peri, A., Ferrari, M., Mosca, F.: How to build patient-specific synthetic abdominal anatomies. An innovative approach from physical toward hybrid surgical simulators. Int. J. Med. Robot. Comp. **7**, 202–213 (2011)
10. Viglialoro, R.M., Condino, S., Gesi, M., Ferrari, M., Ferrari, V.: Augmented reality simulator for laparoscopic cholecystectomy training. In: De Paolis, L.T., Mongelli, A. (eds.) AVR 2014. LNCS, vol. 8853, pp. 428–433. Springer, Cham (2014). https://doi.org/10.1007/978-3-319-13969-2_33
11. Ferrari, V., Viglialoro, R.M., Nicoli, P., Cutolo, F., Condino, S., Carbone, M., Siesto, M., Ferrari, M.: Augmented reality visualization of deformable tubular structures for surgical simulation. Int. J. Med. Robot. + Comput. Assist. Surg. MRCAS **12**, 231–240 (2015)
12. Viglialoro, R., Condino, S., Freschi, C., Cutolo, F., Gesi, M., Ferrari, M., Ferrari, V.: AR visualization of "synthetic Calot's triangle" for training in cholecystectomy. In: 12th IASTED International Conference on Biomedical Engineering, BioMed 2016 (2016)
13. Vaughan, N., Dubey, V.N., Wainwright, T.W., Middleton, R.G.: A review of virtual reality based training simulators for orthopaedic surgery. Med. Eng. Phys. **38**, 59–71 (2016)
14. Sato, Y., Sasama, T., Sugano, N., Nakahodo, K., Nishii, T., Ozono, K., Yonenobu, K., Ochi, T., Tamura, S.: Intraoperative simulation and planning using a combined acetabular and femoral (CAF) navigation system for total hip replacement. In: Delp, S.L., DiGoia, A.M., Jaramaz, B. (eds.) MICCAI 2000. LNCS, vol. 1935, pp. 1114–1125. Springer, Heidelberg (2000). https://doi.org/10.1007/978-3-540-40899-4_116
15. Parchi, P., Condino, S., Carbone, M., Gesi, M., Ferrari, V., Ferrari, M., Lisanti, M.: Total hip replacement simulators with virtual planning and physical replica for surgical training and reharsal. In: Proceedings of the 12th IASTED International Conference on Biomedical Engineering, BioMed 2016, pp. 97–101 (2016)

16. Tepper, O.M., Rudy, H.L., Lefkowitz, A., Weimer, K.A., Marks, S.M., Stern, C.S., Garfein, E.S.: Mixed reality with HoloLens: where virtual reality meets augmented reality in the operating room. Plast. Reconstr. Surg. **140**, 1066–1070 (2017)
17. Hanna, M.G., Ahmed, I., Nine, J., Prajapati, S., Pantanowitz, L.: Augmented Reality Technology Using Microsoft HoloLens in Anatomic Pathology. Archives of Pathology & Laboratory Medicine (2018)
18. Nicholson, D. (ed.): AHFE 2017. AISC, vol. 593. Springer, Cham (2018). https://doi.org/10. 1007/978-3-319-60585-2
19. Rolland, J.P., Fuchs, H.: Optical versus video see-through mead-mounted displays in medical visualization. Presence Teleoperators Virtual Environ. **9**, 287–309 (2000)

# Haptic Stimulation Glove for Fine Motor Rehabilitation in Virtual Reality Environments

Edgar F. Borja$^{(\boxtimes)}$, Daniel A. Lara$^{(\boxtimes)}$, Washington X. Quevedo$^{(\boxtimes)}$, and Víctor H. Andaluz$^{(\boxtimes)}$

Universidad de las Fuerzas Armadas ESPE, Sangolquí, Ecuador
{efborja,dalara4,wxquevedo,vhandaluz1}@espe.edu.ec

**Abstract.** This paper presents a fine motor rehabilitation system for upper limbs by using a virtual reality environment. For this purpose, a glove of stimulating bilateral haptic is built, which allows directly to determine the finger's position through flexibility sensors. Also stimulate the medium and ulnar nerves of hand's palm by using vibratory actuators in charge of feedback to contact with virtual surfaces. This system is based on bilateral communication between the virtual environment in the Unity 3D graphics engine and the haptic glove. It is responsible for analyzing the movements used by the patient and interact with the Oculus Rift and Leap Motion for an increased immersion of the patient in the virtual rehabilitation environment. In addition, it generates vibrating feedback submitted to contact with virtual objects. The connection and transmission of data is done through wireless technologies in charge of creating a reliable and real time communication. The patient performs exercises based on fine motor rehabilitation which they are feedback with haptic glove and validated by algorithms based on Euclidean distance. The experimental results show the correct operation of the glove and the virtual environments oriented to virtual rehabilitation systems.

**Keywords:** Rehabilitation system · Haptic glove · Virtual reality

## 1 Introduction

New Technologies have been integrated into the development of innovative systems that include different types of user interaction and control prototypes [1]. Haptic technology is positioned among the most representative tools. In industry Field this technology has participated in the creation of management and control systems in prototypes of teleoperated mobile robots [2, 3]. Currently the haptic devices have an important role in medicine. Especially in the implementation of rehabilitation systems where the tactile sensitivity and movement are of great importance [4, 5].

Different studies have determined that the inclusion of haptic devices improve the interaction with the user. Providing stimulation to the sense of touch by using force feedback [6, 7]. This kind of system have been used together with virtual interfaces of high immersion for limbs strengthening and recovery of fine motor skills [8]. In the systems of virtual reality to rehabilitation have been integrated infrared cameras or optical tracking sensor. Whose purpose is to provide support in the recovery processes

© Springer International Publishing AG, part of Springer Nature 2018
L. T. De Paolis and P. Bourdot (Eds.): AVR 2018, LNCS 10851, pp. 211–229, 2018.
https://doi.org/10.1007/978-3-319-95282-6_16

[9, 10]. These types of components are integrated into different systems for handling them, through the analysis of signals obtained from the movement of hands [11, 12]. For the development of complete platforms dedicated to rehabilitation is incorporate to these technologies the use of virtual reality glasses. These devices increase the immersion of virtual rehabilitation system [13].

Virtual reality represents a great support in the treatment for patients with motor problems [14, 15]. Virtual environments become an attractive alternative in fine motor rehabilitation therapies. As well as providing a motivational system for the patient to continue with the treatment [16]. Therefore, new studies have been revealed for the creation of treatments through the use of multisensory and high interaction virtual environments, these studies have been of great benefit in the work of rehabilitation specialists. The haptic elements, optical tracking and virtual reality glasses have been incorporated into virtual reality in the treatment of motor problems, as a result, virtual reality is an excellent option by its high innovation and good rehabilitation technique [17, 18].

The implementation of Haptic gloves stands out for its comfort and ease of use; through the integration of different sensors, haptic gloves participate in the development of multiple applications dedicated to fine motor rehabilitation. The signals provided by this type of system allow to analyze problems of coordination, weakness and muscular rigidity [13–19]. This tool has been included in friendly and immersive virtual environments, where the patient interacts in real physical therapy routines with adequate and repetitive exercises, these routines offer an effective recovery of their motor skills [20]. The development of haptic gloves for virtual rehabilitation increase the user's domain on this type of interfaces and increase the realism during the interaction [21, 22].

Methods based on Virtual Reality provide high-impact rehabilitation systems, under clinical experience is possible to demonstrate that strength test and its feedback of upper limb-isolated muscles can be useful in the evaluation and recovery of an injury. For rehabilitation have focused mainly on motor rehabilitation through movements and stimulates which improves the processes of care [23], among the principles of rehabilitation should be supported in promoting repetition, task-oriented training, adequate feedback and an intuitive and patient-friendly environment [24].

Innovative studies present the development of haptic gloves that use different methods to generate tactile stimuli in user hands. A method is the use of motorized mechanisms to give movement to the joints of the hands. In addition, another prototype that has participated in the rehabilitation of the Stroke uses a system of compressed air to generate the movement sensation in the fingers [25, 26].

This work presents a rehabilitation system for loss of sensitivity and fine motor, through the construction of a haptic glove and interaction into a virtual reality environment. The system integrates virtual activities, which promote a new type of cognitive rehabilitation. Thus leaving the traditional processes of therapy with movements of object manipulation making clamp, hand extension and joints flexion. The sensory and data acquisition system is formed by bending gauges distributed in the phalanges and metacarpals as well as the main points of movement of the hand. In addition, the glove has vibrating actuators placed on the middle and ulnar nerves of the palm of the hand. These actuators are responsible for providing a stimulating vibratory feedback to contact with surfaces and virtual objects. The virtual interface is developed in the Unity 3d graphic engine. This interface allows the interaction of the glove with the patient to generate exercises based on skills and surface contact. Finally, communication is done through wireless technologies to obtain a real-time and ergonomic data management system.

This paper details the following developmental stages: Sect. 2 describes the structure of the rehabilitation system, the composition of the haptic glove for vibratory stimulation. The development of the virtual rehabilitation environment, multilayer diagram of the virtual environment is detailed in Sect. 3; Sect. 4 contains the results obtained in this work through the rehabilitation system in the virtual environment. Finally, Sect. 5 details the conclusions obtained during the development.

## 2   Structure of the System

The purpose of the proposed system is to improve the fine motor rehabilitation. As well as generate vibratory stimulation to each of the upper extremity's fine engine regions, depending on the patient's interaction with the surfaces in the virtual environment. The system consists of an architecture consisting of two modules that show in structural form each of the steps and methods used for the rehabilitation session. Figure 1, highlights each of the essential parts of the interaction process between the *interface module* and the *patient module*.

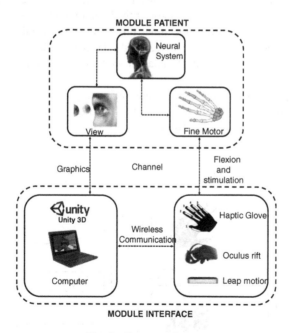

**Fig. 1.** System structure.

The communication process is developed in bidirectional form between two modules, the *interface module* and the *patient module*. These modules are constantly communicated to monitor the displacement and flexion of the phalanges, metacarpals of the hand. As well as generate feedback of haptic vibratory stimulation into the area of affection, generated by interacting with the virtual rehabilitation environment.

The *interface module* is comprised of two blocks: the computer is responsible for providing the rehabilitation virtual environment to the patient, simultaneously executing methods and algorithms of data processing to establish a relational logic between action and the reaction to each movement. The second element corresponding to the interface module is the haptic stimulation glove. This device is fundamental in the process due to it performs the sensing function of flexions of hand's fingers. In addition, it provides haptic vibratory feedback in specific points of glove surface that stimulate the middle and ulnar nerves of the hand; i.e. The glove is responsible for exercising haptic vibratory feedback and monitoring the flexions of fine motor within the system. Oculus Rift generates immersion into the virtual environment. On the other hand, Leap motion traces the hand's displacement that together with the flexion gauges placed into the glove. These gauges sense the fingers's flexion even when Leap motion presents singularity points, which it does not trace the hand, all together provides a greater immersion of the patient in virtual reality.

The *patient module* is formed by three blocks within the rehabilitation process. Vision is responsible for interpreting the virtual environment by recognizing the shapes, profiles and textures. Each one of the images perceived by the eyes are directly sent to the neural system which emits a logical meaning to the observed. As well as it establishes a motor action in the fine motor of the hand to manipulate and interact with the virtual environment. At the same time, this module has a vibratory stimulation feedback in the hand by using the glove. While the haptic glove has an ergonomic architecture between sensing and stimulation systems. It generates an easy-to-use system for patient.

The glove operation is comprised of three main stages, as shown in Fig. 2, each block interacts sequentially and in real time in order to sense the flexions and generate proportional vibrations to the stimulation.

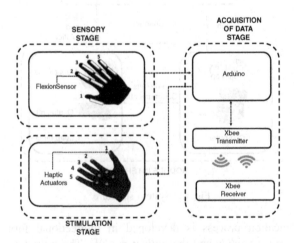

**Fig. 2.** Composition of the haptic glove.

*Sensory Stage,* the flexion sensing stage of the hand's phalanges and metacarpals is formed by nine flexion gauges located; Four flexion sensors between the medial and proximal phalanges in the fingers 2, 3, 4, 5 and five flexion sensors between the proximal and metacarpals phalanges in the fingers 1, 2, 3, 4, 5 of the hand, as shown in Fig. 3. Each one of the hand's fingers play an important role by its movement composition in each of the phalanges and metacarpals, flexion sensors are able to measure the level and flexion moment of the joints in each of the fingers.

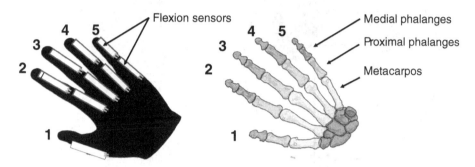

**Fig. 3.**  Location of bending gauges in the glove.

*Stimulation Stage,* the stimulation stage is formed by ten vibratory actuators that generate haptic feedback by using vibratory stimuli proportional to the interaction of patient with the virtual rehabilitation environment. The vibratory actuators are distributed in the ten specific points of the glove that stimulate the median and ulnar nerves of the hand's palm. These nerves are attached to the brachial plexus which is a nerve network that is located at the base of the neck and connects the spinal cord with the peripheral nerves of the hand. This nerve transmits the information motor and sensory of the upper limb as shown in Fig. 4. Each one of the actuators is activated according to the exercise and/or interaction of the patient with the virtual environment receiving haptic vibration stimulation in these nerves. The vibratory actuators are important in the immersion in the virtual rehabilitation environment because their vibratory stimulus in each one of the zones produces concentric movements that give the sensation of touching objects in the virtual environment. Therefore, the glove generates immersion and interaction with the patient, its homogeneous structure and design transform it into an ergonomic system and comfort to use.

*Data acquisition stage,* finally, the communication between the virtual environment and the haptic glove is developed with the implementation of Xbee wireless technology which provides real-time data. As well as eliminates cabling and promotes an ergonomic and immersive system for the patient. This allows a better validation of behavior based on data processing protocols.

On the other hand, the glove presents conductive tracks to acquire the information of the gauges flexion and carry the electric impulses towards the vibratory actuators, by using conductive wire as shown in Fig. 5. The conductive thread facilitates the movement of the hand inside the glove and generates an ergonomic texture in the use of the glove on the part of the patient in the rehabilitation.

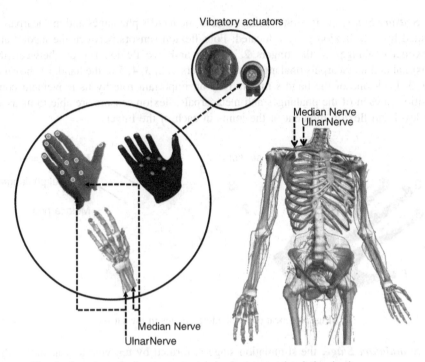

**Fig. 4.** Location of vibrating actuators and sensory stimulation in the nerves.

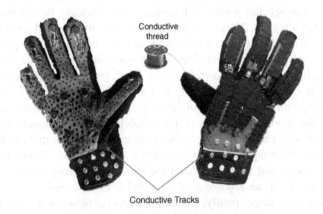

**Fig. 5.** Conductive tracks of the glove.

## 3   Virtual Environment with Stimuli Rehabilitation

The operative scheme of fine motor rehabilitation is developed as a 3D virtual reality application that consists of three stages: input and output; virtual environment and scripts, as shown in Fig. 6.

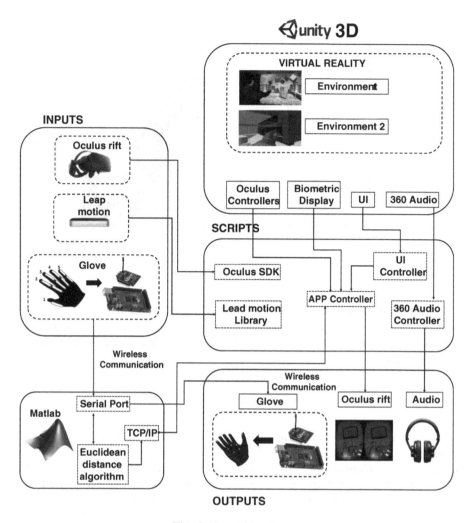

**Fig. 6.** Operative scheme.

The *inputs* stage consists in bending the hand's fingers, the signals of the flexion gauges generate data see Fig. 7, that are acquired and processed in Matlab. Later transferred to Unity 3D through TCP/IP communication, the data of resistance variation are converted to digital through an ADC are interpreted as flexion angles of the fingers in the virtual environment to evaluate the movements of each one of the fingers. In addition to generate feedback and validate the exercise of rehabilitation by using the Euclidean distance algorithm.

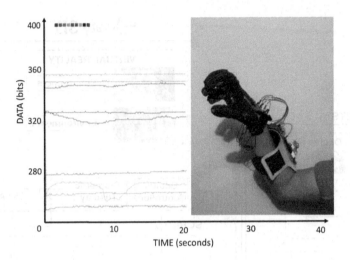

**Fig. 7.** Signs of flex gauges.

Each rehabilitation movement generates digital values of each bending gauge and is stored in a database, through Matlab evaluates the value of data stored in the database and compares it with the value of each finger flexion data in real time using the following equation:

$$D(F_a, F_r) = \sqrt{\sum_{i=1}^{9} (F_{ai} - F_{ri})^2} \qquad (1)$$

where $F_{ai}$ is the flexion of each one of the nine gauges stored in the database of each rehabilitation exercise and $F_{ri}$ is the flexion of each gauge in real time. To finally interpret the Euclidean distance and evaluate it with what type of rehabilitation exercise the patient performed and save it in a *.txt* file to be sent to Unity as a response to the type of exercise and to perform the interaction with the patient.

At the stage of the *outputs* through the interaction of the hand with the virtual environment generates a haptic feedback to the glove. That generates vibrational stimulation in the hand's palm when interacting with the virtual environment in conjunction with Oculus Rift and 360 Audio Surround where the patient experiences greater immersion in the virtual environment.

In the *scripts* stage, communication with the input and output devices is implemented, so that the virtual environment performs the required functionality; The APP controller manages the hand movement and interaction with haptic feedback generating vibratory stimuli.

Finally, the *virtual environment* stage presents 3D environments, which are based on generating an immersion in the patient an immersion where the brain does not distinguish between the real and the virtual to perform the rehabilitation exercise. The haptic glove allows the interaction optimally with the virtual environment getting a greater immersion of the user. The functionality of the virtual rehabilitation environment is described through the multilayer scheme, see Fig. 8. This scheme describes the

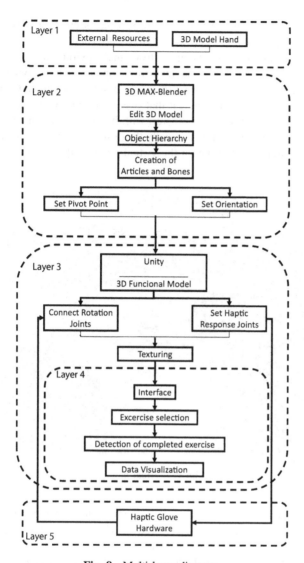

**Fig. 8.** Multi-layer diagram.

interaction between virtual environments, script and hardware; all the components that form this system are linking in an orderly manner. Its contents are presented as follows:

*Layer 1.* This layer defines the materials and resources needed to be used in the design process. For the resources selection was necessary criteria of design and planning for the elaboration of an effective recreational and multisensory system for fine motor rehabilitation. Among these materials you have: images, colors, audio, textures and basic figures, in addition, molds and hand templates were chosen with striking and real features, which will contribute to the creation of high quality virtual models.

*Layer 2.* This layer describes the process of 3d objects creation through specialized design software for modeling such as: 3Dmax and Blender among others. Virtual objects are built using selected resources from the previous layer, which are given shape and realism through mesh and texturing implementation. When the 3d hand model is implemented, it is necessary to create a set of bones and joints, with the motive of giving an adequate movement that overlap to the movement of a real hand. These elements will be strategically ordered with hierarchies and inheritances. Which allow much more realistic movements, finally the design is completed by placing all the bones and articulations created within the virtual hand model see Fig. 9.

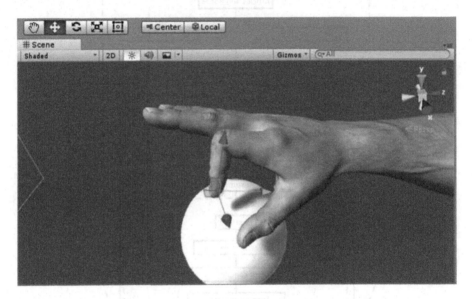

**Fig. 9.** Virtual hand.

*Layer 3.* In this layer all virtual objects are imported into the Unity 3d graphic engine. This tool integrates all the elements created previously with the development and implementation of virtual environments. The graphical engine creates a new texture of virtual objects, which together with their movement show interactive scenarios, with high immersion and real-time functionality. In addition, in this process the virtual objects are linked with script components to give the operation mechanics and allow the interaction with the tasks presented during the rehabilitation sessions see Fig. 10. The main virtual element that participates in the execution of the tasks is the 3D hand model, which allows to interact with the proposed objectives and to carry out routines of rehabilitation exercises within a high immersion system.

**Fig. 10.** Game of rehabilitation.

*Layer 4.* The layer indicates the relationship between script and interaction within the virtual environments by means of the interface, giving the functionality to the rehabilitation system. They run a script that allows the selection of routine of rehabilitation exercises. As well as manage the actions and information in real time within the application execution. In the development of the proposed tasks through scripts generates relevant information for therapies such as: number of successes and failures, the time to finish each task, and characteristic signals of the movements used in fine motor. All data generated in this process will be analyzed and evaluated by a specialist.

*Layer 5.* This layer links the main hardware component, the haptic glove, which performs a digital signals exchange, sending the hand real movements towards the virtual environment and receiving interaction in the form of haptic stimulation when activating the colliders while manipulating virtual objects. Through this interaction the system obtains a multisensory characteristic, this hardware component creates a feedback loop between the virtual environment and the sense of touch at levels of vibratory haptic stimulation, allowing the user to interact and feel real-time events occurring during the use of the rehabilitation system see Fig. 11.

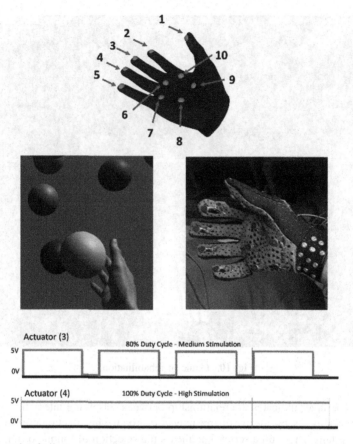

**Fig. 11.** Levels of vibratory stimulation, where the vibratory actuators 3 and 4 intervene when interacting with the virtual object.

## 4  Experimental Results

One of the relevant factors is that the patient, having tactile sensations of what he touches in the virtual rehabilitation environment, his tactile haptic feedback causes the nerves of the hand to begin to generate stimuli to the brain that helps in the rehabilitation since the problems of fine motor skills are caused by difficulties in coordination. Therefore, this section presents some of the results obtained from the virtual application developed, aimed at patient rehabilitation in order to exercise fine motor skills, sensitivity and coordination of movements according to the type of game selected. In Fig. 12, it shows the immersion of the patient in the virtual environment, to perform fine motor rehabilitation therapy. The applications performed stimulate the patient in a visual, tactile and auditory way allowing the interaction with the environment to be as real as possible, that is, the patient is immersed in animations, sounds and vibratory stimuli depending on the selected environment for which Oculus Rift, hearing aids and haptic glove are used.

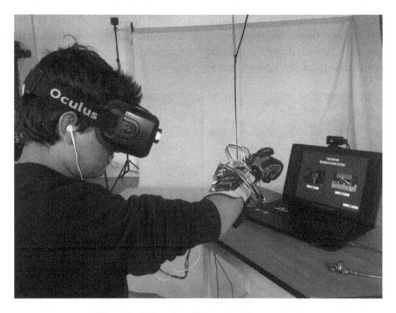

**Fig. 12.** Virtual reality patient immersion.

As described in Fig. 13, shows the developed application consisting of a virtual menu with two games for the patient to select the environment according to the type of rehabilitation that he wishes to perform. It should be noted that in each of the virtual environments the control algorithm used (Euclidean distance) is considered, which allows a real-time response to the type of exercise performed by the patient based on the data processed from the gauges and treated in Matlab.

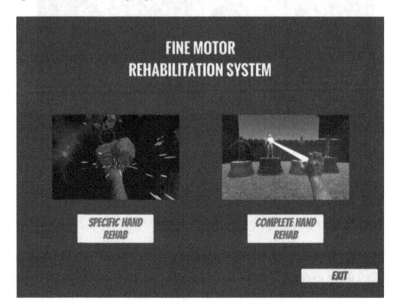

**Fig. 13.** Menú of virtual rehab.

The first game considers a virtual environment with the purpose of destroying stones and passing rings, the same ones that reach the patient in a direct and friendly way by means of which using the specific exercises fist and extension will validate the affection and ability of the patient, see Fig. 14.

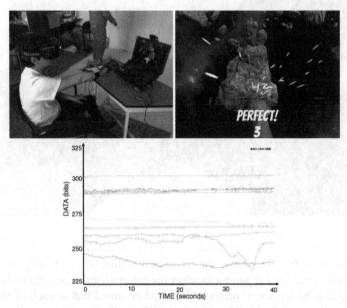

(a)  Fist exercise, in which stones are broken when performing the exercise correctly.

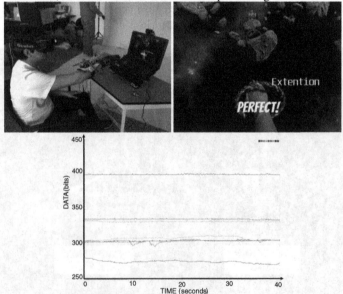

(b)  Extension exercise, in which vibratory haptic vibration is received when passing the ring and doing the exercise correctly.

**Fig. 14.** Expecific hand rehab.

When the patient correctly performs the *fist exercise* see Fig. 14(a), the stone explodes and all the actuators vibrate, so that the haptic glove stimulates the patient's hand, activating all the actuators according to the intensity of the impact (fist-stone); On the other hand, the hand *extension exercise*, see Fig. 14(b), when performed correctly when the hand passes through the ring, the actuators of the haptic glove are activated sequentially with the hand passing through the ring.

In the second game it is oriented to the complete rehabilitation therapy, by means of repetition of the exercises of *grip, flexion, fist* and *extension*, when performing each of the exercises correctly, activate the laser that collides with the specific avatar with each

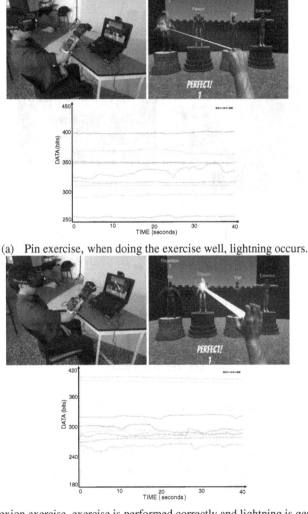

(a)  Pin exercise, when doing the exercise well, lightning occurs.

(b)  Flexion exercise, exercise is performed correctly and lightning is generated.

**Fig. 15.**  Complete hand rehab.

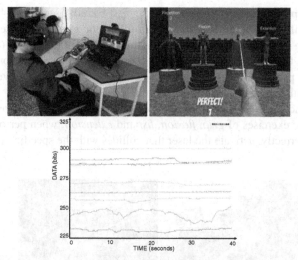

(c)  When doing the fist rehabilitation exercise the beam is generated towards the avatar.

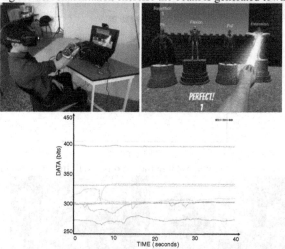

(d)  Extension exercise, by doing it correctly the lightning occurs.

**Fig. 15.**  (*continued*)

exercise, activating the actuators of the haptic glove, to finally visualize in an indicator that the exercise of the therapy was performed correctly see Fig. 15.

The result of system usability is presented. Eight children between 10 and 23 years old completed the SEQ survey. The outcomes (56 ± 0.42) in Table 1 are according to [27]. If SEQ result is within a range of 40–65, the application is considered for rehabilitation. This result indicates that the virtual system has acceptance to be used in rehabilitation.

**Table 1.** SEQ mean and standard deviation

| Questions | Results (N = 8) | |
|---|---|---|
| | Means | SD |
| Q1. How much did you enjoy your experience with the system? | 4,63 | 0,48 |
| Q2. How much did you sense to be in the environment of the system? | 4,75 | 0,43 |
| Q3. How successful were you in the system? | 4,5 | 0,71 |
| Q4. To what extent were you able to control the system? | 3.5 | 0,71 |
| Q5. How real is the virtual environment of the system? | 3,88 | 0,78 |
| Q6. Is the information provided by the system clear? | 4,38 | 0,69 |
| Q7. Did you feel discomfort during your experience with the system? | 4,5 | 0,71 |
| Q8. Did you experience dizziness or nausea during your practice with the system? | 4,63 | 0,69 |
| Q9. Did you experience eye discomfort during your practice with the system? | 4,88 | 0,33 |
| Q10. Did you feel confused or disoriented during your experience with the system? | 4 | 0,71 |
| Q11. Do you think that this system will be helpful for your rehabilitation? | 4,13 | 0,59 |
| Q12. Did you find the task difficult? | 4,63 | 0,48 |
| Q13. Did you find the devices of the system difficult to use? | 3,63 | 0,69 |
| GLOBAL SCORE (Total) | 56 | 0,42 |

## 5 Conclusions

The results in the system of fine motor rehabilitation for extremities through virtual reality environments is an acceptable method for rehabilitation according to the SEQ survey with results (56 ± 0.42), the rehabilitation system shows good experience when interacting in virtual reality environments, which allow patients to overcome problems in the affected areas. The haptic stimulation provided by the vibratory actuators towards the hand generates a tactile response when we manipulate a virtual object, with the aim of creating an attraction and realism for the patient using intuitive graphic environments that allow the development of their sensitivity while the patient recovers from your condition.

**Acknowledgment.** The authors would like to thanks to the Corporación Ecuatoriana para el Desarrollo de la Investigación y Academia – CEDIA for the financing given to research, development, and innovation, through the CEPRA projects, especially the project CEPRA-IX-2015-05, Tele-Operación Bilateral Cooperativo de Múltiples Manipuladores Móviles; also to Universidad de las Fuerzas Armadas ESPE, Universidad Técnica de Ambato, Escuela Politécnica de Chimborazo, and Escuela Politécnica Nacional, and Grupo de Investigación en Automatización, Robótica y Sistemas Inteligentes, GI-ARSI, for the support to develop this paper.

# References

1. Ramírez-Fernández, C., Morán, A.L., García-Canseco, E.: Haptic feedback in motor hand virtual therapy increases precision and generates less mental workload. In: 2015 9th International Conference on Pervasive Computing Technologies for Healthcare (PervasiveHealth), Istanbul, pp. 280–286 (2015)
2. Low, J.H., et al.: Hybrid tele-manipulation system using a sensorized 3-D-Printed soft robotic gripper and a soft fabric-based haptic glove. IEEE Robot. Autom. Lett. 2(2), 880–887 (2017)
3. Li, J., Tavakoli, M., Huang, Q.: Absolute stability of Multi-DOF multilateral haptic systems. IEEE Trans. Control Syst. Technol. 22(6), 2319–2328 (2014)
4. Atashzar, S.F., Shahbazi, M., Samotus, O., Tavakoli, M., Jog, M.S., Patel, R.V.: Characterization of upper-limb pathological tremors: application to design of an augmented haptic rehabilitation system. IEEE J. Sel. Top. Signal Process. 10(5), 888–903 (2016)
5. Jiang, T.T., Qian, Z.Q., Lin, Y., Bi, Z.M., Liu, Y.F., Zhang, W.J.: Analysis of virtual environment haptic robotic systems for a rehabilitation of post-stroke patients. In: IEEE International Conference on Industrial Technology (ICIT), pp. 738–742 (2017)
6. Sanfilippo, F., Pettersen, K.Y.: A sensor fusion wearable health-monitoring system with haptic feedback. In: IEEE International Conference on Innovations in Information Technology (IIT), pp. 262–266 (2015)
7. Otaduy, M.A., Okamura, A., Subramanian, S.: Haptic technologies for direct touch in virtual reality. ACM SIGGRAPH Courses (2016)
8. Molinari, M., Esquenazi, A., Anastasi, A.A., Nielsen, R.K., Stoller, O., D'Andrea, A., Calatayud, M.B.: Rehabilitation technologies application in stroke and traumatic brain injury patients. In: Pons, J., Raya, R., González, J. (eds.) Emerging Therapies in Neurorehabilitation II. Biosystems & Biorobotics, vol. 10, pp. 29–64. Springer, Cham (2016). https://doi.org/10.1007/978-3-319-24901-8_2
9. Iosa, M., Morone, G., Fusco, A., Castagnoli, M., Fusco, F.R., Pratesi, L., Paolucci, S.: Leap motion controlled videogame-based therapy for rehabilitation of elderly patients with subacute stroke: a feasibility pilot study. Top. Stroke Rehabil. 22, 306–316 (2015)
10. Khademi, M., Hondori, H.M., McKenzie, A., Dodakian, L., Lopes, C.V., Cramer, S.: Free-hand interaction with leap motion controller for stroke rehabilitation. In: CHI 2014 Extended Abstracts on Human Factors in Computing Systems, pp. 1663–1668 (2014)
11. Lahanas, V., Loukas, C., Georgiou, K., Lababidi, H., Al-Jaroudi, D.: Virtual reality-based assessment of basic laparoscopic skills using the Leap Motion controller. Surg. Endosc. 31, 5012–5023 (2017)
12. Rodriguez, N.: Teaching virtual reality with affordable technologies. In: Kurosu, M. (ed.) HCI 2016, Part I. LNCS, vol. 9731, pp. 89–97. Springer, Cham (2016). https://doi.org/10.1007/978-3-319-39510-4_9
13. Parreño, M.A., Celi, C.J., Quevedo, W.X., Rivas, D., Andaluz, V.H.: Teaching-learning of basic language of signs through didactic games. In: Proceedings of the 2017 9th International Conference on Education Technology and Computers, pp. 46–51 (2017)
14. Castillejos, D.E., Noguez, J., Neri, L., Magana, A., Benes, B.: A review of simulators with haptic devices for medical training. J. Med. Syst. 40, 104 (2016)
15. Andaluz, V.H., Salazar, P.J., Miguel Escudero, V., Carlos Bustamante, D., Marcelo Silva, S., Quevedo, W., Sánchez, J.S., Espinosa, E.G., Rivas, D.: Virtual reality integration with force feedback in upper limb rehabilitation. In: Bebis, G., et al. (eds.) ISVC 2016, Part II. LNCS, vol. 10073, pp. 259–268. Springer, Cham (2016). https://doi.org/10.1007/978-3-319-50832-0_25

16. Hatzfeld, C., Kern, T.A.: Motivation and application of haptic systems. In: Hatzfeld, C., Kern, T.A. (eds.) Engineering Haptic Devices: A Beginner's Guide. SSTHS, pp. 3–28. Springer, London (2014). https://doi.org/10.1007/978-1-4471-6518-7_1

17. Garner, T.A.: Applications of virtual reality. Echoes of Other Worlds: Sound in Virtual Reality: Past, Present and Future. PSS, pp. 299–362. Palgrave Macmillan, Cham (2018). https://doi.org/10.1007/978-3-319-65708-0_9

18. Bonnechère, B.: Serious Games in Physical Rehabilitation: From Theory to Practice. Springer, Cham (2018). https://doi.org/10.1007/978-3-319-66122-3

19. Hoda, M., Hafidh, B., El Saddik, A.: Haptic glove for finger rehabilitation. In: 2015 IEEE International Conference on Multimedia & Expo Workshops (ICMEW), Turin (2015)

20. Connelly, L., Jia, Y., Toro, M.L., Stoykov, M.E., Kenyon, R.V., Kamper, D.G.: A pneumatic glove and immersive virtual reality environment for hand rehabilitative training after stroke. IEEE Trans. Neural Syst. Rehabil. Eng. **18**(5), 551–559 (2010)

21. Ma, Z., Ben-Tzvi, P.: RML glove—an exoskeleton glove mechanism with haptics feedback. IEEE/ASME Trans. Mechatron. **20**(2), 641–652 (2015)

22. Andaluz, V.H., Pazmiño, A.M., Pérez, J.A., Carvajal, C.P., Lozada, F., Lascano, J., Carvajal, J.: Training of tannery processes through virtual reality. In: De Paolis, L.T., Bourdot, P., Mongelli, A. (eds.) AVR 2017, Part I. LNCS, vol. 10324, pp. 75–93. Springer, Cham (2017). https://doi.org/10.1007/978-3-319-60922-5_6

23. Fira, A.L., Mónica, S.C., Paulino, T., i Badia, S.B.: The benefits of emotional stimuli in a virtual reality cognitive and motor rehabilitation task: Assessing the impact of positive, negative and neutral stimuli with stroke patients. In: 2015 International Conference on Virtual Rehabilitation (ICVR), pp. 65–71 (2015)

24. Sucar, L.E., Orihuela-Espina, F., Velázquez, R.L., Reinkensmeyer, D.J., Leder, R., Hernández-Franco, J.: Gesture therapy: una plataforma de rehabilitación motora de base de realidad virtual. IEEE Trans. Neural Syst. Rehabil. Eng. **22**(3), 634–643 (2014)

25. Polygerinos, P., Stacey, L., Zheng, W., Nicolini, L.F.: Towards a soft pneumatic glove for hand rehabilitation. In: IEEE Intelligent Robots and Systems, pp. 1512–1517 (2013)

26. Yili, F., Qinchao, Z., Fuhai, Z., Zengkang, G.: Design and development of a hand rehabilitation robot for patient-cooperative therapy following stroke. In: IEEE International Conference on Mechatronics and Automation, pp. 112–117 (2011)

27. Gil-Gómez, J.A., Gil-Gómez, H., Lozano-Quilis, J.A., Manzano-Hernández, P., Albiol-Pérez, S., Aula-Valero, C.: SEQ: suitability evaluation questionnaire for virtual rehabilitation systems. application in a virtual rehabilitation system for balance rehabilitation. In: 2013 7th International Conference on Pervasive Computing Technologies for Healthcare and Workshops, Venice, pp. 335–338 (2013)

# Virtual Simulation of Brain Sylvian Fissure Exploration and Aneurysm Clipping with Haptic Feedback for Neurosurgical Training

Sergio Teodoro Vite[1(✉)], César Domínguez Velasco[1],
Aldo Francisco Hernández Valencia[2], Juan Salvador Pérez Lomelí[1],
and Miguel Ángel Padilla Castañeda[1]

[1] Unidad de Investigación y Desarrollo Tecnológico (UIDT),
Instituto de Ciencias Aplicadas y Tecnología (ICAT),
Universidad Nacional Autónoma de México (UNAM), Mexico City, Mexico
sergioteovit@comunidad.unam.mx, miguel.padilla@ccadet.unam.mx
[2] Unidad de Neurología y Neurocirugía, Hospital General de México (HGM)
"Dr. Eduardo Liceaga", Mexico City, Mexico

**Abstract.** The development of simulation systems from surgical procedures has been a research topic in several areas in medicine and engineer applications because it supposes a novel alternative for medical skills acquisition, surgical planning, guide during surgery and postoperative control. At the same time, simulation systems represent significant challenges, regarding conceptual design, mathematical, numeric and computational modelling, and finally the validation of the system. In this paper, we present the advances and methodologies applied for the development of a virtual reality system for medical training in neurosurgery. As the case of study, we present the simulation of an aneurysm clipping procedure in two of the main stages: brain Sylvian fissure exploration and aneurysm clipping.

## 1 Introduction

Neuro-simulation [16] is the term used to describe the study, development and validation of systems capable of recreating nervous system diseases, and their approaches using surgical techniques, through technological resources. This kind of systems can be classified into three types:

a. HPS (Human Patient Simulators): employ physical models or mannequins constructed of tactile special materials that can include sophisticated electronic and computer control systems, such as those described by [13,14,17],
b. computer simulators: this establishes idealized scenarios in which a user must interact with a virtual environment to achieve a series of goals; examples are NeuroTouch [5], from the National Research Council of Canada, vascular neurosurgery simulator by [6] and cerebral aneurysm clipping simulator of [1]. Finally,

L. T. De Paolis and P. Bourdot (Eds.): AVR 2018, LNCS 10851, pp. 230–238, 2018.
https://doi.org/10.1007/978-3-319-95282-6_17

c. hybrid simulators: they make use of mixed reality techniques (augmented reality, augmented virtuality or mixed reality) that combine dummies, virtual models and tracking with cameras. In general, these systems are conceived for planning and guidance in surgical procedures, such as the system reported in [10], which uses the concept of neuro-navigation to guide a user through veins and cerebral arteries superimposed virtually on a nylon mannequin.

Developing computer simulators involves the adoption of important challenges: realistic visual representation of anatomical structures, biomechanical and numerical modelling, and finally the interaction with devices that feedback the users inputs with the computer system. Each one of these challenges can be treated by techniques of computer graphics, mathematical and numerical modelling based on continuum mechanics and robotics.

In neurosurgery, the surgical procedures require high precision and complex interactions, since they carry risks of mortality or permanent damage to the structures of a patient nervous system [18]. Therefore, current simulators are focused on high incidence conditions that represent, help or reliably predict emergency situations. In all these cases, current efforts focus on four primary applications: planning, training, surgical guidance and postoperative control.

A common and high-risk procedure is the repair of cerebral aneurysms. An aneurysm is a weak region of the wall of a blood vessel that causes bulges, which has the direct consequence of impaired blood flow [11]. The most serious complication of a cerebral aneurysm is that it broke, which leads to an accumulation of blood in the surrounding regions of the brain or inside it. The standard procedures for the repair of cerebral aneurysms are clipping (Fig. 1) and endovascular repair.

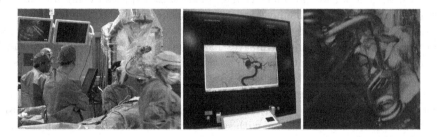

**Fig. 1.** On the left, cerebral aneurysm surgery, the neurosurgeon uses the microscope to explore the brain across the Sylvian fissure. At the centre, angio-TAC showing the presence of a giant brain aneurysm. On the right, clipping to strangle the aneurysm dome (Courtesy, HGM.)

The full clipping technique involves several steps from the pre-operative stage (case of study) to post-operative control after surgery. In the operating room, the procedure consists of marking, skin cutting, the opening of the skull (open craniotomy surgery), and dura mater aperture, to allow the surgeon the use of a microscope and tools to open their way through brain tissues. Finally, clipping step involves placing a metal clip at the base of the aneurysm neck to prevent the stroke. The workflow is shown in the Fig. 2.

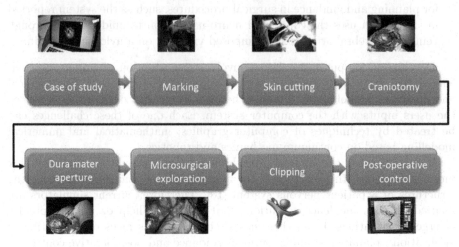

**Fig. 2.** Scheme of the workflow of the cerebral aneurysm repair procedure.

## 2    Methodology

### 2.1    Computational Model

Computational model consists of functional blocks that interact in real time (Fig. 3). In general, we can identify five synchronised spaces during a computer simulation. (1) Graphic display hardware (monitor and GPU) in charge of processing all the visual elements. (2) Virtual models that define the anatomy and surgical instruments (using primitives like points, lines, triangles and hexahedral information). (3) Mathematical models that describe the mechanic of soft and rigid objects (heuristic methods, based on continuum mechanics and hybrid methods). (4) Collision models for detecting interaction between the surgical instruments and tissues. (5) The force feedback model, which provides the user with the sensation of interacting with simulated tissue, such as the brain through the virtual tools.

These modules work with multitasking and multiprocessing architecture. Which means that several processes run concurrently, with a primary process to control the user interface and other processes for visualisation tasks, physics-based simulation (mechanical tissue), the interaction between models (collision detection with SOFA [7] library) and the haptic interaction (OpenHaptics Toolkit [9] with Geomagic Omni Phantom).

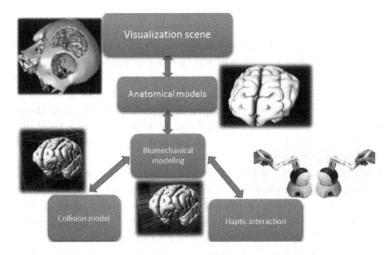

**Fig. 3.** Scheme showing the main modules for the simulation of dynamic objects and their interaction with the user within a simulated environment by computer.

## 2.2 Anatomical Models and Virtual Tools

We obtained reconstructions of the head (face skin, skull and brain), using specialised equipment from HGM (Artis Zee system) to obtain images of angio-TAC and 3D reconstruction software (OsiriX and 3DSlicer). Two models of real patients were reconstructed, a man of 57 years old and a woman with 67, both with diagnoses of aneurysm in non-hemorrhagic stage.

The instruments mechanism were modelled according to the manufacturer's specification sheets. The virtual tools considered up to this stage of the project are syringe, surgical dissector, tweezers and separators, craniotome, surgical spatula, aspirator, dura dissector, microsurgical spreader tips, microscissors, resector, clips, and clip applicator. Some of these tools are shown in Fig. 4.

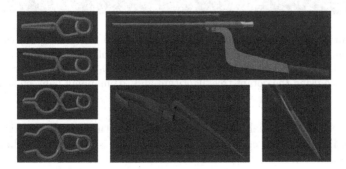

**Fig. 4.** Clips virtual models, opened and closed positions (left). On the right, clip applicator and microscissors. Instruments modelled in Blender at 1:1 scale concerning the manufacturers specification sheets.

## 2.3    Biomechanical Modelling

The biomechanical model aims to establish an interaction, simulation and realism relationship, in which a mapping of the geometric model is carried out from a static space to a dynamic space. Thus, in the simulation, we identified three types of objects: rigid, deformable bodies and particles. In neurosurgery, it is important to represent these three types of objects depending on the structure of interest. Thus, for example, the skull can be considered as a rigid object, the brain as a deformable body and the blood flow as a set of particles that flow through veins and arteries.

In the literature, there are many papers about simulation methods of objects with different physical behavior (rigid, deformable and particles). Commercial and open libraries have been developed to implement different methods of simulation at hardware level (using GPUs and PPPs - units for graphics and physics processing, respectively) and software level. Examples of this libraries are SOFA (Simulation Open Framework Architecture [7]), and Nvidia Flex [2,12].

In this work, we used SOFA for tissue modelling. SOFA is a simulation framework engine for medical applications that implements the concept of multi-model representation based on scene graphs. A scene graph is composed of an arbitrary number of objects that can interact under a set of spatial constraints and equations that describe the biomechanical behaviour of the objects. The great advantage of using multi-model schemes is that each workspace works independently and then synchronise them through an operation called "mapping". Thus, during a simulation, three main spaces are defined: a geometric space of visualisation, a space of collisions (contacts between objects) and a mechanical space on which the biomechanical model operates (Fig. 5).

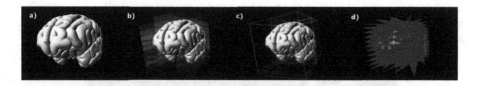

**Fig. 5.** Multi-model representation of a deformable object in SOFA [7]; (a) visual model of the brain, (b) biomechanical space defined as a set of hexahedrons that surround the geometric model (FEM-Finite Element Method/FFD-Free Form Deformation), (c) collision space using the octant tree algorithm and (d) mapping between spaces.

A biomechanical model, widely used in the literature to simulate tissue deformation [3,4] is based on continuum mechanics and is governed by the equation of motion:

$$M\ddot{u} + D\dot{u} + Ku = f_{ext} \tag{1}$$

where $M$ is the mass matrix, $\ddot{u}$ is the acceleration vector due to deformation, $D$ is the damping, $\dot{u}$ the velocity of the deformation, $K$ the stiffness matrix (defined in terms of Young's modulus and Poisson's radius), $u$ the deformation vector and $f_{ext}$ the sum of external forces acting on the boundary of the geometric object.

Several simulation methods exist in the literature to solve (1). One of the most important due to its biophysic realism is the Finite Element method (FEM), which operates over volume elements (tetrahedra or hexahedra). However, depending on the resolution of the geometric object of interest, the algorithms of computational solution can be very slow. Some algorithms, such as FFD (Free-Form Deformation) and mass-tensor, have proven to be quick methods for deformations computation based on the Finite Element approach. In this work, our simulation is based on the FEM-Co-rotational method [8,15] and domain decomposition techniques [3], because in conjunction both offer substantial advantages regarding biomechanical realism and interaction on real-time applications.

## 3   Experiments and Results

### 3.1   Brain Exploration

For the simulation of the microsurgical exploration, we used a 3D generic brain model adapted from an anatomy education software, shown in Fig. 6. This brain was adapted using CAD software to match with an adult (man or woman). This model was decomposed into two regions defined by the Sylvian fissure, with the objective of separate the model into two subregions, on which the biomechanical method was applied separately.

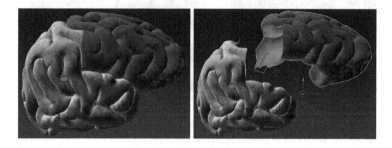

**Fig. 6.** Idealized brain model subdivided into two regions that define the Sylvian fissure. The upper region or frontal lobe is composed of a domain subdivided into hexahedrons of resolution $7 \times 7 \times 7$ and the lower region, or temporal lobe is composed of a domain subdivided into hexahedrons of resolution $10 \times 10 \times 10$. Restriction boxes were defined on each of the regions to fix points where the model does not suffer deformations.

We performed deformation tests of the brain model in the Sylvian fissure region using controlled interactions with the haptic device, applying variable forces in different directions, simulating a microsurgical procedure, as shown in Fig. 7.

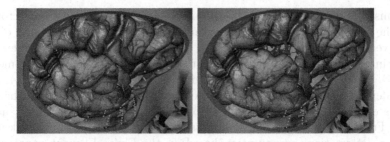

**Fig. 7.** Simulation of soft-tissue deformation of the brain through the Sylvian fissure at closed and opened states.

## 3.2   Aneurysm Clipping

Deformation tests were performed on a generic model of an aneurysm located in the carotid region with the free-form method over FEM, with a subdivision of the space of $7 \times 7 \times 7$, with a Euler-implicit numerical solver, a conjugate gradient as a solution method for the matrix system and uniform mass matrix (Fig. 8). These models were integrated with the haptic device to provide force response and manipulate the aneurysm neck.

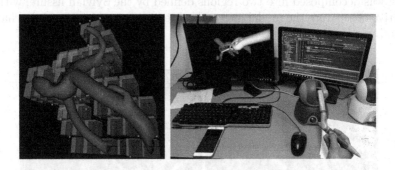

**Fig. 8.** Discretization of the biomechanical space according to an input geometry. At left, an idealised model of a cerebral aneurysm. At right, aneurysm simulation with haptic feedback.

## 3.3   Simulation System

The current simulation system is composed by an idealised brain model divided into two domains delimited by the Sylvian fissure. Textures obtained from a video of a real surgery were applied. Some lighting effects were applied to improve visual realism. Interaction with the user is achieved with two haptic devices, one to manipulate a tool to separate the two lobes of the brain and another for the placement of the clip. The surgical area is currently delimited by the cranial opening, which was defined by an experimented neurosurgeon and subsequently processed with a mesh cutting algorithm based on Boolean operations. Additionally, the system has the environmental audio effect to provide the user with more immersion during the simulation.

All the tests performed were validated with an expert neurosurgeon, which approved the realism of deformation and visualisation.

## 4 Conclusions and Discussion

In this version of the simulation system, the biomechanical behaviour was considered using an FFD-FEM technique, improving the visual and biomechanical realism. With the biomechanical model, we developed a new interaction scheme to simulate the micro-surgical gestures of exploration across the brains Sylvian fissure, which is a critical step during a real surgery. For reconstruction of vascular structures of patient-specific cases, it was not possible to reach a satisfactory result, so that other methods of reconstruction are still being explored. For the force feedback of the tissues need to be calibrated according to experiments with living tissues, mainly brain, bone and vascular structures. Finally, in the state of the current development, we hope to conduct validation studies with residents in neurosurgery and then we will evaluate the usefulness of this kind of systems in other applications, like planning and postoperative control.

**Acknowledgements.** This work was supported by National Autonomous University of Mexico through its Program of Support to Projects for the Innovation and Improvement of Teaching (PAPIME), projects PE109018 and PE109118.

## References

1. Alaraj, A., Luciano, C.J., Bailey, D.P., Elsenousi, A., Roitberg, B.Z., Bernardo, A., Banerjee, P.P., Charbel, F.T.: Virtual reality cerebral aneurysm clipping simulation with real-time haptic feedback. Neurosurgery **11**(Suppl 2), 52–58 (2015)
2. Bender, J., Müller, M., Otaduy, M.A., Teschner, M., Macklin, M.: A survey on position-based simulation methods in computer graphics. Comput. Graph. Forum **33**, 228–251 (2014)
3. Bro-Nielsen, M.: Finite element modeling in surgery simulation. Proc. IEEE **86**(3), 490–503 (1998)
4. Bro-Nielsen, M., Cotin, S.: Real-time volumetric deformable models for surgery simulation using finite elements and condensation. Comput. Graph. Forum **15**(3), 57 (1996)
5. Delorme, S., Laroche, D., DiRaddo, R., Del Maestro, R.F.: NeuroTouch: a physics-based virtual simulator for cranial microneurosurgery training. Neurosurgery **71**(1 Suppl Operative), 32–42 (2012)
6. Dequidt, J., Coevoet, E., Thinès, L., Duriez, C.: Vascular neurosurgery simulation with bimanual haptic feedback. In: Jaillet, F., Zara, F., Zachmann, G. (eds.) Workshop on Virtual Reality Interaction and Physical Simulation. The Eurographics Association (2015)

7. Faure, F., Duriez, C., Delingette, H., Allard, J., Gilles, B., Marchesseau, S., Talbot, H., Courtecuisse, H., Bousquet, G., Peterlik, I., Cotin, S.: SOFA: a multi-model framework for interactive physical simulation. In: Payan, Y. (ed.) Soft Tissue Biomechanical Modeling for Computer Assisted Surgery. Springer, Heidelberg (2012). https://doi.org/10.1007/8415_2012_125

8. Georgii, J., Westermann, R.: Corotated finite elements made fast and stable. In: Faure, F., Teschner, M. (eds.) 2008 Workshop in Virtual Reality Interactions and Physical Simulation "VRIPHYS". The Eurographics Association (2008)

9. Itkowitz, B., Handley, J., Zhu, W.: The OpenHaptics(TM) Toolkit: A Library for Adding 3D Touch^(TM) Navigation and Haptics to Graphics Applications, January 2005

10. Kersten-Oertel, M., Chen, S.S.J., Drouin, S., Sinclair, D.S., Collins, D.L.: Augmented reality visualization for guidance in neurovascular surgery. Stud. Health Technol. Inform. **173**, 225–229 (2012)

11. Lawton, M.T.: Seven Aneurysms: Tenets and Techniques for Clipping. Thieme (2011). https://books.google.com.mx/books?id=wI5kEN8TFpEC

12. Macklin, M., Müller, M., Chentanez, N., Kim, T.-Y.: Unified particle physics for real-time applications. ACM Trans. Graphics **33**, 53 (2014)

13. Mashiko, T., Kaneko, N., Konno, T., Otani, K., Nagayama, R., Watanabe, E.: Training in cerebral aneurysm clipping using self-Made 3-dimensional models. J. Surg. Educ. **74**(4), 681–689 (2017)

14. Musacchio Jr., M.J., Smith, A.P., McNeal, C.A., Munoz, L., Rothenberg, D.M., von Roenn, K.A., Byrne, R.W.: Neuro-critical care skills training using a human patient simulator. Neurocrit. Care **13**(2), 169–175 (2010)

15. Nesmea, M., Faurea, F.: Physically realistic interactive simulation for biological soft tissues

16. Papangelou, A., Ziai, W.: The birth of neuro-simulation. Neurocrit. Care **13**(2), 167–168 (2010)

17. Ryan, J.R., Almefty, K.K., Nakaji, P., Frakes, D.H.: Cerebral aneurysm clipping surgery simulation using patient-specific 3D printing and silicone casting. World Neurosurg. **88**, 175–181 (2016)

18. Yaniv, Z.R., Webster, R.J., Fenz, W., Dirnberger, J.: Real-time surgery simulation of intracranial aneurysm clipping with patient-specific geometries and haptic feedback. In: Proceedings of SPIE, vol. 9415(1), p. 94150H, March 2015

# Augmented Reality System for the Complement of Cognitive Therapeutic Exercise in Children: Preliminary Tests

Edwin Pruna[✉], Ivón Escobar, Andrés Acurio, Henry Cocha, José Bucheli, and Luis Mena

Universidad de las Fuerzas Armadas ESPE,
Sangolquí, Ecuador
{eppruna,ipescobar,adacuriol,hpcocha,
jgbucheli,lemena}@espe.edu.ec

**Abstract.** This paper describes the development of an interactive and motivational tool, to give immersion in the cognitive therapeutic exercise (Perfetti method). This system is implemented with the use of virtual environments developed in the Unity 3D graphic engine. The environments present friendly, novel designs, which are shown to the user in augmented reality with the help of a high-end smartphone and virtual reality headset. In addition, the system helps in the process of recording activities and collecting important data for the monitoring and evolution of the users.

**Keywords:** Augmented reality · Cognitive therapeutic exercise
Unity 3D

## 1 Introduction

A neurological disease is any disorder of the nervous system. Structural, biochemical, or electrical anomalies located in the brain, spinal cord or other nerves can result in a series of symptoms such as paralysis, muscle weakness, lack of coordination, loss of sensation, seizures, confusion, pain and altered levels of consciousness.

Children affected by neurological disease need to carry out a continuous rehabilitation process, to minimize the loss of functionality and to achieve good maintenance of physical state, trying to avoid or alleviate secondary complications to the disease itself [1]. The physical therapy of children especially with slight motor deterioration of the type hemiplegic is one of the elements of an infantile development program in which, the therapists have to incorporate authentic efforts to obtain a stimulating, varied and quality environment, considering that a child needs new experiences and interaction with the outside world in order to learn [2, 3].

Cognitive therapeutic exercise (Perfetti method), is already used several years ago in the treatment of the central and peripheral nervous system; it is based on the conception that the movement does not consist of a simple muscular contraction, but it is given as a result of a more complex process that begins in the brain. In this case, the

L. T. De Paolis and P. Bourdot (Eds.): AVR 2018, LNCS 10851, pp. 239–246, 2018.
https://doi.org/10.1007/978-3-319-95282-6_18

treatment is not only directed to the muscle of the affected area, but it takes into account how the movement is organized at the cerebral level [19].

The choice of the exercise emerges from the valuation, which allows to individualize what elements of the human body are present and what functions or part of it we must recover. The cognitive therapeutic exercise presents several levels, a first level of intervention is directed to channel the attention of the child towards the analysis of the information, mainly of those that have been considered more deficit. A second level is one where exercises are carried out whose aim is to favor the elaboration between the different types of information; in a third level of exercises are those in which the demand is mainly directed to the phase of projection of the information and a fourth level is characterized by exercises that refer to the motor image [20].

In this context, in recent years augmented reality has been incorporated into the development of applications of high visual attraction and immersion [4–7]. Applications of augmented reality and virtual reality are used in innovative systems of motor rehabilitation, where they merge to other technologies such as haptic devices and virtual reality glasses, electromyographic sensors, and others [8, 9]. With the inclusion of different devices, it is achieved to increase the efficiency of the therapies and the level of immersion that the user experiences. This type of system has become very popular, especially in the treatment of children with disabilities [10, 11]. For infants the augmented reality tools are shown as a high-motivational option, their high-detail visual components help to easily capture the attention of minors [12–15]. Many of these systems have been able to implement a high degree of interaction between virtual objects and the user, thus generating effective tools for physical recovery [16–18, 21].

## 2   Structure of the System

A virtual and interactive system of augmented reality is developed to complement the cognitive therapeutic exercise, through reliable patterns by using printed images, the same that will be visible on the board of the test of Perfetti, whose goal is to encourage the fine motor rehabilitation in children.

The system includes striking 3D environments, with which the user will be able to interact in real time. For this work it is considered the level 1 of the cognitive therapeutic exercise, based on figures like triangle, square, circle.

There is a sound feedback with different melodies according to the figure that is selected, these melodies are used for the recognition of figures when the user performs the tasks of identification of figures with the eyes closed. The system block diagram is shown below (Fig. 1).

## 3   System Development

This section describes the development of the system. The operation system diagram is shown in Fig. 2.

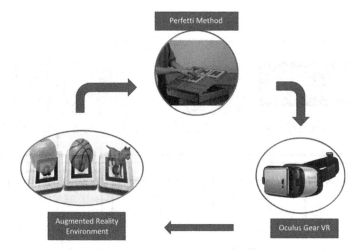

**Fig. 1.** System structure block diagram.

Next, the stages considered in the development of augmented reality system is presented:

**Data Acquisition**

The first stage corresponds to the inputs of the system, it collects the movements that the user performs with the head, this through the camera of the smartphone, which allows to visualize the patterns placed on the pieces of the Perfetti's board.

**Script Development**

The flowchart in Fig. 3 explains the operation of the applications, according to the activities programmed in C#. At the time the application runs, the initialization of variables is made. When the camera is positioned on top of a pattern it will allow a virtual object to appear and at the same time it will be possible to interact with the test and the increased 3D object. Verification is made whether the exercise was completed and when the total number of interactions is completed, a signal will be given to the user indicating that can direct its attention to the following figure. This process is repeated for each piece on the board.

**Environments Design**

Animations of the environments are created in the Unity 3D graphic engine; these virtual environments will be projected on the patterns placed on the pieces of the Perfetti board. The user will be able to view the virtual objects using the Oculus and interact with them at the same time that it is evaluated with the Perfetti test.

## 4  Test and Results

**Test**

Two tests are considered to determine the correct functioning of the implemented system:

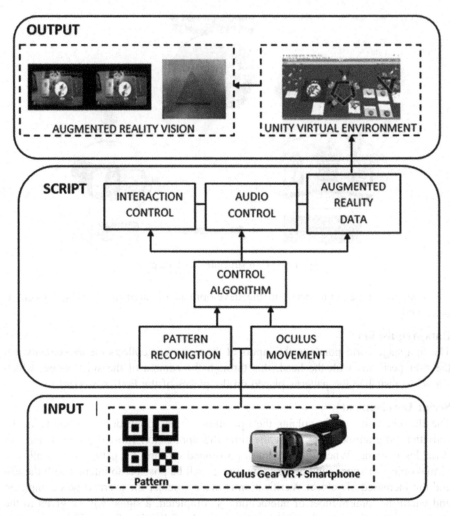

**Fig. 2.** Operating system diagram.

First Test, preliminary experiments were carried out to verify the real-time response of the interaction that the user has with the augmented reality environment and also verify the correct operation of the application. The tests follow the sequence as shown in Fig. 4.

As a second test, the user with closed eyes performs the same task, the tracking the contour of the geometric figure, the system gives auditory feedback (melodies) according to the figure used.

**Results**

In Fig. 4, the first scene presents a virtual reality interface, which allows the user select the number of interactions going to do the test. The next stage presents a reality-increased atmosphere, which shows a button virtual where the user must interact in order

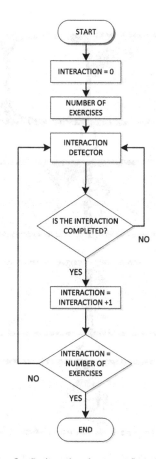

**Fig. 3.** Scripts development flowchart.

to turn others reality increased objects and give the start of activity with the pieces of the test. An indicator is shown with a count variable, which check the number of interactions that should be made. At the time of completing all the interactions, an indication of be finished exercise and user can continue with the next part of the board are shown. With this test is could check that the system has a response speed optimum and suitable for working in real time. The speed with the reality figures are increased is below the 30 fps. The interaction response between user and objects virtual has a proper sensitivity, which allows the user to make the tasks on the board of the test in a fluid way.

Finally, the second test carried out, through the feedback of sound of each figure, allows the user to identify the correct figure (square, triangle, circle, etc.), fulfilling the essence of cognitive therapeutic exercise.

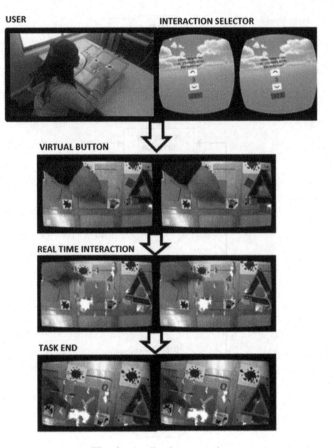

**Fig. 4.** Application operation

## 5   Conclusions and Future Works

These types of virtual systems demonstrate to be a very useful contribution in the use of the Perfetti test. It provides the current version of the test with a novel component and gives immersion to users, with the inclusion of flexible, friendly interfaces and melodies that motivate the user to perform the activities about the test in a better way. In addition, the record of activities about the test is done more accurately and orderly, it provides to the specialist with more reliable and real-time data, the same that helps to make a better evaluation of the results that were obtained in the execution of the test with the augmented reality system.

For future work, more efficient and accurate statistical algorithms will be implemented, by using image processing; allowing an automatic diagnosis after the test is executed. A complete interactive and intelligent system will be developed, which automatically evaluates the activities to be carried out, facilitating the specialist to supervise these processes with much more precise information.

**Acknowledgements.** We thank the "Universidad de las Fuerzas Armadas ESPE" for financing the investigation project number 2016-PIC-0017.

# References

1. Bryan Kolb, I.W.: Fundamentals of Human NeuroPsychology. Macmillan Publishers, Basingstoke (2009)
2. De Campos, A.C., da Costa, C.S., Rocha, N.A.: Measuring changes in functional mobility in children with mild cerebral palsy. Dev. Neurorehabil. **14**, 140–144 (2011)
3. Prosser, L.A., Lee, S.C., Barbe, M.F., VanSant, A.F., Lauer, R.T.: Trunk and hip muscle activity in early walkers with and without cerebral palsy – a frequency analysis. J. Electromyogr. Kinesiol. **20**, 851–859 (2010)
4. Oh, S., Bailenson, J.: Virtual and augmented reality. In: The International Encyclopedia of Media Effects (2017)
5. Rodrigues, J., Cardoso, P., Monteiro, J., Figueiredo, M.: Handbook of Research on Human-Computer Interfaces, Developments, and Applications. IGI Global, Hershey (2016)
6. Hwang, G., Wu, P., Chen, C., Tu, N.: Effects of an augmented reality-based educational game on students' learning achievements and attitudes in real-world observations. In: Interactive Learning Environments, pp. 1895–1906 (2015)
7. Krichenbauer, M., Yamamoto, G., Taketom, T., Sandor, C., Kato, H.: Augmented reality versus virtual reality for 3D object manipulation. IEEE Trans. Vis. Comput. Graph. **24**(2), 1038–1048 (2015)
8. Kerdvibulvech, C., Wang, C.-C.: A new 3D augmented reality application for educational games to help children in communication interactively. In: Gervasi, O., et al. (eds.) ICCSA 2016. LNCS, vol. 9787, pp. 465–473. Springer, Cham (2016). https://doi.org/10.1007/978-3-319-42108-7_35
9. Sobota, B., Korečko, Š., Jacho, L., Pastornický, P., Hudák, M., Sivý, M.: Virtual-reality technologies and smart environments in the process of disabled people education. In: Emerging eLearning Technologies and Applications (ICETA) (2017)
10. Lin, C., Chang, Y.: Interactive augmented reality using Scratch 2.0 to improve physical activities for children with developmental disabilities. In: Research in Developmental Disabilities, pp. 1–8 (2015)
11. Suzuki, K.: Augmented human technology. In: Sankai, Y., Suzuki, K., Hasegawa, Y. (eds.) Cybernics: Fusion of Human, Machine and Information Systems. LNCS, pp. 111–131. Springer, Tokyo (2014). https://doi.org/10.1007/978-4-431-54159-2_7
12. Serrano, C.V., Bonilla, I., Gomez, F.V., Mendoza, M.: Development of a haptic interface for motor rehabilitation therapy. In: Engineering in Medicine and Biology Society (EMBC), 37th Annual International Conference of the IEEE, pp. 1156–1159 (2005)
13. Lin, C., Chai, H., Wang, J., Chen, C., Liu, Y., Chen, C., Lin, C.-W., Huang, Y.-M.: Augmented reality in educational activities for children with disabilities. Displays **42**, 51–54 (2016)
14. Robson, N., Faller, K., Ahir, V., Ferreira, A., Buchanan, J.: Creating a virtual perception for upper limb rehabilitation. Int. J. Biomed. Biol. Eng. **11**, 152–157 (2017)
15. Hsiao, K., Rashvand, H.: Data modeling mobile augmented reality: integrated mind and body rehabilitation. Multimed. Tools Appl. **74**, 3543–3560 (2013)
16. Ravi, D., Kumar, N., Singhi, P.: Effectiveness of virtual reality rehabilitation for children and adolescents with cerebral palsy: an updated evidence-based systematic review. Physiotherapy **103**, 245–258 (2017)

17. Kolar, P., et al.: Clinical Rehabilitation. Alena Kobesová, Prague (2014)
18. De Cecco, M., et al.: Augmented reality to enhance the clinician's observation during assessment of daily living activities. In: De Paolis, L.T., Bourdot, P., Mongelli, A. (eds.) AVR 2017. LNCS, vol. 10325, pp. 3–21. Springer, Cham (2017). https://doi.org/10.1007/978-3-319-60928-7_1
19. Hatem, S., Saussez, G., Faille, M., Prist, V., Zhang, X., Dispa, D., Bleyenheuft, Y.: Rehabilitation of motor function after stroke: a multiple systematic review focused on techniques to stimulate upper extremity recovery. Front. Hum. Neurosci. (2016)
20. Manzanares, M., Galán, C., Morales, N., Guerrero, E.: Sensitive reeducation of the hand. In: Fisioterapia, pp. 114–122 (2004)
21. Lv, Z., Esteve, C., Chirivella, J., Gagliardo, P.: A game based assistive tool for rehabilitation of dysphonic patients. In: Virtual and Augmented Assistive Technology (VAAT), pp. 9–14 (2015)

# Applications of VR/AR
# in Cultural Heritage

# Digital-Assisted Repairing of the Six Steeds in Zhao Mausoleum

Qiang Chen[✉], Zhenyu Ouyang, Chaoying Luo, and Jielong Liu

Institute for the Preservation of Cultural Heritage in Modern Science
and Technology, Xi'an Jiaotong University, Xi'an, China
chenqiangatt@xjtu.edu.cn

**Abstract.** The Six Steeds of Zhao Mausoleum were world-renowned for its realistic style and typical ancient Chinese carving skills. They were carved in memory of the six horses belong to the Emperor Taizong of Tang Dynasty and placed on the north slope of Jiuzong Mountain where the mausoleum of emperor located in. By thousand years efflorescing and destructing, they were seriously damaged, and the majority of the surface details were lost. It is urgent and significant to reconstruct the missing parts and give the entire embossments an integrated vision. Cause of the important historical values and complex artistic surface shape, it is hard to reliably restore the missing parts only using the technical method or artist's method. By combining mathematic method and sculpture modeling method, this paper put forward a way to restore the damaged embossments in virtual space. It is the first time to give the Six Steeds a trustworthy full sight both in the point of artistic style and archaeology; what's more, the output data of the research can convert into real parts via the CNC machining equipment.

## 1 Introduction

The Six Steeds of Zhao Mausoleum located on the north slope of the emperor Tang-taizong tomb in Liquan county Shaanxi province. Because of the importance in art and history, it was included in the list of national treasure which permanently prohibited exhibition abroad. While suffer from thousands of years efflorescing and weathering, these stone relievos were seriously damaged and broken in fragments. A majority of the exquisite carving details were lost in abrasion and hard to distinguish. It is quite urgent for us to restore the missing parts and the lost carving details.

Three problems make the repairing work difficult to deal with. Firstly, all of the Six Steeds were damaged so seriously that lot of geometrical and structural information were lost permanently. Secondly, the missing parts of the embossments are irregular shape, traditional repairing algorithms via revolve axis, symmetry and extended curvatures works badly on this situation. The repairing of large area damaged sculpture should be implemented under the guidance of the transdisciplinary research related to history, archaeology, art and engineering. Third, because of the frangibility of the material and weathered layer, repairing directly on the original relics will cause irreversible secondary damage (Fig. 1).

© Springer International Publishing AG, part of Springer Nature 2018
L. T. De Paolis and P. Bourdot (Eds.): AVR 2018, LNCS 10851, pp. 249–260, 2018.
https://doi.org/10.1007/978-3-319-95282-6_19

Fig. 1. Photographs of the Six Steeds of Zhao Mausoleum.

## 2 Background

At present, related researches on how to recover the missing parts of the Six Steeds were still limited and scanty. In the 1940s, Ziyun Wang and his investigate team casted the Six Steeds molds with plaster and made a copy for each steed [1]. However, as we all know, the casting technique will damage the original copy more or less.

In 2011, based on the unearthed new fragments, experts from US and China jointly repaired and protected two of the Six Steeds collected in Penn Museum [2]. The repairing project employed the IRT and XRD technology and analysed structure strength and material ingredient. They also implemented artistic repairing and got a fine result, but they didn't recover missing parts of the horse legs and saddles. Drilling and glue process had a bad influence of the relics. Related repairing method can be found in the works of J. Hayes at Carleton University in 2015 [3], using the 3D scanning and CNC machining technology, they recovered a seriously damaged relief of parliament buildings national historic site of Canada. Combining the computer added rough machining and handwork finishing modeling, they reached a pleased artistic result. But because of the influence of artist's subjective factor, the repairing result is likely to be instable and inconstant. Similar research can found in the project of restoring the sculpture named "Guerriero di Castiglione" directed by Fatuzzo [4]. They constructed a digital model of the missing horn of the sculpture in CAD software. Although some reference images or historic documents have been used in recovering process, the main modeling mehold was still implemented by hand via keyboard, mouse, graphic board or other kinds of input devices, further deeply artistic style analysis was insufficient. For sculpture shaped relics repairing, reliable results cannot be reached, if we only use the artistic or technique method. Thus, the repairing of the Six Steeds embossments in Zhao Mausoleum needs composite method.

With the development of technology, it is possible to resolve the difficulties above in another way. Combining mathematical theory, computer graphic, virtual reality technology and the theory of heritage conservation, effectiveness, and precision of repairing would be improved observably. This paper talks about how to apply those technique tools in the repairing process, especially for stone carving embossments.

## 3 Method

Facing the problems we described above, this research employed a transdisciplinary method by combining methods from art, history, and technologies. On the one hand, using the artistic and historical document and graphic analysis, we can make sure the artistic style and construction study to be trustworthy. On the other hand, optical measure tools and computer graphic algorithms give precise geometric data.

The detailed technique route map is shown in Fig. 2. Shape certification and repairing parameter quantification are the key links in the route map. The resource data of shape certification comes from: 3D scanning data, old photographs shot in 1920s, related Chinese paintings, sculptures and historical records.

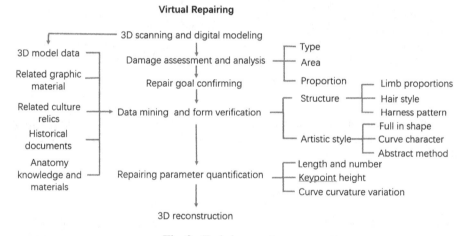

**Fig. 2.** Technique route map.

## 4 Implement Details

### 4.1 3D Scanning and Digital Modelling

In order to preserve details as precise as possible, we employed a wide field optical scanner and a handheld scanner. In addition, we used a digital SLR camera to capture the images as an assistant texture solution. The average geometric precision is 0.01 mm and the dot spacing is 0.2 mm. Final 3D models were shown in Fig. 3.

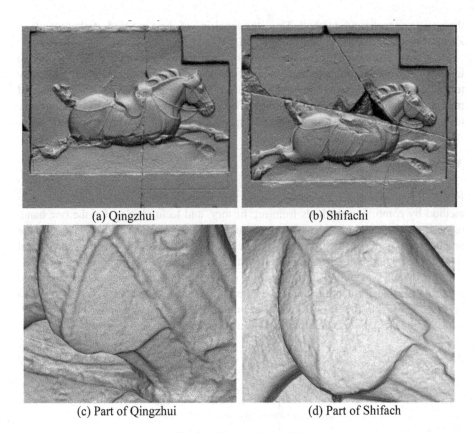

(a) Qingzhui                              (b) Shifachi

(c) Part of Qingzhui                   (d) Part of Shifach

**Fig. 3.** 3D scanning model.

Referred to the photographs and material texture, the appended plaster in repairing history have been carefully recognized and deleted in 3D software. The final scanning data information was shown in Table 1.

**Table 1.** 3D scanning information.

| Number | Number of points (Million) | Number of triangles (Million) | Average point spacing (mm) | Size of data (GB) |
|---|---|---|---|---|
| 1(Shifachi) | 8.4 | 16.5 | 0.2 | 2.56 |
| 2(Qingzhui) | 13.7 | 26.7 | 0.2 | 4.16 |
| 3(Teqinbiao) | 11.3 | 21.9 | 0.2 | 3.41 |
| 4(Baitiwu) | 23.1 | 45.6 | 0.2 | 7.21 |

As the stone relieves were broken in fragments and inlaid on the wall, we can't scan the fracture and back face, in order to enable the geometric Boolean calculation, the mesh surface model have to be thickened to create a closed poly mesh. In addition, we need to realign the fragments and recheck the continuity along the crevice as well. Transform parameters were given in Table 2. Z-axis represents the front side of the embossment, and Y-axis represents the height direction. Rotate pivot is the geometric center.

**Table 2.** Transformation parameters of Baitiwu

| Axis | Move (mm) | Rotate (degree) | Scale |
| --- | --- | --- | --- |
| Axis X | −2.9 | 0 | 1 |
| Axis Y | −4.0 | 0.26 | 1 |
| Axis Z | 1.1 | 0.2 | 1 |

At first, we separated crafts surfaces and fracture surfaces to different parts with the help of mesh mean curvature colorizing technique [5]. Cause the original object surface was severely corroded, and some segmentation work was carefully implemented under the help of manual intervention in Geomagic Studio (Fig. 4).

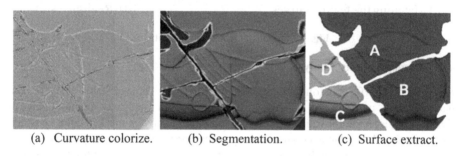

(a)  Curvature colorize.     (b)  Segmentation.     (c)  Surface extract.

**Fig. 4.** Segmentation of 3D model.

Because of the large size and fracture surface weathering, it is hard to align fragments precisely in real world. While, in the digital virtual space, we can handle these debris data easily via 3D software. As shown in Fig. 5(a), we can use the curve features on each fragment to check the alignment result. Using the curvature information, the point cloud related to the line feature can be picked out, then using least-squares methods to figure out the feature curves.

Based on sculpting rules these couples of curves should be blended smooth, in other words, the start points of curve group B should be on the extended curves from the end points of curve group A. To minimize the distance between A and start point of B we can get the moving parameter as shown in Table 2.

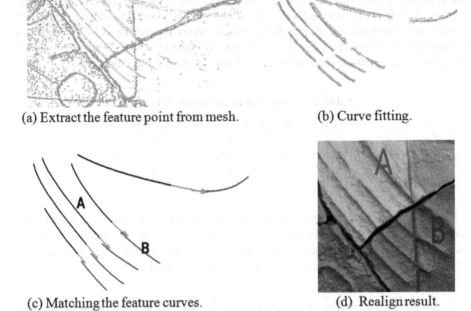

(a) Extract the feature point from mesh.          (b) Curve fitting.

(c) Matching the feature curves.          (d) Realign result.

**Fig. 5.** Fragments realigning of Baitiwu.

### 4.2 Damage Status Analysis

It is a prediction for repairing strategy planning to make damage status analysis. The damage area, portion and damage reason have been analyzed quantitatively in Grasshopper a plugin for Rhin. Then illustrated different area in masked color. As been shown in Fig. 7, the damaged area relating to the horse (colored in purple) are saddle, front left leg, back left leg, back of horsetail. Besides, part of the relief frames has been exfoliated away (Fig. 6).

It is quite easy to recover the missing part on the frame. However, for the area relating to the horse, the repairing process calls for a scrupulous shape verification from artistic style and philological research.

### 4.3 Form Verification

Form verification is to ascertain the original status of the damaged area; it is the key link of the whole research and it affects the artistic effect and reliability of repairing results. The main reference information comes from:
- The 3D scanning data
- Old photographs shot in the early 19th.
- Official publication about the two steeds collected in Penn Museum
- Paintings and sculptures created at the same age or same region to the Six Steeds
- Related research paper and books
- Anatomy documents about horses

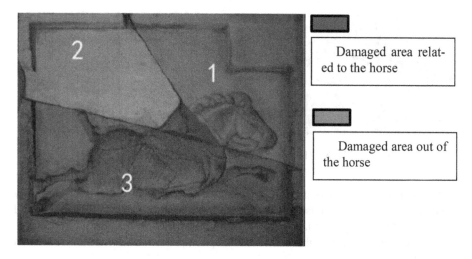

**Fig. 6.** Damage status analysis (Color figure online)

From the fine art point of view, form verification can be separated in graphic construction and molding artistic style. While artistic style reflects artist's character and habit. The constructed elements, length or width of saddle etc. belong to form construction problems (Fig. 8).

Referring to related historical materials [6–8] and images, it is easy to find the intact structure of the saddle used in the Six Steeds. Figure 7 shows the main saddle structure. For the damaged horse legs, using Chinese parallel perspective painting principle, anatomy data and the abstract form, we obtain the leg boundary and bloat shape distribution as the graphics shown in Fig. 9.

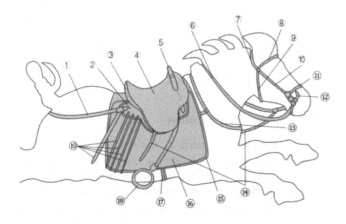

**Fig. 7.** Saddle structure of Shifachi

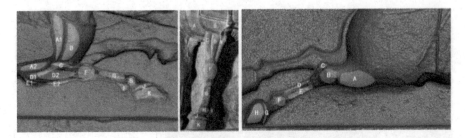

**Fig. 8.** The boundary and structure of horse legs

In order to find the boundary shape style, we cut the whole relief with uniformly spaced plane. (See Fig. 9) It is obvious that the angle θ between sidewall and baseboard is based on the real space relationship. It can be explained by Lambertian reflectance law (see Fig. 10). Because the darker the shape appeared the deeper the space can represent.

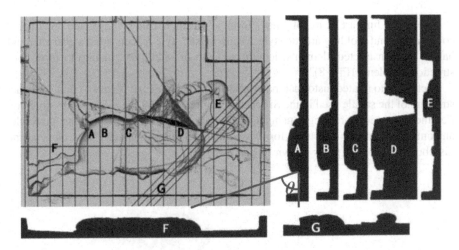

**Fig. 9.** Section shape of Saluzi

### 4.4   Repairing Parameter Quantification

Parameter quantification means we need to translate all the repairing evidence or information to certain value. This is important to guarantee the uniqueness and reliability of the repairing result. By comparing the size of all Six Steeds, we found that the size proportion of parts in Qingzhui and Shifachi is very close (see Fig. 11). Thus, we can use the proportion of Qingzhui to represent the same part of Shifachi, especially the missing parts. Finally, we confirmed that the length of damaged saddle is 193 mm, and the height is 264 mm.

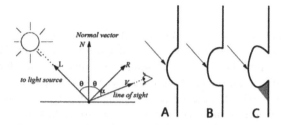

**Fig. 10.** Lambertian law

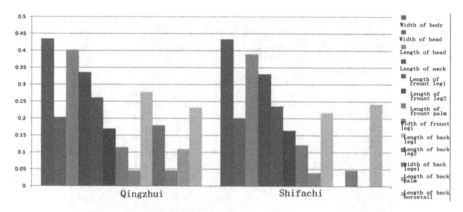

**Fig. 11.** Proportopn of different parts on 'Qingzhui' and 'Shifachi'

As well, we can figure out the height range of some key points via undamaged surface point height value and relief space compression law. We can find the key point of height horse legs and saddle relationship in Fig. 9 meet the condition: 78 mm $\leq$ Hf $\leq$ Hb $\leq$ Hk = 95 mm (Fig. 12).

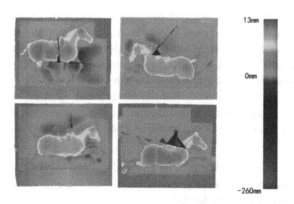

**Fig. 12.** Height space of Teqinbiao, Baitiwu, Qingzhui and Shifachi

### 4.5   3D Reconstruction

Based on the repairing parameter and realigned mesh, we recreated the missing part of the relief in virtual space. At first, we use digital sculpture software Zbrush to extract the fractured face from the original scanning mesh, then reversed the face direction, close the hole, so that we obtained a closed and well-matched poly mesh. Using the clipping function in 3D software, we can copy the undamaged surface and paste them on the damaged relief. It is quite easy and convenient to modify the shape of 3D models in virtual space. Sculpture relics repairing involved large amount of poly mesh editing, the majority work was implemented in digital sculpting software (Fig. 13).

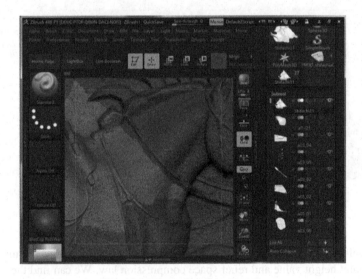

**Fig. 13.**  Edit the mesh in Zbrush.

Firstly, we cut the related undamaged part from Qingzhui, which have been confirmed have the same graphic proportion pattern in previous section. In addition, in order to make sure the repaired parts match the original fracture surface well, we extract the fracture surface from Shifachi to construct closed objects (Fig. 14).

For the situation which have no reference scanning data, we can using the fill hole function in Zbrush to close the hole and draft the shape manually based on repairing parameter using Zbrush modelling techniques. In order to make sure the key point height match the parameter confirmed before, we placed some reference points in the space. There are some strict rules should be obey when we sculpt the missing parts manually (Fig. 15):

(1)  The original model should never be changed.
(2)  The appended object boundary should blend with the original scanning surface.
(3)  Artistic style should keep the same.

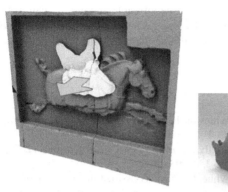
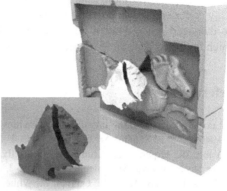

(a) Extract the undamaged part from Qingzhui    (b) Combin the fracture surface with pasted saddle surface

**Fig. 14.** Construction of the missing parts of Shifachi

**Fig. 15.** Finished repairing result.

## 5 Conclusion

Above all, virtual repairing based on modern digital technique gives us a new platform for the protection of sculpture cultural relics. It set an example on culture relics and heritage conservation via combining science technology and art together. Although software tools make the molding fast and convenient, the core problem is how to confirm the lost information as precise as possible. What's more, we should make sure the harmonious on artistic style.

A majority of Chinese traditional sculpture heritage was made of clay, which was easily damaged, and hard to protect. While, using the virtual technique, we can recover the damaged relics without any secondary damage. What's more, for those works, which collected separately overseas, we can combine them together in virtual space.

# References

1. Luo, H.: Review of the investigation activities of the ministry of education art and heritage 1940–1945. J. Nanjing Art Inst. (Art Des.) **4**, 1–5 (2005)
2. Yang, W.: Experts from China and US jointly repairing "Saluzi" and "Quanmaogua"of the Six Steeds of Zhao Mausoleum. Cult. Reli. **2**, 86–95 (2012)
3. Hayes, J., Fai, S., Kretz, S., Ouimet, C., White, P.: Digitally-assisted stone carving of a relief sculpture for the parliament buildings national historic site of Canada, II-5/W3, pp. 97–103 (2015)
4. Fatuzzo, G., Mussumeci, G., Oliveri, S.M., Sequenzia, G.: The "Guerriero di Castiglione": reconstructing missing elements with integrated non-destructive 3D modelling techniques. J. Archaeol. Sci. **38**, 3533–3540 (2011)
5. Guennebaud, G., Gross, M.: Algebraic point set surfaces. ACM Trans. Graph. **26**, 23 (2007)
6. Liu, X.: Jiu Tang Shu, Zhonghua Book Company, Beijing (1975)
7. Dong, G.: Quan Tang Wen, Zhonghua Book Company, Beijing (1983)
8. Sun, J.: Horse saddles and trappings in the tang dynasty. Cult. Reli. **10**, 82–88 (1981)

# Virtual Acoustic Rendering in Old Spaces: Application to an Early-Modern Theatre in València, "L'Olivera"

Sebastián Mirasol-Menacho[1], Ana Planells-Pérez[2], Jaume Segura-Garcia[1(✉)], Santiago Felici-Castell[1], Máximo Cobos-Serrano[1], Rosa Cibrián[1,2,3], Alicia Giménez-Pérez[2], and Joan Oleza-Simó[3]

[1] Dpt Informàtica, ETSE, Universitat de València, Avda Universitat s/n, 46100 Burjassot, Spain
semime@alumni.uv.es, {jsegura,felici,macose2}@uv.es
[2] Dpt Física Aplicada, UPV, Camí de Vera s/n, 46020 Valencia, Spain
anaplape@upvnet.upv.es, agimenez@fis.upv.es
[3] Dpt Filología Hispánica, Universitat de València, Avda Blasco Ibañez 13, 46013 Valencia, Spain
joleza@uv.es
http://www.uv.es/etse/, http://www.upv.es/

**Abstract.** The application of the VR to the renderization of ancient and lost buildings is one important topic in the cultural heritage field nowadays. Moreover, the addition of other senses apart from the graphical view, increases the sensation of immersion in a virtual application. The aim of this paper is to show the work on a virtual acoustic system, based on Unity, FMOD and Csound. This system has been implemented to render binaural auralizations and has been applied to the renderization of an old and lost theatre in València (Spain). This theatre was firstly build in the 16th century, and rebuilt several times until the 18th century. It has been modelled from ancient documents. The auralization of several theatrical excerpts of different Spanish authors of that time is also presented.

**Keywords:** Virtual reality · Virtual acoustics
Acoustical archaeology · Auralization

## 1 Introduction

Virtual acoustics applied to the archaeological area allows to obtain realistic reconstructions of ancient buildings or even recreate previous stages of actual ones. The user is transferred to a free moving space inside or around buildings that were lost or modified over time. Among different examples of integration of the acoustic environment, we can find in [1] an example of the analysis of a lost building including the integration of the graphical model and the acoustic

© Springer International Publishing AG, part of Springer Nature 2018
L. T. De Paolis and P. Bourdot (Eds.): AVR 2018, LNCS 10851, pp. 261–274, 2018.
https://doi.org/10.1007/978-3-319-95282-6_20

model as a virtual acoustic model. This modality of virtual reality allows the user to enjoy a sensory experience, not just seeing how the building was in different ages, but also "taste" the sound in the environment. In this work, an application to an ancient and lost building devoted to the theatrical performance in Valencia (Spain) is analyzed. The innovative aspects of this work are related to the modularity of the acoustic rendering elements applied to the virtual acoustic reconstruction of ancient and lost buildings.

## 1.1    The "Corral de comedies de l'Olivera"

First theatrical performances in Valencia were made in an itinerant way, in outdoor spaces or improvised locations without a specific acoustical conditioning. The first building specifically designed to these performances was promoted by the Hospital of Valencia, an institution which got the monopoly on theatrical activities in the city to fund some expenditures of the hospital related to charity. It was built in 1584. The documentation about this original playhouse is very scarce, but it is known the location. The old "Casa de la Olivera" was in operation for 34 years, until the Hospital decided to tear it down and build a new one, larger, and better adjusted to the functional requirements of the time. For this purpose, some adjoining properties were acquired and the new "Casa de la Olivera" was built [2].

This new theatre was rebuilt in the same place in 1618. The building had a substantially circular geometry with a width of 15 meters and a depth of 13 meters. It had ground floor and two heights and it was covered. It had a maximum capacity for about 1800 spectators. The existing documentation includes detailed studies on the capacity [7] and a schematic plan of its layout in 1678. The ground floor had chairs where were located the nobility, classes para-nobiliary and clergy, some benches behind these chairs and a few terraces in the background. The first floor was divided in 20 rooms that were the most expensive and luxurious seats of the theatre. Finally, the second floor known as the "aposento de les dones" ("cazuela" as it was known at the Spanish "corrales" or playhouses) was reserved exclusively for women. Each of the zones had its own independent access. Figure 1 shows the distribution of chairs in the ground of the theatre.

The stage was formed by a single rectangular platform, surrounded by the public on three sides, behind it was the costumes of the actors and over it a balcony, which was accessed by a staircase at the hidden back of the stage, called "balcony of the apparitions" and used for the representation on an upper level. This "Casa de Comedias" remained in use until 1715 when, due to its poor condition, it was decided to carry out a significant remodelation that was maintained until 1748 when the archbishop forbade any kind of theatrical performance.

In this paper we will show the visual and acoustical reconstruction (VR/VA) of an ancient theatre in Valencia in the 17th century (now lost) and its integration in a virtual environment. This integration has involved several aspects which involved not only the design of the graphical navigator but also the integration with other audio tools like FMOD and/or Csound to allow the 3D audio rendering and the interaction with the virtual acoustic environment. We will discuss

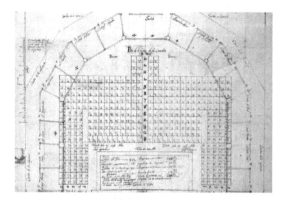

**Fig. 1.** Schematic ground of the "Casa de Comedias" in Valencia from 1678. (Source: General Archive and Photographic of the "Diputación de Valencia")

the acoustic aspects and the auralization of different theatrical excerpts from Spanish playwrights. The paper structures as follows: a methodology section explaining different methodological aspects involved in this project (the development of the graphical and acoustic model, acoustical simulation and calibration, auralization, integration of the model in the graphical and audio engine and final representation), a results section and a final discussion with some conclusions.

## 2 Methodology

The methodology in this work is based on the integration of the graphical engine with the acoustical system to provide the user a complete integrated and interactive reality. The study is applied to the "Corral de comèdies de l'Olivera", an ancient theatre in Valencia. To study this building, different aspects have been considered: the visual/graphical and the acoustical analysis of the model, the integration in a graphical engine (as Unity), the auralization of different theatrical excerpts and the integration of the Unity engine with FMOD and Csound to allow an interactive graphical and acoustical renderization.

### 2.1 Graphical and Acoustical Model

The graphical model was built from four basic studies: one by Sirera [4] , other by Ros [5], other by Mouyen [6–8] and another by Oleza [9], and some old documents containing instructions to the builders. The study by Ros-Andreu [5] included the plan of three floors, two sections and an axonometry. Figure 2 shows all these plans by Ros-Andreu. This architectural study was contrasted by Joan Oleza with the original management documentation of the builders, conserved in the Generl Archive of the Diputación of Valencia, and with the historical evolution of the urban topography at the zone, then the structure, the dimensions and the architectural plans were reformulated. Architect Ana

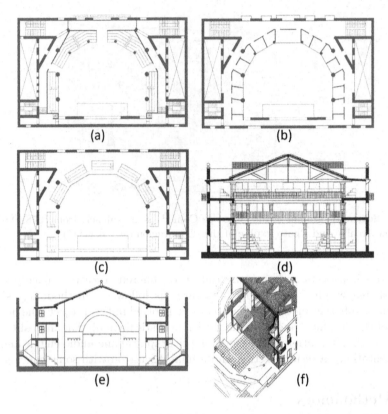

**Fig. 2.** Plans of the Olivera by Ros [3]: (a) ground, (b) first floor, (c) second floor, (d) façade, (e) section from the façade and (f) section towards the stage

Centelles drew the new plans and Architect Francisco Pomares developed a 3D model using Rhinoceros 5. Figure 3 shows two views of the model.

The acoustical model was obtained from a simplification of this graphical model and taking the acoustic characteristics of the materials in the original documentation of the builders. As they wrote, the six large pillars that supported the roof as the other smaller four that supported the "ochavo" (the polygonal galleries at the front side of the stage) were made of 'Godella' stone, but in the first and second floors the pillars material changed to bricks covered with plaster. The walls were made of brick covered with plaster. The beams were made of wood and scaffold. The theatre had ceramic tiles flooring on all floors and iron railings on the upper floors. The grandstands where the spectators stayed were made of wood [10].

In order to do an acoustical study of this theatre, the acoustical properties of these materials were selected from databases as the original materials were lost. The simulation was performed using ODEON software.

**Fig. 3.** Graphical 3D model of the Olivera: (a) view from the 1st floor (from the 'aposentos'), (b) view from the ground floor (from the stalls)

Another important aspect of the model was the integration in the graphical engine and the illumination aspects (this issue will be tackled in the next section).

## 2.2 Dry Recordings and Auralization of Different Theatrical Excerpts

As this building was made in the Golden Age of the Spanish literature, some excerpts of works by Lope de Vega, a reference playwright in the Spanish literature of the Golden Age. This recordings were made in the dry room of the SPAT Lab at the ETSE in the University of Valencia to different professional actors of classical theatre. Figure 4 shows a picture of one of the recording sessions in the Lab. Digital recorder ZOOM H6 was used with 2 additional omni-directional microphones to register the dry recordings for the auralizations.

From the acoustical simulation, different impulse responses (IRs) in different locations were obtained (see Sect. 3.1). These locations were selected as references in every floor. These IRs were splitted in the early and late reverberation, taking as a reference for this room its Early Decay Time (EDT). These pre-processed signals will be later used to filter the anechoic sound of the selected theatrical excerpts.

## 2.3 Integration of the Unity Engine with FMOD and Csound

Unity 5 offers an Audio Spatializer SDK, but even though it has come a long way since the first time it was implemented, it is still quite limited in comparison with other alternatives available. FMOD and Csound are two options, frequently used together with Unity, to achieve what Unity's Audio Spatializer SDK does not cover.

FMOD Studio is an audio content creator tool developed by Firelight Technologies for audio professionals and game developers. It provides a programming API compatible with most of the popular graphic engines, such as the one used in this paper or Unreal Engine. On the other hand, Csound is a tool that is more

**Fig. 4.** Recording session with two performers

appealing to the programmer, since it is an audio programming language. From its release in 1985 until the most recent version (Csound 6), there have been many improvements, such as the addition to the C API of Python, Java, C++ and a few more.

**FMOD** [12]. This tool provides the developer with an easy to use graphical interface that makes 3D audio design as easy as a drag and drop system of the desired sound. FMOD integrates several blocks for 3D spatialization [13] which are very useful for creating sound in a virtual environment (Fig. 5).

First of all we applied a 3D panner that separates each channel of a stereo sound in a right and left mono track and lets the use experiment in real time with different pans and attenuation distances. This is what gives the final user hear a 3D sound in relation with the distance and direction relative to the sound source.

As mentioned before the interior of the building was acoustically modeled, this provided us with impulse responses of different interior parts. These responses could be applied directly to a convolutional reverb, which convolutes the sound with the impulse response on the fly. What this does is to make any kind of noise sound as if it where physically in the point where the impulse response was taken.

All the changes made to the sounds are saved on FMOD's *Master Bank*. This is quite useful, since in the future the user can access any of the sounds independently with all the modifications applied.

**Csound** [14]. This programming language is oriented to digital sound processing. It was originally written by Barry Vercoe back in 1986. The latest version

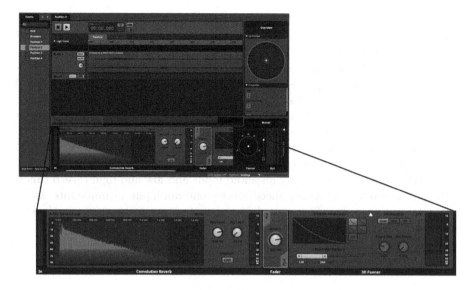

**Fig. 5.** FMOD Studio interface

(Csound 6) was started in 2013 and the current release has improved performance for live performance, allowing only score mode in real-time (this means that the use of different sound sources can be scheduled as in a score).

The possibility to program the audio signal process on a high level language like Python allows a high versatility in the development of systems. Even more if the way to schedule processes is through the score mode in which the tasks are processed in real-time like in a parallel processing system.

Csound is composed by many opcodes that work as a block with inputs and outputs. In this paper we worked with some of Csound's binaural 3D sound opcodes: *hrtfmove2*, *hrtfearly* and *hrtfreverb*. There are two opcodes that work with binaural HRTF [15]. *Hrtfmove* is based on phase truncation processing or minimum phase based processing, on the other hand, *hrtfmove2* uses a Woodworth based spherical head model with more low frequency phase accuracy. Both of these opcodes have left and right stereo outputs meant to be used for headphone reproduction.

When working in closed spaces, such as the one we are studying in this paper, reverberation is a key concept. There are different approaches to recreate an artificial reverberation in a virtual space, but Csound uses a two-stage process with the *hrtfearly* and *hrtfreverb* opcodes [16]. The first of them process early reflections, emulating the reflections of the sound source within the enclosed space. The second opcode process the diffuse reverberation. These do not work directly with the impulse responses taken on site, since some preprocessing is needed in order to get all the necessary parameters.

The *hrtfearly* opcode makes available for the user quite a few parameters in order to be more flexible, but it assumes a shoebox-shaped geometry. Besides the location of the source and listener in the x, y and z planes, and the HRTF datafile, the user can use the default room or specify the length, width and depth. As optional parameters, one can specify high and low frequency absorption coefficients and gain factors of a three band equalizer.

Later diffuse field is processed with the *hrtfreverb* opcode, it can be used standalone or along with *hrtfearly*. The standalone use is recommended when the processing of early reflections is too high. Reverberation is built using a cross-fertilization paradigm to build the late reverb tale, each delay line feeds into the other in order to ad density. The algorithm also uses averaged binaural filters, as well as accurate interaural coherence. Opcode operation is more simple than that of *hrtfearly*, since only an audio input and low and high reverb times. If there is a need for a more advanced reverb, one can input a sample rate, mean free path and an order. These two last parameters are to be used to calculate an appropriate delay for the late tail.

## 3   Results and Discussion

### 3.1   Acoustical Simulation

The acoustical simulation is obtained by determining the materials of this theatre. This is a complex task because this building does not exit nowadays. The building notebook of the theatre [10] used in the construction of 1678, which is located in the Library of the "Diputació de València", contains information about the types of materials, and using the library of materials in ODEON we have assigned the materials to each surface in the model. Table 1 shows the values of absorption coefficients used in this acoustic simulation.

**Table 1.** Absorption coefficients of the materials used in the rehabilitation of 1618

|  | 125 Hz | 250 Hz | 500 Hz | 1000 Hz | 2000 Hz | 4000 Hz |
|---|---|---|---|---|---|---|
| Pilar of stone | 0.19 | 0.23 | 0.43 | 0.37 | 0.58 | 0.62 |
| Pilar of bricks | 0.14 | 0.28 | 0.45 | 0.90 | 0.45 | 0.65 |
| Wooden flooring | 0.14 | 0.10 | 0.06 | 0.08 | 0.10 | 0.10 |
| Wooden tiers | 0.25 | 0.15 | 0.10 | 0.09 | 0.08 | 0.07 |
| Wooden covering | 0.14 | 0.10 | 0.06 | 0.08 | 0.10 | 0.10 |
| Ceramic tiles | 0.21 | 0.54 | 0.74 | 0.34 | 0.28 | 0.42 |
| Brick walls with plaster | 0.08 | 0.09 | 0.12 | 0.16 | 0.22 | 0.24 |
| Iron banister | 0.14 | 0.10 | 0.06 | 0.05 | 0.04 | 0.03 |
| Wooden ceiling | 0.19 | 0.14 | 0.09 | 0.06 | 0.06 | 0.05 |

Figure 6 shows the locations of sources studied in this acoustic analysis in this theatre. We have located 6 sources in the stalls and 2 sources in some balconies in the second floor.

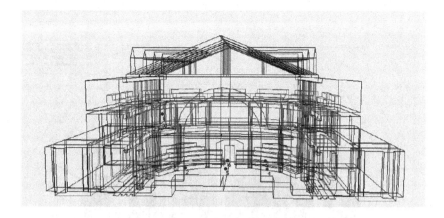

**Fig. 6.** Location of receivers

According to [7], social distribution was reflected in the seating arrangement. Figure 7 shows a graph of this distribution according to this study.

Therefore, we will analyze the distribution of speech transmission index (STI) in the stalls to relate the possible concentration of nobility with the quality of perception.

The ODEON software was used for acoustic simulation. We have made the acoustic tests on a grid in the seating area using a grid of 0.5 m of granularity and 1.2 m high (Table 2).

**Table 2.** Average acoustic parameters in the theatre.

|          | 125 Hz | 250 Hz | 500 Hz | 1000 Hz | 2000 Hz | 4000 Hz |
|----------|--------|--------|--------|---------|---------|---------|
| EDT (s)  | 1.25   | 1.15   | 1.03   | 1.22    | 1.12    | 0.88    |
| RT30 (s) | 1.35   | 1.24   | 1.06   | 1.30    | 1.23    | 0.97    |
| D50      | 0.45   | 0.47   | 0.55   | 0.51    | 0.45    | 0.51    |
| C80 (dB) | 2.2    | 2.8    | 4.0    | 3.0     | 2.5     | 4.3     |
| Ts (ms)  | 86     | 78     | 62     | 76      | 78      | 62      |
| LF80     | 0.272  | 0.274  | 0.240  | 0.258   | 0.272   | 0.268   |

Figure 8 shows the calculation of the STI carried out based on the acoustic simulation of the model, the distribution in the theatre stage (the presence of chairs and audience in the stage or in the boxes has not been taken into account). In this figure we observe a concentration of localities with a good STI in the central area and fanning out, which explains quite clearly the concentration of nobles in this area.

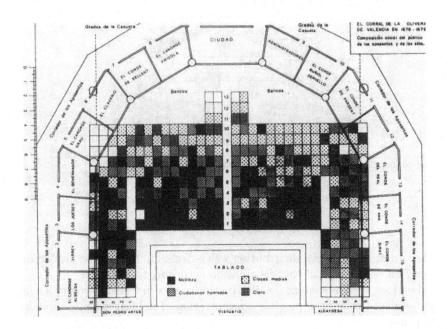

**Fig. 7.** Seating distribution and social sectors in the "Casa de Comèdies de la Olivera", in Valencia, according to Jean Mouyen (1981).

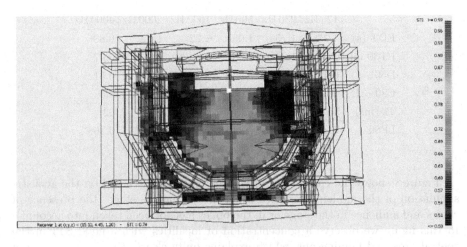

**Fig. 8.** STI distribution in the stalls

## 3.2   Integration of Graphical and Acoustical Models

The architectural model of the lost theatre was developed in 3D from the before mention studies using Rhinoceros 5. After the model was deemed accurate enough by experts in the field it was exported in *Filmbox*(.fbx) format in order to import the model into the Unity. Once the import process was completed and all textures and materials were accounted for, we proceeded to clone the project. This was done so we could have two identical projects, one using FMOD Studio, and another with Csound.

**FMOD.** The integration with unity is very simple, they already have available for the public a plug-in for Unity that connects the *master bank* of any FMOD project to the graphics engine. The only adjustments needed is making sure the FPSController has Unity's *Audio Source* disabled, and FMOD's *Studio Listener* script loaded as a component. Audio sources must do the same, but instead loading FMOD's *Studio Event Emitter* script loaded as a component. Now the user can chose any sound from the *Master Bank* as a source, with all the faders that where applied before in FMOD already applied on the sound source (Fig. 9).

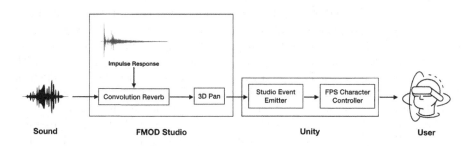

**Fig. 9.** FMOD and Unity integration

**Csound.** Making Csound work with Unity is more complicated than with FMOD. In older versions of Csound, the interface could only be done via the *Open Sound Control* (OSC) protocol as explained by Walsh [25], but it was deemed unstable in Csound 6. Doing further research and testing, the Csound-Unity wrapper developed by Walsh [24] was found to be the easiest way for interfacing both engines. After doing all the preprocessing in order to obtain all the parameters for the before mentioned opcodes, an instrument was implemented for each sound source. This limited all sound computing to Csound, while Unity only sent the controller's position and heading and listened to the audio outputs (Fig. 10).

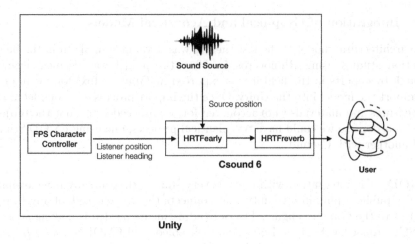

**Fig. 10.** Csound and Unity integration

## 4    Conclusions

The integration of different tools to work with any simulator or game that allows head movement independently of the body has been tested to develop a model of a lost building. On this particular paper, the setup is focused in virtual archeology to provide the user a sensorial experience and the analysis of a lost 16th century theatre in Valencia. The architectural model, which was developed in Rhinoceros 5, has been integrated in Unity Pro 5 in order to obtain visually and acoustically a first-person navigator. Using a developed module to allow head tracking as an input to select HRTFs, the integration with different possibilities as audio engine have been studied. As discussed, in order to achieve full immersion, the acoustic model has also been developed based in the documentation of the archives and different studies, in order to determine the absorption coefficients of the construction materials.

The model built out of the described geometry found in the documentation and texturized based on existing buildings in the same century. The acoustical calibration from the experimental IRs was not possible, but the simulation is based on historical buildings of this type. For that reason, the auralizations and visualizations developed can be considered of general interest.

In this work, we have also considered different options for 3D audio rendering apart from the usual 3D audio in Unity. All these options are related to the use of the impulse responses of any room, specifically applied to the integration of the graphical and acoustical model of the Olivera theatre. These options consider the use of FMOD and/or Csound for auralizing anechoic audio in real-time. In our case, these tools combined allow a powerful engine for theatrical studies in the Spanish Early-Modern theatre. This is the first study for a future database of buildings devoted to the theatrical performance.

**Acknowledgements.** This study has been partially supported by the Spanish Ministry of Economy and Innovation and FEDER funds in the research project with reference BIA2016-76957-C3-R and the Network of Excellence Consolider "Patrimonio teatral clásico español" with reference FFI.2015-71441-REDC.

# References

1. Sender, M., Planells, A., Perelló, R., Segura, J., Giménez, A.: Virtual acoustic reconstruction of a lost church: application to an Order of Saint Jerome monastery in Alzira, Spain. J. Build. Perform. Simul. **11**(3), 369–390 (2017). https://doi.org/10.1080/19401493.2017.1340975
2. Barba, A., Giménez, A.: El teatro principal de Valencia: acústica y arquitectura escénica. Ed. Generalitat Valenciana, Universitat Politècnica de València (2011)
3. Ros Andreu, J.Ll.: L'Efímer en la formació del Barroc valencià, 1599–1632. Doctoral Thesis, Universitat Politècnica de València (1981)
4. Sirera, J.L.: El teatro en Valencia durante los siglos XVI y XVII: la producciónb dramática valenciana en los orígenes de la comedia barroca. Ph.D. Thesis, Universidad de Valencia (1980)
5. Ros Andreu, J.L.: L'Efimer en la formació del Barroc valencià, 1599–1632. Ph.D. Thesis, Universitat Politècnica de Valencia (1981)
6. Mouyen, J.: El corral de la Olivera de Valencia en 1678 y 1682: tentativa de definición sociológica de su público. IIè. Colloque sur les Pays de la Couronne d'Aragon. Pau, Université de Pau (1981)
7. Mouyen, J.: Comedias y comediantes. Estudios sobre el teatro clásico español. Universitat de València (Dpto. Filología Española), Valencia (1991)
8. Mouyen, J.: Las casas de comedias de Valencia. In: Diez Borque, J.M.: Teatros del Siglo de Oro: Corrales y Coliseos en la Península Ibèrica, pp. 91–122. Cuadernos de Teatro Clásico, Madrid (1991)
9. Oleza, J.: La casa de comedias de La Olivera. Reconstrucción virtual de un teatro distinto. XVIII Congreso Internacional de la AITENSO. El personaje dramático en su discurso. Universidad Iberoamericana & El Colegio de México, México, 23–27 de octubre de 2017
10. Capitulació del modo i orde que se ha de tenir en fabricar la Casa de les Comèdies conforme les traces formades per les $SS^o$.s Administradors del Espital General. Archive of the Diputación de Valencia. Published by Juliá, Eduardo: "Nuevos datos sobre la Casa de la Olivera de Valencia" Boletín de la Real Academia Española, XXX, pp. 46–85 (1950)
11. Getting Started with FMOD in Unity. https://www.fmod.com/api. Accessed 15 Feb 2018
12. Lanham, M.: Game Audio Development with Unity 5.X. Packt Publishing (2017). https://www.safaribooksonline.com/library/view/game-audio-development/9781787286450/. Accessed 10 Mar 2018. ISBN: 9781787286450
13. Studio 3D Events. https://www.fmod.org/docs/content/generated/overview/3dstudio.html. Accessed 16 Feb 2018
14. Lazzarini, V., Yi, S., ffitch, J., Heintz, J., Brandtsegg, Ø., McCurdy, I.: Csound: A Sound and Music Computing System. Springer, Heidelberg (2016). https://doi.org/10.1007/978-3-319-45370-5. ISBN: 978-3-319-45370-5
15. Carty, B.: HRTFmove, HRTFstat, HRTFmove2: using the new HRTF Opcodes. Csound J. (9), 28 July 2008

16. Carty, B.: Hrtfearly and Hrtfreverb. Csound J. (16), 24 January 2012
17. ISO3382-1:2009: Acoustics. Measurement of room acoustic parameters. Part 1: Performance spaces (2009)
18. ISO3382-2:2008: Acoustics. Measurement of room acoustic parameters. Part 2: Reverberation time in ordinary rooms (2008)
19. M. S. Developments. http://www.winmls.com. Accessed 13 Dec 2015
20. Vorländer, M.: Auralization: Fundamentals of Acoustics, Modelling, Simulation, Algorithms and Acoustic Virtual Reality. Springer, Berlin (2008). https://doi.org/10.1007/978-3-540-48830-9
21. Savioja, L., Huopaniemi, J., Lokki, T., Väänänen, R.: Creating Interactive virtual acoustic environments. JAES 47(9), 675–705 (1999)
22. Christensen, C.L.: Odeon Room Acoustics Program, Version 10.1, User Manual, Industrial, Auditorium and Combined Editions. Odeon A/S, Lyngby (2009)
23. Dalënback, D.I.: CATT. Acoustics. http://www.catt.se/. Accessed 13 Dec 2015
24. Walsh, R.: Csound wrapper for Unity3d. http://rorywalsh.github.io/CsoundUnity/. Accessed 5 Feb 2018
25. Walsh, R.: Interfacing Csound and unity. Csound J. (19), 14 February 2014

# ViennAR: User-Centered-Design of a Bring Your Own Device Mobile Application with Augmented Reality

Andrea Schönhofer, Sabine Hubner, Perihan Rashed[(✉)], Wolfgang Aigner,
Peter Judmaier, and Markus Seidl

St. Pölten University of Applied Sciences,
Matthias Corvinus-Straße 15, 3100 St. Pölten, Austria
perihan.rashed@fhstp.ac.at

**Abstract.** In many museums it is still common that visitors have to read
static texts from boards to gain information about the exhibits. In times
where almost every visitor carries a smartphone in their pocket, these
devices could be utilized for a more personalized and interactive visitor
experience. In this paper we present a design study for a "Bring your own
device" setting that combines augmented reality (AR) and navigation in
museums. We applied an iterative user centered design approach that
included conceptual design, prototyping, user tests, as well as a field test
in a large museum in Vienna. One of the main results is that a new and
digital form of navigation isn't as essential as the museum thought it
would be. Apart from that the application was well received during the
field test.

**Keywords:** Mobile application · Augmented Reality · Navigation

## 1 Introduction

In general, applying AR in museums is not an entirely novel idea. However,
so far, museums who provide AR content usually offer loaned or permanently
mounted devices with pre-installed apps and content for visitors to experience
AR content. Another recent development is that nowadays almost all museum
visitors carry smartphones in their pockets which could be utilized to enhance
museum experiences. Therefore, we focused on the approach of *bring your own
device* in a museum context. Potential advantages of this approach are that more
museum visitors would have access to additional AR content, lowering the necessary effort for device maintenance, less cost for devices, and the convenience for
visitors to work with their own devices they are used to. Additionally, solutions
are possible that are more personalized and span multiple museums. Potential
disadvantages are, that museums as content providers have less control over the
devices used, software needs to be provided that fits a much broader spectrum
of devices and operating systems, and museums need to provide an easy way for
visitors to install and download software.

© Springer International Publishing AG, part of Springer Nature 2018
L. T. De Paolis and P. Bourdot (Eds.): AVR 2018, LNCS 10851, pp. 275–291, 2018.
https://doi.org/10.1007/978-3-319-95282-6_21

One of the main goals of this paper was to investigate users' needs and requirements and whether it is possible to create an application which will work under common conditions in a museum, e.g., the usually not satisfactory lighting of all exhibits. Therefore, we followed a user-centered design and prototyping approach that included problem analysis, conceptual design, prototypical implementation, and user evaluation phases.

The paper is divided into six sections. The following section discusses related work and the differences to other projects. Following that, section three presents the conceptual design, the methods we used, and their results. The following section explains the process of the prototypical implementation and the used technologies. Section 5 describes the prototype evaluations we conducted in form of a lab test and a field test at the Museum of Natural History in Vienna. Finally, Sect. 6 summarizes our results and gives an outlook to future work.

## 2    Related Work

Generally, AR apps have been on the market for quite some time now. Starting with only 2D representations and 2D target objects which improved to 3D with audio, movements, and interactions. Augmented reality has the potential to bring museums back to life. And this is a reason for museums for using this technology and seek for innovative improvements.

First, we will investigate related work of using AR in the context of museums. This section covers two fields. The first field are scientific approaches on augmented reality in museums. The second field are products used in museums. Generally, there are numerous museum AR apps on the market that could be taken as an example. We specifically picked three examples to exemplify different features compared to the other museum AR apps.

### 2.1    Scientific Literature

A paper that helped consider overlooked points is called "The Loupe" [11]. The Loupe is "a tangible Augmented Reality prototype in form of a magnifying lens, which allows museum visitors to get information in context about museum artifacts" [11]. The goal of this project was to test whether this prototype will increase visitors attention to the objects on display and improve their understanding or not. An issue that was brought up in terms of the design was the case of the prototype. The authors wanted the users to not perceive the iPhone that had the application on it, as a smartphone. Instead, the goal was to perceive it as a learning tool. Consequently, they did put the iPhone into a magnifying lens case, as it "invokes a metaphor and cultural form" [11]. The paper also mentions the technical struggles the developing team went through, for instance the environment of the artifacts and how it plays a role in the identification process of the objects. The authors mention issues like lighting, shadows, and reflections.

Yoon and Wang [17] "explore the accordances of an AR tool on learning that is focused on the science concept of magnets and magnetic fields" [17]. From their point of view, it was obvious that Augmented Reality is helping students construct and enhance their understanding, however, they wanted to understand the reason behind it and proof their hypothesis scientifically. Therefore, they studied the affect of AR on seventy students from the fifth to the seventh grade. In order to proof their hypothesis they created two groups of students, one was learning with the help of AR and the other one without. Their findings supported their hypotheses, since the group of students that was learning through Augmented Reality continued to interact with the magnets much longer than the other group with much more teamwork and engagement. After the students' actions were observed, they were interviewed to get feedback on the product. The interview results scored the highest at being visible and dynamic. In the interview 'visible' stood for allowing users to see things that are normally invisible and 'dynamic' stood for displaying the phenomenon in motion showing changes over time.

## 2.2 Examples Applied in Museums

In July 2016 the History Trust South Australia published an article saying, "[e]veryone is going Pokmon Go crazy in Adelaide and both the South Australian Maritime Museum and National Motor Museum are getting in on the act" [8]. From there, they have decided to provide a 3D AR application when scanning the artifacts displayed as for example shown in Fig. 1. The exhibition that was used as context showcased original sketches and paintings created by Charles Alexandre Lesueur and Nicolas Martin Petit during their exploration voyage of Australia in 1800.

**Fig. 1.** Screenshots of the History Trust South Australia Museum augmented reality app [8].

Another museum that has been using AR for years is the Toronto Royal Ontario Museum. The idea of the application is to help visitors visualize how dinosaurs may have looked like in the past. As you can see Fig. 2, there are different stations where visitors can use permanently mounted iPads to experience AR.

**Fig. 2.** Augmented Reality stations at the Royal Ontario Museum Toronto [7]

In contrast to our project, we do not want to have fixed devices, instead we follow the idea of "Bring your own Device". Therefore, users have the freedom to move around with their devices, see the artifact in 360 degrees and even use their device in groups.

As third example, the Art Gallery of Ontario managed to increase their visitors' interest by introducing AR content [4]. As you can see in Fig. 3, their application allows families and friends to play a treasure hunting game. The user gets six objects that are located in the actual paintings of the exhibition, which they are asked to hunt. Each mission contains six objects, and after each mission, a locked prize gets unlocked and a new mission starts. During this journey, "interactive quiz questions and creative AR puzzles reveal exciting secrets behind the artwork" [13]. The application is based on the Time Tremors television series, which talks about a journey of two kids traveling through time to hunt for historical objects and learn about them. The museum succeeded at motivating many families and groups of friends to visit exhibitions and learn through fun ways. Moreover, during the past two years, the hunting game is spreading globally at international museums [15].

To sum up, the three examples mentioned had their advantages and their disadvantages. The History Trust Museum, offered its app on the visitors' smart phones, however its information representation was very limited. The users were only able to see a 3D model of the fish, without any background information about it. The Toronto Royal Ontario Museum managed to represent its artifact information in a innovative way. The information was only visual and the user was at least able to visualize how a dinosaur would move and look like with flesh. However, there was no sound or any kind of storytelling in the app and the this experience was only stationary, i.e., visitors could not experience AR with their own devices.

Explore and hunt for treasures at the AGO for the ability to collect a rare future Time Treasure!

**Fig. 3.** Time Tremors Game, gaming interaction in groups [15]

# 3    Conceptual Design

In this chapter we will describe the concept of the implemented application and the steps of the process taken until the final user test we conducted.

The application we designed for the Natural History Museum Vienna consists of an graphical intro section which provides an overview of the app itself as well as some background information about the museum, like the most important exhibitions (see Fig. 4). The user is able to see a digital plan of the museum where all of the exhibition rooms are displayed. With the navigation part the user can be guided to the exhibits where augmented reality content is available. The current navigation is implemented as slide show of pictures which show the correct way to the exhibits. The augmented reality part of the application is the centerpiece on which we concentrated the most during the implementation. It consists of a 3D animation which plays automatically when a target was detected. In the animation a virtual "Venus of Willendorf" - which is one of the exhibition highlights in the Natural History Museum in Vienna - tells a story about the history of the museum and two different exhibits (Fig. 4).

## 3.1    Design Process

Before the realization of the application, as described in Sect. 4, interviews with three different museums were conducted and personas and scenarios [10] were created for the target audience. Further steps were a structure for the application, screen designs and a paper prototype [14].

### 3.1.1    Interviews in Museums

The project started in autumn 2016 with a brainstorming session about which interactive experiences we could provide in a museum in the context of a *bring*

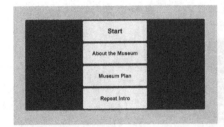

**Fig. 4.** Screenshots of the graphical interface of the application and the 3D animation with the virtual "Venus of Willendorf"

*your own device* approach. This eventuated in three main ideas: deliver additional content to the museum visitors via an application (1) in form of video, audio and text, (2) in form of augmented reality, or (3) as digital navigation through the museum building. These ideas were presented to representatives of three different museums in Austria. After the feedback and insights from the museums we decided to focus on augmented reality and navigation, specifically in the context of the Natural History Museum in Vienna.

### 3.1.2    Target Group, Personas, and Scenarios

Together with the museum, the main target group was defined. These are technically oriented adults aged between 30 and 50 years who own a smartphone, speak either German or English, and are visiting the museum in groups up to three persons. Also adults with hearing and visual impairment belong to the target group. This target group was chosen because in the past there weren't any interactive installations in the museum especially for adults. Out of the target group, we finally specified three different personas and created an individual scenario for each of them [10]. The first persona is a woman with 47 years who planned an interesting and pleasant visit in the museum with her husband and their friends. The second persona is a 43 years old interpreter who is visually impaired. He wanted a visit in the museum with his wife with as hassle-free as possible. Finally, a 30-year-old American woman who works as an assistant professor was the third persona we created. Her goal was to gain new experiences and extend her knowledge.

### 3.1.3    Card Sorting

One of the first methods used to determine the information architecture was card sorting [16]. It is a fast, efficient and cheap method, to structure content needed in our solution. The sessions included 450 values/functions and 9 participants. Our participants were all students and were aged between 20 and 30 years. Each subject was asked to organize the content of the application into groups and come up with meaningful group names (topics), in way that would make sense to them. This helped us understand which features belong together and how they should be grouped. Moreover, it helped us dramatically with our next step of creating wireframes. We were able to organize the needed functions and steps in a logical and efficient way. This resulted in achieving a more user-friendly app. This was a particularly important goal, since the AR technology we used is not well spread nowadays and not everyone knows how to use it.

### 3.1.4   App Structure

In a further step, a page overview diagram was created where all of the planned pages of the application and the interaction between them can be seen (Fig. 5). Museum visitors can first adjust the basic settings like the language followed by an intro page. Afterwards they can get directly to the main page where it is possible to change the settings and get help. From the main page the visitors can view a plan of the museum, see the available services (restaurant, shop, toilet etc.) and all the areas and exhibits as well as the exhibits in the immediate surrounding. From there it is possible to call up the navigation part of the application. For this, it is planned to use iBeacons [1] for automatically determining one's location and support navigation through the museum. Also, additional information about the individual exhibits are available. The AR part of the application can be viewed after the navigation or directly after choosing a certain exhibit and standing there. In the AR part it is possible to take a photo with the 3D animations and share it on other social media platforms like Facebook, Instagram or WhatsApp. Moreover, the full text search can be called up from all pages of the application.

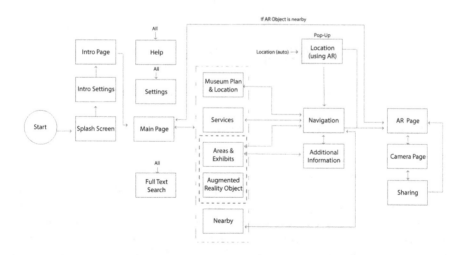

**Fig. 5.** Page structure of the application

### 3.1.5   Lego-Based Prototyping and Paper Prototypes

Before creating the wireframes [12], we created a user journey using lego bricks. This allowed us to visualize the path of each user and to organize the functions of the app. In the next phase we created paper prototypes [14] and tested them at the usability lab of our university with four users. During the user test, we used thinking aloud as main method, i.e., we asked the users to say what is going on in their minds while testing our prototypes instead of us interrupting them with our questions.

### 3.1.6   Screen Designs

To provide a sense of how the application should look like, more polished screen designs were created. Examples can be seen in Fig. 6. The first screen pictures the page "areas and exhibits" of the page structure in Fig. 5 and shows the list of the exhibits where an AR part is available (the list is filtered by AR). The second screen illustrates the AR page of the application. The final look of the page, where the different services of the museum are listed, can be seen in the third screen and the navigation part in the fourth screen.

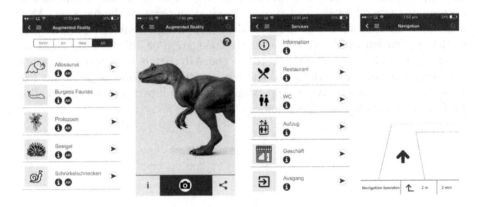

Fig. 6. Screen designs of the final application

## 4   Prototypical Implementation

As already mentioned, one of our main goals was to offer an AR application that can be used on a broad range of different smartphones. In a first step, we looked for technical environments which support at least the two mainly used operating systems iOS and Android [6]. We decided to use the development platform Unity [2] in combination with Vuforia [3] as they support both operating systems, are free to use, and provide a good level of support as well as a lively community. Unity is a game development platform for 3D and 2D games. It can be used to deploy games across mobile, desktop, Virtual Reality/Augmented Reality, consoles or the Web [2]. Vuforia is an AR platform which supports phones, tablets and digital eye-wear across Android, iOS, and UWP. With the version 2017.2, Unity integrated the Vuforia engine into their platform [3].

Another tool we used was Maya, a computer animation and modeling software from Autodesk [5]. We used it for the modeling of the 3D models for the animations of the augmented reality part in the application. First, we not only used Maya for modeling but also for the creation of the animations of the models. Then, they were exported into the Unity 3D-scene. But then we recognized that this procedure prevented us from scaling the 3D-models afterwards in Unity and it was also not possible to bring them into the right position in the 3D-scene anymore. Therefore, we decided to do the whole animations in Unity.

### 4.1 Technical Architecture

One of our ambitions in the project was to avoid the attachment of any markers in the museum like a bar or QR code for the recognition of the AR part. So our original plan was to use the exhibits in the museum themselves as targets for the AR function. With the use of targets, the AR Camera in the Vuforia package is able to track and render the corresponding virtual content for each of the exhibits as well as their positions. Unfortunately, the Vuforia platform at that time only supported the scanning of smaller objects for the use as 3D targets (like toys which could fit on a table). Also, these 3D scans did not work very well as there were often too less features on the objects which could be recognized by the software. After these insights, we decided to use image targets (markers), like the logo of the museum, for the detection of an exhibit as they showed stable recognition performance.

The overall architecture of the implementation can be seen below in Fig. 7. As mentioned before, the 3D-models where designed in Maya and exported to Unity, where the animations where created. Also the GUI for the application was built in Unity. The Vuforia engine supplied the targets, the AR camera as well as the necessary software packages for the augmented reality visualizations. The finished application was then installed on the iOS and Android devices. After opening the AR camera and scanning the image target (marker), the AR animation started to play automatically.

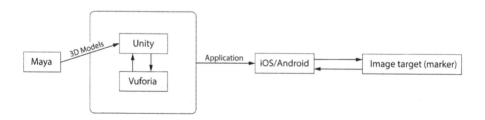

**Fig. 7.** Technical architecture of the implementation

## 5 Evaluation

### 5.1 Lab Test

This section summarizes the outcomes of the first user test we conducted with our working prototype. The underlying user story went as follows: The "Venus of Willendorf" takes the users on a virtual tour, where she would present her favorite artifacts at the museum. While the story is being told, she relates the objects to each other. Her favorite objects at the museum are the famous Bull Figure, the Dom-Pedro-Dose, and the first entrance ticket to the museum (see Fig. 8). The test took place at the usability lab of our university. For this test, we used Android devices. Each user was given the choice to either borrow one of our devices or download the app on the Android smartphone. For this test the following materials/devices were needed: cameras and microphones to record the test, printed room plan of the lab for the navigation, Android devices with the app installed, and the AR targets and their descriptions. The subjects were all students at the university and their age range was between 20 and 45 years.

**Fig. 8.** The first entrance ticket

*Procedure.* The user test was conducted with 7 individual users and a group of 3 users (see Fig. 9). After welcoming the users and installing the app on their smartphones, each one was given a room plan with the artifacts marked on it. The users were also given the option to borrow a device from us, with the app installed. All what they were told was to read the introductory text for the museum tour and to finish the tour till the end. The lab had 4 cameras, therefore the whole test was recorded with audio and video. After the test, the users were surveyed and gave their own feedback on the product.

*Hypotheses and measurement.* The survey questions were divided into three categories. First, questions about the content of the virtual Venus, second, questions about the content of the text panels, and third, general questions about the application. Categories 1 and 2 were evaluated using a Likert-Scale. There were six hypotheses in this test:

1. A museum visit with augmented reality content is more fun.
2. Content conveyed through augmented reality can be remembered better by museum visitors.

**Fig. 9.** User testing the first prototype during the first user test.

3. Scanning an artifact by scanning a sticker works better than by scanning the object itself.
4. Using the app on your own smart-phone is easier than using a borrowed device.
5. Augmented reality content is easier to consume than printed text.
6. Text panels are rather poorly read.

There were six measures for the hypothesis mentioned:

1. How attentively are the text panels next to the objects read?
2. Will the users better notice the content of the text panels or the augmented reality content?
3. How much time do the users need to scan the objects?
4. How much time do the users take for the test?
5. How well do the subjects like the augmented reality content?
6. Are certain things unclear during the test?

*Test Results.* A few technical problems, such as the interruption of the animations, occurred during the test which might have affected the impression of the users. However, the results of the test provided a lot of helpful feedback. For example, the explanation was rated as good and very friendly, the tour was perceived very personal, the subjects liked the idea of a virtual tour, the presentation of the information, the fact that they could listen and see information at the same time, as well as being able to display important places. In terms of critical notes, for some participants it was not clear what needed to be scanned, the zoom function had to be explained, the interruption of the animations was perceived as disturbing, the portrait and landscape function was not clear, and mainly technical problems were noticeable and needed to be improved. Most of the hypotheses were supported and six of the subjects would download the app on their smartphones. Moreover, from the 12 possible points in the final questions, the average score was 9.6 points. These questions were about the story of the museum and information related to the rest of the artifacts in the test. While questions where their content could only be found in the text panels, only an average of 1.75 points was reached. Furthermore, according to the users, borrowing a device or using their own device did not affect their journey. All users expressed that the tour with the Venus, which included text and images, is more fun than just reading printed text and only one user attempted to read the printed text. They also self-reported that for them it is easier to remember the AR communicated content than the usual printed text.

## 5.2   Field Test

This section contains information about a field test we conducted on two consecutive days in January 2018 in the Natural History Museum in Vienna. The main goal of this test was to find out if the developed application is comprehensible and user-friendly. Further, we wanted to know how museum visitors like the application and if the defined hypotheses are supported.

*Experiment Design.* The test was designed in two parts. In the first part, the participants were asked to answer six questions about the story the "Venus of Willendorf" told in the AR animation. In the second part, the test persons were asked general questions and their opinions about the application. The participants where observed by the testing team and observations were captured as notes. Also, the screen of the used devices was recorded during the test to measure any issues and also the testing time.

*Pretest.* Three weeks before the final user test we also executed a pretest in the museum, to check if there are any relevant problems with the application or the test settings which should be fixed before the final test. There didn't occur any technical problems, but we found out that it is necessary to also prepare an English version of the application as a lot of visitors in the museum were tourists who couldn't understand the prepared German version.

## 5.3   Participants

During the two days, the application was tested 20 times, either from an individual test person or from groups up to 6 persons. All participants were visitors of the museum and were asked to voluntarily try out the application we developed. The participants were adults between about 18 and 50 years. 11 of the tests were taken in English and 9 in German.

*Apparatus.* We installed the test setting in an exhibition room of the museum. On a table we prepared different iOS and Android devices (smartphones and tablets) with the developed application. Because of the noise in the museum, we also organized a headset for a better understanding of the audio during the AR animation. The logo of the museum, which served as the marker for the AR animation, was placed on a frame for easier scanning. The whole setup can be seen in Fig. 10. Apart from that, we generated a website with a slide show of pictures which showed the way to the exhibition room with our test setting and also to the "Venus of Willendorf" as well as the first entrance ticket (the two exhibits mentioned in story of the AR animation).

**Fig. 10.** Test person trying out the application at the test setting in the museum

*Procedure.* The test started at the entrance hall of the museum where the potential test persons were divided into two groups. One group received a QR-Code with the URL of the website that included an illustrated description of the way to our test setting, the "Venus of Willendorf", and the first entrance ticket. The other group received a traditional floor plan printed on a sheet of paper where the way to our test setting was marked. Overall, eight QR-Codes and two floor plans were handed out. In the room where the test setting was installed, visitors who came by were asked if they would like to test an application which was developed in cooperation with the museum. Then they could choose one of the prepared devices. After opening the app and starting the screen recording, the devices were passed to the test persons. So they could freely interact with the application. We only helped them if they had any questions or problems during the usage. After they said they are finished, we asked them the prepared questions (see Sect. 5.2). Furthermore, we showed them the different navigation options (website and printed plan) and asked them which of them they would rather use.

*Hypotheses.* There were 5 hypotheses we investigated in this test:

- The tested application has added value for the museum.
- A virtual buddy is able to provide information more deeply.
- The "Venus of Willendorf" is a better virtual buddy than another figure from another section of the museum.
- The application can be used by groups consisting of up to three persons.
- Test persons do not confuse navigation elements with design elements.

*Results.* **Hypotheses.** Four out of the five hypotheses mentioned in the previous paragraph were supported by the results. According to the subjects, using AR made them remember lots of information that was told by the "Venus of Willendorf". One group consisting of six persons used the application without any problems. Only the hypothesis investigating the "Venus of Willendorf" as a better virtual buddy could not be accepted. 6 persons preferred the figure, the rest would like to see other figures as tellers of the story.

**Navigation.** Unfortunately, only two of the persons whom we gave the QR-Code or the floor plan visited the test setting in the exhibition room. One person with a QR-Code and one with the printed plan. A possible reason for this could be that most of the visitors in museums just stroll around the rooms. Another reason could be that they don't wanted to follow the given route. It is also possible that they just couldn't find the way with the help of the website with the illustrated description or the printed floor plan. One insight from the test was, that most of the test persons said that they would prefer the printed plan over the slide show navigation.

**Application with AR animation.** 10 out of 20 visitors who tested the application at our test setting mentioned that they liked the 3D-animation. A further answer from 4 persons was that they liked the easy use of the application. 15 out of 20 persons would install the application on their own smartphones. 6 persons liked the "Venus of Willendorf" as the teller of the story, but the rest would like to have another virtual buddy, as for example a dinosaur or a scientist. Overall, the test worked well without any major problems during the use of the application. The visitors, which are interested in new technologies, would like to use such an application on their own devices in the museum. Only a few small technical problems occurred (see Sect. 6), but conclusively we can say that they did not affect the test persons during the final user test.

# 6   Conclusion and Future Work

One of the two main goals was to determine if it is possible to create an application for the Natural History Museum Vienna which works under typical conditions there. During our first visit in this museums our contact person told us that they would like to have an application for mobile devices which combines AR and navigation. The navigation part was very important to them, because, in their opinion, most visitors have difficulties with finding their way through the museum. They also wanted us to create content with AR that shows information besides the typical static texts from boards along exhibits. The second goal was to find out if visitors would like to have and to use such an application on their own smartphones. Both of these goals were achieved during the process of working with the museum. To validate our solution, a field test was conducted in the museum.

The described application was created with the softwares Vuforia and Unity. Unfortunately, the used version of Unity and Vuforia caused development problems because of software bugs. One big issue was that the AR camera was active the whole time although the according scene in Unity was only just invoked by selecting the start button in the application. Another problem this software bug caused was the combination of the English and German version in one application. The idea was to create a start screen were the users could choose between those two languages, but this was not possible. As a solution we created two different versions of the application. Indeed, since then Unity and Vuforia published new versions which already eliminated that problems, but during the development process of our application it wasn't possible to update the software.

One particularly interesting insight was, that it is not that simple to use an exhibit from the museum as a marker for scanning. We figured out that scanning objects have to have a quite small size, they should be as symmetrical as possible, they should show a high contrast, and they should be rather broad than high. One of the first objects that we tested as a marker was a "Venus of Willendorf" figurine. It is about 11 cm high, mostly brown or beige and her surface is relatively sleek. So the software wasn't able to recognize this object as a marker. As a further object we tried to use a toy dinosaur. This also wasn't much better because it didn't show a lot of contrast at all. After some samplings and research, we decided to use the logo of the museum as a marker for our final user test as it worked fine.

Despite all these problems, the app was well received by the potential users. 15 out of 20 persons would install the application on their own smartphone if they visit the museum. This aspect confirmed one of our goals that was to find out if visitors of the museum would like to have and to use such an application.

During the development process of the concept there was the idea of deploying an extensive application for the Natural History Museum Vienna. The current prototype of this app only contains one marker and one story that the "Venus of Willendorf" tells. In the museum there are 100 objects that are specially highlighted. Step by step those objects and further stories could be implemented in the app. In the concept of the application it was planned to build a 3D navigation to all of these 100 objects and further important places like the restaurant or the elevator. For this implementation an indoor navigation system with iBeacons could be implemented, based on the technical infrastructure we described in [9].

One of the final questions for the visitors was, if there was something in the app they did not like. Two people answered that they don't like that the story stops if they lose the marker. Another question for the users was if they like the "Venus of Willendorf" as their virtual buddy through the story. 16 out of 20 persons would prefer another object like a dinosaur or a scientist. A possible solution for this is that the users can choose between several virtual buddies or different buddies could be used in different sections of the museum.

The project showed that applying AR in the context of museums is a promising approach. But especially when it comes to the bring-your-own-device aspect the technology is not fully developed yet, as it can be seen by the problems occurred during the implementation of such an application.

**Acknowledgements.** We thank the Natural History Museum Vienna, especially Mag. Iris Ott, for supporting us in the conception of the prototype and for facilitating the field test in the museum. This work was supported by the Austrian Federal Ministry of Science, Research and Economy under the FFG COIN program (MEETeUX project, no. 7209770).

# References

1. iBeacon - Apple Developer: https://developer.apple.com/ibeacon/
2. Unity: https://unity3d.com
3. Vuforia | Augmented Reality. https://www.vuforia.com/
4. Home | AGO Art Gallery of Ontario (2014). http://www.ago.net/home
5. Maya | Computer Animation & Modeling Software | Autodesk (2017). https://www.autodesk.com/products/maya/overview
6. Mobile OS market share 2017, August 2017. https://www.statista.com/statistics/266136/global-market-share-held-by-smartphone-operating-systems/
7. Royal Ontario Museum: (2017). https://www.rom.on.ca/en/node
8. SA Museums embrace virtual and augmented reality | History Trust of South Australia (2017). http://corporate.historysa.com.au/media-releases/sa-museums-embrace-virtual-and-augmented-reality
9. Blumenstein, K., Kaltenbrunner, M., Seidl, M., Breban, L., Thür, N., Aigner, W.: Bringing your own device into multi-device ecologies: a technical concept. In: Proceedings of the 2017 ACM International Conference on Interactive Surfaces and Spaces, ISS 2017, pp. 306–311. ACM, New York, (2017). https://doi.org/10.1145/3132272.3132279, ISBN:978-1-4503-4691-7
10. Cooper, A., Reimann, R., Cronin, D., Noessel, C.: About Face: The Essentials of Interaction Design. Wiley, Hoboken (2014). ISBN:978-1-118-76658-3
11. Damala, A., Hornecker, E., van der Vaart, M., van Dijk, D., Ruthven, I.: The Loupe tangible augmented reality for learning to look at Ancient Greek art. Int. J. Mediterr. Archaeol. Archaeom. **16**(5), 73–85 (2016). http://strathprints.strath.ac.uk/57659/

12. Hamm, M.J.: Wireframing Essentials. Packt Publishing Ltd., Birmingham (2014). ISBN:978-1-84969-855-9
13. Xenophile Media Inc.: Time Tremors : AGO, June 2014. https://play.google.com/store/apps/details?id=ca.xenophile.timetremors.agoandroid&hl=en
14. Sefelin, R., Tscheligi, M., Giller, V.: Paper prototyping - what is it good for?: a comparison of paper- and computer-based low-fidelity prototyping, pp. 778–779. ACM, April 2003. ISBN:978-1-58113-637-1, https://doi.org/10.1145/765891.765986
15. Time Tremors: Time Tremors AGO App Trailer - CBC (2014). https://www.youtube.com/watch?v=3CVU318lP24
16. Usability.gov: Card Sorting, October 2013. https://www.usability.gov/how-to-and-tools/methods/card-sorting.html
17. Yoon, S.A., Wang, J.: Making the invisible visible in science museums through augmented reality devices. TechTrends **58**(1), 49–55 (2014). https://doi.org/10.1007/s11528-013-0720-7. ISSN 1559-7075

# Comparing Different Storytelling Approaches for Virtual Guides in Digital Immersive Museums

Marcello Carrozzino[1(✉)], Marianna Colombo[2], Franco Tecchia[1],
Chiara Evangelista[1], and Massimo Bergamasco[1]

[1] Scuola Superiore Sant'Anna, Perceptual Robotics Laboratory,
Institute of Communication, Information and Perception Technologies, Pisa, Italy
{m.carrozzino, f.tecchia, c.evangelista,
m.bergamasco}@santannapisa.it
[2] Department of Filologia, Letteratura e Linguistica,
Università di Pisa, Pisa, Italy
marianna.colombo89@gmail.com

**Abstract.** Virtual museums are becoming increasingly popular, especially thanks to the recent spread of low-cost immersive technologies enabling even small cultural realities to enrich their technology-based offer. The growing availability of computational power and high-quality visual elements enables the use of virtual characters in order to add depth to the virtual visit experience, up to nowadays often limited to the exploration of lifeless environments. This paper presents a pilot study aimed at investigating the positive effects that the use of avatars can provide to a virtual cultural experience, proposing a virtual museum with three different alternatives of storytelling, including one featuring virtual humans, and comparing the results in terms of engagement and understanding of the proposed content.

**Keywords:** Virtual Reality · Immersive technologies · Cultural heritage
Virtual humans · Avatar · Storytelling

## 1 Introduction

The meaning of cultural heritage is constantly evolving. Because of the increasing request of a more engaging experience while learning, the traditional way to communicate culture has been progressively enhanced with the use of new technologies.

The most popular technology used for reenacting past cultures and link them with their original environment is Virtual Reality. Creating 3D virtual worlds for cultural heritage applications is being credited as the most affordable, dynamic and interactive option for integrating environment, objects and knowledge associated with a culture [1]. Bringing together culture and new technologies can improve the learning experience of the non-experts, such as children, students and enthusiasts.

However, 3D virtual reconstructions of sites are often only composed of architectural components, objects and other unanimated elements, thus providing a limited experience to the users. Consequently, the current trend is to populate these virtual

L. T. De Paolis and P. Bourdot (Eds.): AVR 2018, LNCS 10851, pp. 292–302, 2018.
https://doi.org/10.1007/978-3-319-95282-6_22

worlds with *avatars* or virtual humans, that have an appearance and behavior very similar (hopefully identical) to the original historical inhabitants of the reconstructed sites. Such virtual actors may interact with the environment, with one another and with the user by human-like behaviour (moving, speaking, using tools and other artefacts, etc.).[1] These new figures provide a more stimulating way to learn historical facts, as users are typically more involved and their concentration level is stronger.

The aim of this paper is to study of the positive effects that the use of avatars can provide to the educational experience, proposing a virtual museum with three different alternatives of storytelling, including one featuring virtual humans, and comparing the results in terms of engagement and understanding of the proposed content.

## 2    Previous Work

A virtual human is defined as a computer-generated character with the appearance of a human being. This term is used to indicate two virtual figures having different abilities: virtual agents and avatars. A virtual agent is a digital and interactive character, with or without human appearance, presenting several human abilities - like cognition or verbal/non-verbal communication – managed by some form of artificial intelligence. An avatar is a graphical digital representation of a human user, in either a two-dimensional (images, static or moving) or a three-dimensional form (i.e. characters from video games or virtual worlds).

A thorough study of the state of the art about this topic [1] has identified two macro categories of applications: those providing interaction with the users, and the ones that do not. Other possible taxonomies subdivide applications by content, identifying growing levels of immersion and interaction (if present): 2D animated, 3D animated, 3D immersive, Serious games. Users can relate to virtual agents or simply listen to their explanations. Single virtual humans with enhanced interaction capabilities are commonly used [2, 3] as the user's avatar in 3D immersive environments or when the situation requires a single counterpart (like in the case of virtual guides [4]), in other words in circumstances where the VH and the user must interact closely [5]. Multiple avatars [6, 7] (even crowds [8, 9]) are instead opportune to populate virtual reconstructions where the user explores large environments and the VHs are used for increased realism.

Modern cultural heritage application involving VHs nowadays provide a high quality visual interface, at the same time fostering the enhancement of the interaction between the user and the virtual agent, through natural and body language or other means of non-verbal communication. In the case of virtual guides, a high degree of realism and human-like verbal skills and personality traits, are required features in order to maximize their social acceptance and to increase the user engagement. Conclusions from this research point out that the use of virtual actors is able to stimulate a high quality learning experience, especially for young users. Many applications using

---

[1] Virtual Humans in cultural applications: a review. Octavian M. Machidon, Mihai Duguleana, Marcello Carrozzino, p. 1.

virtual actors have been developed following the *edutainment* concept, where learning is associated with having fun.

# 3 The Study

The research hereby presented is related to the investigation about the opportunities provided by virtual humans in digital learning environments dealing with cultural elements. The experiment presents users with an interactive visit of a virtual gallery of art objects, subdivided in rooms each related to a specific historical period, proposing three different types of aid assisting the visit:

- traditional expository panels, where explanations about the artworks are shown in text form;
- narrating voice, simulating a typical museum audio guide;
- virtual human, guiding the users around the virtual gallery.

The development of the application has taken into consideration the typology of contents in order to study the different emotional- cognitive reactions of the users. During the preliminary writing of the texts for the expository panels and the narrating voice, particular attention was paid to the definition of complete and concise information. In the same way, the creation of the virtual model involved an accurate selection of elements (3D models and textures) immediately conveying the idea of the historic period of the rooms.

The virtual gallery, modeled using Autodesk 3D Studio Max, is composed by five rooms:

- Entrance
- Egyptian room
- Classical room
- Medieval-Viking room
- Art gallery

**Fig. 1.** Top-view of the virtual gallery

The entrance is a basic room providing access to the virtual gallery. The Egyptian room includes artworks from the V dynasty (2500–2350 B.C) and the XXVI dynasty (672–525 B.C). The environment features materials coherent with the historic period: hieroglyphics on the walls and rock tiles on the floor, to avoid a too invasive appearance. The Classical room includes sculptures and busts from the period 130–200 B.C. The space is composed by a pink marble colonnade, and other architectural elements textured with white marble, following the appearance of ancient classical temples. The Medieval-Viking room conserves different typologies of items: weapons, shields, coins and chess pieces. The style is rustic; walls are textured with rock bricks and the floor with dark wood. The last room reunites the most important artworks from Renaissance (XIV–XVI sec.) to contemporary age (1789-present). The pieces are key examples of every artistic movement, to help the user understand the history and evolution of the different artistic styles.

The items in the rooms are 3D models downloaded from *Sketchfab*[2]; in particular the British Museum offers several free 3D models of famous artworks with textures, many of which has been used in the Virtual Gallery. Coins and paintings have been modeled texturing simple 3D models with a jpg image of the original artwork. Every room features photometric lights, whose effects have been embedded in the 3D models

**Fig. 2.** Views of the virtual gallery rooms

---

[2] https://sketchfab.com/.

of artworks using lightmaps. The interactive application presenting the three virtual itineraries has been developed with XVR [10], an integrated development environment for the rapid development of Virtual Reality applications.

The structure of the virtual itinerary is composed by a series of viewpoints, which enable the exploration of the virtual gallery in a predefined sequence. Once in a room, the user is free to move around and explore the objects; however, when leaving the room, the next room is always the one predefined in the sequence.

## 4 The Three Itineraries

### 4.1 First Itinerary: Panels

In the first itinerary the learning process is regulated by fluctuating expository panels recalling a traditional museum visit. The fluctuating expository panels have been implemented as billboard, constantly pointing toward the observer. The style of explanations is fluid, not educational: only main concepts are presented in order avoid a decline in the attention level of the user. In the art gallery, panels focus on the meaning of the painting and on the idea of the artist.

During the virtual tour the panels are arranged in strategic points: one at the entrance of each room, with information related to the corresponding historic period, and one near every item, presenting the corresponding description. Panels appear when the user is located at a specific position and disappear when the user proceeds towards the next positions.

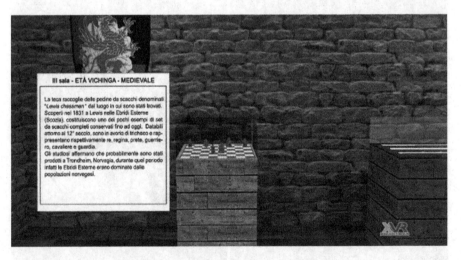

**Fig. 3.** View of the first itinerary, panels

## 4.2    Second Itinerary: Audio Guide

In the second itinerary, the user is guided through the virtual gallery by a narrating voice which describes and explains the content of each room. To keep a high attention level, the voice is young and comfortable. Contents are brief, with some sentences devoted to guide the users during the visit through the rooms, welcoming and inviting the user to proceed to the next. Following the same structure of the first itinerary, the audio content start when the user is placed in a specific position. The audio tracks have been implemented as 3D audio objects placed in the same position of the examined artwork.

## 4.3    Third Itinerary: Virtual Guide

In the third itinerary information is provided by a virtual actor with the same narrative outline of the second itinerary. The integration of the virtual actor in the XVR environment has been made by means of the Speaking Avatar class, an XVR class [11] offering features for the management of character animation and lip-sync with audio files or speech to text, based on the following mid-level tools:

HALCA (Hardware Accelerated Library for Character Animation), a library [12] based on Cal3D allowing to visualize and animate simultaneously several realistic avatars on simple display desktop, HDM's and CAVE-like devices.

SAPI (Speech Application Programming Interface), a Windows API providing a speech recognition feature retrieving text from audio data identifying phonemes and their duration. The Annosoft Speech Recognizer, based on SAPI, creates a text file of the sequences of such phonemes which are furtherly translated into *visemes* (the visual equivalent of phonemes, consisting in basilar postures of the mouth) in order to create a plausible lip sync.

The virtual actor is a young male character whose appearance of the avatar is extremely realistic: he always looks at users and engages with them, with a tone and a

**Fig. 4.** View of the third itinerary, virtual guide

voice coherent with his appearance and his casual outfit. The agent is positioned aside of every item, according to the behavior of a traditional museum guide.

## 5 Pilot User Study

The virtual application has been tested in a non-immersive desktop setup by 15 people, using a combination of mouse and keyboard for their interaction. Users have been divided into three groups, each one following a specific itinerary. Before starting the virtual tour, users had to compile a brief questionnaire aimed to collect personal information and previous knowledge with VR and digital cultural environments.

The user sample is composed of 7 male and 8 female subjects aged between 22 and 32. The education level varies from high school (2 users, 1 M and 1 F), bachelor degree (5 users, 2 M and 3 F), master degree (6 users, 3 M and 3F) and Ph.D. (2 users, 1 M and 1 F).

The duration of the test was different depending on the specific itinerary. The visit of the first itinerary lasts approximately 30 min, as it requires the additional effort of reading the panels, the other two last approximately 20 min, a difference that may has consequences on the attention level. After the visit, users completed a test with specific questions related to the items/artwork exposed in the gallery and questions about their emotional feelings, cognitive experience and engagement during the experience.

Questions relative to feelings, cognitive experience and comprehension had answers ranging from 1 (nothing) until 7 (totally).

The first question was: "How much was your senses involved in the virtual visit?" The diagram in Fig. 1 shows a high engagement level for the third itinerary and a strong variability for the second itinerary with a different interest level. This score could be due to a different academic background. Users with lower experience in virtual museums gave a high score in the test, while users with more competence in virtual cultural heritage gave a low score. Previous experiences in VR field have probably influenced the level of engagement during the virtual experience (Fig. 5).

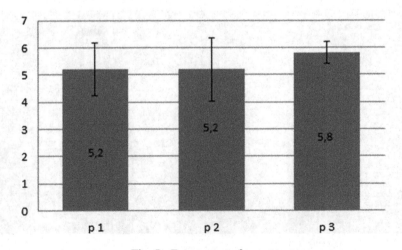

**Fig. 5.** Engagement of senses

The general appearance of the virtual museum involved mainly users experiencing the third itinerary (Fig. 2). This confirms findings of recent studies proving that the presence of a virtual realistic actor can generally increase engagement and attention of the user [5]. The first itinerary received instead the lowest score (4.8): we can argue that the absence of a vocal narration, leading to rely only on vision, made visitors more focused on the task and therefore less available to feel engaged in the environment (Fig. 6).

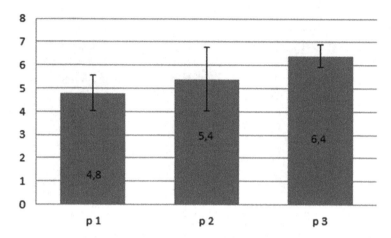

**Fig. 6.** Engagement of the visual experience

A comprehension question followed which was different depending on the itineraries ("Were the information panels clear and easy to read?" for the first one, and "Was the narrating voice clear and the provided information easy to understand?"). Results of this question demonstrate a general accuracy in the composition of the contents, in the planning of the expository panels and the choice of narrating voice (Fig. 3a). The third itinerary achieved the highest score (7): explanations provided by the virtual actor have been deemed complete and able to maintain a higher attention level.

Fourth question was related to pleasantness ("Was the text of the panels appropriate?" for the first itinerary, "Was the narrating voice pleasant?" for the second and "How annoying was the presence of the virtual actor?" for the third; in the latter case, 1 was a positive mark, i.e.: the presence of the virtual actor was not annoying at all. None of the users believed that the virtual agent could be annoying (all of the users gave a mark of 1) (Fig. 7).

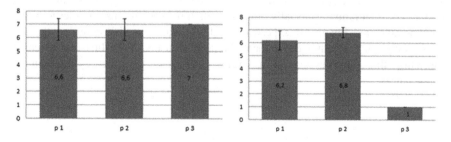

**Fig. 7.** (a) Third question: comprehension of contents (b) Fourth question: accuracy of contents

The last question concerned how much the experience helped the user to understand the content. The first and third itinerary received a very high score (Fig. 4). The second itinerary presents a greater variability of the results; this could be due to a not uniform level of experience in virtual museum of the second group of users that might have an impact on engagement but also on focusing attention (Fig. 8).

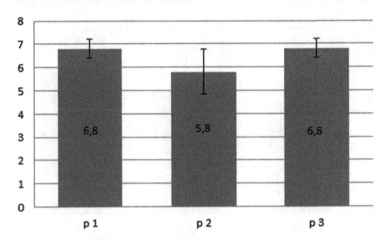

**Fig. 8.** Fifth question: how much the experience helped to understand the contents

The final results demonstrate that the third itinerary is the most complete one, users who visited gallery through the avatar's explanations found it easier and easily understandable. Users who attempted the first and second itineraries found them less clear and not useful for a complete learning process. The research confirms the important role a virtual agent can perform in a didactic application.

A second questionnaire aimed to estimate the efficacy of the implemented storytelling approaches in terms of learning and memory retention, posing two questions for each visited room related to the artworks thereby contained. No relevant differences were found with the partial exception of the users of the first itinerary who on average made more errors than the others. This could probably suggest a better efficacy of the latest two approaches in delivering content and in helping to keep a deeper attention.

At the end of the questionnaire, an open question asked users about suggested improvements. Besides some improvements requested on the visual quality of the environment, some users suggested to improve the quality of the visit with the insertion of more vocal narration, especially in the transition between rooms, in order to create a more organic and integrated experience and stimulate the visitor during the visit. Interestingly, all the gathered comments come from users of the first two itineraries, suggesting that the presence of a virtual guide lead to a better impression of completeness.

# 6 Conclusions

This paper proposes a pilot user study aimed to evaluate the efficacy of the presence of a virtual guide in order to implement an avatar-based storytelling approach to assist users in the visit of a virtual museum.

Preliminary findings confirm the hypothesis that an embodied virtual agent is able to stimulate attention and involvement, and contributes to a better content delivery and learning. We plan to extend this pilot study to a larger number of users, refining the comparison protocol, and to use a complete immersive setup based on head mounted displays.

**Acknowledgments.** This paper is supported by European Union's Horizon 2020 research and innovation programme under grant agreement No. 692103, project eHERITAGE (Expanding the Research and Innovation Capacity in Cultural Heritage Virtual Reality Applications).

# References

1. Machidon, O.M., Duguleana, M., Carrozzino, M.: Virtual humans in cultural heritage ICT applications: a review. J. Cult. Herit. (2018, in press)
2. Kennedy, S., Fawcett, R., Miller, A., Dow, L., Sweetman, R., Field, A., Allison, C.: Exploring canons & cathedrals with open virtual worlds: the recreation of St. Andrews Cathedral, St. Andrews day, 1318. In: Digital Heritage International Congress (Digital Heritage 2013), vol. 2, pp. 273–280. IEEE, October 2013
3. Fanini, B., Pagano, A.: Interface design for serious game visual strategies the case study of "Imago Bononiae". In: Digital Heritage 2015, vol. 2, pp. 623–626. IEEE, September 2015
4. Kopp, S., Gesellensetter, L., Krämer, N.C., Wachsmuth, I.: A conversational agent as museum guide – design and evaluation of a real-world application. In: Panayiotopoulos, T., et al. (eds.) IVA 2005. LNCS (LNAI), vol. 3661, pp. 329–343. Springer, Heidelberg (2005). https://doi.org/10.1007/11550617_28
5. Swartout, W., et al.: Ada and Grace: toward realistic and engaging virtual museum guides. In: Allbeck, J., Badler, N., Bickmore, T., Pelachaud, C., Safonova, A. (eds.) IVA 2010. LNCS (LNAI), vol. 6356, pp. 286–300. Springer, Heidelberg (2010). https://doi.org/10.1007/978-3-642-15892-6_30
6. Bogdanovych, A., Rodríguez, J.A., Simoff, S., Cohen, A., Sierra, C.: Developing virtual heritage applications as normative multiagent systems. In: Gleizes, M.-P., Gomez-Sanz, J. J. (eds.) AOSE 2009. LNCS, vol. 6038, pp. 140–154. Springer, Heidelberg (2011). https://doi.org/10.1007/978-3-642-19208-1_10
7. De Paolis, L.T., Aloisio, G., Celentano, M.G., Oliva, L., Vecchio, P.: Experiencing a town of the middle ages: an application for the edutainment in cultural heritage. In: IEEE 3rd International Conference on Communication Software and Networks (ICCSN), pp. 169–174. IEEE, May 2011
8. Maïm, J., Haegler, S., Yersin, B., Mueller, P., Thalmann, D., Van Gool, L.: Populating ancient pompeii with crowds of virtual romans. In: Proceedings of the 8th International Symposium on Virtual Reality, Archeology and Cultural Heritage-VAST (No. VRLAB-CONF-2008-151) (2007)

9. Carrozzino, M., Piacentini, V., Tecchia, F., Bergamasco, M.: Interactive visualization of crowds for the rescue of cultural heritage in emergency situations. SCIRES-IT-SCIentific RESearch Inf. Technol. **2**(1), 133–148 (2012)
10. Carrozzino, M., Tecchia, F., Bacinelli, S., Cappelletti, C., Bergamasco, M.: Lowering the development time of multimodal interactive application: the real-life experience of the XVR project. In: Proceedings of the 2005 ACM SIGCHI International Conference on Advances in Computer Entertainment Technology, pp. 270–273. ACM, June 2005
11. Brondi, R., Carrozzino, M., Lorenzini, C., Tecchia, F.: Using mixed reality and natural interaction in cultural heritage applications. Informatica **40**(3), 311 (2016)
12. Normand, J.M., Spanlang, B., Tecchia, F., Carrozzino, M., Swapp, D., Slater, M.: Full body acting rehearsal in a networked virtual environment—a case study. Presence Teleoperators Virtual Environ. **21**(2), 229–243 (2012)

# Improvements and Implementations of the Spatial Augmented Reality Applied on Scale Models of Cultural Goods for Visual and Communicative Purpose

Donato Maniello[✉]

Studio Glowarp, Spatial Augmented Reality for Cultural Heritage, Naples, Italy
info@glowarp.com

**Abstract.** This article wants to present the Spatial Augmented Reality technique (hereafter S.A.R.), better known as video mapping, used by the Studio Glowarp on scale models of archeological finds and cultural heritage. The use of S.A.R. technique offers new communication ways for archeology and museum fields. It helps to show fragile or destroyed goods, sometimes far away from the exhibition set, for the listed reasons considered as fragmented and hard to be reached by a bigger audience, become interesting case studies of digital anastylosis. The aim of this paper is to show from a different point of view the S. A.R. method that now can be considered not only as an "artistic" technique but also as a technique serving the cultural heritage, and to recommend it as one of the possible means of the future restoration and of the augmented heritage field.

**Keywords:** Spatial Augmented Reality · Video mapping · Augmented heritage

## 1 Introduction

Recently S.A.R. [1, 2] has been using into the field of the cultural heritage increasingly [3]. Building's façades has always been the perfect set for the application of S.A.R. technology, so this connection has always been existing since its first use.

This "fluid technology", part of the mixed reality [4], allows adapting the multimedia content to the complexity of every kind of surface by matching them and creating a lasting and unique bond with the space around them. S.A.R. may be applied not only to buildings and big areas but also to archeological finds and in general cultural heritage.

Many of these findings are often, for different reasons, far from the place where they were discovered, too fragile to be exposed to the public or to the light, absent because borrowed for exhibitions or even destroyed [5]. The possibilities of mixing S. A.R. and the reproduction of the goods, obtained by traditional techniques or 3D printing, offers new and interesting scenarios for enjoying such goods.

Measures have to be taken when we work on scale models and we want that the real and virtual models are matching, because the small dimensions of the objects, the used resolution, the video projectors involved and the good placement are all fundamental for the final result. The interesting aspect of these applications is that the artistic

L. T. De Paolis and P. Bourdot (Eds.): AVR 2018, LNCS 10851, pp. 303–319, 2018.
https://doi.org/10.1007/978-3-319-95282-6_23

dimension gives way to the ethical dimensions of the performance that turns in a documentary by taking advantage of the typical edutainment perceptual channels [6]. The choral dimension of the vision and the sharing of the emotions in real-time make the S.A.R. more advisable than other exclusive techniques such as V.R. [7].

In fact, more and more often, using only one video projector system and high quality multimedia content, we can turn the surfaces into media-surfaces [8] that ensure the viewer emotional involvement [9] during the performance. The paper focuses on different case studies that refer to different type of scale model mono video projection actions and the work in progress solutions used. The attention to detail is different depending on several variables such as the dimension of the area in relation to the audience distance from it.

An interesting aspect emerged from the use of these methods is the antithesis, between the accurate acquisition of the shape of the objects and the photorealistic restitution of them, as highlighted by other authors. Considering a 3D model, the adherence to the metric data and the relation to the perceived reality are linked by an inverse correlation. For example the reconstruction of complex parts of a building can be avoided using a texture that have to be applied to a low-polygon model, as it happens for the gaming, trying to keep in mind that the Level Of Details, hereafter L.O. D., mainly depends from the distance of the audience from the building and its surface's complexity (Fig. 1).

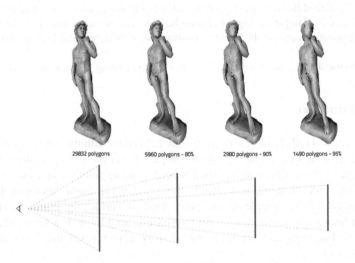

**Fig. 1.** Level Of Detail (L.O.D.) depending on the viewer distance

The 3D model generation can use the Structure for Motion technique, hereafter S.F.M., which turns a smartphone or a camera in a powerful and performing scanner that extract the 3D models from a cloud photos thanks to a specific software. It allows to have very precise and detailed 3D poly-models (High poly, Hp) that are reduced into polygons (Low poly, Lp) by the reverse modelling technique, a method capable of recreating the object according to a classic modelling.

Merlo et al. [10] define a summary scheme that relates the 3D model, visualization and use (Fig. 2). The high fidelity of the model respect to the metric data sacrifices the perceptive prospective, in the same way as the need of having models for the real-time operations sacrifices the metric conformity respect to the observed data.

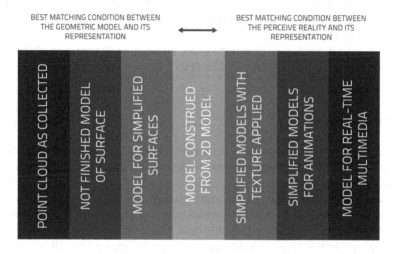

**Fig. 2.** 3D models state of the art chart

## 2  Available Techniques

Today the available techniques that allows that a multimedia content matches with three-dimensional surfaces are different and more and more often used together. Here we will list the ones used and improved by Studio Glowarp, referring to specific works for further consideration [11, 12].

They are intended to recreate the point of view from which the scene is projected. Camera and video projector have different perspectives and the available methods approximately mark the one's viewpoint to display it on the other, correcting it.

Every methods need Layer Masks that provide a guide in the final projection stage, called warping, and, using projective geometry techniques such as homothety, homography and anamorphosis, the virtual model screens the real one, marking the not corresponding parts in order to have the perfect matching. Exists in fact a two-way correspondence between the mapped image and the point of view of the video projector that remains univocal. Depending on the various settings, there are different methods here split in two main categories:

**Basic Methods**

Trace Mapping (M1)
matching established without the texture of the setting.
Photographic Mapping (M2)
matching derived by approximations with the texture of the setting.

**Advanced Methods**

Mapping with 2D scanning (M3)
matching established with the texture of the setting.

Mapping with 3D scanning (M4)
using SFM (Structure For Motion) techniques – matching to be determined once placed the video projector and the texture of the setting.

Virtual mapping (M5)
matching to be defined once placed the video projector and the texture of the setting. It is used when was designed a 3D scene but it has not been realised yet.

## 3  Spatial Display

Where the video projector is placed is an important variable for the final result, because much depends on its positioning and how it lights up the scene. The ideal condition is a front projection with an axis at a right angle to the model surface in order not to twist the screening table. Unfortunately, this chance is very rare because in most cases linked to exhibition purpose; it must not compromise the audience's vision and therefore is placed on the scene in order to satisfy this need. The result is a trapezoidal deformation of the video projection (Fig. 3) and as effect, the final mapping file will be affected by the deformation.

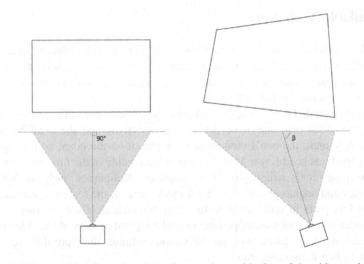

**Fig. 3.** Trapezoidal deformation depending on the positioning of the video projector

The presence of multiple shadows brought to the scene, due to a multi-projective system, or a not well-studied position, can compromise the final quality. Too many shadows on the scene, result of a multi-projection system, or a not well-thought location may preclude a positive result. The aim is to find a middle ground between the positioning of the video projector and a proper lightning of the setting in order to create a mapping file that has the fewest deformations.

Furthermore, it is essential to choose from which point of view, the video projector's or the audience's, should be produced all the video contents, considering that it is almost impossible to choose the first one due to the small dimensions of the scene. In general, there are three different kind of surfaces for the video mapping: planar, non planar or discontinuous surfaces (Fig. 4), each of them with their own features.

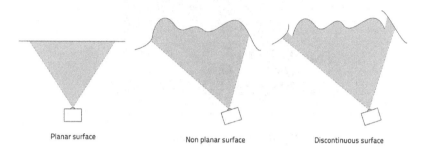

Planar surface          Non planar surface          Discontinuous surface

**Fig. 4.** Different type of used surfaces

## 4   Planar Surface: Scale Model of All Bands by Sol Lewitt

It is possible to create depth on a planar surface using the 2.5D or pseudo3D technique, called in this way because it is symbolically halfway between 2D and 3D. It is a trick very often used by computer graphics and especially by video gaming, an example are the videogames with an isometric graphics that create the illusion of three-dimensionality. Generally it is possible to use the reverse mapping technique, that is a computer project of the scene and its animations, than the model made only of lines was projected on the surface and the outlines are life re-drawn. When the video projection hits the surface, the contents will highlight the drawing and it will look like three-dimensional (Fig. 5).

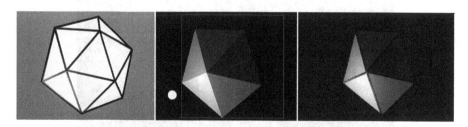

**Fig. 5.** Example of 2.5D video projection

## M2 Method

The 1:2 scale model of the work by the minimalist Sol Lewitt was one of the best achievement (Fig. 6).

**Fig. 6.** Model of Sol Lewitt's work

The M2 method was used for these surfaces taking the picture from a central perspective in order to minimise the deformations and avoid the photogrammetry. We could have used an image of the work for creating the Layer Masks, if the picture was available online or published on a catalogue. These kind of pictures are usually shot from a central point, ready for the use. In fact, using this type of image the virtual and real model coincide under a homothetic logics, provided that the video projector is set centrally to the scene (Fig. 7).

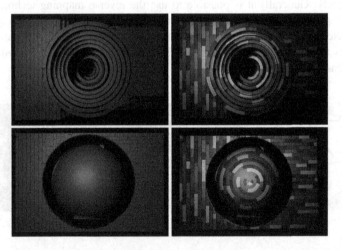

**Fig. 7.** Comparison between the rendering of the scene and the scale model's video mapping

# 5  Non Planar Surface

## 5.1  3D Scale Model of Ostuni's San Francesco Courtyard

This case study is the 1:30 3D scale model of Ostuni's San Francesco Courtyard, realized using traditional techniques and the 3D printing to recreate details like capitals, arches and pilasters (Fig. 8). M2, M3 and M4 methods were used separately in order to obtain the coincidence between the real and virtual model.

**Fig. 8.**  The courtyard 1:30 scale model

## M2 Method

Scale model and cloister are in two-way correspondence between them. For this reason, a photograph taken frontally in the real scene was used to texturize it. Afterwards the photo was correctly scaled, photo-rectified, all the layer masks were created (Fig. 9) and subsequently used only those relating to the foreground, and then the warping phase was performed.

**Fig. 9.**  Courtyard's stages of work

## M3 Method

The positioning of the video projector in front of the scene (Fig. 10) and the scan of the scene using a structured light (Fig. 11) allowed getting an excellent mapping file, as the generated aberrations were almost nil.

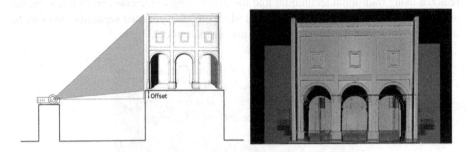

**Fig. 10.** Video projector's position on stage and the final scanning

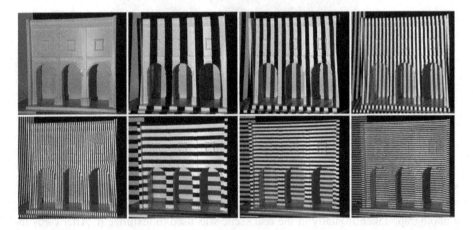

**Fig. 11.** Phases of structured light scanning through vertical and horizontal patterns

The real texture was obtained by modifying the actual photo of the courtyard until it coincided with the mapping file created. We moved on creating layer masks and there was no need to perform the warping.

## M4 Method

The M4 Method was used to have the 3D High poly textured model of the courtyard (Fig. 12). In order to making the best use of the models, the High poly were severely reduced by reverse modelling techniques, re-creating a Low poly unit (Fig. 13). A problem linked to this method is the division of the texture in areas (Fig. 14), called atlas, that reduce the continuity of the image and make difficult the post-production edit.

**Fig. 12.** Overlap between courtyard's Hp and Lp models

| Information | | Information | |
|---|---|---|---|
| Memory: | ca. 3722 KBytes | Memory: | ca. 131 KBytes |
| Points: | 32468 | Points: | 2263 |
| Polygons: | 63183 | Polygons: | 1682 |
| Objects: | 1 | Objects: | 23 |
| OK | Hp | OK | Lp |

**Fig. 13.** Number of Hp and Lp poly compared

**Fig. 14.** Atlas divided (Hp model) and entire (Lp) final texture

For each of the methods here described, we created layer masks using those relating to the foreground only. This kind of file is very important because is used as guideline during the projection phase (Fig. 15). Then, we moved to the final video projection phase and, where necessary, we used the warping (Fig. 16), obtaining an excellent coincidence between the real and the virtual model (Fig. 17).

**Fig. 15.** Courtyard photo-rectified and layer masks

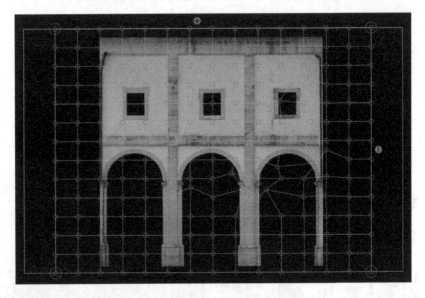

**Fig. 16.** Warping

**Fig. 17.** Final video projection with real texture and layer masks

## 5.2  3D Full Scale Model of Block N XLVI Parthenon North Frieze

Differently from the previous case, where we demonstrate that each method has the possibility to produce a similar mapping file, this case wants to show how the real and virtual models have been overlapped using the M4, M3 and M1 in a coordinated way as listed.

### M4 Method

The acquisition of the volume of the original block located at London British Museum, took place using SFM techniques: with a cloud of 67 photos, the 3D virtual model of the block was reconstructed (Fig. 18), which enabled to fulfil a polyethylene real-scale model got using a "rotational molding", a mold whose shape was obtained by "fall". The just mentioned trick was necessary to have a single block of great dimensions without junctions and at a considerably lower cost compared to a traditional 3D printing [13, 14].

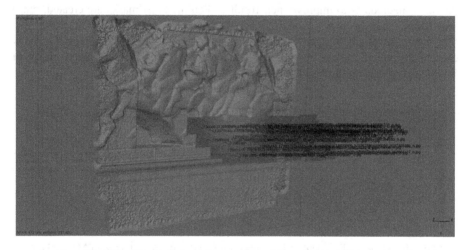

**Fig. 18.**  Cloud of photo for creation of 3D model of the block

### M3 Method

The block was placed on the wall and once delimitated the affected area according to the size of the video projection, so as to have an additional surface to project further contents, it was scanned with the structured light (Fig. 19). We decided to opt for this further step even if we could have used M4 Method immediately because of the complexity of the object.

Due to the fact that any linear geometric elements, as in the case of the courtyard, was missing, and being the block rich in details, it was necessary to choose a method that unambiguously would identify the correct position of the video projector in a virtual environment. It happens because its identification in M4 takes place by imposing the viewpoint features of the video projector manufacturer to the virtual camera, which do not always coincide, thus determining misalignment in the matching phase during the projection.

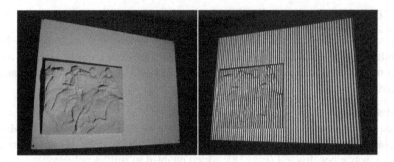

**Fig. 19.** Area projected and structured light scanning of the scene

**M1 Method**

This method is usually adopted to reproduce by tracing the details not collected with the other methods or to improve their results. Then the layer masks are created, but it may happen that this is not enough to have a perfect coincidence. Therefore, the real-time correction of any inaccuracies occurs using M1 method (Fig. 20). Being the block completely white, the real texture was obtained by modifying the image, result of S.F.M. operations on the block until it coincides with the mapping file.

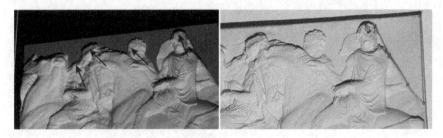

**Fig. 20.** Manual adjustment of layer masks not perfectly coinciding with M1 method

Finally, we created the layer masks, real texture and the warping was used in some parts to match virtual model and real one (Fig. 21).

### 5.3    3D Full Real Scale Model of Apulian Red-Figure Dinos

**M4 Method**

We chose to follow an artisanal approach to reproduce a 1:1 scale model of the Dinos, considering it better than a 3D printing model both for the costs and for results. Since the vase is under a glass and a good shooting almost impossible because of the outside glare, the geometry and texture were captured using the S.F.M. technology, recon-structing the model through measurements that we already had because used in previous publications [15].

The coincidence between the real and virtual model was obtained using the M4-M3 method but only after deciding where to place the video projector (Fig. 22).

**Fig. 21.** Video projection with reconstruction of missing parts

**Fig. 22.** The Dinos reproduction and the video projection

## 6 Discontinuous Surfaces

The last case study was the realization of 1:500 3D scale model of Arenberg's UNESCO mining site in Wallers, France (Fig. 23). Due to the small dimensions of various parts of the model, sometimes a few millimetres, we did not chose a real texture.

Furthermore, the choice of high positioning a single video projector was driven by the following reasons: reducing the shadow devices, streamlining the work phases (more coupled video projectors, greater computing power and confluence problems), prefer a frontal view for the user.

Actually, this positioning brought with it some problems that arose during the phases of acquisition of the mapping file. One of these was the beam of projection that arrived so oblique on the vertical surfaces to affect any possibility to project something without not suffering of excessive deformation. This led to the use of the M3 and M1 methods, as listed, to get the coincidence between the real and virtual models.

**M3 Method**
The structured light scanning of the scene and the location of the video projector allowed obtaining a scanning file that had an evident oblique frame perspective. Starting from that, we had needless difficulties to create the layer masks because the 3D

**Fig. 23.** 1:500 3D model of Arenberg mine

model had been painted using a white polish that produced some curious visual arte-facts that did not permit to identify the geometry of the structure unambiguously (Fig. 24).

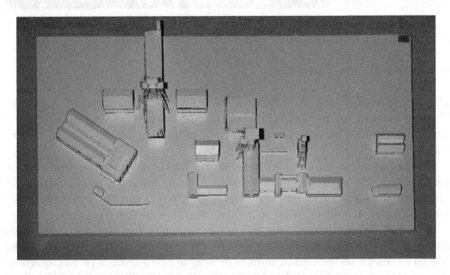

**Fig. 24.** Final result of the structured light scanning

**M1 Method**
Each layer mask was corrected directly on the model in real-time in order to perfectly adjust the masks to the real set. For this particular case, we needed almost a week to reach the correct overlap of all the parts (Fig. 25).

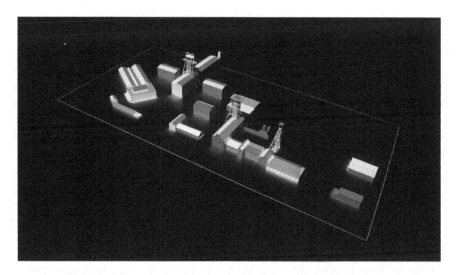

**Fig. 25.** Layer masks projection on 3D model

The creation of layer masks was used as a guide for the creation of all multi-media content (Fig. 26).

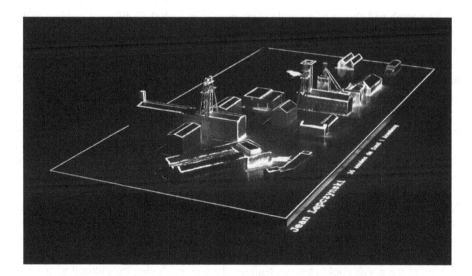

**Fig. 26.** Final Projection on 3D model of one a frame of final work

# 7   Conclusions

The listed methods, perfected over the years by Studio Glowarp, allow the application of S.A.R. on any type of surface and demonstrate how it is possible to achieve perfect adherence between the real and virtual model even on scale models of different complexity. Their combined use shows that there is no single method of proceeding and that it is often necessary to use them in synergy in order to generate a single mapping file and therefore an excellent matching. In particular, the use of this technology brings with it some problems:

- The viewpoints undergo small displacements due to different working temperatures over time. This means that while using the methods M1 or M3, which are the only ones that can generate a file without approximations, as they univocally identify the point of view of the video projector in space, it is possible to find translations of the mapping file when video projected on the scene.
- Most of the working sets will be dismantled and rebuilt in the final work environment. Reassembling the scene even with the same setup, produces inevitable movements such as translations and rotations.
- The previous problems when occur on the scale models simultaneously amplify the sense of error due to the missing coincidence between the real and virtual model. It is necessary to use the warping phase and a constant control over the project settings is required.

The combined choice of multiple video projectors with their different features or the choice of even one of them must be evaluated in relation to the type of surface, the size of the video projection area and the L.O.D. The above-mentioned applications show how the S.A.R. can be used on scale reproductions of archaeological and cultural heritage while keeping high the awesomeness of the performances achieved over the years on the buildings of the city.

The possibilities offered by simple tools now commonly used as the passive sensors for the 3D scanning printing, change the classical museum perception thanks to the easy way in recreating copy of archeological goods or portions of buildings. Whatever the scale of the object is these means offer unexpected and new scenario for the diffusion of multimedia contents.

That is the case of the 3D scan of the famous bust of Queen Nefertiti by the artists Nora Al-Badri and Jan Nikolai and exposed breaching the copyright etiquette at Berlin Neues Museum in 2015 [16]. The artists scanned the bust using a Kinect camera and published it on the web so that everyone could reproduce it using a 3D printer. This action of great artistic value offers an interesting starting on how the paradigms of fruition of the goods could change changing the way of sharing the cultural heritage in the digital age.

The cultural good begins to become non-exclusive and reproducible from anyone. The versatility and limited ease of these means make them ideal tools for virtual restoration and as a valid tool to support traditional museography and museum communication [17].

# References

1. Oliver, B., Raskar, R.: Spatially Augmented Reality. Merging Real and Virtual World. AK Peters, Wellesley (2005)
2. Raskar, R., Welch, G., Fuchs, H.: Spatially augmented reality. In: Proceeding of the First IEEE Workshop on Augmented Reality, pp. 63–72 (1998)
3. Maniello, D., Amoretti, V.: Interference ancient-modern: new strategies for digital enhancement for museums. In: VIIth International Conference Diagnosis, Conservation and Valorizazion of Cultural Heritage, pp. 22–32. A.I.E.S. Beni Culturali (2016)
4. Milgram, P., Takemura, H., Utsumi, A., Kishino, F.: Augmented reality. A class of displays on the reality-virtuality continuum. In: Telemanipulator and Telepresence, pp. 22–32 (1994)
5. Maniello, D., Amoretti, V., Cirafici, A.: 3D data and augmented reality in heritage fruition. A case history. In: World heritage and degradation, XIV International Forum, Smart Design, Planning and Technologies, vol. 69, ID 269. La scuola di Pitagora, Napoli (2016)
6. Trocchianesi, R.: Design a narrazioni per il patrimonio culturale. Maggioli, Sant'Arcangelo di Romagna (2014)
7. Bryson, S., Zeltzer, D., Bolas, M.T., de La Chapelle, B., Bennett, D.: The future of virtual reality: head mounted displays versus spatially immersive displays. In: SIGGRAPH 97 Conference Proceedings, Annual Conference Series, ACM SIGGRAPH, pp. 485–486. Addison-Wesley (1997)
8. Bruno, G.: Superfici. A proposito di estetica, materialità e media. Johan & Levi, Monza (2016)
9. Bruno, G.: Atlante delle emozioni. In: viaggio tra arte, architettura e cinema. Johan & Levi, Monza (2015)
10. Merlo, A., Fantini, F., Lavoratti, G., Aliperta, A., Hernández, J.L.L.: Texturing e ottimizzazione dei modelli digitali reality based: la chiesa della Compañía de Jesús. Disegnare con la fotografia digitale 6(12), 2–3 (2013). Disegnarecon
11. Maniello, D.: Augmented Reality in Public Spaces: Basic Technique for Video Mapping, vol. I. Le Penseur, Brienza (2015)
12. Maniello, D.: Tecniche avanzate di video mapping: la realtà spaziale aumentata applicata al bene culturale, vol. II. Le Penseur, Brienza (2018)
13. Maniello, D., Amoretti, V., Cirafici, A.: The magnificent adventure of a 'fragment': block NXLVI Parthenon North Frieze in augmented reality. SCIRES IT SCIentific REsearch Inf. Technol. 5(2), 129–142 (2015)
14. Maniello, D., Amoretti, V.: Paesaggi digitali in realtà aumentata per una nuova museologia. Romarchè, VII Salone dell'Editoria Archeologica, Roma 5(2), 129–142 (2016)
15. Cassano, R.: Principi imperatori vescovi. Duemila anni di storia a Canosa, pp. 272–273. Marsilio, Padova (1992)
16. http://nefertitihack.alloversky.com
17. Rosa, P.: From museums as a collection to museums as narration. Tecnologie per la comunicazione del patrimonio culturale 4(8), 129–138 (2011). Disegnarecon

# Augmented Reality to Understand
# the Leonardo's Machines

Lucio Tommaso De Paolis$^{(\boxtimes)}$, Valerio De Luca$^{(\boxtimes)}$, and Giovanni D'Errico$^{(\boxtimes)}$

Department of Engineering for Innovation, University of Salento, Lecce, Italy
{lucio.depaolis,valerio.deluca,giovanni.derrico}@unisalento.it

**Abstract.** Augmented reality plays an important role in cultural heritage and education. The magic effect of 3D animated objects can enhance students' interest, attention and engagement in school subjects. Moreover, augmented reality can help understand spatial concepts and the working principles of complex mechanical components. In such context, machines designed by Leonardo Da Vinci are a perfect case study for augmented reality technologies. This paper presents a mobile augmented reality application developed for an exhibit on Leonardo's inventions: it shows the overall structure and the working principles of some machines recognized on the pages of the Atlantic Codex. We used Blender to design the animated 3D models of the machines and the ARToolkit and Vuforia frameworks to superimpose virtual models over Leonardo's sketches framed by the camera of mobile devices. Subjective data about user experience collected through some questionnaires proved how AR applications can improve the dominant learning style in accordance with Kolb's theory.

**Keywords:** Mobile augmented reality · E-Culture
Cultural heritage · Education

## 1 Introduction

Nowadays, information technology is widely adopted in cultural heritage and education. Some years ago, Massive Open Online Courses (MOOCs) were introduced as innovative technologies to disseminate knowledge [1]. Unfortunately, most of them are still based on conservative forms of delivered contents, such as static video, audio and text. Some audio/video streaming systems try to achieve a more strict form of real-time delivery, referred as interactive real-time [2,3]: it allows students to ask questions during a lesson thanks to a reduced playback lag between the event in the real world and the received audio/video. However, it is not enough to hold the students' attention until the end of a lesson.

For this reason, other technologies such as virtual reality (VR) [4] and augmented reality (AR) [5,6] are adopted to enhance the level of attention and engagement of learners. In cultural heritage, learning often assumes the form of informal learning [7]: it is not related to institutional education, which typically

© Springer International Publishing AG, part of Springer Nature 2018
L. T. De Paolis and P. Bourdot (Eds.): AVR 2018, LNCS 10851, pp. 320–331, 2018.
https://doi.org/10.1007/978-3-319-95282-6_24

takes place at school; it takes advantage of intrinsic motivations, such as personal curiosity, which makes it a pleasant activity. Even when it is institutionally sponsored, informal learning is not highly structured or classroom-based [8]. It is often closely related to practical experience, which can take place by exploiting the support of virtual and augmented reality.

Edutainment refers to any form of entertainment aimed at an educational role; it enhances the learning environment and makes it much more engaging and fun-filled [9]. The videogame is one of the most exciting and immediate tools of the edutainment applications since the game enables a type of multi-sensory and immersive relationship of the user through its interactive interface [10]. The reconstruction of a virtual interactive town increases dramatically the possibilities of information exchange and diffusion [11]. The MediaEvo Project aims to develop a multi-channel and multi-sensory platform for edutainment in cultural heritage for the realization of a digital didactic game oriented towards the knowledge of medieval history and society by means of the integration of human sciences and new data processing technologies [12].

The wider diffusion of mobile augmented reality applications [13] has fostered a learning by doing paradigm and has established a direct interaction with users, by turning them from simple passive viewers into active and autonomous participants in the learning process. Augmented reality can be integrated into MOOCs to increase the engagement of students and reduce the dropout rate [14]. It enhances learning attention and motivation thanks to its fascinating graphical content and its engaging interaction modalities.

Augmented reality can provide an important support for various education levels. Children are fascinated by its surprising effects and consequently become also more interested in the topics of school lessons.

In higher order studies it is often employed to enhance the understanding of spatial concepts. Static 2D images in traditional books cannot give an exhaustive idea about the 3D structure of objects. Moreover, in the special case of animated objects, such as mechanical components, fixed images can show neither movements and working principles of objects nor how they could be used.

Some works [15, 16] presented augmented reality applications that help students understand the structure and the spatial extension of geometric 3D objects and also the conceptual connection between a 2D and a 3D representation [17].

Augmented reality allows inspecting an object from several sides: users have just to move their mobile phones to change point of view while framing 3D models. Moreover, in cultural heritage, the joint use of AR and Unmanned Aerial Vehicles, commonly known as drones, has enabled the possibility to explore from different perspectives archaeological sites that are not directly accessible by visitors [18].

The use of augmented reality and cloud computing technology can enrich the scenes of sites with a relevant cultural interest [19]. The main goal is to develop a mobile application to improve the user's cultural experience during the sightseeing of a city of art through the integration of digital contents related to specific sites or historic monuments.

An obvious benefit deriving from augmented reality consists in helping learners to collect and mentally associate several concepts and phenomena. Moreover, augmented visualization of virtual objects over 2D images makes memorization tasks easier: indeed the magic effect of animated 3D objects makes the whole experience more impressive.

One of the drawbacks hampering a wider adoption of augmented reality in education concerns the design of 3D models. Unfortunately, teachers have a deep knowledge about the learning strategies and the typical difficulties of their subjects, but they usually have no expertise on 3D modeling. On the other hand, 3D designers may have no experience about education issues. For this reason, a strict collaboration between these two figures is a key aspect for the concept and the design of successful AR-based educational scenarios.

This paper presents a mobile augmented reality application developed for an exhibit on Leonardo da Vinci's inventions to present machines for which physical models were not available: by recognizing the pages of the Atlantic Codex [20], it shows the structure and the working principles of such machines. Nowadays several sketches of Leonardo's machines are available [20], even though their understanding is not straightforward. They were drawn neither for dissemination nor for educational purposes: they belong to Leonardo's personal notes and are often unclear and incomplete. We exploited augmented reality to visualize 3D reconstructions of Leonardo's machines when the corresponding sketches are framed by a smartphone camera.

The remainder of this paper is structured as follows: Sect. 2 describes Leonardo's machines we chose for our AR application; Sect. 3 describes our Leonardo AR application; Sect. 4 presents some experimental results collected during a public exhibit; Sect. 5 concludes the paper.

## 2   Machines in Leonardo's Sketches

The Leonardo's sketches chosen for our application can be classified according to different levels of understanding. A sketch that is particularly difficult to understand shows the design of a musical instrument, called "Pianoviola", which could be worn on the waist of the body and played like a piano (Fig. 1). The sketch represents several separate mechanical components, such as pulleys and cams, which composed the system. A flywheel was triggered by the legs of a man walking while he was wearing the system. In this way, other mechanical components could get in touch with some strings, which could produce a viola sound. Even though the assembled system is depicted at the bottom of the sketch, a simple look at the notes can give neither a clear global overview of the system nor an idea of its working principles.

Another complex sketch represents a machine transforming alternate motion in perpetual motion (Fig. 2). In particular, Leonardo focused on the effort to lift an object from the ground. When an operator moved a lever back and forth, a rope could wrap around a central rotating pivot.

Another sketch, which is easy to understand, depicts a war machine, called "Bombarda", and the parabolic path of the bullets (Fig. 3).

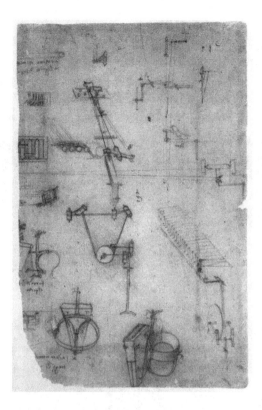

**Fig. 1.** Leonardo's sketch of a pianoviola

**Fig. 2.** Leonardo's sketch of an alternate motion machine

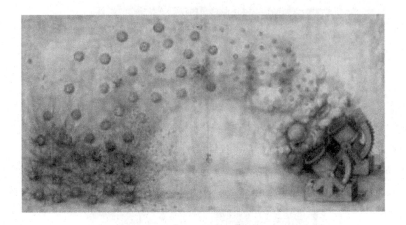

**Fig. 3.** Leonardo's sketch of a bombarda

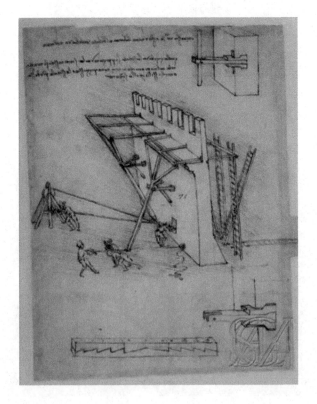

**Fig. 4.** Leonardo's sketch of a lever-based defense system

On the other hand, Leonardo designed a lever-based defense system, which allowed soldiers behind the ramparts of a castle to push away enemies through a simple and quick action (Fig. 4).

# 3   Leonardo AR Application

A correct overlap of virtual objects over the real ones requires the estimation of camera position and orientation (also known as camera pose estimation) [21], which allows the creation of a virtual camera. Pose estimation can be based on artificial markers placed in the real scene (whose position is known a-priori) or on natural feature detection. Markerless AR is more effective than marker-based AR in the education field. Indeed, the use of markerless image targets enables the possibility of associating contextually relevant information directly with real images that are difficult to understand. Fast algorithms can be employed also because AR applications developed for educational purposes do not require high precision and accuracy. On the contrary, in some other contexts, such as industrial environments [22], marker-based AR is still preferred due to difficulties of markerless algorithms in dealing with wider physical areas and variable ambient light.

A comparative study of software development kits available for the development of augmented reality applications in the education field can be found in [23].

We developed an early version of Leonardo application based on ARToolKit [24], but then we switched to Vuforia [25] and exploited its features integrated into the Unity3D environment [26]. ARToolKit and Vuforia were analytically compared in [27].

## 3.1   3D Modelling

Starting from some reconstructions derived from Leonardo's sketches, we designed the 3D models in Blender [28], a well-known free and open source 3D modeling software. Blender's features include 3D modeling, UV unwrapping, texturing, raster graphics editing, rigging and skinning, fluid and smoke simulation, particle simulation, soft body simulation, sculpting, animation, match moving, camera tracking, rendering, video editing and compositing.

We simplified the structural complexity of the models by reducing the number of polygons to make the models suitable for rendering on mobile devices, which have constrained resources in terms of processor, video card and memory.

We enriched some models with animations to better explain the working principles of the represented objects and also to increase the user engagement and the surprise effect.

## 3.2   ARToolkit

The early versions of ARToolkit [29] were designed for desktop applications and could recognize only square marker patterns. Then the framework was extended to support also mobile devices and natural feature tracking (NFT). For markerless tracking, ARToolkit provides the Image Database Management Utility, which performs a training on the image that should be recognized in the augmented scene.

We compiled the mobile applications for both Android and iOS platforms, by using the Android Studio [30] and Xcode [31] environments respectively.

ARToolkit6 [24] NFT accepts only the OpenSceneGraph (OSG) [32] format for 3D models. Since Blender 3D cannot export models in OSG format, we converted them to the FBX format [33], which is used for data exchange among different proprietary and open source 3D modeling applications (3ds Max, Maya, MotionBuilder, Mudbox, etc.). Then we imported FBX models in Autodesk 3ds Max 2014 [34] and exported them in OSG format through the OpenSceneGraph Max Exporter [35].

### 3.3   Vuforia and Unity3D

Vuforia can associate virtual objects with several types of 2D and 3D targets, including both frame markers and markerless image targets. Moreover, it supports multi-target configurations. The framework provides also an extension for the Unity3D game engine [36], which enables an easy porting of the developed applications on different platforms and operating systems.

Vuforia provides developers with an online Target Management System, a cloud environment that processes uploaded target images and extracts patterns or features that will be used for the image identification. The output dataset consists in a XML configuration file that allows the developer to configure trackable features and a binary file containing the trackable database.

We imported in the Unity3D environment the Vuforia database we created for the Leonardo's sketches. Then we created an image target in the scene for each Leonardo's sketch. Every image target represents a sketch on which we want to superimpose a 3D model. It can be selected among those included in the target database imported before. The 3D model of the virtual object was imported in the scene tree as a child of the image target.

## 4   Results

Figures 5, 6, 7 and 8 show the application running on a tablet: when posters depicting Leonardo's sketches are framed by the camera, 3D models are shown superimposed on them.

Visitors had the possibility to use our augmented reality application during an exhibit of some Leonardo's machines at University of Salento. After the experience with the Leonardo AR application, visitors were asked to fill in a twelve-items questionnaire based on the Kolb's Learning Style Inventory format [37, 38].

**Fig. 5.** Augmented visualization for a lever-based defense system

**Fig. 6.** Augmented visualization for a bombarda

**Fig. 7.** Augmented visualization for an alternate motion machine

**Fig. 8.** Augmented visualization for a pianoviola

According to Kolb's theory, each person has a different learning style depending on several factors, such as social environment, educational experiences and basic cognitive structure. In our scenario, we detected three different kinds of learners:

- Visual learners, which are inclined to read text or look at videos, charts and augmented reality contents;
- Auditory learners, which are inclined to listening activities;
- Kinesthetic (or tactile) learners, which are inclined to write notes and to perform manual activities.

For each questionnaire item, visitors had to choose a score among 3 (enough), 2 (not much), 1 (for nothing). The final score allowed us to identify the predominant learning style for each visitor during his/her experience with the mobile AR application. The chart in Fig. 9 represents the obtained statistical results. In particular, we can conclude that augmented reality mainly fosters the visual and kinesthetic style during a learning session.

## Dominant Learning Style

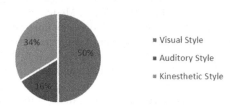

Fig. 9. The dominant learning style during a learning session with Leonardo AR application

## 5    Conclusions and Future Work

In this paper we have presented a mobile augmented reality application that helps understanding the machines designed by Leonardo Da Vinci. The animated 3D models visualized over Leonardo's sketches give a better idea of the structure and the working principles of such machines and enhance people participation and engagement. The experimental data collected during a public exhibit allowed us to evaluate the effect of augmented reality on the dominant learning styles described by Kolb's theory.

We developed an early implementation of the application with ARToolKit, but then we switched to Vuforia and Unity3D. In the current release, 3D models are directly stored in the mobile application package. In future works, for a wider range of 3D models, the application will access the feature database on Vuforia's cloud environment to save space on devices. It will also download from a server the 3D models to superimpose on the recognized features instead of storing them locally in the app package. These architectural changes will enable also the possibility of performing more in-depth tests on a wider scale about usability and user experience.

# References

1. Balaji, B.S., Sekhar, A.C.: The various facets of MOOC. In: IEEE International Conference in MOOC, Innovation and Technology in Education (MITE), pp. 139–142 (2013)
2. Tommasi, F., Melle, C., De Luca, V.: OpenSatRelaying: a hybrid approach to real-time audio-video distribution over the internet. J. Commun. **9**(3), 248–261 (2014)
3. Tommasi, F., De Luca, V., Melle, C.: Are P2P streaming systems ready for interactive e-learning? In: International Conference on Education Technologies and Computers (ICETC), pp. 49–54 (2014)
4. Martín-Gutiérrez, J., Mora, C., Añorbe-Díaz, B., González-Marrero, A.: Virtual technologies trends in education. Eurasia J. Math. Sci. Technol. Educ. **13**(2), 469–486 (2017)
5. Iqbal, J., Sidhu, M.S.: A review on making things see: augmented reality for futuristic virtual educator. Cogent Educ. **4**(1), 632–645 (2017)
6. Koutromanos, G., Sofos, A., Avraamidou, L.: The use of augmented reality games in education: a review of the literature. Educ. Media Int. **52**(4), 253–271 (2015)
7. Lin, A.C., Fernandez, W.D., Gregor, S.: Understanding web enjoyment experiences and informal learning: a study in a museum context. Decis. Support Syst. **53**(4), 846–858 (2012)
8. Marsick, V.J., Watkins, K.E.: Informal and incidental learning. New Dir. Adult Contin. Educ. **89**, 25–34 (2001)
9. De Paolis, L.T.: Walking in a virtual town to understand and learning about the life in the middle ages. In: Murgante, B., et al. (eds.) ICCSA 2013. LNCS, vol. 7971, pp. 632–645. Springer, Heidelberg (2013). https://doi.org/10.1007/978-3-642-39637-3_50
10. De Paolis, L.T., Aloisio, G., Celentano, M.G., Oliva, L., Vecchio, P.: A Game-based 3D simulation of otranto in the middle ages. In: Third International Conference on Advances in Computer-Human Interactions, pp. 130–133 (2010)
11. De Paolis, L.T., Aloisio, G., Celentano, M.G., Oliva, L., Vecchio, P.: Experiencing a town of the middle ages: an application for the edutainment in cultural heritage. In: IEEE 3rd International Conference on Communication Software and Networks, pp. 169–174 (2011)
12. De Paolis, L.T., Aloisio, G., Celentano, M.G., Oliva, L., Vecchio, P.: MediaEvo project: a serious game for the edutainment. In: 3rd International Conference on Computer Research and Development, vol. 4, pp. 524–529 (2011)
13. Petrucco, C., Agostini, D.: Teaching our cultural heritage using mobile augmented reality. J. E-Learn. Knowl. Soc. **12**(3), 115–128 (2016)
14. Chauhan, J., Taneja, S., Goel, A.: Enhancing MOOC with augmented reality, adaptive learning and gamification. In: IEEE 3rd International Conference on MOOCs, Innovation and Technology in Education (MITE), pp. 348–353 (2015)
15. Banu, S.M.: Augmented reality system based on sketches for geometry education. In: International Conference on E-Learning and E-Technologies in Education (ICEEE), pp. 166–170 (2012)

16. Contero, M., Gomis, J.M., Naya, F., Albert, F., Martin-Gutierrez, J.: Development of an augmented reality based remedial course to improve the spatial ability of engineering students. In: Frontiers in Education Conference Proceedings, pp. 1–5 (2012)
17. Álvarez, A., Javier, F., Parra, B., Beatriz, E., Tubio, M., de Paula, F.: From 2D to 3D: teaching terrain representation in engineering studies through augmented reality: comparative versus 3D pdf. In: IEEE Frontiers in Education Conference (FIE) Proceedings, pp. 1–4 (2014)
18. Botrugno, M.C., D'Errico, G., De Paolis, L.T.: Augmented reality and UAVs in archaeology: development of a location-based AR application. In: De Paolis, L.T., Bourdot, P., Mongelli, A. (eds.) AVR 2017. LNCS, vol. 10325, pp. 261–270. Springer, Cham (2017). https://doi.org/10.1007/978-3-319-60928-7_23
19. Vecchio, P., et al.: Cloud computing and augmented reality for cultural heritage. In: De Paolis, L.T., Mongelli, A. (eds.) AVR 2015. LNCS, vol. 9254, pp. 51–60. Springer, Cham (2015). https://doi.org/10.1007/978-3-319-22888-4_5
20. da Vinci, L., Marinoni, A.: Il Codice Atlantico della Biblioteca Ambrosiana di Milano. No. v. 1–4 in Grandi opere in facsimile, Giunti (2000)
21. Zendjebil, I.M., Ababsa, F., Didier, J.Y., Vairon, J., Frauciel, L., Hachet, M.A., Guitton, P., Delmont, R.: Outdoor Augmented Reality: State of the Art and Issues (2009)
22. Blanco-Novoa, Ó., Fernández-Caramés, T.M., Fraga-Lamas, P., Vilar-Montesinos, M.A.: A practical evaluation of commercial industrial augmented reality systems in an Industry 4.0 Shipyard. IEEE. Access **6**, 8201–8218 (2018)
23. Herpich, F., Guarese, R.L.M., Tarouco, L.M.R.: A comparative analysis of augmented reality frameworks aimed at the development of educational applications. Creat. Educ. **8**(9), 1433–1451 (2017)
24. ARToolKit 6. https://github.com/artoolkit
25. Vuforia. https://www.vuforia.com/features.html
26. Unity3D. https://unity3d.com
27. Santos, A.B.D., Dourado, J.B., Bezerra, A.: ARToolkit and qualcomm vuforia: an analytical collation. In: XVIII Symposium on Virtual and Augmented Reality (SVR), pp. 229–233 (2016)
28. Blender. https://www.blender.org
29. ARToolKit. http://www.hitl.washington.edu/artoolkit
30. Android Studio. https://developer.android.com/studio
31. Xcode. https://developer.apple.com/xcode
32. OpenSceneGraph 3D graphics toolkit. http://www.openscenegraph.org
33. FBX Assets File Format. http://images.autodesk.com/adsk/files/fbxassets.pdf
34. Autodesk 3ds Max. https://www.autodesk.com/products/3ds-max/overview
35. OpenSceneGraph Max Exporter. https://sourceforge.net/projects/osgmaxexp/files
36. Grahn, I.: The Vuforia SDK and Unity3D Game Engine: Evaluating Performance on Android Devices (2017)
37. Kolb, D.A.: Experiential Learning: Experience as the Source of Learning and Development. Prentice-Hall P T R, Englewood Cliffs (1984)
38. Kolb, D., Rubin, I., McIntyre, J.: Organizational Psychology: Readings on Human Behavior in Organizations. Behavioral Science in Business Series. Prentice-Hall, Englewood Cliffs (1984)

# Optimization Techniques for Photogrammetry Applied to Cultural Heritage and the Action of Transformation Groups

Fabrizio Bazzurri[1,2] and Massimo A. Picardello[2]([⊠]) [iD]

[1] Nu.M.I.D.I.A. srl, Via Giacomo Peroni 130, 00131 Roma, Italy
fabrizio.bazzurri@gmail.com
[2] Department of Mathematics, University of Rome "Tor Vergata",
Via della Ricerca Scientifica 1, 00133 Roma, Italy
picard@mat.uniroma2.it

**Abstract.** Technology could sensitize end-users to preservation of cultural heritage while stimulating more interest based on a greater involvement. Our approach to this goal is based on a novel gamification and story-telling based on scientific foundations. At the same time, this application can offer the pro-user an interactive visualization suitable to study and verify new theories about the artifacts both on their current state and on its 3D reconstruction, but, at the same time, design a workflow capable to integrate different optimization techniques to adjust data depending on different scenarios. This leads to a unified system able to adapt itself to external requirements in a semi-automatic fashion. Finally, new ways of playful interaction, based on simple mathematical operations, were investigated.

The second-named author is partially supported by MIUR Excellence Department Project funds, awarded MIUR to the Department of Mathematics, University of Rome Tor Vergata, CUP E83C18000100006.

## 1 Introduction and State of the Art

Studying and preserving cultural heritage have always been primary goals. These goals are highly preeminent in Italy, a country with rich historical background and endowed with a large number of archaeological finds and historical artifacts of outstanding quality. It is necessary not only to study and collect data related to artifacts, but also to make them widely known with in-depth scientific analysis and with attractive exhibitions and presentations. In order to give the witness clear and accurate information, but at the same time to encourage him to undertake further investigations and to make him feel as an active part of the cultural environment, these two sides must be always kept in balance.

In recent years, technological progress and continuous growth of ICT gave rise to completely new types of man/machine and man/man interfaces. From the state of the art of just a few years ago, giant steps have been made, above

L. T. De Paolis and P. Bourdot (Eds.): AVR 2018, LNCS 10851, pp. 332–348, 2018.
https://doi.org/10.1007/978-3-319-95282-6_25

**Fig. 1.** A frame output by our real-time app

all in modeling and rendering. Henceforth we shall focus on new technologies for 3D-modeling and visualization of cultural heritage. For the former aspect, there is a significant progress in making use of photogrammetry for 3D-model acquisitions of real-world artifacts: this progress is made possible by the constant increase of computing power even in end-user equipment and non-professional workstations. The latest CUDA programming techniques on graphic processors have significantly shortened the computing time to obtain dense point clouds starting with photographic images. This has promoted photogrammetric techniques to the status of strong competitor of the classical methods based on laser scans, even more so because of higher and higher quality of texturing (Fig. 1).

On the other hand, the visualization of historic artifact has profited of significant advances in real time rendering, that used to be an almost exclusive monopoly of the gaming world, particularly evident in the development of increasingly more refined physically based models for the interaction of different materials with light. This growing interest led to new rendering techniques aimed to more accurate photorealistic output and faster processing time. Visualizations that used to be available only through offline rendering are now achieved in real time with minor compromises on quality. Moreover, we are witnessing a demand for user-experience based on immersive interface and interaction with real world. This push towards virtual reality interfaces led to the marketing of new and advanced Virtual Reality viewers (Oculus and HTC Vive) that can project a virtual world where the viewer is fully immersed and can naturally interact. At the same time, the industry is developing new devices able to generate mixed reality, that is, mixing the true world with virtual elements: these are the augmented reality viewers. These viewers need a much higher computing speed, to support real time rendering of more frames (two instead than one for

VR viewers), and higher frame rates. Indeed, a frame rate of 90 Hz instead of the usual 60 Hz is the minimum in order to avoid motion sickness due to poor synchronization of real movement of the head and the related movement of the virtual camera: at a lower refresh frequency, the projected images are not fluent enough.

All these tools give rise to a new way of interaction with the artifacts, leading to new opportunities and new ethic and formal viewpoints about the individual-vs-community and individual-vs-world approach. These dual approaches give rise to social aggregation and social inclusion of people with physical disabilities. As for the first point, the digitalization process leads to a new way of sharing information and a new way of social aggregation that overcomes geographical and time barriers. However, particular attention must be devoted to the correct use and management of enormous quantity of data produced as time goes by. A rigorous and reproducible workflow is essential for a correct data storage and processing aimed to avoid the inability to adapt to future use of data and to prevent data fragmentation. On the basis of this last point and the available set of technological tools, the adopted procedures should be open-source to favor prototyping and a rich exchange between academic and industrial environments. This leads to different paths: by means of the same data, different applications could be developed for end-users or professionals. A common language (adaptable to various applications) can transfer scientific approach and contents to the end-user. In this way the final application is not based on pure spectacularization neglecting pedagogic aspects (the basis of cultural production). Moreover, the gamification process enables a new interactive communication mode, different from expository or graphic (that is, distinct from narrative or written). This new way of communicating balances the interaction and collaboration respect to the generality of the exposed message. This balance is acceptable because the gamification turns out to be a cognitive tool of significant impact (see [1]. This was also verified on-field by the use of the application, object of this article.

We already observed that the introduction of digital tools in cultural heritage facilitated the social inclusion of people with physical inabilities. Immersive displays and virtual reality allow the access (both in their present state and in historical reconstruction) to site otherwise precluded by physical barriers. Other sites could be easily visited by all the people (with or without physical disabilities) but they are restricted for preservation needs. For this reason, virtual reality is a great tool of social inclusion: the cultural heritage could be shared by all in the same way (no separate paths should be implemented depending on physical abilities) and this identical sharing could destroy (or at least greatly reduce) the psychological and physical barriers and led to social aggregation. Furthermore, on the grounds of preservation of cultural heritage, its digitalization enables two main aspects: studying and archiving. To the former it offers a chance to study and inspect artifacts without damage (and also remotely). The latter aspect is a pivotal starting point for the conservation of the current state of a specific artifact or site.

## 2    A Case Study and Our Workflow

In this Section we present the workflow for interactive rendering of the main hall of the Catacombs of San Senatore at Albano Laziale, developed by the first-named author with the collaboration of Dr. Roberto Libera, Director of Museo Diocesano of Albano, Italy. This archaeological area raises some exciting challenges:

- a correct rendering of light in the scanning process to achieve a neutral texture;
- a suitable split of the processing of surface geometry (normal map) of the fresco and its colored texture.

Moreover, our goal was a virtual reality reconstruction, suitable for full-immersion remote navigation by the visitors, aimed to divulgation, spread of knowledge and user-friendliness. The last issue is a very important challenge with high-impact ethical value, because it makes possible to disabled visitors to enjoy the monument: this is a fundamental reason to design a museum presentation in photorealistic virtual reality.[1]

The flow chart of our procedure, in order to achieve a smooth VR simulation, was subdivided as in Fig. 2.

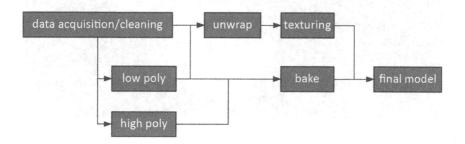

**Fig. 2.** The flowchart

Clearly, the flowchart in Fig. 2 is aimed to create an individual modeled object to be inserted into a scene (for instance, the frescoed wall or a vase or a lamp laying on a table inside the room to render). The first phase consists of capturing/creating the 3D-model and cleaning the data: it starts with a set of photographic images from several viewpoints and extracts from them a dense cloud of 3D-points. The building of those point clouds is based on photogrammetry (without laser or structured light scanners). We limited attention to this

---

[1] This aspect is particularly important for catacombs. A visitor with walking disabilities will not be able to visit a catacomb not equipped with suitable adjustments of the walking path. but these adjustments are often incompatible with the preservation of the archaeological area, or at least very difficult. Virtual Reality allows these persons to experience a full immersion into the archaeological site, with natural interaction.

technique to verify, on-field, the quality of the algorithms and the software currently available. We shot 570 photos (Nikon D7000 equipped with 35 mm lens) of the main hall following some best practices [3]. By making use of Reality Capture as reconstruction software, we obtained in a few hours a dense point cloud (15 millions triangles) on consumer hardware (CPU Intel i7-5820K, 32 Gb RAM, GPU NVIDIA Titan). The number of images as well as the polygon density of the dense point cloud should be higher for final use. For this target, we plan to improve the final visual performance by trying to optimize both the snapshot step and the point cloud management. Our research provided a good enough performance when the data are used only for gamification, but a greater resolution (consequently, a greater number of photos) should be used in order to build up a unified workflow (end-user and pro-user).

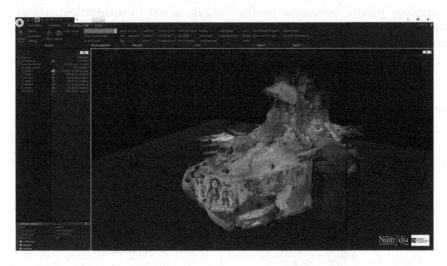

**Fig. 3.** View of Reality Capture screenshot, with the dense point cloud of the main hall of the Catacombs of San Senatore

Note that, during the snapshot step, controlled temperature lamps were used in order to maintain an adequate colorimetric level. Furthermore, we move them as to have a good illumination response. This is really important to get a correct capture of the paintings and to manage the texture during real-time rendering.

A neutral and uniform illumination without shadows allows to insert artificial lights in the rendering phase with photorealistic material response. Furthermore, uniform and "clean" data speed up image post-processing considerably.

This dense cloud is the starting step to generate a *high-poly* (high-resolution) and *low poly* (low-resolution) meshes. These two variants of the meshes allow us to use the same captured 3D-model at the high precision needed for a scientific presentation and at the lower precision but faster processing speed suitable for a virtual visit and interactive remote navigation. The projection of the meshes

**Fig. 4.** Lamps used for snapshot step

onto the texture plane performed by the reconstruction software is highly dependent of the required output quality, and can be scarcely adapted to provide an
adequate rendering performance. For this reason we performed an appropriate
semi-automatic unwrap capable of an optimal compromise between the conflict-
ing goals of preserving the quality and speeding up the rendering. Furthermore
we transferred (baked) the high-resolution topological information to the texture
of the low-poly in a way that allows to add surface details without impacting on
performances (see more details below in the example of the wall).

The unwrap step is very important: it is based on a semi-automatic tweaking
procedure. The way a texture is unwrapped onto a surface has a direct impact
on performance of rendering. To obtain high quality rendering and to take full
advantage of the information obtained from the photos, a high pixel density
should be used. This could be made possible by "subdividing" a surface mapped
on the square $[0, 1] \times [0, 1]$ of texture coordinates, but this procedure associates
many different materials to an individual object, or, in order to achieve better
performance, to many objects (stemming from a subdivision based on materials).
When the number of objects increases, the number of draw calls also does, with a
negative impact on rendering performance. We could counterbalance the negative
impact by making use of a texture with lower resolution than to the one used
for an individual object. We have three degrees of freedom:

– how many sub-objects stem from an individual one;
– texture resolution for an individual sub-object;
– number of operations to perform to transfer all the data to game engine.

We could make an automatic choice of some of these parameters, but the third one is the most time-consuming as it is mostly manual. There is no general rule to optimize these parameters. We can develop appropriate scripts to speed up some factors over others, but some tweaking is always needed depending on the scene. In the scene shown in the figures, we focused our attention to the main fresco and developed an unwrap style aimed to maximize the use of this surface. Furthermore, the main surface should be correctly managed in view of a post-processing phase of restoration. Indeed, a fragmentation of the fresco (unwrapping the main surface to different sectors) is a bad choice here, because it makes more difficult to restore the painting during post-processing.

Figure 5 illustrates a ceremony in the catacombs, built in Virtual Reality for the purposes of illustration addressed to visitors of the museum. The scene includes several objects whose geometric shape and texture has been reconstructed via photogrammetric methods, at least in part: for instance, a capital, a lamp, an amphora and a frescoed wall. The modeling was achieved through photogrammetry in the parts where the original surface of the amphora in Fig. 6 was entirely modeled by means of photogrammetric elaboration. The lamp in Fig. 7 was rebuilt for approximately half of its surface, and only about one fourth of the capital in Fig. 8 was obtained starting with photographs.

The frescoed wall shows a good example of unwrapping. Figure 9 shows four adjacent slices. From left to right, the first slice has been modeled through the high resolution mesh high-poly. The second is based on low-poly. In the third, the mesh is low-poly, but the normal vectors of each polygon of the mesh have been changed: what we see is the rendering based on Phong illumination after replacing at each point the normal vector of the low-poly mesh with the normal vector of the high-poly variant. The data about the normal vectors are embedded

**Fig. 5.** A moment in history reconstructed in Virtual Reality

**Fig. 6.** An amphora entirely reconstructed via photogrammetry

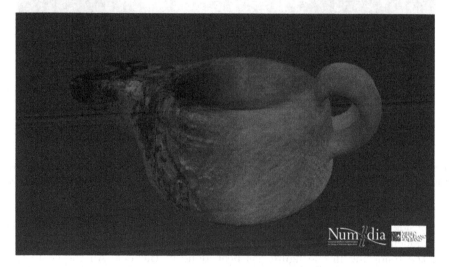

**Fig. 7.** A lamp reconstructed via photogrammetry (on the left) and partial rebuilding (on the right): the texture on the left shows the real color captured by the camera, but the color on the right is a superimposed terra-cotta texture

in the material as a texture, in order to enhance the speed of the rendering phase. In the fourth slice, we did the same, but added a diffusive component of the lighting, based on Lambert illumination rule: the color at each point used in Lambert model is given by the texture of the fresco extracted from the photographic images.

**Fig. 8.** A reconstructed capital: the red part was obtained through photogrammetry, the rest was remodeled and rebuilt (Color figure online)

Beside the simple visual representation, we investigated the chance to use the 3D modeling tool to support the virtual restoration of paintings and artifacts. All the rendering in the figure has been done in Blender. All the geometric, texturing and unwrapping manipulations have been done with proprietary code in Python by the first-named author. We choose Blender because of the following fundamental aspects: its open-source nature, the easiness of its modeling tools, the expandability provided by its API. The mesh obtained from photogrammetry as the base of polygonal modeling allowed the study of new restoration solutions and theories.

The real time rendering was done on Unreal Engine while the VR system was HTC Vive. This choice is due to the quality offered by this game engine over its direct counterpart (Unity). No particular interactions were implemented in the main scene. The main hall dimensions, in fact, are similar to the ones required by the typical installation of room-based virtual reality (4 × 4 meters).

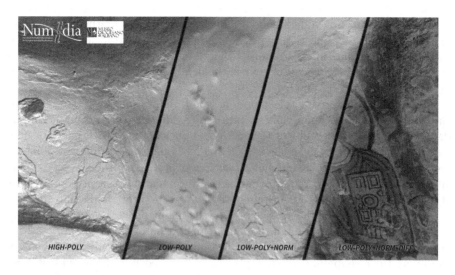

**Fig. 9.** Mixing meshes of various resolutions to obtain different levels of precision on the reconstruction of an ancient wall

Using this installation, the user could easily reach every point of interest in the virtual scene. To focus the attention on the main fresco we used a "fog shield" sited along directions with no interest. Furthermore, the chance to not use the teleportation system (typical for room scale VR with scene much bigger than $4 \times 4$ m) alleviate the need by the user to learn a new interaction technique and facilitate the approach to the experience.

The user starts his visit in the current state of the main hall (as reconstructed from photogrammetry) and after a while he is carried to the reconstruction of the same hall (around VII century AD). Finally, the user is projected in a totally neutral environment where he could interact with some artifact (the amphora, the capital or the lamps) digitally reconstructed from the photogrammetry step. The interaction (thanks to Vive controller) is deliberately simple to stimulate the exploration and the view of artifacts as they could be seen inside the museum cases, with the added opportunity to virtually handle them and to view them all around.

## 3 Toward a Mathematical Approach to the Style of Ancient Pottery

We have seen that some artifacts in the catacombs were partially rebuilt for the purposes of museum exhibition, visualization and illustration. This was necessary as a consequence of incomplete preservation of the original surface. It is important, when we rebuild part of an archaeological find, to preserve the original style as much as possible (see for instance the capital in Fig. 8, where the rebuilding was extensive. But how do we define the concept of *style* so that a computer program can understand it? This last section is a mathematical divertissement about this question, with no claims of expertise in art history, but with the hope of providing stimulus to museum exhibitions addressed to children. Except for this purpose, of course, the definition of style that we are about to present is far too simplistic.

Once an artistic artifact is found in good shape, almost intact, like the amphora in Fig. 6, we may clone it into many different variants by acting on the mesh of the modeled object (let us say, an ancient vase) with linear or nonlinear operators, maybe even choosing a different operator on different points of the mesh. Of course, the latter choice (varying operators), although very simply implemented in Python, requires interactive intervention of a person, because of many constraints (like, for instance, the fact, to be prevented, that after the manipulations a part of the surface of the vase might penetrate another part of its surface). On the other hand, non-linear operators of this type are essential in producing instances of the vase, for instance in adding handles or a beak or modifying their shape and relative positions. But because of the evident complexity, the approach via varying operators will not be analyzed in this simple sketch, but we shall give some examples later.

We should point out the following fact. There are two ways to modify an object in $\mathbb{R}^3$: by modifying the coordinates of world space, hence in particular the object but as a whole, or by applying local changes to its mesh. The former is expressed by the action of a linear operator, the latter is not, and it offers much more adaptability and variety.

However, the manipulation by linear operators is much simpler, and indeed, it is very congenial to photogrammetry, since the camera models in photogrammetry and computer vision are based on similar tools. There are three types of operators to consider, of increasing generality.

The case of least generality is euclidean operators, that is, similarities. These operators consist of compositions of translations, rotations and dilations. Their action changes the object exactly has we would do by physically handling the object with rigid motions, that is, moving it aside, rotating it and bringing it closer or farther away of our eye. Of course, the modified object is still considered, in our mind, the same as before the modification, not true variant: only position and scale have been changed, but not the relative proportions and shapes of its parts.

The case of maximum generality must be expressed in the framework of projective geometry. The vertices of the mesh are vectors $v = (v_1, v_2, v_3) \in \mathbb{R}^3$. Embed them into $\mathbb{R}^4$, but keep the number of parameters equal to three by identifying any two vectors that are non-zero multiples of each other. Then each non-zero vector in $\mathbb{R}^4$ belongs to a different equivalence class, and each equivalence class has a special representative $\tilde{v} = (v_1, v_2, v_3, 1)$, except the classes with representative $\tilde{v} = (v_1, v_2, v_3, 0)$, that (taken all together) form the *plane at infinity*. The set of equivalence classes is called the *projective space* $\mathbb{P}^3$. A projective transformation is a special type of mapping on $\mathbb{P}^3$, or equivalently, a mapping of $\mathbb{R}^4$ that preserves the equivalence classes, that is, that commuted with dilations.

This special mappings are those that are invertible and map collinear triples of points of $\mathbb{R}^4$ into collinear points. It is easy to see that these mappings are expressed by linear operators on $\mathbb{R}^4$ (hence their action is given by a very fast computation in all computer languages), and form a group, called the projective group. Unfortunately, the action of the projective group is transitive on the projective space, and in particular many projective transformations map points at infinity into points at finite (and conversely): that is, the plane at infinity is not preserved. The reason why we wrote "unfortunately" is that transformations that map to infinity a point inside an object give rise to frightening geometric and perspective distortions and shrinkings, that produce unrecognizable variants of the object (say, a vase): nobody would consider these variants as examples of another vase of a similar style. However, we shall soon see that the projective transformations that do not map to infinity points of the vase (or inside its convex hull) provide a large number of interesting and realistic variants of similar type. Once the modeled object is given, the projective transformations that map its convex hull to the convex hull of the transformed object are called *quasi-affine transformations* of the object. The quasi-affine transformations of an object form a group, that we call its quasi-affine group.

The intermediate case between similarities and projective maps consists of those linear operators of $\mathbb{R}^4$ that are invertible and preserve the plane at infinity. These linear operators are called *affine*. When we restrict attention to a three-dimensional subspace $V \approx \mathbb{R}^3$ of $\mathbb{R}^4$ that does not contain the plane at infinity, affine operators consist of linear operators on $\mathbb{R}^3$ followed by translations in $\mathbb{R}^4$. The action of an affine transformation on an object is not a similarity: orthogonality of vectors is not preserved, but parallelism is. So an affine deformation of an object is a variant with a distorted but recognizable geometry. However, affine transformations are still rather rigid. For instance, the amphora of Fig. 6 has a handle and a beak on the opposite side: no affine transformation of the amphora can bring handle and beak to the same side, because the three points given by the barycenter of the handle and the beak and the center of the top opening of the vase are collinear, and collinearity is preserved by affine transformation. Actually, the same is true for any linear operator, so also the projective transformations are rigid in this sense: they not yield twists or twirls. In order to make variants of the vase where handles and beaks get closer, we need more handles. We build a vase with four antipodal handles to illustrate the ideas of this Section: see Fig. 10. The variants of a round vase would be much more realistic once deformed, but we choose to design a square vase in order to make the geometric actions clearer.

Linear transformations preserve the number of handles. This statement is a consequence of the following result:

**Theorem 1.** *Projective transformations preserve the topological genus of a surface.*

So, we can now produce many realistic variants of our vase. Figure 11 shows some examples of quasi-affine transformations of the square vase with four handles.

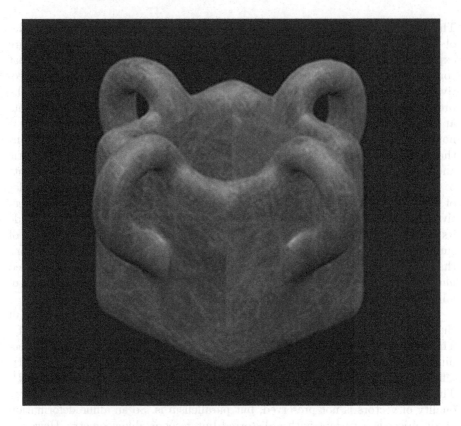

**Fig. 10.** A square vase with four handles, designed for this presentation

Note that these transformations are not affine: indeed, the four vertical corner lines do not remain parallel.

The viewpoint of a mathematician is that there is something in common between all these variants, and we should call this mysterious entity the *style* of the artpiece. In this sense, the style of an object is its orbit under the group of quasi-affine transformation, or in other words the equivalence classes of the relation that states that two objects are equivalent if each of them can be transformed into the other by a affine (or quasi-affine) transformation.

A projective transformation is represented by a four-dimensional matrix,

$$\begin{pmatrix} a_{11} & a_{12} & a_{13} & a_{14} \\ a_{21} & a_{22} & a_{23} & a_{24} \\ a_{31} & a_{32} & a_{33} & a_{34} \\ a_{41} & a_{42} & a_{43} & a_{44} \end{pmatrix}.$$

This matrix gives rise to an affine transformation if its last row is $(0, 0, 0, 1)$: this preserves the plane at infinity in the projective space. The square vase in Fig. 10 is a modification of the unit cube centered at the origin in $\mathbb{R}^3$ with main axes

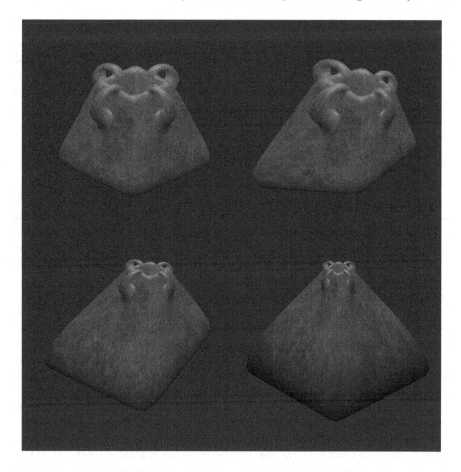

**Fig. 11.** Quasi-affine variants of square vase

given by the three canonical basis vectors $(1, 0, 0, (0, 1, 0), (0, 0, 1)$. Its four variants of Fig. 11 are produced by the action of four projective transformation that are quasi-affine with respect to the unit cube. The upper three by three block in all four is the same as the identity matrix. In the fourth column we set $a_{34} = 0$ in all four, and choose $a_{14}$, $a_{24}$ small and possibly different from matrix to matrix (these entries represent skew, that is, horizontal translations of the top of the vase). The last rows of the four matrices are, respectively, $(a_{41}, a_{42}, a_{43}, a_{44}) = (0, 0, 0.3, 0.8)$, $(0.1, 0.1, 0.3, 0.8)$, $(0, 0.1, 0.5, 0.8)$, $(0, 0, 0.2, 0.25)$. It is easy to see that none of these matrices maps any point of the unit cube to infinity, hence they are quasi-affine on it. By reducing the value of the last entry, we can make the projective transformation become non-quasi-affine, but then a part of the vase is mapped to infinity and Blender is unable to offer an understandable rendering (and so is anybody: the shape becomes unbelievably complex). See [2] for a reference on projective, quasi-affine and affine transformations in photogrammetry.

Since matrix operations are fast, the variants can be created (and rendered) quickly, and will serve a good purpose in interactive museum games meant to lead children to reflect on art and styles. Of course, the game should have bounds in its sliders so as to prevent making the transformations non-quasi-affine, as explained above. But a more fulfilling and satisfactory approach can be obtained by adding local deformations, as explained below.

## 4   Producing Variants of an Artpiece via Non-linear Operators

It is important to realize that quasi-affine transformations, being linear operators, that is, global changes of coordinates in three-dimensional space, on one side have the great advantage of being extremely fast, but on the other side are a bit rigid: the variants of an artpiece under these transformations do not have any twists. So let us show examples of other transformations, nonlinear, that apply to the mesh of vertices of the model (or just to a part of it) and produce twirls or stretches or other deformations. These transformations, that we call *local transformations*, are easily implemented in Blender. Twirls and stretches are great tools to modify a modeled vase into some new variants that appear as instances of the same style, but have very different looks, as shown in Fig. 12. Therefore, our mathematical idea of style extends to include orbits under non-linear transformation groups. The application Blender implements twirls and stretches on the whole mesh of a modeled object, but also on local parts of the mesh: it allows, for instance, to twist a handle or stretch another. New handles can be added via specific creation (or *prototyping*) operators that modify the mesh by replacing parts of it with appropriate predefines shapes: these transformations, however, must be built case by case by operating upon a given mesh, ad so they must be constructed interactively in real time, a demanding and time-consuming process.

A very nice fact (evident in all our Figures) is that also the texture of the object is transformed to a new texture, both by projective transformations and by local transformations. But here the usual meaning of style requires a much wider group of transformations acting on textures: we must accept as realistic variants of textures those obtained by transformations that are continuous but do not necessarily map collinear triples to collinear triples, hence not linear. For instance, a person painted on a vase may have straight arms and legs, but we would consider variants within the same style those where the painted persons have folded arms and legs. Again here, the texture transformation must preserve the convex hull of (planar) objects, and in particular, for every painted person with a given outline, the transformation not only maps outline to outline, but must also map its interior to the interior of the image. However, there are many more constraints, often different from a style to another. For instance, the decoration of several types of ancient vases often splits the surface into horizontal levels (like floors, that is, horizontal curves, perpendicular to the central vertical axis of the vase), and aligned on the same horizontal level several groups

**Fig. 12.** Twisted or stretched variants of square vase.

of persons and animals. Therefore the acceptable texture transformations must preserve these horizontal curves. On the other hand, they do not have to preserve the number of persons at each level. Therefore the "style" of the texture or painting can be considered an equivalence class under a group of transformations that, again, must include local creation and cancellation operations. This becomes a very complicated concept or axiomatic definition, and we stop our presentation here.

# References

1. de Freitas, S.: What-can-Gamification-add-to-cultural-heritage.pdf. http://www.
   digitalmeetsculture.net/wp-content/uploads/2013/07/Sara_de_Freitas_What-can-
   Gamification-add-to-cultural-heritage.pdf
2. Hartley, R., Zisserman, A.: Multiple View Geometry in Computer Vision, 2nd edn.
   Cambridge University Press, Cambridge (2004)
3. Mallison, H., Wings, O.: Photogrammetry in paleontology - a practical guide. J.
   Paleontol. Tech. **12**, 1–31 (2014)

# User Experience of Markerless Augmented Reality Applications in Cultural Heritage Museums: 'MuseumEye' as a Case Study

Ramy Hammady[1]([✉]), Minhua Ma[1], and Anna Powell[2]

[1] School of Computing and Digital Technology,
Staffordshire University, Stoke-on-Trent, UK
ramy.hammady@research.staffs.ac.uk, m.ma@staffs.ac.uk
[2] School of Art, Design and Architecture, University of Huddersfield,
Huddersfield, UK
A.Powell@hud.ac.uk

**Abstract.** This paper explores the User Experience (UX) of Augmented Reality applications in museums. UX as a concept is vital to effective visual communication and interpretation in museums, and to enhance usability during a museum tour. In the project 'MuseumEye', the augmentations generated were localized based on a hybrid system that combines of (SLAM) markerless tracking technology and the indoor Beacons or Bluetooth Low Energy (BLE). These augmentations include a combination of multimedia content and different levels of visual information that required for museum visitors. Using mobile devices to pilot this application, we developed a UX design model that has the ability to evaluate the user experience and usability of the application. This paper focuses on the multidisciplinary outcomes of the project from both a technical and museological perspective based on public responses. A field evaluation of the AR system was conducted after the UX model considered. Twenty-six participants were recruited in Leeds museum and another twenty participants in the Egyptian museum in Cairo. Results showed positive responses on experiencing the system after adopting the UX design model. This study contributes on synthesizing a UX design model for AR applications to reach the optimum levels of user interaction required that reflects ultimately on the entire museum experience.

**Keywords:** User experience · Markerless · UX design model
iBeacon · Cultural heritage

## Abbreviations

UX    User Experience
MAR   Markerless Augmented Reality

# 1  Introduction

Augmented Reality (AR) as a term has evolved through the last decade [1–3]. It has become a promising trend and its potential role in museums has become more widely understood as a part of developments in approaches to museum interpretation [4–6]. With a view to addressing usability for interpretation devices in the museum context, this research has developed a mobile museum guide named 'MuseumEye' that can be employed in museums with a markerless tracking technique. The technique enables the viewer to observe objects and artefacts safely, and in more detail, outside the confines of their glass vitrines. This technique does not require a label or tag to trigger the augmentations [7]. Also, the tracking method used is an integration between MAR and indoor location beacons. The design philosophy here is primarily one of visual communication and user experience. Primary research was conducted in museums to enable the researchers to experience and test their products in an appropriate environment. The factors measured included usability, flexibility and human interactions with the technology. The literature addressed in this research supported identification of the most appropriate technical aspects of the project relevant to tracking systems, for example the functionality of Markerless tracking and the SLAM method. Ultimately, it is hoped that this investigation of user experience will provide a useful model or taxonomy transferrable to other AR applications.

Simultaneous Localization And Mapping (SLAM) is a method that can detect a model's edges from a series of images, without the need for previously identifying the real environment [8]. It is also defined as the process of simultaneously building a static map and estimating the sensor motion [9]. SLAM as a technique is illustrated when a computer with a live camera is attached to it, transforming it into a real-time sensor position [10]. It is also defined as a self-mapping of visual features which are located in the surrounding environment, through a continuous calculation of the camera motions [10]. Other researchers further evolved SLAM by defining a new algorithm that can overcome the challenge of selecting the landmarks' edges [11]. Most Augmented Reality (AR) applications that deploy the mobile devices rely on the recognition of unseen physical objects in the real environment to apply the augmentation in the process. Moreover, the tracking should be accurate and allow the user to interact with the augmentation. Most of the conventional AR applications were built on the basis of the existing marker. However, there are various limitations to the fiducial or visual markers: For instance, the superimposed objects will be lost in tracking if the camera moves fast due to the correlation of the framerate. Visual markers have a limited range for tracking and should remain in sight [8]. Furthermore, they are not scalable for the outdoor environment [12].

SLAM relies on the Markerless Augmented Reality (MAR) as it breaks the boundaries of allocating tags or images on the augmentation area. Markerless tracking has a great impact upon AR user experience. It enhances user interaction and perception with the real world without physical constrains [15]. It can consider any part of the real environment as a marker to position the virtual objects [15]. This tracking system could be achieved using various sensors technologies such as gyroscopes, hybrid vision, GPS triggering, infrared tags or triggers [16, 17, 2]. There has been a considerable amount of tracking research conducted with the monocular camera [18, 10] or with Kinect cameras [19] in order to track complex 3D models in real-time while avoiding occlusion and illumination [15].

There are examples of MAR tracking applications in the museums and galleries sector: A group of scholars created a project named "MapLens" [20] and it is claimed that the method used was Markerless. However, it works by identifying a paper map which has to be facing the user's camera. A further project named "ANR GAMME" was built, based on an iterative design method to guide visitors in museums, which relies on a Markerless tracking. Visitors were, however, required to angle the device's camera towards the painting on the wall to reveal the pre-prepared content [21]. Headsets such as optical see-through displays have also been used in MAR, in the context of cultural heritage, to identify the motivations and needs of museum professionals [22].

In 'MuseumEye', we resolved that one of the most efficient ways to build successful communication between the user's device and our servers was to use IBeacons. These beacons rely on using a low energy connection. The rationale behind using beacons is the large range of connection it usually has compared with infrared tags. It connects with devices via Bluetooth transmission in a range of 70 m [23]. Bluetooth connections can influence devices within their sphere of connections, rather than relying on other ways of connection that require point-to-point correspondence [16]. So MuseumEye contributes on creating a hyper system that combines between creating MAR augmentations on SLAM technology and the indoor location beacons. This system aims to achieve robust connections between the user and the generated visuals.

This study also investigates the user experience concepts and criteria that should be taken into account during the development of AR application in museums. The investigations included a study on the tour requirements and the way the visitor responds during the usage of the AR system. These investigations contributed on creating the UX design model, that able to assist developers to create museum AR applications with enhanced usability aspects, which reflects ultimately on the museum experience.

## 1.1 User Experience (UX) and (MAR)

User Experience (UX) as a term emerged from two decades in the community of Human Computer Interaction (HCI) [24]. UX generally includes several disciplines such as visual design, human factors, information delivery, hologram design, content, sound design, and interaction design, as depicted in Fig. 1. User experience was defined by ISO as a *"person's perceptions and responses resulting from the use and/or anticipated use of a product, system or service"*. It also observes the responses ranging from emotions, perceptions, behaviours to the physical and psychological responses from users prior, during and after experiencing the application [25]. However, researchers and writers have attempted to define UX from different perspectives. For instance, Ellis defines UX as the discipline that instructs the way of changing the product in order to affect the user's feelings and his/her behaviour. It includes the whole experience of using the product/system such as making assessments about user preferences, even identifying moments of delight or frustration [26]. However, Unger and Chandler [27] defined user experience design within a broader definition, which is *"The creation and synchronization of the elements that effect the user's experience with a particular company, with the intent of influencing their perceptions and behaviour"* [27]. These are elements that are manifested in the human senses, such as touch (haptics), hearing and smell. It was difficult for the researchers and designers working in the field to decide upon a definitive definition until Law et al. surveyed 5 definitions. These definitions vary depending on the perspective of the respondent and their nature of work; either academic or industrial, and the scope of their work [24]. Based on the capacity and nature of this system, and the researcher disciplines and backgrounds, this paper uses the following definition: *"UX is a consequence of a user's internal state (predispositions, expectations, needs, motivation, mood, etc.), the characteristics of the designed system (e.g. complexity, purpose, usability, function-ality, etc.) and the context (or the environment) within which the interaction occurs (e.g. organizational/social setting, meaningfulness of the activity, voluntariness of use, etc.)"* [28]. In short, UX surpasses the traditional line of usability and achieving the product goals through creating emotional and perception-based bonds between the human and the product, whether a tangible or nontangible product.

The recent trend of mobile AR applications takes many forms such as head mounted displays, smartphones and tablets. One of the significant objectives of this paper is to discover which elements of user experience should be embraced in the proposed mark-erless augmented reality application, and to build a UX design model which can be used as a workflow to build successful MAR applications that foreground user experience.

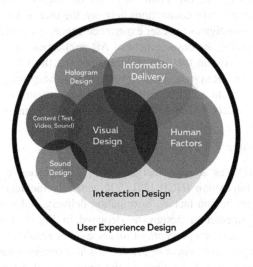

**Fig. 1.** Diagram of User Experience involving cross disciplines (modified from www.interaction-design.org)

## 2   UX Design Process Model

While it is essential to build a workflow that includes all design phases, it proved to be a challenge to articulate the true impact of user experience of the markerless AR application. Due to its novelty in the industry, it was difficult to identify what users want in these applications, and whether they are effective in enhancing the viewing experience. Identifying the user experience in the interactive system is even more complicated than in the traditional systems [29]. The next step, therefore, was to brainstorm a unified workflow that could work as a model for the UX design process and include these (Fig. 2). This model has three phases starting with the design requirements for UX and ended with evaluation.

In the 'requirement phase', there are some information, skills and data needed to be obtained before starting to design and develop the system. The objectives of the system had to be considered alongside the practicalities of building the system, such as providing guidance and visual information to support and not conflict with the museum's existing displays and interpretation resources. Besides this, it was necessary to acquire the information content for the artefacts with which the technology would be used, such as the 3D models, the audio commentaries, relevant images and the existing explanatory text provided alongside the exhibits. The research then took a considerable step forward to address following questions:

- Is this application intuitive and easy to use?
- Does the navigation meet expectations? In another words, is the next move anticipated?
- Are the visuals supported and can they achieve the goals set?
- Is the 3D navigation intuitive?
- Is placing the 3D artefacts within the physical environment intuitive or cumbersome to the viewer's experience and understanding of the exhibits?
- Does the application construct an emotional bond between it and the user so we guarantee the continuity of using it?
- Is the user satisfied and interested to continue using the app alongside his tour?

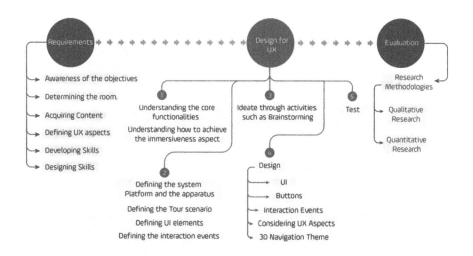

**Fig. 2.** UX design process model

Würstl believed that user experience generally comprises three main areas, 'Usability', 'Look' and 'Feel', and he suggested that usability is one third of these divisions [30]. In the following model we conclude that the UX is a mixture of usability aspects blended with the sensory and emotional aspects. By responding to the previous questions and through first hand research, we were able to devise the user experience aspects of markerless augmented reality applications depicted in Fig. 3. In short, it has two main categories: the **'Utilitarian'** aspects which focus on the main functionalities of the system, and the **'Visual'** aspects that concern the appearance of the application and ways of influencing the look and feel of the system to the user. Regarding the **'Utilitarian'** aspect, it has two main sections: functionality and interaction. The **'Functionality'** section manifests the focus of the system and the main role that the system plays. The MAR app requires a seamless integration of the 3D object in the physical environments to enable the user to have the illusion of being immersed in a mixed environment. It is essential for it to be a lightweight application that does not use too much RAM, and it is recommended that it should consume enough energy from the mobile battery to last the duration of the visit. Moreover, the registration of the 3D objects in the real world should be very accurate to help create a sense of their realness. Customization is a key factor in letting the user feel ownership of the application which, in turn, helps them to build an emotional bond with the system.

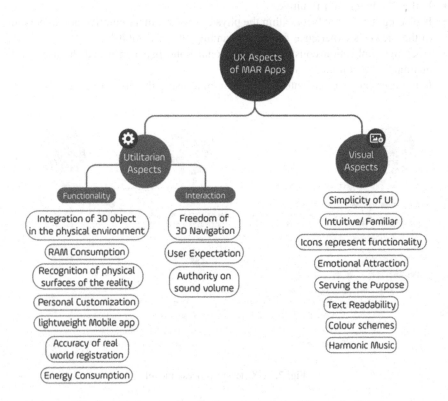

**Fig. 3.** UX aspects of markerless augmented reality applications

The second section includes the '**Interaction**' elements. These are concerned with how the user interact with the system and the responds to the system. It allocates the human to the center of the system and it also considers them to be the most integral part of the communication process between him/her and the system. These aspects necessitate giving the user the privilege of freedom of navigating the 3D object in the physical environment, as the user holds the object in reality. This allows the user to reposition, rotate and rescale the object. This feature was a fundamental reason behind building the application, due to the fragility of many artefacts and the simultaneous benefits to the viewer of being able to access them close at hand. One of the key usability factors of the system is to allow the user to anticipate the next click/move. It is also important to allow the user some authority over his/her device while the application is running, such as controlling the sound volume, pausing, playing and stopping the file.

Concerning the second section, the '**Visual aspects**', the main objective is to construct the emotional bond between the system and the users. To achieve these objectives, it is important to make the user interface as simple as possible, including all UI elements such as buttons, headers, images etc. Familiarity is one of the key aspects in creating an emotional bond between the user and the application; to create the sense that they have used the application before. The idea behind the abstract graphic icon was to represent its function directly without confusing the viewer. This will help to save time when using the device, and make the application more familiar and intuitive to the new user. Design skills are an important part of ensuring the UI achieves an emotional bond in the viewer and that it serves its intended purpose. Some elements require specific consideration to fulfil their role successfully, such as the font size and colours, which can determine the effectiveness of information delivery. Moreover, the colour scheme should be chosen in a way that is relevant to the context of the application, and the same consideration should be applied to the chosen background music for the application, which plays constantly while presenting content.

The second phase, '**Design for UX**', came directly after determining the perquisites of the app. This phase built on the process of design thinking and was developed to fit the integration of user experience with the entire process.

Design for UX starts with gaining a comprehensive understanding of the context in which it will be used (the museum), and the methodology was to build system specifically targeted for this context. This step was accomplished by exploring the museum and talking to museum visitors as an exploratory study. Further knowledge was gained through referring to relevant literature about designing effective museum interpretation, and further research into the technical information of markerless augmented reality. It was also important to gain a full understanding of the objectives of the system and to understand the importance of UX as previously discussed.

The final phase is to define the specifics of certain elements of the system, such as the platform – either android or IOS – in order to prepare the developing tools that fit the targeted device, which can mount the potential system. Identifying the UI elements is important in the designing phase in order to set the interaction events and determine how the system responds to the user. Eventually, this phase ended with drawing the tour scenario for the targeted room, which will be discussed in the next section.

After gaining sufficient knowledge, the next step is to generate ideas. There are some strategies to follow to produce ideas such as brainstorming, SCAMPER [31], Brainwrite, Braindump etc. [32]. These techniques are not only for generating ideas; they can reveal solutions to potential problems. Usually, this stage analyses observations and the information collected in the final stage.

The designing phase is the stage that involves sketching and designing the UI of the application including buttons, and interaction events. During this phase, all of the UX aspects will be addressed and considered. This stage should culminate in a prototype with full functionality and without bugs or errors. Moreover, this prototype should communicate perfectly with the IBeacons in order to mount them in the museum room.

The final stage is testing and this stage is conducted several times in the lab and by both designers and developers in order to reveal any flaws and errors. However, this stage is usually conducted iteratively. Whenever a problem pops up during testing, the system will be taken back to previous stages to get a full understanding of the situation, in order to determine a solution.

The third phase is 'Evaluation' and this phase involves visitors in museums and experts in the field providing valuable feedback. This stage follows a particular methodology to obtain the required feedback and it is divided into two methods: Qualitative and Quantitative research. The workflow of the evaluation phase will be demonstrated in the participation and experiments section.

# 3   'MuseumEye' Project

This project used the SLAM markerless-tracking technique to achieve the most effective way of viewing appropriate to the required augmentation. Most markerless applications currently in the market depend on pointing the device's rear camera to an exhibited image. These images are considered markers to the camera and trigger the augmentations in the AR system to be revealed. Research into the development of augmented reality is now considering similar techniques to marker-tracking, but without using labels or illustrated markers. SLAM markerless tracking relies on placing the augmentations on a surface, requiring the user to point the device's camera to a further surface in order reveal a virtual object or character. The MuseumEye system considers the surface as the origin point to the object, so augmentations look as if they are placed in the real environment and have a realistic appearance.

Some of the tools that used to help us to build MuseumEye included 'Unity', and open source codes such as 'open cvs' and SDK files such as 'ARCore'. These codes and SDKs provide our system with image processing functions such as recognizing and tracking surfaces. Afterwards, the system integrates with the iBeacons which are working as servers for the mobile devices. These beacons are able to allocate the visitor's location then trigger his/her device to be fed with the augmentations, visual and haptic information needed that relevant to the antique's location.

Regarding the 3D antiques, we conducted 3D scanning for the replicas of the antiques then we obtained visual and audio data about the collected antiques. UI designed using Adobe Illustrator and other image editing software such as Adobe Photoshop.

One of the objectives of creating this system was to give the visitor the opportunity to explore a 360-degree view of the exhibited artefact, outside the confines of the glass vitrine, instead of being limited to a predetermined visual perspective. The visitor is given the freedom to see the exhibit from different perspectives, and the navigation tool added to the system allows the user to reposition, rotate and scale the object.

## 3.1   Scenario

The tour design for Leeds museum and the Egyptian museum was created to be a thematic type of tour. It was designed by synchronizing the audio content with the relevant artefacts, to develop an ambient music, which was appropriate to the museum context. Firstly, as seen in Fig. 4, we drew a sensible route in the targeted rooms in both museums, one which would be a closed route to start and end at the same point in a circle shape. Then, as seen in Fig. 5, we designed the tour by adding the visual and audio commentaries fitting the context of the room to make the visitor embrace the virtual content in an interesting manner. As the visitor arrives at the first point, the aim is that he/she will gain the full experience of the AR system.

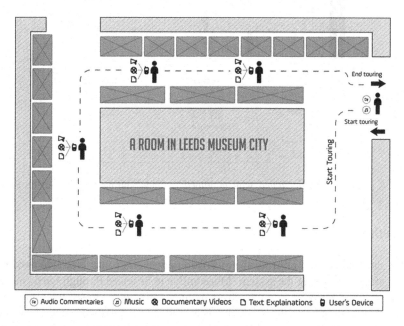

**Fig. 4.** A planned walk Integrated with multimedia content during the visit in Leeds Museum City's room.

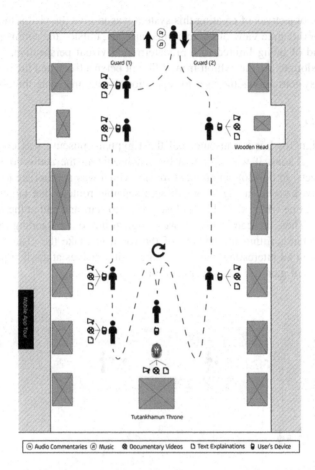

Fig. 5. A planned walk Integrated with multimedia content during the visit in the Egyptian museum's room.

## 4 Method

Briefly, the method embraced for the evaluation process is constituted into two stages, the first stage is exposing the system 'MuseumEye to be tested through Leeds museum. During the experiment, an in direct observation was conducted to see the user's ability to use the system and also the observations extended to target their emotions about the usability factor. 26 from Leeds Museum's visitors were surveyed and the observation outcomes where taken into consideration to amend the UI functions in the next stage. The second stage was conducted at the Egyptian museum in Cairo and 20 participants were employed to test the system for measuring the usability and the user experience.

This following section describes the device that was adopted to operate the AR guided system alongside the experiment settings in both museums. Further, we demonstrate the experiments carried out within the museum conditions, and how the data collection was conducted in details.

## 4.1  Apparatus

Our system benefits from the scalability of devices that can be used to run it. Thus, any android device higher than Android Marshmallow 3.3 can operate our system. The device employed to run our system was Amazon Fire tablet – a cheap device with many advantages. It has 1.3 GHz quad-core processor and rear- and front-facing cameras and unlimited storage with cloud space or with the SD card. It has a display with resolution of (171 PPI/1024 × 600).

## 4.2  Software

'MuseumEye' was built to work as a markerless application which has the benefit of being able to localize the augmented content, such as 3D models of the artefacts, in a pre-determined location. It was not possible to place markers in the museum halls due to the strict standards of the museum settings. It would, in any case, have been cumbersome for users to follow the markers for each item. Thus, markerless-based tracking gives the user the ability to locate the augmentation wherever he/she desires. Moreover, it has the ability to present the augmentations in real-time in the museum's environment.

Once the visitor arrives to the antique's location, the visitor gets notification from the iBeacon servers to open the interface of the application, which brings a live feed camera in front. This interface includes buttons on left and right that comprised of all desired visuals that visitor might needs such as textual, images, audio recordings.

**Fig. 6.** 'MuseumEye' places objects using MAR technology

At the bottom- middle of the UI, a button requesting the visitor to allocate the virtual antique on the ground. So, the visitor can aim to the ground then presses this button, then the antique's augmentation will be placed on the ground with synced audio narratives about the antique. The most interesting part of the augmentations is the freedom of navigation of the chosen object. The user can interact with the 3D object by rotating, repositioning, scaling it with the proper size he/she desires, as depicted in Fig. 6.

'MuseumEye' encompasses of a combination of multimedia content such as audio commentaries, video representations, and different levels of information about the selected item in a text format and a gallery of images. The user is centred in a multimedia panel which acts as an encyclopaedia to assist the visitor in gaining further information. The localization feature was executed in our system by employing IBeacons in the walls of the hall which was chosen for conducting the field-research. These beacons located the users' devices by triangulation, by sending and receiving signals to a specific point. From this point, the user's device starts to receive the bundle of information (2D/3D visualization/video/animation). Depicted in Fig. 7 is the method of employing IBeacons in Leeds City Museum and The Egyptian Museum in Cairo.

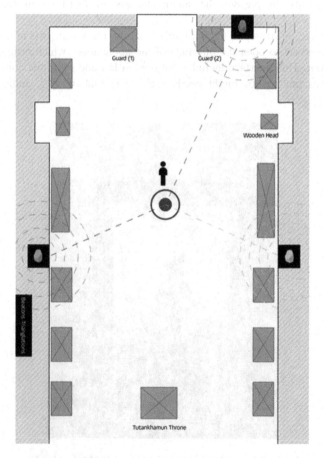

**Fig. 7.** Placing IBeacons in the Egyptian museum's room.

### 4.3   Participants and Experiments

To identify appropriate methods for exploring and testing our system, it was first divided into qualitative and quantitative data, based on the information needed. The quantitative research relied on using quite a large sample of users to identify trends and draw conclusions. Moreover, the qualitative research is needed to get a more in-depth understanding of the context and to acquire valuable information for improving the system. At 'Stage 1' at Leeds city Museum, twenty-six participants were employed for our experiment. What distinguished that sample was the variation of their ages, they were starting from 16 years old to above 60. There was also variation in their levels of education. This varied sample enriched our research findings. The plan was to instruct the chosen participants to use the tablet containing the AR prototype during their regular visit. We briefly demonstrated the system to them individually, then they were asked to start their short tour taking the route described in the previous section. After finishing the planned tour, participants participated in a semi-structured questionnaire (Fig. 8).

**Fig. 8.** Testing MuseumEye at the Egyptian Museum in Cairo.

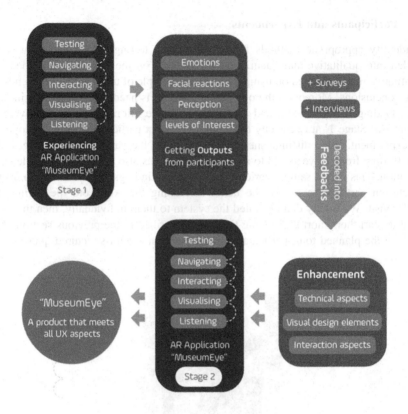

**Fig. 9.** The pathway followed to build 'MuseumEye'

At the Egyptian museum in Cairo the system was setup in the eastern room in the application (product), centring around sense perceptions. While exploring the system in the targeted room, we captured viewers' emotions recognized through comments and facial expressions, and all of these observations were noted and analysed. These observations formed the basis of further questions to the users conducted verbally through interviews, in addition to their nonverbal questions in the questionnaires as depicted in Fig. 9.

Analysis of this user data led to substantial modifications. 'Visual Design': some alterations were accomplished in the interface design such as the button shapes, appearance and fonts. 'Interactivity aspect': the alterations included the navigation gestures and the flow of movement of the 3D model in the space to be more intuitive and familiar to potential users. The application was applied one more time in the Egyptian museum in Cairo, Egypt. At 'Stage 2', the researchers let the application be explored again by the Egyptian museum visitors. Through all of these phases, the application was enhanced to help it to improve on all of the UX aspects that were manifested before.

## 5  Results

After testing the application with 26 participants in Leeds museum and another 20 participants in the Egyptian museum in Cairo, the following results were collated, which present findings from the corresponding questionnaires. The majority of the responses were positive in both museums. In Leeds City Museum, the responses regarding the measured aspects are detailed below in the following table (Table 1):

**Table 1.** Shows the responses of Leeds museum visitors on 'MuseumEye' system.

| Aspects | Strongly Agree | Agree | Neutral | Disagree | Strongly disagree | Average (max = 5) |
|---|---|---|---|---|---|---|
| Immersion aspect | – | 77% | 23% | – | – | 3.76 |
| Useful in Guidance | 15% | 81% | 4% | – | – | 4.11 |
| System easy to use | 19% | 69% | 8% | 4% | – | 3.92 |
| Interesting in museums | 19% | 77% | 4% | – | – | 4.15 |
| Intuitive | 15% | 77% | 8% | – | – | 4.07 |
| Visuals served the purpose | 8% | 92% | – | – | – | 4.07 |

Overall, feedback from the testing phase suggested positive responses to the application as a means of providing guidance and information in the museum. Of the respondents of the Leeds Museum survey, 81% agreed that the application was useful in providing guidance to the museum's exhibits, with 77% agreeing that they felt immersed in the experience of using the application; that it was an interesting way of accessing information in the museum; and that it was intuitive to use.

4% of respondents did not agree that the application was easy to use, and there were a number of low-scoring 'neither agree nor disagree' responses across all questions. These values have been taken into account to improve the functioning of the application for the next phase of evaluation conducted at the Egyptian Museum in Cairo. In the Egyptian Museum, the responses regarding the measured aspects are detailed below in the following table (Table 2):

**Table 2.** Shows the responses of the Egyptian museum visitors on 'MuseumEye' system.

| Aspects | Strongly agree | Agree | Neutral | Disagree | Strongly disagree | Average (max = 5) |
|---|---|---|---|---|---|---|
| Immersion aspect | 55% | 45% | – | – | – | 4.45 |
| Useful in Guidance | 70% | 30% | – | – | – | 4.7 |
| System easy to use | 45% | 45% | 10% | – | – | 4.35 |
| Interesting in museums | 19% | 77% | 4% | – | – | 4.45 |
| Intuitive | 35% | 65% | – | – | – | 4.35 |
| Visuals served the purpose | 55% | 35% | 10% | – | – | 4.45 |

After collating this information it became clear that the most significant different in responses was in relation to the question about the extent to which participants' felt that they were immersed in the experience of using the application. The scores increased in this area from an average of 3.76 out of 5 to an average of 4.45 out of 5. This change may have resulted from the enhancements that were applied to the application after the initial testing phase at Leeds Museum, including amendments to the user interface and some functions relating to user interaction such as exploring the artifact in the 3D view.

It was also notable that the ease of use statement increased in this second testing phase from an average score of 3.92 to 4.35 out of 5, again as a result of enhancements in response to the initial testing phase…. The first version includes some gestures that users did not prefer such as navigation in the images gallery by clicking instead of swiping. Moreover, the level of 3D navigation freedom was very exaggerated. It was cumbersome to navigate the 3D object in 3 coordinates at the same time so we enhance it by freezing axis Y in order to navigate the 3D object around X and Z. Other statements such as the usefulness and intuitiveness of the application also demonstrated an increased score from respondents. It appears from these responses that the enhancements made to the application for the second phase of testing had a beneficial effect on the overall functioning and usability of the application in its museum context.

These results helped to approve the validity of the system after its various stages of enhancements and, in turn, to support the validity of the UX framework that was designed specifically for this system.

The next two graphs show the potential of using Markerless Augmented Reality applications that use SLAM technology to guide visitors in museums, in comparison with the other alternative guides such as human guide, books and audio guides. Participants from Leeds museum chose the preferred guide as the AR guide with 42% against all other guidance methods. However, the analysis showed that the Egyptian museum's visitors chose the AR guide above all guides, with 50% selecting AR as their preferred guide. These results were surprising to us as researchers, and contradicted our preliminary expectations. Conclusions can be drawn here about the likelihood of

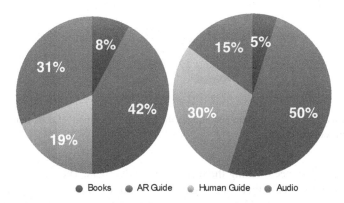

**Fig. 10.** Guide methods chosen by Leeds Museum Visitors (Left) the Egyptian Museum Visitors (Right)

visitors to the Egyptian Museum potentially embracing MAR technology and using mobile devices in their tours (Fig. 10).

The Research conducted at Leeds City Museum and the Egyptian Museum, inCairo, indicates 77% of participants to have felt that using AR technology made the museum-visiting experience a more interesting one. It is interesting to consider the extent to which AR technology might enhance the visitor experience in terms of enjoyment by increasing interest and excitement. It is also important to consider the extent to which visitors' engagement *with the process of using the technology* might surpass and overshadow their engagement with – and understanding of/learning taken from – the exhibits themselves. It seems fair and logical to suggest that excitement will be generated in the visitor by an interpretation device which is capable of 'bringing to life' an exhibit in such a way that the static object is shown to be kinetic and functioning in a new, dynamic context. The way in which it achieves this so effectively – and perhaps one of the most admirable functions of AR – is through its ability to blur the boundaries between reality and artifice. Perhaps the way AR appears to seamlessly meld the real and the illusory is so effective because of the fact that it is, in some respects, delivering reality: It delivers real, lived experience of one kind, in order to enhance real, lived experience of another kind. In this sense, the way it might potentially 'bring to life' an object is truly ground-breaking. The novelty and innovation of this technology's capabilities for animating exhibits in such a way is, arguably, likely to spark visitors' interest and excitement by providing a new type of encounter with the object or artefact, as well as, potentially, by enhancing their understanding and learning.

In light of the question of whether AR technology might limit human-to-human interaction and engagement in the museum, research conducted at both Leeds Museum and The Egyptian Museum, Cairo, asked visitors trialling AR technology to - the extent to which they considered it to actively enhance interaction between themselves and other visitors. Over 70% of participants at both museums agreed that the technology actually encouraged them to interact with others (see Fig. 11). One reason for this might be the fact that, in being a novel form of interpretation, visitors were keen to

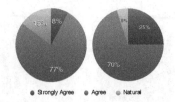

**Fig. 11.** Responds on 'AR system encourages the human interaction' (Leeds museum on Left) (Egyptian museum on right)

discuss their experience of using the technology with others. The extent to which their interaction was to discuss their learning experience, or even the exhibits themselves, is unclear at this stage. It would be interesting to learn whether, if AR was to become an established form of interpretation in museums, this interaction would continue at such a level, or gradually subside.

In summary, AR presents exciting possibilities for museum interpretation. Its communicative capacity combines with its ability to potentially enhance what is seen and heard without having to substantially shift the viewer's field of vision away from an exhibit. This enables the viewer to retain an optimal vantage point for simultaneously viewing the exhibit and learning more about it. It also, potentially, enhances the viewer's understanding of the object's wider context by engaging them in a process of detailed interpretation – the extent to which it might affect visitors' knowledge and understanding of artefacts would be an interesting direction for further research into UX in AR in museums for MuseumEye.

It is also, however, important to remember that for some, new technology can be daunting and even alienating. For others, a more traditional museum-visiting experience might simply be preferred. Perhaps the most successful use of AR in museums would be to implement it as an *option*. By providing an element of choice, visitors would be able to access the technology or to opt for more familiar and established means of engaging with exhibits, depending upon their personal preferences. As a solution to museum interpretation, then, AR might be used in a way that reiterate's Prior's assertion that, 'Perhaps the most innovative and clear-sited museum directors are those who have recognised and exploited the plasticity of the museum idea in order to overlay various levels of aesthetic experience [33].

## 6   Contribution

This paper contributed theoretically by creating the characteristics of the user experience model for augmented reality applications in museums. The UX model process facilitates the procedures needed to identify the visitor's requirement in order to design and develop the system. Also, the UX system contributed to enhance the usability through two field studies and resulted an obvious enhancement on the museum experience. Additionally, the paper contributed practically through building a SLAM markerless AR mobile system 'MuseumEye' that integrated with iBeacons for the indoor spatial allocation purposes. The system surveyed in two museums and resulted positive responses on the usability aspects and for the overall museum experience during the usage of the system. The system passed through several enhancement during the evaluation process by the public contribution to assure the ultimate level of usability.

## 7 Conclusion

This paper has aimed to demonstrate a clear framework of the UX of markerless augmented reality application by manifesting the pathway that was approached for our system in both museums in Leeds, UK and Cairo, Egypt. It emphasized the user experience and usability aspects that should be considered when building a guided system for museums based around mobile devices. The framework has been applied in our system and assessed in two different museums in two different countries. Results show the potential of using AR guides in museums and demonstrate more positive results at the second museum after a series of developments had been put into place after recommended from the first museum visitors: The system was successfully improved based on these public contributions and the valuable feedback received.

Finally, this paper provides insight into the functionality and aesthetic aspects of the user experience of MAR applications which have an impact on the user's enjoyment, motivation, satisfaction and productivity while using the application. It also addresses the optimum levels of user interaction required to best experience the application, and, ultimately, to understand the relationship between AR systems and effective audience engagement in museums.

**Acknowledgments.** The authors would like to thank Leeds museum city staff and the Egyptian museum in Cairo for facilitating our activities. In addition, authors would also like to thank Helwan university and British Council in Egypt and the Egyptian Culture Bureau as the main funding body for our research and all who supported us and gave us the valuable advises to design and develop our system.

## References

1. Azuma, R.T.: A survey of augmented reality. Presence **6**(4), 355–385 (1997)
2. Azuma, R., et al.: Recent advances in augmented reality. IEEE Comput. Graph. Appl. **21**(6), 34–47 (2001)
3. Höllerer, T., Feiner, S.: Mobile augmented reality (2004)
4. Damala, A., Marchal, I., Houlier, P.: Merging augmented reality based features in mobile multimedia museum guides. In: Anticipating the Future of the Cultural Past, CIPA Conference 2007, 1–6 October 2007 (2007)
5. Wojciechowski, R., et al.: Building virtual and augmented reality museum exhibitions. In: Proceedings of the Ninth International Conference on 3D Web Technology, pp. 135–144. ACM, Monterey (2004)
6. Tscheu, F., Buhalis, D.: Augmented reality at cultural heritage sites. In: Inversini, A., Schegg, R. (eds.) Information and Communication Technologies in Tourism 2016, pp. 607–619. Springer, Cham (2016). https://doi.org/10.1007/978-3-319-28231-2_44

7. Teichrieb, V., et al.: A survey of online monocular markerless augmented reality. Int. J. Model. Simul. Pet. Ind. **1**(1), 1–7 (2007)
8. Zhou, F., Duh, H.B.-L., Billinghurst, M.: Trends in augmented reality tracking, interaction and display: a review of ten years of ISMAR. In: Proceedings of the 7th IEEE/ACM International Symposium on Mixed and Augmented Reality. IEEE Computer Society (2008)
9. Molton, N., Davison, A.J., Reid, I.: Locally planar patch features for real-time structure from motion. In: BMVC British Machine Vision Conference (2004)
10. Davison, A.J.: Real-time simultaneous localisation and mapping with a single camera. In: Ninth IEEE International Conference on Computer Vision, Proceedings. IEEE (2003)
11. Eade, E., Drummond, T.: Edge landmarks in monocular SLAM. In: Proceedings of the British Machine Vision Conference. Citeseer (2006)
12. Hammady, R., Ma, M., Temple, N.: Augmented reality and gamification in heritage museums. In: Marsh, T., Ma, M., Oliveira, M.F., Baalsrud Hauge, J., Göbel, S. (eds.) JCSG 2016. LNCS, vol. 9894, pp. 181–187. Springer, Cham (2016). https://doi.org/10.1007/978-3-319-45841-0_17
13. Chekhlov, D., et al.: Ninja on a plane: Automatic discovery of physical planes for augmented reality using visual slam. In: Proceedings of the 2007 6th IEEE and ACM International Symposium on Mixed and Augmented Reality. IEEE Computer Society (2007)
14. Neubert, J., Pretlove, J., Drummond, T.: Semi-autonomous generation of appearance-based edge models from image sequences. In: Proceedings of the 2007 6th IEEE and ACM International Symposium on Mixed and Augmented Reality. IEEE Computer Society (2007)
15. Comport, A.I., et al.: Real-time markerless tracking for augmented reality: the virtual visual servoing framework. IEEE Trans. Vis. Comput. Graph. **12**(4), 615–628 (2006)
16. Proctor, N.: Off base or on target? Pros and cons of wireless and location-aware applications in the museum. In: ICHIM, Paris, France (2005)
17. Azuma, R.T.: A survey of augmented reality. Presence Teleop. Virtual Environ. **6**(4), 355–385 (1997)
18. Barandiaran, I., Paloc, C., Graña, M.: Real-time optical markerless tracking for augmented reality applications. J. Real-Time Image Process. **5**(2), 129–138 (2010)
19. Newcombe, R.A., et al.: KinectFusion: real-time dense surface mapping and tracking. In: 2011 10th IEEE International Symposium on Mixed and Augmented Reality (ISMAR). IEEE (2011)
20. Morrison, A., et al.: Like bees around the hive: a comparative study of a mobile augmented reality map. In: Proceedings of the SIGCHI Conference on Human Factors in Computing Systems. ACM (2009)
21. Tillon, A.B., et al.: A day at the museum: An augmented fine-art exhibit. In: 2010 IEEE International Symposium on Mixed and Augmented Reality-Arts, Media, and Humanities. IEEE (2010)
22. Damala, A., Stojanovic, N.: Tailoring the adaptive augmented reality (A 2 R) museum visit: identifying cultural heritage professionals' motivations and needs. In: 2012 IEEE International Symposium on Mixed and Augmented Reality-Arts, Media, and Humanities (ISMAR-AMH). IEEE (2012)
23. Krzych, J.: Estimote Beacons (2015). http://estimote.com/. Accessed 2016
24. Law, E.L.-C., et al.: Understanding, scoping and defining user experience: a survey approach. In: Proceedings of the SIGCHI Conference on Human Factors in Computing Systems. ACM (2009)
25. ISO: Ergonomics of human-system interaction—Part 210: Human-centred design for interactive systems (2010). https://www.iso.org/obp/ui/-iso:std:iso:9241:-210:ed-1:v1:en. Accessed Feb 2017

26. Ellis, J.C.K.Z.S.N.M.:UX Design 2015 & 2016: successful Trends for digital Products. UXPin inc. (2015)
27. Unger, R., Chandler, C.: A Project Guide to UX Design: For User Experience Designers in the Field or in the Making, 2nd edn. Pearson Education, London (2012)
28. Hassenzahl, M., Tractinsky, N.: User experience-a research agenda. Behav. Inf. Technol. **25**(2), 91–97 (2006)
29. Forlizzi, J., Battarbee, K.: Understanding experience in interactive systems. In: Proceedings of the 5th Conference on Designing Interactive Systems: Processes, Practices, Methods, and Techniques. ACM (2004)
30. Würstl, D.: User Experience consists of Usability, Look and Feel (2009). http://www.katzenbergdesign.net/
31. Dam, R.F., Siang, T.Y.: Learn How to Use the Best Ideation Methods: SCAMPER 2017. https://www.interaction-design.org/literature/article/learn-how-to-use-the-best-ideation-methods-scamper. Accessed 2017
32. Dam, R.F., Siang, T.Y.: Introduction to the essential ideation techniques which are the heart of design thinking (2017). https://www.interaction-design.org/literature/article/introduction-to-the-essential-ideation-techniques-which-are-the-heart-of-design-thinking. Accessed 2017
33. McClellan, A.: Art and Its Publics: Museum Studies at the Millennium. Wiley, London (2008)

# Augmented Reality for the Enhancement of Apulian Archaeological Areas

Doriana Cisternino[✉], Carola Gatto[✉],
and Lucio Tommaso De Paolis[✉]

Department of Engineering for Innovation, University of Salento, Lecce, Italy
{doriana.cisternino,carola.gatto,
lucio.depaolis}@unisalento.it

**Abstract.** In this paper is presented an application of the Augmented Reality technology, for the enhancement of some Apulian archaeological areas, regarding the indigenous population of the Apulia region. The aim is to improve visitors' knowledge about this population, in order to better understand the archaeological areas of the Museo Diffuso "Castello di Alceste", in San Vito dei Normanni (BR), and the site of Fondo Giuliano, in Vaste (LE). A mobile application (for Android and iOS devices) has been developed for non-specialized audience; by focusing on a planimetric map of the archaeological areas, 3D models are superimposed on, and combined with other kinds of contents (texts, images, video, audio), in order to allow the visitors to fully understand the history and all of the features of the ancient sites.

**Keywords:** Augmented reality · Cultural heritage · Archaeology
Messapian civilization

## 1 Introduction

Recently there have been several studies in order to combine ICT (Information and Communication Technology) with the human sciences. This allows the information technology to experiment new fields of development and permits humanistic disciplines to achieve higher results in terms of audience development.

It should be taken into account that in an archaeological context the "absent" is often what has to be told, what can be reconstructed through some trails, but not fully visible.

Therefore, the principal pain is the lack of tangible elements and the need is to "augment" the reality. The best answer to this need comes from Augmented Reality technology (AR): this technology indeed is able to extend the visible, without however replacing the reality with a completely synthetic one. There are several kinds of AR applications in the cultural heritage field: some of them are supposed to improve the user fruition of the site, others are used by specialists in certain studies.

Thanks to its versatility, this technology is exploited both in indoor environments, such as museums, galleries, archives, both in outdoor environments, in particular public places with high historical, naturalistic, cultural value.

© Springer International Publishing AG, part of Springer Nature 2018
L. T. De Paolis and P. Bourdot (Eds.): AVR 2018, LNCS 10851, pp. 370–382, 2018.
https://doi.org/10.1007/978-3-319-95282-6_27

The general trend is actually the experimentation of new forms of involvement for the visitors within cultural places (museums, gallery, archaeological sites): visitor is no longer a passive spectator, but an active part of the cultural experience [1].

This is also the scenario in which we collocate this work: the aim is to create a model that can convey high information about indigenous population, in a simple, dynamic and pleasant way, in order to stimulate the user's interest and encourage learning.

The idea is to develop a mobile application (for Android and iOS devices) based on Augmented Reality technology, in order to allow the visitors to fully understand the history and all of the features of two archaeological contexts:

- the Museo Diffuso "Castello di Alceste", in San Vito dei Normanni (BR);
- the Fondo Giuliano, in Vaste (LE).

The user, simply by using the app on his smartphone, can look for information straightly within an "augmented" archaeological context.

## 2  Related Works

Augmented Reality technology is growing also in terms of involvement in the cultural heritage: indeed, it is a popular technology, not only among the scientific community but also for the general public. Recently several cultural institutes have started to adopt AR systems in order to provide a more interesting and educational experience to visitors. Indeed, the main advantage of AR is that there is a relationship between the user and the real world.

There are numerous examples of research about the use of AR in the cultural heritage field.

In particular, the AR technology can be used as an edutainment tool: edutainment refers to any form of entertainment aimed at an educational role; it enhances the learning environment and makes it much more engaging and fun-filled. The videogame is one of the most exciting and immediate tools of the edutainment applications since the game enables a type of multisensory and immersive relationship of the user through its interactive interface [2, 3].

Some best practices have been analyzed for designing and implementing the application.

De Paolis et al. [4, 5] describe the MediaEvo Project: a reconstruction of a virtual interactive town increases dramatically the possibilities of information exchange and diffusion. The MediaEvo Project aims to develop a multi-channel and multi-sensory platform for edutainment in cultural heritage for the realization of a digital didactic game oriented towards the knowledge of medieval history and society by means of the integration of human sciences and new data processing technologies.

Another example is the use of augmented reality and cloud computing technology [6]; this can enrich the scenes of sites with a relevant cultural interest. The main goal is to develop a mobile application to improve the user's cultural experience during the sightseeing of a city of art through the integration of digital contents related to specific sites or historic monuments.

The i-MiBAC VOYAGER [7] is an AR mobile application that provide virtual reconstructions of "Fori Romani" in Rome. By using GPS tracking the application allows the user visualizing and aligning the 3D reconstruction on the real archaeological ruins. In addition, the app includes a voice-over that illustrate and explain in different languages the history and the description of the ancient buildings while the user is focusing on them.

An indoor solution is the ARTLENS 2.0 [8] application, aimed at integrating AR technology into the Cleveland Museum of Art. By 2013, the app has reached more than 70.000 download. By focusing on real artefacts, the user is able to display augmented contents in order to receive information about it. In addition to this, the Beacon technology has been combined with AR, in order to provide different kinds of path within the museum, according to users' preferences.

The aim of ARCHEOGUIDE [9] is to develop a wearable AR tour guide at cultural heritage site. The user is able to freely explore virtual reconstructions of ancient Olympia in Greece by means of a see-through Head-Mounted Display and wearable computing equipment. According to the user' position and orientation in the site, the appropriate information is visualized through augmented reality.

Another example of an outdoor AR application is PUGLIA REALITY+ [10], aimed at improving the fruition and knowledge of the cultural places in the Apulia region, Italy. By looking at a virtual map, user can collect all of the points of interest, then he\she can decide which ones visit among them. Ones the user reaches that place, he\she can activate the AR for visualizing contents and collecting information about the cultural areas.

AR technology is also used for supporting scientific studies, in order to highlight and make clearer their results. For example, MAAP - Megalithic Art Analysis Project [11] is an AR application, developed by the University College of Dublin in 2017, in order to support the archaeological studies concerned megalithic artefacts. It provides an innovative method of interacting with megalithic art, combining cross-disciplinary research in digital heritage, 3D scanning and imaging, and augmented reality.

## 3   Analysis of the Archaeological Context: Fondo Giuliano and San Vito dei Normanni

In this section we provide a historical analysis of two Apulian archaeological sites, which currently constitute the contents of the application: "Museo Diffuso Castello di Alceste" in San Vito dei Normanni (BR), and Fondo Giuliano site in Vaste (LE). We looked into the historical context in the light of data emerged during the digs campaigns. In this way we defined the contents that are actually object of the application and that the user can visualize them using augmented reality.

### 3.1   Fondo Giuliano Site in Vaste (Lecce)

Fondo Giuliano [12] is an archaeological area located a few miles to the north of Vaste, near Poggiardo (Lecce, Italy). By 1991, archaeological digs brought to light three

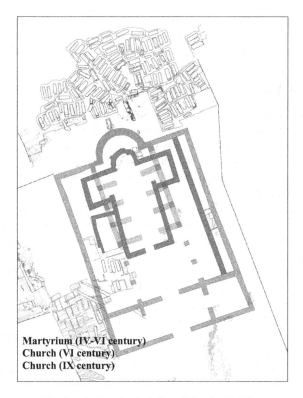

Martyrium (IV-VI century)
Church (VI century)
Church (IX century)

**Fig. 1.** Archaeological site of Fondo Giuliano

places of worship which were built sequentially between $4^{th}$ and $10^{th}$ century [13]. Around it was a large rock-cut necropolis [14] shown in Fig. 1.

The oldest church is defined as *martyrium* because this building was linked to the cult of the relics of a martyr, perhaps St Stephen. The church has a cruciform plan with a small apse; it is 14 m long and 14 m wide. The building retains only the foundation blocks and few floor ruins, while the roof was composed of tiles on wooden trusses.

The presbytery area was bordered by a stone slab balustrade (*cancellum*), decorated with geometric shapes, floral or cross-shaped motifs, and painted in red. Outside the church, leaning against the northern wall of the nave, there was a service environment for liturgical activities or for the preparation of funerary ceremonies.

To the south, instead, there is a wall for delimiting the area of the church and the necropolis located behind it.

According to planimetric data and artefacts found, the first church is dated to second half of the 4th century.

The church was subsequently extended after the Gothic War (535–553 AD). The new church has 3 naves, divided by two rows of eight pillars each, a large semi-circular apse and the narthex; the roof was double pitched with wooden beams covered with tile. The apse was decorated with frescoes with figures of the saints.

The destruction of the second church led to the construction of a new religious complex during the 9th century. It reuses the previous apsidal structure and part of the central nave in which four chapels are created. The roof consisted of a barrel vault.

## 3.2    Castello d'Alceste Site in San Vito dei Normanni (Brindisi)

The second case studies analyzed is the archaeological site of Castello di Alceste, in San Vito dei Normanni (BR). This area is located a few hundred meters south of the modern town, on a slight elevation (108 m). The archaeological dig started in 1995, thanks to the collaboration between the Department of Cultural Heritage of the University of Salento, the Municipality of S. Vito dei Normanni and the Archaeological department of Apulia [15].

The data acquired so far unearthed the existence of two settlements: the first one dated back to the Iron Age (VIII century B.C.) and inhabited by Iapygian population, the second one from the Archaic period (VI-V century B.C.) and inhabited by Indigenous population.

The site provides the precious opportunity to analyse the process of transformation that involves the Iapygian population between the 8th and 6th centuries B.C. [16]

Regarding to the first settlement, it is a small village of huts organized by scattered cores, alternating with free spaces. On the top of the hill, in an area of about 10 ha, traces referable to huts have also been identified, and they can be referred to the typical Iron Age housing structures.

Thanks to the data from the digs, it can be deduced that the village consisted of huts constituted by a single oval-shaped space, of variable width but not exceeding 15 m, with inside a paved in a beaten of earth. The frequentation of the area is also confirmed by the findings of pottery, made in reddish-brown mixture, painted with geometric motifs.

Regarding to the latter settlement, it overlaps with the previous one, and continues to be frequented until the beginning of the 5th century BC. The archaeological traces reflect the presence of a well-organized urban system, inhabited by a society more complex than the previous one [17].

The structures found in this context belong to multi-compartment buildings of quadrangular shape, with stone foundations and tiled roofs. Most of the houses found have a size of 100 \ 150 m$^2$, are characterized by small rooms alternating with courtyards, whose walls are built with irregular blocks about 40 \ 50 cm wide.

Completely different is the construction technique of the so-called Building A (or "Grande Edificio"): this is a much larger structure (more than 16 m long), located on one of the sides of the "square", therefore in a central position compared to the development of the rest of the urban system. This building can be related with public functions, such as ceremonies and rituals, that can also be assumed thanks to the traces of different kinds of pottery (both produced on site and imported from Greece).

# 4   Work Hypothesis

The idea of this study is to enhance the understanding of indigenous ancient culture, in particular for archaeological contexts we have analyzed in the previous section.

Museums often lack of technological systems for presenting archaeological sites in an interesting and appealing way. For this reason, we propose a new approach that allows users to visualize the 3D reconstruction of the archaeological buildings and artefacts that no longer exist. This is made possible thanks to the augmented reality technology. Simply by focusing on a planimetric map of the place with a mobile device, historical contents (3D models, texts, audio) related to the area are provided to the user.

Obviously, this map can be provided to the visitor both in the archaeological site, both inside the related museum.

The application has been created to transcend traditional methods of communication and to allow visitors to interact with the context. Indeed, the application includes all benefits of audio guides and, at same time, it is an innovative and alternative tool of cultural enhancement.

In particular, the visitors will be able to freely see and explore the ancient buildings, something that they cannot do in the real archaeological site, where nowadays only the ruins and remains are visible.

Therefore, the tracking system has been an important subject of discussion and analysis, evaluating in particular the fruition needs within the archaeological site.

The most suitable method is the vision-based system, in particular the markerless one. This fits very well both for indoor place, for example the museum, and outdoor environment, for example the archaeological area. In this case of study, the tracking of 3D models takes place by focusing on a 2D image, such as an aerial photograph of the area.

This choice comes from the study and evaluation of all of the methods [18]: since the scene is still changing in these archaeological contexts (because of the digs), we cannot think about a direct tracking. At the same time a sensor-based tracking could be less suitable for this application, since we want it to work in different places, and to be easy transportable.

These are most of the analysis' topics that led us to design a markerless vision-based application, whose main technical features are subject of the next paragraph.

# 5   Software Evaluation

In this section is reported the description of the app, in terms of software and hardware used to develop a useful tool of fruition. We focus also on the methodology adopted for the implementation of the augmented reality within the mobile app.

We discuss the following topics, as fundamental for designing a good AR application:

- quality of the 3D models, faithful to the historical truth and in line with the archaeological studies;
- balancing of virtual contents with additional textual, audio, video ones;

- identification of the most effective tracking method;
- fast tracking and overlapping of the 3D models over the image;
- choice of an interaction modality for the user;
- pleasant and captivating graphic design.

Based on these factors the precise technical choices were made, especially in relation to software to be used in development.

As far as the 3D models are concerned, we focused on optimizing the quality of the 3D models and rendering, and on balancing these with textual content. Indeed, too high-quality textures, such as too many polygons for each model, can affect the app's functionality. We balanced these factors in order to get the most stable visualization of models in augmented reality application.

Regarding the tracking methodology to adopt, firstly we studied the work's scenario. Most of the times, an archaeological site is an outdoor scenario, such as our cases of study. Although the first and natural/obvious solution was the creation of an AR outdoor application, we have adopted a markerless approach based on image recognition: first the camera pose is calculated then the system acquires additional natural features (Fig. 2) and uses them to update the pose calculation [19].

This choice depends on different factors including accuracy, cost and resolution of tracking system.

**Fig. 2.** Visualisation of the image target features

Thus, as far as the augmented reality frameworks are concerned, the applications presented use Vuforia, a software platform that contains SDK to recognized 2D target (Image Target) in a markerless system, but also 3D objects (Object Target) and Multi-Target [20]. Vuforia allows developers to position and orient 3D models and display them when the target is detected and recognized; the registered 3D object is displayed following the relative camera perspective.

By integrating Vuforia with Unity, the applications have been developed for mobile device, in particular Android and iOS systems.

Unity is a cross-platform game engine aimed at developing video game and virtual and augmented applications for PC, consoles and mobile device [21].

All of the 3D models have been developed on Cinema 4D, a software for 3D modelling, animation, and rendering, produced by the software house MAXON Computer [22].

## 6 Results

### 6.1 Augmented Visualisation of Fondo Giuliano

By analysing the archaeological context of Fondo Giuliano, it is evident that the visitor has a great difficulty in understanding the chronological sequence of ancient buildings only through examination of perimeter wall remains.

This difficulty can be overcome through the augmented reality technology; by means of the developed app, the visitor is able to choose the 3D reconstruction related to each phase of religious building: first phase (second half of the 4th century), second phase (second half of the 6th century), third phase (9th century). By focusing on the aerial photo of archaeological site of Fondo Giuliano, the 3D model of the church is superimposed on the image following the ancient perimeters as shown in Figs. 3 and in 4.

**Fig. 3.** Augmented visualisation of the 3D model on the image target

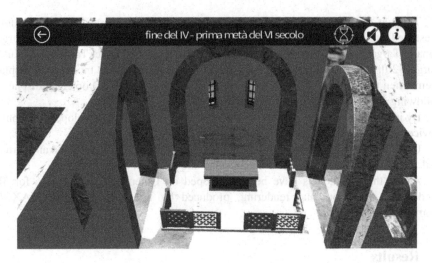

fine del IV- prima metà del VI secolo

**Fig. 4.** Interior spaces of Martyrium (First phase)

Special care was taken in modelling the churches; these have been created with high realism and historical accuracy based on specific bibliography and historical studies conducted by Department of Cultural Heritage of the University of Salento.

By getting closer to the 3D model, the app allows the visitor visualizing the interior spaces and to navigate inside them. Moreover, other kinds of content (texts, images, audio commentaries) are included in the application, which the visitor can choose, or not, to visualize. In particular, each 3D model is provided with information points in order to allow to fully understand the history and all features of the ancient buildings; a voice-over can be activated to explain the history of the places, using specific strategies for accessibility and involvement.

Within the app the descriptions of museum rooms and the archaeological site of Fondo Giuliano are provided for visitors. In this way they have not only a support during their tourist path but also the possibility to learn all features of them before their visit.

### 6.2    Augmented Visualisation of the Castello di Alceste

Regarding the archaeological site of the Castello di Alceste, in San Vito dei Normanni, the app provides the opportunity to switch from the Iron Age settlement to the Archaic settlement, to visualize the 3D reconstruction of the ancient buildings and pottery, and to collect information about specific objects on the scene.

The app's contents have been organized according to the chronological order: this is the most suitable type of organization because it represents what actually happens in the visitor's mind. The app represents a means by which the visitor explores the site, in a time travel through three phases, from the latest backwards.

This is the same process of the archaeologist's work, who top-down in a dig, from the most recent phase to the oldest one. These three phases represent the three main sections of the application, each one identified by its own color range: the site today, the Archaic settlement and the Iron Age settlement.

In order to obtain a target that represents the area of the archaeological site (Fig. 5), we needed to get some aerial photos, by using a DJI Phantom 4 Pro drone.

**Fig. 5.** Image Target

Although the shots obtained from the flight were of high quality, during the implementation it was not easy at all to use the material produced, for two main reasons. The first one is closely linked to the place, since the archaeological site is surrounded by a homogeneous vegetation and consequently, the identifiable features on the photos are not well distributed. The second one is a technical limit imposed by Vuforia's target manager: target's resolution. Indeed, this parameter cannot be higher than 2 MB, even if the photos we acquire were around 7 MB. In order to use one of them, we have drastically lowered their quality.

A crucial moment in the implementation was the design of the interaction's model. It is based on the calculation of the distance between the camera and the object on the scene, in order to provide a dynamic and engaging system of interaction.

We decided to provide a tool able to make the interaction dynamic: when user detects a point of interest over the 3D model, he can get closer to it with the camera; in this way the app answers giving on the screen some information about that object.

The method used is Vector3.distance of Unity; it outputs the distance between two points. In our case it returns the distance between the camera and the 3D object. If the distance is less than a specific value established at the start, the program performs an action, in our case it changes scene, opening a new one with specific information about the object (Figs. 6 and 7).

**Fig. 6.** Augmented visualisation of the 3D models and contents

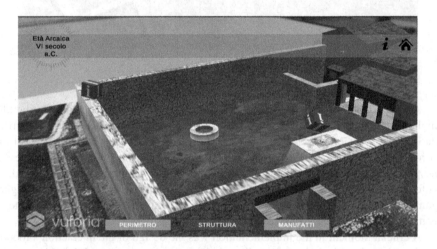

**Fig. 7.** Augmented visualisation of the 3D models on the image target

# 7  Conclusions and Future Work

The presented work is the result of multidisciplinary skills, which have allowed the development of AR mobile application to support and improve the enhancement and fruition of two archaeological areas.

The result is an interactive learning scenario which allows visitors to become an active actor within his\her own fruition trip.

Future work includes the design and integration of other 3D objects belonging to the archaeological sites, such as the necropolis of Fondo Giuliano, or the fortification wall in San Vito. Moreover, the development of tool able to provide on-site fruition without using the image target.

The possibility of using the beacon technology will be investigated in order to give visitors a complete path within the archaeological sites, as well the use of Unnamed Aerial Vehicles (UAVs) [23]. At the same time, we would like to create an interactive map with all of the Apulian archaeological site, in order to give AR contents for each of them.

**Acknowledgment.** This work was carried out thanks of the partnership with IBAM CNR, which provided the 3D models for the area of Fondo Giuliano, the Classical Archaeology Laboratory of the University of Salento and the LIA Laboratory of University of Salento, which provided the 3D models of San Vito and the historic contents used in the application.

The authors would like to thank Giovanni Mastronuzzi, Grazia Semeraro, Massimo Limoncelli and Francesco Gabellone for their helpful collaboration.

# References

1. Bonacini, E.: Il museo partecipativo sul web: forme di partecipazione dell'utente alla produzione culturale e alla creazione di valore culturale. IL CAPITALE CULTURALE. Stud. Value Cult. Herit. **5**, 93–125 (2012)
2. Paolis, L.T.: Walking in a virtual town to understand and learning about the life in the middle ages. In: Murgante, B., et al. (eds.) ICCSA 2013. LNCS, vol. 7971, pp. 632–645. Springer, Heidelberg (2013). https://doi.org/10.1007/978-3-642-39637-3_50
3. De Paolis, L.T., Aloisio, G., Celentano, M.G., Oliva, L., Vecchio, P.: A game-based 3D simulation of otranto in the middle ages. In: The 3rd International Conference on Advances in Computer-Human Interactions (ACHI 2010). IEEE Computer Society Publishing, St. Maarten, 10–16 February 2010
4. De Paolis, L.T., Celentano, M.G., Vecchio, P., Oliva, L., Aloisio, G.: Experiencing a town of the middle ages: an application for the edutainment in cultural heritage. In: The 2011 IEEE International Conference on Information and Education Technology (ICIET 2011), Guiyang, China, 26–28 January 2011
5. De Paolis L.T., Aloisio G., Celentano M.G., Oliva L., Vecchio P.: MediaEvo project: a serious game for the edutainment. In: 3rd International Conference on Computer Research and Development (ICCRD 2011), Shanghai, China, vol. 4, pp. 524–529, 11–15 March 2011
6. Vecchio, P., et al.: Cloud computing and augmented reality for cultural heritage. In: De Paolis, L.T., Mongelli, A. (eds.) AVR 2015. LNCS, vol. 9254, pp. 51–60. Springer, Cham (2015). https://doi.org/10.1007/978-3-319-22888-4_5
7. Mibact.    www.beniculturali.it/mibac/export/MiBAC/sito-MiBAC/Contenuti/MibacUnif/ Comunicati/visualizza_asset.html_198945880.html. Accessed 20 Apr 2018
8. Ding, M.: Augmented reality in museums. In: Arts Management & Technology Laboratory, Heinz College, pp. 3–8 (2017)
9. Vlahakis, V., Karigiannis, J., Tsotros, M., Gournaris, M., Almeida, L., Stricker, D., Gleue, T., Christou, I.T., Carlucci, R., Ioannidis, N.: Archeoguide: first results of an augmented reality, mobile computing system in cultural heritage sites. In: VAST, Proceedings of the Conference on Virtual Reality, Archaeology and Cultural Heritage, ACM, Glyfada, Greece, pp. 131–140 (2001)
10. Bonacini, E.: La realtà aumentata e le app culturali in Italia: storie da un matrimonio in mobilità. Capitale culturale **IX**, 89–121 (2014)

11. Barbier, J., Kenny, P., Young J., Normand, J.M., Keane, M., O'Sallivan, M., Ventresque, A.: MAAP annotate: when archeology meets augmented reality for annotation of megalithic art. In: 23rd International Conference on Virtual Systems and Multimedia (VSMM 2017), Dublin, Irland, pp. 1–8 (2017)
12. D'Andria, F., Mastronuzzi, G., Melissano, V.: La chiesa e la necropoli paleocristiana di Vaste nel Salento. In: Rivista di Archeologia Cristiana, LXXXII, pp. 231–322 (2006)
13. Sistema Museale Vaste-Poggiardo. www.sistemamusealevastepoggiardo.it/
14. Mastronuzzi, G.: Sistema Museale di Vaste e Poggiardo, pp. 38–43. Guida, Maglie (2015)
15. Semeraro, G., Monastero, A.: Itinerario di Visita del Castello di Alceste (S. Vito dei Normanni - BR), S. Vito dei Normanni (2011)
16. Semararo, G.: Le comunità indigene delle Murge salentine. In: Greco, G. (ed.) Segni di appartenenza e identità di comunità nel mondo indigeno, Atti del convegno di Napoli, p. 332, 6–7 luglio 2012
17. D'Andria, F.: Gli insediamenti arcaici della Messapia. Ricerca e valorizzazione di una ricchezza. In: L'area archeologica di Località Castello a San Vito dei Normanni - La ricerca come risorsa, Brindisi, pp. 2–8 (1998)
18. Krevelen, D.W.F., Poelman, R.: A survey of augmented reality technologies, applications and limitations. Int. J. Virtual Real. 9, 1–20 (2010)
19. Kalarat, K.: applying relief mapping on augmented reality: case study on façade of Sino Portuguese architecture. In: 12th International Joint Conference on Computer Science and Software Engineering (JCSSE 2015), Phuket, Thailand, pp. 315–318 (2015)
20. Vuforia. https://vuforia.com
21. Unity. https://unity3d.com
22. Cinema 4D. https://www.maxon.net/it/prodotti/cinema-4d/cinema-4d/
23. Botrugno, M.C., D'Errico, G., De Paolis, L.T.: Augmented reality and UAVs in archaeology: development of a location-based AR application. In: De Paolis, L.T., Bourdot, P., Mongelli, A. (eds.) AVR 2017. LNCS, vol. 10325, pp. 261–270. Springer, Cham (2017). https://doi.org/10.1007/978-3-319-60928-7_23

# Virtual Reality Arcade Game in Game-Based Learning for Cultural Heritage

Saverio Iacono, Daniele Zolezzi, and Gianni Vercelli$^{(\boxtimes)}$

Università degli Studi di Genova – DIBRIS, Genoa, Italy
{saverio.iacono,daniele.zolezzi,
gianni.vercelli}@unige.it

**Abstract.** In this paper we present Puzzle Battle, an arcade VR-based serious game for promoting and reflect on the history of painting art. The idea behind Puzzle Battle is about to see famous artists like Van Gogh or Frida Kahlo fight against each other or against other artists from different eras, in a classic puzzle game. The player will have to impersonate an artist and play in a fun context where he will improve his historical knowledge about the artist and his works by taking advantage of current studies on immersive learning experiences with virtual reality.

**Keywords:** Virtual reality · Game-based learning

## 1 Introduction

The game has a gift. Adults and children through fun activities are able to learn, practice and develop new skills by being in close contact with other people [1]. From childhood both solitaires and multiplayer games lead the infants to collect important information from the surrounding world. Plato said "you can find out more about a person in an hour of play than in a year of conversation" and this is true. While in face-to-face conversation persons can manage their words, during a game's activity where the achievement of the goal leads to a strong rivalry, competition and/or collaboration, people necessarily show themselves for what they are. Nowadays digital technologies have revolutionized almost every aspect of our daily lives; even the game has undergone such revolution.

The global video game market is a consolidated phenomenon, about 116 billion dollars in game software revenues in 2017 (+10, 7% wrt previous year) [2]. Video game represents the perfect union between modernity and the cardinal principles of every game activity. Approximately 2.2 billion of people in this planet [3] through various devices (mobile first), unconsciously or not, are gamers and, thanks to their passion, they move huge amounts of money. According to Prensky [4], video game as well as cinema, literature and television has reached a social status that makes it able to convey messages of all kinds, form the most futile to the most serious and useful. In less than seventy year, the gaming industry has passed from simulation of very simplified space battles and Tic-Tac-Toe's games to complex immersive experiences able to sensitize the public on issues as war (e.g. Valiant Hearts: The Great War from

© Springer International Publishing AG, part of Springer Nature 2018
L. T. De Paolis and P. Bourdot (Eds.): AVR 2018, LNCS 10851, pp. 383–391, 2018.
https://doi.org/10.1007/978-3-319-95282-6_28

Ubisoft) [5] and diseases (e.g. That Dragon, Cancer from Numinous Games) [6]. Aiming to teach something through videogames led to the emergence of serious games, experiences initially idealized by Abt [7] and subsequently popularized in educational and training contexts. Moreover, Michael and Chen [8] said "a serious game is a game in which education (in its various forms) is the primary goal, rather than entertainment". The slow rise of Virtual Reality that we are witnessing from Azuma's "A survey of Augmented Reality" [9] is entering the gaming world through Head Mounted Displays (such as Oculus Rift from Oculus VR, HTC Vive from Valve and PlayStation VR from Sony) provides highly immersive experiences that place the player within the action [10].

The high level of user engagement proposed by current VR-based titles is a convincing indicator that VR-based serious games approach players better, with more rapid learning curves and higher awareness of the problem treated by the game.

Serious Games, to be able to better teach their message, must be (especially as regards simulators) close to the phenomenon represented and VR-based immersive experiences need to be perceived as realistic in order to deeply engage the player in the virtual world.

In this paper, after our experience with gamification and Star Words Project [11], we present Puzzle Battle, an arcade VR-based serious game for promoting and reflect on history of painting art. The idea behind Puzzle Battle is to apply some typical elements of classic puzzle games (such as famous titles *Tetris* [12] and *Puzzle Bobble* [13]) to virtual reality. In this way this game potentially affects a very large audience, from children to adults, because it's based on a playful activity that anyone has played at least once in their life. The experience aims to increase user's knowledge related to art history: the player is placed inside an arena, and she/he must grab tiles falling from the top while solving puzzles depicting very famous paintings (e.g. masterpieces from Leonardo Da Vinci to Frida Kahlo to Salvador Dalì and others). Avatars of such artists are also present close to the arena to challenge the player with the intent to hinder her/him and complete the proposed puzzles before the player. Every time the player solves a given puzzle, the related painting unlocks a part of a virtual tour inside a layered Virtual Museum of Arts, aiming at being aware of the need to support and promote the conservation of cultural heritage.

## 2 Related Work

The simulation and reconstruction of environments for the purpose of training and learning have been studied since '80–90s, namely before the renaissance of virtual reality studies as we understand it today. The concept of serious game itself has benefited from several years of study and where the intuition of Zyda [14] identified how the pedagogical aspect should be subordinated to history and fun to function properly. This is now reflected in the well-known guidelines in which it's reiterated that "Storytelling is a critical component to simulation" until the experience it remains somewhat measurable [15]. Serious Games, to be able to better teach their message, must be (especially as regards simulators) close to the phenomenon represented and virtual reality claims to be perceived as realistic in order to immerse the player in the virtual world. Using virtual reality allows users to freely make decisions and solve concrete problems with their hands. It's important to recreate scenarios that can make the player reflect so that he can choose the best way to achieve the set goal.

The increasing availability of HMD has motivated software houses to look for new ways to spread their messages. Virtual Reality is based on the fidelity of its experiences: the more the videogame will be similar to its real counterpart, the more the player will be involved in the events. There are three types of loyalty [16]:

- Interaction Fidelity: it concerns the level of realism related to the interaction with the gaming world. It's important in a VR experience that orders given through input devices are reactive and represented in the most similar way possible to their real counterpart.
- Scenario Fidelity: refers to how much the proposed scenario, the behaviors, the rules and the properties included in the game are considered realistic.
- Involvement Fidelity: it concerns the level of realism generated by the output systems. The images that are shown on the screen must be able to stimulate player's senses making it totally immersed in the experience.

Huizinga identified in [1] five game's characteristics: (1) playing a game is freedom, (2) playing a game is not real life, (3) place and duration of games are distinguished from ordinary life, (4) playing a game requires an absolute and supreme order, and (5) playing a game is not connected to material interests or profit. Piaget considered play and imitation two fundamental functions in the process of intellectual development of the child [17]. A survey conducted by Mishra and Foster identified a high number of behavioral statements attributable to learning games, later categorized into five categories: cognitive abilities; practical skills, motivation, social skills and physiology [18]. A careful examination of their results reveals that the consensus is general regardless of the field of belonging: games can lead to changes in attitudes, behaviors and skills reinforcing the idea of DGBL's effectiveness as an effective training medium as analyzed by Vogel et al. [19].

A study conducted by Butussi and Chittaro [16] analyzed how a serious game has different levels of involvement depending on the type of screen used. The videogame chosen for experimentation was a simulation that represented an emergency scenario in which the player had to be able to evacuate from an airplane following an accident. The experience created with the game engine Unity 4.6 clearly showed the player how his mistakes could cause serious problems, from being burnt to death. The users were divided into three groups, with three different technologies, a classic 27″ Full HD Asus monitor, a Sony 45° FOV viewer and two 1280 × 720 OLED display at 3 DOF, while for the third group an Oculus Dk2 was used, OLED display with 1920 × 1080 pixel resolution, 100° FOV and 6-DOF tracker.

Among the ninety-six volunteers aged 18 to 36 who participated in the search were non-players, casual players and real gaming fans who claimed to use videogames at least once a day. The results obtained showed a significant difference between the pre-test and post-test preparation. All three groups acquired much more knowledge, but the volunteers who increased their preparation more (albeit slightly) were those who used Oculus Rift. The members of the third group were also those who declared that they felt more involved with the proposed activity and that they had a greater sense of presence within the virtual world. The improvement of all groups demonstrates the educational validity of serious games, especially with regard to highly immersive experiences in VR. Providing a safe environment in which to learn increases the possibility of teaching successfully. After playing the videogame, the participants were more confident than their ability to handle a delicate moment like the evacuation of an airplane. Compared to the other parameters studied, the self-assessment of the participants did not find significantly different results among the groups analyzed. On the contrary, as was foreseeable, the use of a VR display with higher performance has found a greater sense of presence rather than the use of the same software on a mid-range viewer or on a monitor as described also in further studies [20]. The results obtained demonstrate how the use of serious games in VR environments can further increase the benefits of using video games in education and training.

## 3 Puzzle Battle

### 3.1 Methodology and Goals

Puzzle Battle's aim is to improve learning and recognition of the works of a selection of pictorial artists through a game with a highly dynamic gameplay based on the recognition of a picture in its form and composition. It takes advantage of an high degree of involvement that can arise by putting the player in a flow state suitable to memorize what he is looking at and to obtain a fertile mental state for learning [21, 22].

Puzzle Battle is an arcade VR-based serious game for promoting and reflect on history of painting art. As we stated above, the idea behind Puzzle Battle is to apply some typical elements of classic puzzle games to VR. The given experience aims to increase user's knowledge related to art history: the player is placed within a simple arena (as depicted in Fig. 1), and she/he must grab tiles falling from the top while solving puzzles depicting very famous masterpieces of the History of Arts. Avatars of artists are the "competitors", placed close to the arena to challenge the player with the intent to hinder her/him and compete against the player to solve the proposed puzzles before her/him. Every time the player solves a given puzzle, the related painting unlocks a part of a virtual tour inside a layered Virtual Museum of Arts, aiming at being aware of the need to support and promote the conservation of cultural heritage. In this second level, the insertion of extended information about the unlocked paintings enables a deeper experiential learning on cultural heritage.

### 3.2 Game Design

Puzzle Battle's Game Design Document was drawn up following MDA (Mechanics Dynamics Aesthetic) [23] model in which the mechanics are the rules and components at the base of a game system; the dynamics are what happens when the player interacts with the game mechanics, so the interaction action and its effects; aesthetic is user/player's experience, the kind of emotion that the game generates on him, whether it be entertainment, learning or boredom. Competing directly against the artist who has made the work you are trying to reproduce should increase the player's level of emotive engagement. The environment is very simple. The player will be positioned inside a closed arena – a sort of cage – to naturally delimit the room scale: on three of four walls there will be empty frames that must be filled with the correct puzzle pieces. The gaming system is inspired by the mechanics that have characterized the success of Tetris. A system of supplying the pieces with descent from the top is used so that the user can freely manoeuvre the piece to insert it in the frame. The pieces that come down have different sizes and shapes, it will be up to the player to choose which ones to grab and which ones to drop on the ground. Every piece of puzzle that touches the ground will be destroyed automatically. When one of the pieces necessary to complete the puzzle falls to the ground, this will be repeated later. Each game will last two minutes, so it will be essential to identify the correct piece of puzzle needed to complete your picture. If neither of the two challengers were to complete all three proposed paintings, the one who placed the largest number of correct pieces inside the frames will win. The game offers two modes of learning. The first occurs during each challenge: the player coming into contact with the avatars of the opponent will unconsciously learn to associate each painting with the artist who made it. The mode that offers the most information is the Gallery. The gallery looks like a real artistic exhibition that can be visited. Each artist present in the game will have his own room containing the paintings that the player has been able to complete. The cultural aspect present in the Gallery mode is not only given by the presence of paintings of great artistic value, but also by the possibility of learning additional notions related to the picture that one is admiring. At the centre of the room will be a model of a tablet that it will be activated when we are positioned in front of a painting, showing a card containing information such as the pictorial technique used, the story represented or the reasons that led the artist to paint that subject.

**Gameplay and Mechanics Provided**

Slow Motion: the player performing a "combo" can slow down the falling puzzle pieces. Combos are activated when the player is able to grasp, for example, ten pieces of puzzles consecutively without causing them to fall to the ground. Other types of objects may fall apart from the pieces of the puzzle in order to make the challenge more fun. These objects, if grabbed, can be used immediately against the opponent or collected to get a bigger.

Bomb: the player can launch it in the opponent's room to explode part of a newly composed picture.

Chain: taking the chain, the player can throw it in the opponent's area to chain it to the ground for 5 s.

Water Bucket: throwing a water bucket in the opposing room, the pieces will start to fall faster.

Oil Flask: throwing the oil flask in the opponent's field will make the pieces slippery and therefore more difficult to grasp.

Time Stop: it stops the descent of the opponent's pieces.

**Game Mode**

Story Mode: the player will challenge the most representative (CPU-driven) artists around the world and fight to the last piece of the puzzle.

Time Mode: the player tackles the challenge by himself trying to finish the various levels in the pre-established time. When the pieces touch the ground, without being picked up by the player, they will vanish.

Multiplayer: the player can challenge online against other players around the world.

My Pics: the player can import his own images to face the challenge with his photos, since he will already know the content of the image, this mode will present many more pieces to increase the level of challenge.

Gallery: area to review all the paintings unlocked in the game and learn more about their story.

Difficulty: the level is given by the amount of pieces needed to complete a puzzle, the time, the opponent's ability (AI or challenger) and the number of puzzles.

### 3.3 Game Development

Game development is based on the choices previously indicated. The game was conceived for HTC Vive because it is equipped with a stable room scale technology, which involves the possibility of moving in a space previously delimited by a setup operation using Steam VR's free software. The game development software chosen was Unreal Engine 4, as it offers a highly functional development template that can be integrated with custom code, in which a VR pawn is made available that includes, for example, the basic interaction of capture and release.

Autodesk Maya with an educational license was used for modelling blocks to be used as puzzle pieces for prototype development. The game arena used for the demo recalls wrestling's cages and the VR controller is positioned inside the cage. On the walls of the cage are placed four complete pictures of a specific artist, in this case Frida Kahlo, and alongside a frame where to place the piece just collected. To differentiate and initially make it easier to understand what was the right piece to grab and what could be the wrong one, we have turned the pieces into destructible mesh in such a way as to immediately make the mistake and move on to search for suitable pieces among the others. The slowing effect of the objects was obtained by modifying the Linear Damping and the Angular Damping, which is immediately ignored when the object is gripped, so as to allow the player to freely manipulate the object in order to position it in the frame.

About the automatic production of the pieces, the blueprint code is used for the wave and random generation of the pieces from a zone about a distance of 10 m, in order to avoid having to wait too long for the descent of the first pieces or that they are too close and you haven't time to recognize them and take them during descent.

We designed a second environment using Unreal primitives and assets of learning content, simulating a virtual visit, always with a VR pawn in which there are pictures that will be unlocked as you advance in the game and make different choices of characters. Here is a tablet that acts as a guide instead of the traditional captions, showing information on the picture looked at that time (Fig. 2).

**Fig. 1.** Puzzle battle's screenshot

**Fig. 2.** Gallery's screenshot

## 4   Prototype's Experience

We started a first phase of alpha testing in which a small group of people experienced the prototype. We could see that a seemingly simple and consolidated mechanics like Tetris [11] ones assumes a superior degree of difficulty in 3D. In the early learning phase of how you use the game, it seemed more complex than expected to recognize pieces and place them. Having chosen a typology of natural locomotion combined with Teleport, the phenomenon of VR sickness hasn't yet been presented. It's to be assessed when there is an excess of broken puzzle on the ground how much it can affect performance by reducing the frame rate that must not fall below 60. The experience can be affected by giving rise to phenomena of judder or latencies higher than the standard for virtual reality.

## 5   Future Development and Research

The roadmap includes the completion of the spawn code generation of puzzle pieces and a subsequent test to correctly adjust the base stream for a scalable experience, simply by modifying the quantity of the generated pieces and the impact on the framerate of the destructible mesh. Going to compile and gradually insert the planned mechanics, experimenting those that actually work and produce positive aesthetics from the point of view of fun and consequently positive for learning. It is evident how much the current use of the Gallery where most of the knowledge about artists and works is concentrated, has yet to find its deepest collocation in the gameplay systems; now the hypothesized solutions would be forced according to the principle: "Design a serious game only if the content naturally lends itself to gameplay" [14]. To verify the quality of learning we are currently working on ex-post questionnaires and user experience surveys to assess the user experience, matter knowledge, immersivity, skills and challenging levels according to the indicators described in [24]. It is also necessary to analyze the possible changes to the user experience to expand accessibility for people with disabilities.

## References

1. Huizinga, J.: Homo Ludens: A Study of the Play-Element in Culture. Routledge & Kegan Paul, London (1949)
2. NewZoo: Europe, Amsterdam (2017). https://newzoo.com/solutions/standard/market-forecasts/global-games-market-report/
3. McGonigal, J.: Reality is Broken: Why Games Make Us Better and How They Can Change the World. Penguin Group, USA (2011)
4. Prensky, M.: The Digital Game-Based Learning. McGraw-Hill, New York (2001)
5. Ubisoft: Valiant Hearts: The Great War (2014). https://www.ubisoft.com/it-it/game/valiant-hearts/
6. Numinous Games: That Dragon, Cancer (2016). http://www.thatdragoncancer.com/
7. Abt, C.: Serious Games, University Press of America (1971)

8. Michael, D., Chen, S.: Serious Games: Games That Educate, Train, and Inform, Course Technology. Cengage Learning, Boston (2006)

9. Azuma, R.: A survey of Augmented Reality. Presence: Teleoperators Virtual Environ. **6**, 355–385 (1997)

10. Martindale, J.: PlayStation VR dominates third-quarter VR headset sales (2017). https://www.digitaltrends.com/virtual-reality/playstationvr-outsells-htc-vive-oculus-rift/

11. Coccoli, M., Iacono, S., Vercelli, G.: Applying gamification techniques to enhance the effectiveness of video-lessons. J. e-Learn. Knowl. Soc. **11**(3), 73–84 (2015)

12. Pajitnov, A., Pokhilko, V.: Tetris (1984)

13. Taito: Puzzle Bobble (1994)

14. Zyda, M.: From visual simulation to virtual reality to games. IEEE Comput. **38**, 25–32 (2005)

15. Kapp, K., Blair, L., Mesch, R.: Gamification of learning and instruction fieldbook. Wiley, Hoboken (2013)

16. Butussi, F., Chittaro, L.: Effects of different types of virtual reality display on presence and learning in a safety training scenario. IEEE Trans. Vis. Comput. Graph. **24**(2), 1063–1076 (2018)

17. Piaget, J.: Nachahmung, Spiel und Traum: die Entwicklung der Symbolfunktion beim, Klett-Cotta (1975)

18. Mishra, P., Foster, A.: The claims of games: a comprehensive review and directions for future research. In: Proceedings of 91 the 18th International Conference of the Society for Information Technology & Teacher Education, San Antonio, TX (2007)

19. Vogel, J., Vogel, D., Cannon-Bowers, J., Bowers, C., Muse, K., Wright, M.: Computer gaming and interactive simulations for learning: a meta-analysis. J. Educ. Comput. Res. **34**(2), 229–243 (2006)

20. Dalgarno, B., Lee, M.J.: What are the learning affordances of 3-D virtual environments? Br. J. Educ. Technol. **41**, 10–32 (2010)

21. Liu, M., Horton, L., Olmanson, J., Toprac, P.: A study of learning and motivation in a new media enriched environment for middle school science. Educ. Technol. Res. Devel. **59**(2), 249–265 (2011)

22. Nakamura, J., Csikszentmihalyi, M.: The concept of flow. In: Flow and the Foundations of Positive Psychology, pp. 239–263. Springer, Dordrecht (2014). https://doi.org/10.1007/978-94-017-9088-8_16

23. Hunicke, R., Leblanc, M., Zubek, R.: MDA: a formal approach to game design and game research, In: Proceedings of the AAAI Workshop on Challenges in Game AI, vol. 4 (2004)

24. Hamari, J., Shernoff, D.J., Rowe, E., Coller, B., Asbell-Clark, J., Teon, Edwards T.: Challenging games help students learn: an empirical study on engagement, flow and immersion in game-based learning. Comput. Hum. Behav. **54**, 170–179 (2016)

# Virtual Museum, the Exploration of Cultural Heritage with Virtual Reality Techniques

Francesco Settembrini[1]([✉]), Maria Giuseppa Angelini[2], and Domenica Costantino[2]

[1] DICAR, Politecnico di Bari, via Orabona 4, 70126 Bari, Italy
francesco.settembrini@poliba.it
[2] DICATECh, Politecnico di Bari, V.le del Turismo, 8, 74121 Taranto, Italy
{mariagiuseppa.angelini,
domenica.costantino}@poliba.it

**Abstract.** The use of immersive Virtual Reality (VR) technology is a relatively recent trend that is spreading in various areas such as, for example, the digital fruition of cultural heritage. The set of appropriately integrated hardware and software technologies are able to combine three-dimensional models of virtual or real objects obtained, for example, from integrated laser scanner and/or photogrammetric survey. If the user observes a computer monitor there is three-dimensional non-immersive VR to which the user accesses through devices with which he can controls what is displayed onto a flat screen. In the VR a true reality can be simulated, you can navigate and move in real-time in photorealistic environs and interact with the objects presents in them. This paper illustrates the Virtual Museum project, a system of digital fruition of cultural heritage with low-cost virtual reality techniques, under development by AESEI s.r.l. - Spin-off of Polytechnic of Bari. This software, entirely written in C++ language, is compatible with the 64-bit Windows operating systems and interfaces with an Oculus DK2 Head Mounted Display (HMD) device for immersive vision and with the Leap Motion device for gestures recognition.

**Keywords:** Virtual Reality · Virtual Museum · ICV
Cultural heritage management · Leap Motion · Oculus DK2

## 1 Introduction

The need to preserve the historical-artistic memory of cultural heritage that undergo the deterioration phenomenon due to natural or anthropic events and the advent of information technology has led to the development of Virtual Reality (VR) techniques intended as a management tool and display of complex digitized resources.

In recent decades we have witnessed a constant evolution of ICT (Information and Communications Technology) and, in particular, the involvement of such technologies in many sectors, such as that of cultural heritage. The ICT, in fact, allow on one hand to preserve the goods and on the other hand they promote improvements in making them usable.

A European Commission study on the application of ICT to cultural heritage [1, 2] highlights the need for cultural organizations to adopt new technologies to become

© Springer International Publishing AG, part of Springer Nature 2018
L. T. De Paolis and P. Bourdot (Eds.): AVR 2018, LNCS 10851, pp. 392–400, 2018.
https://doi.org/10.1007/978-3-319-95282-6_29

competitive in the current and future scenario [3]. The study shows that, despite the initiatives already implemented, it is necessary to work on many aspects, such as the users involvement, both managers than visitors.

The Virtual Reality (VR) is, at today, an emerging and high specialized category in the field of ICT whose technologies allow to create and display high resolution three-dimensional objects and/or objects with which the user interacts in real time, by experiencing a sensation of immersion and presence in the reconstructed environments [4]. This technology applied to cultural heritage gives the visitor a unique, immersive and engaging experience.

The low-cost availability of increasingly high-performance personal computers and the recent spread of advanced interfaces for man-machine interaction make it possible to explore new and [5], in some ways, still pioneering methods in using the huge wealth of cultural heritages.

For some time now, thanks to the enormous growth of the video-gaming market, which has become a driving force in the ICT sector, it is possible to find advanced devices such as Head Mounted Display (HMD, Fig. 1) [6–8], data gloves, motion trackers, 3D controllers, etc. at ever more accessible costs and with increasingly advanced performance.

**Fig. 1.** Head Mounted Display (HMD) DK2 produced by Oculus (http://www.oculus.com)

If by years, thanks to diffusion of the Internet and the Word-Wide-Web [9], is possible to access to the numerous and prestigious on-line cultural heritage archives, only relatively recently we can do it by adding further elements that can make these explorations exciting besides interesting: these elements are interactivity, immersion and presence, the three fundamental pillars of Virtual Reality.

The trend of information technology has always been aimed at improving man-machine interaction both by inventing new devices and using existing technologies but by perfecting and integrating them with increasingly advanced and intelligent software. For example, if for the interaction with virtual scenarios HTC combines its HMD Vive with light and precise 3D pointing devices (Fig. 2), another company, the Leap Motion [10], allows to interact with virtual scenarios by bare hands, thanks to the use of miniaturized IR stereo-cameras and the use of complex image processing algorithms for hands and gestures recognition (Fig. 3).

**Fig. 2.** HTC Vive system, HMD and 3D pointing controller device (http://www.vive.com)

**Fig. 3.** An example of interaction with virtual environs by means of simple and natural gestures (http://www.leapmotion.com)

It is very likely that, in the future, we will be able to interact with VR environments without the need to wear particular devices (HMD, data-gloves, etc.) because the precision and intelligence of the new devices will recreate the scenarios around users. For example, you could use holographic projection systems for images and devices for tracking and recognizing gestures to allow interaction with virtual environments naturally.

This paper illustrates the Virtual Museum project, a system of digital fruition of cultural heritage using low-cost virtual reality techniques, under development by AESEI s.r.l. - Spin-off of the Polytechnic of Bari. The software part, written in C++ language, is compatible with the 64-bit Windows operating system and interfaces with an Oculus HMD DK2 device and with the Leap Motion device for user interactions with virtual environs, by automatic recognizing of hands and gestures. Oculus DK2 combined with Leap Motion have been used to allow users to touch and interact with objects in the VR scenarios [11].

## 2 Materials and Methods

The AESEI, Spin-off of the Polytechnic of Bari, always attentive to technological innovations, intends to explore the considerable potential inherent in the use of Augmented/Virtual Reality techniques in various application concepts and, in particular, in the field of cultural heritage.

The *Virtual Museum* application is part of this projects, born from the desire to make easily accessible the huge cultural heritage, offering a multimedia exploration that wants to be as interactive and involving as possible. It is a work-in-progress project that, however, also in this first experimental version, allows to delivery of multimedia information contents, enriching them with remarkable interactivity and ease of use.

Virtual Museum is a Windows operating system application written entirely in C++ language in Object-Oriented programming paradigm (OOP), which makes use of an HMD viewer for projection and displaying of scenarios and makes use of the Leap Motion for interactions with virtual environs by mean of hand gestures (Fig. 4).

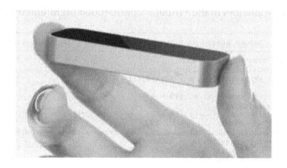

**Fig. 4.** Leap Motion (http://www.leapmotion.com)

The Oculus Rift DK2 is an AMOLED head-mounted display with high contrast, low persistence and high refresh rate (60 fps), with 1080 × 960 resolution for each eye.

Integrated in the HMD DK2 there is a millimetric precision tracking system, consisting of an infrared camera able to detect a series of LEDs positioned on the front and side parts of the HMD visor, according to a very precise and univocally identifiable pattern.

In the HMD there is also an IMU (Inertial Measurement Unit) capable of temporarily replacing the position and set-up information in the event that the HMD exits the range of the camera or in the event that the user looks in the opposite direction of the camera field of view.

The Oculus DK2 driver installed in the operating system in combination with the runtime code calculates the relative position and the rotations along the three coordinate axes of the HMD so as to provide the relative modelview matrices necessary for the correct rendering of the virtual scenario. It also uses pose prediction techniques to guarantee lower latency and a more homogeneous tracking.

By way of example, the SDK function for obtaining modelview matrices is shown below (the functions of the Oculus SDK are highlighted in bold underline):

```
//-----------------------------------------------------------------
//      PURPOSE: Returns position (Pos [3]) and HMD orientation
//          sub-form of quaternion (Orient [4])
//-----------------------------------------------------------------
void __fastcall TFormVrtk::GetHeadPose(float Pos[3], float Orient[4])
{
        double displayMidpointSeconds = ovr GetPredictedDisplayTime(m pOvrSession, 0);
        ovrTrackingState HmdState = ovr GetTrackingState(m pOvrSession,
                displayMidpointSeconds, ovrTrue);

        ovrPosef HeadPose = HmdState.HeadPose.ThePose;
        Pos[0] = HeadPose.Position.x;
        Pos[1] = HeadPose.Position.y;
        Pos[2] = HeadPose.Position.z;
        ovrQuatf orientation = HmdState.HeadPose.ThePose.Orientation;
        Orient[0] = orientation.x;
        Orient[1] = orientation.y;
        Orient[2] = orientation.z;
        Orient[3] = orientation.w;
}
```

Once the position and orientation of the HMD have been obtained, we can use them to set the camera parameters in the virtual scenario (code highlighted in bold underline):

```
//-----------------------------------------------------------------
//      PURPOSE: Render stereo-pair (with asymmetric left/right frustum)
//-----------------------------------------------------------------
int __fastcall TFormMain::Render()
{
        assert(m_pViewers[0] && m_pViewers[1]);

        static int nCurBB = 0, nCurFB = 0;;
// imposto i framebuffers
        m_pViewers[OVR_LEFT]->pFrameBuffer = m_pFrameBuffers[nCurBB][OVR_RIGHT];
// inverto LEFT con RIGHT
        m_pViewers[OVR_RIGHT]->pFrameBuffer = m_pFrameBuffers[nCurBB][OVR_LEFT];
        nCurBB = Circling(nCurBB, 1, NUMFB);
        nCurFB = Circling(nCurBB, NUMFB/2, NUMFB);
        SoPerspectiveCamera *pLCam = (SoPerspectiveCamera*) m_pViewers[0]->getCamera();
        assert(pLCam);
        SoPerspectiveCamera *pRCam = (SoPerspectiveCamera*) m_pViewers[1]->getCamera();
        assert(pRCam);
        float Pos[3], Orient[4];
        FormVrtk->GetHeadPose(Pos, Orient);
        SbRotation HeadPose(Orient[0], Orient[1], Orient[2], Orient[3]);
        pLCam->orientation = HeadPose;
        pLCam->position = SbVec3f(Pos) * float(m ScalePos);
        pRCam->position = pLCam->position;
        pRCam->orientation = pLCam->orientation;
        pRCam->focalDistance = pLCam->focalDistance;
        pRCam->aspectRatio = pLCam->aspectRatio;
        pRCam->nearDistance = pLCam->nearDistance;
        pRCam->farDistance = pLCam->farDistance;
        return nCurFB;
}
```

The Leap Motion, on the other hand, is a device able to identify the position and orientation of the user's hands. It is based on an infrared stereo-camera, in the band of about 850 nm, and a series of IR-LED able to illuminate objects within a range of about 60 cm.

The very wide-angle lenses of the cameras allow you to have a field of view angle of more than 120°, more than enough to capture the user's hands (and gestures) in practically any position (provided, of course, the hands of user are frontally, e.g., obviously, in the field of view of the device).

The runtime software provides the user with the position and orientation information of the hands and also any other parameter that can recognize the gestures by skeletal tracking processes. Also in this case an SDK (Software Development Kit) is available that allows us to integrate the Leap Motion functionalities into our application software.

The Virtual Museum application integrates several libraries for computer graphics (by using SGI OpenInventor [12]), for multimedia (by using the Windows MediaPlayer components but also some open-source libraries such as FFMpeg [13] and OpenAL [14]) and many libraries for data access and retrieval of the cultural heritage informations stored in relational databases (MySQL, SQLite and InterBase RDBMS).

The HMD and Leap Motion devices, appropriately assembled together, are shown in Fig. 5.

**Fig. 5.** Installation of Leap Motion device on top of Oculus DK2 HMD

The Virtual Museum version presented in the paper shows only a small part of the available archive of cultural assets cataloged and stored in the database. In particular, some paintings are exhibited in the virtual environment deliberately kept it simple and essential to allow the usability of the application even with computers that are not particularly performant (Fig. 6).

The user is able to look around in every direction, to approach paintings and analyze them in details, to move freely in the virtual gallery and, when in front of a painting of his interest, to access to the multimedia contribs by mean of simple gestures (thanks to the Leap Motion device) (Fig. 7).

For example, simply touching an artwork, it activates a form that exposes the available multimedia contribs associated to the selected opera: in the case of (Fig. 8) we can see that is available a video-clip for a detailed description of the opera.

**Fig. 6.** Virtual picture gallery of Virtual Museum

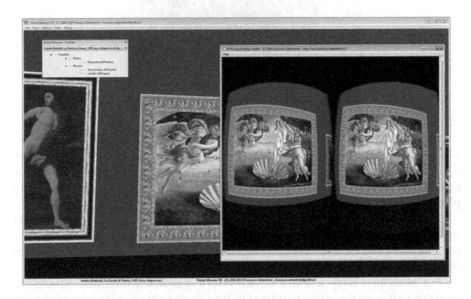

**Fig. 7.** Mirror (on the right) of stereo imaging reproduced by Oculus DK2 HMD

**Fig. 8.** Activation of the form (top left) that presents at the user the multimedia contributions

## 3   Considerations and Future Developments

The usability of cultural heritage with Virtual Reality techniques offers enormous possibilities in terms of simplicity of use, interactivity and, therefore, in terms of participations and user interests, as he/she is always called to be an active part of exploration.

And a more motivated and participative user leads to a better and more effective communication process and a better transmission of knowledge.

It is not difficult to understand the enormous potentialities in the use of VR in the learning processes thanks to contributions of presence, immersion and interaction and, most of all, thanks to the possibilities of experimentations.

As already mentioned, Virtual Museum is a work-in-progress project, the first experiment of AESEI in the field of Virtual Reality, in this case applied to cultural heritage applications. Attentions was focused on the economy and practicality of the fruition system, therefore, low-cost, small, lightweight and simple to use devices were used such as the Oculus HMD DK2 and the Leap Motion device which, when conveniently combined, offer a natural level of immersion and interaction with digital content.

It can certainly be improved both in the interface as in the contents: some authors, for example, have already tried their hand at more creative projects by imagining entering and even interacting with the characters depicted in the same artworks [15, 16]. The aim is to apply these fruition techniques to three-dimensional scenarios to improve the communication process in the explorations of cultural heritage things (e.g. archaeological sites, historical buildings, rock churches, etc.) obtained from integrated techniques such as laser scanners and photogrammetry, appropriately modeled and texturized.

In fact, we want to integrate the Virtual Museum module into the ICV (Intelligent Cloud Viewer) framework, another application developed in-house by AESEI for point-clouds management: developed for 64 bit Windows systems ICV allows to handle point clouds with a virtually unlimited number of points with ease, also on inexpensive computers. Written entirely in C++, ICV integrates different modules implemented by the authors from scratch or by using open-source algorithms specialized in computer graphics (SGI Open Inventor) and in Computational Geometry (CGAL) so that we can, for example, build shaped 3D models directly from point-clouds arising from laser-scanner or photogrammetric processes [17].

# References

1. eCult Vademecum A Guide for Museums to develop a Technology Strategy (2015)
2. eCult Vision Paper on the Use of Technologies for Cultural Heritage (2015)
3. Izzo, F., Mustilli, M., Guida, M.: Realtà aumentata e valorizzazione dei beni culturali. Riflessioni sull'offerta culturale casertana. In: XXVII Convegno annuale di Sinergie - Heritage, management e impresa: quali sinergie? pp. 797–809 (2015). http://hdl.handle.net/11591/334895
4. Jerald, J.: The Vr Book: Human-Centered Design for Virtual Reality. Association for Computing Machinery and Morgan & Claypool, New York (2015)
5. Carrozzino, M., Bergamasco, M.: Beyond virtual museums: experiencing immersive virtual reality in real museums. J. Cult. Herit. **11**, 452–458 (2010)
6. Davis, B.A., Bryla, K., Benton, P.A.: Oculus Rift in Action. Manning, Shelter Island (2015)
7. Hodder T.: Oculus Rift: The Future of Virtual Reality Gaming (How to guide) (2013)
8. Loizides, F., El Kater, A., Terlikas, C., Lanitis, A., Michael, D.: Presenting cypriot cultural heritage in virtual reality: a user evaluation. In: Ioannides, M., Magnenat-Thalmann, N., Fink, E., Žarnić, R., Yen, A.-Y., Quak, E. (eds.) EuroMed 2014. LNCS, vol. 8740, pp. 572–579. Springer, Cham (2014). https://doi.org/10.1007/978-3-319-13695-0_57
9. Parisi, T.: Learning Virtual Reality, Developing Immersive Experiences and Applications for Desktop, Web, and Mobile (2015)
10. Webel, S., Bockholt, U., Engelke, T., Gavish, N., Olbrich, M., Preusche, C.: An augmented reality training platform for assembly and maintenance skills. Robot. Auton. Syst. **61**(4), 398–403 (2013)
11. Barsanti, S.G., Caruso, G., Micoli, L.L., Rodriguez, M.C., Guidi, G.: 3D visualization of cultural heritage artefacts with virtual reality devices. Int. Arch. Photogramm. Remote Sens. Spat. Inf. Sci. **40**(5), 165–172 (2015). https://doi.org/10.5194/isprsarchives-xl-5-w7-165-2015
12. https://web.archive.org/web/20041120092542/http://oss.sgi.com/projects/inventor/
13. http://www.ffmpeg.org
14. http://www.openal.org
15. http://sites.itd.cnr.it/ted03/scrovegni_descrizione.htm
16. https://vrjam.devpost.com/submissions/36821-the-night-cafe-an-immersive-tribute-to-vincent-van-gogh
17. Costantino, D., Angelini, M.G., Settembrini, F.: Point cloud management through the realization of the intelligent cloud viewer software. Int. Arch. Photogramm. Remote Sens. Spat. Inf. Sci. **42**(5), 105–112 (2017). https://doi.org/10.5194/isprs-archives-xlii-5-w1-105-2017

# Applications of VR/AR in Industry

# An Augmented Interface to Display Industrial Robot Faults

Francesco De Pace[(✉)], Federico Manuri, Andrea Sanna, and Davide Zappia

Dipartimento di Automatica e Informatica, Politecnico di Torino,
C.so Duca degli Abruzzi 24, 10129 Torino, Italy
francesco.depace@polito.it

**Abstract.** Technology advancement is changing the way industrial factories have to face an increasingly complex and competitive market. The fourth industrial revolution (known as industry 4.0) is also changing how human workers have to carry out tasks and actions. In fact, it is no longer impossible to think of a scenario in which human operators and industrial robots work side-by-side, sharing the same environment and tools. To realize a safe work environment, workers should trust robots as well as they trust human operators. Such goal is indeed complex to achieve, especially when workers are under stress conditions, such as when a fault occurs and the human operators are no longer able to understand what is happening in the industrial manipulator. Indeed, Augmented Reality (AR) can help workers to visualize in real-time robots' faults. This paper proposes an augmented system that assists human workers to recognize and visualize errors, improving their awareness of the system. The system has been tested using both an AR see-through device and a smartphone.

**Keywords:** Industry 4.0 · Industrial robots
Human-machines interfaces · Augmented reality

## 1 Introduction

The fourth industrial revolution is bringing both new opportunities and challenges. An increasing number of devices is connected and it is capable of exchanging data in real-time. In an industrial context, modern factories are composed by many automated systems, such as industrial robots, that can perform different tasks, improving the overall production. As the market is becoming increasingly competitive, factories are required not only to enhance the products quality but also to reduce manufacturing and maintenance times. As industrial robots are becoming more powerful and efficient, it is possible to imagine a scenario in which robots collaborate actively with human workers. Development in the Artificial Intelligence's (AI) field have allowed the creation of machines able to work in completely autonomy and to recognize the human workers. Whilst these improvements represent important steps to the realization of machines increasingly complex and sophisticated, there is the risk that workers will not be able

© Springer International Publishing AG, part of Springer Nature 2018
L. T. De Paolis and P. Bourdot (Eds.): AVR 2018, LNCS 10851, pp. 403–421, 2018.
https://doi.org/10.1007/978-3-319-95282-6_30

to understand and recognize what machines are doing, compromising the realization of a real active collaboration. In order to understand how to achieve a true collaboration, a new scientific discipline is born: the so-called Human Robot Collaboration (HRC)[1]. HRC tries to understand how to improve the human-robot collaboration using innovative interfaces. Several works have investigated the effectiveness of original technologies in the human-robot collaboration context. From the development of Cascade Convolutional Network [5] to the ingenious use of a motion capture system [2,6], an increasing number of researches are investigating this new topic. In an industrial context, workers should trust robots to obtain a real collaborations system. Creating such a context is a complex challenge: a human-human collaboration system is considered safe because one human can naturally understand the intention of another human. Thus, understanding the robot's intentions becomes a crucial issue. Intentions can be expressed through the actions that the robot is doing (movements, task, and so on): if workers could visualize them, they would be able to understand the robot's purposes, improving their awareness of safety.

AR can indeed be used to achieve this purpose, since it is able to show information contextualized in the real environment. The origin of this visualization technology dates back to the last years of the sixties, when the first AR prototype was proposed by Sutherland [28]. It was not until the early years of the nineties that the AR concept was formalized by Milgram and Kishino [24]: these authors introduced the definition of *Mixed Reality* as a continuum space going from full reality to full virtuality; within this definition it is possible to identify AR as a category where real elements are dominant and are supplemented by virtual elements. Until few years ago, there was a lack of low cost AR devices and this technology was used only in a limited number of cases. Thanks to the technology improvements, not only smartphones provide all the sensors necessary to implement AR applications, but it is also possible to find on the market several AR see-through devices such as the Meta 2 AR headset [15] or the Microsoft Hololens [16]. Thus, the number of AR applications is greatly increased, from educational or cultural heritage applications [30] to industry ones, such as maintenance-assembly-repair processes or product inspection and building monitoring [29]. It should also be noticed that the effectiveness of a new technology can be measured by its market penetration and AR potentially has a much larger market than Virtual Reality (VR), since it allows users to interact with the real world, which is, at least so far, much more complex than the fictitious environments provided by VR.

Since AR technology is becoming more widespread, several researches are trying to figure out how to use it in the HRC context. In [3,7,8], systems based on projected AR have been developed to visualize in real-time the future motions (trajectories, occupied space) of Automated Guided Vehicles (AGV). Moreover, authors in [9,10], are exploring the use of AR for visualizing the robot's arm movement in the real environment. Ameri et al. [9] developed an AR system in which the worker is not only able to detect which is the object that is going to be manipulated by the robot but also the trajectory that the robot will follow.

Being aware of the robot's movements is indeed useful, but there may be circumstances that require the visualization of other data. In [11], forces applied by the robot arm are represented in the real space as 3D vectors centered in the application point. However, the works described above do not take in consideration situations in which robots are affected by faults. In a human-robot collaboration context, humans work side-by-side with manipulators and faults may increase anxiety in the workers because they are not able to understand in real-time which is the cause of the error. It is then quite important to be able to visualize robots' faults in real time.

Since HRC is a quite new scientific discipline, there is still a lack of researches that have tried to figure out how to develop AR systems for the robots faults visualization.

In this paper, a preliminary study regarding the use of AR for detecting and visualizing faults on robotic arms is proposed. The paper is organized as follows: the background of this work and the problem of fault detection in the context of industrial robots are briefly introduced in Sect. 2, followed by a general classification of any possible fault. The subset of faults considered in this work with the set of 3D assets used to describe the faults, are presented in Sect. 3. The hardware and software architecture of the proposed application is explained in Sect. 4. Tests and the analysis of the gathered results are presented in Sect. 5. Finally, conclusions and possible perspectives are discussed in Sect. 6.

## 2   Human-Robot Augmented Collaborative Environment

Fault detection is a subject that has been studied since the first use of industrial robots. However, there is still a lack of straightforward techniques to detect and visualize in real-time shortcomings on the manipulators. As described in [4], factory productivity may be widely affected by faults in industrial manipulators. Nowadays, when a fault occurs on an industrial manipulator, one common procedure used to solve the error is represented by the following work-flow:

- a text file, containing the corresponding error, is saved as a log file;
- technicians use this log file to understand the nature of the problem and try to solve the fault using technical manuals and their experience.

This procedure takes a long time and it is not possible to understand in real-time the nature of the fault. In an Human-Robot Augmented Collaborative (HRAC) environment, human workers can work side-by-side with industrial manipulators, visualizing faults directly in the real environment without the necessity of the procedure explained above. Figure 1 shows this scenario. To achieve this purpose, successful strategies to recognize and solve errors in the shortest possible time must be pursued. Many approaches exist to control the robot's state: in [17–19] neural networks have been used to monitor and isolate industrial manipulator's faults. However, these methods suffer for the requirements of high computational power; moreover, workers are not able to visualize the errors on the robot and consequently they cannot recognize the location of the faults.

AR is indeed suitable to achieve this purpose: thanks to its intrinsic capability to enrich the real environment with additional information, faults can be clearly recognized by workers in real-time. Nowadays, industrial robots work inside security cells, completely separated from the human workers to avoid any possible injury. Normally, when a mechanical robot's fault occurs, the manipulator suddenly stops its movements: this is a safety procedure, used to ensure that unprogrammed actions are not performed by the robot. In a HRAC context, however, the arm robot and the human worker carry out tasks side-by-side and unexpected interruptions in the manipulator's movements may increase anxiety and stress in the operators. This paper represents a preliminary work that investigates which 3D metaphors best represent some faults on industrial manipulators. To achieve this purpose, an AR system has been designed and developed: it is able to correctly align the 3D assets on the robot to highlight the nature of the faults.

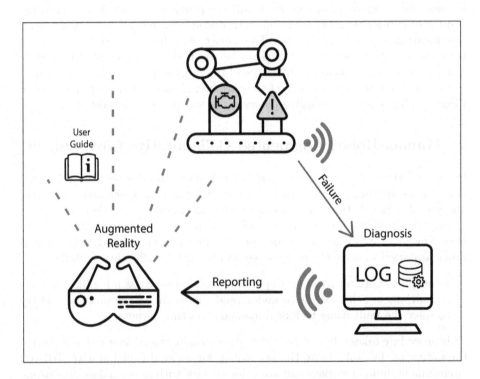

**Fig. 1.** The HRAC scenario: when a fault occurs on an industrial manipulator, it is both saved on a database and it is possible to visualize the augmented fault in real-time.

## 2.1   Classification of the Faults

An industrial manipulator is defined as a $n$-degree-of-freedom ($n$DoF) arm robot: joints are controlled by using either DC or brushless electric motors, their position is sampled by means of encoders whereas the joints' velocity is measured with tachometers. Arm robots are made of sensors, mechanical parts and actuation systems, thus it is possible to classify errors in three main categories [12]:

- faults on the sensors;
- faults on the mechanical structure;
- faults on the actuation system.

The first category regards errors that may occur during the acquisition of data by sensors: it may happen that the values provided by sensors are wrong even if the physical quantity is actually not affected by any error. The second category refers to faults that may occur on mechanical components; for example, a joint is blocked due to a fault in the brakes or a collision among the robot and an unexpected object occurs and the manipulator suddenly stops. Finally, faults on the actuation system may involve the electrical components, such as the motor drivers and the motors themselves. A fourth category can be added considering the overloading fault [13]. Each manipulator is able to raise weights up to a predefined limit; however, if this limit has overcome, the manipulator suddenly stops its movements. This fault may cause stress and displacements in the structure; hence it should be considered as well as the others introduced above.

## 3   AR Interface for Fault Visualization

To improve the sense of safety and reliability of the human workers, errors should be identified and highlighted by graphic metaphors that represent the real problems. In a human-robot collaborative scenario, when the robot suddenly stops for one (or more) of the faults introduced in the previous section, the human worker should be immediately able to both understand the typology of the faults and to visualize them in the proper location. In this project, just the collaborative robots are considered and, moreover, a subset of the faults categories introduced above is contemplated:

- fault on the velocity sensor: velocity can be measured by a tachometer; a fault in the tachometer circuit causes the read velocity to be null;
- fault on the actuation system: fault on a motor may stop the rotation of one of the joints;
- collision detection: a collaborative robot is able to foresee an imminent collision and in that case it comes to a sudden stop; it is then important for the human worker to understand that it has stopped not because of an internal error but in order to avoid the collision;
- overloading fault: the industrial manipulator is not able to raise the payload because the object's weight overcomes the robot's limit.

Each of these faults is represented by a 3D asset, superimposed on the fault's location:

- a 3D circular arrow: this model rotates as long as the angular velocity sensor reads correct data, while it stops (also changing color) when the sensor reads null velocity;
- a 3D motor: when an error occurs on a joint's motor, the 3D model starts to blink;
- a 3D sphere: this asset represents the working-area of the manipulator; when a collision is detected, it starts to blink;
- a 3D anvil with a 3D warning signal: when the manipulator stops its movement due to overloading problems, these assets are superimposed on the payload.

## 4    The System Architecture

In this section the system architecture including hardware and software elements is presented.

### 4.1    Hardware Architecture

The hardware architecture is composed by three different elements: a Personal Computer (PC), an AR Android device and the industrial manipulators. On the PC, the Ubuntu 16.04 LTS distribution has been installed along with the Robot Operating System (ROS) Kinetic version [20]. The PC works as a server, sending both the instruction to control the robot to the industrial manipulator and the data used to correctly align the 3D assets to the Android device (acting as a client) over a TCP connection. Both devices have to be connected to the same LAN network.

### 4.2    Software Architecture

The software architecture is divided in three different parts: the first one is represented by the ROS system used by the server to send data both to the manipulator and to the Android client. Information sent to the robot is used to control it, while data sent to the Android device is used to correctly align the 3D assets in the real environment. In fact, using the ROS system the server is able to get some precious information from the robot (such as its joint's orientation or velocity) and send them to the Android device for properly visualize the 3D models. The second one is represented by the robot controller, used for managing the manipulator's behaviour. Finally, there is the software layer used by the Android client to visualize the 3D assets. It has been developed using Unity3D as Integrated Development Environment (IDE) and the Vuforia Software Development Kit (SDK). With Unity3D is possible to manage 3D objects in a relative simple way whereas the main task of Vuforia is to detect and recognize the marker for correctly positioning the 3D models in the real world. Another advantage of using Unity3D is that it is able to build the developed application into an APK for the Android devices.

## 4.3   Implementation

Since this research project represents a preliminary work, for the development of this project it has been used a 3D model of the Smart-5 Six Comau manipulator (Fig. 2): it is a 6-DoF arm robot, employed for welding operations. The 3D model is directly managed by the client's software, hence only the Android application and the server software using ROS have been developed. To correctly align the 3D robot in the real space, a target (marker), printed on a sheet of format A0, has been used. When the AR device detects the marker, the system can extract some essential information (such as orientation and distance from the camera) to correctly align the 3D assets in the augmented scene.

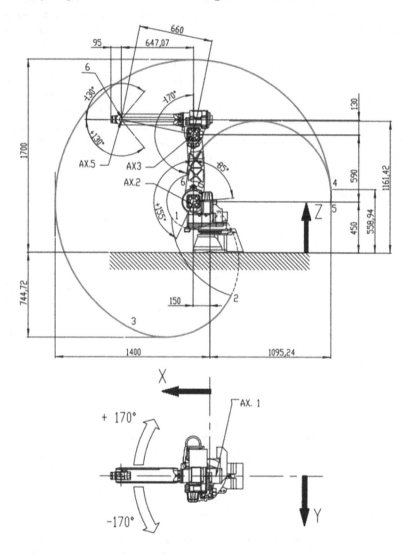

**Fig. 2.** Operational area (red line) of the Comau Smart-5 Six. (Color figure online)

The main purposes of the server software are to wait for connections from a client and to send the robot simulation to it. To establish the connection, the rosbridge_server package has been used. It is part of the rosbridge suite and it provides a WebSocket transport layer. To create a suitable set of animations for the virtual robot, four nodes have been developed using the C++ language. To represent the Smart-5 Six as a 3D asset, an URDF file describing all the characteristics of the robot has been used [31]. At the system bootstrap, the rosbridge_server node is initialized and it creates a websocket connection on a specific IP-port couple. When the client has established the connection on the websocket, the server can send data for controlling the virtual robot starting the corresponding node. Each of the nodes has a similar structure: it publishes on the "join_states" topic a message of type "sensor_msgs/JointStateMessage" containing the data used to describe the state of the robot joints. In this way, it is possible to change the orientation of each of the joints of the robot. The Android device's software manages the visualization of both the 3D metaphors and the virtual industrial robot. For managing a 3D model consistent with the one used in the server, it has been necessary to use the URDF file that describes the characteristics of the Smart-5 Six robot. Unity3D does not support .urdf extensions and the use of an external plugin has been mandatory [21]. With this plugin, it is possible to create a GameObject from the URDF file, obtaining a real 3D representation of the arm robot. It also allows to develop publisher and

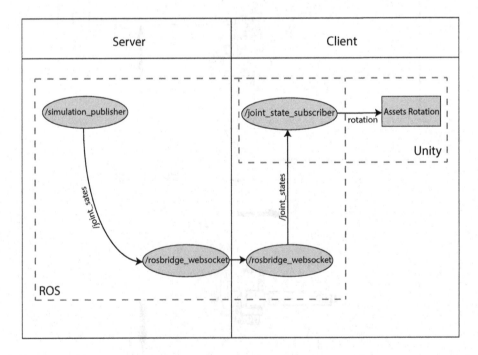

**Fig. 3.** The ROS nodes architecture.

subscriber nodes using the C# language, allowing the Unity3D application to be compatible with the ROS system of the server. When the Android application starts, it establishes a connection with the server using a websocket. Then, a ROS node subscribes to the "joint_state" topic, waiting for incoming data. When data arrive, they are used to rotate the arm robot GameObject created previously from the URDF file. Figure 3 shows the nodes architectures.

## 5   Tests and Results

In order to assess the framework usability and the clarity of the assets, some tests have been held at Politecnico di Torino. The tests were focused on some objective and subjective parameters: specifically, the user's understanding of each problem, the clarity of representation of each problem and the different user experience using AR glasses and smartphone.

Users were students and members of the Polytechnic of Turin. There were 10 testers, 8 men and 2 women, with ages that ranged between 20 and 30 years. A computer science laboratory has been used for the test, with an artificial lighting comfortable for using AR devices. During the test, users had to visualize four different scenes using an AR see-through device, the Epson Moverio BT-200 (with Android 4.0 as operating system) [22] and an Asus Zenfone 2 (with Android 5.0.1 as operating system). Each scene is composed by the virtual Smart-5 Six Comau model and a 3D representation of a fault. At the beginning of the scene, the robot is working normally, making some pre-defined tasks. At a certain random moment, a fault occurs and the robot may stop its movement or may continue its task, depending on the nature of the fault. The scenes are the following (see Figs. 4, 5, 6 and 7):

- Scene 1: this scene focuses on the fault on the velocity sensor. At the beginning the robot is acting normally; when the fault occurs, the virtual manipulator does not stop its movements because this type of error does not affect its motion but the corresponding 3D metaphors (the 3D arrows) stop to rotate and their color changes.
- Scene 2: this scene focuses on the fault of the actuation system. At the beginning the robot is acting normally; when the fault occurs, the virtual manipulator stops its movements and the engine of the blocked joint is highlighted.
- Scene 3: this scene focuses on the collision detection. In this scene there are two different robots, the 3D Smart-5 Six and a 3D AGV that is moving around the environment. At the beginning the 3D Smart-5 Six is acting normally; when it foresees the collision with the AGV, it pauses its movements, letting the AGV pass, and the sphere starts to blink for highlighting the risk of a collision. When the AGV has passed, the robotic arm resumes moving.
- Scene 4: it is the scene that focuses on the overloading problem. At the beginning the robot is acting normally: when it tries to raise a payload that weights more than the robot's limit, the manipulator suddenly stops and an anvil appears, superimposed on the payload.

**Fig. 4.** Scene 1: the 3D arrows used to visualize the joints' angular velocity. (Color figure online)

**Fig. 5.** Scene 2: when the robot stops its movements, the internal blocked engine is highlighted.

**Fig. 6.** Scene 3: when the robot foresees the collision with the AGV, it stops its movements changing the color of the sphere. (Color figure online)

**Fig. 7.** Scene 4: when the robot tries to raise a payload that weights more than its intrinsic limits, a 3D anvil is superimposed on the payload

For each session, two scenes were visualized with the AR glasses and the other two with mobile device: in order to get relevant results, the scenes were randomly selected. Users had to examine the whole scene in order to understand which was the nature of the fault. Users can freely move in the environment, watching the scene from different perspectives. A questionnaire has been created and proposed to the user after the test: prior to performing it, users were individually introduced, firstly with a short tutorial of the application and next with a description of the aim of the project. Testers were all volunteers and their participation were not remunerated. After the starting tutorial, they were placed in front of the target and they had to accomplish the whole test. During the test users had to pay attention to some factors in order to evaluate correctly the fluency, the usability and the utility of the system. After the test, users had to fill the questionnaire, composed by 24 questions.

## 5.1  Results

The questionnaire is divided in four different sections: the first one is about the user's information, computer science knowledge and familiarity with augmented reality. The second section is divided in four sub-parts, one for each scene: the questions are relative to the clarity and the utility of the symbology of the assets used for the faults representation. Since scene 3 is slightly different from the others (the robot stops its movements not because of a fault but because it foresees a collision), the questions relative to it are marginally different from the ones used in scenes 1, 2 and 3. Depending on the typology of the question, three different modality of answers are presented in the questionnaire: double answer (Yes/No), linear scale from 1 (strongly disagree) to 5 (strongly agree) and multiple answer. In the multiple answer typology, users have to choose from the following fault list which one represents the most reasonable error:

- fault on joint position sensor;
- engine block;
- angular speed sensor fault;
- joint block;
- overload;
- fault on current sensor;
- collision detected;
- fault on the actuation system.

In the third section, some questions are proposed to compare the application usability with the devices used, the AR glasses and the smartphone. Finally, in the last section, there is a specific optional area where users can add their comments and feedbacks. The following images (Figs. 8, 9, 10, 11, 12 and 13) summarize the results of the test.

## 5.2  Results Analysis

Tests have been evaluated with a number of participants (10) too small to obtain results with statistical validity. Moreover, subjects of these tests were university students without any background in the robotic domain. Despite this, the proposed study can be suitable to lay the foundations for future developments. Testers have found some hardware-related problems: since the Moverio glasses have a very limited field-of-view (FOV) that is around 23°, subjects could not watch large objects entirely and they were forced to change their point of view. This is a well-known limitation of the see-through devices and only an improvement in the underlying technology could overcome this issue. For each scene, users both had to understand if the robot had a problem and they had to evaluate the intuitiveness of the symbology. Finally users had to understand the nature of the faults.

From Figs. (8, 9, 10, 11, 12 and 13), it is visible that in scene 1 the 70% of testers have reported that the robot has performed its routine without any problem (in fact a sensor fault does not affect the robot's motion). The symbology

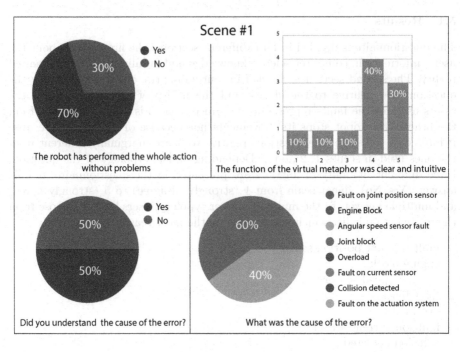

**Fig. 8.** Scene 1 results.

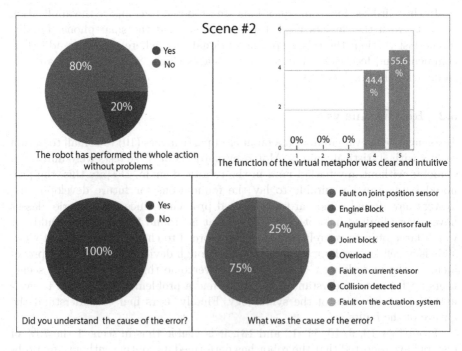

**Fig. 9.** Scene 2 results.

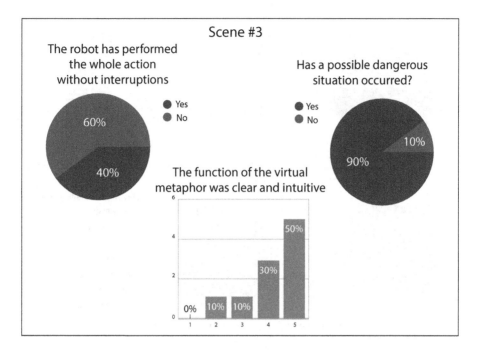

**Fig. 10.** Scene 3 results

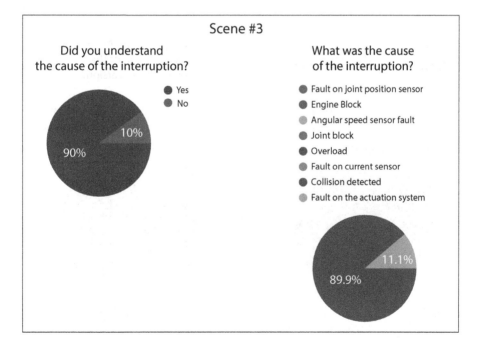

**Fig. 11.** Scene 3 results

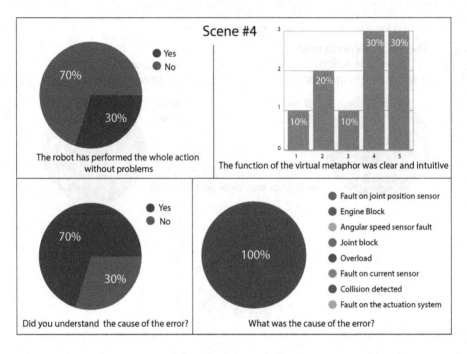

**Fig. 12.** Scene 4 results

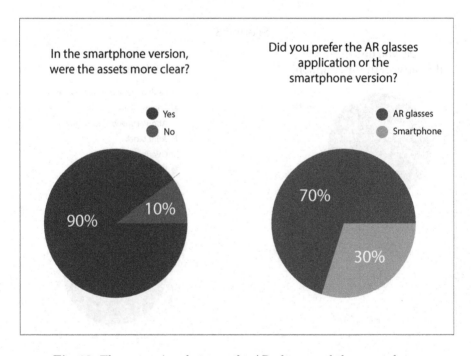

**Fig. 13.** The comparison between the AR glasses and the smartphone.

responses are also important, because 70% of the testers agreed that the virtual arrows have been clear and intuitive in representing speed, but only few users understood the real problem. In fact, it has been confused with the joint block error. It is important to know that this type of error is particular, and for this reason it is very difficult for users without some specific knowledge in robotics to understand it. In the second scene 80% of the testers have recognized that the robot had a problem, and 100% of them agreed or strongly agreed that the symbology was very clear. Furthermore, among the users who understood there was a fault, 25% said that the robot had a joint block and 75% chose engine block. Despite the correct answer was engine block (75%), the latter can be regarded to cause a joint block: hence the remaining 25% of testers understood the nature of the problem but not the real cause. In the third scene, despite only 60% of the users have noticed that the robot stopped its movements when the AGV was passing, 90% of the subjects have understood that a possible dangerous situation was occuring. In fact, 80% of testers have found the sphere symbology intuitive or very intuitive; furthermore, 89.9% of them understood the right cause of the problem. In the fourth scene, although testers have indicated that the symbology should be more intuitive and clear, 70% of them have understood that the fault was due to overloading problem. Finally, subjects have indicated that they would have preferred the smartphone version, since it would have been more comfortable and assets would have been clearer and more understandable.

## 5.3   Additional Test

It has been decided to evaluate the same system with a real robot. The aim is to verify if the visualization of 3D assets is affected by the virtual robot or not. To do this, a humanoid physical robot was used, because it was not possible to use a proper industrial robot. The real robot is the open source 3D printed life-size humanoid robot InMoov [23] although it is not an industrial manipulator, its arm can be seen as an arm robot composed by different joints, each of them controlled by an electric motor. Thus, it is indeed suitable for testing the effectiveness on the 3D assets.

Both the same assets and the same Android devices have been used for this additional test. The main difference with the previous test is that the robot is already blocked because an error has occurred. Ten new testers have been found and again they were not robot technician expert. Subjects had to identify the nature of the faults, visualizing the 3D metaphors superimposed on the real robot. As in the previous session, two scenes were visualized with the AR glasses and the remainder with the mobile device. Figure 14 shows the InMoov robot with a 3D metphor correctly aligned.

The results of this additional test confirm in part the hypothesis introduced at the beginning of this section: in fact, in scene 2 and 4 more than the 80% of the testers understood the nature of the faults, confirming that using a virtual representation of the virtual robot does not affect the effectiveness of the 3D metaphors. Also in scene 1, users faced the same problems found with the virtual version. On the other hand, results show some unexpected results for scene 3: in

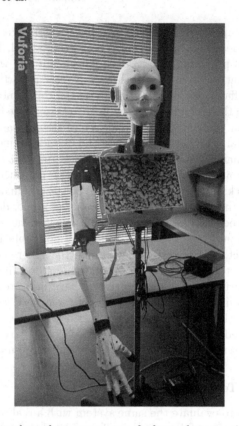

**Fig. 14.** The 3D metaphor, that represents a fault on the actuation system, correctly aligned on the real robot.

the previous collision scene, 90% of the subjects have been able to recognize the correct problem; in the additional test, only 50% of the testers could understand the true nature of the problem. As the robot was already blocked, the 3D collision sphere was already blinking, creating disturbance in the scene. Thus, it is possible to deduce that since there was the absence of an initial correct phase, in which the robot can complete its task without interruptions, users could not compare the initial phase with the fault phase and, consequently, they could not understand the nature of the faults.

Another important result is that using a physical robot users preferred to use the AR glasses despite the 3D assets were the same used for the previous version. Indeed, in the case of the virtual robot, users had difficulties in visualizing all the 3D assets at the same time using the Moverio glasses, because of the well-known limitation of this kind of devices. On the other hand, in the real robot scenario, subjects have been able to focus only on the 3D metaphors, which are much less demanding as the FOV is concerned: thus, in this case they have preferred the Moverio glasses.

# 6    Conclusions

In this paper a new AR fault visualization system has been proposed. In a human-robot collaboration context, human operators work side-by-side with industrial manipulators, hence they have to trust them, especially when faults occur, creating unpredictable scenarios. Thus, the new HRAC environment has been proposed: in this scenario, not only workers carry out tasks close to industrial manipulators but they can visualize faults, by means of 3D metaphors, directly on the true location of the errors. The effectiveness of the proposed 3D assets has been tested: results show that the use of a virtual robot model or of a real one does not affect the clarity of the visualization. Issues were found relative to the representation of the angular speed value: most of the visualization tools for robotic systems, such as RVIZ [25] or OpenHRP [26], represent rotations using 3D arrows [27] and test result seem to hint at possible issues in the application of this typology of interface in an AR environment. One possible explanation might be that some metaphors are suitable only for a completely virtual world, while others can be used also in an AR scenario.

The two experiments differed from the quantity and the dimensions of the 3D assets represented in the scene: this difference has indeed influenced the choice of the most suitable device. In fact, in the case of the virtual model, the limited FOV of the Moverio glasses results into a worse user experience; on the other hand, in the real robot scenario, since the quantity and the dimensions of 3D metaphors to be visualized were less demanding, the Moverio's FOV was sufficient to guarantee a reasonable experience.

Further experiments will be taken to better investigate which metaphors are suitable for representing faults in an augmented reality system, also using some see-through devices, such as the Microsoft Hololens, with a greater FOV.

**Acknowledgements.** This work is co-funded by the regional project HuManS (Human Centered Manufacturing Systems).

# References

1. Bauer, A., Wollherr, D., Buss, M.: Human-robot collaboration: a survey. Int. J. Humanoid Robot. **5**(01), 47–66 (2008)
2. Morato, C., Kaipa, K.N., Zhao, B., Gupta, S.K.: Toward safe human robot collaboration by using multiple kinects based real-time human tracking. J. Comput. Inf. Sci. Eng. **14**(1), 011006 (2014)
3. Coovert, M.D., Lee, T., Shindev, I., Sun, Y.: Spatial augmented reality as a method for a mobile robot to communicate intended movement. Comput. Hum. Behav. **34**, 241–248 (2014)
4. Chen, J., Patton, R.J.: Robust Model-based Fault Diagnosis for Dynamic Systems, vol. 3. Springer, Boston (2012). https://doi.org/10.1007/978-1-4615-5149-2
5. Miseikis, J., Knobelreiter, P., Brijacak, I., Yahyanejad, S., Glette, K., Elle, O.J., Torresen, J.: Robot Localisation and 3D Position Estimation Using a Free-Moving Camera and Cascaded Convolutional Neural Networks (2018). arXiv preprint arXiv:1801.02025

6. Nikolaidis, S., Lasota, P., Rossano, G., Martinez, C., Fuhlbrigge, T., Shah, J.: Human-robot collaboration in manufacturing: quantitative evaluation of predictable, convergent joint action. In: 2013 44th International Symposium on Robotics (ISR), pp. 1–6. IEEE (2013)

7. Chadalavada, R.T., Andreasson, H., Krug, R., Lilienthal, A.J.: That's on my mind! robot to human intention communication through on-board projection on shared floor space. In: 2015 European Conference on Mobile Robots (ECMR), pp. 1–6. IEEE (2015)

8. Matsumaru, T.: Mobile robot with preliminary-announcement and display function of forthcoming motion using projection equipment. In: The 15th IEEE International Symposium on Robot and Human Interactive Communication, 2006, ROMAN 2006, pp. 443–450. IEEE (2006)

9. Akan, B., Çürüklü, B.: Augmented reality meets industry: Interactive robot programming. In: Proceedings of SIGRAD 2010: Content Aggregation and Visualization, 25–26 November 2010, Västerås, Sweden, no. 052, pp. 55–58. Linköping University Electronic Press (2010)

10. Michalos, G., Karagiannis, P., Makris, S., Tokçalar, Ö., Chryssolouris, G.: Augmented reality (AR) applications for supporting human-robot interactive cooperation. Procedia CIRP **41**, 370–375 (2016)

11. Mateo, C., Brunete, A., Gambao, E., Hernando, M.: Hammer: an android based application for end-user industrial robot programming. In: 2014 IEEE/ASME 10th International Conference on Mechatronic and Embedded Systems and Applications (MESA), pp. 1–6. IEEE (2014)

12. Fantuzzi, C., Secchi, C., Visioli, A.: On the fault detection and isolation of industrial robot manipulators. IFAC Proc. Vol. **36**(17), 399–404 (2003)

13. Singh, V. D., Banga, V. K.: Overloading failures in robot manipulators. In: International Conference on Trends in Electrical, Electronics and Power Engineering (ICTEEP'2012)/Planetary Scientific Research Centre, pp. 15–16 (2012)

14. Michieletto, S., Chessa, N., Menegatti, E.: Learning how to approach industrial robot tasks from natural demonstrations. In: 2013 IEEE Workshop on Advanced Robotics and Its Social Impacts (ARSO), pp. 255–260. IEEE (2013)

15. Meta 2 ar headset. Accessed 2018

16. https://www.microsoft.com/it-it/hololens

17. Eski, I., Erkaya, S., Savas, S., Yildirim, S.: Fault detection on robot manipulators using artificial neural networks. Robot. Comput.-Integr. Manuf. **27**(1), 115–123 (2011)

18. Vemuri, A.T., Polycarpou, M.M.: Neural-network-based robust fault diagnosis in robotic systems. IEEE Trans. Neural Netw. **8**(6), 1410–1420 (1997)

19. Ghrieb, A.O., Kourd, Y., Guersi, N.: Supervision of industrial manipulators using ANFIS system. In: 2017 17th International Conference on Control, Automation and Systems (ICCAS), pp. 161–166. IEEE, October 2017

20. http://www.ros.org/

21. https://github.com/siemens/ros-sharp/wiki

22. https://www.epson.it/products/see-through-mobile-viewer/moverio-bt-200

23. http://inmoov.fr/

24. Milgram, P., Kishino, F.: A taxonomy of mixed reality visual displays. IEICE Trans. Inf. Syst. **77**, 1321–1329 (1994)

25. https://github.com/ros-visualization/rviz

26. https://fkanehiro.github.io/openhrp3-doc/en/

27. Hulin, T., Hertkorn, K., Preusche, C.: Interactive features for robot viewers. In: Su, C.-Y., Rakheja, S., Liu, H. (eds.) ICIRA 2012. LNCS (LNAI), vol. 7508, pp. 181–193. Springer, Heidelberg (2012). https://doi.org/10.1007/978-3-642-33503-7_19

28. Sutherland, I.E.: A head-mounted three dimensional display. In: Proceedings of the AFIPS, pp. 757–764. ACM, San Francisco (1968)

29. De Pace, F., Manuri, F., Sanna, A.: Augmented reality in industry 4.0. Am. J. Comput. Sci. Inf. Technol. 6(1), 1–7 (2018)

30. Sanna, A., Manuri, F.: A survey on applications of augmented reality. Adv. Comput. Sci. Int. J. 5(1), 18–27 (2016)

31. https://github.com/siemens/ros-sharp

# Cyber Physical Systems for Industry 4.0: Towards Real Time Virtual Reality in Smart Manufacturing

Emanuele Frontoni[1], Jelena Loncarski[2], Roberto Pierdicca[3(✉)], Michele Bernardini[1], and Michele Sasso[4]

[1] Department of Information Engineering, Università Politecnica delle Marche, Via Brecce Bianche 12, 60131 Ancona, Italy
e.frontoni@staff.univpm.it

[2] Department of Engineering Sciences, Division for Electricity Research, Uppsala University, Box 534, 751 21 Uppsala, Sweden

[3] Dipartimento di Ingegneria Civile, Universitá Politecnica delle Marche, Edile e dell'Architettura, 60100 Ancona, Italy
r.pierdicca@staff.univpm.it

[4] UBISIVE s.r.l., Via Dell'Universit 13, 63900 Fermo, FM, Italy
info@ubisive.it

**Abstract.** Cyber Physical System (CPS) together with Internet of Things, Big Data, Cloud Computing and Industrial Wireless Networks are the core technologies allowing the introduction of the fourth industrial revolution, Industry 4.0. Along with the advances in new generation information technologies, smart manufacturing is becoming the focus of global manufacturing transformation. Considering the competitive nature of industry, it requires manufacturers to implement new methodologies. Realistic virtual models mirroring the real world are becoming essential to bridge the gap between design and manufacturing. In this paper model conceptualization, representation, and implementation of the digital twin is presented, on the real use case of manufacturing industry and in the cyber physical environment. A novel CPS architecture for real time visualization of complex industrial process is proposed. It essentially considers the Simulation technological pillar of Industry 4.0. The results from a real industrial environment show good performances in terms of real time behaviour, virtual reality and WebGL CPS visualization features, usability and readability.

## 1 Introduction

There is a worldwide movement trying to improve the productivity and efficiency in industrial manufacturing by integrating the latest advances in information and communications technology (ICT) [1]. The adoption of emerging ICT technologies will affect the competitiveness of manufacturing and introduce completely new services in the years to come. Governments have recognized the importance of ICT in industry and are launching the different initiatives

© Springer International Publishing AG, part of Springer Nature 2018
L. T. De Paolis and P. Bourdot (Eds.): AVR 2018, LNCS 10851, pp. 422–434, 2018.
https://doi.org/10.1007/978-3-319-95282-6_31

such as the Industrial Internet and the Advanced Manufacturing Partnership in United States, Industrie 4.0 in Germany, and La Nouvelle France Industrielle in France, etc. Industry 4.0 is the 4th Generation of Industrial Revolution and Germany is leading its transformation towards Cyber-Physical System based manufacturing and service innovation [2]. Software and embedded intelligence are being increasingly incorporated in industrial products and systems, and predictive technologies can further intertwine intelligent algorithms with electronics and e-intelligence. These technologies can viably be adopted to autonomously manage and optimize product service needs, predict product performance degradation, etc. There are several technologies involved in this global trend such as: Internet of Things (IoT), Big Data, Cloud Computing, Additive Manufacturing, Autonomous Robots, System Integration, Augmented Reality, Cyber Security, and Simulation. All these technologies will allow businesses to establish global networks that incorporate their machinery, warehousing systems and production facilities in the shape of Cyber-Physical Systems (CPS) [3]. Cyber-Physical Systems comprise smart machines and storage systems capable of autonomously exchanging information, triggering actions and controlling each other independently. The future smart factories will have the capabilities of self-awareness, self-prediction, self-comparison, self-reconfiguration, and self-maintenance [2]. They will allow several important features and will solve many key issues in manufacturing such as meeting the individual customer requirements, dynamic business, optimized decision-making, resource and energy efficiency, better work-life balance, etc. Cyber-Physical Systems (CPS) is defined as transformative technologies that offer integrations of computation, networking, and physical processes. Some of the defining characteristics of CPS include:

1. cyber capability in physical components,
2. high degree of automation,
3. networking at multiple scales,
4. integration at multiple temporal and spatial scales,
5. reconfiguring dynamics [4].

The increasing growth of sensors and networked machines facilitated the growth of high volume data that is known as Big Data. In this environment, CPS can be further developed for managing Big Data and improve the interconnectivity of machines to reach the goal of intelligent and self-adaptable machines [5,6]. There exist several challenges in designing the CPS, due to the close interaction of the physical and cyber world. The events in the physical world need to be reflected in the cyber world, and the decision taken by the cyber world needs to be communicated to the physical world, accurately and in a timely manner [4]. The sensors and actuators provide an interface between the physical and cyber worlds, and policies are needed to adapt to the physical and cyber context. In this regard, CPS consists of two main functional components: (1) the advanced connectivity ensuring the real-time data acquisition and information feedback; and (2) intelligent data management, analytics and computational capability constructing the cyber space.

While CPS has vertical architecture consisting of 3 or more layers for developing and deploying a CPS for manufacturing application, namely the sensor/actuator layer, communication layer, and application (control) layer [7], IoT has horizontal architecture, connecting massive number of devices, monitoring and controlling them in cyber space. Some recent works propose 5-layer architecture (5C) outlined as follows: (1) Smart connection acquiring accurate and reliable data, (2) Data-to-information conversion algorithms to infer information from the data, (3) Cyber level central information hub, (4) Cognition decision support system, (5) Configuration resilience control system [5].

To link better the IoT with the key physical objects, there is the need to develop technological solutions that augment the capabilities of the physical devices with additional functionalities and allow all of them to talk to each other at the same level [8]. The solution has been the introduction of the concept of virtual object, which is the digital counterpart of any physical object and has the fundamental role of bridging the gap between the physical and the virtual world. The concept of digital twin was firstly presented by Grieves [9]. Generally, virtual models of physical objects are created digitally to simulate their behavior in real-world environments [10]. Thus, the digital twin is composed of three components, namely the physical entities in the physical world, the virtual models in the virtual world, and the connected data that tie the two worlds. Is task is to guides the physical process towards the optimized solutions, after the simulation and optimization of manufacturing, design or maintenance process.

This paper is also based on our previous works and experiences on Virtual and Augmented Reality [11–13] and on recent research in the field of industrial engineering and big data analysis [11,14–16].

In this paper CPS and its technologies are presented and studied on the real industry case, transforming it and approaching the Industry 4.0 framework. The smart factory development includes several technologies: Traceability with identification systems (RFID and BLE), Virtual Reality, and Digital Twin. The smart factory implementation will be based on Simulation pillar of Industry 4.0. The concept of CPS will lead to optimized production and maintenance/assistance. The methodology has been implemented and verified in the experimental environment on the example of a real industrial group. The results from a real industrial environment show good performances in terms of real time behaviour, virtual reality and WebGL CPS visualization features, usability and readability. The main contribution is on the real application that proves the effectiveness of this approach for future application of Virtual Reality CPS in the Industry 4.0 scenario. Other contributions are on the data standard for IoT and Virtual environment Interoperability and, finally, on the specialized WebGL implementation for sensor based movement alignments.

Paper is organized as follows: Sect. 2 gives the description of the technologies involved in smart factory implementation in general, Sect. 3 gives the insight to the approach used in this analysis, Sect. 4 gives the experimental results on the real use case of manufacturing industry where the CPS was implemented and tested. Future works with the conclusions are presented in Sect. 5.

# 2     Technologies Enabling the Smart Factory

Smart factories consists of several technologies, where the CPS is the core enabling technology together with IoT and the related tools that include cloud computing, web apps, mobile devices, sensors, and Digital Twins [17].

## 2.1     Cyber Physical System

The CPS concept is composed of technologies that enable the communications and interactions between machines, humans and other components. The definition of CPS generally includes an integration between physical and computational assets [5]. In literature exist many topics on CPS, ranging from cyber security [18], the technologies and the design involved [4], to its importance in building Industry 4.0 [5]. The architecture for building CPSs can be viewed a composition of three to five levels (the 5 C architecture).

## 2.2     Data Transmission

Nowadays, two broadly used communication solutions for the industrial applications are CyberOPC and MTConnect. CyberOPC application protocol is based on reverse AJAX and Java-Script object notation (JSON) remote procedure call (RPC). It was initially created for monitoring computer numerical control (CNC) tools. This protocol adopts streaming techniques for industrial communication technologies over Internet protocol (IP)-based networks, representing an open and performing alternative for monitoring protocols such as OPC and MTConnect [19]. MTConnect Standard is an open-source and royalty-free protocol that enables data transmission from manufacturing equipment, based on eXtensible Markup Language (XML). It allows communication from machine to machine and machine to operator. The two crucial elements are the adapter (data collection element that interfaces a physical sensor with a network connection), and the agent (data aggregator collecting readings from one or more adapters and storing them in a buffer). In this case a python script of the application performs the XML parsing and sends the data to the cloud. The data is then stored in the remote server. MTConnect compatibility on a machine tool provides access to a wide range of variables including motor loads, axis positions, etc. Manufacturing execution system (MES) can use these data to determine the production state of a machine and to determine the overall productive efficiency of a process [17] (Fig. 1).

## 2.3     Enterprise Resource Planning and Manufacturing Execution Systems

ANSI/ISA-95 defines a hierarchy of control between the enterprise resource planning (ERP) systems and control systems. Here MESs assume the role of connecting the office ERPs with the shop-floor equipment, implementing manufacturing operational management (MOM) functions in the enterprise [20]. In the

ISA95 standard, the MTConnect information would fit in the lower levels, while the ERP and other high-level management tools would fit in the upper levels, with the link between them i.e. MES. Current MESs experience several problems: some data need to be entered manually by the operators, lack of real time capability, problems with interoperability and data sharing between different elements, etc. Number of characteristics of a MES need to be considered in order to ensure its compatibility with Industry 4.0, including decentralization, mobility, connectivity, and cloud integration [21].

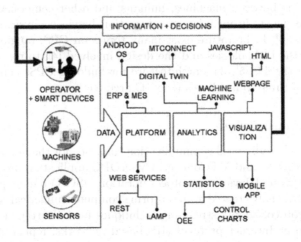

**Fig. 1.** Data flow in the system, the data collected from the operators, machines and sensors is sent to the CPS, and then information produced and decisions from management are returned to the operators who control the machines.

## 2.4  Web Applications and Smart Devices

We have witnessed the potential of mobile devices and applications hosted on the web are growing with impressive speed, and became technologies in daily use. In CPS, users can interact with the web applications directly on their devices, without the need of any additional installation. The application is hosted in the cloud, and users can easily access it from any location using only a web browser. The web app is responsible for both data visualization and data management. The family of smart devices includes mobile device (tablet or smartphone), but also wearables (glasses and smartwatches). They are basically technologies equipped with microchips, sensors and wireless communications capabilities. Mobile devices offer a host of functionality to users, including sensors, connectivity, customizable GUIs, access to the web apps and mobile apps, augmented reality, etc. Both web applications and wearables (Android mobile app and smart glass) are used in the realization of the CPS proposed in this work. Wearable technologies are based on Adaptive Augmented Reality techniques that can enrich the real environment with digital contents, virtual models, simulations in order to facilitate maintenance operations, support remote assistance and the training of the operators, provide instructions that increase the safety, etc. MES.

## 2.5   Cloud Computing and Cloud Manufacturing

The use of Cloud Computing (CC) resources in the context of manufacturing is known as Cloud Manufacturing (CM). CM has many definitions, one of which defines CM as manufacturing focused on providing services-based on resources from its pool of virtualized manufacturing material [22]. CM provides scalability and flexibility at lower costs through sharing resources in the cloud. Information can be shared in the cloud via internet access. Additionally, CM enables a manufacturer to provide access to equipment and production data to any Internet-connected device. This is actually the main advantage of the cloud concept, and the global availability of data has been beneficial to the manufacturing industry. There have been several key CM technologies identified in the literature [22]: *cloud adoption decision* (SMEs are the major category that can benefit from cloud services due its low cost and pay-as-you-go format), *Pay-As-You-Go* (resources are being used for a certain amount of time and the user pays for that usage), *resource virtualization* (conversion of a physical resource to a resource that can be consumed through the cloud), *interoperability* (virtualizing the resources such that they can be used among multiple cloud providers), *security* and *equipment control*.

## 2.6   The Digital Twin Concept

Digital Twin concept refers to a digital models of components necessary to the manufacturing process. The twin concept refers to producing a copy of a part or product and using it for reasoning about other instances of the same part or product [23]. The vision of the digital twin can be described as the vision of a bi-directional relation between a physical artefact and its virtual models. The establishment of such relations between physical parts and their virtual models, offers many benefits such as efficient execution of product design, manufacturing, servicing, etc. Digital Twins are updated in near-real time and are viably used to view, analyze, and control the state of the equipment or process. The digital twin concept was enhanced by the collection and aggregation of large amounts of product and process data; these data enable the construction of simulations of different scenarios, useful to make predictions about behaviors or failures, taking into account the latest data obtained from the physical twin. More information about the digital twin realized in the paper will be given in the following.

# 3   Virtual Object and Digital Twin on Real Use Case

The MES and the ERP developed for this analysis are the enablers of a 3D Digital Twin representing the capital equipment. The Android-based MES, powered by mobile device, web application, and CM, is an ideal platform to ensure the compliance with the I4.0 scenario. CPS presented in this work is envisioned as: the components of the physical factory (machinery and discrete sensing devices which transmit data to the cloud platform using MTConnect), and tooling, products, materials, and people, whose information is supplied directly to the cloud platform using the MES. Finally, the information provided by the Digital Twin can be used by managers, providers, or clients, who then take actions regarding the factory. Tests have been conducted within a scientific joint venture between Universit Politecnica delle Marche and Schnell group, world leading company in the production of automatic machines for reinforcement processing, for the production of electro-welded mesh and software technologies for all shaping centers.

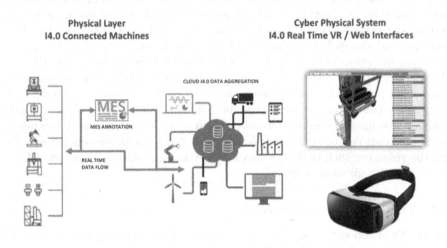

**Fig. 2.** The process schema of the proposed approach: from the real machines connected to the cloud storage system, to the real time visualization interfaces.

### 3.1 Traceability and Identification System

Traceability has been a critical concern for manufacturing systems. The ability of systems to extract valuable data from manufacturing processes is of great importance. Several traceability approaches started with applying RFID technology to industrial systems for tracking individual items in a manufacturing process [24]. The ISO 9000 standard defines "traceability" as "the ability to go back to the past and use or locate the considered entity". This concept can be applied by considering the traceability as the downstream process knowing the input elements it allows to identify a precise product batch, and traceability as the upstream process - starting from the product it is possible to find the origin of the deviation from what was expected. The traceability is implemented as the trace detection, determination of which objects will be detected (generators, batch carriers, serial numbers, etc.), and how the consumption of the materials will be managed.

## 3.2 CPS Real Time Implementation

**Wearables.** The solution was developed and tested as presented in the Fig. 2, related to the field of remote assistance through Smart Glass with the following basic features:

- Communication platform between "Hardware with camera, microphone and speakers" (Vuzix) and mobile app (Android) of the maintainer.
- Management of the assistance ticket through the app: the maintenance technician views the list of tickets, takes charge of one and starts receiving the feedback from the camera of the associated device (with a frame rate of about 10 fps), which will guide the operator to assistance through a voice-chat.
- In the case of insufficient voice prompts, the maintenance technician can send to the operator a series of files that can be viewed through the application.
- All operations can be recorded or recorded (individual screenshots) in order to document operations.

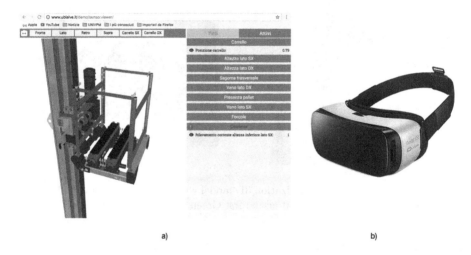

a)                                          b)

**Fig. 3.** Two different interfaces are available for the proposed CPS: (a) web interface with interactive control of the real time CPS and alert monitoring; (b) VR visualization tool of the same environment. A fully working demo version of the web interface is available at the following link: http://www.ubisive.it/demo/sensorviewer/

**Digital Twin.** In this analysis, the digital twin of the forklift in the Fig. 4 was developed on a web based interface totally based on WebGL libraries and able to provide VR visualization. The general schema of the application is reported in Fig. 2 showing how data coming from the real environment (both sensors and actuators) are collected in the cloud I4.0 infrastructure of the company and from here to the visualization tool. All the system was developed for the project with CPS and Maintenance purposes. Two main visualizations engines are available for the proposed CPS: (a) web interface with interactive control of the real time CPS and alert monitoring; (b) VR visualization tool of the same environment. A fully working demo version of the web interface is available at the following link: http://www.ubisive.it/demo/sensorviewer. Figure 3 show an example of these interfaces.

**Fig. 4.** Some images of the visualization 3D model with real-time movements based on data coming from the sensors and actuators. Green sensors or actuators are working fine, while red ones have alert or warning message on going. (Color figure online)

The graphics engine is developed in WebGL and manages the whole rendering phase of the 3D model, both for the static part and for the animated part. The format of the 3D model consists mainly of a .json file. The XML configuration file of the system that has all the data useful for rendering, animation and sensors consists of 4 sections:

1. Camera - Configures and sets the system to default views (the buttons at the top of the system that move the camera);
2. Models - All the components of the 3D model are defined by an ID, and each of them is associated with various "Attributes" (Mesh = the 3D model,

Material = the material applied, Lightmap = Map of light). Essentially it serves to render everything correctly. Visible = 1 identifies that the object must be rendered, Visible = 0 identifies objects that should not be displayed, i.e. "Collider".

3. Materials - Identifies all materials and inherits their parameters.
4. Sensors - There are 2 sub-categories "Template" and "Group". Template is revealing the performance, a PLC communicates a code and from this section it is possible to conclude if the code is related to an error. Group defines all the sensors related to a group, in this case the forklift, and in this section are defined also the calls API of the specific sensors. The APIs are managed from the Esisoftware side, and the structure is the following: the PLCs communicate to a local server and the local server has at the disposal the APIs, where the Polling is done to obtain the data in "Pseudo-realtime".

All the sensors and actuators parameters are the same that are collected on the cloud system for maintenance perspective. Using this data the system simulate all movements and manage all the warning messages with different colours.

## 4    Results and Discussion

To prove the effectiveness of the proposed method we tested different aspects of the system and in particular: (a) a technical test mainly based on real time performances; (b) a preliminary evaluation of on technology acceptance and usability.

### 4.1    Real Time Performances

The following table compares data retrieved from 30 panelists (those who answered also the below mentioned questionnaires) to measure different performances on different devices and to prove the effectiveness of proposed architecture on different end points (7 mobile phones, 11 tablets and 12 laptops).

| CPS & Real Time Metric List | | |
|---|---|---|
| Metric description | Avg | Max |
| CPS interface loading time | 0.89 s | 12.2 s |
| Delay Physical vs Cyber-Physical | 7.6 s # | 8.1 s # |
| CPU usage | 18% | 67% |
| Memory usage | 22 MB | 26 MB |
| WebGL crashes per session | 0.1 | 3 |

Even in the worst cases (mainly coming from old Android Smart Phone versions) performances are acceptable and the total delay with respect to the real environment is never over 15 s. The CPS developed is still under monitoring and we foresee to collect more data about its functioning in the upcoming years. However, given the preliminary results showed, it brings a strong contribution w.r.t. the following issues:

- improved visibility across manufacturing operations: make more informed decisions with a real-time picture of operational status;
- improved utilization: maximize asset performance and uptime with the visibility required for central monitoring and management of the full production and reuse cycle;
- reduced waste: take faster action to reduce or prevent certain forms of waste, thanks to insight on key production metrics;
- targeted cost savings: benchmark resource usage and identify inefficiencies to support operational improvements, mainly in terms of material reuse and sustainability;
- improved quality: detect and prevent quality problems by finding and addressing equipment issues sooner.

## 5    Conclusion and Future Work

In this paper CPS and its technologies are presented and studied on the real industry case, transforming it and approaching the Industry 4.0 framework. The analysis of the technologies that comprises a smart factory was provided, followed by the CPS system including low cost and highly available tools like mobile devices and web services. In particular, the smart factory development includes several technologies: Traceability with identification systems (RFID and BLE), Virtual Reality, and Digital Twin. Digital Twin of the forklift together with Smart Glass providing the remote assistance have been developed, being that the spot of the forklift is inaccessible for the maintenance/assistance. An Android OS application was developed to interact with the operators and collect data from inaccessible places. The app is connected with a cloud database storing historical data and was used to provide visualizations of forklift status using a web application. This information was made available for any device connected to the internet and was updated in real time.

The concept of CPS studied in this work will lead to optimized production and maintenance/assistance. It presents a potential alternative for SME to evolve into the Industry 4.0 age. The results from a real industrial environment show good performances in terms of real time behaviour, virtual reality and WebGL CPS visualization features, usability and readability. The main contribution is on the real application that proves the effectiveness of this approach for future application of Virtual Reality CPS in the Industry 4.0 scenario. Other contributions are on the data standard for IoT and Virtual environment Interoperability and, finally, on the specialized WebGL implementation for sensor based movement alignments.

# References

1. Posada, J., Toro, C., Barandiaran, I., Oyarzun, D., Stricker, D., de Amicis, R., Pinto, E.B., Eisert, P., Döllner, J., Vallarino, I.: Visual computing as a key enabling technology for industrie 4.0 and industrial internet. IEEE Comput. Graph. Appl. **35**(2), 26–40 (2015)
2. Lee, J., Kao, H.A., Yang, S.: Service innovation and smart analytics for industry 4.0 and big data environment. Procedia Cirp **16**, 3–8 (2014)
3. Kagermann, H., Wahlster, W., Helbig, J.: Securing the future of German manufacturing industry. Recommendations for implementing the strategic initiative INDUSTRIE 4 (2013)
4. Khaitan, S.K., McCalley, J.D.: Design techniques and applications of cyberphysical systems: a survey. IEEE Syst. J. **9**(2), 350–365 (2015)
5. Lee, J., Bagheri, B., Kao, H.A.: A cyber-physical systems architecture for industry 4.0-based manufacturing systems. Manuf. Lett. **3**, 18–23 (2015)
6. National Institute of Standards and Technology: Workshop report on foundations for innovation in cyber-physical systems, January 2013
7. Lin, J., Yu, W., Zhang, N., Yang, X., Zhang, H., Zhao, W.: A survey on internet of things: architecture, enabling technologies, security and privacy, and applications. IEEE Internet Things J. **4**(5), 1125–1142 (2017)
8. Nitti, M., Pilloni, V., Colistra, G., Atzori, L.: The virtual object as a major element of the internet of things: a survey. IEEE Commun. Surv. Tutor. **18**(2), 1228–1240 (2016)
9. Grieves, M.: Digital twin: Manufacturing excellence through virtual factory replication. White paper (2014)
10. Qi, Q., Tao, F.: Digital twin and big data towards smart manufacturing and industry 4.0: 360 degree comparison. IEEE Access **6**, 3585–3593 (2018)
11. Pierdicca, R., Liciotti, D., Contigiani, M., Frontoni, E., Mancini, A., Zingaretti, P.: Low cost embedded system for increasing retail environment intelligence. In: 2015 IEEE International Conference on Multimedia & Expo Workshops (ICMEW), pp. 1–6. Turin (2015)
12. Mancini, A., Clini, P., Bozzi, C.A., Malinverni, E.S., Pierdicca, R., Nespeca, R.: Remote touch interaction with high quality models using an autostereoscopic 3D display. In: De Paolis, L.T., Bourdot, P., Mongelli, A. (eds.) AVR 2017. LNCS, vol. 10325, pp. 478–489. Springer, Cham (2017). https://doi.org/10.1007/978-3-319-60928-7_40
13. Pierdicca, R., Frontoni, E., Pollini, R., Trani, M., Verdini, L.: The use of augmented reality glasses for the application in industry 4.0. In: De Paolis, L.T., Bourdot, P., Mongelli, A. (eds.) AVR 2017. LNCS, vol. 10324, pp. 389–401. Springer, Cham (2017). https://doi.org/10.1007/978-3-319-60922-5_30
14. Sturari, M., Liciotti, D., Pierdicca, R., Frontoni, E., Mancini, A., Contigiani, M., Zingaretti, P.: Robust and affordable retail customer profiling by vision and radio beacon sensor fusion. Pattern Recogn. Lett. **81**, 30–40 (2018)
15. Frontoni, E., Marinelli, F., Rosetti, R., Zingaretti, P.: Shelf space re-allocation for out of stock reduction. Comput. Ind. Eng. **106**, 32–40 (2017)
16. Frontoni, E., Marinelli, F., Paolanti, M., Rosetti, R., Zingaretti, P.: Optimal production planning by reusing components. In: 2016 24th Mediterranean Conference on Control and Automation (MED), pp. 1272–1277. Athens, June 2016
17. Coronado, P.D.U., Lynn, R., Louhichi, W., Parto, M., Wescoat, E., Kurfess, T.: Part data integration in the shop floor digital twin: mobile and cloud technologies to enable a manufacturing execution system. J. Manuf. Syst. (2018)

18. Giraldo, J., Sarkar, E., Cardenas, A.A., Maniatakos, M., Kantarcioglu, M.: Security and privacy in cyber-physical systems: a survey of surveys. IEEE Des. Test **34**(4), 7–17 (2017)
19. Torrisi, N.M.: Monitoring services for industrial. IEEE Ind. Electron. Mag. **5**(1), 49–60 (2011)
20. Iarovyi, S., Mohammed, W.M., Lobov, A., Ferrer, B.R., Lastra, J.L.M.: Cyber-physical systems for open-knowledge-driven manufacturing execution systems. Proc. IEEE **104**(5), 1142–1154 (2016)
21. Almada-Lobo, F.: The industry 4.0 revolution and the future of manufacturing execution systems (mes). J. Innov. Manag. **3**(4), 16–21 (2016)
22. Buckholtz, B., Ragai, I., Wang, L.: Cloud manufacturing: current trends and future implementations. J. Manuf. Sci. Eng. **137**(4), 040902 (2015)
23. Schleich, B., Anwer, N., Mathieu, L., Wartzack, S.: Shaping the digital twin for design and production engineering. CIRP Ann. **66**(1), 141–144 (2017)
24. Huang, J., Zhu, Y., Cheng, B., Lin, C., Chen, J.: A petrinet-based approach for supporting traceability in cyber-physical manufacturing systems. Sensors **16**(3), 382 (2016)

# CAD-VR Integration as a Tool for Industrial Assembly Processes Validation: A Practical Application

Claudio Pascarelli[1], Mariangela Lazoi[1(✉)], Gabriele Papadia[1],
Valerio Galli[2], and Luigi Piarulli[3]

[1] Department of Engineering for Innovation, University of Salento, Lecce, Italy
{claudio.pascarelli,mariangela.lazoi,
gabriele.papadia}@unisalento.it
[2] ESI Italia, Bologna, Italy
valerio.galli@esi-group.com
[3] BHGE Nuovo Pignone, Bari, Italy
luigi.piarulli@bhge.com

**Abstract.** Assembly planning and evaluation are important phases of the product development process. The generation of assembly plans is often a lengthy and costly manual process with a direct impact on the time to market. Many attempts to improve this process through the adoption of Virtual Reality have been done in the last twenty years, however the adoption of these approaches in real industrial environments is still immature and not well documented in the available literature. This paper aims at evaluating, through the adoption of a case study research approach, the real benefits coming from the adoption of Virtual Assembly strategies in an industrial company operating in the Oil & Gas sector.

**Keywords:** Virtual Assembly · Virtual Reality · Case study

## 1 Introduction

Manufacturing is an important sector for the economy. Currently, products are increasingly complex, processes highly sophisticated and market demand rapidly evolving. Also, manufacturing enterprises can be globally distributed and linked in terms of materials, information and knowledge flows. To remain competitive, industry must constantly keep pace with new technological opportunities and be open to change existing procedures and systems in favour of more effective and efficient new ones.

The application of Virtual Reality (VR) in manufacturing gives rise to enormous potential and challenges, both for research and industrial applications. In the design field, the benefits of applying VR consists in improving the visualization capability of the product, thanks to the user's coexistence in the same environment of the virtual product model [1] and thanks to the possibility to interact with it [2]. In the field of Operations Management, the greatest benefits are in support of technological and economic modelling of different production planning scenarios [3] and training.

© Springer International Publishing AG, part of Springer Nature 2018
L. T. De Paolis and P. Bourdot (Eds.): AVR 2018, LNCS 10851, pp. 435–450, 2018.
https://doi.org/10.1007/978-3-319-95282-6_32

In manufacturing processes, the most important applications realized are in the field of assembly, in order to reduce the time of the design cycle, predict the quality of assembly and the cost of a product, to provide an environment for the evaluation of inspection methods and the detection of collisions [4].

In all these areas, visualization was the first area of application in which VR was appreciated, since this allows the user, thanks to large displays and stereoscopic vision, to better understand the meaning of the data displayed, or the aesthetics of a new product. In the automotive field, for example, VR has been used to display, in real scale, digital mock-ups (DMUs) of new car models [5] and to display complex engineering data, e.g. from finite element simulations [6].

Although visualization has played an important role in the diffusion of VR in industries, it does not exploit the natural interaction capabilities of VR. The main advantages offered by VR are more evident in all applications where interaction with the virtual product is important. A typical example, in this sense, is virtual assembly, aimed at simulating the entire operating context in which the operator works, during assembly/disassembly operations, in order to identify potential difficulties in reaching or displaying certain components, or in order to evaluate the operator's posture during operations [7, 8].

Assembly planning and evaluation are important components of the product design process in which details about how parts of a product will be put together are formalized. A well designed assembly process should take into account various factors such as optimum assembly time and sequence, tooling and fixture requirements, ergonomics, operator safety, and accessibility, among others [9].

Virtual Assembly is one of most important field of application of VR in -manufacturing. It allows to personnel with expert knowledge, such as assembly workers, to assess in, a virtual environment, an assembly plan before any prototype components are manufactured.

One of the scope of the VMAN (Virtual MANufacturing) project, carried out in the Apulia region (Italy), was to investigate the potential benefits of VR application in the Oil & Gas industry, through its integration with CAx tools.

On the basis of the achieved results in the VMAN project, the paper aims to exploit the innovation potential of CAD-VR integrated applications for the assembly processes planning and evaluation related to Oil & Gas products of BHGE Nuovo Pignone, a Baker Hughes - General Electric company partner of the project, assessing the feasibility of an assembly plan by mean of VR. A single case study [10] based on applicative evidence emerging from qualitative data are discussed in the paper. Evidences and data are collected through the observation of the research and development practice in the VMAN project and from semi-structured interviews. The findings show the necessary steps for immersive Virtual Assembly simulations and their benefits in an industrial company.

The paper has four main sections. In Sect. 2, a literature review provide the paper's background context and analyzed relevant researches in the area of Virtual Assembly. In Sect. 3, the adopted research approach is illustrated. In Sect. 4, the industrial case study is described, in terms of steps performed, technologies exploited and achieved results. Finally, a section for discussions and conclusions ends the paper.

## 2   Literature Review

The assembly process planning consists of determine process steps, equipment and tools required. A good assembly process plan can increase the efficiency and quality, and decrease the cost and time of the whole product manufacturing process, which is important as product and production demand changes rapidly in today's market [11]. If assembly is conducted manually it must be considered that its costs may often account for even half of the total manufacturing expenses [12].

Consequently, assembly sequence planning has been an active research field. Many techniques and methodologies have been developed attempting to automate or to semi-automate the key sequencing process. These approaches go under the name of Computer-aided process planning (CAPP). However, some of these efforts have not been successful in general, and many assembly process plans are still based on traditional methods [11].

Expert assembly planners today typically use traditional approaches in which the three-dimensional (3D) CAD models of the parts to be assembled are examined on two dimensional (2D) computer screens in order to assess part geometry and determine assembly sequences for a new product for which, at the end, physical prototypes are built and assembled by experienced workers to identify any issues with either the assembly process or the product design [9]. When assembly processes are complex, these methods are no more efficient and effective. For such complex assembly operations, VR technology plays a vital role allowing operators to simulate them in an immersive and interactive environment.

Virtual assembly (VA), a key component of virtual manufacturing, is defined as [7]: "The use of computer tools to make or "assist with" assembly-related engineering decisions through analysis, predictive models, visualization, and presentation of data without physical realization of the product or supporting processes."

According to its definition, VA simulations allow designers to perform product assembly/disassembly simulation since the early design phases, therefore long before the first physical prototypes are built.

A great amount of researches has been conducted in the area of VA. In this Table 1, the most cited studies in this field are summarized.

Each study has been classified based on the research results typology: virtual environments (VE), interfaces (IN), methods (ME), reviews (RW), case studies (CS). "Virtual environments" refers to papers that describe whole technological environment developed for VA simulations. "Interfaces" refers to studies on technologies that have been developed to improve the human interaction with the virtual environment to perform manual assembly operations. "Methods" refers to more conceptual studies where new approaches/processes/frameworks/models to perform the design or validation of assembly procedure in virtual environments are presented. "Reviews" refers to papers that review the VA state-of-the-art in scientific literature. Finally, "Case studies", which category includes this paper, refers to studies conducted to demonstrate the potentiality of VA in assisting real assembly processes designs.

Below, additional details on some relevant case study papers are provided.

**Table 1.** Classification of Virtual Assembly studies

| ID | Reference | N^A Ct. | Typology | Main contribution |
|----|-----------|---------|----------|-------------------|
| 1 | Pere et al. - 1996 [13] | 25 | VE | Development of a desktop-based system for mechanical assembly training |
| 2 | Dewar et al. - 1997 [14] | 101 | ME | Presentation of tools to reuse product model database and perform manual assembly |
| 3 | Jayaram et al. - 1997 [7] | 533 | ME/VE | Presentation of concepts behind a VA system (VADE) and the feasibility of the system proved through initial prototypes |
| 4 | Gupta et al. - 1997 [15] | 177 | VE | Development of a desktop system called the virtual environment for design assembly (VEDA) |
| 5 | Stefan et al. - 1998 [16] | 32 | ME | Description of a process for integrating an interactive VR-based assembly simulation of a digital mockup into an existing CAD/CAM infrastructure |
| 6 | Ritchie et al. - 1999 [17] | 76 | ME | Presentation of a new approach, for the preparation of assembly plans for manufactured goods, based on the adoption of immersive VR |
| 7 | Jayaram et al. - 1999 [8] | 532 | VE | Development of a VR based application to facilitate the planning, evaluation and verification of a mechanical assembly system |
| 8 | De Sa and Zachmann - 1999 [18] | 385 | ME | Investigation of steps needed to apply VR for virtual prototyping to verify assembly and maintenance processes |
| 9 | McNeely et al. - 1999 [19] | 660 | ME | Development of a voxel-based approach to haptic rendering that enables 6-DOF manipulation of a rigid object within an arbitrarily complex environment of static objects |
| 10 | Su et al. - 1999 [20] | 45 | ME | Development of collision detection algorithms for objects in a virtual environment |
| 11 | Zachmann - 2000 [21] | 115 | ME/VE | Description of frameworks, concepts, and algorithms and implementation of several modules of a VR system named Virtual Design II |
| 12 | Bullinger et al. - 2000 [22] | 90 | ME | Description of concepts of a planning system that uses VR features to carry out assembly planning operations |
| 13 | Boud et al. - 2000 [23] | 44 | CS | Investigation into the usability of VR for the assembly of a number of component parts into a final product. |

(*continued*)

**Table 1.**  (*continued*)

| ID | Reference | N$^A$ Ct. | Typology | Main contribution |
|----|-----------|-----------|----------|-------------------|
| 14 | Banerjee and Banerjee - 2000 [24] | 37 | ME | Description of a virtual manufacturing lattice structure used to augment the scenegraph to capture manufacturing attributes and behavior of objects |
| 15 | Zachmann and Rettig - 2001 [25] | 79 | ME/VE | Development of multimodal input techniques including speech input and gesture recognition for controlling a VA system |
| 16 | Coutee et al. - 2001 [26] | 74 | IN | Development of an application called HIDRA which integrates haptic feedback into an assembly/disassembly simulation environment |
| 17 | Choi et al. - 2002 [27] | 61 | CS | Demonstration of the applicability and efficiency of a virtual assembly tool |
| 18 | Li et al. - 2003 [28] | 152 | VE | Development of a desktop VR system for maintenance training |
| 19 | Jezernik and Hren - 2003 [29] | 69 | VE | Development of a system for VRML model visualization that enables changes in the configuration file and that automatically reviews the model including the functional behavior |
| 20 | Jayaram et al. - 2004 [30] | 20 | CS | Demonstration and validation of the use of immersive VA in the simulation of factory floor manufacturing processes |
| 21 | Mujber et al. - 2004 [31] | 313 | RW | Overview on virtual reality applications in manufacturing processes |
| 22 | Huagen et al. - 2004 [32] | 24 | ME/IN | Development of a kinematics model of virtual hand to guarantee motion realism, and real-time collision detection |
| 23 | Wan et al. - 2004 [33] | 66 | VE | Development of MIVAS, a Multi-modal Immersive Virtual Assembly System |
| 24 | Seth et al. - 2005 [34] | 44 | IN | Development of an haptic VR interface for mechanical assembly |
| 25 | Wang and Li - 2006 [35] | 47 | ME | Description of a dynamic data model for visualization of industrial assemblies. |
| 26 | Seth et al. - 2006 [36] | 80 | IN | Developed a system known as SHARP for haptic assembly and realistic prototyping |
| 27 | Yao et al. - 2006 [37] | 28 | VE | Development of a system for interactive assembly planning and training in a virtual environment |
| 28 | Wang et al. - 2006 [38] | 52 | VE | Development of a CAD-linked virtual assembly environment that make use of a constraint-based modeling for assembly |

(*continued*)

**Table 1.** (*continued*)

| ID | Reference | N^A Ct. | Typology | Main contribution |
|---|---|---|---|---|
| 29 | Jimeno and Puerta - 2007 [39] | 68 | RW | Review of applications of VR in the field of design and manufacturing processes |
| 30 | Jayaram et al. - 2007 [40] | 67 | CS | Demonstration and validation of the use of immersive VA in the simulation of factory floor manufacturing processes |
| 31 | Brough et al. 2007 [41] | 110 | VE | Development of a VR-based training system for assembly operations |
| 32 | Wang et al. - 2009 [11] | 96 | RW | Review of methodologies and tools for assembly process planning and identification of future trends |
| 33 | Song and Chung - 2009 [42] | 32 | ME | Use of Digital Mockup systems to build virtual models of designs to prevent the interferences and mismatch during precision design stages |
| 34 | Seth et al. - 2011 [9] | 194 | RW | Review of researches on VA, categorization of the different approaches and presentation of critical requirements and directions for future research |
| 35 | Xia et al. - 2012 [43] | 58 | VE | Development of an haptics-based virtual environment system for assembly training of complex products |
| 36 | Qiu et al. - 2013 [44] | 25 | ME | Presentation of a real-time driving model of a virtual human for interactive assembly and disassembly operation in VR |
| 37 | Leu et al. - 2013 [45] | 68 | RW | Review of the state-of-the-art methodologies for developing CAD-based systems for assembly simulation, planning and training in VR |
| 38 | Choi et al. - 2015 [46] | 40 | RW | Review of virtual reality applications in manufacturing industries |

Boud et al. [23] proposed two simple VA tasks: the assembly of a water pump consisting of eight separate components and the "Tower of Hanoi" problem [47] that consists of three rings of different sizes and three pegs that have to be sequentially stacked. Both experiments have been performed by university students on desktop VR environments, with the main aim of investigating whether the ability of VR to permit direct manipulation of assembly components would facilitate the training for assembly.

Choi et al. [27] presented the application of two different IT tools to establish the right assembly sequence of a grill plate and to produce information on assembly efficiency, time, cost, methods, and suggestions for redesign. It was found that the assembly time was improved and, as a result, the production efficiency was enhanced. The assembly operation was simulated in a virtual on-screen environment. This enabled better process planning by showing factory technicians, and discussing with them, the product that they will be building.

Jayaram et al. [30, 40] illustrated some industrial case studies, designed from actual assembly floor projects, that have been conducted as part of the Virtual Assembly Technology Consortium [48]. The test cases provided the university researchers with complex practices and settings in which the technology had to perform and in turn provided the industry partners with focused deployments of cutting edge technology. It also provided a process and opportunity to reflect on the advantages and disadvantages of the existing immersive virtual assembly methods and challenges in adapting them to real-life situations. The authors argued that, even if the case studies were successful, to be VA truly accepted in industry, there were still issues to be addressed in terms of ease of use, portability of the applications, and preparation of the models for the evaluations.

These latter studies can be maybe considered as the only real attempts to prove the ability of immersive VA in supporting real industrial practices. However, these studies are more than ten years old, and, as authors stated, the technology in that period was not able to repeat, in a real industrial environment, what had been done so far in laboratory environments.

Nowadays, we believe that Virtual Assembly related technologies are mature enough to allow useful applications even on an industrial scale and the proposed case study is an attempt to prove this thesis.

## 3 Research Design

The VMAN project, co-funded by the Apulia Region (Italy) and the European Union, started in 2015 and it is currently in its final phase. The project involved large, medium and small enterprises of the Oil & Gas sector, a VR software company, a software developer company, and two research organizations. This project aimed to achieve product and process optimization, in the Oil & Gas industry, through the use of digital technologies (CAD, CAE, CAM and Virtual Reality) and innovative production technologies (Additive Manufacturing). One of the three main goals of the project was to integrate some CAx technologies (CAD, CAE, CAM) into a Virtual Reality environment to support complex industrial products design, assembly, and maintenance activities.

In the context of the VMAN project, it has been developed the case study treated in this paper. It is a single case study [10] describing the specific activities and results of VA research in an industrial company. It is based on applicative evidence emerging from qualitative data are discussed in the paper. Evidences and data are collected through the observation of the research and development practice in the VMAN project and from semi-structured interviews.

The aim of the case study has been to analyze the use of CAD-VR for innovating their combined application in an industrial context mainly for assembly simulation. To address this aim, a real product has been selected: a pump of the oil & gas field. Three main phases of research have been designed: context analysis, information and data collection and simulation. The activities performed for the pump assembly have been analyzed observing the practice of the industrial engineers. When an adequate understanding of the process has been reached, needs of improvements have been collected and a questionnaire, named inside the project "Context Module" has been administered in order to gather useful information for the VA simulation. Finally, activities of simulation have been performed and feedbacks collected. A methodology guiding the activities of simulation has been also proposed.

# 4   Case Study

## 4.1   Assembly Process of a Pump

Among the different Oil & Gas products, the case study exploits the assembly of centrifugal pumps. A centrifugal pump (Fig. 1) is a turbo machine used in the industry to elevate the pressure of a fluid and "push" it into a piping system. Every oil pipeline that transports crude oil has its own transfer pumps. These machines have a power rating of just a few kW to about 20 MW (equivalent to the electric power consumption of about 7000 homes), with weights of up to tens of tons.

**Fig. 1.** Example of BHGE Nuovo Pignone multistage centrifugal pump [49]

The simulation focused on the vertical assembly method of the diffuser and diaphragm assembly, for the first two stages of a pump, which consists of a total of 10 stages. The procedure, that describes step by step the assembly process and the equipment and tools to be used, involved three different assembly phases:

1. tilting phase of the suction flange housing (Fig. 2.1);
2. tilting phase and vertical positioning of the shaft (Fig. 2.2);
3. mounting phase of the diffuser and diaphragm assembly for the first two stages (Fig. 2.3).

Some significant steps of the procedure (one per phase) are represented in the following figure.

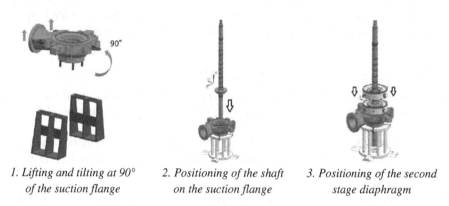

*1. Lifting and tilting at 90°*          *2. Positioning of the shaft*          *3. Positioning of the second*
*of the suction flange*                   *on the suction flange*                   *stage diaphragm*

**Fig. 2.** Significant steps of the simulated assembly procedure

In order to extent VR also for application in the assembly procedure, together with the industrial companies, some specific needs to be evaluated have been defined:

• simulating, by mean of VR, the assembly procedure and verify its feasibility;
• verifying, by mean of VR, that during lifting and tilting of components, the selected anchorage points ensure workers to operate safely, avoiding unwanted overturning.

For achieving these results, the Context Module has been distributed among the company research staff. With the Context Module is asked to provide a detailed description of the assembly cycle, the assembly simulation specific goals and the CAD files used. All the CAD files, in STEP format, of all components, tools and equipment involved in the assembly process are also provided.

### 4.2    Methodology and Equipment for Virtual Assembly Simulations

The main steps of the methodology followed to perform the Virtual Assembly simulations are described below:

1. Information gathering and analysis of the assembly process

As described in the previous paragraph the first step was to obtain by the industrial partner, through the Context Modules, all the relevant information on the process to be performed, on the assembly simulations specific goals, and to retrieve all the necessary CAD models of the components to be simulated.

## 2. Virtual environment preparation

Once obtained the CAD models they have been imported in the simulation environment, previously configured in order to reflect the factory real location, and positioned in the right places.

## 3. Simulation of the assembly process

The assembly process was then performed many times, using the immersive virtual assembly environment and according to the precise procedure provided by the industrial company. The assembly simulation sessions was recorded for further investigations.

## 4. Analysis of the assembly simulations results

During the simulation sessions and at their end, by mean of the recorded videos, the assembly procedure have been analyzed in order to gather possible problems and issues.

About step 3 "Simulation of the assembly process", the assembly simulations (Fig. 3) have been conducted in a virtual environment, available at the Università del Salento, equipped with:

- two workstations with Intel® Core™ i7 processors, 32 GB RAM, Nvidia® Quadro® 8 GB graphic cards;
- a 2,5 x 1,9 m rear projection screen;
- a Full HD OPTOMA® projector;
- an ART® SMARTTRACK® tracking system and controller.
- IC.IDO® software, by ESI Group.

**Fig. 3.** Two frames of the conducted Virtual Assembly simulations

## 4.3  Virtual Assembly Simulations Results

The conducted simulation activities allowed the industrial company to validate, and partially correct, the assembly procedure hypothesized. More in detail the company was able to:

- validate the position of the anchorage points of the lifting eyebolts chosen during the preliminary design phase;
- verify the applicability and correctness of the assembly procedure and in particular of the components lifting and tilting procedure;
- develop an assembly procedure (Visual Instructions) with detailed sequence of steps to be performed;
- modify the design of the equipment in order to improve its ergonomic aspects related to the working position.

Referring to this last point, the operation of tightening an M33 nut (i.e. a nut with a nominal diameter of 33 mm), with an hexagonal open wrench, to clamp the suction flange on the equipment (mounting rod) was simulated. This simulation allowed to identify critical ergonomics aspects of this process step that have been eliminated by modifying the design of the equipment. The figure below shows the design of the pre and post simulation equipment.

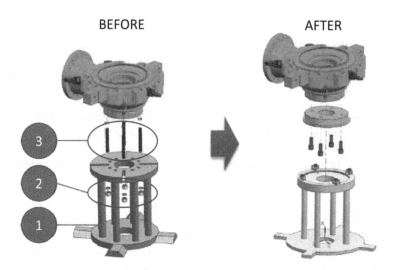

**Fig. 4.** Equipment design before and after the VR simulations

In the preliminary design of the equipment (before VA simulations) there were eight vertical elements (n.1 in Fig. 4), very close to each other. This made it difficult to tighten the nuts and washers (n.2 in Fig. 4) on the tie-beams (n.3 in Fig. 4) in order to secure the flange on the mounting equipment. In fact, during assembly simulations, it was found that the operator had to bend very much in order to have a good view of the

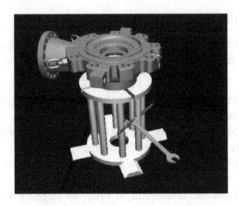

**Fig. 5.** Interference between the tool and the equipment during a simulation

working area. In addition, the accessibility of the hexagonal wrench to the working area was difficult because of continuous interferences between the tool and the equipment (Fig. 5).

All these issues have been eliminated by reducing to four the number of vertical elements in the final design of the equipment and modifying how it was fastened to the flange.

## 5 Discussion

The simulation of the assembly process, performed in a virtual environment, led to real and tangible benefits for the industrial partner:

- it has been able to optimize the initial assumed assembly sequence and the design of some equipment, without the need for physical prototypes;
- it could check for any hazards that cannot be identified in a static/bi-dimensional environment (e.g. effects linked to the choice of incorrect anchorage points on the components).

The archived results were possible thanks to high sense of realism provided by the virtual environment. Because of the combination of realism and environment interaction, Virtual Assembly proved to be an excellent tool to design/verify assembly procedures before their implementation and without the need for physical prototypes, then reducing the costs and shortening the time-to-market of new complex products.

Even thanks to these results, the company is now considering adopting VR technology extensively in order to significantly increase the company's productivity by overcoming the limitations of the current two-dimensional interfaces of CAD tools.

The archived results concerning the benefits of Virtual Assembly were deductible from relevant available literature but not yet sufficiently demonstrated in real industrial contexts, as emerged from the literature review.

# 6  Conclusion

Virtual Reality technology has now matured, and the feasibility of adopting this technology in complex industrial environments has grown its potential. Among different areas of application, Virtual Assembly (i.e. the possibility to evaluate products assembly procedures in a virtual environment long before the first physical prototypes are built) is considered one of the most important ones. Although the first studies in this field are more than 20 years old, the adoption of immersive Virtual Assembly approaches in real industrial environment is still immature and not well documented in the available literature.

In this paper, we have presented a case study representing a real industrial process selected by an industrial company, involved in the VMAN project and operating in the Oil & Gas sector. After an introduction of the assembly process, it is described the methodology with the main steps adopted in the simulation, later the application on an industrial product is reported. The paper results represents a concrete example of how VR can impact positively on the daily operative activities.

As regards limitations and possible future improvements of the conducted case study, it should be noted that in the used technological infrastructure there is no tracking of the left hand in the virtual environment. So, the left hand cannot interact with it and, even if most assembly situations were simulated adequately, this represent a limitation for an even better sense of realism. The second limitation concerns the lack of an haptic feedback system for the operator. Again, this lack limits the sense of realism of the simulations. Both these limitations concerns only the hardware of the adopted virtual environment available and not the software side, already suitable for these improvements. The impacts of these technological improvements, on the Virtual Assembly case study methodology, may be the theme of future researches.

# References

1. Rohrer, M.W.: Seeing is believing: the importance of visualization in manufacturing simulation. In: Proceedings of the 32nd Conference on Winter simulation, pp. 1211–1216. Society for Computer Simulation International. December 2000
2. Schaefer, D., Borgmann, C., Scheffter, D.: Factory planning and the potential of virtual reality. In: Proceedings of AVRII & CONVR, pp. 92–98 (2001)
3. Sung, W.T., Ou, S.C.: Using virtual reality technologies for manufacturing applications. Int. J. Comput. Appl. Technol. **17**(4), 213–219 (2003)
4. Caputo, F., Di Gironimo, G., Marzano, A.: A structured approach to simulate manufacturing systems in virtual environment. In: XVIII Congreso International de Ingegneria Grafica, Barcelona, Spain, 31st May–2nd June 2006
5. Zhou, T., Wu, Y., Wang, Z.: Implementation of virtual reality techniques in car styling. Automot. Eng. **23**(1), 18–20 (2001)
6. Bryson, S.: The virtual windtunnel: a high-performance virtual reality application. In: Virtual Reality Annual International Symposium, 1993, 1993 IEEE, pp. 20–26. IEEE, September 1993
7. Jayaram, S., Connacher, H.I., Lyons, K.W.: Virtual assembly using virtual reality techniques. Comput.-Aided Des. **29**(8), 575–584 (1997)

8. Jayaram, S., Jayaram, U., Wang, Y., Tirumali, H., Lyons, K., Hart, P.: VADE: a virtual assembly design environment. IEEE Comput. Graph. Appl. **19**(6), 44–50 (1999)
9. Seth, A., Vance, J.M., Oliver, J.H.: Virtual reality for assembly methods prototyping: a review. Virtual Reality **15**(1), 5–20 (2011)
10. Yin, R.K.: Case Study Research, Design & Methods, 4th edn. (2009)
11. Wang, L., Keshavarzmanesh, S., Feng, H.Y., Buchal, R.O.: Assembly process planning and its future in collaborative manufacturing: a review. Int. J. Adv. Manuf. Technol. **41**(1–2), 132 (2009)
12. Pintzos, G., Matsas, M., Triantafyllou, C., Papakostas, N., Chryssolouris, G.: An integrated approach to the planning of manual assembly lines. In: ASME 2015 International Mechanical Engineering Congress and Exposition, pp. V015T19A016–V015T19A016. American Society of Mechanical Engineers, November 2015
13. Pere, E., Langrana, N., Gomez, D., Burdea, G.: Virtual mechanical assembly on a PC-based system. In: ASME Design Engineering Technical Conferences and Computers and Information in Engineering, Irvine, CA, pp. 18–22, August 1996
14. Dewar, R.G., Carpenter, I.D., Ritchie, J.M., Simmons, J.E.: Assembly planning in a virtual environment. In: Innovation in Technology Management-The Key to Global Leadership. PICMET 1997: Portland International Conference on Management and Technology, pp. 664–667. IEEE, July 1997
15. Gupta, R., Whitney, D., Zeltzer, D.: Prototyping and design for assembly analysis using multimodal virtual environments. Comput.-Aided Des. **29**(8), 585–597 (1997)
16. Steffan, R., Schull, U., Kuhlen, T.: Integration of virtual reality based assembly simulation into CAD/CAM environments. In: Industrial Electronics Society, 1998, IECON 1998, Proceedings of the 24th Annual Conference of the IEEE, vol. 4, pp. 2535–2537. IEEE (1998)
17. Ritchie, J.M., Dewar, R.G., Simmons, J.E.: The generation and practical use of plans for manual assembly using immersive virtual reality. Proc. Inst. Mech. Eng. Part B: J. Eng. Manuf. **213**(5), 461–474 (1999)
18. De Sa, A.G., Zachmann, G.: Virtual reality as a tool for verification of assembly and maintenance processes. Comput. Graph. **23**(3), 389–403 (1999)
19. McNeely, W.A., Puterbaugh, K.D., Troy, J.J.: Six degree-of-freedom haptic rendering using voxel sampling. In: Proceedings of the 26th Annual Conference on Computer Graphics and Interactive Techniques, pp. 401–408. ACM Press/Addison-Wesley Publishing Co., July 1999
20. Su, C.J., Lin, F., Ye, L.: A new collision detection method for CSG-represented objects in virtual manufacturing. Comput. Ind. **40**(1), 1–13 (1999)
21. Zachmann, G.: Virtual reality in assembly simulation-collision detection, simulation algorithms, and interaction techniques (Doctoral dissertation, Zachmann, Gabriel) (2000)
22. Bullinger, H.J., Richter, M., Seidel, K.A.: Virtual assembly planning. Hum. Factors Ergon. Manuf. Serv. Ind. **10**(3), 331–341 (2000)
23. Boud, A.C., Baber, C., Steiner, S.J.: Virtual reality: a tool for assembly? Presence: Teleoper. Virtual Environ. **9**(5), 486–496 (2000)
24. Banerjee, A., Banerjee, P.: A behavioral scene graph for rule enforcement in interactive virtual assembly sequence planning. Comput. Ind. **42**(2–3), 147–157 (2000)
25. Zachmann, G., Rettig, A.: Natural and robust interaction in virtual assembly simulation. In: Eighth ISPE International Conference on Concurrent Engineering: Research and Applications (ISPE/CE2001, vol. 1, pp. 425–434, July 2001
26. Coutee, A.S., McDermott, S.D., Bras, B.: A haptic assembly and disassembly simulation environment and associated computational load optimization techniques. J. Comput. Inf. Sci. Eng. **1**(2), 113–122 (2001)

27. Choi, A.C.K., Chan, D.S.K., Yuen, A.M.F.: Application of virtual assembly tools for improving product design. Int. J. Adv. Manuf. Technol. **19**(5), 377–383 (2002)

28. Li, J.R., Khoo, L.P., Tor, S.B.: Desktop virtual reality for maintenance training: an object oriented prototype system (V-REALISM). Comput. Ind. **52**(2), 109–125 (2003)

29. Jezernik, A., Hren, G.: A solution to integrate computer-aided design (CAD) and virtual reality (VR) databases in design and manufacturing processes. Int. J. Adv. Manuf. Technol. **22**(11–12), 768–774 (2003)

30. Jayaram, U., Jayaram, S., DeChenne, C., Kim, Y.J., Palmer, C., Mitsui, T.: Case studies using immersive virtual assembly in industry. In: ASME 2004 International Design Engineering Technical Conferences and Computers and Information in Engineering Conference, pp. 627–636. American Society of Mechanical Engineers, January 2004

31. Mujber, T.S., Szecsi, T., Hashmi, M.S.: Virtual reality applications in manufacturing process simulation. J. Mater. Process. Technol. **155**, 1834–1838 (2004)

32. Huagen, W., Shuming, G., Qunsheng, P.: Virtual grasping for virtual assembly tasks. In: Third International Conference on Image and Graphics (ICIG 2004), pp. 448–451. IEEE December 2004

33. Wan, H., Gao, S., Peng, Q., Dai, G., Zhang, F.: MIVAS: a multi-modal immersive virtual assembly system. In: ASME 2004 International Design Engineering Technical Conferences and Computers and Information in Engineering Conference, pp. 113–122. American Society of Mechanical Engineers, January 2004

34. Seth, A., Su, H.J., Vance, J.M.: A desktop networked haptic VR interface for mechanical assembly. In: ASME 2005 International Mechanical Engineering Congress and Exposition, pp. 173–180. American Society of Mechanical Engineers, January 2005

35. Wang, Q.H., Li, J.R.: Interactive visualization of complex dynamic virtual environments for industrial assemblies. Comput. Ind. **57**(4), 366–377 (2006)

36. Seth, A., Su, H.J., Vance, J.M.: SHARP: a system for haptic assembly and realistic prototyping. In: ASME 2006 International Design Engineering Technical Conferences and Computers and Information in Engineering Conference, pp. 905–912. American Society of Mechanical Engineers, January 2006

37. Yao, Y.X., Xia, P.J., Liu, J.S., Li, J.G.: A pragmatic system to support interactive assembly planning and training in an immersive virtual environment (I-VAPTS). Int. J. Adv. Manuf. Technol. **30**(9–10), 959–967 (2006)

38. Wang, Q.H., Li, J.R., Gong, H.Q.: A CAD-linked virtual assembly environment. Int. J. Prod. Res. **44**(3), 467–486 (2006)

39. Jimeno, A., Puerta, A.: State of the art of the virtual reality applied to design and manufacturing processes. Int. J. Adv. Manuf. Technol. **33**(9–10), 866–874 (2007)

40. Jayaram, S., Jayaram, U., Kim, Y.J., DeChenne, C., Lyons, K.W., Palmer, C., Mitsui, T.: Industry case studies in the use of immersive virtual assembly. Virtual Reality **11**(4), 217–228 (2007)

41. Brough, J.E., Schwartz, M., Gupta, S.K., Anand, D.K., Kavetsky, R., Pettersen, R.: Towards the development of a virtual environment-based training system for mechanical assembly operations. Virtual Reality **11**(4), 189–206 (2007)

42. Song, I.H., Chung, S.C.: Synthesis of the digital mock-up system for heterogeneous CAD assembly. Comput. Ind. **60**(5), 285–295 (2009)

43. Xia, P., Lopes, A.M., Restivo, M.T., Yao, Y.: A new type haptics-based virtual environment system for assembly training of complex products. Int. J. Adv. Manuf. Technol. **58**(1–4), 379–396 (2012)

44. Qiu, S., Fan, X., Wu, D., He, Q., Zhou, D.: Virtual human modeling for interactive assembly and disassembly operation in virtual reality environment. Int. J. Adv. Manuf. Technol. **69**(9–12), 2355–2372 (2013)

45. Leu, M.C., ElMaraghy, H.A., Nee, A.Y., Ong, S.K., Lanzetta, M., Putz, M., Zhu, W., Bernard, A.: CAD model based virtual assembly simulation, planning and training. CIRP Ann. **62**(2), 799–822 (2013)
46. Choi, S., Jung, K., Noh, S.D.: Virtual reality applications in manufacturing industries: past research, present findings, and future directions. Concurr. Eng. **23**(1), 40–63 (2015)
47. Kotovsky, K., Hayes, J.R., Simon, H.A.: Why are some problems hard? Evidence from Tower of Hanoi. Cogn. Psychol. **17**(2), 248–294 (1985)
48. Virtual Assembly Technology Consortium (VATC). https://vrcim.wsu.edu/pages/vatc/
49. GE Oil & Gas. https://www.geoilandgas.com/refinery-petrochemical/refinery-petrochemical-fertilizer/ddhm-high-pressure-diffuser-barrel

# Immersive Environment for Training on Industrial Emergencies

Mauricio Rosero, Rai Pogo, Edwin Pruna$^{(\boxtimes)}$, Víctor H. Andaluz,
and Ivón Escobar

Universidad de las Fuerzas Armadas ESPE, Sangolquí, Ecuador
{mgrosero4, rapogo, eppruna, vhandaluz1,
ipescobar}@espe.edu.ec

**Abstract.** This work presents the development of an interactive virtual environment for training in emergencies that may arise in industrial environments. This environment contains equipment and usual structures in production plants with a high risk index, simulations of accidents and potential hazards that must be overcome by the user. The application has been created using a CAD tool and the Unity3D graphics engine that, combined with peripheral input devices, provide a high level of immersion, all in order to recreate the sensations that the person could feel in case of facing an adverse situation that requires the user knowledge and skills in security issues and protocols.

**Keywords:** Virtual reality · Unity3D · Industrial emergency · Security training

## 1 Introduction

The process industry has inherent risks that endanger the integrity of the people, environment and equipment that make part of it.

The process industry has inherent risks that endanger the integrity of the people, environment and equipment that are part of it. Every year, thousands of people die or become invalid due to work-related accidents, many of which could be avoided if operators are adequately trained in safety and procedures to follow in case of emergencies. Human error has been a determining factor in up to 80% of work accidents in the petrochemical, construction, mining and nuclear industries due to limited safety knowledge [1–3, 14].

Field operators have a priority role in safeguarding the safety of their environment through their behavior and reactions, by taking a risk or by mitigating it. Even though a company has taken all the necessary precautions by preparing the workplace and providing training and protective equipment to staff, workers' decisions are what make the difference at the time of a disaster. Their ability to identify risks, analyze their magnitude quickly, and make a reasonable decision are factors that determine the risk of a situation of danger [2, 14, 15]. These skills, in part, are obtained through the training received, which is taught through manuals, videos or demonstrations that are not totally efficient because they are theoretical and poorly illustrative, as well as lacking a realistic impact and according to their importance [3–5, 9].

© Springer International Publishing AG, part of Springer Nature 2018
L. T. De Paolis and P. Bourdot (Eds.): AVR 2018, LNCS 10851, pp. 451–466, 2018.
https://doi.org/10.1007/978-3-319-95282-6_33

In this context, virtual reality has been widely used in a big number of fields, including training for firefighters, mine safety, surgical procedures, safety equipment operation, construction industry and civil engineering education [3, 6–8]. Specifically, for the process industry, have been created environments with simulations of several concrete events, where the user can visualize everything that is happening around him [11]. This allows him to understand the scheme of the process and the plant, beyond the level of representation of these through two-dimensional planes [11, 12]. This characteristic of virtual environments allows the reproduction of the feelings and emotions that could be felt in reality. Eventually, these aspects result in a more comprehensive training with an effective and enduring knowledge acquisition [10, 14]. All of this has made virtual reality a common tool in industries that try to improve their competitiveness and productivity by giving it a wide variety of uses [13, 15].

This article proposes an interactive virtual environment that contains industrial processes with a high risk index, properly signaled according to ANSI and OSHA regulations, where the operator will be faced with several hazards and accidents that must be overcome by him; It will require his theoretical knowledge of safety, his ability to identify abnormal conditions in the plant and his speed in decision making, which will be put into practice during the execution of the tasks. The level of immersion of the user in the application is very high because it has realistic details and sounds that complement the experience, besides the possibility of using their hands within the environment to fulfill the required objectives. The user may experience the same feelings of anxiety, fear or concern he feels in dangerous situations and learn to deal with them, with the advantage that his physical integrity is not exposed and that he can repeat the process as many times as he wants. This training gives the user experience in handling the above situations and enables him to better respond to them in reality. For the creation of the environment, it is considered a CAD tool to develop 2D and 3D graphics, which can be exported to a software of characterization and animation of virtual objects and thus achieve the desired interactive environment.

This article is organized in V sections including Introduction. Section 2 describes the system structure. Section 3 details the development process of the application. In Sect. 4 results and discussion are presented and finally the conclusions are exposed in Sect. 5.

## 2  System Structure

This work presents the development of an application in an interactive virtual environment for the training of operators of industrial plants on emergencies and security, through the use of visual immersion in a virtual plant that presents the emulation of inherent emergencies of the process industry. In addition, the application allows safety education for industrial plants, mainly in the interpretation of preventive and informative signs.

Training in safety and emergencies is carried out from the activation of events, within the virtual environment, which suppose hazards to the operator and to the plant. These events occur when a process variable has exceeded its operating limits, leading to industrial accidents.

The proposed safety and emergency training system makes use of various software and hardware tools that, when integrated with each other, provide immersion and interaction between the environment components and the user.

The interaction between the peripheral devices and the programs used is shown in Fig. 1.

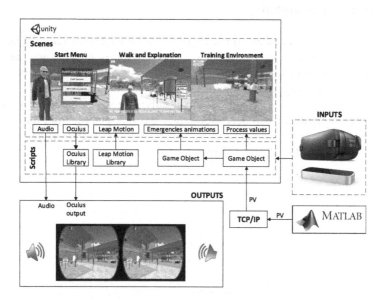

**Fig. 1.** System structure

In the input stage, the HMD Oculus Rift and the gestural controller Leap Motion are considered. The HMD allows immersion by tracking user movements and changing the angle of vision accordingly. Leap Motion is responsible for the recognition of hands to be able to use them within the environment and thus access to various functions of the same by the user.

In the scripts stage, the communication between Unity3D, Matlab and the input devices is managed, and the behavior of each of the components of the environment is modeled to they respond according to the actions performed by the user, by this way, a functional environment in which industrial variables such as temperature, pressure, level, etc. are simulated. These industrial variables are the basis for the generation of accidents and emergencies within the environment, because overlimiting them will trigger a dangerous event that the user must face in the shortest possible time.

The behavior of simulated industrial variables in the virtual plant varies according to data sent from Matlab, which acts as a manager of the plant's events. The data received are displayed on the indicators and transmitters of the plant processes, for which operating ranges are defined, which, when overcome, generate industrial emergencies. The communication between Unity 3D and Matlab is implemented through the TCP/IP protocol, which makes possible the real-time communication between the two used programs for the sending of data in a unidirectional or bidirectional way, thus obtaining control of the events of the plant externally, from the same computer or remotely through an Ethernet, Wi-Fi or internet network.

The output stage contains the sounds of the components of the virtual plant and its alarms, besides the visual immersion in the virtual environment.

## 3 Virtual Environment

For the creation of the virtual environment, two systems are considered suitable for the simulation of emergencies and industrial accidents, given their high risk indices and the inherent dangers they suppose. The first system consists of two industrial boilers that use diesel, for which they need a service tank and pumps that propel the fuel towards them, in this way the boilers provide steam steadily; The second system consists of a large capacity compressor, two heat exchangers and fuel pumps, from these components a source of constant compressed air is obtained. The P&ID diagrams of these processes are presented in Fig. 2 and Fig. 3, respectively.

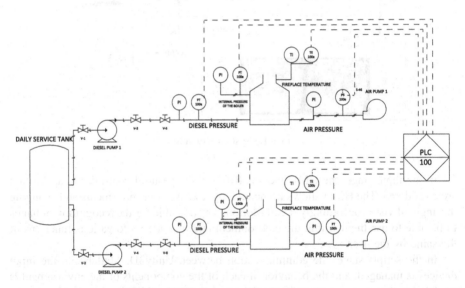

**Fig. 2.** P&ID diagram of the boilers system

The selected systems are combined to form a virtual industrial plant with a high degree of detail to obtain the user's immersion.

Figure 4 shows the diagram that describes the process used to implement the VR application, which consists of several stages, and is based on the design of its components through various specialized programs in the creation and characterization of 3D objects. In addition, the data corresponding to the industrial variables of the virtual plant are managed from Matlab.

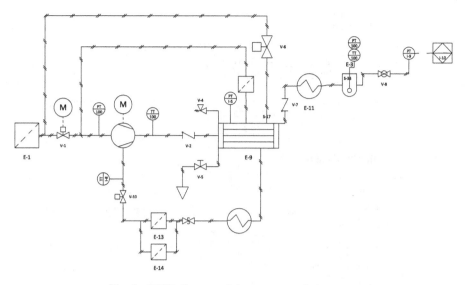

**Fig. 3.** P&ID diagram of the compressed air system

## 3.1 Preliminary CAD Design

This design stage presents the creation and interconnection of instruments and equipment, using CAD tools such as AutoCAD Plant 3D, a program oriented to the design of industrial plants, which allows to generate, modify and interconnect the components of the piping and instrumentation diagram using three-dimensional and realistic objects, as shown in Fig. 5.

The digitized environment in which the user will be immersed in order to perform security training, requires the highest level of detail and realism possible to be able to meet the goal of obtaining high impact training. For this reason, it is necessary to use other programs such as SolidWorks, Inventor, 3DSMax, among others, to create some of the instruments that make up the plant, this contributes to improve the user experience by having a more detailed design and close to reality. For this reason, additional components have been designed in SolidWorks, such as a level transmitter for one of the plant tanks, see Fig. 6.

## 3.2 Unity3D Design

The design implemented in AutoCAD Plant 3D is imported in FBX format in Unity3D and must be characterized in its totality, for which it is necessary to create the materials corresponding to each object and its subsequent assignment. An important aspect to improve the level of detail, and therefore of immersion, is the creation of the place where the plant is located, its details, lighting, shadows, etc. These details do not affect the functionality of the processes, but provide greater user comfort and credibility to the environment, see Fig. 7.

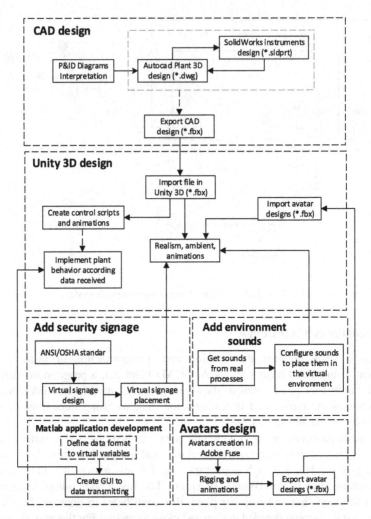

**Fig. 4.** Flow diagram of the application creation process

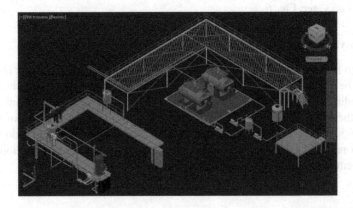

**Fig. 5.** AutoCAD Plant 3D design

**Fig. 6.** Level transmitter developed in a CAD software

**Fig. 7.** Virtual environment developed in Unity 3D

### 3.3   Addition of Security Signage

Training in industrial emergencies includes the recognition and interpretation of preventive and informative safety signs, which are always present in the process industry. For this, several signs are added in the places that merit them, which follow ANSI and OSHA international standards. This feature of the environment provides greater expertise for the user to face an accident, or simply to be able to act safely in a dangerous environment. In Fig. 8, one of the added signs is shown, which indicates risks to hazardous materials, in this case diesel, given by the National Fire Protection Association (NPFA).

### 3.4   Environment Sounds Addition

The characteristic sounds of some industrial equipment such as pumps, boilers and compressors are important to maintain the realism of the environment. These are implemented within a limited area so that, if the user moves away, it is heard with a lower intensity progressively. A sound area corresponding to the diesel pumps in

**Fig. 8.** NPFA security sign

operation, which propagates in spherical form, is shown in Fig. 9 and is intensified or attenuated according to the proximity of the user to it. These sounds are obtained from real industrial processes and are located strategically so that they contribute to increase the realism of the VR application.

**Fig. 9.** Sound component for diesel pumps

### 3.5    Avatars Design

The environment becomes more interactive by having characters that perform tasks within the application and with which it is possible to interact. For this reason, four avatars are developed in Adobe Fuse (see Fig. 10), which is a program specialized in the creation of these and also allows to do the necessary rigging to be able to create animations with ease. The avatars have an aspect according to the environment and will mainly perform patrolling tasks, as well as providing information to the user about the virtual plant.

Patrol routes for the avatars are implemented using empty game objects like targets that must follow cyclically as shown in Fig. 11. When the avatar departs towards a target, the distance between this and that target is calculated constantly taking into account the current coordinates of both of them. When the distance is minimal between

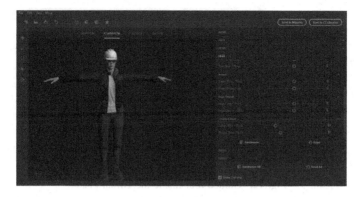

**Fig. 10.** Avatar developed in Adobe Fuse

**Fig. 11.** Patrol route for an avatar

the avatar and the current target, the same procedure is repeated for the next goal. This is how the developed avatar is kept patrolling within the environment in a closed path.

Using the created patrol routes, it is implemented a guided tour and explanation of the environment functionalities, as shown in Fig. 12. This feature offers an approach to the environment before the security training. At this point, the avatar fulfills the role of user guide, which is responsible for providing the most relevant information about the virtual plant and about the tasks that must be accomplished during the training. The information is presented through dialogues and also text boxes.

### 3.6 Matlab Application Development

The data that govern the behavior of the virtual plant are managed from an application that has a graphical interface developed as a Matlab GUI, as shown in Fig. 13. From this application all the industrial variables of the environment are controlled in a local or remote way through the TCP/IP protocol. Industrial emergencies can be generated by entering and sending the values of the industrial variables individually or with the buttons that have the preloaded data needed for it. These data are sent in a standard

**Fig. 12.** Guided tour inside the virtual plant

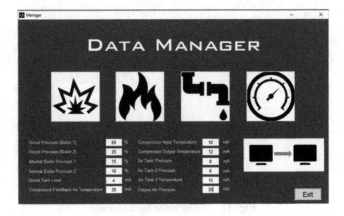

**Fig. 13.** Matlab application interface that manages the environment data

current range for the transmitters and in percentage for the analogue indicators of the plant. Thus, when a data sent exceeds the operation limit, an emergency or accident in the environment is generated.

## 4 Results and Discussion

The VR application developed focuses on the generation of industrial emergencies and user reactions to them in a given period. In addition, security signs are located in places that merit them for interpretation as part of the training. In this way training for emergencies and industrial safety is complete and effective.

The developed application presents a menu that allows access to a guided tour inside the virtual plant or to the security training directly, see Fig. 14.

The guided tour inside the virtual plant, as shown in Fig. 15, offers an overview of the environment as such and an approach to the purpose of the application, for which an explanation is implemented, accompanied by dialog boxes that are presented while

**Fig. 14.** Start menu

**Fig. 15.** Guided tour inside the virtual plant

the avatar that guides the route moves through the virtual plant with the user behind it. This feature makes the application more attractive to the user and more complete for the training.

The virtual environment for training consists of two fully defined systems, as shown in Fig. 16.

In order to demonstrate the performance of the application, experiments are presented that consist on the change of the values of the industrial variables controlled in the virtual plant and the visualization of them in the corresponding transmitters and/or indicators, besides the event that generate these values. The values sent from Matlab to Unity3D for the industrial variables are shown in Fig. 17. (a) Diesel pressure at the pump of 25 bar, (b) Compressed air temperature of 25 °C and (c) Level of 10 inches in a diesel tank.

(a) Constant steam generation system

(b) Constant compressed air generation system

**Fig. 16.** Virtual plant systems for emergencies training

Emergencies arise from certain values of the industrial variables that are outside the limits of operation of the processes. Figure 18 shows the emergency that generates a diesel pressure value of 100 bar corresponding to the drive of one of the pumps located in the constant steam generation system. This pressure value causes a leakage in the pipeline, for which there are two possibilities depending on the user's reaction: (a) The user identifies the valve to close to stop the flow of diesel to the boiler within the set time and does not occur any event or (b) The user does not comply with the action required to mitigate the emergency within the set time and an explosion occurs in the boiler.

(a) Measurement of a pressure variable corresponding to 25 bar

(b) Measurement of a temperature variable corresponding to 25 °C

(c) Measurement of a variable level corresponding to 10 inches

**Fig. 17.** Transmitters and indicators that show the values of plant variables

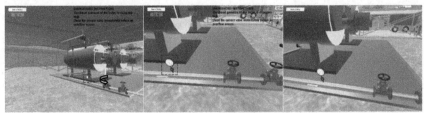

(a) The closing of the correct valve prevents an explosion in the boiler

(b) An explosion occurs in the boiler if the correct valve is not closed

**Fig. 18.** Generation of an industrial emergency from a pressure value of 100 bar in the boiler diesel pipeline

In Fig. 19, an emergency generated by a flammable material is shown in a pipe in the area of the constant compressed air system, which results in a fire. The value generated to detonate this emergency corresponds to a temperature value of 200 °C which can be displayed on the corresponding transmitter. This emergency requires the user to take the nearest fire extinguisher to put out the fire within the set time.

**Fig. 19.** Generation of an industrial emergency from a temperature value of 200 °C

# 5   Conclusion

An immersive VR application has been implemented for the operators and students training and education in cases of emergencies and industrial safety. The immersion that provides the application to the users is accomplished with a high level of detail in the design of the 3D objects implemented for the conformation of the industrial plant.

With the use of this application the user can be instructed on procedures to follow in case of accidents in the industry, in addition an education about security signs that are present in production plants all the time. One of the benefits of using a VR application for training is the impact it can produce on users, which translates into more effective and perpetual training than conventional training provided by enterprises or educational institutions.

Finally, the developed VR application can help develop the skills of field operators and engineering students in industrial safety issues by providing useful and enduring knowledge over time, which can reduce the consequences of imminent hazards and accidents in a considerable percentage in the process industry.

# References

1. Sacks, R., Perlman, A., Barak, R.: Construction safety training using immersive virtual reality. Constr. Manag. Econ. **31**(9), 1005–1017 (2013)
2. Zhao, D., Lucas, J.: Virtual reality simulation for construction safety promotion. Int. J. Inj. Control Saf. Promot. **22**(1), 57–67 (2014)
3. Shikdar, A., Sawaqed, N.: Worker productivity, and occupational health and safety issues in selected industries. Comput. Ind. Eng. **45**(4), 563–572 (2003)
4. Khan, F., Abbasi, S.: Major accidents in process industries and an analysis of causes and consequences. J. Loss Prev. Process Ind. **12**(5), 361–378 (1999)
5. Garrett, J., Teizer, J.: Human factors analysis classification system relating to human error awareness taxonomy in construction safety. J. Constr. Eng. Manag. **135**(8), 754–763 (2009)
6. Le, Q., Pedro, A., Park, C.: A social virtual reality based construction safety education system for experiential learning. J. Intell. Robot. Syst. **79**(3–4), 487–506 (2014)
7. Nedel, L., de Souza, V., Menin, A., Sebben, L., Oliveira, J., Faria, F., Maciel, A.: Using immersive virtual reality to reduce work accidents in developing countries. IEEE Comput. Graph. Appl. **36**(2), 36–46 (2016)
8. Choi, S., Jung, K., Noh, S.: Virtual reality applications in manufacturing industries: past research, present findings, and future directions. Concurr. Eng. **23**(1), 40–63 (2015)
9. Peña, A., Ragan, E.: Contextualizing Construction Accident Reports in Virtual Environments for Safety Education, pp. 389–390 (2017)
10. Ford, J., Schmidt, A.: Emergency response training: strategies for enhancing real-world performance. J. Hazard. Mater. **75**(2–3), 195–215 (2000)
11. Manca, D., Brambilla, S., Colombo, S.: Bridging between virtual Reality and accident simulation for training of process-industry operators. Adv. Eng. Softw. **55**, 1–9 (2013)
12. Nazir, S., Totaro, R., Brambilla, S., Colombo, S., Manca, D.: Virtual reality and augmented-virtual reality as tools to train industrial operators. Comput. Aided Chem. Eng. **30**, 1397–1401 (2012)

466     M. Rosero et al.

13. Andaluz, V.H., et al.: Immersive industrial process environment from a P&ID diagram. In: Bebis, G. (ed.) ISVC 2016. LNCS, vol. 10072, pp. 701–712. Springer, Heidelberg (2006). https://doi.org/10.1007/978-3-319-50835-1_63
14. Zhou, Z., Irizarry, J., Li, Q.: Applying advanced technology to improve safety management in the construction industry: a literature review. Constr. Manag. Econ. 31(6), 606–622 (2013)
15. Crichton, M., Flin, R.: Training for emergency management: tactical decision games. J. Hazard. Mater. 88(2–3), 255–266 (2001)

# Intelligent Oil Field Approach Using Virtual Reality and Mobile Anthropomorphic Robots

José E. Naranjo[1] (iD), Paulina X. Ayala[1], Santiago Altamirano[1],
Geovanni Brito[1], and Marcelo V. Garcia[1,2(✉)] (iD)

[1] Universidad Técnica de Ambato, UTA, Ambato, Ecuador
{jnaranjo0463, ep.ayala, santiagomaltamirano,
geovannidbrito, mv.garcia}@uta.edu.ec
[2] University of the Basque Country, UPV/EHU, Bilbao, Spain
mgarcia294@ehu.eus

**Abstract.** The need to implement architectures with a high degree of scalability, a low level of error and the preservation of the integrity of human beings in the oil industry, has led to the development of technologies that use tele operation, in addition to graphic interfaces that reach a total immersion of the user. To achieve this, it is necessary to use tools such as augmented reality and virtual reality, which help to make the transparency of any system infinite. This research presents the design of a tele-operation system that allows periodic inspections of equipment, maintenance tasks, or training of new personnel in the Well-Pads located in Petroamazonas EP, Ecuador. The transmission of data has been made through the MQTT protocol in order to use the lowest possible bandwidth and consume few resources. In the local site several environments of augmented reality and virtual reality have been implemented, this allows to transmit the skill of the operator to the slave robot through the senses of kinesthesia, sight and hearing implementing an operation based on the concept of Intelligent Oil Field.

**Keywords:** Intelligent Oil Field · Augmented reality · Virtual reality
Teleoperation · Mobile manipulator

## 1 Introduction

Digitization is changing the way oil production and exploration companies operate. Leaders in the oil business are increasingly using big data and digital technology to improve the efficiency of the processes [1]. The areas of maintenance, production and operations are those that mostly benefit from technological advances and data-driven functions, however, few of these are interconnected to show the real picture of the operation of an oil and gas field.

These limitations have led to the development of new automation architectures that allow creating the so-called Intelligent Oil Fields (IOF) that entirely visualize the tasks that are being carried out, accessing immediately to key information about risks in addition to enhance the levels of automation inherent to each industry [2, 3]. The Intelligent Oil Field allows to maintain team relations, tracking of events, collaboration of processes and predictive analysis in real time.

© Springer International Publishing AG, part of Springer Nature 2018
L. T. De Paolis and P. Bourdot (Eds.): AVR 2018, LNCS 10851, pp. 467–478, 2018.
https://doi.org/10.1007/978-3-319-95282-6_34

On the other hand, due to the continuous technological development of this industry, communication networks capable of carrying out a fluid process without interruptions with a high level of security are needed. MQQT (Message Queue Telemetry Transport), instant messaging protocol developed by IBM, is based on a publish/subscribe model [4], supports all types of platforms and a variety of programming languages, it is ideal for the implementation of distributed automation systems due to its low consumption of resources and band width. In the traditional model of industry, each member of the value chain has unique and confidential information for the rest of the members, despite this, nowadays it is possible to integrate both knowledge and information systems [5], giving rise to tools such as Augmented Reality (AR) to get the right information, in the right place at the right time [6]. With the use of this technology we can implement the so-called IOF. It is intended that the operator, through a tele-operated robot, visualize the appropriate information of the equipment being inspected, eradicating the need to be exposed to unstable environments besides developing a better way to visualize data and identify risks through online access to specific information and multimedia content [7].

As described in previous paragraphs, this article proposes the implementation of an IOF architecture through a tele-operated manipulator system for inspection, equipment maintenance, risk identification and personnel training in the oil and gas industry. Through remote control, the proposed system allows the KUKA youBot robot to be controlled by integrating the LeapMotion gestural control device and a head mounted display (HMD) in a 3D graphic engine, whose interface developed in both AR and Virtual Reality (VR) lets the operator to know the status, risks and necessary maintenance of the equipment. The communication has been implemented through the MQTT protocol, which real-time response enables the development of an efficient system with low consumption of resources.

This article is divided into 6 sections including the introduction. In Sect. 2 the State of the Art is analyzed. The Case Study is presented in Sect. 3. The Control System is explained in Sect. 4, while the development of the interfaces in Augmented and Virtual Reality is presented in Sect. 5. Finally, Sect. 6 develops the Conclusions and Future Work.

## 2   State of the Art

### 2.1   Kuka youBOT Robot

This type of mobile manipulator can be defined as a machine with several degrees of freedom, whose application is intended for industrial technological development. Its use is focused specifically for repetitive tasks and precision tasks, besides being designed to perform in environments inaccessible to human beings [8, 9]. It is made up of three parts: (i) omnidirectional platform; (ii) robotic arm with five degrees of freedom and (iii) two-finger clamp.

## 2.2   Tele Operation System

The objective of this type of systems is to transfer the skills of the human being to a robot, i.e., allow an operator to have full control of the activities performed by a slave robot through the senses of touch, sight and hearing [10]. The main parts that conform this system are: (i) Local site: place from which the operator sends work orders to the slave; (ii) Remote site: field of action and intervention of the slave; (iii) Interface: is the set of devices that allows a functional connection and, (iv) Communication channel: is the means by which orders are sent from the master device to the slave device [11].

## 2.3   MQTT Protocol

It is a protocol based on a subscription publishing architecture with a message-broker to communicate to both the publisher and the subscriber [12]. See Fig. 1. Due to its low bandwidth consumption, this protocol is oriented to the communication of sensors, it can also be implemented in most embedded devices with few resources. One of the most notorious examples of this protocol, is the Facebook Messenger application for both iOS and Android. The MQTT architecture follows a star topology, in which the broker has a capacity of up to 10,000 clients. The visualization of the messages in this protocol are of JSON type [13].

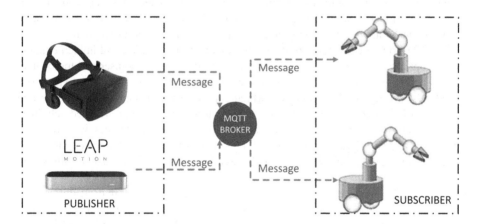

**Fig. 1.** MQTT architecture.

## 2.4   Augmented Reality

The perception of a real environment, which has been modified by virtual objects or computer-generated information is known as Augmented Reality (AR). *Paul Miligram y Fumio Kuishino* [14] created a continuum of virtuality, which describes the oscillation that exists between what can be defined as completely virtual and what is completely reality, where AR is closer to reality and Augmented Virtuality (AV) is closer to a purely virtual environment as can be seen in Fig. 2.

# REALITY-VIRTUALITY CONTINUUM

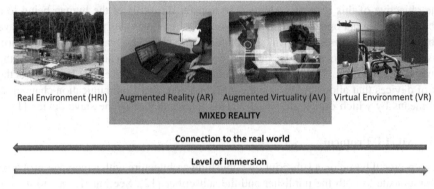

**Fig. 2.** Miligram´s reality-virtuality continuum.

The purpose of AR is based on simplifying the user's life by displaying information, not only to his immediate surroundings, but also to any indirect view of the real-world environment. The data provided by the virtual object, are of great help for operators who have to maintain, monitor the status of equipment or identify risks in industries whose environments are difficult to access and potentially dangerous to their integrity. Contrary to what is generally thought, AR is not only focused on the sense of sight, it can be applied to all the senses such as: hearing, smell and touch.

In order to make AR fully exploited and efficient, the creation and implementation of appropriate techniques for an intuitive interaction between the user and the content of AR application is necessary. For this reason, there are four interaction ways classified as: (i) Tangible AR interfaces, which support a direct interaction with the real world; (ii) Collaborative AR interfaces, which support remote and localized activities; (iii) Hybrid AR interfaces, that combine the use of several devices with different interfaces; and (iv) Emerging multimodal interfaces, that combine the perception of real objects with natural language forms and behaviors such as speech, touch, gestures with natural hands or gaze [15].

On the other hand, when it is needed to develop an AR system, five categories must be taken in count (fixed indoor systems, fixed outdoor systems, mobile indoor systems, mobile outdoor systems, and mobile indoor and outdoor systems [7]) and be very critical with each of its characteristics in order to select the system that best matches the needs and requirements of the user.

## 3    Case Study

Due to the geographical distribution of countries with large oil reserves, remote access to the process is essential when monitoring the status of equipment or making decisions regarding production. These types of industries are made up of several blocks of oil production, i.e., a surface that reduces the environmental impact of the process through oil wells drilled horizontally. These production blocks are called Well-Pad.

The case study focuses on Petroamazonas EP, an Ecuadorian public company dedicated to the exploration and production of hydrocarbons. It is in charge of the operation of 21 blocks, located in the eastern basin and in the coast area of Ecuador.

The proposed system has been simplified to the set of Well-Pads of a single block; this is because the implementation in all the blocks would be a costly and long-term task. For this research, Block 18 has been selected, here, 30 oil wells with a sensor to collect temperature, vibration and pressure data are grouped.

Electrosumergible pumping is the main method of extraction of crude oil. When found on the surface it is stored in a central pipe called the production manifold. In this central pipe, the crude from all the wells that are part of a Well-Pad is collected. This process comes to an end when the crude is sent to the Central Processing Facility (CPF), which is located several kilometers away from the Well-Pads.

The aim of the case study is to use the KUKA youBOT robot in each Well-Pad in order to carry out maintenance tasks, equipment inspection and risk identification, having a human operator as a monitoring and execution tool located in the CPF. The LeapMotion device is used to detect movement orders of the robotic arm and omnidirectional platform. With the implementation of this system it is intended to change the vision with respect to robots and contemplate them as eyes, ears and hands of the operator. In the control system, the operator interacts with the robot and with the medium that is being inspected through a collaborative interface, which uses the AR as a tool to increase transparency in the local site, leading to a significant improvement in the effectiveness (fewer errors) and efficiency (less time to complete the activities) of the proposed tasks. In order to obtain the feedback of the robot states, speed sensors, position sensors and a video camera have been implemented in the KUKA youBOT. See Fig. 3.

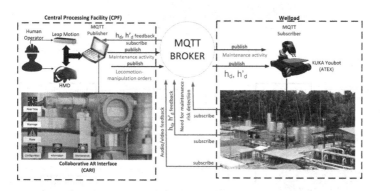

**Fig. 3.** Teleoperation system architecture.

# 4 Control System

Through the kinematics of a manipulator robot, the position and speed of both its omnidirectional platform and its robotic arm can be established. This kinematic model is determined by (1), in which $J(q)$ represents the Jacobian matrix and $v(t)$ express the speed of the mobile manipulator.

$$\dot{h}_{(t)} = J_{(q)}v_{(t)} \tag{1}$$

$J$ (q) determines the relationships between the speeds of the joints and those of the end effector of the robot. It can be obtained by partial derivation of the different functions that comprise the direct kinematics, specifically in the end effector position. Thus, the position of the end effector is expressed by means of a vector in which each component will appear as a multivariate scalar function based on the joint variables as shown in (2). The Jacobian matrix can then be constructed as a composition of the partial derivative by columns of function F(q), this is demonstrated in (3).

$$F(q) = \begin{pmatrix} F_x(q_1, q_2, \ldots \ldots \ldots, q_n) \\ F_y(q_1, q_2, \ldots \ldots \ldots, q_n) \\ F_z(q_1, q_2, \ldots \ldots \ldots, q_n) \end{pmatrix} \tag{2}$$

$$J(q) = \left( \frac{\partial F}{\partial q_1} \middle| \frac{\partial F}{q_2} \middle| \ldots \ldots \cdot \frac{\partial F}{q_n} \middle| \right) \tag{3}$$

It is at this moment where the LeapMotion device intervenes, sending the slave the desired speed for the manipulation mode, see (4), or in turn the position for the locomotion mode as shown in (5).

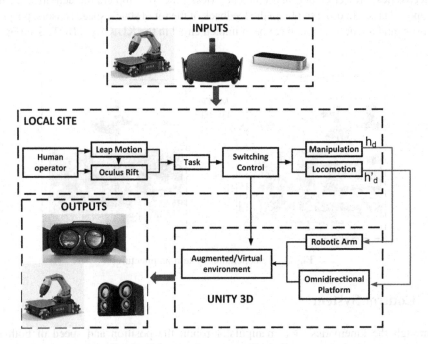

**Fig. 4.** Teleoperation system block diagram.

$$\dot{h}_d = \begin{bmatrix} \dot{h}_l & \dot{h}_m & \dot{h}_n \end{bmatrix}^T \tag{4}$$

$$h_d = \begin{bmatrix} h_l & h_m & h_n \end{bmatrix}^T \tag{5}$$

The Tele operation system implemented through the Unity 3D graphic engine is presented in Fig. 4, a switching control has been developed, where the operator, depending on the action he needs to perform, can choose between controlling the omnidirectional platform or the robotic arm. In addition, the operator can select the work environment that best suits its needs, either VR or AR.

## 5 Augmented and Virtual Reality

Virtual Reality and Augmented Reality are two essential technologies for the transition from Conventional Industry to Industry 4.0, these allow companies to embark on their path towards digitalization. Both use Virtual Reality (VR) or incorporate virtual elements to reality (AR) that provide knowledge and useful information for the optimization of processes.

Once the operator begins to interact with the proposed system, he is automatically immersed in the real oil plant having the remote control of the KUKA youBOT robot. The "slave" has been programmed so that, according to the data obtained through the sensory device LeapMotion, it could move within the programmed environment or at the same time the working activities of the robotic arm could be initiated. This has been achieved through the development of the sense of kinesthesia which allows the operator to perform coordinated movements of his hand (these have been previously established by the control system) so that the locomotion and manipulation of the KUKA youBOT robot can be governed.

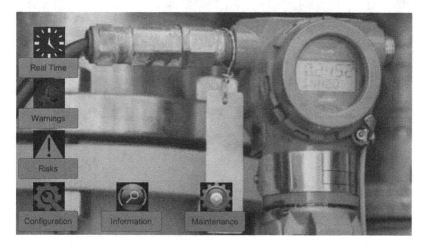

**Fig. 5.** Augmented reality menu.

a) Augmented Reality Menu          b) Oil refinery and KUKA youBot-Unity 3D

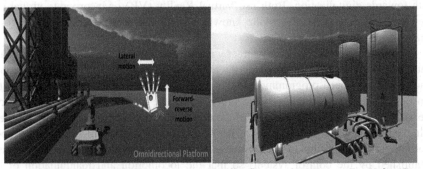

c) KUKA youBot Training          d) Oil refinery and KUKA youBot-Unity 3D

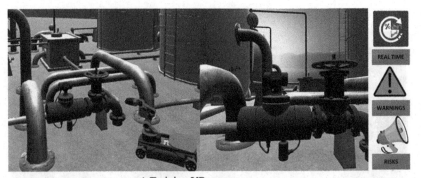

e) Training VR menu

**Fig. 6.** Augmented reality and virtual reality experiment

Through the identification of the equipment, all the necessary information is displayed on screen in real time allowing data entry, operation and remote monitoring. By means of AR and through the video transmission implemented in the slave, the operator can visualize a menu, in which due to the digitalization of the movement of his hands he can select among: see the process in real time, see the warnings, inspect the risks presented by the equipment, navigate through a configuration panel, obtain information on the element or perform maintenance actions. In addition, the proposed system, issues a warning when the date of a preventive maintenance approaches and an alarm when this date has been surpassed. See Fig. 5.

Furthermore, a menu with training options for both the use of the slave robot and for equipment maintenance and risk detection has been implemented. With this, what is proposed is to train the operator to make decisions under any circumstances. Refer to Fig. 6a.

If the operator decides to select the slave robot training, he will be directed to a VR environment, in which the necessary control movements for an efficient development of the proposed tasks will be deployed. This is demonstrated in Fig. 6b and c.

This type of training allows to run simulations of the possible real scenarios for which the personnel must be prepared, helping them to explore, understand and react physically and psychologically in a similar real situation. In addition, virtual reality can be used for the interpretation or analysis of complex information. It allows workers to have a broader view of concepts or processes, which could not be observed directly in the real world due to the risks present in this kind of industries. Each movement to be carried out by the slave robot is assigned to a specific hand movement, developing the sense of kinesthetics of the workers and helping them to understand the dimensions of the surrounding environment.

On the other hand, when the operator selects the option to train in terms of risk detection and equipment maintenance, a menu similar to the one developed in AR will be shown, with the difference that these options will be implemented in VR environment, as shown in Fig. 6d. and e.

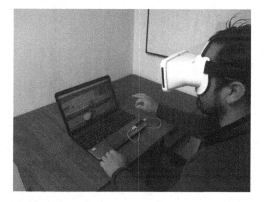

**Fig. 7.** Operator immersed in the VR interface

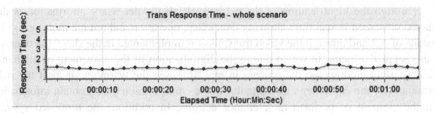

**Fig. 8.** AR interfaces response time

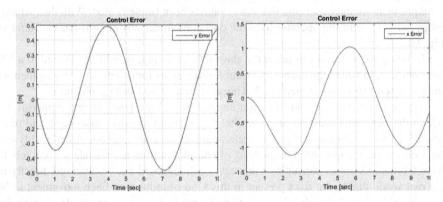

**Fig. 9.** X-Y control errors

**Fig. 10.** End effector efficiency

# 6    Conclusion and Future Work

A tele operation system for maintenance, risk detection and operator training has been presented at Petroamazonas EP, an Ecuadorian public company dedicated to the carburiferous sector. This research has achieved an efficient immersion of the operator due to the implementation of both AR and VR for the daily development of tasks, in addition to preserving their health avoiding their interaction with dangerous environments.

It also includes the option to force variables or to make data entries from its own interface, allowing to visualize data in real time of the identified equipment through communication with existing control systems. The operators designated for the implementation of this system present a great development in their sense of kinesthetics, showing an optimal management and control of the slave through the interface in AR and VR as shown in Fig. 7.

By using the new approach of the IOF, the oil industries are free to design a new, more productive oilfield where collaboration, event management and better measurement exist. With this technology, the vision of training operators and developing more efficient processes, at the right cost, with less implementation risk and greater flexibility, becomes a conceivable objective for any company.

When talking about augmented reality interfaces, it is necessary to take into account the response time and delays inherent to the proposed system. Due to the use of the MQTT protocol, whose consumption of resources and bandwidth is very low, an efficient response time has been achieved as shown in Fig. 8.

Since the visual feedback obtained by the operator that it is immersed in an augmented reality interface has a suitable quality, the control errors are not greater than one meter both on the X axis and the Y axis, establishing that the decision of having used MQTT as a data transmission channel has been accurate. See Fig. 9.

On the other hand, when evaluating the manipulation activities, the sent handling orders versus the executed orders were taken as a reference. 6 inspections were carried out, 150 orders were sent and 135 were satisfactorily completed. These results show an end effector efficiency of 90% assuring compliance of each task with a permissible error range. See Fig. 10.

For future research it is proposed to improve the transparency of the system through different sensing modalities. On the other hand, it is proposed to compare the data transmission rate of the MQTT protocol with other light data consumption protocols in order to verify if there is a better choice to transmit AR and VR information.

**Acknowledgments.** This work was financed in part by Universidad Tecnica de Ambato (UTA) under project CONIN-P-0167-2017, by DPI2015-68602-R (MINECO/FEDER, UE), UPV/EHU under project PPG17/56 and GV/EJ under recognized research group IT914-16 and Government of Ecuador through grant SENESCYT-2013.

# References

1. Shukla, A., Karki, H.: Application of robotics in onshore oil and gas industry-a review Part I. Rob. Auton. Syst. **75**, 490–507 (2016)
2. Liaw, J., Tsai, P.: Target prediction to improve human errors in robot teleoperation system. In: 2017 International Conference on Applied System Innovation (ICASI), pp. 1094–1097. IEEE (2017)
3. Shukla, A., Karki, H.: Application of robotics in offshore oil and gas industry—a review Part II. Rob. Auton. Syst. **75**, 508–524 (2016)
4. Tang, K., Wang, Y., Liu, H., Sheng, Y., Wang, X., Wei, Z.: Design and implementation of push notification system based on the MQTT protocol. In: Proceedings of 2013 International Conference on Information Science and Computer Applications (ISCA 2013), pp. 116–119 (2013)
5. Garcia, M.V., Irisarri, E., Perez, F., Estevez, E., Orive, D., Marcos, M.: Plant floor communications integration using a low cost CPPS architecture. In: 2016 IEEE 21st International Conference on Emerging Technologies and Factory Automation (ETFA), pp. 1–4. IEEE (2016)
6. Milgram, P., Takemura, H., Utsumi, A., Kishino, F.: Augmented reality: a class of displays on the reality-virtuality continuum. In: Telemanipulator and Telepresence Technologies. International Society for Optics and Photonics, vol. 2351, pp. 282–293 (1995)
7. Regenbrecht, H., Baratoff, G., Wilke, W.: Augmented reality projects in the automotive and aerospace industries. IEEE Comput. Graph. Appl. **25**(6), 48–56 (2005)
8. Reyes, F.: Robotica: Control de Robots Manipuladores, 1st edn. Alfaomega Grupo Editor, Mexico (2011)
9. García, M.V., Irisarri, E., Pérez, F., Estévez, E., Marcos, M.: Automation architecture based on cyber physical systems for flexible manufacturing within Oil&Gas industry. Rev. Iberoam. Automática Informática Ind (RIAI), **15**(2), 156–166 (2018). https://doi.org/10.4995/riai.2017.8823. Directory of Open Access Journals
10. Salcudean, S.E., Wong, N.M., Salcudean, S.E., Hollis, R.L., Wong, M., Hollis, R.L.: Design and control of a force-reflecting teleoperation system with magnetically levitated master and wrist. Robotics **11**(6), 844–858 (1995)
11. Andaluz, V.H., Quevedo, W.X., Chicaiza, F.A., Varela, J., Gallardo, C., Sánchez, J.S., Arteaga, O.: Transparency of a bilateral tele-operation scheme of a mobile manipulator robot. In: De Paolis, L.T., Mongelli, A. (eds.) AVR 2016. LNCS, vol. 9768, pp. 228–245. Springer, Cham (2016). https://doi.org/10.1007/978-3-319-40621-3_18
12. Asaad, M., Ahmad, F., Alam, M.S., Rafat, Y.: IoT enabled monitoring of an optimized electric vehicle's battery system. Mob. Netw. Appl. **1**, 1–12 (2017). https://doi.org/10.1007/s11036-017-0957-z
13. Bandyopadhyay, S., Bhattacharyya, A.: Lightweight Internet protocols for web enablement of sensors using constrained gateway devices. In: 2013 International Conference on Computing Networking and Communications. (ICNC), pp. 334–340. IEEE Computer Society, Washington, DC (2013)
14. Handbook of Augmented Reality, Springer (2011)
15. Carmigniani, J., Furht, B., Anisetti, M., Ceravolo, P., Damiani, E., Ivkovic, M.: Augmented reality technologies, systems and applications. Multimed. Tools Appl. **51**(1), 341–377 (2011)

# Real–Time Virtual Reality Visualizer for Unmanned Aerial Vehicles

Fernando A. Chicaiza[1](✉), Cristian Gallardo[2](✉),
Christian P. Carvajal[1](✉), Washington X. Quevedo[2](✉),
Jaime Santana[1](✉), Vicente Morales[2](✉), and Víctor H. Andaluz[1](✉)

[1] Universidad de Las Fuerzas Armadas ESPE, Sangolquí, Ecuador
{fachicaiza,vhandaluz1}@espe.edu.ec,
chriss2592@hotmail.com
[2] Universidad Técnica de Ambato, Ambato, Ecuador
cmgallardop@gmail.com, waxshoxp@gmail.com,
jvmorales99@gmail.com

**Abstract.** The visualization of tele-operated and autonomous executions in the field becomes difficult if the real environments are located in remote areas or present potential dangers for visualizing clients. This work proposes an application based on virtual reality to recreate in real time the execution tasks of a UAV, which is operated remotely or autonomously on a real environment. To achieve a third level of immersion, the reconstruction of the real environment where the field tests are executed is considered, offering the possibility of knowing the real scenario where the tests are executed. The consideration of using commercial UAV development kits is taken into account to obtain internal information, as well as to control the drone from client devices. The results presented validate the unification of 3D models and the reconstruction of the environment, as well as the consumption of vehicle information and climate parameters.

**Keywords:** Virtual Reality · Real time visualization · 3D models
Reconstructed scenario

## 1 Introduction

Unmanned Aerial Vehicles have generated important socio-economic impacts [1]. Given the cost and ease of operation of this type of vehicles, myriad applications have been able to be executed, where the characteristics of the rotary wing vehicles have allowed carried out specific tasks in several fields [2]: (i) In disaster scenarios, coordination of the relief efforts requires communication, where drones can reconstruct high/resolution maps of the affected area, work as temporary mobile access points for extending the coverage on affected areas, tag points of public saturation and so on [3]; (ii) in the agriculture field, UAVs can integrate specialized cameras to transmit information to cloud-based data analytics so that farmers can know the quality of crop growth or detect potential plagues [4]; (iii) For environmental applications, drones can be used for fire detection, pollution detection, water management, as well as for monitoring gases, temperature, humidity, and so on; (iv) For mining companies, unmanned vehicles can obtain accurate volumetric information for excavations and reconstruction of uneven terrain; (v) In the civil and engineering field, drones can mean a solution for the monitoring of pipelines, roads, and cables; (vi) In borders or menace fields, these type of vehicles can collect information about the environment or detect possible threats. Likewise, (vii) rotating wing vehicles can be a support for path planning and coordination, sending aerial image information to other terrestrial robots [5].

On the other hand, at present the most common commercial application is object detection, using data gathered from data sources such as cameras or radars. Given the possibility of capturing photography with metadata, the use of an integrated camera over an aerial vehicle facilitates the overflight view of an environment either in online or offline mode. This information collected enables the digital reconstruction of a real scenario, where the more digital information is obtained, the better details will have the reconstruction. Works as [6, 7] demonstrate the usefulness of UAVs for the reconstruction of environments, where applications such as the recreation of buildings, digitization of large objects and reconstruction of uneven terrain can be carried out [8]. The environments digitalization makes it possible to analyse large terrains, the structural state of a building after natural disasters or environmental characteristics. To take this type of captures, commercial drones offer a range of proprietary applications to optimize the process of information collection, although they are limited to working in open space free of obstacles. To solve this limitation, solutions such as the addition of external sensors, control with a different software to the default one or merge the control techniques with teleoperation can be taken into account.

Depending on the application and the required dexterity, the UAV control can be integrated by a manual control, an automatic control (on the ground or embedded in the drone), or a mixture of both. In the first case, the manual control is related to the straightforward control which the operator can execute on the vehicle, either through a remote control or by gestures that the vehicle recognizes. Research as [9] demonstrate this type of control, having as direct command the user's hands, where the gestures are used to modify the control actions. In this way, the aim is to reduce the complexity in the command of a vehicle located remotely. In contrast, the automatic control is based on the information of sensors and positioning devices to carry out the tracking of a pre-programmed path. In this aspect, several works have done the approach to the stability and robustness of the controllers, which generate the control actions according to the reading of information of the environment [10]. Finally, the difficulty in executing tasks which require high precision can force the merger of the teleoperated controls and the automatic control [11]. Tasks in confined spaces, environments reconstruction or involving dangerous environments could require this unification of controls, where teleoperation can provide operator skills to repetitive and tedious executions. Teleoperation is accessible given the trend of commercial UAVs, however, including a different control to the default one becomes a difficult task if the vehicle does not make it possible to access the command controls or its internal information [12].

Commonly, the communication system between the local controller and the vehicle is transparent to the user [13, 14]. This can be an advantage for users using the UAV for a specific task, however, it can be a limitation when it is required to validate more robust controllers or it is required to know vehicle's internal information. In this regard, several companies have chosen to create open software kits for external developers, which can use computer tools to access configurations and functionalities of the vehicle.

This work proposes the extraction of flight characteristics of a UAV executing tele operated or autonomous tasks, information which is processed for the location of a digitized vehicle on a reconstructed virtual environment. The environment reconstruction is based on the collection of photographic information of the real environment where the tests are executed. Through processing techniques, it is gotten a virtual layout similar to the real one to use it as a reference in a videogames engine. Given the information provided by the photographs with metadata and GPS data provided by the aerial vehicle, the simulated vehicle maintains a position similar to the real one, allowing to visualize in a virtual environment the executions which are executed in the field. In addition to this, the development of communication interfaces to connect clients who consume information from the unmanned aerial vehicle is proposed.

The work is distributed as follows: The Introduction and Problem Formulation are presented in the first and second sections, respectively. Section 3 analyses the blocks necessary for the construction of the application, while Sect. 4 presents the operation mode of the implemented program. Finally, the experimental results and the conclusions are presented in the last Sects. 5 and 6.

## 2  Problem Formulation

Although it can be obtained flight history of a vehicle after execution, a real-time recreation involves obtaining preset parameters, as well as updated data periodically. In this way, a remotely located user could know both the instrumentation and flight parameters of a vehicle which maintains real executions in real scenarios. In a more intuitive way, users located remotely could access the instrumentation of the vehicle, move on a three-dimensional reconstructed scenario, obtain more attractive views, interpret controllers and their way of working in front of disturbances, and so on.

The tasks simulation performed by a UAV on a reconstructed environment requires the consumption of the aerial vehicle data, as well as information on the weather and current time of execution. In order to solve this problematic, this work proposes the fusion of a set of sub-stages shown in Fig. 1. In this way, the reconstruction of the environment where the tests are executed is carried out off-line, being a prerequisite before starting with the simulation.

In contrast, the speeds injected into the UAV and the positions obtained as a result are acquired in real time, so that the behaviour of the vehicle can be emulated on the reconstructed environment. The position information is transmitted in a GPS (Global Positioning System) format, so that it can have a high accuracy of reconstruction. All the information provided (off-line and on-line) is used for flight simulation, taking into account weather conditions and time zones.

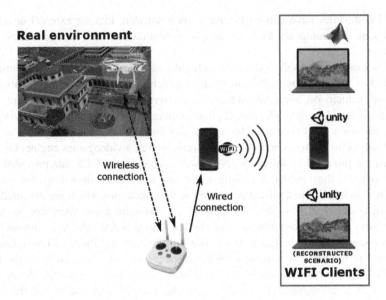

**Fig. 1.** Stages to achieve execution in a reconstructed virtual environment

## 3   System Structure

The structure of the system shows all the blocks required to implement the application, shown in Fig. 2. Without displaying a specific hierarchy, the structure of the system is made up of five blocks which integrates the game objects (models and resources deployed in the scenes of the game), scripts to modify the behaviour of each of the game objects, a digital reconstruction of the scenario where the experimental tests are executed, information input devices to control the user's journey throughout the application, and finally, output devices in which the result of the fusion of all the blocks is shown.

Following the flow of information, *(i) The Inputs* are related to all the information provided by HTC VIVE devices, Gear VR, aerial vehicle instrumentation information and/or some input mode generated on the web. The input devices provide control actions to move the avatar within the scenes, navigate through the menus and zoom in to visualize the instrumentation of the vehicle. Likewise, raw data is acquired from the information provided by the aerial vehicle to modify the behaviour of the 3D model which represents the robotic system.

Consequently, *(ii) External Data Block* provides georeferenced information and climate status. In order to emulate the real scenario where the experimental tests are executed, this type of information provides characteristics of the field, such as level of precipitation, humidity, wind speed, light intensity, and so forth, data which allows to include additional variables to the simulated environment. Also, the block provides time information to include it in the dashboard.

The *(iii) Scripting Block* is made up of fragments of code used to manage the input devices, control the game objects and provide outputs dependent on the execution of the user. Libraries such as SteamVR plugin and Oculus Library manage the local input devices, allowing to generate excitations to manipulate the objects located in the environment, as well as to detect user displacements within the virtual built scenarios. Besides, the raw information provided by the drone is processed to adapt it to the requirements of Unity 3D. In this way, an information decoder is responsible for discriminating data on positioning, height, attitude, electronic and mechanical state of the drone and other internal parameters of the vehicle. Through this decoding, a module of interact and collisions can determinate the position where the digitized drone should be located. In the same way, alarms can be activated by detecting malfunctions in the instrumentation of the vehicle. In contrast, the data provided by external information (date, time and weather) is used for the adjustment of light, climate effects, and

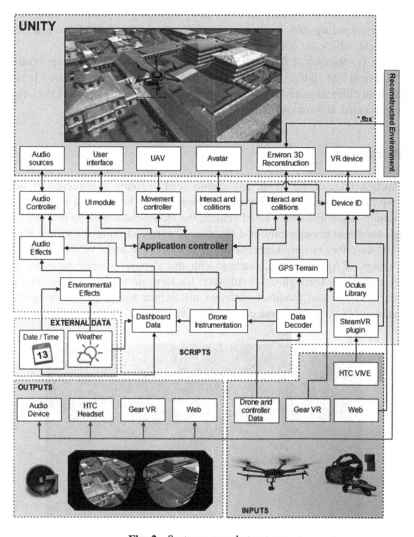

**Fig. 2.** System general structure

adaptation to local time. Besides allowing to generate audio effects, this information is displayed in the dashboard to know the real climatic conditions in which the experimental tests are being executed in the field. The information provided by the aforementioned blocks and blocks that directly control the game objects of the UAV, User Interface, Avatar, and Environment 3D reconstruction are managed by the Application Controller, identified by the diagram as the main scripting module.

The *(iv) Unity Scenes* contain various elements required to build the virtual environment. In this work, three-dimensional models built in CAD software are included, as well as digitally reconstructed models by means of photography. In the same way, the selection of an avatar allows improving the user's immersion in the application, where its displacement is subject to the changes generated by the input devices. In addition, a dashboard is presented where it can be displayed the vehicle's internal information, as well as climatic variables and positioning information. Each of the 3D models, virtual reality devices, interfaces, and audio sources are defined generically as game objects, which are controlled by the scripting block.

Finally, *(v) the Output Block* allows the visualization of the entire application in a visual, haptical and audible way. Given the flexibility that the application presents to connect with different methods of information consumption, the result of the simulation can be presented at a remote or near site.

## 4  Workflow

The functionalities of the whole application need to follow a sequence of stages to reach the final scenario, for which a set of three blocks is proposed that integrate the CAD design of the unmanned aerial vehicle, the reconstruction of the real environment through overflight photography, and the general construction of the virtual stage. *The first block* describes the requirements for the design of the aerial vehicle in a computer-aided design (CAD) software, starting with the physical specifications of the real prototype (Fig. 3). Through CAD software, the three-dimensional model that will be textured, coloured and modified (defining hierarchies and pivots) is designed to be compatible with the video game engine (Fig. 4).

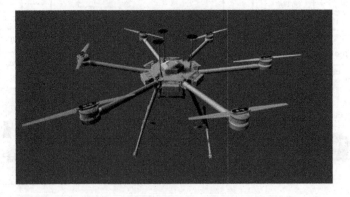

**Fig. 3.** Three-dimensional UAV model without texturization

On the other hand, *in the second layer*, the information collected through aerial photography allows reconstructing the real environment. The characteristics of photography with metadata allows identifying positioning information and height of the site overflown, which may contain elevations of the terrain, buildings, roads, and so forth. By means of an orthophoto processor, the three-dimensional design can be obtained preserving or not the colour characteristics, with export options in different formats compatible with the videogames engine, in this case, *.fbx.

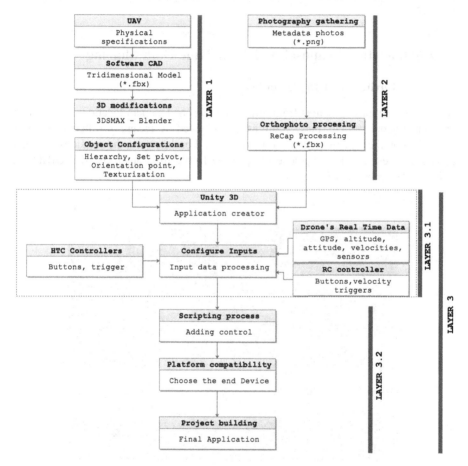

**Fig. 4.** Development of the virtual reality interface

The *(iii) third layer* is divided into two parts, both running entirely in Unity and related to both the acquisition of data from the real aerial vehicle and the process of scripting and generation of the application. Sublayer 3.1 describes the processing of the input information that the application has, where button activation, user movement, rotation, and so on are provided by the virtual reality devices; while the information of positioning, altitude, attitude, and other instrumental information is generated by communication methods described below. The import of both the 3D model of the UAV and the reconstructed environment allows the use of field information to recreate the execution in a completely simulated environment, which integrates the internal characteristics of the UAV, as well as information on the climate status of the real environment. This process is facilitated through the use of scripting, where the input information is adapted and the user is easily transferred to the virtual reality environment. Finally, the resulting application is compiled depending on the output hardware, being applications based on operating systems for computers or Smartphones.

## 5   Digitalization Proposal and Real Time Data Sharing

### 5.1   Real Environment Digitalization

A 3D model requires captures from different angles and camera locations. Through an unmanned aerial vehicle, these captures are achieved by means of different missions depending on the type of captures to be obtained. For this work, the missions used that present the best results to achieve the proposed objectives are DOUBLE GRID and CIRCULAR, presented in Fig. 5.

**Fig. 5.** Configuración de misiones para captura de fotografías

For a suitable three-dimensional reconstruction, photographs taken from different angles in the same location are used, so that heights and depths can be estimated through the rotation variation of the camera. Through the information acquired from the metadata of each image, the Autodesk ReCap Photo software reconstructs a three-dimensional scene similar to the real one. Figure 6 shows the result of the 3D reconstruction of a building, based on a set of approximately 600 photographs.

**Fig. 6.** Reconstruction of real environments

## 5.2   Real Time Data Sharing

The developed application requires a communication bridge between the virtual scenarios and the real-time information of the unmanned aerial vehicle. In this way, a communication bridge based on Wireless Fidelity is developed, generating an Access Point Service by means of a smartphone. The service allows the connection of devices based on mobile or computer operating systems. In this way, the smartphone application allows to command the UAV from a remotely located device, as well as visualizing the internal parameters of the vehicle to know its behaviour in the execution of tasks. Figure 7 shows the operating scheme of the communication bridge developed.

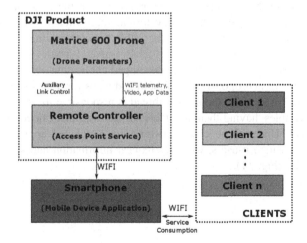

**Fig. 7.** Bilateral communication scheme implemented

## 6  Bilateral Communication Bridge

The standard communication presented by the Matrice 600 is composed of a controller device which generates an Access Point (AP) mode, providing a wireless network to which the robot and any device can connect to. The connection of the mobile device to the AP allows consumption of UAV status information (position, altitude, attitude, and instrumentation), as well as generating control actions to manoeuvre it.

As mentioned above, although the price of this UAV is accessible and at the same time it has functionalities which allow working in the research area; by default the developer does not provide libraries to connect computers or other devices to the UAV, since the standard communication is shown in Fig. 8.

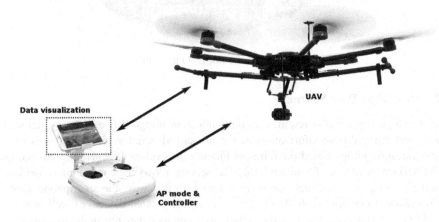

**Fig. 8.** Standard communication Phantom 3 PRO

As a solution to this problem, it is proposed to use the Software developer Kit provided by the company, in order to develop an application which runs on a smart-phone with Android 4.4+ operating system, within the connection infrastructure of the DJI product, Fig. 9.

Figure 10 presents schematically the developed application, where two threads are presented running asynchronously. The first thread waits for user actions to modify the behaviour of the UAV, while the second thread is responsible for requesting the states of the drone variables, having them available for any user that can connect through the TCP/IP protocol. Under these characteristics, the developed application presents a support for consecutive n-users, who can request information and send control commands in parallel (Fig. 11).

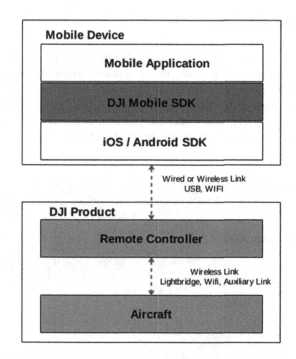

**Fig. 9.** Connection infrastructure

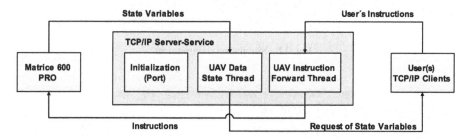

**Fig. 10.** TCP/IP service architecture

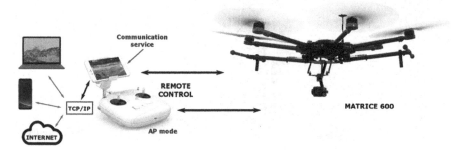

**Fig. 11.** Communication structure proposed

# 7    Experimental Results

This section presents the experimental results obtained from the simulated recreation of a field execution. Figure 12 presents the simulation, where the reconstructed environment, the three-dimensional model of the drone, the avatar, and the information provided by the inputs are visualized, considering that the vehicle is in standby. Because the UAV drive is in idle mode, instrumentation features such as battery charge status, landing gear status and so on can be displayed (Fig. 13).

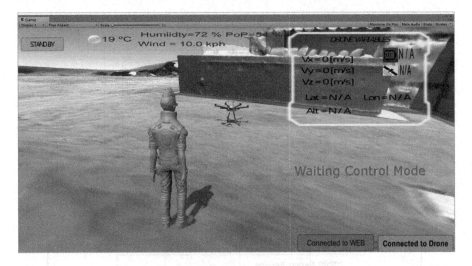

**Fig. 12.** Simulation environment

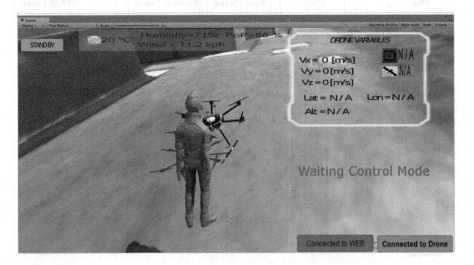

**Fig. 13.** Instrumentation parameters visualization

Considering that the client devices can control and visualize the internal parameters of the UAV, two control modes can be executed to modify the behaviour of the vehicle: by tele operation and controlled autonomously. In this way, the results are presented in two parts.

## 7.1  Teleoperated Control Visualization

The teleoperated control refers to the use of the UAV's controller, where autonomous actions are not taken into account. In this way, the control actions the user in the field generates through the remote controller can be visualized, where the button is highlighted in the virtual environment, as shown in Fig. 14. The functionalities presented by the application allow the avatar to be moved throughout the reconstructed environment so that the behaviour of the vehicle can be monitored throughout the workspace. Figure 15 shows a third person capture of the avatar located in different locations to demonstrate the flexibility of the application. As additional parameters, the climatic conditions are displayed on the display dashboard, which allows modifying the environment and adapting it to wind, rain, light, and so forth conditions.

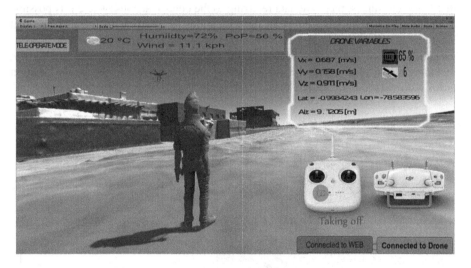

**Fig. 14.** Taking off visualization

## 7.2  Autonomous Control Visualization

Unlike the teleoperated control, the autonomous control visualization includes more parameters related to the execution of the proposed task. Parameters such as control actions, control errors and total errors can be displayed through the inclusion of buttons. Since the application only consumes information, the autonomous control stage is dependent on the executions carried out in the field. Within the information parameters

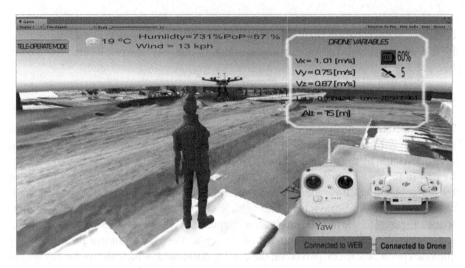

**Fig. 15.** Yaw modification visualization

that Unity consumes, there are data referring to the control actions, where it is possible to discriminate positioning errors in the executions, contrasting the desired and real locations of the UAV. Figure 16 shows the real-time recreation of the autonomous execution carried out by the Matrice 600, where the flight parameters are shown, including a plot of the control actions injected into the vehicle to reduce the position errors.

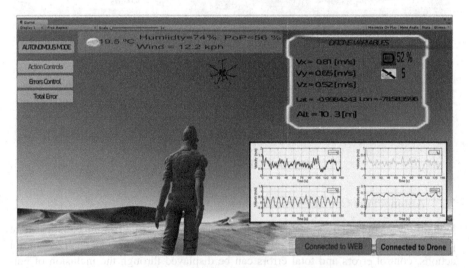

**Fig. 16.** Autonomous controlled execution

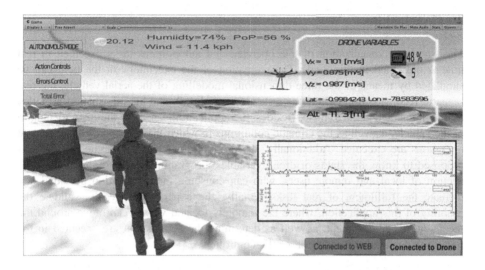

a)    First autonomous execution visualization example

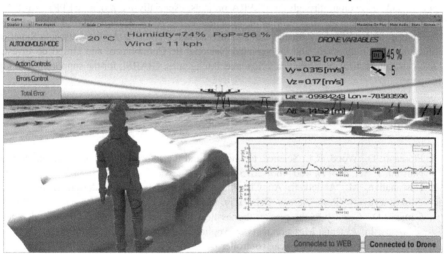

b)    Second autonomous execution visualization example

**Fig. 17.**  Path tracking programmed in the autonomous controller

The graphical inclusion of the programmed path in the autonomous control over the videogame engine, allows understanding the controller reactions. In this way, Fig. 17 (a, b) shows the displacement of the drone on the desired positions, showing also the variation of position of the avatar, which observes in first person the aerial vehicle actions.

# 8 Conclusions

The simulated visualization of tele operated and autonomous tasks executed in real time is presented in this work. The recreation of the executions in the field can be simulated by means of the three-dimensional modelling of the aerial vehicle, the real scenario reconstruction (where the tests are carried out), and the information provided by the unmanned aerial vehicle. Besides, the application can show the instrumentation of the vehicle, as well as the climatic conditions in which the tele operated and remote operations are executed. Additionally, the programming and use of the DJI SDK is proposed to know the status of drone variables, programming which allows the connection of local and remote users, who can consume the information provided and recreate the fulfilment of real tasks. Finally, the experimental results validate the usability of this application, where the remotely located viewer can move around the reconstructed environment, as well as determine the actions that are executed in the field to understand the operation of the controllers.

**Acknowledgments.** The authors would like to thanks to the Corporación Ecuatoriana para el Desarrollo de la Investigación y Academia–CEDIA for the financing given to research, development, and innovation, through the CEPRA projects, especially the project CEPRA-XI-2017-06; *Control Coordinado Multi-operador aplicado a un robot Manipulador Aéreo*; also to Universidad de las Fuerzas Armadas ESPE, Universidad Técnica de Ambato, Escuela Superior Politécnica de Chimborazo, and Universidad Nacional de Chimborazo, and Grupo de Investigación en Automatización, Robótica y Sistemas Inteligentes, GIARSI, for the support to develop this paper.

# References

1. Floreano, D., Wood, R.J.: Science, technology and the future of small autonomous drones. Nat. Int. J. Sci. **521**(1), 460–466 (2015)
2. Hassanalian, M., Abdelkefi, A.: Classifications, applications, and design challenges of drones: a review. Prog. Aerosp. Sci. **91**(1), 99–131 (2017)
3. Câmara, D.: Cavalry to the rescue: drones fleet to help rescuers operations over disasters scenarios. In: Antenna Measurements & Applications (CAMA), vol. 2015(1) (2015)
4. Andaluz, V.H., et al.: Nonlinear controller of quadcopters for agricultural monitoring. In: Bebis, G., et al. (eds.) ISVC 2015. LNCS, vol. 9474, pp. 476–487. Springer, Cham (2015). https://doi.org/10.1007/978-3-319-27857-5_43
5. Chmaj, G., Selvaraj, H.: Distributed processing applications for UAV/drones: a survey. In: Selvaraj, H., Zydek, D., Chmaj, G. (eds.) Progress in Systems Engineering. AISC, vol. 366, pp. 449–454. Springer, Cham (2015). https://doi.org/10.1007/978-3-319-08422-0_66
6. Daftry, S., Hoppe, C., Bischof, H.: Building with drones: accurate 3D facade reconstruction using MAVs. In: Robotics and Automation (ICRA), vol. 2015, no. 1, pp. 3487–3494 (2015)
7. Balletti, C., Guerra, F., Scocca, V., Gottardi, C.: 3D integrated methodologies for the documentation and the virtual reconstruction of an archaeological site. Digit. Heritage **5**(1), 215–222 (2015)
8. Francesco, N., Fabio, R.: UAV for 3D mapping applications: a review. Appl. Geomat. **6**(1), 1–15 (2014)

9. Sarkar, A., Patel, K.A., Ram, R.G., Capoor, G.K.: Gesture control of drone using a motion controller. In: Industrial Informatics and Computer Systems (CIICS), vol. 2016(1), pp. 1–5 (2016)
10. Andaluz, V.H., Chicaiza, F.A., Meythaler, A., Rivas, D.R., Chuchico, C.P.: Construction of a quadcopter for autonomous and teleoperated navigation. In: Design of Circuits and Integrated Systems (DCIS), vol. 2015(1), pp. 1–7 (2015)
11. Andaluz, V.H., Quevedo, W.X., Chicaiza, F.A., Varela, J., Gallardo, C., Sánchez, J.S., Arteaga, O.: Transparency of a bilateral tele-operation scheme of a mobile manipulator robot. In: Augmented Reality, Virtual Reality, and Computer Graphics, vol. 9768, no. 1, pp. 228–245 (2016)
12. Kothari, M., Postlethwaite, I., Gu, D.-W.: UAV path following in windy urban environments. J. Intell. Robot. Syst. **74**(3–4), 1013–1028 (2014)
13. Kendoul, F., Yu, Z., Nonami, K.: Guidance and nonlinear control system for autonomous flight of minirotorcraft unmanned aerial vehicles. J. Field Robot. **27**(3), 311–334 (2010)
14. Cai, G., Chen, B.M., Dong, X., Lee, T.H.: Design and implementation of a robust and nonlinear flight control system for an unmanned helicopter. Mechatronics **21**(5), 803–820 (2011)

# Autonomous and Tele-Operated Navigation of Aerial Manipulator Robots in Digitalized Virtual Environments

Christian P. Carvajal[✉], María G. Méndez[✉], Diana C. Torres[✉],
Cochise Terán[✉], Oscar B. Arteaga[✉], and Víctor H. Andaluz[✉]

Universidad de Las Fuerzas Armadas ESPE, Latacunga, Ecuador
chriss2592@hotmail.com, {mgmendez,dtorres,hcteran,
obarteaga,vandaluz1}@espe.edu.ec

**Abstract.** This paper presents the implementation of a 3D virtual simulator that allows the analysis of the performance of different autonomous and tele-operated control strategies through the execution of service tasks by an aerial manipulator robot. The simulation environment is development through the digitalization of a real environment by means of 3D mapping with Drones that serves as a scenario to execute the tasks with a robot designed in CAD software. For robot-environment interaction, the Unity 3D graphics engine is used, which exchanges information with MATLAB to close the control loop and allow for feedback to compensate for the error. Finally, the results of the simulation, which validate the proposed control strategies, are presented and discussed.

**Keywords:** Environment digitalization · Service robotic · Aerial manipulators

## 1 Introduction

In recent years, the robotics has taken boom in different application fields, introducing sustainable solutions to solve problems within multiple areas as military, industry, medicine, among many areas, taking advantage of the new technologies that allow to optimize the intelligence and the mobility of the robotic prototypes [1, 2]. The services that present the different types of robots depend on how they are structured mechanically, presenting a wide variety of robotic systems as they are terrestrial, aquatic, spatial, air, among others; and simultaneously each of these using shaped systems of locomotion of wheels, of paws, wings, helices, type caterpillar, between other [3, 4]. In this way, the mobile robotics incorporates applications to give support to the human being, appending robots that allow execute tasks that require greater precision and time optimization within the industrial field [5]. The vast majority of these robot's work in structured environments and partially structured environments, with the purpose of accomplishing tasks of transport, navigation, handling and translation of objects from one place to another [3, 5]. Although a vehicle can reach physical objectives, the lack of a robotic arm can be a limiting factor to run more complex tasks and precision tasks. In order to fulfill these tasks, the robotic systems can incorporate arms to their mechanical structure [6].

© Springer International Publishing AG, part of Springer Nature 2018
L. T. De Paolis and P. Bourdot (Eds.): AVR 2018, LNCS 10851, pp. 496–515, 2018.
https://doi.org/10.1007/978-3-319-95282-6_36

The physical unification between an air vehicle and a set of robotic arms is commonly known as aerial manipulator (VMA), and can be simple (a single arm), dual (two arms) or multiple arms [7]. Given the versatility presented by this type of vehicles, different tasks such as welding, transport of long objects, manipulation of elements placed in heights. The tasks can be executed given by the amount of redundancy presented by the robotic system. Works as [8] present real applications of this type of robotics sets, posing a solution for the adjustment of valves located at a distance or to heights that a human operator cannot access. Also, applications oriented to the service robotics can be developed [10]. In this aspect, [9] presents the use of a simple aerial manipulator for Perching and Door-opening tasks, showing the capabilities that can have this kind of vehicles in difficult tasks to run with a terrestrial robot. Besides, the applications that can be run with this type of robot require robust controllers that unify the mobile part with the robotic arm [11]. Focuses on the design, modeling and control of a mobile prototype manipulator, proposing an innovative configuration in order to guide this vehicle to applications indoor. Jobs as these emphasize the need to incorporate advanced control strategies to this type of robotic systems, which may vary according to the type of method that one glides to use [12].

Control strategies that are used in aerial manipulators are commonly studied from a general perspective, using the kinematics that conform the robotic system configuration [13]. Depending on the type of control required, the whole robotic can be analyzed jointly or separately (robotic arm and Air Vehicle), where the points of interest are dependent on this type of analysis. An unmanned air vehicle with two arms can be analyzed cinematically as three different robots (UAV, the right arm and left arm), as a UAV and a pair of arms, or as a single system with the point of interest in the middle of the ends operational of each arm [13, 14]. The cinematic model depends directly on this analysis, which contains the features of movement of a vehicle that can be used both for simulation and experimentation. Commonly, controllers require simulators to validate the generation of responses from the control strategy, where by facility many of the times is used the mathematical software where develops the control system. However, own graphs limitations of the Mathematical Software impede any precise assessment of the implementation, forcing them to seek better alternatives to resolve these shortcomings [15].

A simulation alternative can be implemented across platforms for the development of video games, such as Unity, Unreal, cryEnGINE, highlighting to Unity 3D for various relevant characteristics. In spite of that Unity 3D is an engine of videogames, the facilities of connection with external software and import of external information makes it an attractive solution for engineering applications [16]. Compatibility with different formats, low latency of exchange of data in real time, the versatility to interact with other software, supports integrated for video cards, physics engines, and support for devices of virtual reality. Are the characteristics that make Unity a highly, scalable and useful engine for simulation [17, 18]. In this context, various virtual environments can be designed for simulation tests, either using elements of the graphics engine or 3D models designed in another software. However, many of the times the requirements of simulation pose have similar environments to the reality to determine visually the performance of the task. In this way, the import to the simulation should not be provided only with reconstructed three-dimensional models, but also reconstructions made by photography, taking into consideration that all models require a format compatible with Unity [18].

The inclusion of rebuilt environments on a video games platform help visually to evaluate the performance of controllers, as well as to understand the functioning of imported 3D models. In this aspect, works like [19, 20] and [20] pose reconstruction methods of real environments such as buildings, plots or archaeological sites. The literature indicates a large amount of works related to reconstruction based on image, where the capture methods vary from vision by satellite to the use of manned and unmanned aerial vehicles. The addition of environments reconstructed presents advantages at the moment of knowing the real environments where the implementation is to be carried out, where features such as potentially dangerous areas, structural obstacles, fauna and flora and uneven terrain. Can be identified. In this context, this article proposes the virtualization of real environments for the autonomous navigation and tele-operated in an aerial robot, with the purpose of creating an alternative to the experimental tests combining Virtual Reality with a CAD software and a mathematical software. The simulation of all these parameters in a virtual environment close to reality allows you to interact with the 3D model of an aerial robot, which runs the trajectory tracking for the evaluation process for the different schemes of autonomous control.

This work is divided into 5 sections, including the introduction. In Sect. 2, it presents the approach the problem, while Sect. 3 presents the diagram multilayer. The kinematic model and the development of control strategies are presented in Sect. 4. The results simulated obtained are presented in Sect. 5 and finally, in Sect. 6 presents the conclusions of the work.

## 2    Problem Formulation

To execute experimental tests in purpose to evaluate control algorithms to perform different tasks with an aerial manipulator robot it is indispensable to be provided with the physical prototype; considering the high inversion not only in acquiring the robot but also to cover needs for use, maintenance and acquisition of licenses for program it, of equal way one adds the inconvenience caused by meteorological conditions of the environment where the experimental tests are executed, i.e., speed of the wind, temperature, turbulence, rain, between other meteorological conditions; affecting in a significant way the tests with the robot; To the different limitations mentioned that is includes the fact that is experimenting with the robot, i.e., the prototype will be put to multiple tests in which the it risk its physical integrity and therefore its functioning during the experimental procedure. Taking into account the problematics that are generated when performing experimental tests, is seen feasible evaluate the control strategies in a simulator, the which provides of way visually the operation of the aerial manipulator, incorporating features and configurations own the robot to correctly simulate their actual behavior; allowing functionally analyzing the stability and robustness of different advanced control strategies for autonomous and/or tele-operated navigation tasks.

At present it makes use of simulators that allow to reproduce the behavior of various aerial robots, most of them targeting for the most of them focused for the pilots' training or tests of autonomous control, i.e., simulators ranging from simple systems of training to sophisticated systems that allow to simulate the automatic control of the robot aerial; in [21–23] is performed flight tests self-nomos a UAV, presenting results of behavior in a visual manner with the help of the pretender Flight Gear that incorporates a wide variety of models of ships to select. Similarly, there are aerial vehicles that integrate their own simulator, e.g., DJI, offers a unique experience by controlling in a 3D environment The Phantom or other prototypes of the company DJI, allowing to familiarize with the control knobs and the different applications that incorporates the commercial platform, the main requirement of the simulator is to have connected the prototype physically in the computer in order to run the simulation [24, 25]. On the other hand, there are software like Stage that simulates a large variety of mobile robots, sensors and objects environmental, taking as original purposes; *(i)* Allowing the rapid development of control algorithms which eventually commanding real robots; and *(ii)* allowing experiments of robots without access to hardware and without real environments [26].

The different existing simulators have their own limitations as they are not flexible in terms of the number of robots that can be integrated into the environment and make use of not real scenarios; limitations that must be taken into account to make a more robust evaluation of the different control strategies. Therefore, it is proposed to develop a 3D simulator that requires its own characteristics consuming real ambient meteorological data, such as temperature, wind speed, weather conditions, among other data; the simulation scenario will be a digitized environment using the 3D mapping method with drones obtaining a georeferenced DTM (Digital Terrain Model), providing an environment close to reality and with GPS data of the location of the mapped terrain. At the same time, the simulator allows to implement different advanced control strategies for an aerial manipulator, consisting of a rotary wing air vehicle and two robotic arms at the bottom of the platform, the robot will be modeled in a CAD software, considering all the appropriate configurations to resemble a real aerial manipulator.

## 3 Estructure System

In Fig. 1, the proposed scheme for the simulator's implementation is presented, which is developed under the UNITY 3D platform. The system consists of Environment Simulation, programming SCRIPTS to control each game object of the system, input devices, Output devices and external sources that help the development of the virtual simulator.

The *Environment of Simulation* contains 3D models whit allows to create the virtual simulation environment. The characteristics of the environment are assigned, such as weather, gravity, audio data and other physical properties that simulate a real environment. The environment incorporates an aerial manipulator designed to perform control tests for autonomous or tele-operated navigation tasks, where the task is

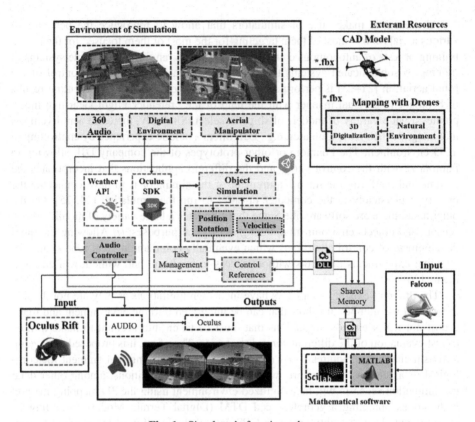

**Fig. 1.** Simulator's function scheme.

selected prior to the simulation within an interactive menu for the user. In addition, it allows to write the position and initial orientation in which the robot is placed.

The *External Resourses* are defined by 3D models: (i) Aerial manipulator developed in a CAD software with all the characteristics and appropriate configurations that a real aerial manipulator has and (ii) the 3D model of the terrain digitized by means of the 3D mapping technique with drones; achieving a simulation scenarios similar to the real and performing the control tests on it.

The set of *SCRIPTS* contains blocks of code which allow communication with input and output devices of the system. For the interaction with the virtual reality input device (OCULUS), the propietary library of the device (SDK) is used, making it possible to establish communication with the equipment in order to visually and aurally feedback the execution of the proposed task of the manipulator aerial. The climate data will be consumed from a Weather API, thus obtaining the status of the digitized terrain climate, to be incorporated in the simulation environment so that it influences the aerial manipulator control test; finally, the diagram contains SCRIPTS that allow the link with the mathematical software through the use a dynamic-link library (DLL) that generate a shared memory (SM) for the exchange of data between different software. By means of the SM the control actions are injected to the aerial manipulator and in the same way the position and rotation data of the robot is found, are read and later sent to the mathematical software, obtaining in this way the feedback of the simulation to compensate the control errors.

# 4 Virtual Simulator Environment Development

For the development of the application and its functionalities, 4 stages are defined as shown in Fig. 2. The stages of development are separated by: *(i)* 3D design of the aerial manipulator modeled from a CAD software, *(ii)* 3D digital model of the simulation environment, *(iii)* import of each 3D model and the respective programming to each game object that are port of the simulator and *(iv)* the control writing proposed for the aerial manipulator, which is done from Matlab mathematical software. All the layers are indispensable for the correct execution of the presented system. In this way, a simulator with sufficient characteristics to evaluate advanced control algorithms is developed.

## 4.1 3D Aerial Manipulator Design

The design of a computer or machine is done in a CAD software such as Solid-Works, which allows to create solid objects to be assembled allowing to obtain 3D models complete. Figure 3. presents the block diagram of the steps to obtain the final model of the aerial manipulator used for simulation in the virtual environment.

The design of the aerial manipulator is composed of an airborne platform and two robotic arms placed in the bottom of the main structure. The robot is previously modeled individually in SolidWorks, obtaining as a result a file of assemble *.sldasm. In accordance with the assembly, it is required to establish hierarchies of the aerial manipulator, including the number of items and restrictions of relative position of each part that makes up the robot. For the orientation and location of the parts of the model, points of reference are determined. Finally, the design is converted in a compatible model with the platform of UNITY 3D, using the software 3DS Max that allows to export the file obtained from SolidWorks to a file with the extension *.fbx.

### 4.1.1 Structural Analysis

The behavior of the structure of the aerial manipulator is modeled by the finite element method (FEM) [27], that allows to predict failures due to load conditions to which the design is subjected, showing the distribution of stresses in the material, stresses, allowable values of tensions, security factor, modulus of elasticity, tendency to deform, vibrate. The tasks necessary to perform the structural analysis are: *(i) Pre-process*, consists of the definition of geometry, generation of the mesh and assignment of properties to the materials. For the aerial manipulator, it is considered to be made up of carbon fiber Hexcel 3 K [28]; *(ii) structural analysis*, point and torque forces are applied, finally, *(iii) Post process*, in this analysis we observe the maximum and minimum values of the tension that the aerial manipulator supports, in order to avoid exceeding its elastic limit, static displacement, unit deformation and safety factor. The results of the post-process are indicated in Table 1.

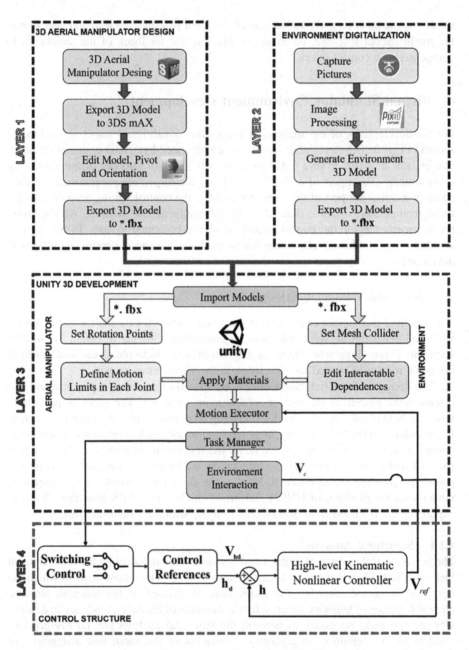

**Fig. 2.** Multilayer Diagram-Design of the 3D Simulator.

In the analysis, an applied force of 25 [N] and a moment of 5 [Nm] was considered; it is obtained as a result that the aerial manipulator does not have stresses that exceed the elastic limit, the maximum displacement value of the manipulator is 22.6 [cm],

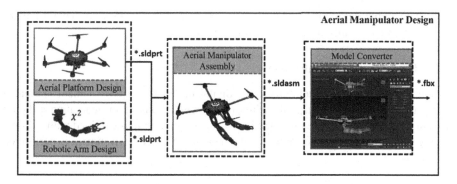

**Fig. 3.** Scheme of the design of the manipulator aerial 3D

**Table 1.** Result of structural analysis of the aerial manipulator

| Analysis Type | Aerial Manipulator | Results | Min. and Max. values |
|---|---|---|---|
| Nodal Tension (von MISES) | | | Max.Value 810390272 (N/m^2) Min Value 9.11 (N/m^2) |
| Static Displacement | | | Max.Value 226.31 mm Min Value 0 mm |
| Unitary Deformation | | | Max. Value 0.06834 Min Value 0 |
| Security Factory | | | Max. Value 263,472,256 Min Value 2.96 |

according to the deformation analysis it is determined that it does not have a unitary deformation and finally the Safety factor is constant over the entire surface.

## 4.2   Environment Digitalization

In the second stage of development, the digital model of the environment is created using the method of 3D mapping with drones, which consists in generating a digital terrain model (MDT) by means of the processing of photographs obtained with a drone. In Fig. 4, a block diagram of how the 3D mapping of a real environment is performed is shown.

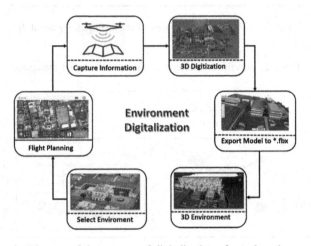

**Fig. 4.** Diagram of the process of digitalization of a real environment.

The digitalization of the environment starts for choosing the place and analyze it in such a way that is known the appropriate height to overfly with the drone and capture as many photos as possible of the place of interest, also consider conditions in which the terrain is suitable and without much presence of people, animals or other objects that affect the model. Finally, it is necessary take into account an appropriate hour in which a good photographic is captured without the presence of shadow of the environment of interest to map. For the lifting of photographic information, it is indispensable count on a drone that allows flight routes to be planned and incorporates in its physical part a camera with high resolution characteristics. Pix4D offers software and applications which facilitate the lifting and processing of information of a terrain, since it has a developed flight planning App for optimal mapping data with the drone (Pix4Dcapture) and desktop application to generate the 3D model from the information obtained by the UAV.

By means of the restored information of the terrain to be mapped, drone flight plans are set in the application as is shown in Fig. 5, The Smartphone application allows to zoom in on the site of interest and store the photographic images taken sequentially. The flight plans more used for 3D mapping are the Double Grid, Circular and Free Flight.

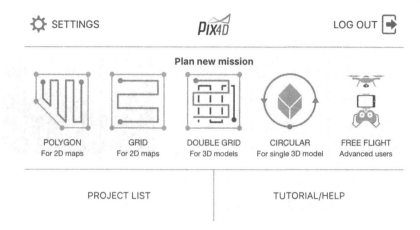

**Fig. 5.** Type of mission plans in PIx4D.

*Remark 1:* The "Double Grid" flight plan is used for the wide-land model in places where there is a large number of elevations or buildings. The "Circular" flight plans are combined combining flights with "Free Flights" to capture images of difficult places.

*Remark 2:* In consideration of the capture of photographs suitable for the 3D model, the angle of inclination of the camera must be adequate, thus achieving the total capturing of all details present in the terrain Figure 6.

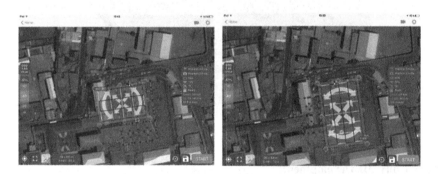

**Fig. 6.** Lifting photographic information with the drone.

Once is captured as many photos of the terrain, the images are processed in the software Pix4D, Fig. 6. In which all the images obtained with the drone are added. These images possess metadata, storing the referenced information of each photograph and the characteristic of the photo acquired through the flight. The processing of information takes time as it is responsible for processing each image and assemble the 3D model of the land (Fig. 7).

**Fig. 7.** Digital processing of the information raised in Pix4D.

With the digitized model, it is finally exported in *.fbx format, readable format for the UNITY 3D platform, the digitized terrain will represent the simulation environment of the aerial manipulator Fig. 8.

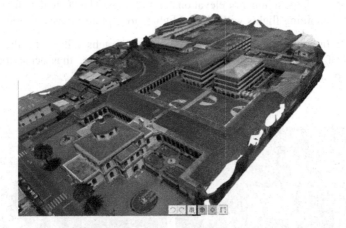

**Fig. 8.** 3D digital model of the terrain in format *.fbx.

### 4.3 Unity 3D Development

At the stage of the application development in Unity 3D, they are imported the 3D models that are part of the simulator. In the case of the aerial manipulator, the rotation points of each joint are placed and defines the minimum and maximum values of each part of the robot Fig. 9 can work are defined. For the creation of the scenario, the 3D model of the digitized terrain is imported, adding physical properties to be able to move and collide objects Fig. 10.

An operation interface is developed where the user selects the type of task to be performed with the aerial manipulator, sending the data of the selected task to Matlab in a shared way to carry out the control Fig. 11, in the same way the system allows to locate the manipulator to establish the initial conditions of the Robot.

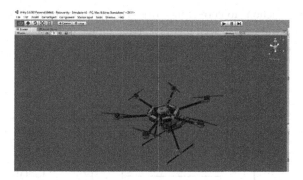

**Fig. 9.** Import model of the aerial manipulator to Unity 3D.

**Fig. 10.** Import of the digital terrain model to Unity 3D.

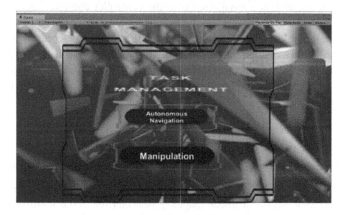

**Fig. 11.** Task management menu.

## 4.4 Control Structure

Control is designed under the Matlab software, allowing the programming of control algorithms. The control structure is feedback with the behavior of the aerial manipulator within the virtual environment. In the same way, the controller sends the respective control actions to correct the error. The control scheme proposed according to Fig. 12 in which it can be seen that depending on the task, Matlab will execute the appropriate control to comply with the user's order.

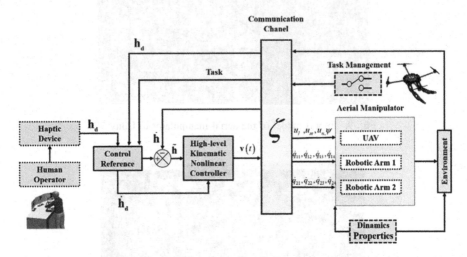

**Fig. 12.** Aerial manipulator control scheme for tele-operation and autonomous control.

The control stage is formulated in such a way that the operator can interact to control the robotic arms manually with a haptic device, through which direct reference commands are given to the controller to reach the object of interest with the aerial manipulator. If the task is a navigation one, the controller automatically generates the references so that the aerial manipulator can be positioned autonomously in the position desired by the operator. For the purpose of aerial manipulator control, the kinematic model is used which results in the location of the final effectors according to the configuration of the robotic arms and the location of the air vehicle (or its operational coordinates as functions of the generalized coordinates of the two robotic arms and the operational coordinates of the air vehicle), represented by:

$$\dot{\mathbf{h}}(t) = \mathbf{J}(\mathbf{q}_q, \mathbf{q}_{a1}, \mathbf{q}_{a2})\mathbf{v}(t) \tag{1}$$

where, $\dot{\mathbf{h}}(t)$ is the velocity vector of the final effectors represented by, $\mathbf{v} = [\mathbf{v}_q \mathbf{v}_{qa1} \mathbf{v}_{qa2}]^T$ is the mobility control vector of the mobile manipulator and $\mathbf{J}(\mathbf{q}_q, \mathbf{q}_{a1}, \mathbf{q}_{a2})$ is the Jacobin matrix that defines a linear mapping between the aerial manipulator velocity vector and the velocity vector of the final effectors. The kinematic model is composed of a set of twelve speeds represented in the spatial reference frame $\langle Q \rangle$. The movement of the airborne mobile manipulator is guided by the three linear speeds $u_l$, $u_m$ and $u_n$, y, and is defined in a spatial frame of reference and the angular velocity $\omega$, as shown in the Fig. 13.

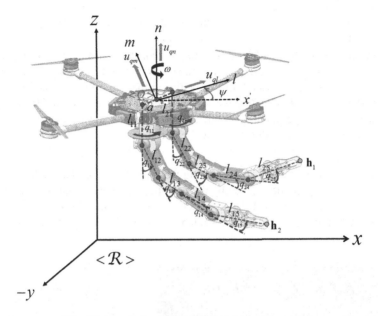

**Fig. 13.** Analysis of Aerial Manipulator Kinematics.

The kinematic model of the manipulator is defined as follows:

$$\begin{bmatrix} \dot{h}x_1 \\ \dot{h}y_1 \\ \dot{h}z_1 \\ \dot{h}x_2 \\ \dot{h}x_2 \\ \dot{h}x_2 \end{bmatrix} = [\mathbf{J}(\mathbf{q}, \psi)][ul\ um\ un\ \omega\ \dot{q}_{11}\ \dot{q}_{12}\ \dot{q}_{13}\ \dot{q}_{14}\ \dot{q}_{21}\ \dot{q}_{22}\ \dot{q}_{23}\ \dot{q}_{24}]^{\mathbf{T}} \tag{2}$$

where, $\mathbf{J}(\mathbf{q}) \in \Re^{mxn}$ con $m = 6$ y $n = 12$ represents the Jacobian matrix that defines a linear mapping between the velocity vector of the mobile aerial manipulator $\mathbf{v} \in \Re^n$ where $\mathbf{v} = [u_l\ u_m\ u_n\ \psi\ \dot{q}_{11}\ \dot{q}_{12}\ \dot{q}_{13}\ \dot{q}_{14}\ \ \dot{q}_{21}\ \ \dot{q}_{22}\ \ \dot{q}_{23}\ \ \dot{q}_{24}\ ]^T$ and the speed vector of the operating end $\dot{\mathbf{h}} \in \Re^m$ where $\dot{\mathbf{h}} = \begin{bmatrix} \dot{h}_{x1} & \dot{h}_{y1} & \dot{h}_{z1} & \dot{h}_{x2} & \dot{h}_{y2} & \dot{h}_{z2} \end{bmatrix}^T$.

## 5 Experimentals Results

To carry out the simulation tests, it is necessary to implement a control law based on the kinematics (2) of the aerial manipulator described in the previous section, which is defined as:

$$\mathbf{v} = \mathbf{J}^{\#} \left( \dot{\mathbf{h}}_{\mathbf{d}} + \mathbf{K_1} \tanh\left(\mathbf{K_2}\, \tilde{\mathbf{h}}\right) \right) \tag{3}$$

where $\dot{h}_d$ is the reference velocity input of the aerial mobile manipulator for the controller; $\mathbf{J}^{\#}$ is the matrix of pseudoinverse kinematics for the aerial mobile manipulator; while that $\mathbf{K}_1 > 0$ and $\mathbf{K}_2 > 0$ area gain constants of the controller that weigh the control error respect to the inertial frame $<R>$; and the **tanh**(.) represents the function saturation of maniobrability velocities in the aerial mobile manipulator [14].

With the purpose of validating the performance of the simulator and the control law implemented, two experiments are carried out, in which the behaviour of the aerial manipulator is observed within the virtual environment.

## Experiment 1:

The first experiment consists of designating that the aerial manipulator positions itself autonomously at a point designated by the operator, enters the simulator waiting for all the necessary data to be loaded and selects what we want following the developed menu of the simulator including the Matlab part to establish the data link (Fig. 14).

a)    Start of the virtual simulator                    b) Data management in Matlab

**Fig. 14.** Beginning of the communication between Matlab and Unity.

Once the communication with Matlab is loaded and established, the aerial manipulator is selected in the simulator menu Fig.15.

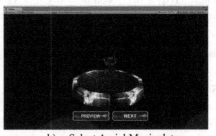

a)    Simulator Menu.                          b)    Select Aerial Manipulator.

**Fig. 15.** Data loading from the simulator and the aerial manipulator.

With the selection of the aerial manipulator for experiment 1, proceed to the "Task Management" menu and select the Autonomous Navigation Task Fig. 16, establishing the initial conditions of the aerial manipulator and the desired position to be reached autonomously Fig. 17.

**Fig. 16.** Selection autonomous navigation in task management menu.

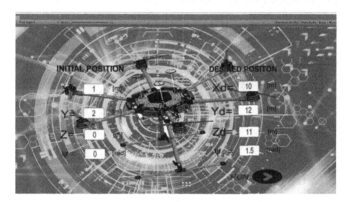

**Fig. 17.** Initial conditions of the aerial manipulator and the desired positions.

The data entered in the simulator are received in Matlab and the proposed task is executed, in Fig. 18, indicating the stroboscopic movement of the aerial manipulator movement within the virtual environment, observing the speeds applied and the positions of the current operating ends of the aerial manipulator.

**Experiment 2:**
The second experiment consists of the execution of a teleoperation task to transport an object from one place to another, using haptic devices to control the operating end of each robotic arm and at the same time command the mobility of the aerial platform. In the Task Management menu, we choose the Manipulation option and the user proceeds

**Fig. 18.** Autonomous control operation for positioning the aerial manipulator in the virtual environment.

to tele-operate the robot, managing to hold the object with the operating ends of the manipulator as shown in Fig. 19.

When the operator is able to hold the desired object with the operating ends, he proceeds to transport it, controlling in this case the speeds towards the aerial platform to move to the point desired by the user Fig. 20.

a)    Handling of an object.

b) User teleoperating the Aerial manipulator.

**Fig. 19.** Teleoperation of the aerial manipulator to transport an object.

a)    Transport of object with the aerial manipulator.

b) Handling of the aerial manipulator with the Haptic device.

**Fig. 20.** Transport of an object through control with a Haptic device.

## 6    Conclusions

To make the 3D simulator of an aerial vehicle and two robotic arms, several 3D design tools were linked, in the digital terrain model Unity is used in conjunction with a CAD software obtaining an environment very close to the real one. In the handling of the manipulator, a haptic device is used which simulates the transport and handling of objects with the different control strategies verifying the ability to respond to disturbances as meteorological data from a real environment.

**Acknowledgements.** The authors would like to thanks to the Corporación Ecuatoriana para el Desarrollo de la Investigación y Academia–CEDIA for the financing given to research, development, and innovation, through the CEPRA projects, especially the project CEPRA-XI-2017-06; *Control Coordinado Multi-operador aplicado a un robot Manipulador Aéreo;* also to Universidad de las Fuerzas Armadas ESPE, Universidad Técnica de Ambato, Escuela Superior Politécnica de Chimborazo, and Universidad Nacional de Chimborazo, and Grupo de Investigación en Automatización, Robótica y Sistemas Inteligentes, GI-ARSI, for the support to develop this work.

# References

1. Andaluz, Víctor H., et al.: Robust control with dynamic compensation for human-wheelchair system. In: Zhang, X., Liu, H., Chen, Z., Wang, N. (eds.) ICIRA 2014. LNCS (LNAI), vol. 8917, pp. 376–389. Springer, Cham (2014). https://doi.org/10.1007/978-3-319-13966-1_37
2. Jayawardena, C., Kuo., Unger, I., Igic, A., Wong, R., Watson, C., Stafford, R., Broadbent, E., Tiwari, P., Warren, J., Sohn, J., MacDonald, B.: Deployment of a service robot to help older people. In: IEEE/RSJ International Conference on Intelligent Robots and Systems (2010)
3. Andaluz, Víctor H., Ortiz, Jessica S., Sanchéz, Jorge S.: Bilateral control of a robotic arm through brain signals. In: De Paolis, L.T., Mongelli, A. (eds.) AVR 2015. LNCS, vol. 9254, pp. 355–368. Springer, Cham (2015). https://doi.org/10.1007/978-3-319-22888-4_26
4. Doriya, R., Chakraborty, P., Nandi, G.: Robotic services in cloud computing paradigm. In: 2012 International Symposium on Cloud and Services Computing (2012)
5. Pillajo, C.: Calculation of SCARA manipulator optimal path subject to constraints. In: II International Congress of Engineering Mechatronics and Automation (2013)
6. Naldi, R., Gentili, L., Marconi, L.: Modeling and control of the interaction between flying robots and the environment. IFAC Proc. Vol. 43(14), 975–980 (2010)
7. Fumagalli, M., Naldi, R., Macchelli, A., Forte, F., Keemink, A., Stramigioli, S., Carloni, R., Marconi, L.: Developing an aerial manipulator prototype: physical interaction with the environment. IEEE Robot. Autom. Mag. 21(3), 41–50 (2014)
8. Orsag, M., Korpela, C., Bogdan, S.: Valve turning using a dual-arm aerial manipulator. In: Unmanned Aircraft Systems (ICUAS), vol. 2014(1), pp. 1–7 (2014)
9. Tsukagoshi, H., Watanabe, M., Hamada, T., Ashlih, D., Iizuka, R.: Aerial manipulator with perching and door-opening capability. Robot. Autom. (ICRA) 2015(1), 4663–4668 (2015)
10. Marconi, L., Basile, F., Caprari, G., Carloni, R., Chiacchio, P., Hurzeler, C., Lippiello, V., Naldi, R., Nikolic, J., Siciliano, B., Stramigioli, S., Zwicker, E.: Aerial service robotics: the AIRobots perspective. In: 2nd International Conference on Applied Robotics for the Power Industry CARPI (2012)
11. Fumagalli, M., Naldi, R., Macchelli, A., Forte, F., Keemink, A.Q., Stramigioli, S., Carloni, R., Marconi, L.: Developing an aerial manipulator prototype: physical interaction with the environment. IEEE Robot. Autom. Mag. 21(3), 41–50 (2014)
12. Albers, A., Trautmann, S., Howard, T., Nguyen, T.A., Frietsch, M., Sauter, C.: Semi-autonomous flying robot for physical interaction with environment. In: IEEE Conference on Robotics, Automation and Mechatronics (2010)
13. Guerrero-Sanchez, M., Abaunza, H., Castillo, P., Lozano, R., Garcia-Beltran, C., Rodriguez-Palacios, A.: Passivity-based control for a micro air vehicle using unit quaternions. Appl. Sci. 7(1), 13 (2016)
14. Ortiz, Jessica S., et al.: Modeling and kinematic nonlinear control of aerial mobile manipulators. In: Zeghloul, S., Romdhane, L., Laribi, M.A. (eds.) Computational Kinematics. MMS, vol. 50, pp. 87–95. Springer, Cham (2018). https://doi.org/10.1007/978-3-319-60867-9_11
15. Andaluz, Víctor H., et al.: Modeling and control of a wheelchair considering center of mass lateral displacements. In: Liu, H., Kubota, N., Zhu, X., Dillmann, R., Zhou, D. (eds.) ICIRA 2015. LNCS (LNAI), vol. 9246, pp. 254–270. Springer, Cham (2015). https://doi.org/10.1007/978-3-319-22873-0_23
16. Wang, S., Mao, Z., Zeng, C., Gong, H., Li, S., Chen, B.: A new method of virtual reality based on Unity3D. In: 8th International Conference on Geoinformatics (2010)

17. Oliveira, M., Pereira, N., Oliveira, E., Almeida, J. E., Rossetti, R.J.: A multi-player approach in serious games: testing pedestrian fire evacuation scenarios. In: Oporto, DSIE15, January 2008
18. Indraprastha, A., Shinozaki, M.: The investigation on using Unity3D game engine in urban de-signstudy. J. ICT Res. Appl. 3(1), 1–18 (2009)
19. Geiger, A., Ziegler, J., Stiller, C.: StereoScan: dense 3d reconstruction in real-time. In: Intelligent Vehicles Symposium (IV), vol. 2011(1), pp. 1–6 (2011)
20. Flores, D.A., Saito, C., Paredes, J.A., Trujillano, F.: Aerial photography for 3D reconstruction in the Peruvian Highlands through a fixed-wing UAV system. In: Mechatronics (ICM), vol. 2017(1), pp. 1–7 (2017)
21. Kurnaz, S., Cetin, O., Kaynak, O.: Adaptive neuro-fuzzy inference system based autonomous flight control of unmanned air vehicles (2018)
22. Sorton, E., Hammaker, S.: simulated flight testing of an autonomous unmanned aerial vehicle using FlightGear (2018)
23. Kurnaz, S., Cetin, O., Kaynak, O.: Fuzzy logic based approach to design of flight control and navigation tasks for autonomous unmanned aerial vehicles. J. Intell. Robot. Syst. 54, 229–244 (2018)
24. Psirofonia, P., Samaritakis, V., Eliopoulos, P., Potamitis, I.: Use of Unmanned Aerial Vehicles for Agricultural Applications with Emphasis on Crop Protection: Three Novel Case - studies (2018)
25. Trujano, G.B.R.R.F., Chan, B., Beams, G., Rivera, R.: Security Analysis of DJI Phantom 3Standard (2016)
26. Gerkey, B.P., Vaughan, R.T., Howard, A.: Tools for multi-robot and distributed sensor systems. In: Proceedings of the International Conference on Advanced Robotics (ICAR 2003), Coimbra, Portugal, pp. 317–323, 30 June–3 July 2003
27. Figueroa, R., Müller-Karger, C.: Effort analysis by the finite element method in the artificial foot design process. In: IV Latin American Congress on Biomedical Engineering 2007, Bioengineering Solutions for Latin America Health, pp. 732–735 (2007)
28. Xu, Y., Hoa, S.: Mechanical properties of carbon fiber reinforced epoxy/clay nanocompos-ites. Compos. Sci. Technol. 68(3–4), 854–861 (2008)

# Virtual Training for Industrial Automation Processes Through Pneumatic Controls

Jessica S. Ortiz[1]([☒]), Jorge S. Sánchez[1]([☒]), Paola M. Velasco[1]([☒]),
Washington X. Quevedo[1]([☒]), Christian P. Carvajal[1]([☒]),
Vicente Morales[2]([☒]), Paulina X. Ayala[2]([☒]),
and Víctor H. Andaluz[1]([☒])

[1] Univeridad de las Fuerzas Armadas ESPE, Sangolquí, Ecuador
{jsortiz,jssanchez,pmvelasco,wjquevedo,
vhandaluz1}@espe.edu.ec, chriss2592@hotmail.com
[2] Universidad Técnica de Ambato, Ambato, Ecuador
jvmorales99@gmail.com, ep.ayala@uta.edu.ec

**Abstract.** This work presents the implementation of virtual environments oriented to managing pneumatic controls applied to industrial processes in order to strengthen training and teaching-learning processes. The implemented application enables the multi-user immersion and interaction with the aim to accomplish predefined tasks to be developed within lab environments and virtualized sceneries for industrial processes. Obtained results show how easy it is to interact with the proposed multi-user environment.

**Keywords:** Virtual Reality · Training · Capacitation · Industrial processes
Multi-user

## 1 Introduction

The technological age of society has made changes in several areas such as industry, health, training, education. A world which has been inserted in daily life has been generated, transforming habits, customs, and personal preferences [1, 2]. Education is not far from these constant changes which have created a notorious difference between traditional education and modern education. The traditional approach was focused on transmitting knowledge unilaterally through a teaching process subject to didactic and pedagogical methodology limitations [3]. This approach is replaced by modern education which allows transmitting knowledge bilaterally through a teaching-learning process. In this approach, the teacher-student interaction is performed in an active way through modern pedagogical tools [4, 5].

The implementation of Information and Communication Technologies, ICTs, complement and transform education through a group of techniques, tools, and advanced devices, which allow the student to access, generate, and transmit information and knowledge [6]. The implementation of ICTs has developed applications such as interactive rooms, virtual labs, simulators, and more. These apps let innovation processes to be oriented toward several environments in order to promote building more dynamic and interactive learning spaces [7–9]. In recent years, education has implemented Virtual Reality, VR, and Augmented Reality, AR, applications, with the

© Springer International Publishing AG, part of Springer Nature 2018
L. T. De Paolis and P. Bourdot (Eds.): AVR 2018, LNCS 10851, pp. 516–532, 2018.
https://doi.org/10.1007/978-3-319-95282-6_37

aim of introducing students to immersive and multi-sensorial environments, in which students interact within a virtual environment that stimulates the teaching-learning process, allowing the teacher to complement knowledge given [10–12].

VR allows learning in different knowledge areas to be complemented, such as medicine, marketing, and engineering, thus enabling the future professional to interact with real environments through simulators [13, 14]. On the engineering field, applications which are focused in automatization, control and instrumentation, are presented. Here, theoretical knowledge is complemented with practice through the manipulation and control of equipment and electronic devices [12–14]. The development of emulators for industrial processes allows the student to complete training by interacting with equipment and processes in the industry, allow the student to know, analyze, and implement real processes within virtual environments. Therefore, the interaction and immersion in 3D animation, standardized regulations management, and communication with industrial teams, is important [15–17].

Engineering majors must be closely related to the latest technological tendencies applied to the industry. However, the existing budget limitations in the universities stop the implementation of laboratories for each area of studies. That is why, taking advantage of Virtual Reality sources on this work, the implementation of a VR environments with pneumatic controls is proposed. This application has two parts: *(i) Virtual Lab* oriented to developing practices in subjects for industrial control, pneumatic and hydraulic matters, where it is possible to manipulate each lab component and carry out lab classes guided by the teacher, who can also work with multi-user feature as an advantage. Then, it is possible to interact with all lab users as an essential part in the teaching-learning process, and *(ii) Industrial environment*, where VR industrial environments are developed; this make it easy to include the student into a virtual environment where it is possible to identify the process, thus, the student has a work experience in an industrial facility, following regulations and safety procedures, and has the possibility to manipulate and operate machinery during the process. In addition, the student can all acquired knowledge for solving a real problem that may occur in the industrial plant.

This article is divided into 5 Sections including the Introduction. Section 2 describes the system description of the working environment; Sect. 3 describes the multi-layer scheme of the virtual environment development application. Section 4 shows the methodology and discussion that validate the proposal; and finally, the conclusions are detailed in Sect. 5.

## 2 System Description

Figure 1 illustrates the description of the developed VR application. It represents the interaction of four main blocks: Scene, Inputs, Scripts, and Outputs. Their interaction generate a didactic learning environment and practices on the pneumatic controls field.

In the *Scene Block* is the Home, Laboratory and Tannery environment *(i) Home* contains the selection of scenes and certain additional configurations available to the user; *(ii) Laboratory*, preestablished practices with pneumatic controls are established, while in; *(iii) Tannery*, specific tasks related to maintenance, repairing and/or installation

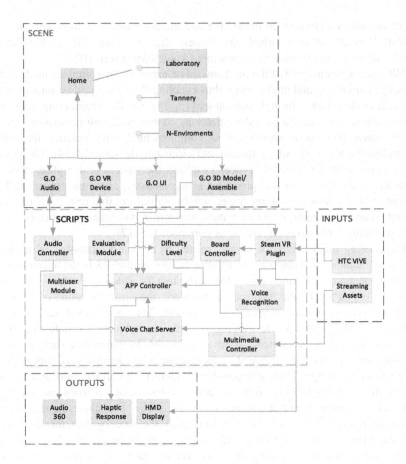

**Fig. 1.** System description diagram

of pneumatic control systems are conducted, an analog practice compared to Laboratory. The system is scalable since it allows to add different scenes according to required needs. The elements which participate in each scene can be generalized through Audio Game Objects, VR Device, UI, and 3D Model/Assemble. All these respond to specific control modules, depending on the work objective that each scene has.

In the *Scripts block*, a group of interconnected control modules can be found. These modules enable to define the behavior of each developed environment. The SteamVR Plugin and Multimedia Controller manage the HTC VIVE and Streaming Assets inputs respectively. Meanwhile, the SteamVR Plugin gathers data from the sensors of HTC VIVE Glasses in order to be used by the APP Controller as an input method, and at the same time, reflected in the G.O VR Device. In order to detect the user's voice commands, a connection with the Voice Recognition module is established, which connects to the Voice Chat Server for transmitting audio to every user within the environment. Using this module requires a simultaneous multi-user connection when sending and receiving environment data. The connection is provided by the Multiuser Module.

Several modules have been developed for scenes to work, such as (i) the Evaluation Module in charge of establishing the user's score after performing a task in the selected environment, and (ii) Difficulty Level which contains the programing for the two difficulty levels in the system. The Board Controller has an additional functionality through the HTC VIVE Controller which is allowing the user to write on a virtual board and project audio visual content through the Multimedia Controller module. The Audio Controller module manages audio sources generated between the object interaction and user's communication. Data is sent to G.O Audio, and as Audio 360 when it is released.

The ideal HTC VIVE Glasses for the current application can be found in the *Inputs Block* since their work space requires 12 m$^2$ and has a tracking system for the HTC VIVE Controllers. The Streaming Assets are also present as external audiovisual resources regarding the application. They are available locally or in the network.

In the *Output Blocks*, a relation among components takes place, such as Audio 360, Haptic Response, HMD Display, which come from HTC VIVE glasses, the hardware used. The Audio 360 module reproduces environment sounds, Haptic Response provides a haptic feedback when interacting with an object, and HMD Display represents images captured by the camera according to the user's interaction within the environment.

## 3  System Development

To conduct an industrial practice or experience within a virtual environment, the physical-technical features must be as real as possible, for instance, size, shape, and functionality of the elements which interact under a specific practice. This way, the user can be provided with the required immersion for the development of a specific task. With this premise, Fig. 2 shows the elaboration and implementation sequence for a virtual lab. This sequence is divided in four stages.

In the *first layer*, modeling elements and objects is considered, which is developed through: (i) 3D design; it is necessary to design in 3D each system element and object according to the lab to be implemented (valves, resistors, capacitor, pistons, engines, pumps, among others). For the modeling, a design software supported by the computer (CAD) is used; the modeling makes it possible to analyze the physical characteristics (size, shape, texture, among others) of each element and device. There are tools such as SolidWorks, Autodesk Inventor, AutoCAD, among others, which allow the user to design the necessary elements to conduct a practice, and (ii) Mechanical Interrelations; this stage considers position and movement transmission interrelations of each object in the virtual environment. The coordinated interaction between two or more objects participating in a specific task will depend on these interrelations.

On the *second layer*, work is done on 3D models developed in the previous stage. The following aspects are considered in this stage: *(i)* 3D features edition; in this stage, the system axis to work with are established as a reference to new objects. Modeling software is used in this phase such as 3DSMAX or Blender. Device parts are distinguished; each element is treated differently since pieces are static elements which provide no response but are present during the practice, and devices which are dynamic

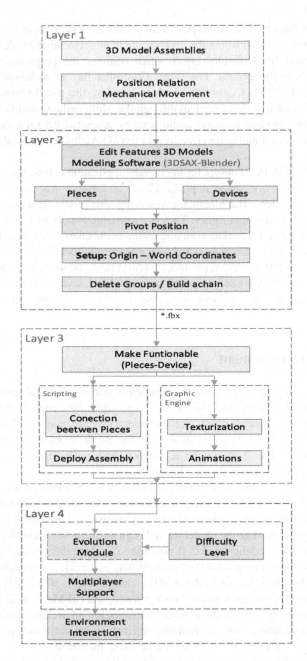

**Fig. 2.** Component interrelation diagram

elements that respond to input stimuli and provide visual or auditive output response; *(ii)* Pivot set-up; the individual pivot point for each piece and device is set. This point is generally located outside the object. Therefore, it is convenient to place this point in each object's geometrical center, so they can rotate or turn around their own axis; *(iii)* Origin placement; the global reference system is determined in this stage. In addition, a reference to the local coordinates system of each object in respect to the global coordinates system is made, as part of the good practices in editing 3D models. Finally, this layer considers; *(iv)* Groups deletion; there are three ways to group objects to be exported: blocks, groups and chains (hierarchies). By default, files are exported in blocks. To develop this application, files are exported in chains since hierarchies, and movement transmission of pieces and devices are kept. These files are exported with the *.fbx. extension.

For models to be functional, Scripting and Graphic Engine tools are used. Thereby, the *third layer* has been subdivided into two subsections (a) Scripting, where the following are developed: (a.1) Connection scripts; a code is implemented for objects to be able to connect and interact with each other, and physical principles which rule the response of each object are implemented; (a.2) Deploy Assembly, this process allows observing the behavior and responses of objects connected to each other. The second subsection considers layer (b) Graphics Engine in which the following stages are considered: (b.1) Texturization where color and realism is given to elements and objects so they behave as real ones; and finally (b.2) Animation in which dynamic elements get animated so as to display certain variation on the interaction among objects.

The *fourth layer* consists of assessment stages and multi-user interaction, where the following is considered: (i) Assessment module where the functioning assessment algorithm for a specific process or practice is implemented, considering different difficulty levels in order for every process or practice to be enrich the teaching-learning process with experiences; and (ii) Multiplayer support which implements the module for each user to make use of the previously developed blocks. This module allows users to interact with each other within the same environment.

## 4 Methodology and Discussion

This section describes the performance of the 3D virtual application developed, which considers two environments that allow the interaction and immersion of the user in order to strengthen the teaching-learning process in the area of engineering, specifically in pneumatic controls. The developed environments can be selected by the user according to the level of learning, see Fig. 3.

Figure 4 shows the requirement for the input of student personal information in order to keep a record of access to the virtual environment and to identify the type and manner of compliance with the activities planned by the teacher in the implemented work environments.

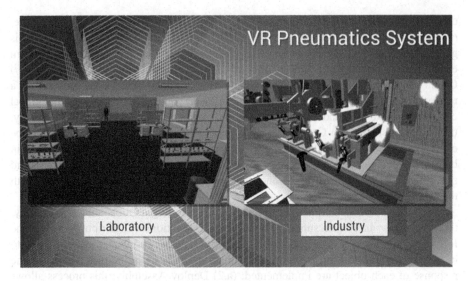

**Fig. 3.** Working environment selection

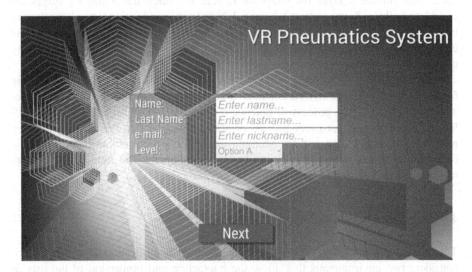

**Fig. 4.** Entering personal information

A. **Virtual Laboratory** oriented to the development of guided laboratory classes in order to recognize, manipulate and control the different equipment-materials related to the area of pneumatic controls. Figure 5 shows the scenario developed.

The stage is equipped with materials found in real laboratories, with a wide variety of single-acting actuators, double-acting actuators, regulating filters, pressure gauges, limit switches, exhaust valves, pushbutton valves, simultaneity valves, compressors,

**Fig. 5.** Virtual laboratory scenario

festo work tables, as illustrated in Fig. 6, so that students can assemble different pneumatic circuits without any limitation of equipment or materials.

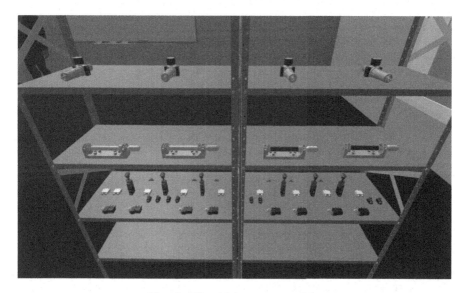

**Fig. 6.** Virtual laboratory materials

Figure 7 illustrates the multi-user interaction, which aims to enable several users (teachers and students) to interact in the same environment.

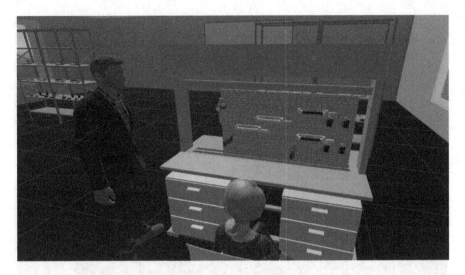

**Fig. 7.** Multi-user interaction

The task is selected and displayed by the teacher to the students through a virtual pneumatic diagram as illustrated in Fig. 8, which shows the necessary analog virtual machines and construction instructions, allowing the student to follow a series of steps to complete the task correctly. The diagram shows a drive sequence A+B+A–B–.

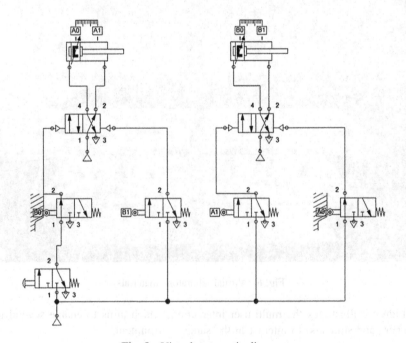

**Fig. 8.** Virtual pneumatic diagram

The level of difficulty of the system will increase according to the teacher's instructions or due to the student's performance in the construction of pneumatic diagrams, in initial levels the system will indicate the type and location of the elements as shown in Fig. 9; and as the level of difficulty increases the indications of help will decrease until it disappears allowing the student to construct the pneumatic diagrams completely alone.

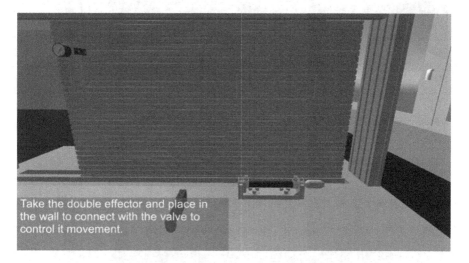

**Fig. 9.** Visual and textual help at difficulty levels

Once the construction of the pneumatic circuit is finished, the process of DEPLOY is started, which allows to check the correct functioning of the circuit, i.e., if the circuit assembly is in good working order, the animation of valves, pistons and other elements simulating the air flow will be observed as shown in Fig. 10a; if the circuit assembly is incorrect an error message will be displayed, illustrated in Fig. 10b.

The system allows the teacher to supervise the work done by each student from their respective module using locomotion techniques such as tele-transportation (see Fig. 11a), and also allows bilateral communication with the student via voice chat as illustrated in Fig. 11b.

The Audio 360 system implemented allows listening to sound effects such as reverberation, echo, distortion, among others, which is generated when the audio source is far from the audio Listener, which makes the experience is immersive and intuitive for the exchange of information by voice. In addition, the system includes a virtual whiteboard, where the teacher through a virtual marker can make pneumatic diagrams, explain different methodologies or techniques, allowing the teacher to interact with the student without restrictions of the system, e.g., generate a pneumatic

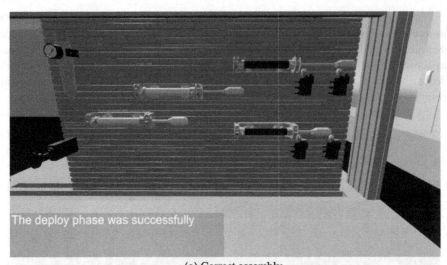

The deploy phase was successfully

(a) Correct assembly

The deploy phase was not successfully, because you need to place 1 end stroke switch in the red field

(b) Incorrect assembly

**Fig. 10.** Checking with DEPLOY (Color figure online)

diagram in order to evaluate the student as shown in Fig. 12a. The same whiteboard is used as a projection screen for multimedia resources hosted on the web or locally. In the first interaction, a YouTube video is presented, showing the safety instructions for the entry and use of the laboratory (see Fig. 12b).

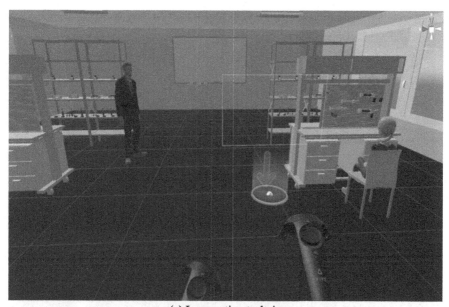

(a) Locomotion technique

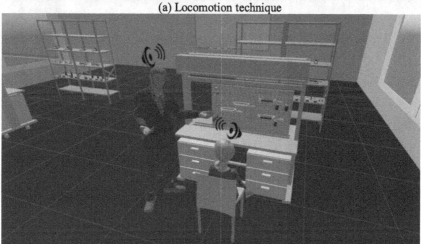

(b) Chat of voice

**Fig. 11.** Teacher supervision

B. *Industrial Environment,* an industrial environment was developed oriented to the tanning of animal skins for the manufacture of clothing. The main objective of the application is to familiarize the student with real industry environments, making it easier for the student to immerse and interact in work environments where it is possible to identify the process to be controlled, in this way the student acquires a work experience, following safety rules and procedures, see Fig. 13.

(a)   Teacher Interaction

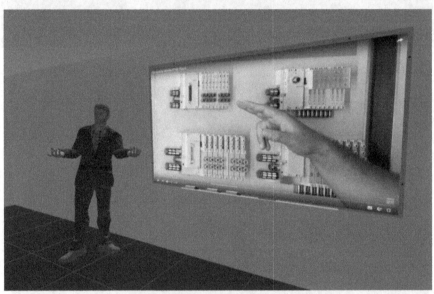

(b) Projection of multimedia resources

**Fig. 12.**  Virtual whiteboard

The virtual industrial process illustrated in Fig. 14, allows the student to become familiar with the handling and operation of tanning process machinery, applying knowledge acquired in the area of pneumatic controls to the solution of real problems that may arise in the industrial plant. The task performed in the industrial environment

**Fig. 13.** Tanning process of animal skins

**Fig. 14.** Task in industrial environment

is like to that performed in the laboratory, but industrial elements are used and implemented in complex systems. Inside the industrial plant, multiple machines are used to finish the leather, one of them is the pneumatic ironing machine that removes wrinkles or imperfections from the leather, its function is based on pneumatic pistons which execute a control sequence based on the temperature, this is opened or closed flattening the leather and heating to the desired temperature.

To complete the task, proceed as follows: *(a) Step 1*, the user must place the safety elements and equip himself with the work tools (see Fig. 15a); *(b) Step 2*, locate the work area in order to suspend the process where the intervention will be performed (see Fig. 15b); *(c) Step 3*, proceed to assemble the parts according to the diagram with the specific tools (see Fig. 15b). Figure 15c; *(d) Step 4*, review the implementation and check that there are no missing or excess elements see Fig. 15d; *(e) Step 5,* activate the machinery and verify the correct operation of the implementation and the synchronization with the system Fig. 15e; *(f) Step 6*, clean the work area and consider the finished task see Fig. 15f.

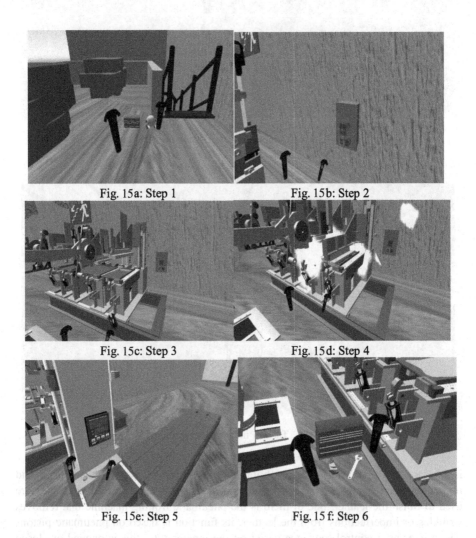

Fig. 15a: Step 1          Fig. 15b: Step 2

Fig. 15c: Step 3          Fig. 15d: Step 4

Fig. 15e: Step 5          Fig. 15 f: Step 6

**Fig. 15.** Process step

# 5  Conclusions

This work developed a Virtual Reality application in order to improve training and teaching-learning processes on the industrial procedures management field, specifically pneumatic controllers. The virtual app considers: *(i) Virtual Lab*, in which users take guided lab classes in order to manipulate and control simple pneumatic controllers' procedures, while in *(ii) Industrial Environment* allows users to become familiar with real environments in which they must develop their skills and abilities within real environments.

**Acknowledgement.** The authors would like to thanks to the Corporación Ecuatoriana para el Desarrollo de la Investigación y Academia – CEDIA for the financing given to research, development, and innovation, through the CEPRA projects, especially the project CEPRA-XI-2017-06; Control Coordinado Multi-operador aplicado a un robot Manipulador Aéreo; also to Universidad de las Fuerzas Armadas ESPE, Universidad Técnica de Ambato, Escuela Superior Politécnica de Chimborazo, and Universidad Nacional de Chimborazo, and Grupo de Investigación en Automatización, Robótica y Sistemas Inteligentes, GIARSI, for the support to develop this paper.

# References

1. Bakir, N.: Technology and teacher education: a brief glimpse of the research and practice that have shaped the field. TechTrends **60**(1), 21–29 (2016)
2. Holland, J., Holland, J.: Implications of shifting technology in education. TechTrends **58**, 16–25 (2014)
3. Zovko, M.E., John, D.: Humanism vs. competency: traditional and contemporary models of education, pp. 1–11 (2017)
4. Kang-Ning, Z., Shi-Min, S., Hai, Y.: College teaching quality evaluation based on system dynamics model. In: MATEC Web of Conferences, vol. 61 (2016)
5. Boekaerts, M.: Engagement as an inherent aspect of the learning process. Learn. Instr. **43**, 76–83 (2016)
6. Park, D., Dosoon, K., Changyu, H.: NCS academic achievement and learning transfer ARCS motivation theory in ICT in the field of environmental education through interactive and immersive learning. J. Korea Soc. Digit. Ind. Inf. Manag. **11**(3), 179–200 (2015)
7. Majumdar, S.: Emerging trends in ICT for education & training. Gen. Asia Pacific Reg. IVETA (2015)
8. Kaware, S.S., Sunil, K.S.: ICT application in education: an overview. Int. J. Multidiscip. Approach Stud. **2**(1), 25–32 (2015)
9. Mihai, A., Andronie, M.: Information and communication technologies (ICT) used for education and training. Contemp. Read. Law Soc. Justice **6**(1), 378 (2014)
10. Freina, L., Ott, M.: A literature review on immersive virtual reality in education: state of the art and perspectives. In: The International Scientific Conference eLearning and Software for Education, vol. 1. "Carol I" National Defence University (2015)
11. Burkle, M., Michael M.: Virtual learning: videogames and virtual reality in education. In: Virtual and Augmented Reality: Concepts, Methodologies, Tools, and Applications, pp. 1067–1087. IGI Global (2018)

12. Andaluz, V.H., Castillo-Carrión, D., Miranda, R.J., Alulema, J.C.: Virtual reality applied to industrial processes. In: De Paolis, L.T., Bourdot, P., Mongelli, A. (eds.) AVR 2017. LNCS, vol. 10324, pp. 59–74. Springer, Cham (2017). https://doi.org/10.1007/978-3-319-60922-5_5

13. Gavish, N., Gutiérrez, T., Webel, S., Rodríguez, J., Peveri, M., Bockholt, U., Tecchia, F.: Evaluating virtual reality and augmented reality training for industrial maintenance and assembly tasks. Interact. Learn. Environ. 23(6), 778–798 (2015)

14. Ortiz, J.S., Sánchez, J.S., Velasco, P.M., Sánchez, C.R., Quevedo, W.X., Zambrano, V.D., Arteaga, O., Andaluz, V.H.: Teaching-learning process through VR applied to automotive engineering. In: International Conference on Education Technology and Computer, pp. 36–40 (2017)

15. Castro, J.C., et al.: Virtual reality on e-Tourism. In: Kim, K.J., Kim, H., Baek, N. (eds.) ICITS 2017. LNEE, vol. 450, pp. 86–97. Springer, Singapore (2018). https://doi.org/10.1007/978-981-10-6454-8_13

16. Huang, Y.C., Backman, K.F., Backman, S.J., Chang, L.L.: Exploring the implications of virtual reality technology in tourism marketing: An integrated research framework. Int. J. Tour. Res. 18(2), 116–128 (2016)

17. Yap, H.J., Taha, Z., Dawal, S.Z.M., Chang, S.W.: Virtual reality based support system for layout planning and programming of an industrial robotic work cell. PLoS ONE 9(10), e109692 (2014)

18. Potkonjak, V., Gardner, M., Callaghan, V., Mattila, P., Guetl, C., Petrović, V.M., Jovanović, K.: Virtual laboratories for education in science, technology, and engineering: a review. Comput. Educ. 95, 309–327 (2016)

# Multi-user Industrial Training and Education Environment

Víctor H. Andaluz[1](✉), Jorge S. Sánchez[1](✉), Carlos R. Sánchez[1](✉),
Washington X. Quevedo[1](✉), José Varela[1](✉), José L. Morales[2](✉),
and Giovanny Cuzco[3]

[1] Univeridad de las Fuerzas Armads ESPE, Sangolquí, Ecuador
{vhandaluz1,jssanchez,crsanchez9,wjquevedo,
juvarela}@espe.edu.ec
[2] Escuela Superior Politécnica de Chimborazo, Riobamba, Ecuador
j_morales@espoch.edu.ec
[3] Universidad Nacional de Chimborazo, Riobamba, Ecuador
gcuzco@unach.edu.ec

**Abstract.** Currently, virtual reality is presented as a solution to the difficulties for teaching and training in industrial processes in the technical area, so a virtual environment was developed where trainers, users, teachers and students interact as the case may be to carry out processes in the automotive industry such as engine assembly and car body assembly. By carrying out these processes in a virtual environment, the aim is for users to gain skills and become familiar with the activities to be carried out in real life. The easy usability of accessories and the user-friendliness of the immersion in the virtual environment makes the participants have a good experience and in the future show their interest in continuing to use a virtual environment for training or acquiring new knowledge.

**Keywords:** Virtual reality · Automotive engineering · Unity3D
Multipurpose training

## 1 Introduction

Virtual Reality, VR, has a significant growth in recent times, providing an immersive experience by creating a virtual space that interacts with the human [1, 2] in collaborative training and learning environments imitating a real-life process or situation [3]. VR environments are obtained using immersive multimedia technology that generates scenes that can be viewed by the user through devices such as: Oculus Rift VR, HTC Vive [1], Samsung Gear VR, or smartphones [2]. To capture the movements of users in VR environments can be used devices such as Wii Mote, Wii MotionPlus, Kinect by Microsoft [3], RealSense by Intel, among others, all devices use different technologies such as video cameras, depth sensors, accelerometers, gyroscopes, pressure sensors, etc. that combined with different actuators achieves the stimulation of the senses in the virtual environment.

© Springer International Publishing AG, part of Springer Nature 2018
L. T. De Paolis and P. Bourdot (Eds.): AVR 2018, LNCS 10851, pp. 533–546, 2018.
https://doi.org/10.1007/978-3-319-95282-6_38

VR-based applications aim to simulate the real world with virtual environments; VR has been applied in areas such as medicine; for anatomy and surgery training [4]; aerospace engineering, for maintenance and repair activities [5]; graphic design, for product design and manufacturing [6], as well as in the automotive industry where the development of virtual environments has been found, mainly oriented to the following fields: *(i) Design* where VR can be used for layout and concept evaluation during an early stage of the development process [7]; *(ii) Virtual Prototyping (VP)*, physical models can be replicated in VR that allow for cost and time reduction derived from omitting the construction of physical models; *(iii) Virtual Manufacturing (VM)* encompasses the processes of modeling, simulation and optimization of critical operations in a process related to automotive engineering; *(iv) Training* in automotive maintenance and service tasks [8] and skills enhancement in immersive 3D environments [9]; *(v) Virtual Assembly (VA)* facilitates the assembly and disassembly of virtual objects, complementing the training process.

In this context, the applications that are developed in VR can be oriented to the processes of teaching–learning [10], in the academic part and to the training - qualification in the industrial scope, these processes previously mentioned can be applied individually or in collaborative works between users, for which it is considered: (i) environments with a user in which tasks that can be performed individually are considered such as assembly of mechanical parts, doors [11], spot welding, precision welding [12, 13], electronic control units, alternators [14], among others; and (ii) Multiuser environments, where more than one agent interacts with each other in the development of a task, these environments aim to strengthen collaborative work [9], in the development of collaborative work VR-Studio [15] of the Volkswagen group is one of the pioneers, however, multi-user environments have not been properly explored in the industry.

This article presents the implementation of a multi-user virtual reality application focused on the assembly process in the area of automotive engineering. The developed application allows interacting in a controlled 3D environment with other virtual users from different points in order to meet the training tasks of industrial processes.

The structure of the publication consists of six sections, in the first the introduction indicates the work that has been done with virtual reality and its advantages. The second part focuses on the problems that exist at the time of teaching and training of the technical part. The third section shows the structure of a virtual environment in which industrial processes are developed, the fourth part describes how the virtual environment was developed and how it works, the analysis of results and the experimental part are shown in the fifth section.

## 2   Problem Formulation

In engineering, by complementing the theoretical part with the practical part, it is intended that future professionals are competent when making decisions. Academically, most higher education institutions do not have sufficient means to achieve meaningful learning through the teaching-learning process. The lack of laboratories and workshops in which the knowledge acquired in the classroom can be applied (theory) represents a disadvantage in the training of students. In the field of engineering, certain industrial processes such as assembly lines or the technical path of an oil field allow students to become familiar with these processes and develop skills that allow high reliability and efficiency during the process.

At this point, it is worth mentioning that in professional life, training is essential because having highly trained personnel allows companies to adapt quickly to new market conditions. This ability of companies depends to a large extent on the ability of operators at all hierarchical levels to act in a self-organised manner in unknown situations and to find creative solutions [16, 17].

Another disadvantage for the realization of industrial processes is the traditional laboratories without adequate maintenance of modules and equipment, deterioration of physical space and lack of investment to acquire upgrades, among others [18]. These problems can be solved through the virtualization of laboratories, with an open structure that allows the manipulation of all the devices, in addition to optimizing the physical space and the use of different modules present in industrial processes, as well as the execution of emergency events, so that virtual teaching can focus on induction and professional training [19].

The development of industrial processes in a virtual environment can be individual or multi-user, additionally allows for teacher-student, student-student interaction, thus achieving the optimization of resources. In this context, it is proposed to develop a virtual environment for multi-user training in industrial processes, as shown in Fig. 1.

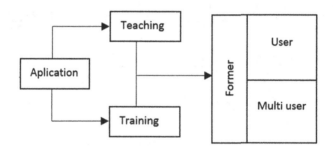

**Fig. 1.** Multi-user training structure

In the specific case of an assembly line in the field of automotive engineering. Assembling a bodywork or assembling an engine involves knowing the function of each of its components (theoretical support) so that during the assembly an established order can be followed and the process can be carried out efficiently (practical support).

The implementation of virtual environments is intended to optimize resources in teaching-learning processes of higher-level students (engineering or technology) and the training of technical staff in the automotive area, and to standardize industrial processes with virtual reality. New processes can be experimented with without the need to stop the operation of the plant. Finally, constant training for the expansion of skills together with work experience will enable us to meet the high requirements in the field of engineering.

## 3 Application Structure

The virtual application is implemented considering a block scheme, in which the following are considered: the block of the scenes, the input and output blocks, and the block of the scripts, see Fig. 2.

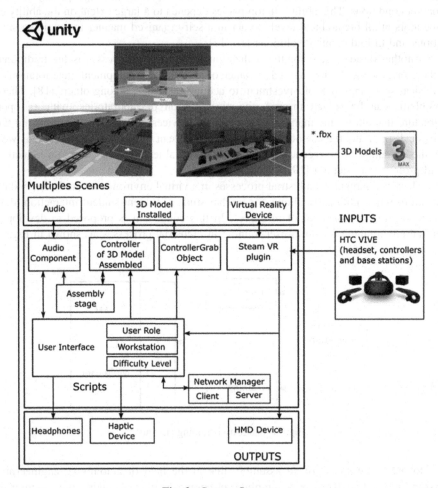

**Fig. 2.** System Structure

The **Scenes** block has the menus and modules that control the 3D components and are linked by a controller to the activity to be performed (engine assembly or body assembly), considering the physical details and assembly characteristics such as rigidity, vibration and strength, among others. In addition, it is composed of several interaction environments, because the system offers different assembly stages in the same production line.

In the **Inputs** and **Outputs** blocks, all the devices that allow the user to interact with the virtual environment are considered, using HTC VIVE glasses, which have headset, controllers and base stations (infrared cameras) as input devices, and headphones, HMD device and haptic device with which the output responses that allow the user to dive can be appreciated. For the operation of this hardware in the 3D graphic engine, connection complements are required, which perform the communication of the input and output devices with a specific action, for what is considered the steam vr plugin. The audio modules allow to generate the sound effects in each assembly station (welding, painting, knocking), which are sent to the virtual environment to obtain sound effects according to the location of the audio listener with respect to the audio source (echoes, noise and attenuation), and to the user through the headphones.

In the **SCRIPTS** block, modules are generated that allow the coordinated interaction between the aforementioned blocks and the elements that facilitate the operation of the system, for which the following modules are considered: (i) Manipulation Scripts: The controller grab object is used to rotate or reposition the manipulated object by means of signals from an input device; on the other hand, when the user needs to place the 3D models in a destination or assemble a finished product depending on the workstation. The controller of 3D Model Assemble is configured, which generates haptic responses in the HTC VIVE; (ii) Interface Scprits: presents the user-configurable options, the user role, the workstation and difficulty level can be selected; in the user roles, the user can choose between teacher and student, obtaining access to specific features depending on each role.

For the workstation, the assembly of an engine or the installation of a bus body is available; and, there are three levels of difficulty, which modify the behavior of 3D Model Assemble and module evaluation; and finally (iii) Scripts for the module of Network manager: which provides multi-user support, so that several users on each Assembly Stage module can intervene in real time on the same assembly line, in addition to the audible voice exchange of each user, this module is linked to the user interface, in which you can choose between teacher or student, by default, the teacher has server and student privileges.

## 4   Export the Models CAD to 3D Graphics Engine

The application of virtual reality for training and multi-user training in a production line of engine assembly and implementation of a bus body, has been built through a multi-layer scheme in order to achieve the necessary immersion and interaction in a virtual environment that fits the reality, see Fig. 3. Thus, we have the following layers:

*Layer 1:* 3D Models Built, to build the 3D elements that make up the virtual environment is used CAD software, because this tool allows creating 3D models identical to reality, considering the physical and mechanical characteristics to be analyzed in the implementation of the production line, the tool used is SolidWork because it has the necessary characteristics in a single package.

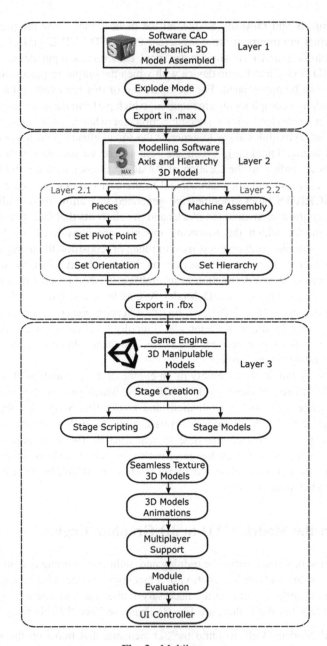

**Fig. 3.** Multilayer

*Layer 2:* Fix Axis and Hierarchy 3D Models, after building the 3D models, the game engine requires conditioning these elements, this includes 2 sublayers: Sublayer 2.1, the pivot point of each piece is fixed at the origin of the same and the orientation of the local reference system is changed to the global reference system, necessary for the manipulation of the elements when the user performs the manipulation and movement tasks in the activity being performed; and Sublayer 2.2, in which the hierarchies between the parts that make up the model are established, this is necessary to carry out the animation and transmission of movement required for the task that can be the assembly of the engine or the assembly of the carriageway. for this layer the elements are edited in 3DS Max, because it is a tool widely used in workflows, between modelling software and game engine.

*Layer 3:* Once the 3D models have been built and conditioned, they are exported to the Unity3D environment to carry out the programming that provides animation and realism to the objects, and allows the user to interact with the virtual environment. First, the workstations of the production line are built and virtual spaces are assigned; for the installation of the bodywork, several stations are available: chassis welding, bodywork welding, painting, engine installation and operation tests; for each station, scripts are programmed to control the behavior of each workstation; and, the respective 3D models of each workstation are located in the space assigned on the production line. See Fig. 4.

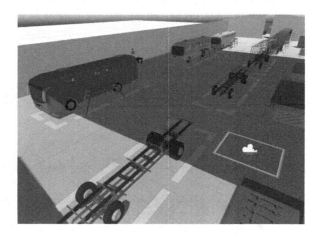

**Fig. 4.** General assembly line

The graphic characteristics of the materials of each object are assigned, using photographs of real textures with which the seamless technique (image editor) is applied, which allows the texture to be homogenized (smoothed contour), thus obtaining an object with a realistic and uniform photo texture, see Fig. 5. In this stage the animation of the mobile elements that take part in the tasks of the workstations is carried out, the physical changes of: texture (painting), colour and shape (welding) are programmed. In addition, visual effects are included for each of the tasks, e.g., in the case of welding, the sparks resulting from consuming the melting material are shown and for the painting station, the aerosol effect of the paint particles in the air is programmed, using the game engine particle system.

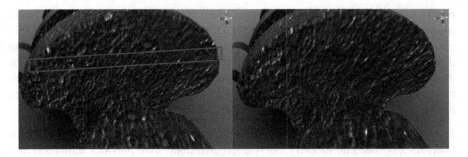

**Fig. 5.** Seamless texture.

Subsequently, the application is configured so that several users can interact in the same environment at the same time through multi-user support, and the characteristics are limited according to the user's role and the activities they can carry out on each workstation. The network administrator module allows an object to be manipulated by several operators, following the Unity structure. Users generate their own movements and transmit it to the server, allowing all users to recreate it, on the other hand, assembly line models are running on the server and their status is transmitted to all users, as shown in Fig. 6.

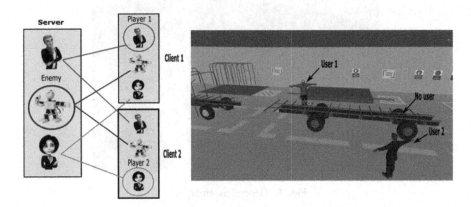

**Fig. 6.** Unity structure vs implemented structure

Finally, the evaluation module is developed that considers the level of difficulty, task execution times, efficiency in the use of materials, initial state of the task and final product, with which the performance is quantified using the evaluation algorithm that differentiates the status of student or operator. The teacher to provide feedback through the student's correction and grading activities uses the results obtained. In addition, a control panel is implemented so that the user can manage all the scenes and activities that are carried out in the assembly stations; these tools are accessible by means of graphic interface components (buttons, text boxes, sliders and others), that the user can use using the HTC VIVE controls; and they allow visualizing the information about attendance, status and results of the objectives of each stage of the assembly line, this information is segmented depending on the type of user.

## 5  Experimental Results

In order to evaluate the multi-user application it is proposed to execute several experiments in which each command and component developed in the virtual environment is used.

To start the application the menu is set up, in which the operator chooses the industrial process he wishes to carry out. See Fig. 7.

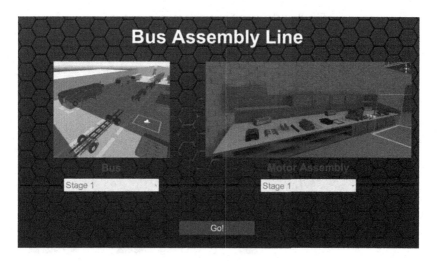

**Fig. 7.** Home de la app

Within the industrial process of the bodywork there are 5 stages: welding, bodywork assembly, equipment, painting and testing stage; each of them contains a specific task for the operator. In the welding area the operator proceeds to weld the part of the car bodywork, within the virtual environment you can count on other users within it, one of them can be the supervisor of the production part while the other users are operators in the same task, each user has the possibility of intercommunicating with each other to make questions or ask for help with the task they are running. The welding of the bodywork has a maximum time of execution, during which the objective must be fulfilled in order to proceed in a repetitive way with the welding of the bodywork. The experiment carried out inside the bodywork in the welding area can be seen in Figs. 8, 9 and 10.

At the end of the process, the product is available for use in another part of production. For the development of the mechanical part within the system menu, you enter the option of assembling the vehicle's engine, the user or users present in the

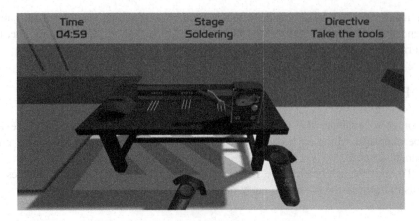

**Fig. 8.** Selection of materials to start the task.

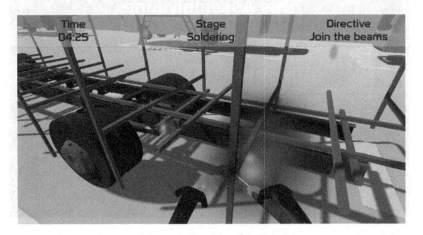

**Fig. 9.** Performing the welding task.

production stage make the incorporation of the parts that are part of the engine, simultaneously in the environment you can count on multiple users who exchange information among them. Figures 11 and 12 show the results of the experiment carried out for the engine assembly.

At the end of production, it unifies the products developed in each sub-stage, thus fulfilling the objective of obtaining a final product. In order to unify the products, the equipment option is entered, a stage in which all the necessary equipment is placed to obtain the final product of production. Figure 13 shows the result of the experiment carried out in the bus equipment stage.

The results presented below indicate the efficiency of the usability of virtual environments to carry out an industrial process, in our specific case: a body assembly line. To this end, the SUS [20] summary assessment method is used. in which a Likert style scale is obtained [21] that generates a single number, represented by an average composed by the usability of the global system under study.

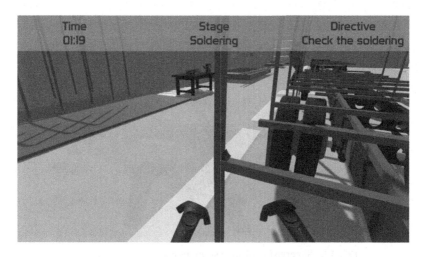

**Fig. 10.** Verify welding task.

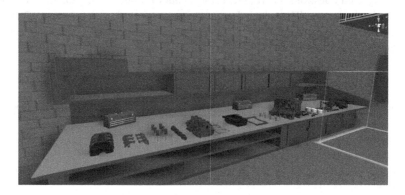

**Fig. 11.** Engine assembly stage.

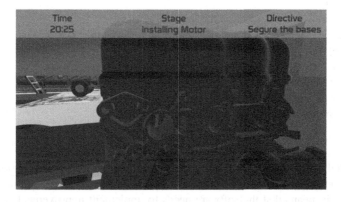

**Fig. 12.** Attaching the engine bases to the bus bodywork.

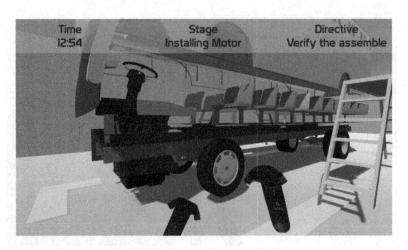

**Fig. 13.** Supervision of the assembly between bus and motor.

The selected questions are 10, see Table 1, out of 50 that frame the most consistent and polarized answers. The selected points have a correlation of between 0.7 and 0.9. The weighting ranges from 1 to 5, meaning complete disagreement and complete agreement respectively.

**Table 1.** Questionnaire results

| Questions to ask | Punctuation | Operation |
|---|---|---|
| How complex was the handling of accessories in a virtual environment? | 4 | 4–1 = 3 |
| I consider this system very user friendly? | 2 | 5–2 = 3 |
| I think that before using the system an induction would be necessary? | 5 | 5–1 = 4 |
| I think I would need technical support to use the system? | 2 | 5–2 = 3 |
| I think that the experience in the virtual environment is very close to reality? | 4 | 4–1 = 3 |
| I found too many inconsistencies in this system? | 2 | 5–2 = 3 |
| I think that the majority of industrial processes can be taken to virtual reality? | 4 | 4–1 = 3 |
| I find it uncomfortable to use the system for an industrial process? | 3 | 5–3 = 2 |
| I have found it very safe to use the system? | 4 | 4–1 = 3 |
| Would you need previous training to operate the system? | 2 | 5–2 = 3 |
| **Total** | | **30** |

The total number, obtained from the sum of the operation in each question results in 30. Based on this result, the SUS score is calculated and expressed by a multiplication of 2.5, which means that the software needs to implement improvements to achieve a higher usability feature score.

The assessment of a virtual environment by users is important because it allows them to identify possible shortcomings and at the same time increase the use of headsets such as HTC VIVE, so that the immersion in a virtual environment becomes an experience that facilitates learning and training in new tasks.

# 6 Conclusions

By using VR you can reproduce industrial processes that are related to engineering. Virtual environments can be used for the collaborative teaching-learning process because it is multi-user and optimizes resources. When carrying out processes involving the assembly, in our case the assembly of a bodywork in a virtual environment offers the advantage of repeating the process until the expected results are achieved, that is to say that users become familiar with the process.

The constant training in the technical area to carry out procedures and the updating of knowledge allows certain industrial processes to be carried out efficiently. In a virtual environment the interaction between users to carry out an activity avoids taking risks, it should be stressed that the experience in a virtual environment must be as close as possible to real life.

From the experiments carried out for the present investigation it was concluded that the users were familiarized with the activities to be carried out during an industrial process, in our case with a body assembly line. During the dives in the virtual environment the users had no difficulty in manipulating the controls and following the instructions. Significant learning was achieved by complementing theoretical knowledge and practical through a process.

**Acknowledgements.** The authors would like to thanks to the Corporación Ecuatoriana para el Desarrollo de la Investigación y Academia –CEDIA for the financing given to research, development, and innovation, through the CEPRA projects, especially the project CEPRA-XI-2017-06; *Control Coordinado Multi-operador aplicado a un robot Manipulador Aéreo;* also to Universidad de las Fuerzas Armadas ESPE, Universidad Técnica de Ambato, Escuela Superior Politécnica de Chimborazo, and Universidad Nacional de Chimborazo, and Grupo de Investigación en Automatización, Robótica y Sistemas Inteligentes, GI-ARSI, for the support to develop this work.

# References

1. Niehorster, D.C., Li, L., Lappe, M.: The accuracy and precision of position and orientation tracking in the HTC vive virtual reality system for scientific research. Iperception **8**(3), 1–23 (2017)
2. Fernández-Palacios, B.J., Morabito, D., Remondino, F.: Access to complex reality-based 3D models using virtual reality solutions. J. Cult. Herit. **23**, 40–48 (2017)
3. Carfagni, M., et al.: Fast and low cost acquisition and reconstruction system for human hand-wrist-arm anatomy. Procedia Manuf. **11**, 1600–1608 (2017)

4. Jang, S., Vitale, J.M., Jyung, R.W., Black, J.B.: Direct manipulation is better than passive viewing for learning anatomy in a three-dimensional virtual reality environment. Comput. Educ. **106**, 150–165 (2017)
5. Dini, G., Mura, M.D.: Application of augmented reality techniques in through-life engineering services. Procedia CIRP **38**, 14–23 (2015)
6. Berg, L.P., Vance, J.M.: Industry use of virtual reality in product design and manufacturing: a survey. Virtual Real. **21**(1), 1–17 (2017)
7. Lawson, G., Salanitri, D., Waterfield, B.: Future directions for the development of virtual reality within an automotive manufacturer. Appl. Ergon. **53**, 323–330 (2016)
8. Borsci, S., Lawson, G., Broome, S.: Empirical evidence, evaluation criteria and challenges for the effectiveness of virtual and mixed reality tools for training operators of car service maintenance. Comput. Ind. **67**, 17–26 (2015)
9. Ortiz, J.S., Sánchez, J.S., Velasco, P.M., Sánchez, C.R., Quevedo, W.X., Zambrano, V.D., Arteaga, O., Andaluz, V.H.: Teaching-learning process through VR applied to automotive engineering. In: Proceedings of the 2017 9th International Conference on Education Technology and Computers, pp. 36–40. ACM, December 2017
10. Stratos, A., Loukas, R., Dimitris, M., Konstantinos, G., Dimitris, M., George, C.: A virtual reality application to attract young talents to manufacturing. Procedia CIRP **57**, 134–139 (2016)
11. Rüßmann, M., et al.: Industry 4.0. The Future of Productivity and Growth in Manufacturing. Boston. Consulting Group, pp. 1–5, April 2015
12. Doshi, A., Smith, R.T., Thomas, B.H., Bouras, C.: Use of projector based augmented reality to improve manual spot-welding precision and accuracy for automotive manufacturing. Int. J. Adv. Manuf. Technol. **89**(5–8), 1279–1293 (2017)
13. Quevedo, W.X., et al.: Virtual reality system for training in automotive mechanics. In: De Paolis, L.T., Bourdot, P., Mongelli, A. (eds.) AVR 2017. LNCS, vol. 10324, pp. 185–198. Springer, Cham (2017). https://doi.org/10.1007/978-3-319-60922-5_14
14. Mårdberg, P., Yan, Y., Bohlin, R., Delfs, N., Gustafsson, S., Carlson, J.S.: Controller hierarchies for efficient virtual ergonomic assessments of manual assembly sequences. Procedia CIRP **44**, 435–440 (2016)
15. Purschke, F., Schulze, M., Zimmermann, P.: Virtual reality-new methods for improving and accelerating the development process in vehicle styling and design. In: Computer Graphics International, pp. 789–797 (1998)
16. Abele, E., Reinhart, G.: Zukunft der Produktion [Future of Production]. Carl Hanser, Munich (2011)
17. Adolph, S., Tisch, M., Metternich, J.: Challenges and approaches to competency development for future production. J. Int. Sci. Publ. – Educ. Altern. **12**, 1001–1010 (2014)
18. Moody, J.A.O., Alonso, R.E.S., Barbosa, J.J.G., Morales, G.R.: Virtual laboratories for training in industrial robotics. IEEE Lat. Am. Trans. **14**, 665–672 (2016)
19. Cáceres, C.A., Amaya, D.: Desarrollo e interacción de un laboratorio virtual asistido y controlado por PLC. Entre Cienc. Ing. **10**(19), 9–15 (2016)
20. Sauro, J., Lewis, J.R.: When designing usability questionnaires, does it hurt to be positive? In: Proceedings of the SIGCHI Conference on Human Factors in Computing Systems, pp. 2215–2224. ACM, May 2011
21. Likert, R.: A technique for the measurement of attitudes. Arch. Psychol. **22**, 55 (1932)

# Robust Motion Estimation Based on Multiple Monocular Camera for Indoor Autonomous Navigation of Micro Aerial Vehicle

Wilbert G. Aguilar[1,2]($\boxtimes$), José F. Manosalvas[1], Joan A. Guillén[1], and Brayan Collaguazo[1]

[1] CICTE Research Center, Universidad de las Fuerzas Armadas ESPE, Sangolquí, Ecuador
wgaguilar@espe.edu.ec
[2] GREC Research Group, Universitat Politècnica de Catalunya, Barcelona, Spain

**Abstract.** This paper is focusing on the development of a system based on computer vision to estimate the movement of an MAV (X, Y, Z and yaw). The system integrates elements such as: a set of cameras, image filtering (physical and digital), and estimation of the position through the calibration of the system and the application of an algorithm based on experimentally found equations. The system represents a low cost alternative, both computational and economic, capable of estimating the position of an MAV with a significantly low error using a scale in millimeters, so that almost any type of camera available in the market can be used. This system was developed in order to offer an affordable form of research and development of new autonomous and intelligent systems for closed environments.

**Keywords:** Computer vision · Cameras array · Quadrotor · Motion estimation
Path planning · MAV · Control system

## 1 Introduction

In recent years we have witnessed a great increase in technological advances, such as the creation of faster processors and small or new materials for batteries that allow a greater capacity of energy storage [1]. These advances help to develop new forms of control for image processing [2, 3], and the exploitation of resources and applications based on unmanned aerial vehicles [4–6].

Most motion estimation systems are quite expensive features of cameras, frames per second, type of lens, among others. Many systems use technologies that are barely found in our environment, for this reason it is necessary to find an affordable method that is easy to install and that demonstrates reliability.

There are several ways to estimate the position of an AVM in a workspace, with the help of external devices such as: on-board systems, external cameras [7], stereo cameras [8], RGBD cameras [9–12] or a LIDAR system [13]. The method described in

© Springer International Publishing AG, part of Springer Nature 2018
L. T. De Paolis and P. Bourdot (Eds.): AVR 2018, LNCS 10851, pp. 547–561, 2018.
https://doi.org/10.1007/978-3-319-95282-6_39

this document is based on the use of RGB monocular cameras mounted on an aluminum structure that acts as a support for the system. In addition to a safety net for protection.

This document is organized as follows: Sect. 2 shows a description of the related works. The proposed motion estimation system is explained in Sect. 3. Section 4 explains the motion planner and trajectory tracking. Section 5 focuses on the explanation of the structure of the system and the processing of images. Section 6 will focus on the process of system calibration, the application of the motion planner and the trajectory tracking of the MAV. The experimentation and results are presented in Acknowledgement. Finally, Conflicts of Interest is intended for conclusions and future works.

## 2 Related Works

The robotic and computer vision communities have developed several techniques for estimating and tracking [14–16] the position of an air vehicle using monocular cameras [17–20], laser scans [21] and stereo cameras [22], in addition to the formulation of algorithms for the processing of data obtained from feedback devices [23, 24]. These devices are implemented on board the UAV, considering the payload they can raise, limiting for micro UAVs.

In our proposal, we use a $2 \times 2$ array of stationary cameras placed parallel to the ground with their angle of view pointing downwards. The image captured by each camera is necessary to be intercepted with the images captured by the adjacent cameras, in such a way that a panoramic image of vertical and horizontal type is generated.

The detection of the UAV is based on the implementation of visual markers on board an aerial vehicle. In the literature, control systems for UAVs are presented using multiple cameras and visual markers for detection [25]. In this context, the RAVEN system (Real-time indoor Autonomous Vehicle test Environment) [26] was developed by MIT ACL (Aerospace Control Lab) which estimates the UAV information by measuring the position through markers installed on board the aircraft by means of the optical sensor of the cameras, although the system has a resolution of up to 1 mm of precision requires expensive equipment, limiting its application. In addition, the position estimation of a quadrotor using two cameras towards the ground has been implemented [27], in which two cameras are positioned one against the other in such a way that the six degrees of freedom (DOF) of the UAV can be estimated. In [28] a visual control system for a micro helicopter is developed, using two stationary cameras with its optical sensor pointing upwards, the aircraft has on board four black spheres used as position reference elements. Mak et al. [29] proposes a location system for a revolving wing MAV (Micro Air Vehicle) that uses three LEDs incorporated in the aircraft, a USB webcam captures the image of the LEDs and by means of an image analysis the position of the MAV is estimated.

Our system proposes the use of inexpensive cameras, together with physical filters Mylar so that it can easily obtain the image of the visual markers incorporated in the top of the air vehicle, discriminating external signals to the system for further processing to allow by applying an algorithm to obtain the position and yaw rotation of the aircraft.

For the autonomous navigation of the MAV in closed environments it is necessary to apply the concepts of visual feedback, in our project a system can be composed of several elements: an array of cameras with physical Mylar filters, visual markers (LEDs) mounted on the aircraft, computer for reception, processing and sending of information and the micro air vehicle Fig. 1.

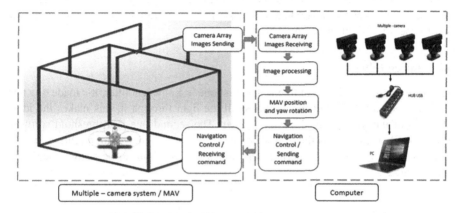

**Fig. 1.** System configuration.

The arrangement of cameras has four elements in charge of visual feedback, these capture the visual markers through the processing of images and through the application of an algorithm the position and yaw rotation of MAV can be estimated. It should be considered that the number of cameras increases the performance of the system, as well as its accuracy and robustness, however the computing load for the computer processor becomes heavier. This system has an arrangement of cameras and mounting of suitable visual markers so that their observability and performance is guaranteed.

## 3   Motion Estimation System

The proposed system contains five principal parts which are: frame, cameras, image filter (Physic and software), markers and algorithms.

### 3.1   Frame

The frame is the structure which should cover the whole workspace, serve as an anchor point for a safety grid and provide a fixed amount of the cameras. This mount should design in such a way that the camera image sensor is the most parallel to the ground. The camera image should show all the wished area.

### 3.2 Cameras

This system was made thinking in a low cost alternative, for this reason the algorithm just need an array of any USB cameras to work. The cameras should be adapted to the application, in our case, the PS3 Eye camera was perfect, it has a 60 fps frame rate, $640 \times 480$ resolution, a good lens quality giving sharper images and the cost was under $ 20 in our midst, but has one problem, the cameras use a lens with IR blocking filter, this means, we cannot use any kind of marker that use infrared light, for this reason we had to use a red light in our markers.

### 3.3 Image Filter

This system uses two kinds of filters. The first one is a physical filter, it's made of a thin Mylar sheet, and this layer block almost all the light through it, this makes the identification of the markers in the image easier. The second one is a threshold software filter, this filter transforms the grayscale image to a binary image, highlighting just the markers in the image. The filtering step allows the algorithm to be accurate and runs faster (Fig. 2).

**Fig. 2.** Physic filter on a ps3 eye camera lens and threshold filter.

### 3.4 Markers

There are two kinds of visual markers, the active ones and the passive ones, the difference between them is the active markers are a light source it selves and the passive just reflects the light form another light source. How its mentioned in [3] the passive markers have many advantages over the active like the light weight and the facility to incorporate into ours MAV, but, in order to get the Wright function of these markers these camera systems have great features, this means an expensive system We are using an active marker system which is easily recognizable by any kind of cameras through the filters (Fig. 3).

**Fig. 3.** Active markers on an isosceles triangle distribution.

### 3.5 Algorithm

This system uses three different algorithms for the image processing to get the X, Y, Z coordinates and the yaw orientation. The first one is the image filtering which helps in the identification of shapes and increase the accuracy of the measurement. The second one is an algorithm for recognizing shapes and count them, this is for identification of the markers in the MAV, get the information of the motion and the orientation. The third one is to get the average measure of the cameras array.

The procedure for operating the system begins with the configuration of the camera array, once the visual markers are activated on board the MAV, the cameras capture the image and send it to the computer where they are processed and the position and yaw rotation of MAV is estimated. The operation in general is shown in Fig. 4.

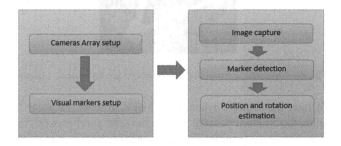

**Fig. 4.** Operation procedure.

## 4  System Structure and Image Processing

Once we have the binary image filtered we can work with it. The first step is the identification of the MAV, the markers are set in a specific configuration in such a way that if we connect the three circles in the image we get an isosceles triangle, but if there are not three dots in the image we conclude that the MAV is not in the image, for those that use the shape count function in the OpenCV library [30].

The next step is to find the moments of each one of the markers, the markers can change in shape or size because of the brightness, angulations of the MAV or the flight height. The OpenCV [30] library has a function to calculate the moments of each shape in the image, later, knowing the moments, we can calculate the exact center of each one with the Eq. 2:

Central moments:

$$mu_{ji} = \sum_{x,y} \left(array(x,y).(x-\bar{x})^j.(y-\bar{y})^i\right) \tag{1}$$

Mass center:

$$\bar{x} = \frac{m_{10}}{m_{00}}, \bar{y} = \frac{m_{01}}{m_{00}} \tag{2}$$

$m_{01}$ : summation of the moments in X
$m_{01}$ : summation of the moments in Y
$m_{00}$ : *totalmass*

Once we get the exact center of each shape, we can match with a line the centers and get an isosceles triangle as is shown in the Fig. 5, then we calculate the moments and the center of the new shape, in this case are the center of the triangle which represent the center of the MAV.

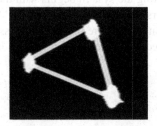

**Fig. 5.** New image matching the vertex to get an isosceles triangle

We already have the X and Y value of the MAV, now we are going to calculate the height or Z value, this value is calculated from the separation between the two markers in the base of the isosceles triangle. The separation of these two markers will increase or decrease in a mathematical reason, the closer the MAV is to the camera, the bigger is the separation of the markers and vice versa, this property was exploited to calculate the height. Figure 7 and Eq. 4 show the interpolation process and the curve that adjusts to the calculation of the height as a function of the pixels acquired by camera 0. It is recalled that this process must be performed for each of the remaining cameras.

Now we calculate the yaw value of the MAV, we have to recognize the front of the MAV, the third marker is used to this. In an isosceles triangle is known that two of the vertices are in a same separation of the center of the triangle and one have a bigger or smaller separation in the center of the triangle in comparison of the base vertexes. Now we know which of the three markers the front is and we do have the center of the triangle, with these two points we can calculate the yaw value in function of the X axis of the work space frame. With the center point (Px1, Py1) and front point (Px2, Py2) of the MAV we apply the arc-tan of the slope generated by these points and the Eq. 3 and get directly the yaw value.

$$\theta = \tan^{-1}\left(\frac{Py_2 - Py_1}{Px_2 - Px_1}\right) \tag{3}$$

The only one value real is the yaw, it is given in degrees, the X, Y, Z value is expressed in pixels and we need to make a processing in order to transform them to millimeters. This process is explained in the next section.

## 5  System Calibration, Experiments and Results

The system calibration is needed to get the relation between the pixel's value got by the image processor and the real value, this process is needed just once as long as the position of the cameras has not changed.

Because of the way in which the cameras are located in the work volume, it produces that, although it does not change the real position in X or Y, but the height do, in the processing of the image it shows data as it would have displaced, this effect is generated by the angle of view of the camera, if an object occupies a position in a certain pixel of the sensor, this position varies in the sensor as it approaches or moves away from the objective, although they remain aligned with the initial position.

During the data collection procedure, marks were positioned on the ground in known positions (all of them with the range of the work area and constant intervals), the target is placed on these marks at different heights and perform data capture. The data that was taken are the x, y, z real values and the data generated by the image processing that are x, y and the distance between the markers, previously explained and expressed in pixels. An example of first interpolation for curve adjustment is shown in Fig. 6 and the data obtained for the realization of this process are presented in Table 1.

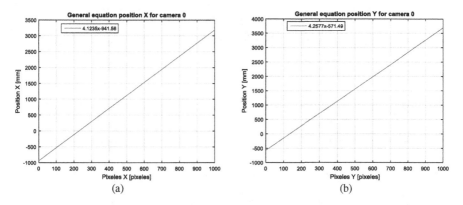

**Fig. 6.** First interpolation and curve adjustment for camera 0 to 0 mm of height. (a) interpolation for X. (b) interpolation for Y.

**Table 1.** Reference EC_1: Data obtained from experimental sample for camera 0.

| Pixels X | Pixels Y | Pixels Z | Position X | Position Y | Position Z |
|----------|----------|-------------|------------|------------|------------|
| 269 | 171 | 39,01281841 | 200 | 150 | 0 |
| 317 | 207 | 39 | 400 | 300 | 0 |
| 366 | 240 | 36,23534186 | 600 | 450 | 0 |
| 412 | 275 | 39,01281841 | 800 | 600 | 0 |
| 508 | 345 | 37,21558813 | 1200 | 900 | 0 |
| 556 | 381 | 39,45883931 | 1400 | 1050 | 0 |
| 603 | 418 | 38,20994635 | 1600 | 1200 | 0 |

The values shown in the Table is a sample of the data obtained with the camera 0

For this type of system we have to ensure two principal features. The first one is the height is not in function of the x or y value, is an independent variable, this means that if the MAV is moving through a plane in the same height, the difference between the markers is the same. The second one is similar to the first one, is ensure that the x value is not in related to the y value or vice versa, the x and y value should be just related to the height, if the x value is related to the y value it means that the camera it's not calibrated, you can see in the image camera a distortion of the image [31].

Once determined that the variables X and Y are not related, it is possible to generate an algorithm for determining the real position of the MAV.

We analyze the data obtained by generating a graph of real height vs. distance between marks, with this first graph is obtained a polynomial equation in which the distance between pixels obtained from the image processor can be substituted and get the real height as we shown in the Fig. 7 and Eq. 4.

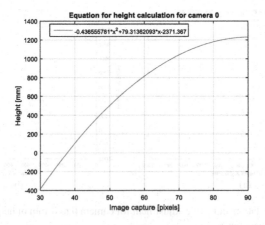

**Fig. 7.** Curve adjustment for height calculation with camera 0

Equation for height calculation for camera 0:

$$Height_0 = -0.436555781 * pixel_0^2 + 79.31362093 * pixel_0 - 2371.367 \qquad (4)$$

Now with the real height at which the MAV is located, the position of X and Y is determined by a process very similar to the previous one, but a little more extensive, next the process of the X axis is explained, since for the y axis it is exactly the same.

The data obtained from the real position vs. the position in pixels obtained from the image processor is reviewed, a graph is generated and it can be seen that the relationship between these two variables is practically linear, an equation can be obtained and with the pixel value substituted the real position is obtained, we will call this equation EC_1.

The problem is that in EC_1 the coefficients vary depending on the height varies, that is, each height variation corresponds to different coefficients. To solve this problem, we obtain all the equations of position previously mentioned, for each height it will be a different EC_1 equation as is shown in Table 2, since they all have the same shape, it is possible to generate a graph of coefficients vs. height, as each equation has two coefficients, it can be generated in two different graphs, from which two new equations are generated which we will call EC_2 and EC_2'.

**Table 2.** Reference EC_2: Data obtained from experimental sample for camera 0

| X values | | | Y values | | |
|---|---|---|---|---|---|
| Height | Equations for X | | Height | Equations for Y | |
| 0 | 4,213503836 | −941,56452 | 0 | 4,25773567 | −571,494707 |
| 150 | 3,935839349 | −825,695733 | 150 | 4,02940526 | −521,4978996 |
| 300 | 3,704813811 | −735,146038 | 300 | 3,75704895 | −462,7015883 |
| 450 | 3,544239168 | −682,249628 | 450 | 3,50872979 | −401,302091 |
| 600 | 3,136782509 | −547,039491 | 600 | 3,11770667 | −316,200084 |
| 750 | 3,038786615 | −519,442275 | 750 | 2,93483469 | −282,5260269 |
| 900 | 2,72245905 | −389,064212 | 900 | 2,68690092 | −211,3153242 |
| 1050 | 2,419677921 | −285,89768 | 1050 | 2,3364677 | −129,7567457 |
| 1200 | 2,253482326 | −248,150967 | 1200 | 2,10437151 | −122,4729272 |

With these two new equations, it is possible to obtain the coefficients of the equation EC_1 as a function of the height and finally replace the position in pixels obtained by the image processor and have the real position. From Table 2 we obtain the graphs shown in Fig. 8, where these are interpolated to find the final coefficients for the position calculation in X and Y.

The PS3 Eye cameras were used for the computer vision system, which have the following characteristics: 60 fps (frame per second) to 640 × 480 pixels, USB interface, 85° viewing angle, all four cameras are connected to a USB 3.0 HUB and to this a computer described later. The Mambo Drone is connected by Bluetooth

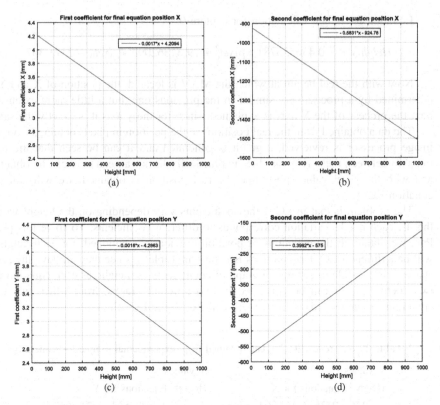

**Fig. 8.** Second interpolation and obtaining final coefficients. (a) First coefficient for X; (b) Second coefficient for X; (c) first coefficient for Y; (d) second coefficient for Y.

communication to the aforementioned computer with the following features: Intel Core i7 6500U 2.5 GHz processor and 16 GB DDR3 RAM running Linux.

The computer is intended for image processing, position estimation and yaw rotation of the MAV and algorithm processing. The open-source OpenCV [30] library developed by Intel Corporation, Willow Garage and currently maintained by Itseez, is a library of programming functions aimed primarily at computer vision in real time.

The evaluation metrics are: Absolute error, the difference between the calculated value and the real value, for each of the coordinate tests performed. Relative error percentage, represents the quotient between the absolute error and the real value, for each of the coordinates tests performed. Example of experiments performed are shown in Figs. 9 and 10.

Table 3 shows the results of the tests performed. Figure 11 show the comparison curves between calculated or analytical results and real values taken as reference.

The results shown in Table 2 of the difference between the real values and values calculated by the implemented algorithm, show a minimum divergence since these numbers have units in millimeters, the values in bold are due to minimum and maximum values taken as a reference and in addition to the fisheye effect of each camera,

(a)                                 (b)

**Fig. 9.** Example test one: real reference values. (a) position coordinates X and Y; (b) position coordinate Z.

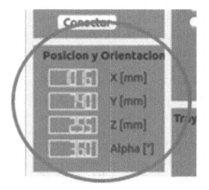

**Fig. 10.** Example test one: calculated values.

**Table 3.** Test performed.

| Test | Real value [mm] | | | Calculated value [mm] | | |
|------|------|------|------|------|------|------|
|      | X    | Y    | Z    | X    | Y    | Z    |
| 1    | 200  | 150  | 100  | 170  | 166  | 150  |
| 2    | 200  | 1350 | 200  | 210  | 1350 | 220  |
| 3    | 600  | 450  | 300  | 580  | 450  | 305  |
| 4    | 600  | 1050 | 400  | 590  | 1060 | 400  |
| 5    | 1000 | 750  | 500  | 1016 | 740  | 490  |
| 6    | 1200 | 600  | 650  | 1200 | 594  | 630  |
| 7    | 1200 | 900  | 1050 | 1202 | 904  | 1030 |
| 8    | 1600 | 300  | 1100 | 1610 | 280  | 1090 |
| 9    | 1600 | 1200 | 1150 | 1629 | 1240 | 1140 |
| 10   | 1800 | 1350 | 1200 | 1810 | 1350 | 1150 |

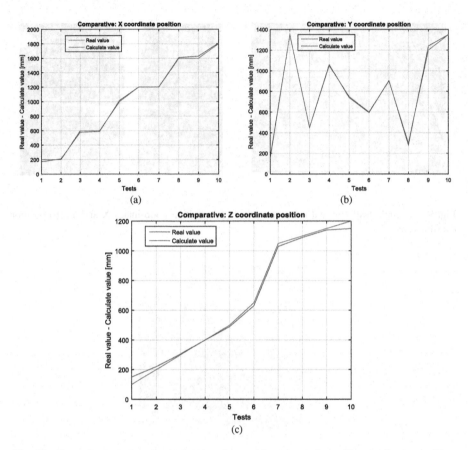

**Fig. 11.** Example test two: calculated values. (a) comparative: X coordinate position; (b) comparative: Y coordinate position; (c) comparative: Z coordinate position.

this is solved by performing a calibration of each camera before image acquisition. Video results are provided on: https://www.youtube.com/watch?v=qczOkf3xpHo.

## 6    Conclusions and Future Works

This document is experimentally verified the optimal and robust performance of our system, through the image detection of an MAV by means of a matrix of monocular cameras as visual feedback devices, and in turn the position estimation in X coordinates and Y and altitude of the aircraft, as well as its yaw rotation.

It can be determined that the proposed system is flexible since it can be used with any type of quadrotor and in turn can expand its workspace includes more cameras to the system.

The physical filter placed in each camera achieves its objective of discriminating signals external to the system, allowing the processing of images with two digital filters one to convert the image to gray scale and the second to convert it into binary.

As a future work, a real-time route planning algorithm [32–34] will be implemented with the implementation of real or virtual obstacles, so that the MAV will follow up on this trajectory.

**Acknowledgement.** This work is part of the project "Perception and localization system for autonomous navigation of rotor micro aerial vehicle in gps-denied environments, VisualNav-Drone", 2016-PIC-024, from the Universidad de las Fuerzas Armadas ESPE, directed by Dr. Wilbert G. Aguilar.

**Conflicts of Interest.** The authors declare no conflict of interest.

# References

1. Kim, H., Park, K.-Y., Hong, J., Kang, K.: All-graphene-battery: bridging the gap between supercapacitors and lithium ion batteries. Sci. Rep. **4**, 13 (2014)
2. Aguilar, W.G., Luna, M., Moya, J., Abad, V., Parra, H., Ruiz, H.: Pedestrian detection for UAVs using cascade classifiers with meanshift. In: 11th International Conference on Semantic Computing (ICSC), San Diego. IEEE (2017)
3. Aguilar, W.G., Luna, Marco A., Moya, Julio F., Abad, V., Ruiz, H., Parra, H., Angulo, C.: Pedestrian detection for UAVs using cascade classifiers and saliency maps. In: Rojas, I., Joya, G., Catala, A. (eds.) IWANN 2017. LNCS, vol. 10306, pp. 563–574. Springer, Cham (2017). https://doi.org/10.1007/978-3-319-59147-6_48
4. Aguilar, W.G., Angulo, C.: Real-Time Model-Based video stabilization for microaerial vehicles. Neural Process. Lett. **43**(2), 459–477 (2016)
5. Aguilar, W.G., Angulo, C.: Real-time video stabilization without phantom movements for micro aerial vehicles. Eurasip J. Image Video Process. **1**, 1–13 (2014)
6. Aguilar, W.G., Luna, Marco A., Moya, Julio F., Abad, V., Ruiz, H., Parra, H., Lopez, W.: Cascade classifiers and saliency maps based people detection. In: De Paolis, L.T., Bourdot, P., Mongelli, A. (eds.) AVR 2017. LNCS, vol. 10325, pp. 501–510. Springer, Cham (2017). https://doi.org/10.1007/978-3-319-60928-7_42
7. How, J.P., Behihke, B., Frank, A., Dale, D., Vian, J.: Real-Time indoor autonomous vehicle test environment. IEEE Control Syst. **28**(2), 51–64 (2008)
8. Di Fulvio, G., Frontoni, E., Mancini, A., Zingaretti, P.: A stereovision system for dimensional measurements in industrial robotics applications. In: IEEE/ASME 10th International Conference on Mechatronic and Embedded Systems and Applications (MESA), Senigallia, Italy (2014)
9. Henry, P., Krainin, M., Herbst, E., Ren, X., Fox, D.: RGB-D mapping: Using Kinect-style depth cameras for dense 3D modeling of indoor environments. Exp. Robot. **31**(5), 647–663 (2012)
10. Aguilar, W.G., Rodríguez, Guillermo A., Álvarez, L., Sandoval, S., Quisaguano, F., Limaico, A.: On-Board visual SLAM on a UGV using a RGB-D camera. In: Huang, Y., Wu, H., Liu, H., Yin, Z. (eds.) ICIRA 2017. LNCS (LNAI), vol. 10464, pp. 298–308. Springer, Cham (2017). https://doi.org/10.1007/978-3-319-65298-6_28

11. Aguilar, W.G., Rodríguez, Guillermo A., Álvarez, L., Sandoval, S., Quisaguano, F., Limaico, A.: Visual SLAM with a RGB-D camera on a quadrotor UAV using on-board processing. In: Rojas, I., Joya, G., Catala, A. (eds.) IWANN 2017. LNCS, vol. 10306, pp. 596–606. Springer, Cham (2017). https://doi.org/10.1007/978-3-319-59147-6_51

12. Aguilar, W.G., Rodríguez, Guillermo A., Álvarez, L., Sandoval, S., Quisaguano, F., Limaico, A.: Real-Time 3D modeling with a RGB-D camera and on-board processing. In: De Paolis, L.T., Bourdot, P., Mongelli, A. (eds.) AVR 2017. LNCS, vol. 10325, pp. 410–419. Springer, Cham (2017). https://doi.org/10.1007/978-3-319-60928-7_35

13. Kohlbrecher, S., von Stryk, O., Meyer, J., Klingauf, U.: A flexible and scalable SLAM system with full 3D motion estimation. In: IEEE International Symposium on Safety, Security, and Rescue Robotics (SSRR), Kyoto, Japan (2011)

14. Andriluka, M., Roth, S., Schiele, B.: Monocular 3D pose estimation and tracking by detection. In: IEEE Conference on Computer Vision and Pattern Recognition (CVPR), San Francisco, USA (2010)

15. de La Gorce, M., Fleet, D.J., Paragios, N.: Model-based 3D hand pose estimation from monocular video. In: IEEE Transactions on Pattern Analysis and Machine Intelligence, vol. 33, no. 9, pp. 1793–1805 (2011)

16. Vincent, L., Pascal, F.: Monocular model-based 3D tracking of rigid objects: a survey. Found. Trends® Comput. Graph. Vis. 1(1), 1–89 (2005)

17. Aguilar, W.G., Salcedo, Vinicio S., Sandoval, David S., Cobeña, B.: Developing of a video-based model for UAV autonomous navigation. In: Barone, D.A.C., Teles, E.O., Brackmann, C.P. (eds.) LAWCN 2017. CCIS, vol. 720, pp. 94–105. Springer, Cham (2017). https://doi.org/10.1007/978-3-319-71011-2_8

18. Aguilar, W.G., Verónica, C., José, P.: Obstacle avoidance based-visual navigation for micro aerial vehicles. Electronics 6(1), 10 (2017)

19. Aguilar, W.G., Casaliglla, Verónica P., Pólit, José L., Abad, V., Ruiz, H.: Obstacle avoidance for flight safety on unmanned aerial vehicles. In: Rojas, I., Joya, G., Catala, A. (eds.) IWANN 2017. LNCS, vol. 10306, pp. 575–584. Springer, Cham (2017). https://doi.org/10.1007/978-3-319-59147-6_49

20. Aguilar, W.G., Angulo, C., Costa-Castello, R.: Autonomous navigation control for quadrotors in trajectories tracking. In: Huang, Y., Wu, H., Liu, H., Yin, Z. (eds.) ICIRA 2017. LNCS (LNAI), vol. 10464, pp. 287–297. Springer, Cham (2017). https://doi.org/10.1007/978-3-319-65298-6_27

21. May, S., Droschel, D., Holz, D., Fuchs, E., Malis, S., Nuchter, A., Hertzberg, J.: Three-dimensional mapping with time-of-flight cameras. J. Field Robot. (JFR) 26, 11–12 (2009)

22. Konolige, K., Agrawal, M.: FrameSLAM: From bundle adjustment to real-time visual mapping. IEEE Trans. Robot. 25, 5 (2008)

23. Gold, S., Ping Lu, C., Rangarajan, A., Pappu, S., Mjolsness, E.: New algorithms for 2D and 3D point matching: pose estimation and correspondence. Patt. Recognit. 31, 1019–1031 (1999)

24. Aguilar, W.G., Verónica, C., José, P.: Obstacle avoidance for low-cost UAVs. IEEE 11th International Conference on Semantic Computing (ICSC), San Diego (2017)

25. Hyondong, O., Dae-Yeon, W., Sung-Sik, H., Hyunchul, D., Tahk, M.-J., Tsourdos, A.: Indoor UAV control using multi-camera visual feedback. J. Intelligent & Robot. Syst. 61(1–4), 57–84 (2011)

26. Valenti, M., Bethke, B., Frank, D., McGrew, A., Ahrens, J., How, S., Vian, J.: The MIT indoor multi-vehicle flight testbed. IEEE International Conference Robot Automation (2007)

27. Altug, E., Ostrowski, J.P., Taylor, C.J.: Control of a quadrotor helicopter using dual camera visual feedback. Int. J. Robot. Res. 24(5), 329–341 (2005)

28. Yoshihata, Y., Watanabe, K., Iwatani, Y., Hashimoto, K.: Multi-camera visual servoing of a micro helicopter under occlusions. In: Proceedings on the IEEE/RSJ International Conference on Intelligent Robots and Systems, pp. 2651–2620 (2007)
29. Mak, L.C., Whitty, M., Furukawa, T.: A localization system for an indoor rotary-wing MAV using blade mounted LEDs. Sens. Rev. **28**(2), 125–131 (2008)
30. Garage W., Intel Corporation. OpenCV. https://opencv.org/. Accessed 20 Oct 2017
31. Bradski, G., Kaehler, A.: Learning OpenCV: Computer vision with the OpenCV library, Sebastopol (2008)
32. Aguilar, W.G., Morales, S.: 3D environment mapping using the Kinect V2 and path planning based on RRT algorithms. Electronics **5**(4), 70 (2016)
33. Aguilar, W.G., Morales, S., Ruiz, H., Abad, V.: RRT* GL based optimal path planning for real-time navigation of UAVs. In: Rojas, I., Joya, G., Catala, A. (eds.) IWANN 2017. LNCS, vol. 10306, pp. 585–595. Springer, Cham (2017). https://doi.org/10.1007/978-3-319-59147-6_50
34. Aguilar, W.G., Morales, S., Ruiz, H., Abad, V.: RRT* GL based path planning for virtual aerial navigation. In: De Paolis, L.T., Bourdot, P., Mongelli, A. (eds.) AVR 2017. LNCS, vol. 10324, pp. 176–184. Springer, Cham (2017). https://doi.org/10.1007/978-3-319-60922-5_13

# Pose Estimation Based on Monocular Visual Odometry and Lane Detection for Intelligent Vehicles

Juan Galarza[1], Esteban Pérez[1], Esteban Serrano[1], Andrés Tapia[1], and Wilbert G. Aguilar[2,3(✉)]

[1] DECEM Department, Universidad de las Fuerzas Armadas ESPE,
Sangolquí, Ecuador
[2] CICTE Research Center, Universidad de las Fuerzas Armadas ESPE,
Sangolquí, Ecuador
wgaguilar@espe.edu.ec
[3] GREC Research Group, Universitat Politècnica de Catalunya,
Barcelona, Spain

**Abstract.** A fundamental element for the determination of the position (pose) of an object is to be able to determine the rotation and translation of the same in space. Visual odometry is the process of determining the location and orientation of a camera by analyzing a sequence of images. The algorithm allowed tracing the trajectory of a body in an open environment by comparing the mapping of points of a sequence of images to determine the variation of translation or rotation. The use of Lane detection is proposed to feed back the Visual Odometry algorithm, allowing more robust results. The algorithm was programmed on OpenCV 3.0 in Python 2.7 and was run on Ubuntu 16.04. The algorithm allowed tracing the trajectory of a body in an open environment by comparing the mapping of points of a sequence of images to determine the variation of translation or rotation. With the satisfactory results obtained, the development of a computational platform capable of determining the position of a vehicle in the space for assistance in parking is projected.

**Keywords:** Monocular visual odometry · Lane detection · Hough transform
Egomotion · Pose

## 1 Introduction

A fundamental element for the determination of the position (pose) of an object is to be able to determine the rotation and translation of the same in space. A simple and widely studied tool is the Monocular Visual Odometry. The present work uses an algorithm for plotting an object within an open environment using OpenCV 3.0 on Ubuntu.

Once the Monocular Visual Odometry algorithm is understood in its entirety, implementing additional mechanisms to improve system performance against disturbances and environmental conditions such as imperfections in the road, low visibility conditions, among others deemed necessary. The use of Lane detection is proposed to feed back the Visual Odometry algorithm, allowing more robust results.

© Springer International Publishing AG, part of Springer Nature 2018
L. T. De Paolis and P. Bourdot (Eds.): AVR 2018, LNCS 10851, pp. 562–566, 2018.
https://doi.org/10.1007/978-3-319-95282-6_40

## 2 Related Work

There are works such as [1] where the authors present a system capable of recovering the trajectory of a vehicle from the video input of a single camera at a very high frame-rate. The overall frame-rate is limited only by the feature extraction process, as the outlier removal and the motion estimation steps take less than 1 ms with a normal laptop computer. The algorithm relies on a novel way of removing the outliers of the feature matching process.

Other jobs such as [2] where is it proposed a semi-direct monocular visual odometry algorithm that is precise, robust, and faster than current state-of-the-art methods. The semi-direct approach eliminates the need of costly feature extraction and robust matching techniques for motion estimation. The algorithm operates directly on pixel intensities, which results in subpixel precision at high frame-rates.

There are works focused on urban environments such as [3] where it develops a system for Monocular Simultaneous Localization and Mapping (Mono-SLAM) relying solely on video input. The algorithm makes it possible to precisely estimate the camera trajectory without relying on any motion model. The estimation is completely incremental: at a given time frame, only the current location is estimated while the previous camera positions are never modified. Authors perform high precision camera trajectory estimation in urban scenes with a large amount of clutter. Using an omnidirectional camera placed on a vehicle, they cover one of the longest distance ever reported, up to 2.5 km.

In articles like [4] specific applications are analyzed as a real-time algorithm for computing the ego-motion of a vehicle relative to the road. The algorithm uses as input only those images provided by a single omnidirectional camera mounted on the roof of the vehicle. The front ends of the system are two different trackers. The first one is a homography-based tracker that detects and matches robust scale-invariant features that most likely belong to the ground plane. The second one uses an appearance-based approach and gives high-resolution estimates of the rotation of the vehicle. This planar pose estimation method has been successfully applied to videos from an automotive platform.

The work presented in [5] present an algorithm for detecting marks of road lane and road boundary with a view to the smart navigation of intelligent vehicles. The experimental results show the effectiveness of the proposed algorithm on both straight and slightly curved road scene images under different day light conditions and the presence of shadows on the roads.

In works such as [6], review of lane detection and tracking algorithms developed in the last decade is discussed. Several modalities are considered for lane detection which include vision, LIDAR, vehicle odometry information, information from global positioning system and digital maps. The lane detection and tracking is one of the challenging problems in computer vision.

Other papers such as [7–10] describe methodologies and approaches for lane detection, with a focus on vehicle safety and the development of navigation systems and other real time applications.

The existing state of the art will be used as the initial basis to begin with the short-term development of a functional platform applicable to real environments.

# 3  Our Approach

Visual odometry is the process of determining the location and orientation of a camera by analyzing a sequence of images. Other authors such as [11] state that Visual odometry (VO) is the process of estimating the egomotion of an agent (e.g., vehicle, human, and robot) using only the input of a single or multiple cameras attached to it. Application domains and robot) using only the input of a single or the egomotion of an agent (e.g., vehicle, human, Visual odometry (VO) is the process of estimating include robotics, wearable computing, augmented reality, and automotive. The term was chosen for its similarity to wheel odometry, which incrementally estimates the motion of a vehicle by integrating the number of turns of its wheels over time. Likewise, VO operates by incrementally estimating the pose of the vehicle through examination of the changes that motion induces on the images of its onboard cameras. For VO to work effectively, there should be sufficient illumination in the environment and a static scene with enough texture to allow apparent motion to be extracted. Furthermore, consecutive frames should be captured by ensuring that they have sufficient scene overlap. Egomotion is defined as any environmental displacement of the observer [12].

When images are to be used in different areas of image analysis such as object recognition, it is important to reduce the amount of data in the image while preserving the important, characteristic, structural information. Edge detection makes it possible to reduce the amount of data in an image considerably. However the output from an edge detector is still a image described by it's pixels. If lines, ellipses and so forth could be defined by their characteristic equations, the amount of data would be reduced even more. The Hough transform was originally developed to recognize lines, and has later been generalized to cover arbitrary shapes [13].

The algorithm for detecting straight lines can be divided into the following steps:

1. Edge detection, e.g. using the Canny edge detector.
2. Mapping of edge points to the Hough space and storage in an accumulator.
3. Interpretation of the accumulator to yield lines of infinite length. The interpretation is done by thresholding and possibly other constraints.
4. Conversion of infinite lines to finite lines.

The finite lines can be superimposed back on the original image. The algorithm traces the trajectory of a body in an open environment by comparing the mapping of points of a sequence of images to determine the pose.

The general method of lane detection is to first take an image of road with the help of a camera fixed in the vehicle. Then the image is converted to a grayscale image in order to minimize the processing time. Secondly, as presence of noise in the image will hinder the correct edge detection. Therefore, filters should be applied to remove noises like bilateral filter, gabor filter, trilateral filter Then the edge detector is used to produce an edge image by using canny filter with automatic thresholding to obtain the edges. Then edged image is sent to the line detector after detecting the edges which will produces a right and left lane boundary segment. The lane boundary scan uses the information in the edge image detected by the Hough transform to perform the scan. The scan returns a series of points on the right and left side. Finally pair of hyperbolas is fitted to these data points to represent the lane boundaries. For visualization purposes the hyperbolas are displayed on the original color image

## 4    Experiments and Results

The algorithm for Monocular Visual Odometry allowed tracing the trajectory of a body in an open environment by comparing the mapping of points of a sequence of images to determine the variation of translation or rotation. The algorithm was programmed on OpenCV 3.0 in Python 2.7 and was run on Ubuntu 16.04. The frames of the video were extracted and stored for further processing.

The results obtained are presented below (Fig. 1):

**Fig. 1.** Monocular Visual Odometry. Experiments and results.

The algorithm for lane detection the algorithm allowed to detect and graph the lanes of a properly signalized road, under favorable climatic conditions. The algorithm was programmed on OpenCV 3.0 in Python 2.7 and was run on Ubuntu 16.04. The frames of the video were extracted and stored for further processing.

The results obtained are presented below (Fig. 2):

Video results are provided on https://www.youtube.com/watch?v=kcRcAlmljKQ.

**Fig. 2.** Lane detection. Experiments and results.

# 5  Conclusions

The algorithm allowed tracing the trajectory of a body in an open environment by comparing the mapping of points of a sequence of images to determine the variation of translation or rotation.

Based on the results obtained in tests, it is concluded that the lane detection means appropriate tool for improving the proposed algorithms for Monocular Visual Odometry. With the satisfactory results obtained, the development of a computational platform capable of determining the position of a vehicle in the space for assistance in parking is projected.

# References

1. Scaramuzza, D., Fraundorfer, F., Siegwart, R.: Real-time monocular visual odometry for on-road vehicles with 1-point RANSAC. In: IEEE International Conference on Robotics and Automation, pp. 4293–4299 (2009)
2. Forster, C., Pizzoli, M., Scaramuzza, D.: SVO: Fast semi-direct monocular visual odometry. In: Proceedings of IEEE International Conference on Robotics and Automation, pp. 15–22 (2014)
3. Tardif, J.-P., Pavlidis, Y., Daniilidis, K.: Monocular visual odometry in urban environments using an omnidirectional camera. In: IEEE/RSJ International Conference on Intelligent Robots and Systems, pp. 2531–2538 (2008)
4. Scaramuzza, D., Siegwart, R.: Appearance-guided monocular omnidirectional visual odometry for outdoor ground vehicles. IEEE Trans. Robot. 24(5), 1015–1026 (2008)
5. Saha, A., Das Roy, D., Alam, T., Deb, K.: Automated road lane detection for intelligent vehicles. Glob. J. Comput. Sci. Technol., 12(6) (2012)
6. Kumar, A.M., Simon, P.: Review of lane detection and tracking algorithms in advanced driver assistance system. Int. J. Comput. Sci. Inf. Technol. 7(4), 65–78 (2015)
7. Kim, Z.: Robust lane detection and tracking in challenging scenerios. IEEE Trans. Intell. Transp. Syst. 9(1), 16–26 (2008)
8. Kaur, G., Kumar, D.: Lane detection techniques: a review. Int. J. Comput. Appl. 112(10), 975–8887 (2015)
9. Bar Hillel, A., Lerner, R., Levi, D., Raz, G.: Recent progress in road and lane detection: a survey. Mach. Vis. Appl. 25(3), 727–745 (2014)
10. Somasundaram, G.: Lane change detection and tracking for a safe-lane approach in real time vision based navigation systems. Ccsea 2011, 345–361 (2011)
11. Scaramuzza, D., Fraundorfer, F.: Tutorial: visual odometry. IEEE Robot. Autom. Mag. 18(4), 80–92 (2011)
12. Warren, R.: The perception of egomotion. J. Exp. Psychol. Hum. Percept. Perform. 2(3), 448–456 (1976)
13. Space, T.H.: Line detection by hough transformation. Transformation 2, 2–8 (2009)

# Human-Computer Interaction

# Towards Assisting Interactive Reality

## Interactive Reality for Education, Data Analysis and Industry

Ahmet Kose[(✉)], Aleksei Tepljakov, and Eduard Petlenkov

Department of Computer Systems, Tallinn University of Technology,
Ehitajate tee 5, 19086 Tallinn, Estonia
ahmet.kose@ttu.ee

**Abstract.** This paper addresses an interactive virtual reality based application of a physical environment. The application presents notable aspects for education, data analysis and industry since the physical building serves as a research and development center. As the project based on physical environment, one of the main target for the work is also concentrated to give high presence feeling for end-users. The developed application is verified in real time. We also introduced our findings in real-time data communication, detection and analysis of human behavior in immersive environment, control systems integration to VR. Data analysis part of the research is linked to human behaviors based on the perception of computational intelligence methods. The activities in immersive environment are engaged to entertaining and joyful learning approaches. Some ideas for further development are also described.

**Keywords:** Virtual Reality · Real-time communication
Human behavior · Architecture modelling · Intelligent systems
Data analysis

## 1 Introduction

Recent significant growth in computer science and technology has complemented computer–simulated environments such as Virtual Reality (VR). Revolutionary growth in computational power in the last few decades gave rise to interactive graphical representation. The rise in high-end human computer interface including VR enhances to immerse completely in virtual environment (VE). The advent of low-cost head-mounted display (HMD) devices such as Oculus Rift [1] and HTC Vive [2] made this technology accessible at large and featured VR with user real-world position and orientation tracking. Therefore, present advancement in VR technology allows to induce a persistent effect of presence in a visual world [3]. Virtual environments (VE) have proven effective in a number of scientific, industrial and medical applications such as [4–7] are employed to, including but not limited to: computer-simulated environments, visualizations of complex data, joyful learning tools etc.

© Springer International Publishing AG, part of Springer Nature 2018
L. T. De Paolis and P. Bourdot (Eds.): AVR 2018, LNCS 10851, pp. 569–588, 2018.
https://doi.org/10.1007/978-3-319-95282-6_41

VR can be considered a very convenient tool to complement learning aspects, particularly for education in engineering. One of great example to point out is as an extension of VR – Virtual Labs (VLs) are usually referred to computer based simulations. They offer similar vision and methods of work to their traditional counterparts [8]. VLs can give access to large number of users at once. Users likewise gain an experience by interacting with accurate replications of physical objects or artificial equipment in VLs. In our earlier work [9], we have introduced the fully immersive environment based on the physical architecture. The architecture includes significant amount of laboratories in diversified fields, particularly conducted with engineering fields. The facility is also used as a research and development center of Tallinn University of Technology [10]. Replication of the building is shown in Fig. 1.

**Fig. 1.** Exterior visualization based on a real-life building [9]

In this work, we advance interior design of the building. We also present the improved replication of the architecture to deliver VLs experience linked to two laboratories – Electronics laboratory and control systems laboratory. Besides that, novelty approach of the framework in this paper is real–time data communication between the game engine and third party software to apply accurate mathematical models for replications of laboratory equipment. As a remarkable benefit of this framework, interactions by users receive real–time feedback with realistic perspective as original objects. Therefore, the VR based interactive application gives better understanding of control systems and allow users to have more efficient learning experience than existing familiar VR based applications.

We now outline the main contribution of the present paper.

First, we create 3D models of objects located in the facility. We also apply texturing to maximize a persistent effect of presence in a visual world. Next, we import created and rendered models to the game engine where we actually create the application. In following section, we describe current problems based on the real-life objects in educational facilities and we introduce our framework to alleviate conditions and alternate laboratories. Then, we provide the description of the proposed VR environment with the complete interaction configuration.

Next, we present the novel developments related to the real-time implementation. Finally, we report and address the initial findings related to the human behavior while the user experiences the application and outline some related items for future research. We also describe our vision to apply computational intelligence methods linked to human behavior in this framework.

The structure of the paper is as follows. In Sect. 2, the replication process of large scale building is described. In Sect. 3, the reader is introduced to human-computer interaction conducted with the immersive environment. Process of real-time data communication with digital twins (DT) objects are explained in Sect. 4. The concept of human behavior is addressed in Sect. 5. Finally, conclusions are drawn in Sect. 6.

## 2    Replication of Large Scale Building

Successful immersive applications based on realistic environment minimize difference among physical and virtual environments. Hence, authors considered to create the virtual environment based on physical conditions precisely. The presented application integrates interactive graphical presentation of the physical building, data communication in real-time, corresponding mathematical models and feasibility study of computational intelligence methods. Although the physical building is unique and extended features are relevant, the process for composing the architecture replica is familiar with existing VR applications. The process is as follows:

(a) Environmental Creation and System Design,
(b) Modeling and Texturing,
(c) Software and Hardware Integration,
(d) Optimization.

Unreal Engine 4 was employed to create the virtual environment as the engine is well known, feature-complete and capable solution for VR development purposes [11]. Robustness, compatibility and low maintenance cost could be considered as some of prior advantages for the preferred physics engine. Overall, using primary game engines is relevant to benefit prominent VR development methods such as the concept of object oriented programming, graphics, reusable code with libraries [12]. Those benefits are also used to create communication tool between software linked to the project. The chosen engine allows to create realistic environments and simulate realistic affects. Head tracking devices are in charge of dynamic altering for the vision of users. Hence users can also feel lifelike interaction during experiencing the application.

As a matter of fact, the teleportation feature is considered to be very suitable tool for the application like other large scale environments. That feature allows users to move independently and effortless in computer simulated realistic facility during investigating the environment. Furthermore, independent movement may also grant users to sense self-learning activities in VE. The user can still interact and during continuous movements.

In what follows, we outline primary stages of the recreation process in a separate subsection.

## 2.1   3D Modeling

In this phase, the 3D model, texturing and rendering of the building were progressed. Creating replication of components for virtual environment is a remarkable part of the process. The whole concept is accomplished to receive high efficiency for supervised and unsupervised human learning. The floor plan of facility is utilized used for accurate virtual environment based on physical assets. Features of those assets are referred for 3D modeling, texturing and rendering by using Autodesk Maya software [13]. 3D models of physical objects were developed using polygon shape and modified using functions such as extrudes, append etc. Reactions of those models to the lighting depend on information from the materials. The physics engine can respectfully identify the material components and map file (Textures) with film-box (FBX) file format. Texture map is directly related to the quality of the model for the physics engine. In addition, Using Level of Detail (LOD) feature is utilized to simplify the 3D models. LOD is useful to reduce the number of polygons for rendering. It is important to receive better vision on VR devices with better performance. Overall, the design should ensure the virtual quality to maximize impact of presence feeling during the experience [14]. Whereas, existing objects in virtual environment should be presented with

**Fig. 2.** Screenshots from two rooms in the VR based application

high rendering aspect. Therefore, we likewise preferred to avoid emissive color contents for replicated objects. Some replication of rooms are shown in Fig. 2.

## 2.2 Recreation of Environment and Software Management

Visualization is applied in various fields related to such as education, product visualization, interactive multimedia and in architecture etc. It is claimed in [15] that visualization is useful to construct intellectual procedures. The virtual environment is employed for multiple purposes such bridging Cyber-Pyhsical Systems (CPS) to VR interface, self-learning activities, physiological and psychological aspects of virtual reality. Although creating an environment is the most time consuming of stage in process, significant accuracy would reduce harder rework. At first, terrain is an essential part of environment where the artificial building lies on. Otherwise the user would be in fully infinitive virtual environment where the presence feeling may not be applied. Flexible massive terrain is done by the Landscape tool in preferred game engine which can be applied for different platforms [16]. Fundamental parts such as walls, columns etc. are inserted in physics engine according to suggested scale compatibility of physics engine (1 unreal unit is equal to 1 cm) [17]. Repeating some fundamental parts are applicable regarding the floor plan. Once modeling and texturing are processed, all the content is created in the physics engine. In other words, we assembly all the artificial models based on physical world in the immersive environment. The principle logic of the application is referred to predefined VR class of the engine: Motion Controller Pawn, HUD, VR Game-mode, Player Controller.

Some users are still inexperienced in using HMD devices. Some difficulties such as insecure emotions were observed occasionally thereof. In addition, it was not pleasant to be isolated from the physical world. Therefore, we decided to benefit from Open Source Computer Vision (OpenCV) library to employ a webcam in virtual environment. The plugin enables to display physical environment at same time while the user experiences in VR. The screenshot of implementation is depicted in Fig. 3. The library also allows to develop Mixed Reality (MR) environments. MR is usually represented in three forms. Those forms can be defined as Augmented Reality (AR), Augmented Virtuality (AV) and VR. In AR, the virtual and real content can be implemented through the physical world by mixing and registering. AV is slightly closer to VR, which refers to approaching physical objects in to a virtual world. Real objects can be integrated to the virtual world, hence it is possible to interact with them synchronously in MR [18]. MR extension of the application will be implemented during further developments.

The application is served with Oculus Rift and HTC Vive. Therefore, users can experience physical mobility in real room scale, real-time positioning and tracking with advanced display resolution. Integrating two most common VR devices also allows us to compare usability and efficiency for the VE. Although authors also proceed with Oculus Rift, HTC Vive is employed more frequently. Independent navigational benefits, convenient hand-held controllers, high resolution display are some facts to prefer HTC Vive. The HMD provides $1080 \times 1200$

**Fig. 3.** Display of physical environment while VR based experience

resolution per eye, and the 9-DOF with 2 lighthouse base stations for tracking. Also the HMD set has two sets of controller. The controller features 24 sensors, dual-stage trigger and multi-function trackpad [19]. Developing with the engine and running the serious game require specific hardware and software requirements. The application run on a PC equipped with a 4.00 GHz Intel i7-6700 processor, 32 GB RAM, and an NVidia GTX 980 graphic card. HTC Vive HMD used for running the project.

## 3   Human Computer Interaction in Immersive Environment

Research and development abilities directly connected with growth in computational power. In other words, the ability to deal with more complicated problems has become within reach while computer science and technology expands significantly [20]. Educational facilities, particularly education in engineering also have been complemented with the recent growth. Researchers have been able to investigate theoretical knowledge and present findings in greater complex levels. It is important to point out that the formal verifications of theoretical findings are presented most commonly with mathematical models. On the other hand, majority of courses including education in engineering are usually introduced by traditional teaching approaches in classroom settings. Moreover, if those approaches are also merged with recent findings, the content of courses can be filled up heavily with math intensive, also remain abstract. The adversity might likely cause failures to enlighten the realities of different types of system implementations [21]. Unlike education served by traditional way, practices linked to laboratory based environments may provide remarkable educational benefits. For instance, students who enroll to experiments are able to investigate the resulting dynamics immediately. Besides that, practical objects can give access to them in order to interact with some physical parameters of the sample system. Therefore, those advantages would lighten students regarding some physical phenomena that are inconvenient to perceive by only a theoretical point of view thought in classroom [22]. Consequently, in this framework, authors likewise concentrate to conduct practical objects with the VR based application in order to obtain efficient and joyful learning experience.

### 3.1 Interactions

Human–Machine Interaction (HMI) is one of notable research topics. The efficiency of learning process is directly conducted with the interactivity. The interactivity encourages students to play a more active role and to get involved in learning process [22]. However, assuring quality of practice in interactive laboratories might be rather difficult problem with correlation between complexity of laboratory equipment and its cost. Furthermore, the magnificent increasing number of students in engineering enforces the limited capacity of laboratories. Hence, large groups of students must then be divided into smaller groups for direct guidance, which significantly increases the workload of the academic staff [23]. Interactive graphical representation of physical equipment can be sufficient approach to avoid previously mentioned difficulties. In addition, accurate simulated replications can complement important aspects of learning different types of systems dynamics. Students likewise can understand dynamics of systems and validate their theoretical knowledge with prototypes [24]. As a matter of fact, merging interactions in virtual reality, brings different perspective to HMI. In other words, HMI can be obtained to maximize in artificial reality conditions [25].

One of the main attitude of VR development is allow user to interact as much as they desire. It gives them independent movement, thinking and improving themselves with support of VE. Moving in the scene of VR can be operated through HMD controller using teleportation, physical movement etc. Users can direct any locations where navigation maps are implemented. Recently, immersive environments have been enriched with interactive graphical user interfaces that let students manipulate the experiment parameters and, explore their evolution [26]. Meanwhile, researchers accomplished several VR based applications in educational aspects to avoid if not relief continuous difficulties to engage students with experiments [27–30]. In general, large amount of students can gain an experience at once by interacting with replications of physical objects within limitations of accurate system identifications, if it is possible to run VR based applications simultaneously.

The presented VR based application allows users to interact by handles are provided with VR device. Although basic interactions have already implemented on previous contribution, major parts of present work is linked to HMI. Previously, we provided an questionnaire to participants who had experienced the replication of the architecture [9]. According to results, we experienced that there is no major differences between real building and virtual replica. Basic interactions in the application also engaged their attention. However, we also observed that functionalities of virtual environment were limited. They would like to demonstrate practical activities. Therefore, presented VR based application concentrate to grant users to have efficient learning experience and minimize limitations. In order to let users experience with real-time applications, we provide an experiment with visual representation of sound source comes through reality. Besides that, we created accurate replications of laboratory equipment supplied with mathematical models. We employ those objects in real-time to give better understanding of control systems. Lastly, we have assembled a vehicle controlled via hand tracking technology and replicated in VR to illustrate. The VR application hereby is complemented with practical activities. Those applications are described in following sections.

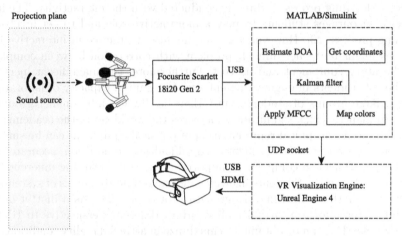

**Fig. 4.** Experimental configuration and signal flow

## 3.2   Experimental Study–Synesthesia

Synesthesia is the act of experiencing one sense modality as another. For example, a person may vividly experience flashes of colors when listening to a series of sounds. Virtual Reality allows to achieve this transition easily, since it can be used to present the spatial whereabouts of the sound source as well as visualize the sound content in a meaningful way. The ultimate goal of the experiment is to provide means for inducing voluntary synesthetic experiences through the VR based application. In our earlier work [31], we have reported initial findings related to acoustic localization and sound processing based on prerecorded data. In further work [3], we describe the revised technical solution meant to deliver the synesthetic experience to the listener in real time. The process of the experimental setup as follow; First, we apply an acoustic localization method to the problem of locating the sound source. We also apply a Kalman filter to reduce motion noise generated by the uncertainty of sound source location prediction. Next, for consistency, we summarize the method for extracting dominant features from the audio spectrum of the sound source and mapping those to the object representing the sound source in the VR environment. Then, we provide the description of the proposed VR system prototype and the complete experimental configuration is shown in Fig. 4. Finally, we present the novel developments related to the real-time implementation thereof. The real-life experimental layout is shown in Fig. 5. Most importantly, the experiments allowed us to gain deeper insight into the effect generated by introducing sound visualization with source localization in a VR environment. It is also of interest to repeat the experiment to analysis human behavior with corresponding artificial sensing. To provide a further illustration of the visualization part, we moved the prototype to Re:creation Virtual and Augmented Reality laboratory [32] located in the same building. Therefore, the real-time migrated experiment to the laboratory where the application is launched is shown in Fig. 6. In this figure, one can observe a snapshot of the visualization resulting in a speaker in the real environment pronouncing the word "hats". It can be noticed, as mentioned previously, the sound "s" with the jet color mapping results in a yellow sphere being produced.

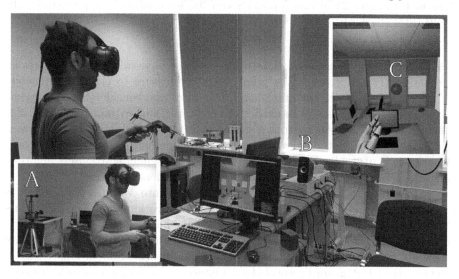

**Fig. 5.** Experimental real-time prototype setup. Elements on image: A—Microphone array; B—Emulated sound source (Bluetooth speaker); C—Spherical visualization as it appears in the recreated room VR environment

## 4   Real Time Data Communication

Learning management systems are utilized commonly within distance education in the last years. Although the usage of those systems can be addressed to complement educational aspects, they do not usually ensure any possibility of illustrating scientific phenomena [33]. Hence, experiment devices could be linked to advance alternative methods. Due to paradigm conducted to distance education, particularly in scientific and technical areas, creation of virtual and/or remote laboratories have become high priority for educational facilities to be universal, successful and advanced environment [34]. Remote Labs (RLs) are broad facilities which use physical devices and plants at distance [35]. RLs have

**Fig. 6.** The migrated experiment presents visualization resulting from pronouncing the word "hats" (Color figure online)

an advantage to receive real time feedback from physical objects with realistic perspective. Moreover, RLs grant flexibility feature to change parameters of implementation. On the other hand, RLs also have considerable limitations. Experiments in RLs cannot be carried out in parallel since equipment is in charge of corresponding. In other words, a student who is not conducting an experiment can only watch the student who is performing an experiment remotely, if only laboratory is utilized with observation tools. Limitation of active users in a time might also cause the drop of motivation among students.

In order to gain the main advantage of RLs into VR based applications successfully, we created a real-time data communication tool. The Blueprints Visual Scripting system in Unreal Engine is a complete game-play scripting system based on the concept of using a node-based interface to create game-play elements from within Unreal Editor [36]. The Blueprint system allowed us to create a User Datagram Protocol (UDP) interface [37] to communicate between MATLAB and the physics engine based on a custom C++ class. To avoid problems with Blueprint multi-threading in Unreal Engine 4, the implementation uses a custom class variable to transfer data between threads to avoid a racing condition in requesting/getting new data from the UDP socket. With this approach, reliable communication via a UDP socket at high sampling rates such as $f_s = 1\,\mathrm{kHz}$ is easily achieved.

The complete visualization thus comprises the following components:

- A C++ class based UDP socket implementation available to the UE4 Blueprint scripting system;
- All necessary animations are scripted in UE4 Blueprints and are based on the information received via the UDP socket from MATLAB software;
- The area where the equipment is located is recreated in the virtual environment.

Since HTC Vive is used, the corresponding UE4 VR template is employed and thus the user can navigate inside of the virtual environment. The main idea here is to synchronize the user real-world location and that in the VR environment.

### 4.1 Digital Twins into Education

The framework is dedicated to creating virtual objects for real-time experiments. The concept of DT is creating and interacting a digital representation of the real world objects by the means of optimization and simulation tools, which are fed with real and updated data [38]. In addition, the concept of DT from the VR perspective in this paper is referred to realistic replications of corresponding original objects by identifying mathematical models of the system to maximize the feeling of physical interaction in immersive environment. Initially, we model objects located in educational facilities such as laboratory, because this allows us to obtain highly accurate mathematical models of their dynamic systems. Thus, the educational value of the complete visualization should be high. A specific goal is to mathematically model and implement physically accurate interactions between the user and the virtual objects. Future goals also include modeling real-life industrial objects for implementing specialized virtual training, also decreasing cost of research and development aspects.

### 4.2 Digital Twins Approach of Control Systems in Immersive Environment

Hereinafter, the process of the development of several DT is provided. The original real-life control objects that served as reference for the DT were produced by Inteco [49]. So far, three objects have been modeled: The Magnetic Levitation System, the 3D Crane, and the Inverted Pendulum. The diagram showing the prototyping configuration is depicted in Fig. 7. The process of the development as follows:

**Mathematical Modeling.** It is previously mentioned in Sect. 3 that mathematical models are applied to achieve accurate replications. In our case, the purpose of mathematical modeling is to establish a dynamic relationship between the states of the system and also the inputs. States and inputs represent some physical parameters of the system. The usual "box" models are commonly used for modeling approaches. In this work, we have proceed with grey box and black box modeling. The grey box model can be defined as the structure of the model is known and the model is derived from physical laws. Certain parts of the model are approximated adequately for modeling purposes. In addition, black box modeling is usually referred to the system does not provide relevant information about its physical structure [39]. Hence, the model is complemented by fitting experimental data to identify mathematical model of the system accordingly.

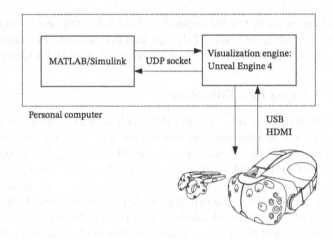

**Fig. 7.** Process of the application for real-time platform

To accomplish accurate modeling of physical objects in this work, we followed two methods: We sample meaningful data by the sensors of the real-life control object. The devices are also connected to the desktop computer through a data acquisition device. We analyze video to derive data in the way to validate our findings. More precisely, we record a video clip contains motion of a certain part of the control object to analyze. We also take into account that stability is not required for control objects. The reason for that introduced virtual objects in the frame of DT should be able to illustrate various related concepts. Thus, DT of physical objects are complemented with a proportional-integral-derivative (PID) controller which is also used frequently for industrial applications [40].

**Interaction Implementation.** The efficiency of learning process is directly conducted with the interactivity which can be considered the primary component of an immersive VR environment. Therefore, the process of DT objects are composed to ensure efficient laboratory instruction. Set points of control objects are changeable to give a better understanding of the system for the user. Besides that, one of the most interesting part of replicated objects give access the user to interact directly with moving parts of virtual objects. Controllers of employed VR device are used to maximize the feeling of physical interaction which causes disturbances in the controlled systems. From the user perspective, such interactions are of curiosity driven experimental nature. Applying responses to interaction mechanics are challenging. Hence, we repeat revisions the mechanics of DT by the subject-based evaluation method until results have become satisfactory.

**3D Modeling and Prototyping in Real Time.** 3D modeling of those objects are implemented the similar process with the creation of virtual environment which detailed in Sect. 2.1. It is likewise important to point out that creation of objects are completed in other modeling software – Blender 3D modeling

**Fig. 8.** Physical object -ML and its 3D model

software [41]. The reason for that to compare two different 3D modeling software according to our needs as well as expectations. One of physical objects and its 3D model is shown in Fig. 8. Previously mentioned UDP communication plugin in Sect. 4 for the game engine that makes real-time simulation possible with Matlab. In order to progress the prototyping in real time, we export validated mathematical models to the game engine as C++ code and/or featured visual scripting method discussed in Sect. 4. By this approach, we enhance flexibility in terms of amount of inputs and outputs for the system and corresponding mathematical models of dynamics. UDP plugin as well as exported modules can also be reused in any project. Once, we set up Matlab via Simulink Desktop Real-Time toolbox and the application via the game engine, created prototypes in the same platform are effectively used to teach control system design. The platform includes modeled objects described in Sect. 4.2 enables to work as a group or as a single user. For instance, the application can run simultaneously if Matlab is set up another computer. Besides that, meanwhile a student is experiencing the virtual object, another student can modify the mathematical model if it is desired. Figure 9 presents the replication of inverted pendulum while the user experiences interactivity in VR based application.

### 4.3   Implementation of Digital Twins for Hand Tracking Technology Based Vehicle

In what follows, to illustrate DT aspect, we have created a vehicle controlled via Leap Motion [42]. First, we assembled the vehicle and attached an arduino board to join interactive electronic objects. Since arduino is known as an open-source electronic prototyping platform, the project has been accomplished adequately. As soon as the assembling phase was completed, we wanted to complement the vehicle with hand tracking device. Finally, the controller was optimized in order to run the vehicle with its replication simultaneously. The completed vehicle is shown in Fig. 10. Practically, Leap Motion is designed to be embedded directly

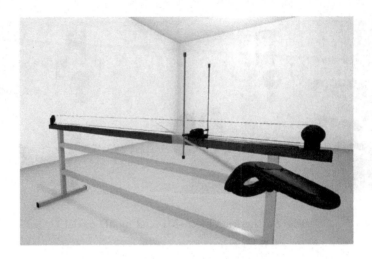

**Fig. 9.** Inverted Pendulum in immersive environment

into VR/AR headsets. Therefore, we suppose that merging such technology in physical object with its DT would serve for demonstrating purposes. Once, the vehicle is completed, its 3D model was created with relevant texturing and rendering aspects. The process of 3D model has been similar to the immersive environment. Next, the 3D model is exported to the game engine where the VR based application is placed. To present a relevant output, we prepared a small track to run both at same time in physical facility and immersive environment. The starting point has been chosen the same reference as well as the track for racing is shown in Fig. 11. Lastly, to validate the achievement, we let users experience the object in both environment. According to their feedback, we ensure that virtual replica has been modeled and functioned successfully the way how the physical is operated. It was exciting to be able to drive the vehicle and meanwhile, to understand how the hand tracking technology works. Most of the participants were attracted by virtual object rather than its physical asset.

## 5    Merging Big Data Visualization and Analysis with VR

Big Data has taken attention of all the industries including, educational facilities, public sector, commercial companies [43]. Investigation of large data-sets usually require visual analytic. On the other hand, the challenge of meaningful visualization of Big Data increases exponentially with significant growth of computational power. Actual challenge is not only to process provided huge amount of data but to process data with high diversity. Although traditional visualization tools have been enforced to extend, they have already reached to their limits when encountered with very large data which are evolving continuously [44]. Therefore, it is necessary to investigate present possibilities to clarify traditional blended techniques such as Virtual Reality (VR). In our perspective, we aim to

**Fig. 10.** The physical vehicle joined with leap motion and arduino

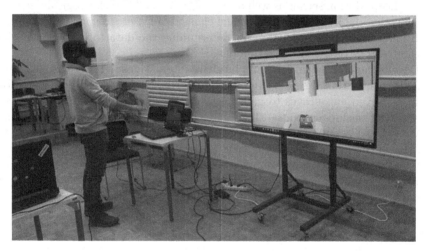

**Fig. 11.** Digital replication of the physical vehicle controlled via leap motion

use dynamic modeling to alleviate difficulties linked to data visualization. The dynamic modeling can ensure to make short time predictions and proactively start downloading the part of the system or process that have to be visualized next. This will make possible high quality and smooth visualization of Big Data based complex systems. Therefore, VR models of real systems and processes will be much more realistic and immersive.

## 5.1 Methodology

Visualization of complex processes (for example chemical processes on atomic level, movements of the layers of the Earth during millions of years etc.) requires downloading huge amounts of data. When working in spatial and geographical domains, simulations and VR can lead to better discovery [45]. In order to alleviate the problem of visualization of Big Data with VR, accurate mathematical model of human behavior using computational intelligence methods can be applied. One of the key issue that investigating a solution to predict user's behavior. The prediction might allow to preload the necessary data from a large visualization dataset. In addition, the solution would also benefit VR based applications to provide a seamless immersive experience to the user. In order to gain the following highly important advantages in complex visualizations, it is notable to engage with key issues which need to be investigated as follows:

1. Development of fast and accurate tracking of human movement in virtual reality, the CAVE [7] and similar VR and AR visualization systems. In addition, to increase accuracy, it would be beneficial to use Microsoft Kinect and the Leap Motion sensor as well as any other available technological means for collecting data for modeling specific elements of user's behavior.
2. Human movement prediction for determining the data to be preloaded into the memory of the visualization device.
3. Development of meaningful and intuitive interactions with the visualizations. This ensures that the data can be explored efficiently and in a way that allows to and even encourages to gain new insights into complex interconnections and relationships given the three-dimensional representation of the data in a virtual reality environment. New efficient forms of perception are expected to arise in this context.
4. Creating a collaborative immersive environment where data scientists can interact with the data and among themselves to increase the efficiency of the data study.

## 5.2 System Identification and Modeling

It is apparent that accurate mathematical model of human behavior in VR requires significant amount of time and effort. In order to process efficiently in the framework of this research, we created a prototyping platform with similar vision described in Sect. 4.2. The platform is also implemented with three software packages: Unreal Engine 4 is employed as the visualization platform while the user experiences the virtual facility with interactive equipment. Motion capture is achieved using present HMD technology which provides access to user movement data. UDP serves as a communication plugin between the game engine and software environment that makes real-time data communication and simulation possible. To proceed with modeling of user head and controller movement, the data of user is sent out to MATLAB to analysis and apply computational intelligence methods. Authors already investigated possible system identification modeling in [39, 46, 47] including artificial neural networks for different contents. In addition to that in [48], novel findings are introduced in various VR applications of data analysis including video cuts, panorama thumbnails, panorama video synopsis, and saliency-based compression. Those findings will be considered for our research. The present configuration and future aspect can be seen in Fig. 12. The project is in the stage of collecting sufficient amount of data sets to employ computational intelligence methods completely.

**Fig. 12.** Data analysis of behavior, (a) Present configuration (b) Forthcoming setup

# 6  Conclusions

In this paper, the general framework towards developing a full-scale interactive VR based application has been introduced. First, the procedure of recreating the architecture was presented– we have described replication of physical assets, creation of virtual environment based on the physical building and integration of hardware devices. In this contribution, the real-time solution was implemented in a VR environment. We created the virtual environment to also demonstrate real-time experiments. The real-time data communication is employed to complement virtual objects in terms of interactivity and accuracy. Those experiments were successful and provided important insights into the development of interactive VR based application. Moreover, recent developments of VR based learning aspects linked to virtual laboratories were reviewed. As a result, the application enhances remarkable advantages of using VR technology in practice. It is also actively used for learning aspects at the present time. Provided feedback from users validate the significant potential in order to benefit from DT approach in VR. Since the present application is envisioned to be used for real-time educational and industrial applications, further development efforts also should be exhibited to different systems. Besides that, the results of proposed dynamic modeling of human behavior is in the stage of collecting sufficient amount of data to apply computational intelligence methods and further results for this research will be presented in future.

# References

1. Oculus VR, LLC. Oculus Rift (2017). Accessed 20 Apr 2017
2. HTC Corporation. HTC Vive (2017). Accessed 20 Apr 2017
3. Kose, A., Tepljakov, A., Astapov, S.: Real-time localization and visualization of a sound source for virtual reality applications. In: 2017 25th International Conference on Software, Telecommunications and Computer Networks (SoftCOM). IEEE, September 2017
4. Psotka, J.: Immersive training systems: virtual reality and education and training. Instr. Sci. **23**(5–6), 405–431 (1995)
5. Donalek, C., Djorgovski, S.G., Cioc, A., Wang, A., Zhang, J., Lawler, E., Yeh, S., Mahabal, A., Graham, M., Drake, A., Davidoff, S., Norris, J.S., Longo, G.: Immersive and collaborative data visualization using virtual reality platforms. In: 2014 IEEE International Conference on Big Data, pp. 609–614, October 2014
6. Draganov, I.R., Boumbarov, O.L.: Investigating Oculus Rift virtual reality display applicability to medical assistive system for motor disabled patients. In: 2015 IEEE 8th International Conference on Intelligent Data Acquisition and Advanced Computing Systems: Technology and Applications (IDAACS), vol. 2, pp. 751–754. IEEE (2015)
7. Cordeil, M., Dwyer, T., Klein, K., Laha, B., Marriott, K., Thomas, B.H.: Immersive collaborative analysis of network connectivity: CAVE-style or head-mounted display? IEEE Trans. Vis. Comput. Graph. **23**(1), 441–450 (2017)
8. Guimaraes, E.G., Cardozo, E., Moraes, D.H., Coelho, P.R.: Design and implementation issues for modern remote laboratories. IEEE Trans. Learn. Technol. **4**(2), 149–161 (2011)
9. Kose, A., Petlenkov, E., Tepljakov, A., Vassiljeva, K.: Virtual reality meets intelligence in large scale architecture. In: De Paolis, L.T., Bourdot, P., Mongelli, A. (eds.) AVR 2017,Part II. LNCS, vol. 10325, pp. 297–309. Springer, Cham (2017). https://doi.org/10.1007/978-3-319-60928-7_26
10. Tallinn University of Technology. Mektory (2017). Accessed 20 Mar 2018
11. Epic Games. Unreal Engine. Accessed 3 June 2016
12. Torres-Ferreyros, C.M., Festini-Wendorff, M.A., Shiguihara-Juarez, P.N.: Developing a videogame using unreal engine based on a four stages methodology. In: 2016 IEEE ANDESCON, pp. 1–4. Institute of Electrical and Electronics Engineers (IEEE), October 2016
13. Autodesk Maya Software. Features (2017). Accessed 25 May 2017
14. Jing, X.: Design and implementation of 3d virtual digital campus - based on unity3d. In: 2016 Eighth International Conference on Measuring Technology and Mechatronics Automation (ICMTMA), pp. 187–190. Institute of Electrical and Electronics Engineers (IEEE), March 2016
15. Bresciani, S.: The design process: a visual model. In: 2015 19th International Conference on Information Visualisation, pp. 354–359. Institute of Electrical and Electronics Engineers (IEEE), July 2015
16. Unreal Engine. Creating landscapes (2017)
17. Ue4/maya lt: Set up grid in maya lt/maya to match unreal engine 4, 2008-2016
18. Jayawardena, A.N., Perera, I.: A framework for mixed reality application development: a case study on Yapahuwa archaeological site. In: 2016 Sixteenth International Conference on Advances in ICT for Emerging Regions (ICTer), pp. 186–192. Institute of Electrical and Electronics Engineers (IEEE), September 2016

19. Dempsey, P.: The teardown: HTC vive virtual reality headset. Eng. Technol. **11**(7), 80–81 (2016)
20. Reichenbach, T., Vasiljevic, G., Kovacic, Z.: Virtual Reality Control Systems (2010)
21. Marti, P., Velasco, M., Fuertes, J.M., Camacho, A., Buttazzo, G.: Design of an embedded control system laboratory experiment. IEEE Trans. Ind. Electr. **57**(10), 3297–3307 (2010)
22. Dormido, R., Vargas, H., Duro, N., Sanchez, J., Dormido-Canto, S., Farias, G., Esquembre, F., Dormido, S.: Development of a web-based control laboratory for automation technicians: the three-tank system. IEEE Trans. Educ. **51**(1), 35–44 (2008)
23. Ionescu, C.M., Fabregas, E., Cristescu, S.M., Dormido, S., De Keyser, R.: A remote laboratory as an innovative educational tool for practicing control engineering concepts. IEEE Trans. Educ. **56**(4), 436–442 (2013)
24. Dormido Bencomo, S.: Control learning: present and future. Ann. Rev. Control **28**(1), 115–136 (2004)
25. Combefis, S., Giannakopoulou, D., Pecheur, C., Feary, M.: A formal framework for design and analysis of human-machine interaction. In: 2011 IEEE International Conference on Systems, Man, and Cybernetics, pp. 1801–1808. Institute of Electrical and Electronics Engineers (IEEE), October 2011
26. Saenz, J., Chacon, J., de la Torre, L., Visioli, A., Dormido, S.: A virtual and remote lab of the two electric coupled drives system in the university network of interactive laboratories. In: 2015 American Control Conference (ACC). IEEE, July 2015
27. Liang, Y., Liu, G.-P.: Design of large scale virtual equipment for interactive HIL control system labs. IEEE Trans. Learn. Technol., 1 (2017). https://doi.org/10.1109/TLT.2017.2731772
28. Badesa, F.J., Morales, R., Garcia-Aracil, N.M., Sabater, J.M., Zollo, L., Papaleo, E., Guglielmelli, E.: Dynamic adaptive system for robot-assisted motion rehabilitation. IEEE Syst. J. **10**(3), 984–991 (2016)
29. Donner, P., Buss, M.: Cooperative swinging of complex pendulum-like objects: experimental evaluation. IEEE Trans. Robot. **32**(3), 744–753 (2016)
30. Khan, S., Jaffery, M.H., Hanif, A., Asif, M.R.: Teaching tool for a control systems laboratory using a quadrotor as a plant in MATLAB. IEEE Trans. Educ. **60**(4), 249–256 (2017)
31. Tepljakov, A., Astapov, S., Petlenkov, E., Vassiljeva, K., Draheim, D.: Sound localization and processing for inducing synesthetic experiences in virtual reality. In: 2016 15th Biennial Baltic Electronics Conference (BEC), pp. 159–162, October 2016
32. Tallinn University of Technology. Official website of Re:creation Virtual and Augmented Reality Laboratory (2018). Accessed 1 Mar 2018
33. Saenz, J., Chacon, J., De La Torre, L., Visioli, A., Dormido, S.: Open and low-cost virtual and remote labs on control engineering. IEEE Access **3**, 805–814 (2015)
34. Atanasijevic-Kunc, M., Logar, V., Karba, R., Papic, M., Kos, A.: Remote multivariable control design using a competition game. IEEE Trans. Educ. **54**(1), 97–103 (2011)
35. Wannous, M., Nakano, H.: NVLab, a networking virtual web-based laboratory that implements virtualization and virtual network computing technologies. IEEE Trans. Learn. Technol. **3**(2), 129–138 (2010)
36. Epic Games. Blueprints Visual Scripting (2017). Accessed 25 May 2017
37. Madhuri, D., Chenna Reddy, P.: Performance comparison of TCP, UDP and SCTP in a wired network. In: 2016 International Conference on Communication and Electronics Systems (ICCES), pp. 1–6. IEEE, October 2016

38. Kuts, V., Modoni, G.E., Terkaj, W., Tähemaa, T., Sacco, M., Otto, T.: Exploiting factory telemetry to support virtual reality simulation in robotics cell. In: De Paolis, L.T., Bourdot, P., Mongelli, A. (eds.) AVR 2017, Part I. LNCS, vol. 10324, pp. 212–221. Springer, Cham (2017). https://doi.org/10.1007/978-3-319-60922-5_16

39. Kose, A., Petlenkov, E.: System identification models and using neural networks for ground source heat pump with ground temperature modeling. In: 2016 International Joint Conference on Neural Networks (IJCNN). IEEE, July 2016

40. Tepljakov, A., Gonzalez, E.A., Petlenkov, E., Belikov, J., Monje, C.A., Petráš, I.: Incorporation of fractional-order dynamics into an existing PI/PID DC motor control loop. ISA Trans. **60**, 262–273 (2016)

41. Blender Foundation. Blender 3d modeling package (2018). Accessed 25 Mar 2018

42. Leap Motion Inc., Leap Motion. Accessed 3 Feb 2018

43. Jin, X., Wah, B.W., Cheng, X., Wang, Y.: Significance and challenges of big data research. Big Data Res. **2**(2), 59–64 (2015)

44. Ali, S.M., Gupta, N., Nayak, G.K., Lenka, R.K.: Big data visualization: tools and challenges. In: 2016 2nd International Conference on Contemporary Computing and Informatics (IC3I). IEEE, December 2016

45. Moran, A., Gadepally, V., Hubbell, M., Kepner, J.: Improving big data visual analytics with interactive virtual reality. In: 2015 IEEE High Performance Extreme Computing Conference (HPEC). IEEE, September 2015

46. Kose, A., Petlenkov, E.: Identification, implementation and simulation of ground source heat pump with ground temperature modeling. In: 2016 15th Biennial Baltic Electronics Conference (BEC). IEEE, October 2016

47. Vassiljeva, K., Tepljakov, A., Petlenkov, E., Netsajev, E.: Computational intelligence approach for estimation of vehicle insurance risk level. In: 2017 International Joint Conference on Neural Networks (IJCNN). IEEE, May 2017

48. Sitzmann, V., Serrano, A., Pavel, A., Agrawala, M., Gutierrez, D., Masia, B., Wetzstein, G.: Saliency in VR: how do people explore virtual environments? IEEE Trans. Vis. Comput. Graph. **24**(4), 1633–1642 (2018)

49. INTECO: Official website of INTECO, LLC (2018). http://www.inteco.com.pl/. Accessed 12 Mar 2018

# Explorable Representation of Interaction in VR/AR Environments

Jakub Flotyński$^{(\boxtimes)}$, Adrian Nowak, and Krzysztof Walczak

Poznań University of Economics and Business,
Niepodległości 10, 61-875 Poznań, Poland
{flotynski,walczak}@kti.ue.poznan.pl, adrian.nowak700@gmail.com
http://www.kti.ue.poznan.pl/

**Abstract.** Synthetic 3D content, which is the main element of virtual and augmented reality applications, typically includes objects, which react to interaction with users and other objects. Interaction may result in changes of the objects' geometry, structure and appearance. Representation of 3D content covering temporal properties can be useful in application domains that benefit from analysis of users' and objects' behavior, such as education, training, e-commerce, marketing and merchandising. However, the available approaches do not enable exploration of 3D content with regards to its time-dependent properties. The main contribution of this paper is temporal representation of interaction. The representation is based on semantic web standards and ontologies, which enable use of general as well as domain knowledge for exploration of content. The representation is discussed in the context of an immersive virtual car showroom implemented using headsets and motion tracking devices.

**Keywords:** Semantic web · Ontologies · Headsets · Motion tracking

## 1 Introduction

Virtual reality (VR) and augmented reality (AR) applications become increasingly popular in various application domains, such as education, training, prototyping, e-commerce, marketing and merchandising, e.g., [15,39]. Widespread use of VR and AR has been enabled by the availability and falling prices of various presentation and interaction systems, such as glasses, headsets, haptic interfaces as well as motion tracking and capture systems.

The primary element of any VR/AR application is 3-dimensional (3D) content, which consists of 3D objects typically including various geometrical, structural and presentational elements. 3D content may evolve over time due to interactions between content objects as well as between content objects and users. Such changes of 3D content may encompass creation of new objects as well as modification and removal of existing objects. Furthermore, different devices may be utilized by users to interact with 3D content, e.g., flysticks, haptic devices,

© Springer International Publishing AG, part of Springer Nature 2018
L. T. De Paolis and P. Bourdot (Eds.): AVR 2018, LNCS 10851, pp. 589–609, 2018.
https://doi.org/10.1007/978-3-319-95282-6_42

eye and motion tracking devices. An essential requirement in multiple practical VR/AR applications is the capability of exploration of time-dependent interactive 3D content. Exploration could be performed while or after using the content, on-demand (with queries), and it could cover all the aforementioned aspects—users, objects, devices and time. Examples of temporal exploration of interactive 3D content pertain to visualization of processes, thus they may be found in virtually every domain, e.g., exploration of users' behavior and preferences while shopping for marketing purposes, exploration of instructors' activities while using machines for training purposes, exploration of physicians' activities in medical operations and substances' behavior in chemical experiments for teaching purposes. In addition, explorable 3D content representation conforms to the current trends in the development of the web, in which content is created by users who are simultaneously producers and consumers (prosumers), and it is further described using metadata and semantics to enhance queries in indexing, searching and processing of the content.

A number of solutions have been developed to enable modeling of interactive 3D content with animations triggered by interactions. The solutions may be divided into several groups. The first group encompasses libraries (e.g., Away3D [10], Java3D [42] and Direct3D [40]), which enable programming of interactions and animations with imperative languages, such as ActionScript, Java and C++. The second group includes declarative 3D formats, such as VRML [59], X3D [60] and XML3D [18], which enable interactions with content using sensors, animations based on key frames and interpolation as well as interactions and animations described by imperative scripts. The last group comprises 3D modeling environments and game engines, which enable both programming of interactions as well as programming and manual modeling of animations, e.g., Blender [28], 3ds Max [9] and Unity [54].

However, although the available solutions enable modeling of interactive animated 3D content varying over time, the 3D content is not suitable for on-demand exploration with users' queries, covering temporal (time-dependent) content properties. This significantly limits the use of the approaches in multiple applications that require analysis of users' and objects' behavior. This problem can be overcome by applying the semantic web to 3D content creation. The research on the semantic web aims at the evolutionary development of the current web towards a distributed database linking structured content described by ontologies [12]. The use of the semantic web standards, such as the Resource Description Framework (RDF) [62], the Resource Description Framework Schema (RDFS) [63], the Web Ontology Language (OWL) [61] and the Semantic Web Rule Language (SWRL) [58] as well as ontologies for 3D modeling has gained increasing attention in the recent years. In contrast to the available 3D formats, the semantic web standards permit 3D content representation based on widely used concepts as well as concepts specific to arbitrary domain, thus making the content more intelligible to both average users and domain experts. The formalism provided by the semantic web could enable precise and comprehensive 3D content exploration by querying about the states of the content in different moments and periods. For example, a 3D city model could be queried about buildings in the city at different moments in time; a 3D educational chemical experiment could be queried about the substances produced at different moments; a running 3D engine could be queried about the presentation and description of its states and fuel consumption at different moments.

However, the available semantic 3D content representations do not use these opportunities, as they are static – they do not evolve over time even if the content does, i.e. even if a semantic representation specifies possible interactions and changes of content properties, it is not altered after the interactions occur. Therefore, the dynamic (time-dependent) nature of the 3D content cannot be subject to semantic exploration.

The main contribution of this paper is temporal representation of interaction for 3D content. The representation is based on the semantic web standards (RDF, RDFS, OWL and SWRL) as well as 4D-fluents [65]. The representation is an extension of the semantic 3D content representation presented in our previous works [23,25]. That representation has encompassed geometrical, structural and presentational 3D components and properties that are constant over time. The new representation extends the previous works with concepts necessary for representation of interaction and interaction results—time, interacting users and objects. The use of the semantic web in our approach have important advantages over the previous approaches to 3D content representation and modeling. First, it enables on-demand exploration (e.g., by users, search engines and analytical tools) and representation of content based on general and domain knowledge. This makes the content intelligible to average users and domain experts who are not IT-specialists. Second, it can be processed with standard reasoning engines to infer tacit content properties on the basis of the explicitly specified properties, e.g., to infer assignment of 3D objects to classes based on the objects' properties. This can liberate 3D content authors from determining all content properties. Due to the use of ontologies, which have been intended as shared terminological and assertional assets, the representation can be used in collaborative VR/AR environments, in which multiple users commonly create time-dependent 3D content using common concepts and various devices.

The remainder of this paper is structured as follows. Section 2 provides an overview of the current state of the art in semantic representation of 3D content as well as semantic temporal representation of different content types. The proposed temporal ontology-based representation of interaction is described in Sect. 3. In Sect. 4, we outline the developed virtual car showroom, in which the representation can be used for marketing and merchandising purposes. In Sect. 5, we discuss an example of an ontology-based interaction representation in the car showroom, followed by a query-based exploration of the 3D content. Finally, Sect. 7 concludes the paper and indicates possible future research.

## 2   Related Works

### 2.1   Semantic Representation of 3D Content

An overview of semantic representation of 3D content has been presented in a few papers [13,27,37,53,56,57]. In this section, the distinction between domain-independent and domain-specific approaches to 3D content representation is discussed.

**Domain-Independent 3D Content Representation.** Domain-independent semantic 3D content representations are based on concepts whose meaning is specific to 3D graphics and animation, e.g., texture, dimensions, coordinates and level of detail [1,6,19,33,52] as well as VR/AR environments, e.g., interfaces, markers and models [48,49]. In [33], an ontology providing elements and properties equivalent to elements and properties specified in X3D has been proposed. Moreover, a set of semantic properties have been proposed to enable representation of 3D scenes with domain knowledge. The ontology proposed in [16] enables semantic representation of non-manifold 3D models. In [17], an approach to generating virtual environments upon mappings of domain ontologies to 3D world ontologies has been proposed. Another approach to semantic modeling of 3D content has been proposed in [24,64]. The approach enables separation of concerns between domain experts, developers and graphic designers. In addition, 3D content can be created with queries to semantic scenes. In [66], a framework for decoupling components in real-time interactive systems with ontologies, and the concept of semantic entities in VR applications have been discussed. In [51], a method of 3D model indexing for content-based 3D model retrieval has been proposed. The method uses an ontology for representing the geometry, structure and appearance of 3D models.

**Domain-Specific 3D Content Representation.** Domain-specific 3D content representations are based on concepts whose meaning is not directly related to 3D graphics and animation, but it is specific to an application or domain, e.g., virtual museum [46] and interior design [7,43]. An ontology for representing virtual humans has been described in [30]. A virtual human is linked to geometrical descriptors (covering vertices and polygons), structural descriptors (covering levels of articulations), 3D animations of face and body and behavior controllers (animation algorithms). In [38], abstract semantic representation of events and actions in AI simulators has been presented. In [32], semantic representation of 3D crowd simulation is proposed. Data semantics is described for the three elements: the structure, topology and height coordinates of 3D scenes. In [14], semantic attributes are selected by users to describe 3D models with different strengths, e.g., animals may be scary to varying degrees. In CityEngine, modeling of 3D content is based on semantic rules that specify elements of the content, such as shapes and textures, as well as operations on the content, such as extrude and split [31]. In [45], an approach facilitating modeling of content behavior has been proposed. The approach provides temporal operators and enables expression of primitive and complex behaviors. A tool-supported design approach to modeling object behavior in X3D scenes has been presented in [44]. A rule-based ontology framework for feature modeling and consistency checking has been explained in [67]. The proposed ontology-based approach addresses mainly modeling of elementary content animations, without support for temporal content exploration. In [47], an approach to spatio-temporal reasoning on semantic descriptions of evolving human embryo has been proposed. The approach leverages RDF, OWL and SPARQL as well as an ontology describing stages, periods and processes. In [55], an approach to semantic description of 3D molecular models has been proposed. The approach combines different input (e.g., interaction using different haptic and motion tracking devices) and output (e.g., presentation in 2D and 3D) modalities to enable presentation and interaction suitable for particular types of content and tasks to be done.

## 2.2  Temporal Content Representation

Reasoning on temporal data has been extensively studied in the domain of knowledge representation and—later—in the semantic web. The research has lead to the development of multiple solutions. The most expressive approaches considered in this paper are rule-based temporal content representations compliant with the first-order logic—the situation calculus [36] and the event calculus [35,50]. In particular, they permit reasoning on numerical domains, which enables analysis of relations between moments and intervals of time. However, in comparison to the remaining solutions, which are based on the semantic web, processing of rules is typically more time-consuming, and, in general, it is undecidable, which means that for some problems, it cannot be determined whether the reasoning algorithm will stop and give a solution.

Several more recent approaches have been developed to enable temporal content representation using the semantic web standards. Temporal description logics extend OWL with temporal operators such as *always* and *sometimes* [8]. Another approach, Temporal RDF, extends the RDF graph with information about time [29]. Versioning of ontologies is an approach, in which new versions of an ontology are created every time the described state of affairs changes [34]. The drawback of this solution is the lack of links between the versions of objects stored in different versions of the ontology, which prevents temporal reasoning on the objects using standard libraries. In the approach based on n-ary relations, for every temporal property, an additional object is created and linked with the primary objects linked by the property as well as with a time interval [41]. The problems associated with the use of the aforementioned semantic approaches have been summarized in [11,65].

## 2.3  4D Fluents

Another solution, which avoids the aforementioned shortcomings of the semantic approaches, are 4D-fluents [65], whose concept is depicted in Fig. 1. A *fluent* is a property that varies over time. The approach transforms a time-independent domain into a time-dependent domain. Informally, the result of the transformation of a statement *two objects are linked by a property* is a statement *two objects are linked by a property within a time interval*. This is achieved by using the concept of *time slices* (instances of the `TimeSlice` class), which are temporal counterparts to the primary objects, associated with *time intervals* (instances of the `TimeInterval` class). In the approach, representation of an object that has several different values of a property within different intervals includes several time slices of the object that are associated with the intervals and are assigned the particular property values. Formally, the following steps must be completed to add temporal information to the statement: `object1` is linked to `object2` by `property`.

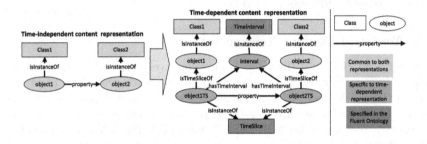

**Fig. 1.** The concept of 4D fluents

1. For both `object1` and `object2`, create an instance of the `TimeSlice` class (`object1TS` and `object2TS`) and set the `isTimeSliceOf` property of both the time slices to their primary objects.
2. Create an `interval` object that is an instance of the `TimeInterval` class, and set the `hasTimeInterval` property of the time slices to `interval`.
3. Link the time slices by `property` as the primary objects were linked.

For instance, to express that Joe was leading a department in 2017, it is necessary to create: time slices for both Joe and the department, and link them by the leads property; and next, to create the interval representing the year 2017, and assign it to the time slices. Similar steps, except for creating `objectTS2`, have to be done to express temporal unary relations (assignment of objects to classes), e.g., a car was being repaired for one week, and to express temporal datatype properties (properties with literal values, such as string, integer and float), e.g., the speed of a train was 100 km/h for 2 min.

4D-fluents introduce less additional data in comparison to n-ary relations, do not require extension of the main semantic web standards (RDF, RDFS, OWL, SWRL and SPARQL), and enable temporal reasoning with the available engines. Hence, they also respect the classes of computational complexity and possible problems that may be described and solved in OWL [4]. This is an important advantage in comparison to the rule-based solutions, which are undecidable in general. Due to these arguments, 4D-fluents have been selected as the basis for the semantic interaction representation.

# 3   Explorable Interaction Representation

## 3.1   Overview of the Approach

The main contribution of this paper is the *explorable representation of interaction* in VR/AR environments, which is based on 4D-fluents. The general idea of using the representation is depicted in Fig. 2. The representation is a T-Box (terminological component), which specifies a conceptualization (classes and properties). The representation is the set of ontologies that consists of: the *fluent ontology*, the *VR ontology*, a *domain ontology* and a *mapping ontology*. The ontologies are encoded using the semantic web standards: RDF, RDFS, OWL and SWRL. The ontologies enable semantic representation of interactions between different VR objects as well as between users and VR objects. In addition, they permit representation of results of interactions covering changes of the geometry, structure and appearance of VR objects. The ontologies are explained in detail in the next section.

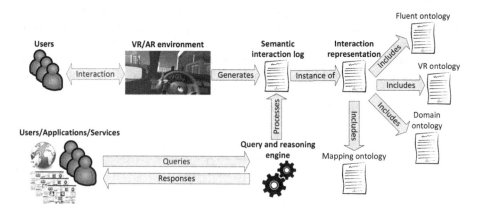

**Fig. 2.** The concept of using the explorable representation of interaction in VR/AR environments

The interaction scheme and data flow in a VR/AR environment based on the interaction representation is as follows. While users and VR objects are interacting within the VR/AR environment, the environment is generating a *semantic interaction log*. A log is an A-Box (assertion component), which is an instance of the interaction representation. A log specifies individuals described by classes and properties specified in the interaction representation. While the fluent ontology and the VR ontology are common to all logs, independently of the VR/AR environment and its use cases, the mapping ontology is designed specifically for a particular environment, and an individual domain ontology is generated for a particular use of the environment. The log represents interactions that occurred during the use of the environment—between the users and VR objects, and between different VR objects—as well as the results of the interactions. Interaction logs may be generated by imperative procedures, e.g., encoded in Java and C#, or by declarative assertion rules. The example assertion rules implemented in Prolog:

```
assert(TimeSlice(newUserTS)) ← forefingerTouches(userTS, carTS)
assert(TimeSlice(newCarTS)) ← forefingerTouches(userTS, carTS)
assert(isIn(newUserTS, newCarTS)) ← forefingerTouches(userTS, carTS)
```

Create new time slices of a user and a car, once the user touches the car. The last assertion states that the user gets into the car. The semantic interaction log created during the use of the environment can be further explored by other users, applications and services (in particular, on the web) by sending queries. Queries may be encoded, e.g., in SPARQL, and they are processed together with the interaction log by a *query and reasoning engine* for the semantic web standards.

### 3.2   Ontologies of the Representation

The main advantages of the proposed interaction representation over the other 3D formats, programming languages and libraries is the possibility of using domain and general knowledge for content description, possibility of on-demand exploration of content with temporal queries as well as the compliance with the current trends and standards in the development of web-based VR/AR environments. These advantages have been achieved due to the use of the semantic web standards and ontologies. The ontologies of the interaction representation are depicted in Fig. 3 and described below.

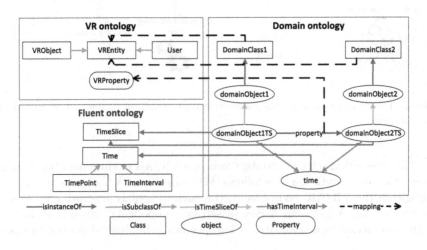

**Fig. 3.** The explorable representation of interaction

1. The *fluent ontology* includes classes that have been derived from the 4D-fluents approach (cf. Section 2.3). TimeSlice is the class of VR objects that are described by temporal OWL datatype or object properties. Another class—Time—has two sub-classes—TimePoint and TimeInterval—to distinguish between instant interactions, which happen at a moment in time (e.g., clicking and touching), and periodic interactions, which happen for an interval (e.g., dragging and scrolling). The fluent ontology has been created once, and it is common to all VR/AR environments based on the interaction representation.

2. The *VR ontology* includes generic (low-level) classes and properties that are specific to 3D graphics and animation, e.g., meshes, textures, position, interpolation, gestures, etc. Like the fluent ontology, the VR ontology is common to all VR/AR environments based on the interaction representation. This ontology is hidden from domain experts, who explore interaction logs, behind the mapping ontology. The details of the VR ontology are out of the scope of this paper, and have been explained in our previous works in the context of building time-independent VR content [22].

3. A *domain ontology* represents a time-dependent state of affairs in a particular use of a VR/AR environment. A domain ontology includes domain (high-level) classes, domain properties (OWL datatype and object properties) as well as domain objects, which are instances of domain classes, described by domain properties. Different domain ontologies may be used in the interaction representation, e.g., to represent cars in a virtual showroom, buildings in a virtual city and exhibitions in a virtual museum. A domain ontology is being generated by the environment while it is running—users are interacting with the environment, and different objects are interacting within the environment. The following elements are generated to express temporal properties (unary and binary) of a domain object interacting with a user or with another object.

   – If the interaction or its results require a temporal assignment of the domain object/user to a class (unary property) or a temporal assignment of an OWL datatype (binary) property to the domain object/user, a time slice of the domain object/user is generated. If the interaction or its results require a temporal assignment of an OWL object (binary) property to the domain object/user, a time slice of the domain object/user as well a time slice of the linked domain object are generated. The time slices are instances of the TimeSlice class and represent the domain objects/user at different moments or within different intervals. For instance, individual time slices can be generated for a user selecting a car to express the selection activity (at a moment) and to express the fact of sitting inside the car (for an interval) after the selection. The time slices are mapped to VR classes and properties (specified in the VR ontology) to be presentable in the VR/AR environment. First, they can be indirectly mapped through linking them to domain classes (which are directly mapped to VR classes and properties) using the isTimeSliceOf and isInstanceOf properties. Such mapping determines presentational properties that do not change over time—are common to all time slices of the domain objects. Second, the time slices can be directly mapped to VR classes and properties to have independent presentations—as the domain objects may have different presentations at different moments and within different intervals.

- An appropriate moment (instance of `TimePoint`) or an interval (instance of `TimeInterval`) is generated respecting the time in which the domain object/user was interacting with the other domain object.

The details of the method of generating domain ontologies, which are a mutable part of interaction logs, are out of the scope of this paper, in which we focus on the interaction representation and generated logs.

4. A *mapping ontology* includes two types of classes and properties. The first type are VR classes and properties that are specific to the particular VR/AR environment, e.g., the mesh and texture of a particular car, gestures recognized by a particular device, etc. Such environment-specific classes and properties are sub-classes and sub-properties of generic, environment-independent classes and properties, which are specified in the VR ontology. They extend the environment-independent classes and properties with some OWL restrictions on VR properties, e.g., a car mesh is assigned a particular face set and a texture.

The second type of classes and properties specified in the mapping ontology link domain classes and properties (specified in the domain ontology) to environment-specific VR classes and properties (specified in the mapping obtology), e.g., a car is represented by the car mesh, and a car selection is done by touching it. In general, a particular domain class or a domain property may be mapped to different hierarchies of environment-specific VR classes and properties. The way in which they are mapped determines the further reuse of the VR classes and properties for representing different interactions and their results in the environment.

Like the VR ontology, the mapping ontology is typically not directly used by domain specialists exploring interaction logs, unless the exploration should cover graphical and animational details. A mapping ontology is created once for a particular environment by a graphics designer, and together with the VR ontology, it provides a reusable *library* of 3D concepts mapped to domain concepts. A mapping ontology is not explicitly depicted in Fig. 3, but it is denoted by the dashed arrows. Creation of a mapping ontology is out of the scope of this paper and has been explained in our previous works in the context of building time-independent VR content [20].

The proposed interaction representation can be applied to diverse applications and domains—by selecting (or creating) an appropriate VR ontology and creating the library of specific interactive 3D models (a mapping ontology).

## 4    Virtual Car Showroom

A virtual car showroom has been implemented to illustrate the explorable representation of interaction. The showroom is an application based on the Unity game engine [54][1]. It uses an Oculus Rift headset [3] and a Leap Motion device [2]. Unity has been selected as it is a widely-used tool for creating VR applications with various presentation and interaction devices. The Oculus Rift HMD enables immersive presentation of 3D content, while the Leap Motion hand tracking system enables interaction with 3D cars using hand gestures.

The following commands are triggered by gestures recognized by the Leap Motion to enable navigation and interaction with cars within the showroom.

1. *Select a car*, which is executed by indicating the car using the forefinger of the right hand (Fig. 4a). In the 3D scene, several different cars are accessible.
2. *Open the main menu*, which is executed by showing the open left hand (Fig. 4b). The menu enables changing the color of the car, watching the car from around, getting in the car, and getting out the car.
3. *Change the color of the car*, which is executed by selecting a color from the palette from the main menu using the forefinger of the right hand (Fig. 4c). The selected color is applied to the body of the car.
4. *Watch the car from around*, which is executed by selecting a direction of rotation around the car from the main menu using the forefinger of the right hand (Fig. 4d).
5. *Get in the car*, which is executed by selecting a place to sit down inside the car from the main menu (Fig. 4e).
6. *Get out the car*, which is executed by showing the thumb of the left hand pointing up (Fig. 4f).

## 5   Example of Explorable Interaction Representation

This example presents the use of the explorable interaction representation to analyze customer's behavior in the virtual car showroom. A semantic interaction log has been generated during the visit of a customer in the showroom. The log is an instance of the interaction representation. It consists of the fluent ontology, the VR ontology, a domain ontology, and a mapping ontology, which are implemented in RDF, RDFS, OWL and SWRL. Only the domain ontology of the log was being expanded while using the environment. The other ontologies were not being altered. This section is divided into descriptions of the particular ontologies followed by a description of possible use cases of content exploration. The method of the log generation is not presented, as it is out of the scope of the paper.

*The fluent ontology.* The fluent ontology (Listing 1.1) is not specific to the showroom and may be reused in all VR/AR environments built upon the interaction representation. It specifies the `TimeSlice` class (line 1), whose instances

---

[1] The following 3D models have been used in the environment:
   https://www.cgtrader.com/dennisp
   https://free3d.com/3d-model/single-road-20861.html
   https://www.3dcadbrowser.com/download.aspx?3dmodel=102858
   https://free3d.com/3d-model/concrete-barrier-301778.html

(a)    (b)

(c)    (d)

(e)    (f)

**Fig. 4.** Interactions triggered by gestures in the virtual car showroom: selecting a car
(a), opening the main menu for the car (b), changing the color of the car (c), watching
the car from around (d), getting in the car (e), getting out the car (f). (Color figure
online)

are assigned to their primary objects using the `isTimeSliceOf` property (2).
We have extended the primary concept of time in 4D fluents (cf. Section 2.3)
by distinguishing between `TimePoint`—for instant interactions, e.g., touching
and pinching, and `TimeInterval`—for periodic interactions, e.g., dragging and
scrolling (3–4). While time points are described by the `value` date-time property,

time intervals are described by the **start** and **end** date-time properties (5–6). Both points and intervals may be assigned to time slices (7).

**Listing 1.1.** The fluent ontology used in the interaction representation (the RDF Turtle format)

```
1  :TimeSlice rdf:type owl:Class.
2  :isTimeSliceOf rdf:type owl:ObjectProperty; rdfs:domain :TimeSlice; rdfs:range owl:
      Thing.
3  :Time rdf:type owl:Class.
4  :TimePoint, :TimeInterval rdf:type owl:Class; rdfs:subClassOf :Time.
5  :value rdf:type owl:DatatypeProperty; rdfs:domain :TimePoint; rdfs:range xsd:dateTime.
6  :start, :end rdf:type owl:DatatypeProperty; rdfs:domain :TimeInterval; rdfs:range xsd:
      dateTime.
7  :hasTimePoint, :hasTimeInterval rdf:type owl:ObjectProperty; rdfs:range :TimePoint, :
      TimeInterval.
```

***The VR ontology.*** The VR ontology provides a semantic 3D format. Like the fluent ontology, the VR ontology is common to all VR/AR environments using the interaction representation. The VR ontology has been comprehensively described in [22]. Hence, in this paper, it is only briefly discussed to illustrate the low-level representation of the domain concepts (Listing 1.2). The main class of the ontology is **VREntity**, which may be a **VRObject** or a **User** described by coordinates (1–3). A specific subclass of **VRObject** is **Mesh3D**, which is described by **faceSet** (4–5). Specific subclasses of **User** are leveraged for gesture recognition— forefinger and open hand (6–7). The gestures are used to touch VR objects in the environment (8–9). The VR concepts are typically not directly used in the domain ontology, except concepts whose meaning is widely known, e.g., **User**.

**Listing 1.2.** A fragment of the VR ontology of the interaction representation in the virtual car showroom (the RDF Turtle format)

```
1  :VREntity rdf:type owl:Class.
2  :VRObject, :User rdf:type owl:Class; rdfs:subClassOf :VREntity.
3  :x, :y, :z rdf:type owl:DatatypeProperty; rdfs:domain :VREntity;  rdfs:range xsd:float.
4  :Mesh3D rdf:type owl:Class; rdfs:subClassOf :VRObject.
5  :faceSet rdf:type owl:DatatypeProperty; rdfs:range :Mesh3D.
6  :UserWithGesture rdf:type owl:Class; rdfs:subClassOf :User.
7  :UserWithRightForefinger, :UserWithRightHand rdf:type owl:Class; rdfs:subClassOf :UserWithGesture.
8  :touches rdf:type owl:ObjectProperty.
9  :forefingerTuches, :openHandTouches rdfs:subPropertyOf :touches.
```

***The domain ontology.*** The domain ontology (Listing 1.3) has been generated while visiting the showroom, so it is specific to the particular use of the environment. In this example, the domain ontology is presented a posteriori—after the visit, and it includes all the interactions occurred. The ontology represents VR objects at a high level of abstraction based on general, widely used concepts, which allows for content exploration by users without knowledge of 3D graphics and animation. The main classes of the ontology represent different types of cars and seats inside the cars (3–5). The customer (Joe) and the cabriolet are OWL individuals (6–8), like the other objects in the ontology, which has been skipped to shorten the listing. The whole visit of Joe in the showroom took place from 10:00 to 10:12. The following interactions have taken place between Joe and VR objects.

1. *Joe selected the cabriolet to watch it in more detail at 10:01* (Fig. 4a). To report the selection in the log, time slices have been generated for both Joe

and the cabriolet (9–10). The selection interaction is represented by the binary selects property, which links users and cars (11). According to the 4D fluents approach, the slices are associated with the same time (12). As a selection is an instant interaction, a point in time is given.

2. *Joe changed the color of the cabriolet from yellow to red at 10:05* (Fig. 4b,c). This interaction is represented by an nary property encoded using a Painting- Descriptor (14–15). A descriptor is a time slice. It indicates the new (red) color of the car. It is linked to a time slice of Joe (13) and a time slice of the cabriolet (16). Painting is an instant interaction, thus all the time slices are assigned the common point in time (17). Once the color of the car is changed, additional time slices of the cabriolet are generated to represent its two versions: previous–yellow and new–red, within the appropriate intervals (18–19).

3. *Joe was watching the cabriolet from 10:06 to 10:07* (Fig. 4d). As this interaction is periodic, the time slices of Joe and the cabriolet are associated the interval (20–22), as opposed to selecting and painting the cabriolet.

4. *Joe was sitting on the front left seat of the cabriolet from 10:08 to 10:10* (Fig. 4e,f). Like watching the cabriolet, sitting is a periodic interaction. However, it is between a Joe time slice and a time slice of the left front seat, which is a sub-object of the cabriolet (23–26).

**Listing 1.3.** A fragment of a domain ontology of the interaction representation in the virtual car showroom (the RDF Turtle format)

```
1    Prefixes: ':', 'fo', 'vr' - domain, fluent and VR ontology
2
3    :Car, :CarSeat rdf:type owl:Class.
4    :Cabriolet,:Coupe,:Limusine,:SUV rdf:type owl:Class; rdfs:subClassOf :Car.
5    :LeftFrontSeat, :RightFrontSeat, :LeftBackSeat, :RightBackSeat rdf:type owl:Class;
         rdfs:subClassOf :CarSeat.
6    :joe rdf:type vr:User, owl:NamedIndividual.
7    :cabriolet rdf:type :Cabriolet, owl:NamedIndividual; :includes :
         cabrioletLeftFrontSeat, :cabrioletRightFrontSeat.
8    :cabrioletLeftFrontSeat, :cabrioletRightFrontSeat rdf:type :LeftFrontSeat, :
         RightFrontSeat.
9    :joeSelecting rdf:type vr:User, fo:TimeSlice; fo:isTimeSliceOf :joe; :selects :
         cabrioletBeingSelected; fo:hasTimePoint :pointSelecting.
10   :cabrioletBeingSelected rdf:type :Cabriolet, fo:TimeSlice; fo:isTimeSliceOf :
         cabriolet; fo:hasTimePoint :pointSelecting.
11   :selects, :watches rdf:type owl:ObjectProperty; rdfs:domain vr:User; rdfs:range :Car.
12   :pointSelecting rdf:type fo:TimePoint; fo:value "2018-03-27T10:01:00"^^xsd:dateTime.
13   :joePainting rdf:type vr:User, fo:TimeSlice; fo:isTimeSliceOf :joe; :paints :
         paintingDesc; fo:hasTimePoint :pointPainting.
14   :paintingDesc rdf:type :PaintingDescriptor; :paintedCar :cabrioletBeingPainted; :
         color "red"^^xsd:string; fo:hasTimePoint :pointPainting.
15   :PaintingDescriptor rdf:type owl:Class; rdfs:subClassOf [ rdf:type owl:Restriction;
         owl:onProperty :paintedCar, :color; owl:qualifiedCardinality "1"^^xsd:
         nonNegativeInteger; owl:onClass :Car, xsd:string ].
16   :cabrioletBeingPainted rdf:type :Cabriolet, fo:TimeSlice; fo:isTimeSliceOf :cabriolet
         ; fo:hasTimePoint :pointPainting.
17   :pointPainting rdf:type fo:TimePoint; fo:value "...T10:05:00".
18   :cabrioletYellow, :cabrioletRed rdf:type :Cabriolet, fo:TimeSlice; fo:isTimeSliceOf :
         cabriolet; fo:hasTimeInterval :intervalYellow, :intervalRed; :color "red"^^xsd:
         string.
19   :intervalYellow, :intervalRed rdf:type fo:TimeInterval; :start "...T10:00:00"^^xsd:
         dateTime, "...T10:05:00"; :end "...T10:05:00", "...T10:12:00".
20   :joeWatching rdf:type vr:User, fo:TimeSlice; fo:isTimeSliceOf :joe; :watches :
         cabrioletWatched; fo:hasTimeInterval :intervalWatching.
```

```
21   :cabrioletWatched rdf:type :Cabriolet, fo:TimeSlice; fo:isTimeSliceOf :cabriolet; fo:
         hasTimeInterval :intervalWatching.
22   :intervalWatching rdf:type fo:TimeInterval; :start "...T10:06:00"; :end "...T10:07:00
         ".
23   :joeInCabriolet rdf:type vr:User, fo:TimeSlice; :sitsOn :
         cabrioletLeftFrontSeatWithJoe;fo:hasTimeInterval :intervalJoeInCabriolet.
24   :cabrioletLeftFrontSeatWithJoe rdf:type :LeftFrontSeat, fo:TimeSlice; fo:
         isTimeSliceOf :cabrioletLeftFrontSeat; fo:hasTimeInterval :
         intervalJoeInCabriolet.
25   do:sitsOn rdf:type owl:ObjectProperty.
26   :intervalJoeInCabriolet rdf:type fo:TimeInterval; fo:start "...T10:08:00"; fo:end "
         ...T10:10:00".
```

***The mapping ontology.*** On the one hand, unlike the fluent and VR ontologies, the mapping ontology (Listing 1.4) is specific to the virtual car showroom. On the other hand, unlike the domain ontology, it has been developed once for the environment and may be reused in all cases of visiting the showroom. Mapping of the domain concepts to the VR concepts enables uniform semantic representation of content and exploration of content at both high and low levels of abstraction. In addition, it permits implementation of a semantic 3D browser that could directly interpret the low-level semantic 3D format without using non-semantic 3D formats. Every `Cabriolet` in the showroom, which is a domain concept, is a `CabrioletMesh` with a face set specified (2–3). Every touch of a VR object by a forefinger is a selection of the object, while every touch by an open hand seats the user on the object (4–5). An SWRL rule states that sitting on an object determines the `x`, `y` and `z` coordinates of the user with regards to the coordinates of the object (6).

**Listing 1.4.** A fragment of a mapping ontology of the interaction representation in the virtual car showroom (the RDF Turtle format)

```
1   Prefixes: ':', 'do', 'fo', 'vr' - mapping, domain, fluent and VR ontology
2   do:Cabriolet rdfs:subClassOf vr:CabrioletMesh.
3   vr:CabrioletMesh rdf:type owl:Class; rdfs:subClassOf vr:Mesh3D, [ rdf:type owl:
         Restriction; owl:onProperty vr:faceSet; owl:hasValue "..." ].
4   vr:forefingerTuches rdfs:subPropertyOf do:selects.
5   vr:openHandTouches rdfs:subPropertyOf do:sitsOn.
6   do:sitsOn(?user, ?seat), vr:x(?seat, ?x), vr:y(?seat, ?y), vr:z(?seat, ?z), swrlb:add
         (?z2, ?z, 10) -> vr:x(?user, ?x), vr:y(?user, ?y), vr:z(?user, ?z2).
```

***Temporal exploration of interactions.*** Temporal exploration of interactions in the virtual car showroom is possible with queries (e.g., encoded in SPARQL) to the generated semantic interaction logs. Such exploration can provide information about customers' preferences, which could be further used for marketing purposes, in particular—for presenting personalized offers. Examples of exploration cover the following use cases:

1. *How much time do customers spend to watch the particular cars outside and inside?* This information could be used to categorize customers between the groups more appreciating the external presentation and more appreciating the functionality as well as the comfort of the cars.
2. *From which places inside are the particular cars watched by particular customers?* This information could be used to distinguish whether the particular customers are usually drivers or passengers.

3. *Which cars are watched by the same customers?* This information could be used to arrange the space in the showroom.
4. *What are the most popular colors selected by customers for the particular cars?* This information could be used to properly paint the cars to increase their attractiveness to customers.

# 6   Discussion

3D content representations that are alternative to the proposed ontology-based interaction representation are: imperative programming languages with libraries (e.g., C++ with OpenGL [5] and Direct3D [40]), declarative 3D formats (e.g., X3D [60] and XML3D [18]) as well as declarative programming languages (e.g., Prolog). Inference-based content creation is not available in imperative languages, including languages used in 3D modeling environments and game engines. In imperative languages, inference must be implemented in advance. This requires more effort in implementation from content authors, who must consider possible consequences of explicitly specified content properties in the context of a particular use case. In addition, 3D content implemented using imperative languages is unsuitable for query-based exploration.

Declarative 3D content formats have not been intended for knowledge inference. Moreover, they permit only low-level representation of content based on concepts specific to 3D graphics and animation. Declarative 3D content formats do not enable conceptual (high-level) representation of content specific to an application or domain. In addition, they offer limited means of expressing temporal content properties, which are typically interpolators and time sensors for some content properties. Finally, like imperative languages, declarative 3D formats have not been intended for query-based processing, except strictly syntactical analysis (e.g., based on XQuery), which does not enable exploration of domain semantic properties of 3D content.

In contrast to the aforementioned approaches, declarative logic programming languages enable knowledge inference at different levels of abstraction. Like in the case of ontologies, such languages are processed by reasoning engines, which liberates content authors from specifying all content properties and from implementing reasoning algorithms on their own. Moreover, on the one hand, due to the use of rules (implications), which may express arbitrary links between properties of classes and objects, such languages have higher expressiveness than ontologies encoded in RDF, RDFS and OWL. On the other hand, reasoning on rules is undecidable, which may prevent generating results in general. In comparison to logic programming languages, the use of the semantic web approach (based on description logics) may benefit from the known decidability and computational complexity of OWL profiles [4]. While both the semantic web standards and logic programming languages permit processing of numerical values describing points and intervals in query processing, the use of the latter may be preferred when such values should also be processed in reasoning, as explained in [21, 26].

# 7   Conclusions and Future Works

The use of semantics for building VR/AR applications gains increasing attention in the research community. However, the available methods and tools do not enable representation of VR content with regards to its temporal properties managed by various interactions between content objects as well as between content objects and users. The development of the current web towards the semantic web offers new technologies that can be used to solve this problem.

In this paper, the representation of interaction for VR/AR environments has been proposed. The representation is based on the semantic web standards, and it offers several advantages over the previous approaches. First, it may be created using concepts related to an arbitrary domain, thus being intelligible to average users and domain experts without technical skills. Second, it enables content exploration with queries, including the past, current and possible future states of the content. Hence, a 3D scene evolving over time can be treated as a responsive dynamic database. Third, it permits inference of tacit knowledge, which liberates content authors from determining properties that may be implied by other related properties. Finally, due to the use of ontologies, which provide a common space for shared terminology, the representation is suitable for the use in collaborative VR/AR environments.

The possible directions of future research encompass several aspects. First, plugins for generating interaction logs in widely used modeling tools and game engines (e.g., Unity and Unreal) could be developed. Second, the development of user-friendly graphical tools for query-based content exploration could benefit from the syntax of the semantic web standards, which is relatively simple in comparison to the syntax of 3D formats and programming languages. Such tools could further improve the overall dissemination of VR/AR environment, in particular on the web. Finally, the representation should be evaluated in terms of the size and complexity of temporal interactive 3D scenes as well as the performance of query execution and reasoning.

# References

1. 3D Modeling Ontology (2018). http://3dontology.org/
2. Leap Motion (2018). https://developer.leapmotion.com/documentation
3. Oculus Rift (2018). https://support.oculus.com
4. OWL 2 web ontology language profiles (second edition). http://www.w3.org/TR/owl2-profiles/#Computational_Properties. Accessed 07 Mar 2018
5. OpenGL. https://www.opengl.org/. Accessed 20 Mar 2015
6. Albertoni, R., et al.: Ontology-based searching framework for digital shapes. In: Meersman, R., Tari, Z., Herrero, P. (eds.) OTM 2005. LNCS, vol. 3762, pp. 896–905. Springer, Heidelberg (2005). https://doi.org/10.1007/11575863_111
7. Albrecht, S., Wiemann, T., Günther, M., Hertzberg, J.: Matching CAD object models in semantic mapping. In: Proceedings ICRA 2011 Workshop: Semantic Perception, Mapping and Exploration, SPME (2011)

8. Artale, A., Franconi, E.: A survey of temporal extensions of description logics. Ann. Math. Artif. Intell. **30**(1–4), 171–210 (2001). https://doi.org/10.1023/A:1016636131405

9. Autodesk: 3ds Max (2017). http://www.autodesk.pl

10. Away3D: Away3D (2017). http://away3d.com

11. Batsakis, S., Petrakis, E., Tachmazidis, I., Antoniou, G.: Temporal representation and reasoning in OWL 2. Semant. Web **8**, 1–20 (2009). http://www.semantic-web-journal.net/system/files/swj855.pdf

12. Berners-Lee, T., Hendler, J., Lassila, O., et al.: The semantic web. Sci. Am. **284**(5), 28–37 (2001)

13. Catalano, C.E., Mortara, M., Spagnuolo, M., Falcidieno, B.: Semantics and 3D media: current issues and perspectives. Comput. Graph. **35**(4), 869–877 (2011)

14. Chaudhuri, S., Kalogerakis, E., Giguere, S., Funkhouser, T.: Attribit: content creation with semantic attributes. In: Proceedings of the 26th Annual ACM Symposium on User Interface Software and Technology, UIST 2013, pp. 193–202. ACM, New York (2013)

15. Ciptawilangga, Y.: Online merchandising and ecommerce with virtual reality simulation of an actual retail location, US Patent App. 12/474, 202, 2 December 2010

16. De Floriani, L., Hui, A., Papaleo, L., Huang, M., Hendler, J.: A semantic web environment for digital shapes understanding. In: Falcidieno, B., Spagnuolo, M., Avrithis, Y., Kompatsiaris, I., Buitelaar, P. (eds.) SAMT 2007. LNCS, vol. 4816, pp. 226–239. Springer, Heidelberg (2007). https://doi.org/10.1007/978-3-540-77051-0_25

17. De Troyer, O., Kleinermann, F., Pellens, B., Bille, W.: Conceptual modeling for virtual reality. In: Grundy, J., Hartmann, S., Laender, A.H.F., Maciaszek, L., Roddick, J.F. (eds.) Tutorials, Posters, Panels and Industrial Contributions at the 26th International Conference on Conceptual Modeling - ER 2007, CRPIT, Auckland, New Zealand, vol. 83, pp. 3–18. ACS (2007)

18. DFKI, Computer Graphics Lab of the Saarland University, I.V.C.I.: XML3D (2017). http://xml3d.org

19. Falcidieno, B., Spagnuolo, M., Alliez, P., Quak, E., Vavalis, E., Houstis, C.: Towards the semantics of digital shapes: the AIM@SHAPE approach. In: EWIMT (2004)

20. Flotyński, J.: Semantic modelling of interactive 3D content with domain-specific ontologies. Procedia Comput. Sci. **35**, 531–540 (2014). 18th International Conference on Knowledge-Based and Intelligent Information and Engineering Systems

21. Flotyński, J., Krzyszkowski, M., Walczak, K.: Semantic composition of 3D content behavior for explorable virtual reality applications. In: Barbic, J., D'Cruz, M., Latoschik, M.E., Slater, M., Bourdot, P. (eds.) EuroVR 2017. LNCS, vol. 10700, pp. 3–23. Springer, Cham (2017). https://doi.org/10.1007/978-3-319-72323-5_1

22. Flotyński, J., Walczak, K.: Semantic multi-layered design of interactive 3D presentations. In: Proceedings of the Federated Conference on Computer Science and Information Systems, Kraków, Poland, 8–11 September 2013, pp. 541–548. IEEE (2013)

23. Flotyński, J., Walczak, K.: Conceptual knowledge-based modeling of interactive 3D content. Vis. Comput. **31**, 1–20 (2014)

24. Flotyński, J., Walczak, K.: Ontology-based creation of 3D content in a service-oriented environment. In: Abramowicz, W. (ed.) BIS 2015. LNBIP, vol. 208, pp. 77–89. Springer, Cham (2015). https://doi.org/10.1007/978-3-319-19027-3_7

25. Flotyński, J., Walczak, K.: Customization of 3D content with semantic meta-scenes. Graph. Model. **88**, 23–39 (2016)

26. Flotyński, J., Walczak, K.: Knowledge-based representation of 3D content behavior in a service-oriented virtual environment. In: Proceedings of the 22nd International Conference on Web3D Technology, Brisbane, Australia, 5–7 June 2017, Article no. 14. ACM, New York (2017)
27. Flotyński, J., Walczak, K.: Ontology-based representation and modelling of synthetic 3D content: a state-of-the-art review. In: Computer Graphics Forum, pp. 1–25 (2017)
28. Foundation, B.: Blender (2017). http://www.blender.org
29. Gutierrez, C., Hurtado, C., Vaisman, A.: Temporal RDF. In: Gómez-Pérez, A., Euzenat, J. (eds.) ESWC 2005. LNCS, vol. 3532, pp. 93–107. Springer, Heidelberg (2005). https://doi.org/10.1007/11431053_7
30. Gutiérrez, M., García-Rojas, A., Thalmann, D., Vexo, F., Moccozet, L., Magnenat-Thalmann, N., Mortara, M., Spagnuolo, M.: An ontology of virtual humans: Incorporating semantics into human shapes. Vis. Comput. **23**(3), 207–218 (2007)
31. Hu, X., Liu, X., He, Z., Zhang, J.: Batch modeling of 3D city based on Esri cityengine. In: Smart and Sustainable City 2013, ICSSC 2013, IET International Conference on IET (2013)
32. Jiang, H., Xu, W., Mao, T., Li, C., Xia, S., Wang, Z.: A semantic environment model for crowd simulation in multilayered complex environment. In: Proceedings of the 16th ACM Symposium on Virtual Reality Software and Technology, pp. 191–198. ACM (2009)
33. Kalogerakis, E., Christodoulakis, S., Moumoutzis, N.: Coupling ontologies with graphics content for knowledge driven visualization. In: VR 2006 Proceedings of the IEEE conference on Virtual Reality, Alexandria, Virginia, USA, 25–29 March 2006, pp. 43–50 (2006)
34. Klein, M., Fensel, D.: Ontology versioning on the semantic web. In: Proceedings of the First International Conference on Semantic Web Working, SWWS 2001, pp. 75–91. CEUR-WS.org, Aachen, Germany (2001). http://dl.acm.org/citation.cfm?id=2956602.2956610
35. Kowalski, R., Sergot, M.: A Logic-based calculus of events. In: Schmidt, J.W., Thanos, C. (eds.) Foundations of Knowledge Base Management, Topics in Information Systems, pp. 23–55. Springer, Heidelberg (1989). https://doi.org/10.1007/978-3-642-83397-7_2
36. Kowalski, R.A., Sadri, F.: The situation calculus and event calculus compared. In: ILPS, vol. 94, pp. 539–553 (1994)
37. Latoschik, M.E., Blach, R.: Semantic modelling for virtual worlds - a novel paradigm for realtime interactive systems? In: Proceedings of the ACM VRST 2008, pp. 17–20 (2008)
38. Lugrin, J.L., Cavazza, M.: Making sense of virtual environments: action representation, grounding and common sense. In: Proceedings of the 12th International Conference on Intelligent User Interfaces, IUI 2007, pp. 225–234. ACM, New York (2007)
39. Lui, T.W., Piccoli, G., Ives, B.: Marketing strategies in virtual worlds. SIGMIS Database **38**(4), 77–80 (2007). https://doi.org/10.1145/1314234.1314248
40. Microsoft: Direct3D 11.1 features (2017). https://msdn.microsoft.com
41. Noy, N., Rector, A., Hayes, P., Welty, C.: Defining n-ary relations on the semantic web. https://www.w3.org/TR/swbp-n-aryRelations/. Accessed 06 Mar 2018
42. Oracle: Java3D (2017). http://www.oracle.com
43. Otto, K.: Semantic virtual environments. In: Special Interest Tracks and Posters of the 14th International Conference on World Wide Web, Chiba, Japan, 10–14 May 2005, pp. 1036–1037 (2005)

44. Pellens, B., De Troyer, O., Kleinermann, F.: CoDePA: a conceptual design pattern approach to model behavior for X3D worlds. In: Proceedings of the 13th International Symposium on 3D web technology, Los Angeles, 09–10 August 2008, pp. 91–99 (2008)

45. Pellens, B., Kleinermann, F., De Troyer, O.: A development environment using behavior patterns to facilitate building 3D/VR applications. In: Proceedings of the 6th Australasian Conference on Interactive Entertainment, IE 2009, pp. 8:1–8:8. ACM (2009)

46. Pittarello, F., De Faveri, A.: Semantic description of 3D environments: a proposal based on web standards. In: Proceedings of the Eleventh International Conference on 3D Web Technology, Web3D 2006, pp. 85–95. ACM, New York (2006)

47. Rabattu, P.Y., Massé, B., Ulliana, F., Rousset, M.C., Rohmer, D., Léon, J.C., Palombi, O.: My Corporis Fabrica Embryo: an ontology-based 3D spatio-temporal modeling of human embryo development. J. Biomed. Semant. **6**(1), 36 (2015). https://doi.org/10.1186/s13326-015-0034-0

48. Rumiński, D.: An experimental study of spatial sound usefulness in searching and navigating through ar environments. Virtual Real. **19**, 223–233 (2015). https://doi.org/10.1007/s10055-015-0274-4

49. Rumiński, D., Walczak, K.: Semantic contextual augmented reality environments. In: The 13th IEEE International Symposium on Mixed and Augmented Reality (ISMAR 2014), ISMAR 2014, pp. 401–404. IEEE (2014)

50. Shanahan, M.: The event calculus explained. In: Wooldridge, M.J., Veloso, M. (eds.) Artificial Intelligence Today. LNCS (LNAI), vol. 1600, pp. 409–430. Springer, Heidelberg (1999). https://doi.org/10.1007/3-540-48317-9_17

51. Sikos, L.F.: 3D model indexing in videos for content-based retrieval via X3D-based semantic enrichment and automated reasoning. In: Proceedings of the 22nd International Conference on 3D Web Technology, Web3D 2017, pp. 19:1–19:7. ACM, New York (2017). https://doi.org/10.1145/3055624.3075943

52. Spagnuolo, M., Falcidieno, B.: The role of ontologies for 3D media applications. In: Kompatsiaris, Y., Hobson, P. (eds.) Semantic Multimedia and Ontologies. Springer, London (2008). https://doi.org/10.1007/978-1-84800-076-6_7

53. Spagnuolo, M., Falcidieno, B.: 3D media and the semantic web. IEEE Intell. Syst. **24**(2), 90–96 (2009)

54. Technologies, U.: Unity (2017). http://unity3d.com/5

55. Trellet, M., Ferey, N., Baaden, M., Bourdot, P.: Interactive visual analytics of molecular data in immersive environments via a semantic definition of the content and the context. In: 2016 Workshop on Immersive Analytics (IA), pp. 48–53. IEEE (2016)

56. Tutenel, T., Bidarra, R., Smelik, R.M., De Kraker, K.J.: The role of semantics in games and simulations. Comput. Entertain. (CIE) **6**(4), 57 (2008)

57. Van Gool, L., Leibe, B., Müller, P., Vergauwen, M., Weise, T.: 3D challenges and a non-in-depth overview of recent progress. In: 3DIM, pp. 118–132 (2007)

58. W3C: SWRL (2004). http://www.w3.org/Submission/SWRL/

59. W3C: VRML (2017). https://www.w3.org/MarkUp/VRML/

60. W3C: X3D (2017). http://www.web3d.org/getting-started-x3d

61. W3C: OWL. http://www.w3.org/2001/sw/wiki/OWL. Accessed 24 Mar 2015

62. W3C: RDF. http://www.w3.org/TR/2004/REC-rdf-concepts-20040210/. Accessed 24 Mar 2015

63. W3C: RDFS. http://www.w3.org/TR/2000/CR-rdf-schema-20000327/. Accessed 24 Mar 2015

64. Walczak, K., Rumiński, D., Flotyński, J.: Building contextual augmented reality environments with semantics. In: Proceedings of the 20th International Conference on Virtual Systems and Multimedia, Hong Kong, 9–12 September 2014 (2014)

65. Welty, C., Fikes, R.: A reusable ontology for fluents in OWL. In: Proceedings of the 2006 Conference on Formal Ontology in Information Systems: Proceedings of the Fourth International Conference (FOIS 2006), pp. 226–236. IOS Press, Amsterdam (2006). http://dl.acm.org/citation.cfm?id=1566079.1566106

66. Wiebusch, D., Latoschik, M.E.: Enhanced decoupling of components in intelligent realtime interactive systems using ontologies. In: Software Engineering and Architectures for Realtime Interactive Systems (SEARIS), Proceedings of the IEEE Virtual Reality 2012 Workshop (2012)

67. Zaid, L.A., Kleinermann, F., De Troyer, O.: Applying semantic web technology to feature modeling. In: Proceedings of the 2009 ACM Symposium on Applied Computing, SAC 2009, pp. 1252–1256. ACM (2009)

# An UE4 Plugin to Develop CVE Applications Leveraging Participant's Full Body Tracking Data

Carlo Luongo[✉] and Paolo Leoncini

CIRA Italian Aerospace Research Centre, Capua, Italy
{c.luongo, p.leoncini}@cira.it

**Abstract.** This technical paper describes a software framework that has been conceived in order to develop collaborative, immersive Virtual Reality applications with the distinctive ability to be fed by real-time full-body tracking data of the multiple collaborating participants. This feature has a key role both to improve the mutual awareness in the visually immersive CVE, and to exploit complete body poses for human-centered joint activities and related assessments. By following recent trends of VR research application development, the framework has been based on a popular game engine (Unreal Engine 4) and leverages its powerful built-in facilities for networked, multiplayer applications and for character skinning. The paper illustrates the implemented techniques for real-time size-independent mannequin animation that could be usefully applied for the same task to different game engines or VR development environments, and also describes the data management strategies devised for an efficient implementation of a CVE architecture dealing with full-body tracking data flows.

The knowledge gained during this engine-specific work will be useful for the future definition of an engine-independent communication framework for CVEs among single-user VR applications, based on heterogeneous game engine technologies, that is a strongly-felt need for promoting collaboration among VR research groups and in multi-partner industrial projects.

**Keywords:** Collaborative Virtual Environment · Virtual reality
Unreal Engine · Skeletal animation · Skeleton tracking · Natural user interface
Motion capture · Motion tracking

## 1 Introduction

Since their availability as free to use a/o open-source code, flagship game engines have soon become a common, powerful, and productive development environment even for VR applications. In particular, VR research labs have been migrating their experimental applications to, and have started new projects with, these new development environments that are far more productive, extensible/customizable, easy to use (IDE GUI), and feature-rich, at almost no money charge (unless of largely profitable projects), with the additional plus of the multi-target deployment including mobile platforms. In the forefront, there are Unreal Engine and Unity 3D; just behind as popularity, CryEngine, the recent Amazon Lumberyard (desktop) and Sumerian (based on WebGL/WebVR).

© Springer International Publishing AG, part of Springer Nature 2018
L. T. De Paolis and P. Bourdot (Eds.): AVR 2018, LNCS 10851, pp. 610–622, 2018.
https://doi.org/10.1007/978-3-319-95282-6_43

Not exactly at the high development level as the cited engines, plain WebGL/WebVR, A-Frame, and BabylonJS, whilst requiring more programming than the flagship engines, are nevertheless good examples of extensible, multi-platform, feature-rich libraries for modern VR application development.

On the other hand, Collaborative Virtual Environments (CVEs), or, in game engine terminology, networked multiplayer VR, is a cool topic in what they allows two or more persons to join in a common virtual working environment in order to carry out some joint activity otherwise not possible for a single one. These might include the simulation of an actual work, e.g. for Design-for-Maintainability or training to maintenance tasks (immersive, first person Virtual Maintenance Trainer), or to do some assessment task whose value raises when accomplished through an in-context opinion exchange (collaborative immersive design reviews, subjective tests in comfort and ergonomics). While in co-located form (all participants in the same physical environment) collaboration is a meaningful plus, it becomes invaluable when distant people are involved [4].

One of the distinctive features of a CVE for industrial use is the ability to bring the full motion ability of a human body into the common VE, for several reasons. Besides benefits of the improved mutual awareness of the participants, one of the most relevant needs for full-body tracking is that participants' body dimensions and poses could be key for a simulated task to be feasible or not (let's imagine a manual disassembly check in a narrow aircraft area). Likewise, large disparities in body dimensions between collaborating workers could make difficult to accomplish a joint task. Thus, VE's devoted to industrial uses really benefits from full-body tracking, both in single and multi-user flavours.

The main game engines have built-in networking multiplayer facilities, which make the development of CVEs much easier than with past technologies. Despite this, getting full-body, multi-person motion real-time capture data in a CVE application is not directly supported in the cited game engines, and even less in the multiple player scenario. Whilst possible through the several extension approaches available in every such new-gen development environment (visual programming, scripting, low-level programming), devising and implementing such a feature is delegated to specific needs for industrial use of these VR development tools.

## 2 The Reference Hardware Setup

In an immersive and collaborative virtual application, each participant dresses a head mounted device that typically shows the virtual scene and provides 6-DOF tracking data of the head. In order to provide these devices with a frame stream, that shows the reconstructed virtual scene, a dedicated machine for each participant, with adequate graphic capabilities, is required. To achieve the fully-wireless objective of the system, the connection between the HMD device and the graphic machine is made using wireless VR adapter such as TPCast [8].

Moreover, one or more additional views of the scene may be required. Nonparticipating viewers may display the point of view of an off-scene third person observer on a large screen in order to enjoy the virtual experience. As for HMD devices, also for the off-scene spectators a dedicated machine is needed.

The software application is composed by a server software and a number of client software, one for each actor, which means both in-scene participants and off-scene spectators. Therefore, the hardware cluster is composed by a workstations used to run the server software and two or more computer machines, one for each actor, for the collaborative purpose. For each in-scene spectator an HMD device and a TPCast device are also required. The reference tracking system is described in [1] and is connected to the software cluster through a Fast Gigabit Ethernet Switch (Fig. 1).

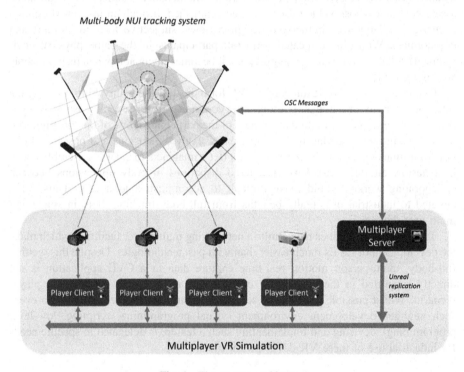

**Fig. 1.** The system architecture

## 3   The Development Framework

The software engine used to develop the VR applications is Unreal Engine 4. Unreal Engine 4 is a framework of tools to develop high-quality games, real-time VR and AR applications across different platform such as PC, console and mobile devices.

### 3.1   The Unreal Engine 4 Programming Model

Unreal Engine 4 supports two ways to add logic and specific behaviors to the applications: C++ development and blueprint scripting [9]. Using C++ the programmer can extend the base classes of the framework to create new types of actors, components and so on, that can be added to the scene or used in the scripts.

This approach is suited for the low-level development of tools and building blocks for which the use of a visual scripting language may result hard.

A very powerful and intuitive way to customize the application logic is the blueprint scripting technique. The Blueprints Visual Scripting system in Unreal Engine is a gameplay scripting environment with a node-based interface that permit the creation of gameplay elements. This technique implements the object-oriented paradigm, so a blueprint script, or simply blueprint, extends the base classes in order to create new types of objects in the engine.

# 4 The Skeletal Animation Software Plugins Set

In order to permit a rapid and simple integration of the virtual reality application with the reference tracking system, the software framework described in this work was developed using UE4 plugins. A plugin is a package of C++ code and UE4 contents that implements specific functionalities and that can be used into more than a single project. This is the best way to encapsulate reusable and specific software component, decoupling them from the application logic. Therefore, the plugin set developed in this work contains only the code needed by the application to interact with the tracking system, to provide the tracking information of the HMD devices and to manage the avatar mannequins.

## 4.1 The Avatar Animation Technique

The main objective of the proposed plugin set is to represent each real participant by a virtual mannequin whose pose reflects the real one. The multi-NUI tracking system provides the state of the skeleton for each person that is in the tracking area, so the software framework have to translate these states into a realistic pose of the avatar meshes. This work relies on the use of the skeletal animation technique as the method to change the pose of the avatar skeleton according to the live captured person's pose.

Skeletal animation is a technique in which a 3D model to be animated, in this case a human character, is composed by two main elements: a mesh that models the shape of the avatar and a skeleton that is a hierarchy of connected nodes, or bones that controls the mesh pose (Fig. 2).

The skeleton is a tree of bones, so each bone, except the root, has a parent and zero or more children. Each bone is fully described by a $4 \times 4$ transformation matrix that define a reference frame for his children. This hierarchical approach of the reference systems, defined by each bone, permits to model any movement of a limb by a rotation matrix applied to the root bone of that limb, so, for example a movement of an arm is obtained rotating the shoulder bone (Fig. 3).

A bone is typically used to model a joint of the real skeleton. The number of bones used to define a skeleton is a function of the movement's complexity that is needed to be replicated in the virtual world and of the capacity of the tracking system to capture these movements. For example, if the system is unable to capture the state of each

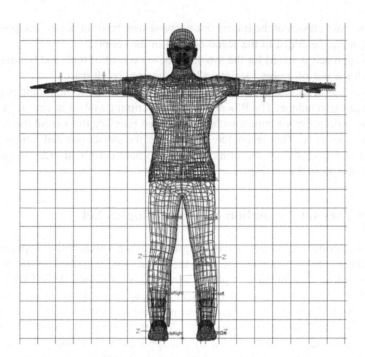

**Fig. 2.** Skeleton structure in "T" pose

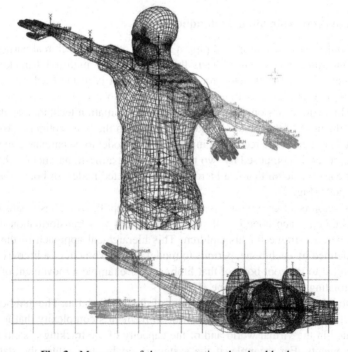

**Fig. 3.** Movement of the arm rotating the shoulder bone

finger there is no reason to increase the complexity of the skeleton to match the real hand structure. In this case, a simplified model is preferable.

In order to understand the relationship between the bones and the real physical skeleton is useful to define the concept of physical bone. For each couple of bones, or joints, of the virtual skeleton $(B_i, parent(B_i))$ the physical bone $P\text{-}B_i$ is the fixed length segment that connects $B_i$ and $parent(B_i)$. It represents which we usually call "bone" in the real life.

For the skeletal animation purpose, the skeleton is modeled in order to have the rotation matrix of each bone $Bi$ oriented with the Y-axis along the direction of $P\text{-}B_i$, so along the direction of the segment that connects the bone $B_i$ and its parent (Fig. 4).

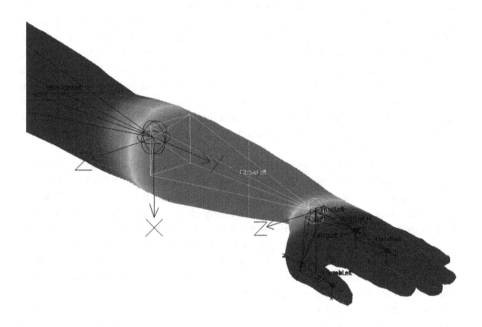

**Fig. 4.** Bone axis orientation and mesh weights

This convention ensures that the positions, in the world space, of the skeletal joints define the Y-axis orientation of the rotation matrix of each bones.

The remaining degree of freedom, the bone roll that is the rotation of the X-Z plane around the Y axis in the local frame of each bone, is usually chosen according to the tracking system. For example, if in "T" pose the tracking system returns the left elbow joint with the Z-axis directed towards the front of the person, is proper to have the same roll angle also into the skeletal model definition. In this way a re-alignment of each captured skeleton is avoided, resulting in a computational speed-up.

## 4.2   Character Rigging

A preliminary operation, called rigging, has to be done on the avatar model in order to define how the skeleton and the mesh are connected. In order to define the relationship between the pose assumed by the skeleton and the shape assumed by the mesh, a set of weights for each vertex is computed. During the rendering phase, the position of each vertex is computed as a function of the weighted arithmetic mean of the transformation matrixes of the bones. Therefore, these weights model how much the movement of a bone, or of a set of bones, influences the deformation of the mesh. For example the position of a vertex near the elbow is influenced by the humerus and the radius while a vertex in the middle of the arm is influenced only by the humerus bone. Figure 4 shows the influence of the bone on the near mesh by a color scale in which the red color indicates the maximum dependency while the blue color the minimum one. The definition of these vertexes weights is typically done with skeleton and mesh in a reference pose: usually a "T" or an "I" pose. In order to closely reproduce the participant's pose, the choice of a particular skeleton structure is very important. If the skeleton model in the reference pose, for example in the "T" pose, is different respect to the skeleton tracked by the sensors, in terms of numbers of bones, relationships among them or relative positions and rotations, an unwanted additional mesh deformation appears due the "distance" between the tracked skeleton, in "T" pose and the skeleton that controls the mesh in the same pose.

As mentioned above, the hierarchical relationship among bones permits that each bone defines a local reference space for its children. Assuming that the length of each P-$B_i$ is fixed during the application execution, which means that each physical bone is inextensible, incompressible and unbreakable, any change of position of a bone can be obtained applying a rotational matrix of its parent bone. In this way it is also possible to represent a participant by a mannequin with a different scale factor. For example, a participant may be a children or a teenager while the avatar may be an adult. If the skeleton's movements are modeled applying only rotations, the length of the physical bones are irrelevant in order to replicate the pose in the virtual scene. The change of position of the participant in the scene is realized moving only the root node of the skeleton structure in the scene coordinate system. However, in the applications that requires dimensional compliance, it is necessary to use an avatar with a scale factor corresponding to the real participant's body size.

Assuming that in the world reference frame the Z-axis is pointing up, a single scale factor in the Z dimension is needed to match properly the height of the root node in the initial pose with the position of the corresponding joint in the real scene. The root bone is typically placed near the hip bone. Therefore, during the initial acquisition, the application computes the ratio between the height of the hip bone of the avatar in "T" pose and the height of the hip of the participant in upright position. This scale factor is applied subsequently to the Z coordinate of the root node in order to move correctly the avatar.

### 4.3 The System Architecture

The software application is a distributed single server-multi client application. The server instance is delegated to manage the mannequin's instances in terms of their creation and deletion and to receive the state updates. To do this, the server have to listen the messages sent by the multi-NUI tracking system (Fig. 1). The communication protocol used to transport this information is Open Sound Control (OSC) [7].

The server stores a map of connected clients in order to bind the data acquired by the specific HMD device to the corresponding mannequin. Moreover, it stores a reference to the third-person clients that are not connected to a VR device and does not represent a participant in the scene (Fig. 5).

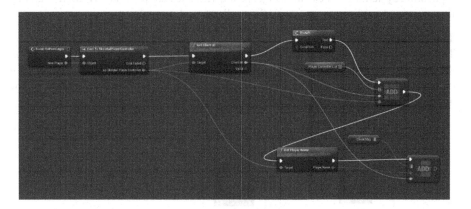

**Fig. 5.** Skeletal Manager Blueprint: Event graph section for clients registration

A client instance for each participant is executed on the machine that drives the corresponding HMD device. The client instance receives from the server the state of mannequins in the scene and renders them. The client also draws the whole virtual scene, so it draws all the graphic objects that compose the virtual world in which the scene is set. Moreover, a client instance for each off scene third person observer is needed. In this case, the point of view that is not connected to the position of the HMD device may be fixed or linked to a navigation mode based on a classic input device such as a keyboard, a mouse or a joypad controller that is locally connected to the client.

### The Communication Plugin

The communication between the server instance and the tracking system is developed by the OSC plugin. This C++ plugin implements a receiving system that exposes to the blueprint scripting system a receiver actor and a receiver component that can be added to the application to receive the OSC messages. In the case of actor receiver, this have to be spawned in the scene while the receiver component can be added as member of another actor class or as member of its derivate class, for example a pawn or a character.

The tracking system sends to the application server three type of OSC messages: creation, deletion and update. This messages use the OSC bundle structure that permits to collect, in a single macro-message, a set of messages. In this way, by a single OSC operation, the whole state of a skeleton is sent. A creation message is sent when a new participant joins the scene entering in the tracking area. The tracking system assigns a unique identifier to each participant and marks with it the corresponding messages. A deletion message, carrying in the participant's identifier, is sent when a participant leaves the scene going out from the tracking are. Since their creation, the tracking system send periodically to the server an update message for each participant. These messages contain the state of the skeletons in terms of a $4 \times 4$ transformation matrix for each bone. An instance of a special pawn is spawned by the skeletal manager for each received creation message. In order to propagate the state of these pawns to the clients, the UE4 replication system is used. The Unreal Engine supports natively a replication system by which same objects and variables are periodically aligned among the connected application instances (both clients and server).

### The Animation Plugin

The purpose of this plugin is to implement a set of assets and functionalities to permit the mannequins management in an easy way. This plugin is composed by a set of UE4 contents each of them has a dedicated purpose. Figure 6 shows the assets of the animation plugin and the dependencies among them.

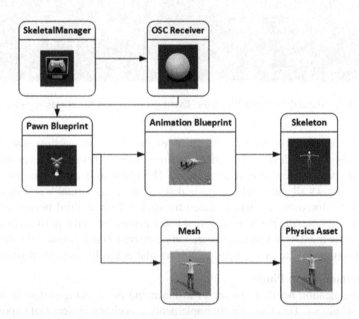

**Fig. 6.** Animation plugin dependency graph

### The Skeletal Manager

The skeletal manager extends the GameMode base class, as such it is executed only by the server instance. The aim of a GameMode class is to define the main application rules. In this sense, the skeletal manager implements the main mannequins' management: it receives the messages from the tracking system, spawning an OSC receiver actor; it decodes them and accordingly with their content, spawns and destroys the pawns that implement the participant's avatar (Fig. 7).

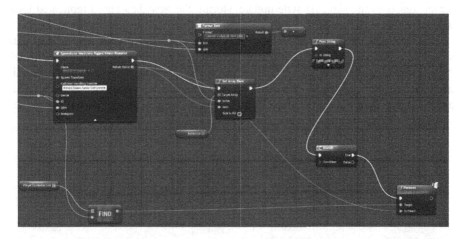

**Fig. 7.** Skeletal Manager Blueprint: Event graph section for pawns spawning

Another key class involved in the client-server application management is the Player Controller. While only the server executes the GameMode, or its derived class, only the client executes the player controller. It represents the real player in the software. The aim of the PlayerController is to manage the input received locally from the input devices such as keyboard, mouse, HMD controllers and so on. It also has a reference to the PlayerState that stores the state information of the player.

Another ability of the PlayerController is to "possess" a pawn. More than one pawn can exists but players can possess one of them at most. According to the UE4 camera responsibility chain, if the player controller possess a pawn, the client camera that define the client rendering point of view, is the camera view of the first CameraComponent in the pawn. In this way, the SkeletalManager set the point of view for each participant.

*The Mannequin's Pawn Class*

A pawn object implements the participant's avatar. According with the Unreal Engine programming model, a pawn is a special type of actor that can be possessed by a PlayerController. Therefore a pawn is the class type that have to be used to implement an actor of the application that can be controlled by a real player, in this case by a participant that moves in the tracking area. The mannequin's blueprint pawn derives by the pawn base class and implements the dispatching of the skeleton state to the clients. This class is linked to an animation blueprint that, in turn, is linked to the skeletal asset. The animation blueprint is responsible for the mesh deformation according to the pose of the skeleton. To do that, the skeleton state has to be shared between the pawn blueprint and the corresponding animation blueprint. Moreover, this data flow must cross the client-server application architecture. The pawn blueprint is devoted to the client-server synchronization. This blueprint has two different behaviors as a function of the context of execution. An object of this class is in fact executed both on the server and on the clients but the execution flow is different. The instance executed on the server, reacts to the skeleton state update, storing the new data into a replicated local data structure.

The instance on the clients instead updates periodically, at each tick, a local data structure of the corresponding animation blueprint reading the data from the replicated data structure mentioned above. In this way, the clients-server synchronization is delegated to the replication infrastructure implemented by the engine (Fig. 8). This architecture ensures that the animation blueprint receives the updated pose of the skeleton, only on the client, where the rendering process occurs.

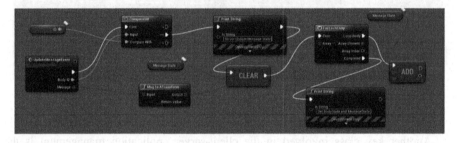

**Fig. 8.** Mannequin's pawn blueprint: Dispatching of the skeleton state by a replicated data structure

The animation blueprint is suited for giving animation to the actors. In order to deform a mesh according to the skeleton pose, a skeletal mesh component as a member of the pawn class can be used. This could be more proper than the proposed approach, based on the animation blueprint, but the current unreal engine version does not support the collision detection functionality for the skeletal mesh component.

In order to implement the physic interactions among the participants and the virtual objects in the scene, the collision detection is indispensable. Therefore, for now an animation blueprint linked to each pawn is needed.

*The Animation Blueprint*

The animation blueprint is composed by two graphs: the event graph and the animation graph. Therefore it exposes a function called "UpdateJointList" by which the pawn blueprint sets the updated skeleton's pose. Figure 8 shows the event graph of the animation blueprint. The Update stage sets the skeleton state into a local variable that is elaborated during the rendering process firing the update animation event.

The animation blueprint has two internal variables: the JointList, that contains the transformation matrixes for each bone, and the BasePosition, that contains the coordinates, in the world space, of the root bone.

When the update animation event occurs, the JointList is converted to a map. This data structure is a map of couples - bone name and rotation matrix and is referenced as

"Pose" in the script. The Pose map permits to be available the skeleton state to the animation graph that accesses only to the local variables. The animation graph simply sets the data red from the Pose map to the skeleton structure, using the Transform Bone function of the Skeletal Controls function set implemented by the engine.

In order to permit the physics simulation, and so the collision detection, a Physics Asset is assigned to the Skeletal Mesh component. A Physics Asset is composed by a set of rigid bodies and constraints used by the physics simulation engine to model the actor. In this case, these rigid bodies are capsules with the main axis coinciding with the corresponding physical bone and the size proportional to the size of the influence area of the bone, as specified during the skeleton definition.

## 5 Conclusions and Further Developments

This paper has illustrated techniques, and described a data management architecture, to manage full-body tracking data in networked multiplayer Collaborative Virtual Environment applications based on the Unreal Engine 4 game engine development environment. Besides pursuing the specific purposes of the research group, this work has constituted an opportunity for an in-depth knowledge of a modern game engine technology, a development approach VR application that will certainly never go back.

By leveraging the gained engine-specific insight, the next step in this research line will aim to try to define an engine-agnostic, body tracking-rich communication protocol for CVE applications. This will allow heterogeneous engine technologies, all supporting a common set of basic mechanisms and techniques (skinning, etc.), to join a collaborative session where players' avatar will be coherently represented in the common virtual environment. The benefits of this approach will include the freedom for distantly-collaborating research groups to retain their favorite technology for the development of VR applications, and, in industrial contexts, the opportunity to collaborate among project partners each one retaining its own CAx tools and visualization systems (e.g. for design reviews) once they will adopt to the new sharing protocol.

In a more general vision, a possible future development could be the creation of a partnership among VR research teams that share this kind of approach, to achieve the interoperability of different VE systems, each one implemented with their specific technologies.

## References

1. Leoncini, P., Sikorski, B., Baraniello, V., Martone, F., Luongo, C., Guida, M.: Multiple NUI device approach to full body tracking for collaborative virtual environments. In: De Paolis, L. T., Bourdot, P., Mongelli, A. (eds.) AVR 2017. LNCS, vol. 10324, pp. 131–147. Springer, Cham (2017). https://doi.org/10.1007/978-3-319-60922-5_10
2. McCaffrey, M.: Unreal Engine VR Cookbook: Developing Virtual Reality with UE4. Addison-Wesley Professional (2017). ISBN 978-01346491
3. Sherif, W., Whittle, S.: Unreal Engine 4 Scripting with C++ Cookbook. Packt Publishing (2016). ISBN 978-1785885549

4. Madathil, K.C., Greenstein, J.S.: An investigation of the efficacy of collaborative virtual reality systems for moderated remote usability testing. Elsevier (2017)
5. Sewell, B.: Blueprints Visual Scripting for Unreal Engine: Build professional 3D games with Unreal Engine 4's Visual Scripting system. Packt Publishing (2015). ISBN 978-1785286018
6. Satheesh, P.V.: Unreal Engine 4 Game Development Essentials. Packt Publishing (2016). ISBN 978-1784391966
7. The Open Sound Control Protocol. http://opensoundcontrol.org/introduction-osc
8. TPCAST. https://www.tpcastvr.com
9. Unreal Engine 4 Programming Guide. https://docs.unrealengine.com/en-US/Programming

# A Low-Cost Full Body Tracking System in Virtual Reality Based on Microsoft Kinect

Nicola Capece, Ugo Erra$^{(\boxtimes)}$, and Giuseppe Romaniello

Dipartimento di Matematica, Informatica ed Economia,
Università degli Studi della Basilicata, Potenza, Italy
{nicola.capece,ugo.erra,giuseppe.romaniello}@unibas.it

**Abstract.** We present an approach based on a natural user interface and virtual reality that allows the user's body to be visualized and tracked inside a virtual environment. Our aim is to improve the sensation of virtual reality immersion through low-cost technology such as HTC Vive and Microsoft Kinect 2. The system has been developed using the Unity 3D game engine and C# language. Our approach has been validated through the implementation of an application for 3D mesh painting where the user is able to interact through hand gestures to select a color from the 3D color palette, rotate the 3D mesh and paint it.

**Keywords:** Mesh painting · Virtual reality · Natural user interface
Human computer interaction

## 1 Introduction

In recent years, virtual reality (VR) has received increasing interest from both consumers and researchers. Through the latest generation of commercial systems based on head mounted displays (HMDs), such as HTC Vive, Oculus Rift and Samsung Gear, VR has left the research labs and is slowly entering the homes of consumers [3,8]. More and more technologies have been developed in the field of VR. Although there have been many improvements in terms of tracking and graphics rendering, the physical representation of the user in VR environments has been a poorly considered problem. Most VR systems do not allow the perception of the user's body inside a 3D scene. As such, the immersion level is drastically lowered. Some devices allow the user to use their hands to interact with the scene through the device's controllers [25]. Although this type of solution improves significantly the user's immersion level inside the 3D scene, it is still far from reality: just think about the controllers floating in midair instead of being in the user's hands [27]. Moreover, such a solution would make it difficult to interact with the scene using another type of controller or through a system based on a natural user interface (NUI).

Our idea is based on three core concepts: immersive VR [4,29], motion capture (MoCap) [16,17] and the NUI [11,31,32]. Immersive VR mainly comprises

© Springer International Publishing AG, part of Springer Nature 2018
L. T. De Paolis and P. Bourdot (Eds.): AVR 2018, LNCS 10851, pp. 623–635, 2018.
https://doi.org/10.1007/978-3-319-95282-6_44

two factors: presence and immersivity [28]. Presence is intended as the level of psychological realism the user is subject to, or as the intuitivism whereby the user can interact with the simulation and the coherence of the evolution of the simulation itself compared with the user's expectations. Immersivity is the ability to involve the cognitive resources of the user, isolating the user from external stimuli. Our aim is to improve these two VR aspects. MoCap consists of a technology and methods that are used to record and reuse the movements of the human body. In general, this operation is performed through sensors positioned at specific points on the user. The combination of VR and MoCap can be performed through the use of an NUI [15]. An NUI is a special type of interface developed to be used without traditional instruments such as mouse, keyboards and physical controllers. It is called *natural* as it is based on the movements of the user's body. A base example of an NUI is a smartphone's touchscreen, which allows the user to move from one page to another of a document using the finger to scroll like a paper book.

In this paper, we propose a prototypical system that enables the user's body to be simulated in a virtual environment and uses NUI for interactions. The idea is to use an avatar, represented through a humanoid 3D model, positioned below an HMD in the object space, which will reproduce the user's movements in real time by allowing the user to see his/her body and allowing the user to use several features through recorded gestures. To validate the proposed solution, we have created a prototype that, through a special sensor, reads and replicates the user's movements, allowing the user to control a 3D avatar. We have also tested this approach in a specific case study where the user manipulates and colors 3D models in the VR environment.

The remainder of this paper is structured as follows: Sect. 2 provides an overview of related works. Section 3 provides background information on the implementation details and technologies used. Section 4 shows our approach and Sect. 5 the VR-NUI mesh painting system. Finally, we end with some ideas for future work in Sect. 6.

## 2    Related Works

Enhancements of VR characteristics such as immersivity and presence have been the subjects of recent studies. De la Peña et al. [20] describe the concept of immersive journalism, a type of information in which news can be visualized and perceived in an interactive way by users. The fundamental idea is to allow the users, which are represented by a digital avatar, to enter the news. The sensation of presence, obtained through an immersive system, offers the user the possibility of accessing images, sounds and emotions that come from the news. The proposed approach is based on three core concepts: place illusion, plausibility and virtual body ownership. Presence is the strong sensation of being in the space represented by the virtual system. It is a static property of an experience, while plausibility concerns dynamic events involved in the news perceived through VR. Another very important component is virtual body ownership, which increments the level of immersion inside the virtual scene. To demonstrate this, a scenario was developed giving the sensation of being in an interrogation room in the Guantanamo Bay prison [2].

In the context of NUI, several approaches in various research fields have been developed. Brancati et al. [5] proposed a wearable system based on augmented reality for the dynamic enjoyment of cultural heritage through smartglasses. The system was developed to use both indoors and outdoors and equipped with a fully touchless interface that allows the user to query dynamically the surrounding environment. The user can navigate inside the cultural heritage and visualize the most important touristic attractions visualized through overlapped icons on the user's field of view. Users can interact with tourists and cultural information through icons using their fingertips. To interact with the application, the user uses a fingertip, which is recognized and overlapped with a virtual pointer by the system. Erra et al. [10] describe an NUI-based system that exploits augmented reality to simulate a dressing room. A 3D model, which represents the dress that the user wishes to wear, is overlapped to the user through an RGB capture-camera used to create a virtual mirror. In this way, the user is able to move and decide whether the dress is suitable and fits well. The development of this application was designed using Unity 3D Pro and Kinect 2 for Windows. The tracking body system inside the dressing room is similar to the one proposed by us; however, in our context, the user has a greater feeling of immersion due to the HMD. Our goal is to take advantage of low-cost hardware resources such as Kinect 2 and HTC Vive to provide a high sense of immersion within the virtual environment. This feeling is due to the fact that the user can perceive the movements of his/her body and move in the same way he/she would do in the real world.

## 3   Background

The proposed software system consists of two different applications. The first one has been developed to manage the Kinect device, the second one to manage the HTC Vive HMD device and the rendering of the 3D scene. Developing two different applications has been necessary to keep the management of the two separate devices simple. The applications communicate through a client–server architecture. In particular, on the server side has been developed an application that interfaces itself to Microsoft Kinect and provides data on the user's movement in the local network. A client–server architecture allows us to expand this type of application to a multi-user use, for example, to allow users to meet in the network using multiple Kinect devices remotely in real time and to also use the data generated by Kinect on devices that do not support it natively, such as smartphones.

Our system has been developed using the Unity 3D game engine, which is based on the *GameObject* hierarchy. Each *GameObject* has a spatial position and orientation, and it is possible to assign to it a 3D model, scripts, sounds, animations, physics and so on. Unity allows developers to use C# and JavaScript programming languages; in our project, we use C#. Furthermore, Unity is able to manage public variables in its scripts, which are visualized directly in the engine's user interface and allow the values to be modified without having to specify them in the code; in this way, the values can be modified at run time, and the effects of the changes can be visualized in real time. The development of our system became easier through the use of Unity 3D, which is already equipped with libraries that allow easy interface with external devices such as HTC Vive and Microsoft Kinect 2.

Basically, the HTC Vive has a refresh rate of 90 Hz and a field of view equal to 110° to adapt perfectly to the user's field of view. It allows stereoscopic display through the use of two screens, one for each eye, and has a resolution equal to $1080 \times 1200$ for a total resolution equal to $2160 \times 1200$. Also, it has several sensors that interact with the base stations to track the position of the screen inside room scale. Other sensors are a proximity sensor, a gyroscope and an accelerometer. For the development of the NUI, we have used a Microsoft Kinect device, which is equipped with a depth camera, an infrared camera and an RGB camera. The working principle of Kinect 2 is based on the time-of-flight camera, which, through the emission of a continuous wave signal, can acquire a depth map with a resolution of $512 \times 424$, and through the RGB camera can acquire images in Full HD [33]. The device is able to detect and reliably track the range of human sizes, ranging from children to adults. Its horizontal field of view is 60° and the vertical is 70°. To get good tracking quality, the optimal distance within which the user must be is about 1.4 m, because the distance in which the device operates ranges from 0.8 m to 4.2 m [26]. In the closest position to the camera, the user has a margin of movement of about 1 m each side, while in the furthest position he/she can move about 2.9 m each side. Through its sensors, the Kinect is able to build a point cloud, through which it can recognize a human shape, identify the joints and their spatial positions and reconstruct the user's movements in a movement area of about $10 \, \text{m}^2$ [14].

The visualization in the VR environment based on HTC Vive enables the user to use room-scale technology [18], which allows the physical space to be converted into virtual space and the user to move freely inside it. Moreover, the user has the perception of his/her position in the real environment, and this allows the user to orientate better and avoid worrying about possible obstacles within the real space. The use of HTC Vive inside Unity 3D is enabled through an external plugin called SteamVR. This plugin contains a set of scripts that allow interaction with the device's sensors. It also allows management of the *GameObjects* of the HMD and access to spatial transformation, components and properties, to integrate them into our scripts and to access HTC Vive's software development kit libraries.

To replicate user movements onto a 3D avatar, first it is necessary to perform two operations, called *rigging* and *skinning* [22]. The first procedure is used to identify the model's joints such as hips, ankles and knees, which will be connected using the representation of real *bones*. The second procedure defines a proximity area that indicates how much the displacement at a joint affects

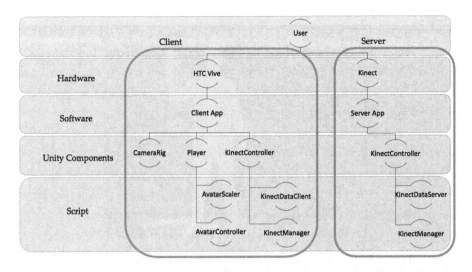

**Fig. 1.** The architecture of our approach. In the left green rectangle are shown the components of the client-side application, whose aim is to manage the HTC Vive, while the right green rectangle shows the server-side application, whose components manage the Kinect device. (Color figure online)

the neighboring joints; for example, the displacement of a joint that represents the hand influences the displacement of the wrist and other joints connected to it. Furthermore, the ability of this device to recognize joint movements gives it the ability to recognize certain gestures that can be used through appropriate scripts to perform certain actions [19,23,30].

## 4   System Architecture

Figure 1 shows the application's client–server architecture. As we can see, on the server and client side is present a component called *KinectController*, which on the server (Fig. 2) tracks the user's movements and makes them public on the network, while on the client (Fig. 3), it receives the data and interprets the data. The avatar is managed through a component called *Player*, which contains a 3D model reference and the scripts *AvatarScaler* and *AvatarController*. The first script performs the avatar resizing, based on the user's dimensions using the Kinect data generated in the tracking phase. In particular, the user's height and width are obtained by computing the distance between the shoulders and between the hips, and the lengths of the user's arms and legs [21]. The second script uses the data extracted from Kinect, through the *KinectManager* component, to create the avatar's animation through a direct kinematic chain [7]. Two more components are associated with the *Player*. They are responsible for the physics management and the skeletal identification that are needed to perform the animation. The avatar is a hierarchical model, which is organized in a tree

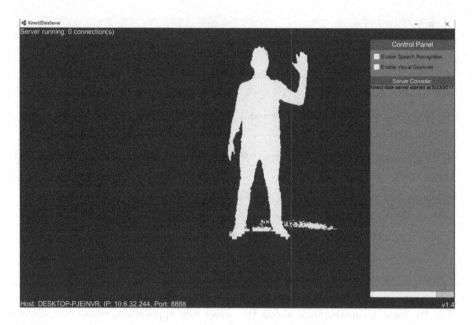

**Fig. 2.** The management Kinect system (server side) developed by [13]. The client–server architecture offers us the possibility to extend the multi-user approach, as well as the possibility to use multiple Kinect devices (see Sect. 6) in future work.

structure: the root is represented by the center of the hips, at which all the other branches are connected through the spine, the lower limbs and the intermediate nodes. The leaves are represented by the head, fingers and toes. To position the HMD in relation to the avatar's head, the positions of the user and the 3D model must be synchronized before the start of tracking. We have computed the user's pelvis position through the HMD's position. The component that determines the offset is called *HipsOffset*, which replicates the HMD's position value; this value, together with the positions of the avatar's head and pelvis, is used by a *HeightConfigurator* to calculate the *HipsOffset*'s position. At the avatar's head vector is subtracted the pelvis vector; this value is subsequently subtracted from the user's pelvis vector. The final result is assigned to the *HipsOffset*, which is updated for rendering the next frame. *AvatarController* contains an attribute that represents the offset of the avatar in relation to the coordinates captured by Kinect; this is the position of the user's hips in relation to the sensor, converted into Unity 3D system coordinates. The server-side application manages the Kinect device. The application is based on previous work [13], and its aim is to retrieve information from the sensor and make it available on the network through the *KinectController* component. Data reading is performed by the client through the *KinectDataClient* and *KinectDataServer* components, which use the Unity 3D application programming interface to send and receive the data on the network.

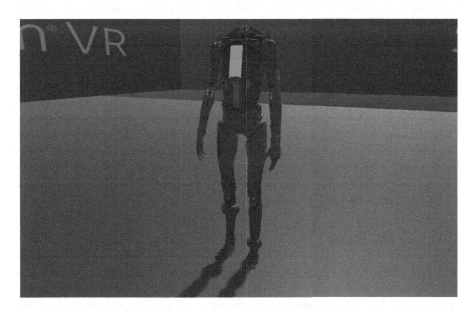

**Fig. 3.** The client-side system. The figure shows the 3D model used to simulate the avatar. The model is shown without its head and is named Adam [1].

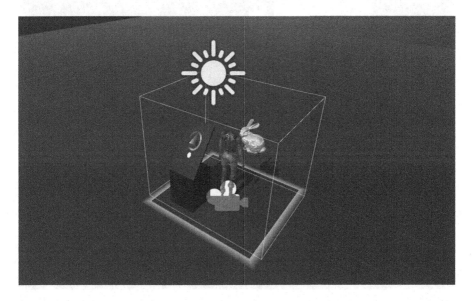

**Fig. 4.** The basic scene consists of a directional light and a plane. The figure also shows the coloring mesh, the body avatar and the color palette. (Color figure online)

From the point of view of the user, he/she perceives the presence of the avatar in the VR as if it is his/her body. Moreover, the user can notice how, for example, the avatar's feet position and the user's feet overlap, as well as how basic interactions such as hitting objects in the scene using the hands or feet will produce a reaction as similar as possible to the one that would occur in the real world, increasing the level of immersion. The user starts the simulation through the gesture "raise your right hand." When the user is detected, the system computes some parameters to adapt the avatar to the user's dimensions. Then the avatar will be positioned on the 3D space in which the user is located. The user's position is detected through HTC Vive's position in the room scale. Subsequently, the user will have full control of the avatar, which will reproduce the user's movements. The basic scene is composed of two principal components, a plane and a directional light (Fig. 4).

## 5   Case Study

We developed a mesh painting system that uses body tracking to test our system. The application consists of two modules: Main Scene and Dynamic Canvas. The Main Scene (Fig. 5) contains the 3D model on which the color is applied, the

**Fig. 5.** Another image of the Main Scene described in the text. In this context is used a perspective camera, which provides the VR scene rendering information at the HMD.

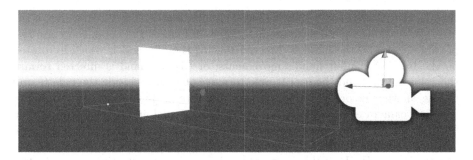

**Fig. 6.** The Dynamic Canvas, in particular the *Quad* and the canvas camera. The rendered texture's UV coordinates are associated with the coloring 3D mesh. (Color figure online)

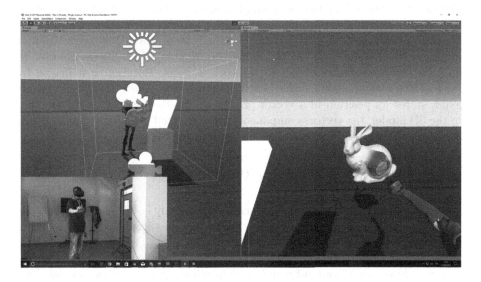

**Fig. 7.** An example of interaction with the 3D mesh painting virtual environment.

color selector and the scripts for management of the graphical user interface, the model and the selected color. In contrast, the Dynamic Canvas (Fig. 6) contains the canvas camera [24], which is needed to overlap the 3D model with the coloring texture, a background and the object that contains the generated color. The 3D palette enables the user to select a color. Once the color is selected, the user can rotate the 3D model and color it using only the user's hands. The right hand is responsible for coloring the 3D model, while the left hand is responsible for the 3D model rotation and the color selection. The interaction happens when a punch gesture by the user is detected. To determine whether the user's hands were directed toward the 3D object, we used a ray casting approach [6]. In essence, when the user places the right hand near the 3D model and closes the hand, a ray is projected from the center of the hand. On the first surface hit by the ray, the selected color is applied as a circular cursor (Fig. 7). However, if the user places the left hand near the 3D model and closes the hand, there are two possible cases: (i) the hand is directed toward the 3D model, which is rotated on the basis of the left hand's movements; or (ii) the hand is directed toward the color palette, and the user is able to move the cursor inside the palette and choose another color. The color of the model takes place using two cameras. The first camera is directed toward the coloring model and provides the data to the HMD, while the second camera is directed toward an element called *Quad*, which is associated with the coloring models texture. Since the first camera is responsible for HMD visible scene rendering, it is a perspective camera, while the second is an orthographic camera. When the user places the right hand in the shape of a punch to apply the color on the model, for each frame an object is created called *BrushEntity*, which represents the color unit, positioned between the *Quad* and the orthographic camera. On the *Quad* is applied a Render Texture, whose UV map is associated with the 3D model's coordinates. When the coloring gesture is detected by the system, the 3D space position of the hand is converted into the UV space coordinates, which allows the user to position the *BrushEntity* object to the correct point. Rotation is managed by *ModelRotator* component, which, when it detects the punch gesture of the left hand, stores its position in a vector. To determine the rotation angle to apply to the 3D model, the vectors components are converted into Eulers angle, which initializes the quaternions to realize the rotation.

## 6    Conclusions and Future Work

We have presented a system for simulating a users body in VR using interactions based on an NUI. We have validated our approach through a mesh painting system. The system was developed through the Unity 3D game engine. Future work will include the use of multiple Kinect devices (made possible by the client–server architecture of our software), which will be positioned on several sides of the room scale, to allow the user to perform body rotation of 360° inside the virtual environment instead of always staying frontally to the Kinect. Since both the HTC Vive and the Kinect are based on infrared technology, the signals of the two devices could clash. To avoid this, we have developed an optimal setup that consists of positioning the HTC Vive's base station above 2 m in height and connected by cable instead of wireless, with the Kinect positioned below 1 m in height. In this way, interference is greatly reduced, if not totally avoided. The described system has proven to be effective, allowing interactions to a good degree of precision with the virtual environment without the need for additional controllers or sensors. The perception of one's body is valid, and the movements are faithful, leading to a high sensation of immersion within the virtual environment.

However, although the Kinect is a low-cost tracking system, there are hardware limits; for example, it is impossible for the user to turn around an object, which would result in interruption of the tracking by the device. Furthermore,

Kinect's hand-tracking ability is very low, in effect limiting the possibility of using single fingers to make choices. Kinect does not allows the user's position to be tracked in 3D space, which would certainly have simplified its ability to integrate with an HMD. To achieve this, more invasive and expensive tracking systems would be needed.

In future work, we will transfer this system into other contexts to evaluate the benefits of tracking a user's body in virtual environments. For instance, we want to test this approach with a 3D information visualization tool used for the comprehension of object-oriented software systems [9,12]. Finally, we could also widen the set of 3D controllers, to derive insights into which type of user interface could be most beneficial for body tracking inside virtual environments.

# References

1. Adam Humanoid 3D model. https://unity3d.com/pages/adam
2. Gone Gitmo. http://gonegitmo.blogspot.it/
3. Anthes, C., Garca-Hernndez, R.J., Wiedemann, M., Kranzlmller, D.: State of the art of virtual reality technology. In: Proceedings of the 2016 IEEE Aerospace Conference, pp. 1–19, March 2016
4. Biocca, F., Delaney, B.: Immersive Virtual Reality Technology. Communication in the Age of Virtual Reality, pp. 57–124 (1995)
5. Brancati, N., Caggianese, G., Frucci, M., Gallo, L., Neroni, P.: Experiencing touchless interaction with augmented content on wearable head-mounted displays in cultural heritage applications. Pers. Ubiquit. Comput. **21**(2), 203–217 (2017)
6. Capece, N., Erra, U., Romano, S., Scanniello, G.: Visualising a software system as a city through virtual reality. In: De Paolis, L.T., Bourdot, P., Mongelli, A. (eds.) AVR 2017. LNCS, vol. 10325, pp. 319–327. Springer, Cham (2017). https://doi.org/10.1007/978-3-319-60928-7_28
7. Ceylan, D., Li, W., Mitra, N.J., Agrawala, M., Pauly, M.: Designing and fabricating mechanical automata from mocap sequences. ACM Trans. Graph. **32**(6), 186:1–186:11 (2013)
8. Desai, P.R., Desai, P.N., Ajmera, K.D., Mehta, K.: A review paper on oculus rift-a virtual reality headset
9. Erra, U., Scanniello, G., Capece, N.: Visualizing the evolution of software systems using the forest metaphor. In: 2012 16th International Conference on Information Visualisation, pp. 87–92, July 2012
10. Erra, U., Colonnese, V.: Experiences in the development of an augmented reality dressing room. In: De Paolis, L.T., Mongelli, A. (eds.) AVR 2015. LNCS, vol. 9254, pp. 467–474. Springer, Cham (2015). https://doi.org/10.1007/978-3-319-22888-4_35
11. Erra, U., Malandrino, D., Pepe, L.: A methodological evaluation of natural user interfaces for immersive 3D graph explorations. J. Vis. Lang. Comput. **44**, 13–27 (2018)
12. Erra, U., Scanniello, G.: Towards the visualization of software systems as 3D forests: the CodeTrees environment. In: Proceedings of the 27th Annual ACM Symposium on Applied Computing, pp. 981–988. SAC 2012. ACM, New York (2012)
13. Filkov, R.: Kinect v2 examples with MS-SDK. https://rfilkov.com/2014/08/01/kinect-v2-with-ms-sdk/x

14. Greuter, S., Roberts, D.J.: Spacewalk: movement and interaction in virtual space with commodity hardware. In: Proceedings of the 2014 Conference on Interactive Entertainment, pp. 1–7. ACM (2014)
15. Kaushik, D., Jain, R., et al.: Natural user interfaces: trend in virtual interaction. arXiv preprint arXiv:1405.0101 (2014)
16. Moeslund, T.B., Granum, E.: A survey of computer vision-based human motion capture. Comput. Vis. Image Underst. 81(3), 231–268 (2001)
17. Moeslund, T.B., Hilton, A., Krüger, V.: A survey of advances in vision-based human motion capture and analysis. Comput. Vis. Image Underst. 104(2–3), 90–126 (2006)
18. Niehorster, D.C., Li, L., Lappe, M.: The accuracy and precision of position and orientation tracking in the HTC vive virtual reality system for scientific research. i-Perception 8(3), 2041669517708205 (2017)
19. Patsadu, O., Nukoolkit, C., Watanapa, B.: Human gesture recognition using kinect camera. In: 2012 International Joint Conference on Computer Science and Software Engineering (JCSSE), pp. 28–32. IEEE (2012)
20. De la Peña, N., Weil, P., Llobera, J., Giannopoulos, E., Pomés, A., Spanlang, B., Friedman, D., Sanchez-Vives, M.V., Slater, M.: Immersive journalism: immersive virtual reality for the first-person experience of news. Presence Teleoperators Virtual Environ. 19(4), 291–301 (2010)
21. Preis, J., Kessel, M., Werner, M., Linnhoff-Popien, C.: Gait recognition with kinect. In: 1st International Workshop on Kinect in Pervasive Computing, pp. 1–4. New Castle, UK (2012)
22. Razzaq, A., Wu, Z., Zhou, M., Ali, S., Iqbal, K.: Automatic conversion of human mesh into skeleton animation by using kinect motion. Int. J. Comput. Theory Eng. 7(6), 482 (2015)
23. Ren, Z., Yuan, J., Meng, J., Zhang, Z.: Robust part-based hand gesture recognition using kinect sensor. IEEE Trans. Multimed. 15(5), 1110–1120 (2013)
24. Ritschel, T., Botsch, M., Müller, S.: Multiresolution GPU mesh painting. In: Eurographics (Short Presentations), pp. 17–20 (2006)
25. Seibert, J., Shafer, D.M.: Control mapping in virtual reality: effects on spatial presence and controller naturalness. Virtual Real. 22(1), 79–88 (2018)
26. Sell, J., O'Connor, P.: The xbox one system on a chip and kinect sensor. IEEE Micro 34(2), 44–53 (2014)
27. Siriborvornratanakul, T.: A study of virtual reality headsets and physiological extension possibilities. In: Gervasi, O., et al. (eds.) ICCSA 2016. LNCS, vol. 9787, pp. 497–508. Springer, Cham (2016). https://doi.org/10.1007/978-3-319-42108-7_38
28. Slater, M., Linakis, V., Usoh, M., Kooper, R., Street, G.: Immersion, presence, and performance in virtual environments: an experiment with tri-dimensional chess. In: ACM Virtual Reality Software and Technology (VRST), vol. 163, p. 72. ACM Press, New York (1996)
29. Small, D.E.: Immersive virtual reality. Technical report, Sandia National Laboratories (SNL-NM), Albuquerque, NM, United States (2011)
30. Tang, M.: Recognizing hand gestures with microsofts kinect. Department of Electrical Engineering of Stanford University:[sn], Palo Alto (2011)
31. Villaroman, N., Rowe, D., Swan, B.: Teaching natural user interaction using OpenNI and the Microsoft Kinect sensor. In: Proceedings of the 2011 Conference on Information Technology Education, SIGITE 2011, pp. 227–232. ACM, New York (2011)

32. Yeo, H.S., Lee, B.G., Lim, H.: Hand tracking and gesture recognition system for human-computer interaction using low-cost hardware. Multimed. Tools Appl. **74**(8), 2687–2715 (2015)
33. Zennaro, S., Munaro, M., Milani, S., Zanuttigh, P., Bernardi, A., Ghidoni, S., Menegatti, E.: Performance evaluation of the 1st and 2nd generation kinect for multimedia applications. In: 2015 IEEE International Conference on Multimedia and Expo (ICME), pp. 1–6, June 2015

# Mid-Air Interaction vs Smartphone Control for First-Person Navigation on Large Displays: A Comparative Study

Spyros Vosinakis[✉]

Department of Product and Systems Design Engineering,
University of the Aegean, Konstantinoupoleos 2, 84100 Syros, Greece
spyrosv@aegean.gr

**Abstract.** User navigation in 3D environments through public large-screen installations is mostly supported by mid-air interactions using motion sensors such as Microsoft Kinect. On the other hand, smartphones have been also used as external controllers of large-screen installations, and they might as well be effective in supporting 3D navigations. The aim of this study is to examine whether a smartphone-based control is a reliable alternative to mid-air interaction for 4-DOF fist-person navigation. We setup an experiment, where users had to navigate and complete a given task in two different scenes using three input modalities. The input modalities and interaction techniques were a known Kinect-based navigation method using body tilt and shoulder rotation, a smartphone-based control though tilting and rotating the device, and a traditional keyboard-based input used as a basis of comparison. We measured quantitative data through automated monitoring of users' actions in the environment (time to finish the task, number of collisions, total collision time and distance travelled), as well as subjective user ratings through questionnaires. The results indicate that smartphone control performs at least as good as mid-air interactions with Kinect, and it was the preferred method of input in the majority of the users.

**Keywords:** 3D navigation · Large screens · Smartphone · Kinect
User study

## 1 Introduction

Advances in 3D graphics technology and natural user interfaces have enabled the development of public interactive installations with virtual reality content. These environments are usually presented on large displays placed indoors or outdoors, and users can explore and interact with them in a natural and intuitive way. Currently, most public installations affording 3D interactions are found in museums and cultural institutions for the dissemination of cultural heritage, e.g. by presenting virtual restorations of ancient cities, buildings or monuments [1, 2]. Other possible uses of these systems include interacting with works of art [3], exploring geographical [4] or historical [5] information, presenting 3D content [6], interacting with scientific visualizations [7], navigating in virtual city models for urban planning [8], etc.

© Springer International Publishing AG, part of Springer Nature 2018
L. T. De Paolis and P. Bourdot (Eds.): AVR 2018, LNCS 10851, pp. 636–654, 2018.
https://doi.org/10.1007/978-3-319-95282-6_45

An important interaction found in almost any interactive 3D environment is the navigation and viewpoint control of the user, as 3D applications naturally require frequent movements and viewpoint changes. Navigation is a mentally demanding process for inexperienced users, because it involves continuous steering of the virtual body, as well as wayfinding abilities. As far as steering is concerned, a difficult challenge is a meaningful translation of the input device into respective movements in the 3D world [9]. In most 3D installations the navigation is from a first-person point of view and involves the virtual walkthrough of interior and exterior spaces.

User interaction and navigation with 3D environments in public installations is being supported with solutions 'beyond the desktop', usually based on natural user interfaces. Initially, the techniques involved handheld devices, such as WiiMote, or other custom controllers, e.g. [10]. However, the use of controllers in public settings raises issues of security and maintenance. More recently, public installations have taken advantage of low-cost vision and depth sensing technology and support mid-air interactions, i.e. body or arm gestures without the need of any additional handheld or wearable device. The most commonly used such sensor is Microsoft Kinect, which can detect body motion of up to four users in real time and translate them into respective virtual environment actions. Several techniques for first-person navigation using Kinect have been proposed and tested in laboratory or public settings, e.g. [2, 11]. A secondary, less used option is Leap Motion controller, which is considered faster and more accurate but is limited to hands-only interaction. Leap Motion needs to be in near distance from the users' hands and therefore it is more appropriate for seated users, which is somehow limiting for public installations.

An alternative approach for interacting with large screens that has been recently proposed is the use of a mobile device as a controller [12]. Most people carry a modern mobile device (smartphone or tablet) with them with satisfactory processing and graphics capabilities and equipped with various sensors. They could easily download (e.g. via a QR code) and run a dedicated app that turns their device into a navigation controller, and use it for interacting with a public installation. The use of mobile devices as controllers has some possible further advantages compared to mid-air interactions. First, it may lead to more personalized experiences, as the application would be able to track and remember individual users, and it could also deliver custom content on their devices. Second, it allows the presence of other people next to the one interacting with the application. On the contrary, the interference of visitors near a person using a Kinect-based installation is restricted, as it may lead to erroneous detection.

The aim of this study is to test whether a smartphone used as a controller can be a reliable alternative to Kinect for 3D navigation in public installations. We compare the user experience and performance between mid-air bodily interactions using Kinect and tilt-based interactions using a smartphone in two environments and respective scenarios: a small museum interior, in which the user has to closely observe the exhibits, and a large scene with buildings, rooms and corridors, in which the user has to effectively navigate to selected targets. The interaction techniques used in this study have been selected and adapted based on the results of previous research. A testbed environment developed for the study automatically measured the time spent to complete each scenario, the path travelled, the number of collisions and the total collision time. Furthermore, subjective ratings and comments for each interaction technique have been collected by the users through questionnaires and follow-up discussions. We present the results of our study and a discussion about their implication for the design of novel interaction techniques for virtual reality applications presented on public displays.

## 2 Related Work

### 2.1 Interaction with Large Displays

User interaction with public installations bears significant differences from typical desktop interaction, i.e. with keyboard and mouse, and poses interesting challenges. The display screen is considerably larger compared to common computer displays, and in some cases users can see virtual scenes and characters in nearly realistic size. The usage time in public installations is usually short to avoid building up queues while other people are waiting to interact [13]. There is a large variety of prospective users, from children to elderly people, having different previous experience with digital technology and different expectations as well. Therefore, there is a need for interfaces that are intuitive and easy to learn and remember. People often come in couples or groups, and they prefer to have a shared experience. Finally, given that users interacting with an installation are being publicly seen, they tend to avoid embarrassing or unnatural body postures and movements [14].

There is a variety of solutions regarding large displays in public settings. The display screen may be horizontal, e.g. on a table surface, or vertical, e.g. projected on a wall or displayed in one or multiple vertical screens. The most common interaction modalities with large screens are [15]: (a) touch or multitouch, adopting similar metaphors to the ones used in modern mobile devices, (b) tangible, where users interact by moving physical objects on the screen, (c) using external devices connected wirelessly to the system, such as game controllers or other custom devices, and (d) based on the movement of the users' body.

User navigation and viewpoint control in 3D environments is a special kind of interaction, for which not all aforementioned modalities are suitable. In the 3D environment the user is supposed to walk and look forward and, thus, the vertical screen is a more natural mapping compared to a horizontal surface. As such, the horizontal systems (multi-touch tables or tangible interfaces) are not suitable. Next, the steering technique is essentially a 3D interaction involving movements and rotations in the 3D space and, as such, the use of touch input on a 2D surface is not as natural and intuitive as in 2D interactions. Direct manipulation of the viewpoint through touching and dragging is not feasible due to the extra dimension (the depth) and usually alternative techniques (such as virtual joystick) are used for navigation in 3D environments using touch screens [16]. Furthermore, the navigation task requires from the user to be able to look at the whole screen while steering his/her avatar's body, and, therefore, the user needs to have some distance from the large screen not being able to touch it. Based on these restrictions, the most prominent solutions for 3D navigation seem to be the use of an external controller and the bodily mid-air interactions.

## 2.2  Kinect-Based Navigation Techniques

Various interaction techniques have been implemented using Kinect sensor for controlling an avatar's position in 3D environments, and numerous studies have been set up recently to assess their effectiveness and usability in field or laboratory settings.

Roupe et al. [17] studied the suitability of Kinect for first-person navigation in urban environments. Their interaction technique was to lean the body forwards or backwards to walk and to turn the shoulders to rotate. The study showed that most participants perceived this navigation interface as easy and non-demanding, and it supported a better understanding of size proportions compared to traditional interfaces.

In another study [18], a gestural navigation system developed in Kinect is compared to keyboard-and-mouse navigation. Their navigation technique is based on the hands; users use both hands to indicate navigation speed and direction following a "broomstick" metaphor. The performance between the two interaction modalities was similar and the user preference was also balanced.

Dias et al. [19] present a user study that compares two methods for first-person navigation in 3D environments using Kinect. The first method is using the 'bike' metaphor with two hands to control the speed and direction of travel, like holding the handlebar of a bike, and the second requires a single hand to control the view, in a way similar to moving a mouse cursor. The results indicated that the free hand control was better in terms of performance and satisfaction.

In a larger study, a number of different techniques for navigating using Kinect have been evaluated [20]. The techniques have been designed to be non-tiring and did not involve the hands of the user, which can be used for other actions. They included body motions such as walking in place, bending the knees, leaning the bust forwards or sideways, rotating the shoulders, etc. The results did not indicate a single interaction that stands out, but led to various interesting observations. Rotating and leaning the bust showed to be better techniques for rotation, whilst for waking there were advantages and drawbacks in all three techniques that have been used (stepping, bending knees, leaning the bust forward).

Finally, Ibanez et al. [21] present another comparative study of interaction techniques using Kinect for virtual environment walkthrough. Six different approaches have been tested, which involved both body and arm motions. The results were in favor of a technique that combines leaning the body forward for walking and rotating the shoulders for turning.

## 2.3  Smartphone-Based Navigation Techniques

A number of researchers have investigated the use of mobile devices as external controllers for interacting with large screens. The idea itself is not new. Smartphones have been used as custom controllers in video games [22], and there have been various proposed interaction techniques with public displays using smartphones, e.g. [23, 24].

Jimenez and Lyons [25] have studied three different techniques for interacting with large displays using smartphones. These are: (a) pressing directional buttons displayed on screen, (b) using multitouch gestures and (c) tilting the device horizontally or vertically. The task was two-dimensional; users had to solve a Tangram puzzle using the smartphone as controller. The results indicated that the use of buttons and the multitouch approach performed better than the tilt-based input.

In another small study [26] three similar interaction modalities for smartphones have been compared, but in a different context; the device was used as a controller for playing games. This time the tilt-based interface clearly outperformed the other two modalities. It was considered more fun and was the first choice for most players.

Liang et al. [27] explore the use of three interaction styles for navigating 3D environments using mobile devices. The styles used in the study are: pressing virtual buttons, using discrete touch gestures (similar to flicking pages) and using continuous touch input to control the speed. Tilt-based input was been included. The results showed that the continuous input and the button press yielded better results compared to the discrete touch gestures.

Berge et al. [7] presented a natural technique for navigating in 3D using a smartphone, based on moving and rotating the device with a single hand. The technique has been compared to the widely-used keyboard & mouse input and to a 3D mouse. The results showed that after a number of trials the performance of the smartphone input is comparable to the 3D mouse, and that most users find it more attractive and stimulating compared to the other two solutions.

Finally, VRMController [28] is another proposed smartphone-based solution for navigating in VR environments. The user navigation is controlled with a combination of continuous touch input and turning the device left or right. The technique outperformed a game controller (Xbox) in the task of exploring a 3D space and searching for hidden items.

### 2.4    The Focus of This Work

Up to date and to the best of our knowledge, the only comparative evaluation of Kinect and smartphone for interacting with large displays has been presented in [14]. However, the tasks were two-dimensional (searching a map and browsing bar charts) and as such, they are significantly different from the task of first-person navigation in 3D environments, which is the focus of this work.

Furthermore, most studies evaluating interaction techniques for Kinect and smartphones are considering only two degrees of freedom (DOF) for first-person navigation: walking forwards/backwards and rotating left/right. The only exceptions were the VRMController [28],which included moving sideways as a third DOF, and the work of Berge et al. [7], which also added the fourth DOF of looking up and down. Our claim is that the two extra DOFs are useful for virtual walkthroughs, and thus they have been included in the interaction techniques used in this study.

This paper presents the results of a comparative study between Kinect and a smartphone for first-person navigation in 3D environments. For these two input modalities, we have implemented respective techniques based on the results of previous studies: a mid-air interaction that involves leaning and rotating the upper body, and a technique based on tilting and rotating the handheld device. The implemented techniques are using 4DOF for navigating in the environment and have been tested in two different settings.

# 3 Interaction Techniques

The interaction techniques used in this study are for three input modalities: keyboard, Kinect and smartphone. Although the aim of the study is to compare Kinect-based with smartphone-based input, we decided to include also keyboard input in the experiments for two reasons: (a) to use it as a basis for comparison, since most users, especially gamers, are already familiar with keyboard-based navigation in 3D environments, and (b) to help users familiarize with the scenes used in the scenarios, so that their focus in the other two techniques is on steering the virtual body rather than wayfinding. Due to the latter reason, all participants in the experiment began with the keyboard input.

All three interaction techniques use 4 DOFs for first-person navigation and viewpoint control. Specifically, in each interaction users can switch between the following navigation modes, and for each mode, they control two DOFs. The navigation modes are:

- **walk/turn:** users walk forwards or backwards and turn to the left or right,
- **walk sideways (strafe):** users walk forwards, backwards or sideways, and
- **look around:** users look up or down and turn to the left or right.

The extra 2 DOFs of walking sideways and looking up/down have been added, because there are cases in which they are useful during virtual walkthroughs in various application areas. Walking sideways may be helpful for browsing a collection of artefacts arranged horizontally in a virtual museum or exhibition, and looking up or down may also be required for focusing on details in reconstructed monuments or buildings.

The interaction techniques for Kinect- and smartphone-based input designed for this study are based on approaches that have been found effective and usable in previous studies. For the Kinect-based input, the technique has been based on the leaning and twisting approach that produced the best results in [21], and was also one of the prevailing techniques in [20]. For the smartphone-based input, the technique used tilting and rotation of the device, which has also been found usable in [7, 26, 28].

The interaction techniques for the three input modalities (Fig. 1) are:

- **Keyboard.** For the 'walk/turn' mode the cursor keys are used: up and down moves the viewpoint forwards and backwards respectively; left and right rotates the view. For the 'walk sideways' mode, the ALT key combined with the cursor keys is used: up and down moves the viewpoint forwards and backwards, left and right moves it sideways, respectively. For the 'look around' mode, the CTRL key combined with the cursor keys is used: up and down turns the viewpoint upwards or downwards respectively; left and right rotates it.
- **Kinect.** In the 'walk/turn' mode, the user has to lean her body forwards or backwards to move to that direction, and to rotate her shoulders to the left or right to rotate the view. The velocity increases or decreases linearly depending on the amount of leaning or rotating. In the 'walk sideways' mode, the user has to raise slightly one arm (either left or right) by bending her elbow. Leaning forwards or backwards moves the viewpoint to that direction, and leaning sideways moves it to the respective side. In the 'look around' mode the user raises slightly both arms,

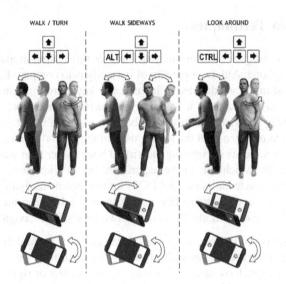

**Fig. 1.** The interaction techniques for the three input modalities (keyboard – top, Kinect – middle, smartphone – bottom) and the three navigation modes (walk/turn – left, walk sideways – middle, look around – right).

leans forwards or backwards to look down or up respectively, and rotates her shoulders to turn to the left or right.

- **Smartphone.** The device is being held by both hands in a horizontal direction (landscape), and the two edges of the screen work as buttons. In the 'walk/turn' mode, the user tilts the device forwards or backwards to move to that direction and rotates it like a steering wheel to turn left or right. Again, the velocity depends on the amount of twisting or turning the device. In the 'walk sideways' mode the user presses one button (either left or right) and moves forward or backwards by tilting the device and sideways by turning it like a steering wheel. In the 'look around' mode, the user presses both buttons and tilts or rotates the device to turn the view to that direction.

## 4   Testbed Environment

A testbed environment has been designed and implemented for the purpose of this study. The environment supports first-person navigation in 3D scenes using the three interaction modalities and respective techniques described in the previous section. While the user is navigating, the environment can monitor her activity and record various data for evaluation, including travel path, duration and collision. The testbed environment is based on the Unity game engine. Its architecture is presented in Fig. 2.

A first-person controller component has been implemented to translate user input into respective actions in the environment. The controller takes as input the navigation type (walk/turn, walk sideways or look around) and two values for the associated

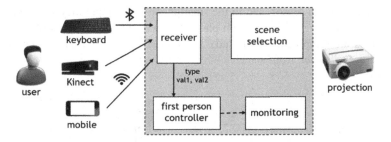

**Fig. 2.** The architecture of the testbed environment.

DOFs, and performs the appropriate translations and rotations of the viewpoint. The controller is treated by the game engine as a physical body and, as such, it collides with the ground and other objects of the scene in a way similar to avatar-based navigation in first-person games. The environment can switch between various scenes and place the controller in the designated starting position of each scene.

For each of the three modalities, a receiver reads the input required for the technique, generates the navigation type and pair of values, and transmits them to the first-person controller. During keyboard input, it simply checks the status of the cursor, ALT and CTRL keys. For Kinect, it reads the rotation values of the spine joint and the two elbow joints of the user skeleton as interpreted by the sensor. Finally, the smartphone runs a simple controller app that transmits the values of the accelerometers and the status of the two buttons to the receiver through Internet using UDP packets.

A small pilot study has been set up to calibrate the testbed environment prior to the main study. Our aim was to adjust the movement and rotation speed of the first-person controller based on user preferences. We asked four users to use the three interaction modalities and navigate around a scene. After some initial familiarization, they were asked to propose any adjustments to the navigation and rotation speed. The speeds were then recalibrated on the fly and the process was repeated until the users felt more comfortable with the interface. All users reached similar desired values, which were significantly slower from the initial values of the testbed. Based on these results, the movement and rotation speeds of the testbed environment have been adjusted to almost 60% of their original value.

## 5   User Study

### 5.1   Equipment and Setting

The study took place in the laboratory. The testbed environment was running on a PC with Intel Xeon CPU 3.70 GHz, 16 Gb Ram and NVIDIA Quadro K4200 graphics card, and the scene was displayed on a projection screen through an Epson EB-X24 Projector.

Each user participating in the study was at a distance of about 2.5 m from the projection screen for all three modalities. In the keyboard-based input users were seated using a wireless keyboard, in the Kinect-based input users were standing in front of a

Kinect 2 (Xbox One) sensor, and in the smartphone-based input they were standing at the same spot holding a Xiaomi mi4i phone that was running the controller app. Figure 3 shows the setup of the user study in terms of screen dimensions, sensor placement and user distance from screen.

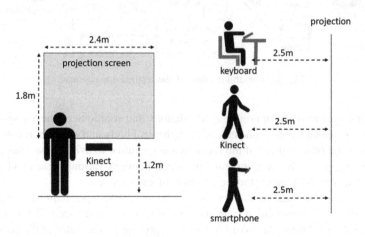

**Fig. 3.** Setup of the experiment. Left: projection screen dimensions and placement and sensor placement. Right: distance between user and projection screen in the three modalities.

Three different scenes have been prepared and used in the testbed environment. These were:

- **Familiarization:** a simple scene for letting users familiarize with each interaction technique. It displays a digitized version of the Stonehenge site.
- **Buildings:** a scene with interior and exterior parts showing abandoned buildings with rooms and corridors. Users have to walk around a building, and to carefully maneuver their virtual body through narrow doors.
- **Museum:** a small interior scene showing a digitized version of the Picture Gallery of the Hallwyl Museum. Users have to walk slowly through the corridors and focus on specific exhibits.

Figure 4 shows two users interacting with the 3D environment using Kinect and smartphone as input, and the buildings and museum scenes used in the study.

### 5.2 Participants

Twenty-two (22) users participated in the study, 11 male and 11 female, most of which were students and faculty from our department. The age span was wide (between 20 and 50), but the majority of users were under 30 (M: 25.4, SD: 7.8).

The participants' experience with computer games and 3D environments was quite balanced. Eleven (11) users reported that they had large or very large experience, six (6) had none or little experience, and five (5) medium.

**Fig. 4.** Two users interacting with the 3D environment using Kinect (a) and smartphone (b) and the two scenes used in the study: museum (c) and buildings (d).

## 5.3   Procedure

The study employed a within-subjects design, so each subject used all three interaction modalities in both scenes, i.e. 6 trials per user. The procedure was the following.

First, users have been introduced to the purpose and procedure of the study, and they had to fill an initial questionnaire with their gender, age and experience with games and 3D environments.

Next, they had to use the three interaction modalities and follow the requested scenarios. All users started with keyboard input, and then they continued with the other two modalities, but with different order. Half of the users interacted first using Kinect and then using the smartphone, and the other half in reverse order to counterbalance possible order effects.

For each interaction modality, the users had to navigate in all three scenes. Initially they were placed in the familiarization scene and were let free to navigate around using the interface, until they felt comfortable with it. Then, they continued to the buildings scene where they had to perform a specific task: they had to enter a building and move to designated positions in three specific rooms. Third was the museum scene, where they had to move around and focus on four specific exhibits by trying to bring them to the center of the screen as close as possible. In both scenarios, the target positions were shown to the users by the evaluators during their navigation, so the actual challenge was to steer their virtual body to the designated targets. At the end of each modality, users filled a questionnaire with their subjective ratings and comments for the interface and interaction technique.

Finally, users were asked to choose between Kinect-based and smartphone-based navigation as their preferred method and give any conclusive comments.

Each user session lasted around 35 min.

## 5.4 Collected Data

The measures used in this study have been selected to provide qualitative and quantitative data about user experience and performance for each interaction technique.

Users provided their subjective ratings for each interaction technique through questionnaires in 5-point Likert scales. Specifically, they had to rate: (a) ease of use, (b) learnability, (c) satisfaction, (d) comfort, and (e) accuracy. These questions have been selected and adapted from popular usability questionnaires.

Furthermore, the testbed environment automatically collected the following measures for each task, i.e. twice for each interaction technique: (a) time to complete task, (b) number of collisions, (c) total collision time, and (d) path. The user collision with a wall or obstacle during her navigation is considered an error, and, therefore, we decided to include the number of collisions and the total time the user was colliding (e.g. whilst sliding on a wall) as an indication of unsuccessful steering. The recorded path can provide a qualitative overview of the navigation quality of each user, and also allowed the calculation the total travelled distance.

Finally, users had to select their preferred input modality between Kinect and smartphone.

# 6 Results

At the end of the experiment, the collected data have been analyzed to provide insight on the usability and performance of each interaction modality. We calculated mean values, standard deviations and 95% confidence intervals for each of the collected measures. The time, collisions and distance data have been further analyzed using one-way analysis of variance (ANOVA) to test for statistically significant differences among the three modalities, and post-hoc Tuckey HSD tests for pairwise comparisons have been run where needed. Being non-parametric due to the use of the Likert-scale, the subjective ratings have been further analyzed for statistically significant differences using pairwise Wilcoxon signed-rank tests.

## 6.1 Time, Collisions and Distance Travelled

The mean values and 95% confidence intervals of task time (sec.), number of collisions, collision time (sec.) and distance travelled (meters) for the tree input modalities are presented in Fig. 5.

Regarding the total time to task, there was a statistically significant difference between the three input modalities in the buildings scene ($F_{(2,63)} = 5.44$, $p = 0.007$) and no statistically significant difference in the museum scene. Post-hoc Tuckey HSD tests revealed that in the buildings scene the total time using keyboard was significantly lower compared to Kinect ($p = 0.02$) and that the total time using smartphone was also significantly lower compared to Kinect ($p = 0.013$).

In the total number of collisions, the keyboard outperformed the other two modalities. Specifically, the analysis of variance indicated statistically significant difference for the buildings ($F_{(2,63)} = 15.03$, $p < 0.001$) and the museum ($F$

(2,63) = 13.33, p < 0.001) scenes. Post-hoc Tuckey HSD tests showed that in both scenes the number of collisions using keyboard were significantly lower compared to Kinect (p = 0.001 in both scenes) and smartphone (p = 0.001 in both scenes).

Regarding the total collision time, there was a significant difference between the three modalities in the buildings scene (F(2,63) = 8.34, p < 0.001) and no statistically significant difference in the museum scene. The post-hoc Tuckey HSD tests for the collision time in the buildings scene showed that using the keyboard the total collision time was significantly smaller compared to Kinect (p = 0.001). No statistically significant difference has been found between keyboard and smartphone.

Finally, for the total distance travelled, the ANOVA tests revealed statistically significant differences in both scenes (buildings scene: F(2,63) = 5.86, p = 0.004, museum scene: F(2,63) = 9.50, p < 0.001). The post-hoc analysis in both scenes revealed that using the keyboard users travelled significantly less distance compared to smartphone (buildings scene: p = 0.004, museum scene: p = 0.001). No statistically significant difference has been found between keyboard and Kinect.

## 6.2   Subjective Ratings

The results of the 5-point Likert questions for the subjective measures in each inter-action modality are summarized in Fig. 6 with averages and 95% confidence intervals.

The analysis using Wilcoxon signed-rank tests identified some significant differences among the modalities in terms of satisfaction, comfort and accuracy. Specifically, in satisfaction the smartphone scored significantly better than the keyboard (p = 0.016), and in accuracy, keyboard control has been rated as significantly better than both other modalities (p = 0.005 for Kinect, p = 0.041 for smartphone). Furthermore, regarding comfort users considered smartphone significantly better than Kinect (p = 0.003).

Looking at the mean scores of the subjective ratings, one can easily see that keyboard scored at least as good as the two other modalities, with the exception of satisfaction. In satisfaction, the mean scores were 3.40 (SD: 1.11) for keyboard, 3.73 (SD: 1.29) for Kinect and 4.14 (SD: 1.10) for smartphone. Furthermore, in all ratings the mean scores for smartphone were slightly higher compared to those of Kinect.

Finally, regarding the preferred input modality between Kinect and smartphone, the majority of users voted for the latter. Seven (7) users (31.8%) preferred Kinect, whilst fifteen (15) users (68.2%) preferred the smartphone-based input (Table 1).

## 6.3   User Comments and Observations

During the study, we collected various user comments about the three interaction modalities through their written responses in the questionnaires or while discussing with them after the experiment. Furthermore, we took note of a number of remarks while observing the users during their tasks. The most important findings are the following.

Unlike keyboard, with Kinect and smartphone-based input users could not keep their virtual body completely inanimate. Slight movements of the human body or rotations of the phone caused slow movements of the viewpoint, which the majority of

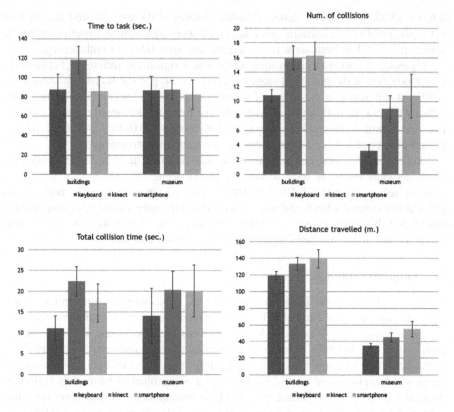

**Fig. 5.** Mean values of total time to finish the task in seconds (upper left), number of collisions (upper right), total collision time in seconds (lower left) and total distance travelled in meters (lower right) in the buildings and museum scenes. Error bars represent 95% confidence intervals.

**Table 1.** Subjective user preference between Kinect and smartphone input (number of users and percentage).

| Input modality | Num. | % |
|---|---|---|
| Kinect | 7 | 31.82% |
| Smartphone | 15 | 68.18% |

the users disliked. We noticed that some experienced users intentionally switched to 'look around' mode when they wished to stop the viewpoint motion.

Some inexperienced users found the smartphone-based and Kinect-based modalities too sensitive. They were not familiar with the analog control of velocity (i.e. to change proportionally to the amount of leaning or rotating), and they had the tendency to make large movements, which in turn lead to higher velocities and less sense of control. On the other hand, more experienced users managed to get control of the techniques much easier.

This difference between keyboard and the other two modalities is also evident in the recorded user paths. With keyboard, users tended to make shorter, more abrupt and linear movements, whilst with the analog control devices they made longer and smoother movements. This may partially explain the fact that although the mean times to task between keyboard and smartphone were comparable, users travelled significantly more distance with the latter. Figure 7 shows the recorded paths of a user (female, 22 y.o., experienced gamer) for the six trials.

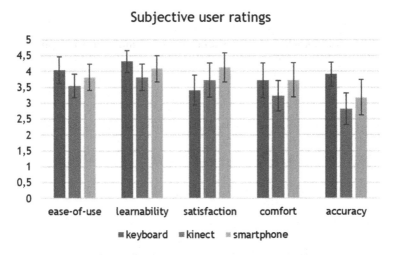

**Fig. 6.** Mean values of subjective user ratings regarding ease-of-use, learnability, satisfaction, comfort and accuracy. Error bars represent 95% confidence intervals.

Some users did not move backwards when using Kinect or smartphone and when asked, they claimed that they forgot they had this option! Also, a few users did not find the strafe motion very useful.

Regarding Kinect-based input, some users confused the shoulder rotation with sideways leaning, leading to difficulties in steering their virtual body.

Regarding smartphone-based input, there were users who forgot to rotate it like a steering wheel and turned the device to the left or right. Also, a lot of users tended to hold the device diagonally (tilted to the front), because they claimed that this is the usual way they hold a smartphone. They preferred this position to be the 'resting' position of the virtual body instead of holding it vertically. One user commented that he would prefer an interaction technique for one hand instead of two.

Finally, we noticed some tendencies among user groups. Users who reported no experience with games and 3D environments seemed to prefer the Kinect input, while experienced gamers were much more enthusiastic with the smartphone. Also, the preference of input modality among female users was almost equally divided (6 for smartphone and 5 for Kinect), whilst with male users it was in much stronger favor of smartphone-based input (9 for smartphone and 2 for Kinect).

**buildings-keyboard    buildings-kinect   buildings-smartphone**

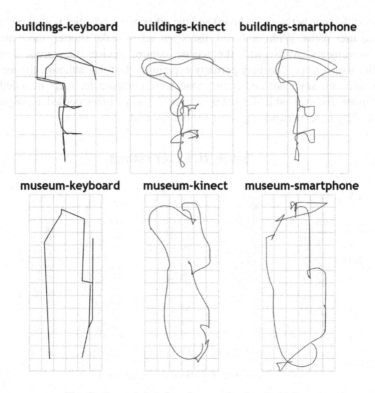

**museum-keyboard    museum-kinect   museum-smartphone**

**Fig. 7.** Recorded paths of a user for the six trials.

## 7  Discussion

According to the results of this study, it appears that smartphone-based interaction performs at least as good as Kinect-based, it is considered more comfortable, and it was also the preferred choice for most participants. This is an indication that smartphones could be used as reliable alternatives to bodily mid-air interactions for 3D navigation in public settings. This finding is in accordance to the results of the study presented in [7], where the smartphone is considered an attractive and stimulating solution for inter-active applications in public settings. However, a further issue that needs to be investigated is whether visitors of museums and other public institutions are willing to download specific apps and use their personal phone as a controller.

The only statistically significant difference found between Kinect and smartphone in all metrics used in this study was in the time to complete the task in the buildings scene, where it took significantly longer using Kinect. This is possibly due to the fact that users had to pass through narrow doors in the buildings scene and they needed to make slow and accurate movements to achieve that. It seems that with the smartphone input they could manage it better, which is also evident in the mean values of the total collision time for the buildings scene (22.40 s for Kinect and 17.20 s for smartphone).

Another interesting observation is that although the participants found the keyboard more accurate as an input device, they rated Kinect and smartphone as more satisfying. A number of users spontaneously commented that they had fun using them. This finding indicates that the natural ways of interacting with a 3D environment are usually more playful and motivating, even if the traditional means give more sense of control. Similar results have been reported in various other studies, e.g. [29].

A further issue that needs to be looked at is the sensitivity of the input devices and the ability to freeze the viewpoint. This is especially important for virtual heritage applications, where users need to stop and look at the details of the scene. Possible solutions to that issue are either to provide a special gesture or button that stops all movement, or to make the interaction techniques less sensitive to small movements.

An important issue that has been made clear during the study is that inexperienced users are in need of assistance when using new interfaces and input modalities, which has been also found in previous studies (e.g. [30]). Users with small or no experience in 3D games and first-person navigation felt quite confident using the keyboard but with the other two modalities they sometimes reported having little sense of control. Interactive systems of this kind should preferably be designed to monitor user performance and, in case they detect non-expected behavior, to offer assistance in a non-intrusive way, e.g. through messages, indications, mini-maps, etc.

Finally, the fact that inexperienced users and females have a more positive stance towards bodily interaction compared to the rest of the population is an issue that needs to be further researched. In the work of Roupe et al. [17], it has also been found that new users found Kinect easier to use than gamers, and also that female users found bodily interaction more comfortable compared to male.

# 8 Conclusions

This paper presented a comparative study between Kinect-based and smartphone-based first-person navigation techniques for large-screen 3D environments. The aim of the study was to examine whether the user's smartphone can be used as a reliable alternative to bodily mid-air interactions in a public installation. The participants had to use the aforementioned modalities along with the traditional keyboard input in two scenarios: a scene with abandoned buildings that involved walking in exterior and interior settings and steering the virtual body through corridors and doors, and the interior of a museum room, where users had to closely look at specific exhibits. The results of the study indicate that the smartphone-based input is at least as reliable as Kinect-based. It was preferred by most participants, it is considered more comfortable, it has been rated higher in all subjective ratings, and it produced significantly shorter task completion times in the first scenario.

An important advantage of a modern smartphone compared to typical game controllers is that its interface can be fully customized, e.g. by adding custom virtual buttons on the screen or by supporting various multitouch gestures. As such, it is more adaptive to afford multiple interaction modalities with a virtual reality application.

An issue that needs further research regarding the design of 3D navigation techniques is the support of secondary actions. Often navigation has to be combined with other actions, such as selecting an object, browsing information, etc. Therefore, the bodily or tilt-based interactions for navigation should leave room for other actions that can be performed in parallel.

Furthermore, this study has been based mostly on relatively young people, and possible issues regarding elderly individuals and their ability to effectively navigate using the proposed bodily interaction has not been taken into account.

In the future, we are planning to further explore the prospects of combining smartphone-based interactions with virtual environments in public settings. We aim to extend our smartphone-based interaction technique by improving its sensitivity and comfort, by adding non-intrusive user assistance through voice messages and icons, and by testing various forms of feedback, e.g. audio and vibration.

# References

1. Fanini, B., D'Annibale, E., Demetrescu, E., Ferdani, D.: Engaging and Shared Gesture-based Interaction for Museums: The case study of K2R international Expo in Rome. In: Proceedings of Digital Heritage 2015, pp. 263–270. IEEE (2015)
2. Rufa, C., Pietroni, E., Pagano, A.: The Etruscanning project : Gesture-based interaction and user experience in the virtual reconstruction of the Regolini- Galassi tomb. In: Proceedings of 2013 Digital Heritage International Congress, pp. 653–660 (2013)
3. Castro, B.P., Velho, L., Kosminsky, D.: INTEGRARTE: digital art using body interaction. In: Proceedings of the Eighth Annual Symposium on Computational Aesthetics in Graphics, Visualization, and Imaging (2012)
4. Häkkilä, J., Koskenranta, O., Posti, M., He, Y.: City landmark as an interactive installation: experiences with stone, water and public space. In: Proceedings of the 8th International Conference on Tangible, Embedded and Embodied Interaction, pp. 221–224 (2014)
5. Grammenos, D., Drossis, G., Zabulis, X.: Public Systems Supporting Noninstrumented Body-Based Interaction. In: Playful user Interfaces, pp. 25–45, Springer, Singapore (2014)
6. Krekhov, A., Emmerich, K., Babinski, M.: Gestures from the point of view of an audience : toward anticipatable interaction of presenters with 3D content. In: Proceedings of CHI 2017, pp. 5284–5294. ACM (2017)
7. Bergé, L.P., Perelman, G., Raynal, M., Sanza, C., Serrano, M., Houry-Panchetti, M., Cabanac, R., Dubois, E.: Smartphone-based 3D navigation technique for use in a museum exhibit. In: Proceedings of ACHI 2014, The Seventh International Conference on Advances in Computer-Human Interactions, pp. 252–257 (2014)
8. Cristie, V., Berger, M.: Game engines for urban exploration: bridging science narrative for broader participants. In: Nijholt, A. (ed.) Playable Cities, pp. 87–107, Springer, Singapore (2017). https://doi.org/10.1007/978-981-10-1962-3_5
9. Bowman, D.A., Koller, D., Hodges, L.F.: Travel in immersive virtual environments: an evaluation of viewpoint motion control techniques georgia institute of technology. In: Proceedings of the 1997 Virtual Reality Annual International Symposium, pp. 45–52. IEEE (1997)
10. Vosinakis, S., Xenakis, I.: A virtual world installation in an art exhibition: providing a shared interaction space for local and remote visitors. In: Proceedings of Re-thinking Technology in Museums (2011)

11. Cho, N., Shin, D., Lee, D., Kim, K., Park, J., Koo, M., Kim, J.: Intuitional 3D museum navigation system using kinect. In: Park, J., Barolli, L., Xhafa, F., Jeong, H.Y. (eds.) Information Technology Convergence. LNEE, vol. 253, pp. 587–596. Springer, Dordrecht (2013). https://doi.org/10.1007/978-94-007-6996-0_62
12. Baldauf, M., Adegeye, F., Alt, F., Harms, J.: Your browser is the controller: advanced web-based smartphone remote controls for public screens. In: Proceedings of the 5th ACM International Symposium on Pervasive Displays, pp. 175–181. ACM (2016)
13. Hornecker, E., Stifter, M.: Learning from interactive museum installations about interaction design for public settings. In: Proceedings of OzCHI 2006, pp. 135–142 (2006)
14. Kurdyukova, E., Obaid, M., André, E.: Direct, bodily or mobile interaction? comparing interaction techniques for personalized public displays. In: Proceedings of 11th International Conference on Mobile and Ubiquitous Multimedia (MUM 2012). ACM (2012)
15. Ardito, C., Buono, P., Costabile, M.F., Moro, A.: Interaction with large displays: a survey. ACM Comput. Surv. 47(3), 1–38 (2015)
16. Jankowski, J., Hulin, T., Hachet, M.: A study of street-level navigation techniques in 3D digital cities on mobile touch devices. In: Proceedings of 3DUI 2014, IEEE Symposium on 3D User Interfaces, pp. 35–38, IEEE (2014)
17. Roupé, M., Bosch-Sijtsema, P., Johansson, M.: Interactive navigation interface for Virtual Reality using the human body. Comput. Environ. Urban Syst. 43, 42–50 (2014)
18. Ren, G., Li, C., O'Neill, E., Willis, P.: 3D freehand gestural navigation for interactive public displays. IEEE Comput. Graph. Appl. 33(2), 47–55 (2013)
19. Dias, P., Parracho, J., Cardoso, J., Ferreira, B.Q., Ferreira, C., Santos, B.S.: Developing and evaluating two gestural-based virtual environment navigation methods for large displays. In: Streitz, N., Markopoulos, P. (eds.) DAPI 2015. LNCS, vol. 9189, pp. 141–151. Springer, Cham (2015). https://doi.org/10.1007/978-3-319-20804-6_13
20. Guy, E., Punpongsanon, P., Iwai, D., Sato, K., Boubekeur, T.: LazyNav: 3D ground navigation with non-critical body parts. In: Proceedings of 3DUI 2015, IEEE Symposium on 3D User Interfaces, pp. 43–50. IEEE (2015)
21. Hernandez-Ibanez, L.A., Barneche-Naya, V., Mihura-Lopez, R.: A comparative study of walkthrough paradigms for virtual environments using kinect based natural interaction. In: Proceedings of the 22nd International Conference on Virtual System & Multimedia (VSMM), pp. 1–7 (2016)
22. Vajk, T., Coulton, P., Bamford, W., Edwards, R.: Using a mobile phone as a "Wii-like" controller for playing games on a large public display. Int. J. Comput. Games Technol. 2008 (6), 6 (2008)
23. Du, Y., Ren, H., Pan, G., Li, S.: Tilt & touch: mobile phone for 3D interaction. In: Proceedings of the 13th International Conference on Ubiquitous Computing, pp. 485–486. ACM (2011)
24. Shirazi, A. S., Winkler, C., Schmidt, A.: Flashlight interaction: a study on mobile phone interaction techniques with large displays. In: Proceedings of the 11th International Conference on Human-Computer Interaction with Mobile Devices and Services - MobileHCI 2009. ACM (2009)
25. Pazmino, P.J., Lyons, L.: An exploratory study of input modalities for mobile devices used with museum exhibits. In: Proceedings of the 2011 Annual Conference on Human Factors in Computing Systems – CHI11, pp. 895–904. ACM (2011)
26. Joselli, M., Da Silva, J. R., Zamith, M., Clua, E., Pelegrino, M., Mendonça, E., Soluri, E.: An architecture for game interaction using mobile. In: Proceedings of the 4th International IEEE Consumer Electronic Society - Games Innovation Conference, IGiC 2012, pp. 1–5. IEEE (2012)

27. Liang, H.N., Trenchard, J., Semegen, M., Irani, P.: An exploration of interaction styles in mobile devices for navigating 3D environments. In: Proceedings of the 10th Asia Pacific conference on Computer human interaction - APCHI 2012, pp. 309–313. ACM (2012)
28. Liang, H., Shi, Y., Lu, F., Yang, J., Papangelis, K.: VRMController: an input device for navigation activities in virtual reality environments. In: Proceedings of the 15th ACM SIGGRAPH Conference on Virtual-Reality Continuum and Its Applications in Industry, pp. 455–460. ACM (2016)
29. Brondi, R., et al.: Evaluating the impact of highly immersive technologies and natural interaction on player engagement and flow experience in games. In: Chorianopoulos, K., Divitini, M., Hauge, J.B., Jaccheri, L., Malaka, R. (eds.) ICEC 2015. LNCS, vol. 9353, pp. 169–181. Springer, Cham (2015). https://doi.org/10.1007/978-3-319-24589-8_13
30. Burigat, S., Chittaro, L.: Navigation in 3D virtual environments: effects of user experience and location-pointing navigation aids. Int. J. Hum Comput Stud. 65(11), 945–958 (2007)

# Distributed Data Exchange with Leap Motion

Mirko Pani[1] and Fabio Poiesi[2(✉)]

[1] Department of Information Engineering and Computer Science,
Università degli Studi di Trento, Trento, Italy
mirko.pani@studenti.unitn.it
[2] Technologies of Vision, Fondazione Bruno Kessler, Trento, Italy
poiesi@fbk.eu

**Abstract.** Collaborative virtual environments can connect people in social virtual spaces even when they are geographically distant from each other. Hand interactions are fundamental to enable natural collaboration and immersive experiences as they are a visually intuitive means of communication. However, scalability is challenging as numerous participants typically produce a large volume of visualisation data that may overload a single node if the management is centralised. In this paper we propose a transmission strategy where the high-throughput visualisation data (e.g. hand joints) is exchanged amongst participants in a distributed fashion. We use a level-of-detail strategy to further reduce the network traffic accounting for spatial distances amongst participants in the virtual space. We design an experiment where we analyse the network traffic in a virtual environment with up to seven participants whose hands are tracked using Leap Motion. We show that the proposed method can effectively reduce the network traffic of visualisation data when compared to a centralised approach.

**Keywords:** Collaborative virtual environments
Distributed communication · Level of detail · Hand tracking
Leap Motion · Unity3D

## 1 Introduction

Virtual Reality (VR) experiences are evolving from being limited to a single participant to being a multi-user collaborative reality [16]. Applications, such as education [15], manufacturing [14], engineering and construction [18], medics [19] and video gaming [8], have shown great interest in collaborative VR. Effective and immersive collaborations are guaranteed if users can interact in VR using their hands in an intuitive manner. Commercially available products, such as HTC Vive and Oculus Rift, provide remote controllers to permit hand-based interactions. However, hand visualisation in VR does not yet appear to be natural as these remote controllers do not track hand joints [10,21]. To achieve total

© Springer International Publishing AG, part of Springer Nature 2018
L. T. De Paolis and P. Bourdot (Eds.): AVR 2018, LNCS 10851, pp. 655–667, 2018.
https://doi.org/10.1007/978-3-319-95282-6_46

**Fig. 1.** Collaborative virtual environment where two groups of participants are interacting via hand gestures. Visualisation data exchanged amongst clients occurs peer-to-peer and using a strategy based on levels of detail. Clients that are close to each other exchange data at a higher level of detail. Because hand gestures of distant clients (e.g. those in the background) are barely visible, their visualisation data will not be transmitted to the clients near to the camera. This strategy allows a more effective communication in populated virtual environments as we can noticeably reduce the data transmitted over the network and managed by the host of the VR session.

immersion and to open up new opportunities in VR, technology developments are shifting towards in-air hand tracking using devices such as Leap Motion [4]. Figure 1 shows an example of collaborative virtual environment (CVE) where participants interact using hand gestures. Unfortunately, there are still several challenges that prevent an uncompromising experience using hand-free interactions in VR, such as transmission latency, high computational demand and hand tracking robustness [17, 22].

Interactions in CVEs are typically managed at network level via an *authoritative server* [22, 24]. An example is Unity3D that provides the High Level API to design CVEs based on authoritative mechanism [2]. The server has the authority to update the states of the objects in the environment, namely *mutable objects* (e.g. position of a player, colour of an object), upon the requests received from the clients. We refer to the term *client* to underline the role of a participant within a network that communicates either with the server or directly with another participant. The authoritative mechanism provides data consistency on each client and the advantage of being robust against malicious players' behaviours (e.g. game cheating). However, CVEs that are designed using an authoritative server are hardly scalable. The larger the number of users that join the same CVE, the larger the delay of state updates and the more likely visualisation lags [11]. A solution to promote scalability is via peer-to-peer communications (i.e. the communication between two clients does not involve a server), at the expenses of more sophisticated strategies to handle state updates and prevent cheats [24]. Leap Motion produces high-frame rate hand visualisation data that leads to high throughput when the visualisation data is exchanged over a network populated by several clients [6, 22]. To mitigate the problem of high throughput, one can employ different data transmission strategies based on peer-to-peer or hybrid communications. Hybrid approaches use server and peer-to-peer communications interchangeably, and are typically employed in massively multiplayer online games (MMOGs) [13, 20]. One can also use an area-of-interest (AOI) based approach where a VR space is divided into zones and data is transmitted peer-to-peer amongst users that are located within the same zone [12].

In this paper we propose a scalable mechanism to exchange visualisation data amongst clients in collaborative virtual environments[1]. Our solution uses the ordinary authoritative mechanism to update the states of mutable objects, but a distributed strategy to handle high-throughput visualisation data exchanges. Differently from AOI-based approaches where the data transmission between clients is either active or inactive without accounting for levels of detail, we use clients' relative distances in the VR space to dynamically variate the resolution of transmitted visualisation data. We will show that our distributed approach effectively reduces the network traffic amongst clients when exchanging the visualisation data as opposed to a centralised approach. We evaluated our approach by implementing it on Google Cardboard devices (or simply Cardboard) [1] and by using Leap Motion [4] for hand tracking. We used Unity3D cross-platform game engine as development environment [9].

## 2    Proposed Approach

A set of participants that interact in the same virtual environment exchange visualisation data under reciprocal requests of levels of detail that depend on their spatial distance in the VR space. In the next sections we will describe the proposed communication mechanism.

### 2.1    Communication Mechanisms

The communication amongst participants is decoupled to handle data differently based on its type. The authoritative server handles client enrollments, while peer-to-peer communications handle high-throughput visualisation data produced by Leap Motion.

A user that initiates a VR session can be both the host and a client. The host is in charge of (i) updating the states of the mutable objects that require synchronisation amongst clients and (ii) managing client enrollments/disenrollments. When a client enrolls to a VR session, the host broadcasts its IP and port addresses (enclosed in a broadcast message) to the other connected clients. When a client disenrolls, the host informs the connected clients that a client has left the virtual environment. These broadcast messages are used by each client to store and maintain the network addresses of the connected clients updated on

---

[1] Project webpage: tev.fbk.eu/distributedLeapMotion.

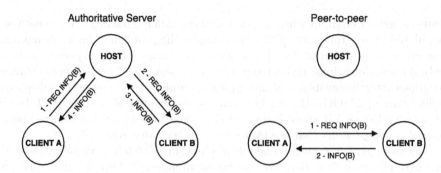

**Fig. 2.** Difference between authoritative and peer-to-peer mechanisms. Requests (REQ) and information (INFO) exchanged over the network are halved in the case of peer-to-peer communications.

their internal *Sync Table*. Each client has the same copy of the Sync Table and can use this global knowledge to establish peer-to-peer communications to exchange visualisation data with the other clients. This is an important element because when devices like Cardboard are used for CVEs, they have limited computational capability and battery duration. With peer-to-peer communications high-throughput data does not go through the host thus reducing its computational load.

Figure 2 shows an example where the requests and the information exchanged over the network are halved in the case of peer-to-peer communications.

## 2.2 Distance-Based Level of Detail

Data that represents hand gestures are typically sampled at a high frame rate to visualise natural movements. However, when hand gestures in VR are seen from far, details might be unnoticeable. Typically, levels of detail are used in these situations to define multiple representations of a model with decreasing resolution in order to reduce the rendering cost for distant or less important objects [23].

We design a request-based mechanism to handle levels of detail dynamically. Clients that are involved in an interaction, reciprocally request their desired level of detail to other clients based on their spatial distance in the VR space: the closer the two clients, the higher the details of the visualisation data they request. The queried clients that accept this request will transmit their visualisation data at the requested levels of detail. A system based on requests can also provide the possibility to extend this distance-based criterion to additional criteria, for example based on network or rendering capacity. In this work we analyse the case of distance only.

Figure 3 shows five clients that are connected to the same VR space, one is the host/client and the others are clients. The top part of the figure shows an example with four levels of detail:

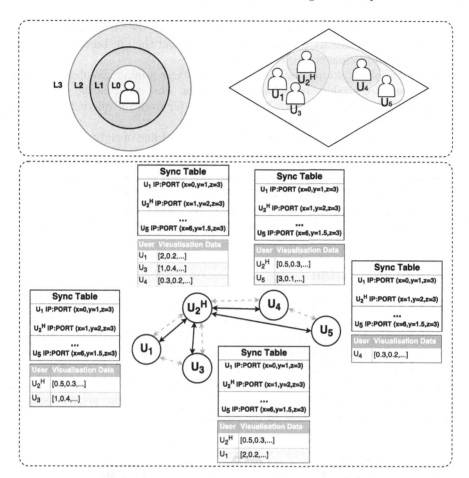

**Fig. 3.** Five clients are connected to the same VR space, one is the host/client and the others are the clients. On the top, four levels of detail are defined: L0 defines the maximum level of detail, L1 and L2 define intermediate levels of detail, and L3 defines no data transmission. The lower part of the figure illustrates the connections (i.e. black arrows) the server uses to broadcast the information about enrollments/disenrollments that are then used to update the Sync Table on each client. Each client uses the information included in this Sync Table to establish peer-to-peer connections with other clients. Green arrows show the peer-to-peer connections between clients to exchange high-throughput visualisation data. (Color figure online)

**L0** defines the maximum level of detail where no approximations of the hand joints are applied. This could be the case where two or more clients interact "face to face" and highly-detailed joint movements are necessary to visualise gestures accurately;

**L1** defines an intermediate level of detail where a subset of joints are transmitted, while ensuring that a well approximated hand motion can still be perceived.

This could be the case where the client requesting the visualisation data is not interacting directly with the queried client, but their distance is such that their hand movements are still visible;

**L2** defines another intermediate level of detail where a minimal subset of joints is transmitted to show basic hand movements. This could be the case where the client requesting the visualisation data is far from the queried client and its hands are barely visible;

**L3** defines no data transmission as clients are out of line of sight.

The connections (i.e. black arrows) the server uses to broadcast the information about enrollments/disenrollments are also used to update the Sync Table on each client. Each client uses the information included in this Sync Table to establish peer-to-peer connections with other clients. Green arrows show the peer-to-peer connections between clients to exchange high-throughput visualisation data.

## 3    Implementation

We have implemented our proposed distributed approach in a scenario where each client can experience VR using Cardboard and interact with Leap Motion. We implemented the client-host requests using the Unity3D's native authoritative mechanism provided through the High Level API (HLAPI) [2]. Peer-to-peer visualisation data exchanges are managed by the proposed distributed request-based mechanism. We use the UDP protocol for timely delivery of data. Each client periodically listens for incoming UDP packets over the network socket. Figure 4 illustrates an overview of the implementation.

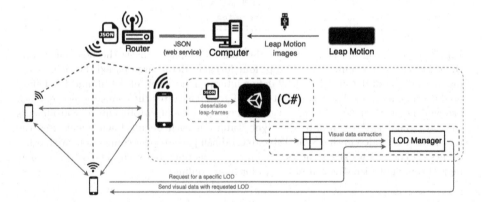

**Fig. 4.** Illustration of the proposed distributed mechanism. Each client is connected to the Leap Motion's web service that is hosted on a computer and leap-frames are transmitted using JSON format. The client deserialises the JSON-formatted leap-frames using C# classes of Unity3D. Requests are dealt by the level of detail (LOD) manager. The clients send visualisation data at the requested level of detail. The figure shows three conceptual blocks: green for the local Leap Motion connection, blue for the local processing of the hand visualisation and red for remote hand visualisation. (Color figure online)

## 3.1   Message Handling

To enable effective communications, we define a protocol that specifies the structure of the messages exchanged between the host and clients to update the Sync Table, and between clients to send requests and transmit visualisation data at different levels of detail. Table 1 lists the messages defined by our protocol.

The protocol functions in the following way. A client joins a VR session through HLAPI. The host assigns a unique identifier (*NetID*) to this client and broadcasts a message informing the connected clients that an enrollment has occurred. Each message is composed of a header and a payload. The header uses the first three bytes of the message to define the type of data carried by the payload. When a client connects, the host sends an 'AIP' message to inform clients that a new entry in the Sync Table should be added. When a client disconnects, the host sends a 'RIP' message to inform the clients that a client should be removed from the Sync Table.

The clients are responsible for requesting the visualisation data to other clients. For example, if client A wants visualisation data of client B, A will send a request message 'RQ' to B requesting the visualisation data at the desired level of details (i.e. based on their distance). When B receives the request, B encapsulates the visualisation data in a message 'AK' and sends it to A. This procedure is repeated periodically at a pre-defined frequency to show hand movements. Algorithm 1 details the overall message handing procedure.

**Table 1.** Messages defined in the communication protocol

| Header | Syntax | Description |
|--------|--------|-------------|
| AIP | [AIP]:<ip>,<port>,<netID> | Message the host sends to inform clients to add a new entry in the Sync Table |
| RIP | [RIP]:<netID> | Message the host sends to inform clients to remove the entry of the disconnected client from the Sync Table |
| RQ<n> | [RQ<n>]:<netID> | Message a client sends to another client to request visualisation data at a specific level of detail |
| AK<n> | [AK<n>]:<HandsParam>,<netID> | Message a queried client sends to a requesting client that contains the visualisation data at a specific level of detail in the payload; <HandsParam> integer value that defines the type of hand contained in the payload (0: left, 1: right, 2: both) |

**Data:**
$t_1$ = Time.Now; $t_2$ = Time.Now;
$\Delta_s$ = 0.2s; $\Delta_r$ = 0.3s;
m = message; c = client;
LOD = level of detail;
Handle(m) = message handling as defined in Table 1;
**while** *true* **do**
    **if** *($t_1$ - Time.Now)* $> \Delta_s$ **then**
        handData = getHandsData();
        $t_1$ = Time.Now;
    **end**
    **if** *($t_2$ - Time.Now)* $> \Delta_r$ **then**
        **for** *c in ConnectedClients* **do**
            LOD = calculateDistance(localClient, c);
            requestHandData(c, LOD);
        **end**
        $t_2$ = Time.Now;
    **end**
    **if** *m == received* **then**
        Handle(m);
    **end**
**end**

**Algorithm 1.** Message handling procedure.

## 3.2    Leap Motion (Visualisation) Data

Leap Motion does not yet support its direct connection to Cardboard [22]. There-fore we connect Leap Motion to a computer and use the native Leap Motion web service to transmit the hand tracking data to Cardboard.

On the computer, Leap Motion software periodically sends hand interaction elements, such as position and orientation of joints, the list of tool and pointable objects detected in the current frame, etc., through *leap-frames* that are encoded with JSON format [3]. Leap-frame transmission rate is typically greater than 60 frames per second [6]. When the leap-frames are received by Cardboard, all the hand interaction elements are used by Unity3D on each client to enable the interactions with mutable objects and to trigger the object physics. These interactions are centrally managed by the authoritative server.

Because the appearance of a hand can be represented only by the position of its joints, we use a subset of these elements to visualise hands on Cardboard. This subset of elements can then be further reduced using levels of detail and in our case we use four levels of detail (Sect. 2.2): L0, L1, L2 and L3. L0 defines the highest level of detail, L1 and L2 are intermediate levels, and L3 defines no data transmission. We use the *CapsuleHand* format to represent Leap Motion hands, which models the hand structure using a set of capsules (i.e. joints) connected by cylinders [5]. Note that our communication approach is independent from this computer-Cardboard connection because hand joints' data is handled at network level as it were processed on Cardboard and the JSON-encoded leap-frames are reconstructed in the same way as they were processed natively.

Figure 5 illustrates how these capsules are defined at different levels of detail and how visualisation data are organised to be efficiently accessed. One hand is represented at L0 with 240 bytes, at L1 with 120 bytes and at L2 with 12 bytes.

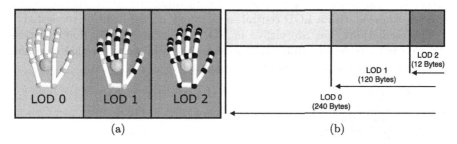

**Fig. 5.** Example of three levels of detail with associated bytes count for the Leap Motion hand. Yellow joints are encoded and transmitted, black joints are ignored. (Color figure online)

## 4   Experiments

We evaluated the proposed method by performing two experiments. Firstly, we measured the number of bytes transmitted during a simulated collaborative VR session. Secondly, we used multiple smartphones as Cardboard devices and measured their transmission latency within a local wireless network. In all the experiments, we compared the performance of our distributed approach against a centralised (i.e. authoritative) approach, and by enabling and disabling the level of detail strategy, namely LOD and NO LOD, respectively. All experiments involved up to seven clients connected to the same VR space. One of the clients was the host. In order to stress the system, we streamed sequences of leap-frames corresponding to two tracked hands, i.e. 480 bytes per leap-frame.

### 4.1   Network Traffic

To measure the network traffic, we designed a simulation where the seven clients were positioned in the VR space randomly. The VR space was 20 × 15 Unity3D units. The level of detail regions had radii of 4, 8, 12 and >12 Unity3D units to define L0, L1, L2 and L3, respectively. Because the VR space was limited and because the duration of the experiment was 150 s, we could simulate several combinations of relative distances between clients and hence trigger transmissions with different levels of detail.

Figure 6 shows the trends of the total number of bytes transmitted as a function of the duration of the experiment. When we account for the level of detail, we can effectively reduce the network traffic using the proposed distributed approach as opposed to the centralised approach. Interestingly, when the level of detail is not used, i.e. the visualisation data are exchanged amongst clients regardless their distance, the centralised approach generates less network traffic than the distributed one. This happens because, although the centralised approach is used, the level of detail strategy led to an effective reduction of bytes when clients are distant from each other. For example, if client A is located in L3 with respect to B, B will request visualisation data using the NO LOD distributed strategy, whereas with a LOD centralised strategy no data will be requested.

The oscillations that are visible in NO LOD strategies are due situations where clients are distant from each other in the VR space. In this case data transmissions are fewer or even absent sometimes.

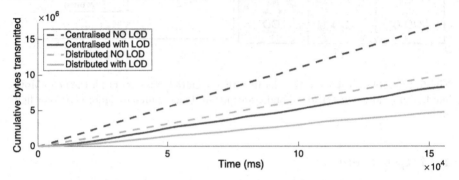

**Fig. 6.** Cumulative network traffic measured in bytes in the case of seven clients. Centralised and distributed approaches that consider level of detail (with LOD) and that do not consider it (NO LOD).

## 4.2 Transmission Latency

In this experiment we evaluated the latency of the data transmission. We quantified the latency as the delay measured by a client to send the request to another client and to receive the data. We tested scenarios with three, five and seven clients connected via wireless. We used Google Nexus 5X, Huawei Honor 8 and Nvidia Shield for the scenario with three clients, these three devices plus two Huawei P10+ for the scenario with five clients and these five devices plus two computers for the scenario with seven devices. Nvidia Shield was used as the host in all scenarios.

Figure 7 shows the average latency as a function of the number of clients corresponding to each scenario. The exact values of average and standard deviation are reported in the legend of the graph. The average latency measured when visualisation data are exchanged with the distributed strategy is smaller than the latency measured with the centralised strategy. The use of levels of detail reduces in general the latency. We can observe that the variance is in general fairly large and this is due to background threads of the devices that delay the processing of the received packets.

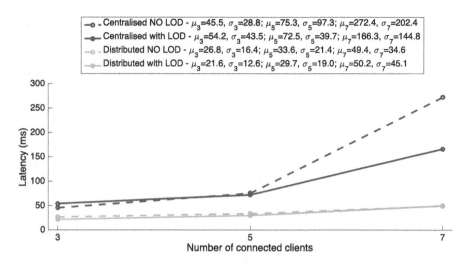

**Fig. 7.** Average latency as a function of the number of clients corresponding to centralised and distributed approaches that consider level of detail (with LOD) and that do not consider it (NO LOD). The network latency is the average of latency measurements collected over a period of three minutes.

### 4.3   Qualitative Analysis

Figure 8 shows a scenario where five clients are within the same VR space and visualisation data are exchanged using the proposed distributed mechanism with levels of detail. The left-hand figure is a screenshot taken from a Cardboard device, while the right-hand figure is a screenshot taken from a desktop computer. The distance between clients is such that they create two groups of data exchange: one group of two clients (left-hand figure) and one group of three clients (right-hand figure). In each group there is one client waving its hands. With this configuration L0 (max resolution) is applied between clients of each

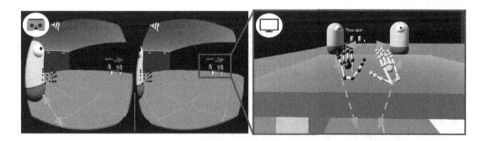

**Fig. 8.** Scenario where five participants are within the same VR space and visualisation data are exchanged through the proposed distributed mechanism using levels of detail. The green arrows illustrate whom the visualisation data is shared with. The video of this experiment can be found on the project webpage. (Color figure online)

group and L3 (no data) is applied between clients of different groups. The green arrows illustrate whom the visualisation data is shared with. From the Cardboard's view we can see the group of three clients in the background and we can observe that their hands' movements would not be visible even if their visualisation data were transmitted to the clients of the other group.

## 5   Conclusions

We have presented a distributed mechanism to exchange Leap Motion (visualisation) data in collaborative virtual environments. We developed a solution where the distance between users is used to select the level of detail at which the visualisation data are exchanged. We created a protocol to share messages that include the reciprocal knowledge about the position of clients and the requests of the level of detail. These messages are exchanged via UDP for timely delivery. We have evaluated our approach in both simulated and real-world scenarios using Google Cardboard, and showed that the proposed method outperformed the centralised approach provided in Unity3D. Although Google Cardboard was used in our tests, the proposed distributed mechanism can also be employed on other VR devices.

Future research will involve the reduction of request messages between clients by implementing requests with durations. Instead of sending one request for each leap-frame we will explore how to send a request for a group of leap-frames. Then we will explore how to utilise our strategy to transmit other visualisation data, such as Kinect point cloud [7]. In this way clients will be able to project their scan in the VR space and make use of the distributed mechanism with levels of detail to reduce the number of points transmitted over the network.

**Acknowledgments.** This research has received funding from the European Union's Horizon 2020 research and innovation programme under grant agreement number 687757.

## References

1. Google Cardboard. vr.google.com/cardboard. Accessed May 2018
2. High Level API. docs.unity3d.com/Manual/UNetUsingHLAPI.html. Accessed May 2018
3. Leap-Frame. developer.leapmotion.com/documentation/java/devguide/Leap_Frames.html. Accessed May 2018
4. Leap Motion. leapmotion.com. Accessed May 2018
5. Leap Motion hand assets. developer.leapmotion.com/documentation/csharp/unity/Unity_Hand_Assets.html. Accessed May 2018
6. Leap Motion latency. blog.leapmotion.com/understanding-latency-part-1. Accessed May 2018
7. Live Scan 3D. github.com/MarekKowalski/LiveScan3D. Accessed May 2018
8. Second Life. secondlife.com. Accessed May 2018
9. Unity 3D. unity3d.com. Accessed May 2018

10. VibeHub. youtu.be/azUXUr6rWSc. Accessed May 2018
11. Abdulazeez, S., Rhalibi, A., Al-Jumeily, D.: Evaluation of scalability and communication in MMOGs. In: Proceedings of Consumer Communications and Networking Conference, Las Vegas, USA, January 2016
12. Ahmed, D., Shirmohammadi, S.: A dynamic area of interest management and collaboration model for P2P MMOGs. In: Proceedings of the IEEE Symposium on Distributed Simulation and Real-Time Applications, Vancouver, CAN, October 2008
13. Carlini, E., Ricci, L., Coppola, M.: Reducing server load in MMOG via P2P Gossip. In: Proceedings of Workshop on Network and Systems Support for Games, Venice, IT, November 2012
14. Choi, S., Jung, K., Noh, S.: Virtual reality applications in manufacturing industries: past research, present findings, and future directions. Concurr. Eng. **23**(1), 40–63 (2015)
15. Freina, L., Ott, M.: A literature review on immersive virtual reality in education: state of the art and perspectives. In: Proceedings of eLearning and Software for Education, Bucharest, RO, April 2015
16. Greenwald, S., Corning, W., Maes, P.: Multi-user framework for collaboration and co-creation in virtual reality. In: Proceedings of Conference on Computer Supported Collaborative Learning, Philadelphia, US, June 2017
17. Guna, J., Jakus, G., Pogacnik, M., Tomazic, S., Sodnik, J.: An analysis of the precision and reliability of the Leap Motion sensor and its suitability for static and dynamic tracking. Sensors **14**(2), 3702–3720 (2014)
18. Hilfert, T., Konig, M.: Virtual reality applications in manufacturing industries: past research, present findings, and future directions. Visual. Eng. **4**(3), 1–18 (2016)
19. Khademi, M., Hondori, H., McKenzie, A., Dodakian, L., Lopes, C., Cramer, S.: Free-hand interaction with leap motion controller for stroke rehabilitation. In: Proceedings of Human Factors in Computing Systems, Toronto, ON, May 2014
20. Kim, K., Yeom, I., Lee, J.: HYMS: a hybrid MMOG server architecture. IEICE Trans. Inf. Syst. **87–D**, 2706–2713 (2004)
21. McMahan, R., Alon, A., Lazem, S., Beaton, R., Machaj, D., Schaefer, M., Silva, M., Leal, A., Hagan, R., Bowman, D.: Evaluating natural interaction techniques in video games. In: 2010 IEEE Symposium on 3D User Interfaces, Waltham, US, March 2010
22. Pretto, N., Poiesi, F.: Towards gesture-based multi-user interactions in collaborative virtual environments. In: International Archives of the Photogrammetry, Remote Sensing and Spatial Information Sciences, vol. XLII-2/W8, Hamburg, GE, pp. 203–208, November 2017
23. Schmalstieg, D., Gervautz, M.: Demand-driven geometry transmission for distributed virtual environment. Comput. Graph. Forum **15**(3), 421–431 (1996)
24. Yahyavi, A., Kemme, B.: Peer-to-peer architectures for massively multiplayer online games: a survey. ACM Comput. Surv. **46**(1), 1–51 (2013)

# Conceptual and Technical Aspects of Full-Body Motion Support in Virtual and Mixed Reality

Vlasios Kasapakis[1]([✉]), Elena Dzardanova[2],
and Charalabos Paschalidis[1]

[1] Department of Cultural Technology and Communication,
University of the Aegean, Mytilene, Greece
{v.kasapakis, ctml6021}@aegean.gr
[2] Department of Product and Systems Design Engineering,
University of the Aegean, Hermoupolis, Greece
lena@aegean.gr

**Abstract.** Full-body motion support has been extensively utilized as a *means to an end*, rather than an impactful factor of concepts such as Body Ownership Illusion (BOI) and the immersive virtual experience. In addition, technical setups are seldom co-related to a study's findings, even though system, equipment and implementation quality are fundamental components that may vastly affect user experience. This study presents a Mixed Reality (MR) environment in which 21 participants had to interact with real objects accurately represented in the virtual space, while having full-body motion control of their avatar with the use of Inverse Kinematics. Sense of presence, BOI, perceived realism and equipment invasiveness were examined in regard to having full-body motion control and real-virtual object handling. Preliminary results indicate that full-body motion support increases BOI, however with high levels of BOI, presence and overall engagement are not concomitant to perceived realism of the virtual environment and experience.

**Keywords:** Virtual Reality · Mixed Reality · Full-body motion support
Body Ownership Illusion

## 1 Introduction

First-person perspective, as the result of head-tracking solutions is, by all accounts, the cornerstone of an immersive Virtual Reality (VR) experience. Its effects go beyond the functional purpose of a 360° view of the virtual environment (VE); above all, it recreates the *egocentric* [1, 2] perspective by which we are wired to perceive the world, where *all* is in relation to the *ego*, or in relation to a *head*, as the cognition's locality. *Egocentricity*, by default, requires a vessel, since it must be contained and distinguished as an autonomous entity, able to receive stimuli in a predictable manner and make use of proprioception mechanisms. In the physical world we hardly ever reflect on its presence or functionalities. In virtual spaces however, existence of a distinguishable vessel is not an intrinsic requirement and when it is (e.g. to allow forms of

© Springer International Publishing AG, part of Springer Nature 2018
L. T. De Paolis and P. Bourdot (Eds.): AVR 2018, LNCS 10851, pp. 668–682, 2018.
https://doi.org/10.1007/978-3-319-95282-6_47

interaction) it does not need to abide by physical laws. When we do attach a virtual body, limbs or any kind of visible, anthropomorphic functionalities (e.g. tools positioned and animated as if held) to the *egocentric* point of view, we are basically subduing to the normality of the human body and its cognitive and physical attributes, capabilities and limitations [3–5]. In short, we are adding elements of perceived physical realness.

Two main points derive from the above understanding, the first being that the *body* – both the real one and any virtual representation of it – is or should be the focal point of VR-related research. The second being that immersive VR, along with its *bodies*, as a field of research, equally tangles between the applicatory and the conceptual; there is no escaping the numerous technological prerequisites and there is no ignoring the socio-affective conceptualizations. All this relates to the fact that full-body motion support, the ability to correlate a real body's movements to those of an avatar, in real-time, is nothing short of groundbreaking, even though as a technological affordance it has been around for quite some time. However, advancements of the past decade, on all fronts of tracking and motion capture technology (e.g. computational power, accuracy, latency, 3D graphics, etc.) have essentially gone unnoticed when it comes to the perpetual inquiries of the virtual experience. It might still be too early to rely on full-body motion support for the dissemination of mind-twisting concepts relating to the *body* in VR, a simpler enquiry however, of *how does it feel to motion control a virtual entity*, is long overdue.

Our emphasis on the *body* and sequentially on the full-body motion support affordance, derives from the acknowledgment that even though users' transcendence into the VE is achieved via cognitive associations, making it a mental process, those associations are always in reference to the human *body*. The *egocentric* view sets off proprioception mechanisms and everything that follows is about feeding and toying with that initial illusion. Having this in mind it is evident that every single development, research and experiment conducted, is an attempt to satisfy human bodily perceptions, or in some cases examine what we can get away with. For instance, field of view, display quality and frame rate have more to do with how the human eyesight and visual processing function, rather than achieving the best solutions technologically possible. Offering the latter could in fact be problematic or even, simply put, useless, as for example, there is a limit to the frames per second the human eye can catch.

The above observations arose during an experimental setup of a Mixed Reality (MR) environment with a game-based scenario, in which participants were provided with full-body motion support with the use of Inverse Kinematics (IK). Apart from other findings, it was noticed that relating studies, particularly those that also apply full-body motion support, do not directly inquiry participants of any affective or user experience impacts that such an affordance poses. Absence of such inquiries does not necessarily affect a study's findings; it could be characterized however as a missed opportunity to establish the importance and possible effects of providing users with free movement and real-time motion control of their avatar, especially when studying concepts such as *Body Ownership Illusion* (BOI). Therefore, although full-body motion support has been extensively utilized in VR-related research, seldom it is co-examined within a set of impactful components of the, by default, multi-variable immersive virtual experience. Finally, there is often a lack of a clear juxtaposition between the technical setup used and a study's findings, considering that one technical setup may vastly differ from the next, either based on equipment quality standards or overall architecture of available solutions. In fact, liberties are often taken with descriptive terms such as *full-body*, regardless of whether the technical setup meets necessary requirements for such terms to be applicable.

The main objective of this paper was an in-depth investigation of the technical and conceptual parameters of implementing full-body motion support in MR. An experimental setup was designed and comparatively executed in the real and in the virtual space. Participants were asked to throw ten small boxes into a larger box, and then repeat the task whilst immersed in a virtual space, in which the real boxes were also virtually represented as accurate 3D models, and motion tracked in real time. To address objectives, the study investigated the use of IK as an alternative to full-body suits, as well as the overall impact of the implemented technical setup. In addition, participants' *sense of presence* and BOI were examined in regard to having full-body motion control over their avatar, while playing against a non-player character (NPC) opponent and experiencing an audience's (NPCs) reaction to their performance.

The remainder of the article is structured as follows: Related research wherein full-body motion support was implemented is reviewed in Sect. 2. A detailed presentation of the specifics of the technical setup and the experimental scenario are presented in Sect. 3. Section 4 presents and discusses the evaluation results, further elaborating on all relevant concepts and research-oriented suggestions. Finally, Sect. 5 concludes the article and draws directions for future work.

## 2   Research Related to Full-Body Motion Support

In a sense, VR-related research is dominated by matters of the *body* – real and/or virtual – and its functionalities, although not all studies fully or consciously acknowledge this; regardless of whether they are examining aspects from a technological standpoint or as part of conceptualizations such as *presence* and BOI. In addition, the immersive virtual experience comes with an immense set of technological prerequisites, therefore, addressing variant shortcomings of available technical setups is of great importance. Following, we review all known cases where full-body motion support has been utilized. When relevant, technical setups are briefly reviewed in relation to the above observations.

Waltemate et al. [6] applied optical motion capture and had users control an avatar via a full-body suit, to examine sickness levels and perceived avatar control, due to motion tracking latency. The experimental setup required participants to perform squats, whilst reviewing their "reflection", mainly their avatar, in a CAVE setting, thus the setup is simulation of typical physical training with a mirror. An important critique of this study's technical setup is that CAVEs are regarded as semi-immersive and do not require a Head Mounted Display (HMD), they are therefore substantially differentiated from the typical immersive experience. Moreover, they are not transferable, as the authors themselves acknowledge, therefore highly improbable to be exploited commercially. Apart from latency-related objectives, there is no mention of whether and how utilization of full-body motion support impacted users and there is also no indication of testing other movements apart from squatting or of any attempt in locomotion.

Dzardanova et al. [7, 8] made use of full-body motion support and although their study relates to BOI, participants themselves maneuvered their avatar via a controller. The motion-controlled avatar was handled by an actor and it was part of the experimental setup experienced by the participants and not applied to. Here too there is a lack of discussing how the technical setup and, subsequently, locomotive limitations affected users.

Wilson et al. [9] examined a known issue regarding accurate finger tracking whilst in a full-body suit tracked by an optical motion capture system. Their solution however was not followed-through with any test-out or experimental setup. Normand et al. [10] on the other hand, provided an interesting experimental setup, having two remote users share a VE to rehearse a play via their respective avatars. One individual was equipped with a full-body suit, whereas the other was maneuvering the avatar via wands and Inverse Kinematics (IK). Their research paid great attention to the task in hand (e.g. directorial efficiency of the virtual rehearsal), yet possible impacts of the technical setup in regards to BOI, virtual social interaction as well as to the excellent opportunity of comparing between a full-body suit and IK were unattended.

In a very interesting research, Lugrin et al. [11] equiped participants with full-body motion support and examined how avatar appearance, from least to most anthropomorphic, affected levels of BOI, essentially testing-out the *Uncanny Valley* hypothesis[1]. Their technical setup, with the use of IK, was adequately justified and their overall research objectives provided substantial insight in regards to BOI and human-like representation in virtual spaces. Considering the scale of their experimental setup as well as the multiple experimental conditions, additional inquiries regarding affective or other impact of full-body motion support could have overloaded rather than enriched their work. However, this was a unique study in which users were provided with significant freedom of movement and locomotion, as well as interaction with virtual elements in an elaborately designed environment. Thus, as a technical and as an experimental setup, it provided great opportunity for examining effects of full-body motion support in VR in regards to BOI and overall affective impact and user experience.

The experiment conducted by Kilteni et al. [12], in 2013, bears perhaps the closest resemblance to the one presented in this paper. Apart from full-body motion support – although with the use of a full-body suit – there was also object handling, since participants had to interact with a real drum whilst viewing the interaciton in real-time in the virtual setting. An NPC, as a second character present, was also used. Although the study's findings are of high importance in regards to the Proteus Effect[2] [13] and BOI, the full-body motion control was not exploited in full. Participants were seated for the entirety of the experiment and no questions were asked in regards to how having the ability to motion control an avatar affected the overall experience and their level of BOI.

---

[1] The Uncanny Valley hypothesis refers to the sudden drop in viewer empathy and immediate sense of discomfort when a humanoids' physiological resemblance comes very close to the human form, yet not enough, making for an aesthetically displeasing imitation.

[2] The Proteus Effect is an observed phenomenon of individuals subconsciously conforming their behavior to better suit their avatars overall appearance and physiology, regardless of how much it differs from their own.

Finally, there are researches where it is stated that participants were provided with full-body motion support, however, this claim only holds to a limited extent. For instance, in the Gonzalez-Franco et al. [14] study there was no feet support, whilst in other cases [15–18] participants were seated or standing still and in essence experienced the virtual setting and occurrences passively, without performing any noteworthy movement or locomotion to justify the use of a full-body motion tracking system, let alone a full-body suit.

The common denominator of the researches presented above is that full-body motion support is often utilized as a tool and a *means to an end*, rather than an area of research of its own. Considering the importance of freeing users within the virtual space and the variant commercial solutions either already available or currently under development aiming at liberating movement within the virtual space, studying the effects of that freedom or, alternatively, limitations of it, should be, at this point, deeply incorporated in VR-related research. For instance, the study and experiment conducted by Roth et al. [19], headed towards this direction, by comparing efficiency of full-body suits to solutions based on IK. This is particularly important as a full-body suit is in many ways time-consuming and counterintuitive when it comes to experimental setups, by requiring detailed and individualized calibration for each participant and by being too 'invasive' when it comes to users' perception of a free and relaxed body. Roth et al. compared the two tracking methods and results indicate that they achieve equally high levels of BOI. However, since IK is lighter and lowers perceived "task load" [19], it becomes a more attractive marker-based motion capture solution. This finding is also in accordance with market and industry trends, providing yet another reason to accordingly adjust in-house, laboratory-based, technical setups.

## 3   Experimental and Technical Setup

### 3.1   Overview of Experimental Setup

The experiment's setup drew inspiration from game-based VR/MR scenarios, typically employed for sports training and locomotion activities to enhance player performance or simulate training conditions [20]. Upon reviewing similar setups, related research as it was presented above, as well as our own research objectives, the experiment's scenario had to incorporate the following technical features:

- full-body motion support in real time using optical motion capture systems, allowing users to perform complex locomotion
- real-time use of real objects, accurately represented in the VR world
- interaction between real and virtual objects
- real-time auditory and visual feedback

These led to the design of a technically challenging MR environment, yet the goal-oriented and gamified task remained simple and easy to follow-through for participants. Apart from testing the technical setup, we wished to investigate overall performance and engagement, therefore non-player characters (NPCs) were introduced as potential sources of affective impact.

The resulting experimental setup was experienced by twenty-one participants (14 females) who visited the MR environment, shown in Fig. 1a and b, with the use of an Oculus Rift HMD. Human-like female and male avatars were assigned to female and male participants, respectively. Each participant was equipped with full-body motion support and their task was to throw, one by one, 10 small boxes across the room (approx. 2 m distance) targeting a bigger transparent box (see Fig. 1a and b) within a timeframe of 60 s. The 10 boxes, as well as the bigger box were real and accurately represented in regard to dimensions and position. Prior to the virtual experience, each participant had to execute the task once in the physical world without any immersive equipment, using the exact same boxes. Upon completing the task in the real world, participants were immediately immersed in the MR environment to experience the virtual version. Within the MR, a virtual scoreboard projected participants' score (number of successful hits) and the 60 s timer (Fig. 1a). Participants could also see their virtual hands and feet when looking down. A NPC, as the opponent, was positioned opposite to the participants, whilst the scoreboard projected the opponent's scores as well. Finally, three more NPCs stood on the left side of participants, as an audience, and either cheered or made sounds and animations in derision of participant poor performance (see Fig. 1a).

## 3.2    3D Modelling and Development

The 3D space, the small boxes, and the bigger basket were designed and created with Cinema 4D based on real-world coordinates and dimensions for accurate representation [21]. The 3D space was designed bigger than the original laboratory where the experiment took place (approx. 9 m$^2$) to avoid a sense of claustrophobia during the virtual experience (see Fig. 1a and b).

(a)                                                    (b)

**Fig. 1.**  (a) Real experimental space; (b) Virtual experimental space.

The avatars, motion controlled by participants, were created with Adobe Fuse[3] and imported into Mixamo[4] for rigging. The engine used for the technical setups was Unity 3D[5], into which all 3D models were imported upon completion. With Unity 3D, two scenes were created, wherein the first scene, functioning as an anteroom (see Fig. 2a and b), participants were given some time to try the full-body motion support by taking some random steps and picking up the boxes positioned in front of them. A virtual mirror allowed them to study their avatar's reflection and responsiveness to their movements. Once participants comfort with the environment, the system and the motions, as well as comprehension of the assigned task was confirmed, the next scene was activated by the research team. Thereafter, without taking the HMD off, participants saw the virtual space where the main experimental session was executed.

(a)                                              (b)

**Fig. 2.** (a) Anteroom; (b) Main experiment space

### 3.3 Effects and Performance Feedback

All participants wore a set of headphones to experience a consistent ambient sound (resembling city noise). Moreover, both groups received auditory and visual feedback upon each attempt of hitting the basket-box. Specifically, a light lit up as green or red for each successful or unsuccessful attempt, accompanied by a positive or negative buzzer sound. Participants were handling real objects represented in the virtual space and since the headphones used were not noise-cancelling, the natural sounds caused by box collision or during object impact with the ground were noticeable.

---

[3] https://www.adobe.com/products/fuse.html.

[4] https://www.mixamo.com/.

[5] https://unity3d.com/.

## 3.4    Implementing Real Objects

There are two steps involved in the representation of real objects and their trajectories in a virtual space in real time. Accurate 3D representation is the first one, which entails the creation of 3D model replicas of the real objects used [21]. 3D creation has to take into account objects' real dimensions, physiology – if necessary – and real to virtual space position concurrence (location and rotation). For the experiment presented here, the objects used, which were 10 small (10 cm × 10 cm) cubical boxes and one larger (50 cm × 50 cm), hollow, cubical box with its top removed, were carefully measured and thus accurately 3D represented by setting the Cinema 4D unit measurement to meters.

The second step is far more complex as objects' trajectory of movement in the real world has to be virtually represented in real time by motion tracking the real objects. This was achieved by using Blade, the Vicon's optical motion capture system. Each object was assigned with five retroreflective markers (see Fig. 3a), which when grouped together can be set as a single *prop* in Vicon Blade (11 objects - 11 *props*). *Props*, meaning a fixed set of five markers, are then tracked by Vicon Blade (see Fig. 3b), therefore achieving simultaneous motion tracking of each of the real objects in real time. This process was successfully executed and followed by the transference of objects' motion into Unity 3D and assignment of each one to the 3D model created during the first step with the use of a custom script[6] which integrated the Vicon Datastream SDK[7] (see Fig. 3c). An important note is that the 3D models which are representing the real objects used, must have the same pivot point as the location of the first marker selected during the Vicon Blade *prop* creation process. This ensures proper transfer and matching of an object's rotation and location in relation to the space.

## 3.5    Full-Body Motion Support

Vicon's motion capture system supports full body motion transfer to Unity 3D using Pegasus[8], which is a middleware software. However, during this particular implementation, certain issues arise. First, a full-body suit is required, which, as already discussed above, affects perceived task-load and confines participants' sense of freedom and comfort during movements. Moreover, a full-body suit requires detailed calibration, which can take up to several minutes and could therefore become problematic for an experimental setup with a substantial number of participants. To address these issues, Inverse Kinematics (IK) were used.

IK, in large, follow the same process as the one implemented for the motion tracking of the real objects, described above. Specifically, 4 retroreflective markers are assigned to each area of the body that needs to be motion tracked. These areas are the hands, feet and head of participants. Then, the 4 markers of each area are grouped and set into Vicon as a single *prop*, making five *props* in total. These *props* were assigned to the rigged

---

[6] The script used to register 3D objects location and rotation to the virtual space based on the real objects positions can be found at: http://zarcrash.x10.mx/Program.cs.

[7] https://www.vicon.com/products/software/datastream-sdk.

[8] https://www.vicon.com/products/software/pegasus.

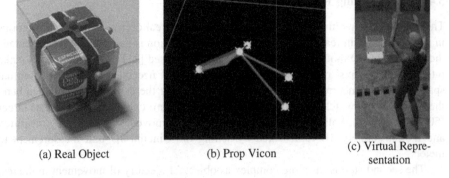

| (a) Real Object | (b) Prop Vicon | (c) Virtual Representation |
|---|---|---|

**Fig. 3.** (a) Object equipped with retroreflective markers; (b) *Prop*; (c) Virtual representation of objects trajectory.

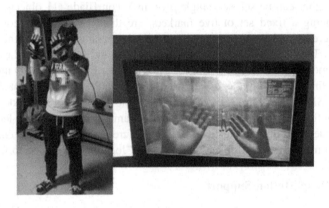

**Fig. 4.** Player equipped with props for full body motion support via inverse kinematics.

avatars using the Final IK[9] software. After successfully tracking the *props'* motion, Final IK calculates and "fills in" the rest of the body's motion (see Fig. 4)[10].

The experimental setup provided insights with respect to several aspects of user experience. However, this article focuses solemnly on full-body motion support and its implicated parameters as those were described in the first two sections. Specifically, upon reviewing related research, it was noted that utilization of full-body motion support is treated as a tool, rather than an area of research, even when research objectives are investigating *sense of presence* and BOI. Our analysis is a preliminary nudge towards a different route of investigation when applying such systems. Before providing an analysis of full-body motion support, our methodology of data gathering,

---

[9] http://www.root-motion.com/final-ik.html.

[10] A video demonstration of the experiment can be found at: https://www.youtube.com/watch?v=wB1qg34T7ws.

both qualitative and quantitative, as well as the results most relevant to the article's scope, are presented.

# 4   Methodology and Evaluation

The experiment was advertised around the university campus and our final sample consisted of 21 undergraduates (14 females) between the ages of 18 to 45. Participants had no prior association with the research team or the laboratory were the experiment was executed and they received no credit or payment for their participation.

Upon arrival, each participant was showed to the laboratory were the experiment would be taking place, briefed over the experimental scenario and presented with the equipment that would be used, which included the HMD, the props that would be worn on their hands and feet for the IK, as well as the boxes. Head props were already attached onto the HMD.

Once the equipment was on, participants were immersed into the anteroom and upon confirmation of comfort, the next scene of the main experiment was activated. Whilst in the anteroom they had the opportunity to ask questions and interact with the researchers who were there in the laboratory space, yet once in the main experimental scene, they were asked to proceed without any further assistance. During the experiment both their real and virtual behavior and performance was documented and screen-recorded for later analysis and for captivating *thinking aloud* occurrences. Upon completing their given task within the virtual space, they could take off the equipment and were immediately showed to a different area. Finally, they were handed a questionnaire.

## 4.1   Questionnaires

A five-level Likert item questionnaire (20 **Questions**[11]) covered 4 areas of enquiry:

(a)   level of *presence* (9 **Q**)
(b)   effect of external stimuli (3 **Q**)
(c)   realism of virtual environment (3 **Q**)
(d)   body ownership illusion (5 **Q**)

Questions were included making specific reference to the affordance of having full-body motion control over an avatar and possible invasiveness of external stimuli and of the equipment used during the virtual experience. At that time, these questions were part of what seemed to be a valid scope of inquiry and only after the completion of the experiment was it realized that full-body motion support has not been previously correlated to VR conceptualizations and that the technical setups implemented are only mildly juxtaposed against a study's findings.

As presented in Table 1, *sense of presence* was confirmed for all 21 participants. The majority of questions was based on previous studies and presence questionnaire

---

[11] Original questionnaires were in Greek.

**Table 1.** Presence

| No | Question | Median | Average |
|----|----------|--------|---------|
| Q1 | I felt that I was in the virtual world | 4 | 4,38 |
| Q2 | I felt surrounded by the virtual world | 4 | 4,43 |
| Q3 | I felt like I was acting from within the virtual world and not externally controlling a virtual character | 4 | 3,71 |
| Q4 | How much were you able to control events? | 3 | 3,67 |
| Q5 | How responsive was the environment to your movements and actions? | 4 | 3,76 |
| Q6 | How natural did your interactions with the environment feel? | 3 | 3,24 |
| Q7 | To what extent did the virtual environment engage your senses? | 4 | 3,90 |
| Q8 | How much did the visuals of the environment affect you? | 4 | 4,05 |
| Q9 | How much did the audio of the environment affect you? | 5 | 4,14 |

related research [16, 22]. Moreover, the VE mechanics were responsive to participant movement and action, achieving high levels of sensory feedback.

An area of inquiry dealt with external stimuli that could disrupt overall immersion and *sense of presence* (see Table 2). Therefore, three questions were posed investigating: (Q10) possible impact of events (e.g. sounds and individuals present) of the surrounding environment, meaning the laboratory were the experiment took place, (Q11) awareness of the equipment worn, which included the HMD and the *props* placed on participants' hands and feet, and (Q12) possible sensorial confusion relating to the fact that they had to interact with real objects and perform locomotive tasks in the real world, whilst receiving only virtual feedback of these interactions.

Results were positive for object handling (Q14), yet marginal for Q13, where participants juxtaposed the virtual experience to the one experienced earlier in the real world and for Q15 examining overall realism of the virtual environment.

As already mentioned, five questions were posed to determine level of BOI (Table 4). The first two are often found in relating studies where participants are asked to establish level of ownership when looking down towards their avatar's torso and legs (Q16) and when seeing their avatars reflection through a virtual mirror or reflective surface (Q17). Both question scores were marginal. Three additional questions were posed, which were original and, to the best of our knowledge, have not been introduced in other studies. These are the key questions of the present article as they enquire participants whether (Q18) the head-tracking motion control, (Q19) the full-body motion support and (Q20) the hand-tracking motion control responsiveness affected their level of BOI. Results were significantly higher for this set of questions in comparison to the Q16 and Q17.

## 4.2    Results Discussion

Participants regarded interactions with the environment as marginally natural (Q6), for which higher scores were expected considering they were equipped with full-body

**Table 2.** Effect of external stimuli

| No | Question | Median | Average |
|---|---|---|---|
| Q10 | I was fully aware of my real surroundings (e.g. sounds, other individuals etc.) | 2 | 2,05 |
| Q11 | I could feel and was aware of the Oculus Rift and the rest of the equipment attached to my body | 2 | 2,57 |
| Q12 | How inaccurate or confusing was sensory input during your virtual experience? | 3 | 3,00 |

**Table 3.** Virtual environment realism

| No | Question | Median | Average |
|---|---|---|---|
| Q13 | How much did your experience in the virtual environment resemble the real-world version? | 3 | 2,67 |
| Q14 | How compelling was the sensation of the moving objects in the virtual environment? | 4 | 4,00 |
| Q15 | The virtual world seemed completely real | 3 | 2,95 |

**Table 4.** BOI

| No | Question | Median | Average |
|---|---|---|---|
| Q16 | When looking down, I felt like the virtual body I saw was my own, even though it didn't look like me | 3 | 3,00 |
| Q17 | When looking in the mirror, I felt like the virtual body I saw was my own, even though it didn't look like me | 3 | 3,10 |
| Q18 | The virtual head's real-time responsiveness to the movements of my own head enhanced the feeling that the virtual body is my own and I am controlling it | 4 | 3,81 |
| Q19 | The virtual body's real-time responsiveness to the movements of my own body enhanced the feeling that the virtual body is my own and I am controlling it | 4 | 3,81 |
| Q20 | The virtual hands' real-time responsiveness to the movements of my own hands enhanced the feeling that the virtual body is my own and I am controlling it | 4 | 4,00 |

motion support and thus had free movement and significant locomotive control over their avatar, as well as real to virtual object support. In regard to audio (Q9), the resulting high scores were expected as an overall positive impact was repeatedly stated during experiment sessions. This relates to the headphones used, which were not noise-cancelling, therefore the natural sounds caused by real object collision and floor impact in the physical world were transmitted "into" the VR experience and at cases perceived as if generated from within it, which we consider further enhances MR realism.

Results of Q10 and Q11 indicate that participants were fully immersed, and that the equipment did not disrupt immersion. This is promising in regard to IK being a more suitable full-body motion support solution, since, even though the present study does not provide a comparison to a full-body suit, as a technical setup it is easier to apply and calibrate. For Q12 however, participant perceived sensory input was marginally accurate, a question that we consider relates to Q6. Furthermore, Q12 and Q6 may also be examined along with questions relating to the VE's overall realism, presented in Table 3, specifically Q13 and Q15. To summarize, four questions investigating naturalness of interactions (Q6), possible sensory input confusion (Q12), real to virtual task comparison (Q13) and overall realism (Q15), indicate that the affordances provided, (a) full-body motion support and (b) real-virtual object handling of which neither bared latency issues, along with (c) high quality non-invasive equipment and (d) high-quality MR audio feedback, were not sufficient to achieve seamless transition between real and virtual elements and events in a MR environment. Having an in-depth understanding of the possible technical-related impacts or impediments is crucial and our main goal was to review as many relating factors as possible. For instance, a number of participants reported minor motion errors occurring between participant and avatar body parts (e.g. virtual hand rotation not matching perfectly real hand's position) or general inconsistencies (e.g. participants feeling taller in VR). These were however *thinking aloud* observations and thus it is unverifiable whether and to what extent all participants experienced either these or similar inconsistencies. We consider that during any given VR experience, not all participants may be able to pinpoint or articulate what feels *off*. When directly asked most participants reflect on the positive aspects of the experience, which in this case was enjoyment of object interaction and avatar motion control. By co-relating all relevant data, we conclude that the marginal degree of perceived realism did not have a negative impact on overall task engagement or performance when compared to the non-immersive sessions executed in the physical world.

Results regarding achieved levels of BOI are also significant, especially when reviewed against related studies and research. Based on the preliminary results presented here we conclude that the specific full-body motion support system used as part of the MR environment as was, increased levels of BOI and should therefore be regarded as an impactful factor. However, we also hypothesize that full-body motion support is dependent on the technical setup and equipment employed and thus, it may either increase or disrupt achieved levels of BOI. Further investigation is required as the majority of related studies, where full-body motion support has been utilized, do not check achieved levels of BOI against all relating factors and in fact it is rather obscure what these factors may be, since technical setups are not properly (or at all) evaluated.

## 5   Conclusions and Future Work

The most important and most relevant to this article's scope conclusions relate to full-body motion support. First, from a technological standpoint, IK is considered a more appropriate motion capture solution over a full-body suit. Further experimentation where IK is compared to other motion capture techniques is required to solidify this stance, however, considering the currently available motion capture methods and their respective disadvantages, IK seems to be simpler to set, faster to put on and calibrate and also, it leaves a greater room for capturing complex user locomotion and movement when compared for instance to depth sensor-based systems.

As an overall affordance for interactive VEs, full-body motion support should presumably elevate perceived realism of the VE and the interactions performed. Even more so when real to virtual objects are integrated making for a stimulating MR experience. However, these affordances do not seem sufficient for achieving high levels of perceived realism of the VE or of the manual interactions incorporated. Comparison of variant experimental conditions is required to, above all, establish which factors are fundamental for perceived realism to begin with and perhaps detect impeding presumptions of and therefore approaches to MR. For instance, our future work will entail comparison of different levels of body motion control in relation to perceived BOI to provide a definitive understanding.

In regard to BOI, our preliminary results indicate that full-body motion support may increase levels of perceived ownership. However, we consider that a far more important conclusion is that *illusion of ownership* is a multifactorial process and should be investigated as such, taking into account all that is or might be affecting the *body* and therefore designing experiments and questionnaires, and collecting data accordingly. *Illusion* is certainly an appropriate term in relation to Botvinick and Cohen's real world experiment [23], however within the virtual space *body ownership* is not a momentarily experienced event, or a quick trick of the brain, but rather a spectrum of cognitive perception, one that is unclear whether users fully comprehend or have the resources to articulate and these are the very reasons for which the *Proteus Effect* or the *Uncanny Valley* hypothesis are so fascinating. They convey a certain mystique that draws attention back to the *body* as the primordial mediator between (socio-)cognitive perception and everything else.

# References

1. Slater, M., Usoh, M., Steed, A.: Depth of presence in virtual environments. Presence Teleoper. Virtual Environ. **3**, 130–144 (1994)
2. Tversky, B., Hard, B.M.: Embodied and disembodied cognition: spatial perspective-taking. Cognition **110**, 124–129 (2009)
3. Nowak, K.L., Biocca, F.: The Effect of the agency and anthropomorphism on users' sense of telepresence, copresence, and social presence in virtual environments. Presence Teleoper. Virtual Environ. **12**, 481–494 (2003)
4. Riva, G.: From virtual to real body: virtual reality as embodied technology. J. Cyber Ther. Rehabil. **1**, 7–22 (2008)
5. Schubert, T., Friedmann, F., Regenbrecht, H.: Embodied presence in virtual environments. In: Paton, R., Neilson, I. (eds.) Visual Representations and Interpretations, pp. 269–278. Springer, London (1999). https://doi.org/10.1007/978-1-4471-0563-3_30
6. Waltemate, T., Hülsmann, F., Pfeiffer, T., Kopp, S., Botsch, M.: Realizing a low-latency virtual reality environment for motor learning. In: Proceedings of the 21st ACM Symposium on Virtual Reality Software and Technology, pp. 139–147 (2015)
7. Dzardanova, E., Kasapakis, V., Gavalas, D.: Affective impact of social presence in immersive 3D virtual worlds. In: Proceedings of the IEEE Symposium on Computers and Communications (ISCC), pp. 6–11 (2017)

8. Dzardanova, E., Kasapakis, V., Gavalas, D.: The effect of social context on virtual reality. Consum. Electron. Mag. (2018, in press)
9. Wilson, B., Bounds, M., Tavakkoli, A.: A full-body motion calibration and retargeting for intuitive object manipulation in immersive virtual environments. In: Proceedings of the 9th Workshop on Software Engineering and Architectures for Realtime Interactive Systems (SEARIS), pp. 1–5 (2016)
10. Normand, J.M., Spanlang, B., Tecchia, F., Carrozzino, M., Swapp, D., Slater, M.: Full body acting rehearsal in a networked virtual environment—a case study. Presence Teleoper. Virtual Environ. **21**, 229–243 (2102)
11. Lugrin, J.-L., Latt, J., Latoschik, M.E.: Anthropomorphism and illusion of virtual body ownership. In: Proceedings of the 25th International Conference on Artificial Reality and Telexistence and 20th Eurographics Symposium on Virtual Environments, pp. 1–8 (2105)
12. Kilteni, K., Bergstrom, I., Slater, M.: Drumming in immersive virtual reality: the body shapes the way we play. Trans. Vis. Comput. Graph. **19**, 597–605 (2013)
13. Yee, N., Bailenson, J.: The proteus effect: the effect of transformed self-representation on behavior. Hum. Commun. Res. **33**, 271–290 (2007)
14. Gonzalez-Franco, M., Perez-Marcos, D., Spanlang, B., Slater, M.: The contribution of real-time mirror reflections of motor actions on virtual body ownership in an immersive virtual environment. In: Proceedings of the IEEE Virtual Reality Conference (VR), pp. 111–114 (2010)
15. Normand, J.-M., Giannopoulos, E., Spanlang, B., Slater, M.: Multisensory stimulation can induce an illusion of larger belly size in immersive virtual reality. PLoS One **6**, e16128 (2011)
16. Kilteni, K., Normand, J.-M., Sanchez-Vives, M.V., Slater, M.: Extending body space in immersive virtual reality: a very long arm illusion. PLoS One **7**, e40867 (2012)
17. Banakou, D., Groten, R., Slater, M.: Illusory ownership of a virtual child body causes overestimation of object sizes and implicit attitude changes. Proc. Natl. Acad. Sci. **110**, 12846–12851 (2013)
18. Peck, T.C., Seinfeld, S., Aglioti, S.M., Slater, M.: Putting yourself in the skin of a black avatar reduces implicit racial bias. Conscious. Cogn. **22**, 779–787 (2013)
19. Roth, D., Lugrin, J.-L., Büser, J., Bente, G., Fuhrmann, A., Latoschik, M.E.: A simplified inverse kinematic approach for embodied VR applications. In: Proceedings of the IEEE Virtual Reality Conference (VR), pp. 275–276 (2016)
20. Miles, H.C., Pop, S.R., Watt, S.J., Lawrence, G.P., John, N.W.: A review of virtual environments for training in ball sports. Comput. Graph. **36**, 714–726 (2012)
21. Kasapakis, V., Gavalas, D., Dzardanova, E.: Creating room-scale interactive mixed-reality worlds using off-the-shelf technologies. In: Proceedings of the IEEE International Conference on Advances in Computer Entertainment, pp. 1–13 (2017)
22. Witmer, B.G., Singer, M.J.: Measuring presence in virtual environments: a presence questionnaire. Presence **7**, 225–240 (1998)
23. Botvinick, M., Cohen, J.: Rubber hands 'feel' touch that eyes see. Nature **391**, 756 (1998)

# Defining Size Parameters for Touch Interaction in Substitutional Reality Environments

Christian Mai[(✉)], Christian Valenta, and Heinrich Hußmann

LMU Munich, Media Informatics, Munich, Germany
{Christian.Mai,Hussmann}@ifi.lmu.de
http://www.medien.ifi.lmu.de

**Abstract.** The physical support of touch interaction for a 2D interface when wearing a fully immersive head-mounted display (HMD), e.g., by using the kitchen table in a home environment, improves the user's quality of interaction. To define interface parameters - button size, adaption over time- we conducted a user study. In two experiments with 30 participants in total, we compared the ability of the HMD user's pointing to targets on a 2D surface without visual feedback, with visual feedback of the touched position and a real-world baseline. As a result, we give estimates for button dimensions, interaction design based on the learning curve of the user and present insights on the tested feedback modalities. We show that providing no feedback has limitations, presenting the touched position helps to increase accuracy and a head-mounted finger tracker has advantages but also comes with restrictions.

**Keywords:** Head-mounted displays · Touch interaction
Pointing task · Haptic feedback · User interface design

## 1 Introduction

The growing distribution of consumer-grade head-mounted displays, like the Oculus Rift[1], leads to many situations in which HMDs are used in real-world (RW) environments. In contrast to the past decades these environments are not highly equipped laboratories, but the user's offices or homes. These environments offer limited space with a number of physical objects in the movement area and the motion tracking system is mostly limited to controllers and head. Further, the user is surrounded by people acting in the RW which might interfere with the users VR experience.

The limited space for physical moves of the HMD user in these everyday environments is one of the major challenges. Several concepts are addressing this: (A) research on locomotion in virtual reality (VR) [16], (B) redirected walking techniques [24] and (C) augmented virtuality [30] or substitutional [27]

---

[1] https://www.oculus.com/rift.

© Springer International Publishing AG, part of Springer Nature 2018
L. T. De Paolis and P. Bourdot (Eds.): AVR 2018, LNCS 10851, pp. 683–701, 2018.
https://doi.org/10.1007/978-3-319-95282-6_48

**Fig. 1.** Conditions during the haptical supported pointing task from left to right: No Feedback (NO_FB), rendering the touched position (TOUCHPOINT_FB), continuous visual feedback of the hand provided by handtracking (HAND_FB) and the real world baseline (RW_BASELINE)

environments. We focus on the concept (C), as (A) often leads to an unnatural abstraction of walking, e.g., swinging the arms to mimic the walking movement [25] and (B) still needs more movement space then a standard living room can offer.

There are several examples using concept (C) like Intel's project Alloy[2], which maps virtual objects onto furniture of a living room. Another example is the integration of a large touch surface to support interaction with the virtual world when controlling a large ship[3]. The authors argue in this paper that the lifespan of a ship is several decades, therefore instead of changing the whole physical bridge, the visualization in an HMD is easy to replace, and the RW needs some new touch surfaces. In a household, the touch surface might be even simpler by using a smartphone or tablet, or it might incorporate a transportable interactive projector like the Sony Xperia touch[4]. So it makes good sense to assume that there are physical touch surfaces available, even with touch sensing technology, but the user is interacting with a visual overlay from a virtual reality simulation.

When using existing physical surfaces to support touch interaction, the user immersed in VR will benefit from (1) a gain in precision - the haptic feedback of the physical table limits one degree of freedom for the touch -, (2) a more consistent and larger space for movement - the integration of physical objects in the VR shows the HMD user where to move without danger - (3) an increased feeling of being present in the VR - more senses are integrated into the VR experience [28] - (4) an environment supporting combined interaction between real and virtual world - the physical touch surfaces can be used as a shared frame of reference for RW bystanders and HMD users by either knowing what kind of interaction is coupled with a physical object or by presenting the same information on the surface for the HMD and the RW user.

Existing research and industrial development show that technically substitutional environments are possible, as the merged reality demo from Intel's project Alloy. Therefore we focus on the unaddressed question of the user interface (UI)

---

[2] https://www.youtube.com/watch?v=Ku9gjx5ECuY.

[3] http://e2c2.ict.usc.edu/blueshark-environment/.

[4] https://www.sonymobile.com/de/products/smart-products/xperia-touch/.

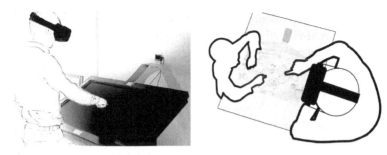

**Fig. 2.** Left: An HMD user acting in the virtual world with haptic feedback. Right: A short term interaction between a RW user and a HMD user with a shared frame of reference by using a mobile projector with touch recognition.

design for these types of systems in detail. In particular, we are addressing the precise definition of the button size and take into account the learning curve of the user for the UI design. The primary challenge arising is that the HMD blocks the users' view on their real hands and therefore the pointing accuracy is reduced. So we are interested in the requirements on the interface design and the compensation possibilities for the blocked view by different feedback methods, described further down.

We expect that touch interaction is possible in principle even if the HMD user does not see his/her own hands, as the human visuomotor system can compensate for such disturbances. We also expect that humans can deal with perceiving the hand in a position not matching precisely with the RW position. Such differences can arise when using a head-mounted finger tracker, e.g., due calibration reasons or the visual limitations introduced by the properties of the HMD [1,3,12,17].

To define button sizes and consider the adaption phase of the user to the respective systems constraints, we conducted a user study. We measured the pointing accuracy in a carefully calibrated system on a 2D touch surface (Fig. 2).

We decided on three feedback conditions plus a baseline condition (Fig. 1). The three feedback conditions differed in how we presented visual feedback to the user during a pointing movement, as described by MacKenzie [21]:

**NO_FB:** The user does not get any visual feedback of the hand or the touch point on the 2D surface.

**TOUCHPOINT_FB:** The user gets feedback on the interaction by a visual presentation of the point on the 2D surface where the touch happened.

**HAND_FB:** The users' hands are tracked by a head-mounted finger tracker and presented in the VR.

**RW_BASELINE:** The user conducts the task in the RW environment.

With our study, we were able to derive the following contributions:

- Detailed insights into the ability of the user to adapt the hand-eye coordination to the limitations introduced by the respective condition.

- Guidelines that help researchers and practitioners in designing user interfaces for substitutional virtual reality environments with targets positioned relative to physical surfaces.

## 2    Related Work

The usage of an HMD introduces two restrictions to the users' hand-eye coordination. One restriction is related to perceptual issues, generating an underestimation of distances when looking at a stereoscopic picture within an HMD [1,23] and the other one is not seeing the own hand when touching an object. Recent studies focusing on interaction with stereoscopic images on 2D touch surfaces in the RW looked into the effects when touching at a 2D surface while the object is rendered with positive or negative parallax, which means it looks like floating behind or in front of the 2D surface of the touchscreen monitor. The focus in this RW interaction is different from the usage of HMD environments, as they focus on occlusion problems and parallax effects and the real hand is visible all the time [7,32].

Studies that use HMD displays to assess interaction with the virtual world mostly focus on different aspects of factors influencing size and distance estimation, as summarized in the literature review of Renner et al. [26]. But it could be shown in different pointing tasks that an adaptation for the systems disturbances by the user is possible [1,4,13,22,29]. These studies do not match our target system of touching at a 2D surface as some of them did not offer a physical target for haptic feedback and/or the participants in the pointing task used a stylus and not their fingers.

### 2.1    Background: Hand-Eye Coordination in 3D Pointing Tasks

The concept we are aiming for is based on the idea of pointing at objects while not being able to see one's hand directly. In this chapter, we introduce how human pointing movements work to motivate that quasi-blind pointing at objects is possible. Further, the description of pointing movements helps us to understand and design the system, as we derive the feedback systems from it.

A goal-directed ballistic movement of the hand to touch a particular point can be divided into two phases. The first phase does not need visual guidance, the second phase, the actual touch, needs visual guidance for readjustment of the finger to the target [21]. Therefore in an RW scenario with undisturbed visual guidance the highest accuracy is expected. We can expect a high-end absolute tracking system to give a comparable accuracy. However, these systems are costly and difficult to use, which is why we do not consider them to be available in consumer grade hardware.

In a pointing movement without visual feedback of the hand, an open loop task, the proprioceptive system, is used to lead the hand to the target location [21]. In this case the users only have the visual information about the target location to plan the ballistic movement of the hand. Without continuous visual feedback a person does not have the possibility to refine the hand and finger position in the second phase of the pointing movement [21], which creates a deviation in the touch accuracy according to the precision in the first phase.

In our system, we always have the haptic feedback given by the touch surface. Further, when using touch-sensitive surfaces like tabletop displays or tablets, the system receives the touched position on this surface, so it can help the user to adapt to the distortions introduced by the HMD. The possible usage of this principle will be discussed in the following section.

## 2.2  Influence of Feedback on a Pointing Task

Many studies suggest that feedback helps the user to adapt the distance perception to the distortions introduced by the HMD system in an egocentric pointing task [1,3,12,17]. In contrast to that, the lack of visual feedback lets the users' accuracy drift [6] and therefore will not be described further but also tested in the condition NO_FB as it might get important when either tracking systems do not operate reliable or are not available at all. For us, the relevant feedback modalities are visual feedback, haptic feedback, and combinations of them.

Most of the studies using a pointing task present the visual feedback of the hand during the whole touch gesture [1,4,12] which therefore matches a closed loop pointing task. It was shown that visual feedback helps to improve the adaptation of the visuomotor system to the HMD distortions in a minimal amount of attempts [1,17] to a significantly higher accuracy [1,5,17]. Therefore continuous optical feedback would give the highest possible accuracy after some touch attempts and is tested as the condition HAND_FB.

A purer form of feedback is to present visual feedback of the touch position on the touched surface only (Fig. 2, bottom left). This does not create a closed loop for pointing, as the user has no continuous visual feedback of the fingertips. But we assume that there will be an adaptation of the visuomotor system for the visual disturbances in the first phase of the ballistic movement that does not need visual guidance [21]. Furthermore, users remember the touched position and adapt their motor planning at the following touch to the visually estimated delta [14,20]. This might compensate for the lack of the second phase of the pointing task to a certain amount and is tested in the condition Touchpoint_FB.

If visual and haptic feedback are presented together, it is essential to know how they influence the visuomotor systems adaptation process and how they influence each other. On the one hand, there is some tolerance for the divergence between visual and haptic depth cues [9,31]. This might help to compensate some issues that are introduced by the inaccuracies of the finger tracking system (Fig. 2, bottom right). Further, it is known for a 3D pointing gesture that giving haptic feedback is essential to determine the depth at the end of the correction phase, the second phase of the pointing task [31]. These effects might be helpful for all conditions, but we are not focusing on examining them. However, they are used in different applications to provide haptic feedback for the user [2,9].

## 3   Experiments

The experimentation on defining the parameters for touch interaction in a substitutional environment was divided into two experiments. This decision was based on a pre-study in which the participants reported to feel the physical effort in their arms after having gone through all conditions after another. In the following, we describe the visual parameters and the apparatus that was the same for both experiments. Both experiments included the Touchpoint_FB condition to indicate the validity of the experiment.

*Visual Parameters.* The findings on factors influencing the perception of distance and size in a virtual environment are very well described by Renner [26]. In fact, there are several factors known to affect size and distance estimation, but it is difficult to put them on a simple numeric scale. Therefore we only report on the parameters we considered when adjusting the HMD system to each user and the method we used.

We measured the interpupillary distance (IPD) in two ways. The first is by using the integrated IPD measuring method of the Oculus runtime (version 0.8). The second measurement was by using an IPD measuring template from Eye-Net Ltd.[5]. Both were conducted according to the given instructions. The mean of both methods was used. Further, all adjustable parameters of the Oculus were checked to be the same in the runtime environment as set at the hardware to guarantee a matching field of view (FOV) between the virtual cameras and the perceived FOV by the user.

The subjects were tested for their leading eye by using the Dolman, also called hole in the card, test[6]. The subjects had normal or corrected to normal vision during the experiment. None of the subjects reported any known disorders with their visual system. We used the graded circle test of a Rendot® stereotest[7] to measure the stereoacuity of the participants without any salience.

*Apparatus.* In our experiment we used a 42 multi-touch table with WXGA resolution with 1366 Pixel resolution in width (x-axis) and 768 Pixel in height (y-axis) and an optical tracking system with mm accuracy for touch recognition just above the surface. The size of the display and touch surface was 1.015 m × 0.57m. The table was slightly tilted towards the user (Fig. 3). We used the Oculus Rift Development Kit 2 [11] with the Oculus Head tracking system and the SDK Version 0.8. The camera was attached to the screen as shown in Fig. 3, left. The frame rate of the system was 75 Hz throughout the experiment. For the HAND_FB condition, a Leap Motion finger tracker was used with the official head mount and the Orion Beta SDK 3.1.1. We decided to use a head-mounted finger tracker, as they are not as intrusive and complicated to use as gloves and

---

[5] https://www.eye-net.com/media/cms/pdf/anl_neu_optiker.pdf.

[6] https://www.usaeyes.org/lasik/library/Dominant-Eye-Test.pdf.

[7] http://www.visionassessment.com/1005.shtml.

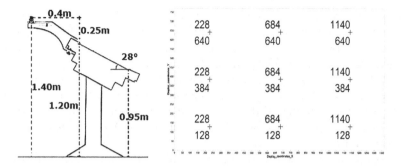

**Fig. 3.** Drawing of touch table dimensions (left) and the target positions in pixel coordinates on the screen (right). (Color figure online)

they are not bound to a specific area like external tracking systems, e.g., Vicon optical tracking[8], as they move with the user.

The table, wall, floor, and room were 3D-modeled in their dimensions according to their real counterpart. The textures were approximated manually. The visualization for the Oculus Rift and the touch table was rendered with Unity 5.3.1. The visualized background on the screen in the real task and the virtual representation was a 50% grey. The target cross was 30 * 30 pixels in red.

To map the virtual representation of the touch surface to the real surface used in our study, the tracking camera was mounted in a defined position relative to the table. The virtual and the RW were overlayed with their origin of coordinate systems in the center of the camera.

Nine different target positions on the screen are defined by coordinates. The screen coordinates start with (0,0) at the bottom left (Fig. 3, right).

During the experiment the target ID and the according position of a pointing event to that target was recorded in pixel values. The metric distance to the target was calculated by using the scale known from the value pixels per centimeter.

### 3.1   Experiment on Comparing NO_FB and TOUCHPOINT_FB

*Participants.* 14 male and 6 female with a mean age of 28 (SD = 9.9) participated in the experiment. The subjects were students and employees from different departments at the LMU Munich. 13 of the participants had minor experiences with HMDs, and the rest had no experience. One subject was left handed.

Between the different conditions, the subjects had time to take a break for a few minutes. The total time for each subject to participate in the experiment was about 40 min including pre-questionnaire, instructions, experiment, and breaks.

---

[8] https://www.vicon.com/.

*Method.* The experiment was conducted as a $2 \times 9$ within-subject design. The independent variables are the two feedback conditions (NO_FB vs. TOUCH-POINT_FB) and the nine target positions (Fig. 3). The dependent variable was the distance from the touch position by the user on the touch screen to the presented target cross center. In between the two feedback conditions the RW condition was conducted as a baseline for the system. In between conditions the participants took off the HMD and played with a tennis ball to avoid carry-over effects and the so called negative aftereffect [15]. All subjects completed all feedback conditions.

The experiment started with the welcoming of the subjects and the explanation of the procedure of the experiment and its goal. They were informed that no personal data is recorded during the study. They were instructed to touch with the fingertip of the index finger of their dominant hand exactly at the center of the cross, lift their hand after touching and go on to the next target. They were asked to concentrate and touch as accurately as possible. The subjects should move quickly, but still feel comfortable. If they got hectic or too slow, they were requested to adapt their speed and keep the focus on precision. They were allowed to rest in between the conditions. After that their dominant eye and stereo acuity was determined. They were told about simulator sickness and possible symptoms and were informed to stop their session at every time if they felt uncomfortable [18].

Then they put on the HMD while standing in front of the touch table. They had to touch at the center of the red target cross. The target disappeared after the touch happened and the next target appeared. Therefore only one target was visible at the same time. All nine targets were touched in a randomized order before one target was touched a second time. This we call a block which will be relevant to identify the adaption phase. The same target was never requested to touch two times in a row. Every subject performed 180 touches per feedback condition.

## 3.2   Results on Comparing No_FB and TOUCHPOINT_FB

*Outliers.* The collected data included unintended touches that occurred by accidentally hitting the touch surface in between two touches. We chose a distance of more than 20 cm to be an unintended touch, as this is the shortest distance between two target centers. 42 touches were excluded for the condition NO_FB, 33 for Touchpoint_FB and 38 for the RW_BASELINE.

The data was processed by using a repeated measures ANOVA. As Mauchly's test of sphericity was violated in all cases, the degrees of freedom were corrected by the Greenhouse-Geisser estimates to compensate for this. As posthoc a Tukey multi comparison (p = .5) was calculated with Bonferroni correction.

*Identifying the Adaption Phase.* We started the analysis of the results with an analysis of adaption phases, as we want to exclude the adaption phase from the analysis for the final UI design. As one can see for the condition

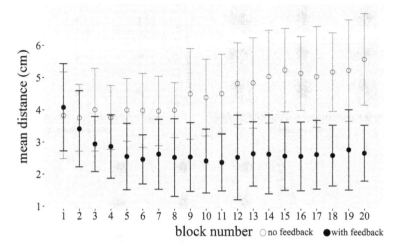

**Fig. 4.** Touch accuracy over blocks during the NO_FB condition with mean and 95% confident intervals. Each block comprises a touch to each target and therefore 9 touches. (Color figure online)

TOUCHPOINT_FB in Fig. 4 (black, solid circle), there seems to be a adaption phase, as the mean distance value drops from the first to the fourth block. A repeated measures ANOVA comparing the mean touch distance between the trials showed a significant difference in touch accuracy between the blocks $(F(5.915, 112.377) = .505$, p $< .05$; ŋ^2 $=.225)$.

The post hoc tests showed that block 1 was highly significantly different from all following blocks, except the block number 2 at p $< .05$. Block 2 showed a significant difference to most other blocks but block 1, 3 and 4 at p $< .05$. Block 3 only showed a significant difference to block 1 at p $< .05$. Block 4 showed no difference to the other blocks. The mean touch distances declined from 4.1 cm (SD $= 1.4$ cm) in block 1, 3.4 cm (SD $= 1.2$ cm) in block 2 to 2.9 cm (SD $= 0.9$ cm) in block 3. This is an improvement of 30% from touching each target for the first time (block 1) to the third time (block 3). Therefore we expect 2 touches to a target to be sufficient to learn to compensate for the introduced disturbances.

The first two blocks will be excluded for the further analysis to describe requirements on the UI design. The resulting dataset for the TOUCHPOINT_FB condition includes 3207 touches. This dataset without block 1, block 2 and without outliers will be called the dataset after the training phase.

*Comparison of Overall Touch Accuracy of the Conditions.* To quantify the differences when implementing on-screen feedback after the users adapted to the system, we compared the touch distributions between the two conditions. A Quantile-Quantile plot showed that the processed data has no normal distribution. A Wilcoxon Signed Rank test indicated that the scores for the NO_FB were

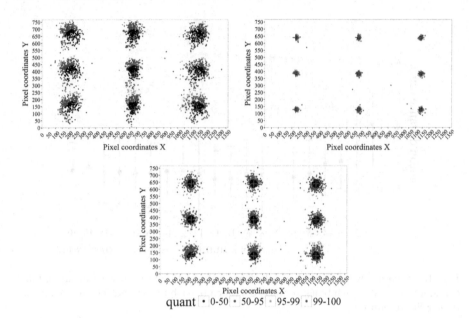

quant • 0-50 • 50-95 • 95-99 • 99-100

**Fig. 5.** Distribution of all touches, without outliers and the adaption phase. Top left: NO_FB, Top right: RW_BASELINE, Bottom: TOUCHPOINT_FB. The shown target crosses are oversized for better visibility

significantly higher than the scores for the TOUCHPOINT_FB (p < .001). The mean touch accuracy without feedback was 4.5 cm (SD = 2.3 cm), with feedback it was 2.7 cm (SD = 1.9 cm).

As one can see in Fig. 4 (brown circle, no fill), there is no adaptation of the user to the condition NO_FB over time, as there is a drift to higher touch deviation. Further, as no threshold is visible, we assume that users are not aware of the drift and the deviation gets worse over time. Therefore we did not consider the NO_FB condition in the further analysis as it has a high potential for failure. As regards to the completeness, in the RW_BASELINE condition, the users could achieve in average 0.7 cm (SD = 0.4 cm) in accuracy for 99% of the touches (Fig. 5, top right).

*Influence of Target Position on Touch Precision.* Using an ANOVA, as described at the beginning of this section, we found a significant difference in touch accuracy between the positions ($F(3.668, 69.697) = 3.334, \mathrm{p} < .05$; ŋ^2 = .149).

The Bonferroni corrected post hoc comparison showed that there is a significant difference between the lower left target (M = 3.0 cm, SD = 1.1 cm) and the middle target (M = 2.2 cm, SD = 0.8 cm) for the condition TOUCHPOINT_FB in the dataset after the training phase.

The difference is rather small, therefore we do not expect a relevant effect for the user's interaction precision.

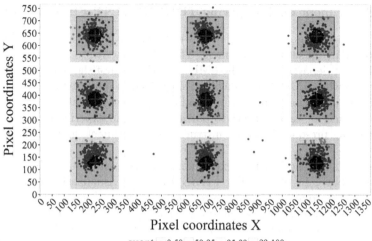

Pixel coordinates X

quant • 0-50 • 50-95 · 95-99 • 99-100

**Fig. 6.** Distribution of all touches, without outliers and without the adaption phase for the TOUCHPOINT_FB condition. The squares represent the size for buttons depending on the accepted failure rate.

*Variability of Touches in Horizontal and Vertical Display Direction and Resulting Target Size.* In the previous sections, the touch distribution was calculated as circular shapes around the center of the targets. But as one can see in Fig. 5 TOUCHPOINT_FB (bottom), the centroid of touches to the targets might be shifted from the actual target, which would give the possibility for improvement by individual calibration [8]. Also, the variability of the touch precision could be bigger on the y-axis compared to the x-axis, which could be supported by buttons of other shapes than squares.

The mean deviation of the centroid of touches to each target in the condition with feedback along the x-axis is 0.4 cm (SD = 0.3 cm), and along the y-axis it is 0.1 cm (SD = 0.2 cm). In comparison to the touch area this deviation is very small, therefore we do not expect a benefit from implementing such a system.

The acceptance of missing a button can help to reduce the target size. As one can see in Fig. 6, the acceptance of 5% touches that would miss the button will influence the necessary size for a button visible.

To generate a minimal target size we compared the maximum deviation of the touches in x-direction to the deviation of the touches to the different targets in y-direction for the 99% closest points. A t-test between the two directions showed significant differences ($t(8) = -1.1663$, $p = 0.027$)) with a mean of 9.8 cm (SD = 1.3 cm) deviation in x- and 10.7 cm (SD = 0.6 cm) in y-direction. For 99% hit success the bounding box would need to be x = 14.9 cm and y = 15.6 cm (Fig. 6). For 95% successful touches the button would need to be x= 11.2cm and y= 11.4cm.

### 3.3    Experiment on Comparing TOUCHPOINT_FB and HAND_FB

*Participants.* 6 male and 4 female subjects with a mean age of 26 (SD = 3) participated in our second experiment. The subjects were students and employees from different departments at the LMU Munich. Two of the participants had no experiences with HMDs, and the other subjects had minor experience. Between the different conditions, the subjects had time to take a break for a few minutes. The total time for each subject to participate in the experiment was about 40 min including pre-questionnaire, instructions, experiment, and breaks.

*Methods.* The method in this experiment was the same as in the experiment described above. In the condition HAND_FB the visualization of the tracked fingers and the touch position on the touchscreen was compared by visualizing the touch position on the touch surface and the fingers within the HMD. In case there was a mismatch between the physical position of the fingers on the screen and the virtual representation it was manually calibrated by putting the real finger on the middle of a target and moving the virtual finger to match the touched position visually.

The rest of the experiment is analog to the methods of the experiment on comparing NO_FB and TOUCHPOINT_FB in the section above.

### 3.4    Results of Experiment on Comparing TOUCHPOINT_FB and HAND_FB

*Outliers.* The collected data includes unintended touches that occurred by accidentally touching the surface in between two touches. We chose a distance of more than 20 cm to be an unintended touch. 13 touches were excluded for the condition TOUCHPOINT_FB and 19 for the condition HAND_FB.

*Insights on Validity of Results Between the Experiments.* To get an insight on the validity of the two experiments we compared the TOUCHPOINT_FB condition from both experiments. There was not a significant difference in the scores for TOUCHPOINT_FB from the first (M = 2.6 cm, SD = 3.5 cm) and TOUCHPOINT_FB from the second (M = 2.7 cm, SD = 2.8) experiment ($t(4143) = 1.7895$, p = 0.07). Further a t-test only tests for differences and does not proof equality, the difference of 0.1 cm with the given sample size is very small. Therefore we expect a good validity for the experiment. Also, the number of outliers is similar to 1.7 outliers per participant in the experiment presented above and 1.3 in this experiment.

*Identifying the Adaption Phase.* Similarly to the experiment presented above, a adaption phase can be detected for the TOUCHPOINT_FB condition on the table. A paired t-test showed significant difference between the distance to the target between the first (M = 3.12 cm, SD = 1.9 cm) and second (M = 2.6 cm, SD = 1.5 cm) block of touches ($t(89) = 2.0969$, p = 0.039). For the condition with finger representation, no adaption phase could be determined.

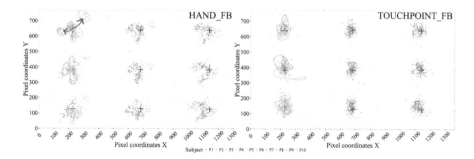

**Fig. 7.** Touches per subject. Left: HAND_FB. Right: TOUCHPOINT_FB. The contours show exemplarily the distribution of touches for each subject.

*Relative Spreading of Touches and Shift of Touch Centroids.* The plot of the touch distribution for each subject in Fig. 7 shows that the area needed to cover all touches appears to be much bigger in the HAND_FB condition (Fig. 7, left), then for the TOUCHPOINT_FB condition (Fig. 7, right). A paired t-test shows a highly significant difference for the mean touch distribution between the TOUCHPOINT_FB condition (M = 4.3 cm, SD = 1.9 cm) and HAND_FB condition (M = 5.6 cm, SD= 2.7 cm) (t(320) = $-5.5486$, p = 0.001). But the distribution of touches for every single subject is smaller in the condition HAND_FB, see the following paragraph.

It is visible in Fig. 7 that the touches in the TOUCHPOINT_FB condition are spread around the targets equally for all subjects (Fig. 7, right). In the HAND_FB condition, the subjects show clusters of touches that do not overlap as much as in the TOUCHPOINT_FB condition. A drift of the centroid of touches to a specific direction and amount is visible (Fig. 7, left). This drift is individual for each subject.

*Variability of Touches in Horizontal and Vertical Display Direction and Resulting Target Size for HAND_FB.* In the following we only analyze the condition HAND_FB, as the TOUCHPOINT_FB condition was compared in a previous section. A paired t-test of comparing the distribution of touches in x- (M = 3.8 cm, SD = 1.1 cm) and y- (M = 4.9 cm, SD = 2.3 cm) direction shows a significant difference (t(89) = $-3,97$, p = 0.001). For the acceptance of 5% missed buttons this leads to a target size of 7.8 cm in x- and 10.1 cm in the y-direction.

### 3.5    Limitations

Although our user study was designed with great care, there are some limitations to it. The mounting for the leap motion finger tracker on the is costume made based on the instruction provided by Leap Motion. But we still had to calibrate for each subject manually. This calibration was done before the experiment and carefully tested. However, during the experiment the calibration might have been lost when the HMD moved relative to the users head.

Further, the number of participants was rather small. As we did not find a remarkable difference between the first and the second study, we argue that our results still give a very good estimation for the pointing accuracy.

Also system inherent attributes might influence the results. Other HMD models might have a different influence on the size and distance estimation. Also pointing to a surface above the head height and different orientation of the surface to the user might lead to deviating results. However, the latest are extreme cases and might be considered for further studies.

## 4    Discussion of the Study Results

The results of the experiment give indications for the definition of button sizes as well as the interaction design for a system enabling touch interaction in substitutional virtual reality environments scenarios. In the following we present guidelines based on the results of our experiment that help to design such systems closely coupled to the users' needs.

*Keep in Mind the Limitations of the Feedback Modality.* In our study, we tested the conditions without restrictions of the HMD (RW_BASELINE) and the three different visualization possibilities no feedback at all (NO_FB), feedback about the touched position on the touch surface (TOUCHPOINT_FB) and continuous visual feedback given by a head-mounted finger tracking system (HAND_FB). The different systems have different requirements on the UI and interaction design.

Interaction in the NO_FB condition is possible. However, this interaction mode puts strong limitations on the interface design, since the touches have a large distribution and a steady drift over time. Further, the distribution of touches gets larger over time, as it was shown in studies with pointing to targets in 3D space before [6]. Therefore not presenting any feedback might only be an option for short-term interactions with a separation of the targets based on directions relative to the user, like left and right or up and downwards.

The TOUCHPOINT_FB helped to improve accuracy as we expected from similar studies in different interaction scenarios before [1,3,12,17]. Therefore existing surfaces with touch detection should be included in the interaction whenever possible. Examples could be but are not limited to tablets, touchscreens or other devices that include tracking like mobile projection system -e.g., Sony Xperia touch-. However, in contrast to our assumption based on the results of MacKenzie [21], the resulting mean deviation of 2.7 cm for the touches is much higher than in a RW scenario with 0.7 cm of deviation.

Further, we could show that the representation of the touchpoint does not only improve the accuracy in the course of the interaction but further prevents a drift of the touches centroid over time. This leads to a reliable touch input for the interaction design.

When accepting 5% touches that miss the desired button, it is possible to fit nine bounding boxes lateral to the users forward direction and five bounding boxes on the used screen along the users forward direction. That leads to 45 hit zones in total for the on-screen touch feedback. This would be enough to design a usable keyboard for text input.

HAND_FB by the usage of a head-mounted finger tracker enables interaction within the limitations of the used finger tracker. In our system, the finger tracker helped to increase the touch accuracy. This is highly dependent on the used head-mounted finger tracking system. Therefore not the definition of buttons sizes but the finding for interaction design is the interesting outcome for this condition in our study.

We could show a drift in the centroid of touches that most likely was introduced due to our manual calibration process. Although we checked the calibration on different targets before the study, the calibration might have been lost during the study by movements of the HMD relative to the users head. Therefore the hand-eye coordination was affected. This is less a problem in purely VR systems as the user does not recognize the shift. But it is a problem for detecting precisely the touch on a target positioned relative to the real-world surface as it changes the calibration. We therefore suggest to include an algorithm that continually recalibrates the finger tracker, e.g., by a technique introduced by Buschek and colleagues [8].

Surprisingly the distribution of touches was not much smaller in the HAND_FB then in the TOUCHPOINT_FB condition. The main reason for that is occlusion of the finger by the user's hand when pointing at a surface. Therefore no absolute tracking of the finger is possible for the tracking system. Therefore the underlying algorithms of the tracking systems assume a finger position as it was trained. Most likely this is the decision between a straight and a bent finger. As a result, we suggest using buttons that have a portrait format. This would lead to a UI that has more buttons in the horizontal direction than in the vertical direction relative to the user. To prevent the occlusion it might help to position buttons in a way that leads to a hand position with the back of the hand perpendicular to the users head.

Further, the head-mounted finger tracker needs to be carefully calibrated to match the user's fingers precisely. Otherwise, the visual position of the finger, the physical feedback of the touch surface and the position of the target relative to the touch surface will not match, which results into a confusion of the user. Also, incomprehensible reactions of the systems can happen as the users see their fingers touching the correct button, but the physical finger hits the button next to it that is positioned relative to the physical touch surface. We calibrated our system in a somewhat naive way, by asking the users about their perception of the finger position and moving it if a mismatch was reported. A calibration process with about 10 touches to known targets to find the delta between touch position and target position could be used to improve this calibration.

*Adaptation of the UI for the User Over Time.* The TOUCHPOINT_FB helped, as expected from related work, to improve the touch accuracy over the trials. The maximum accuracy is reached after about 18 touches, where the user had touched each target two times. As a result, the user should either be trained to use the system, or the size of targets should adapt over time. The last concept could be implemented through bigger buttons at the beginning of the interaction that shrink over time. But this also means that there is less space for targets on the screen at the beginning of the interaction. Taking this into account on could imagine the presentation of a login screen with login buttons distributed over the whole display or a game during the start of the system. This game could be designed as a multi-level game that offers more and smaller buttons in the second step of the procedure.

*Pay Attention When Using Head-Mounted Finger Tracking.* As we reported above, the user's hand in a pointing task has a high potential to introduce inaccuracies by shadowing the finger. Therefore in systems with head-mounted finger tracking, the buttons should be positioned in a way that the user can touch them with the back of his/her hand perpendicular to his/her line of sight.

*Position of Buttons has a Minor Influence on Accuracy.* The TOUCH-POINT_FB condition did not show lower accuracy in the border areas of the field of view, e.g., due to lens distortion in the HMD, as we expected from related work [26]. The inaccuracy might not be present in comparison to earlier experiments due to the significantly better visual systems which are known for improved size and distance estimation in consumer grade HMDs [10, 19]. Also, the higher demand on the natural motion when reaching to a target further away [21] in combination with the missing visual feedback during the pointing task therefore seemed not to influence the users pointing accuracy. This also means that it is possible to transfer the findings made in our study to other touch screen systems. We assume the results to be consistent for systems with small deviations in size, position, and tilt of the touch surface, as long as the interaction is in the arms reach distance for the user. However, there might be extreme positions in which the human motor system comes to a boundary of the ability to move precisely, like the extreme case of leaning backward and pushing a button above or in the back of the user.

## 5   Future Work

The system setup used in this work is a minimal setup for the least complicated UI with static targets. More complex UIs might have moving or moveable UI elements, which might lead to different results for button sizes which should be researched in the future. During the everyday use of a substitutional environment, the user might interact with surfaces at particular points in time during the room-scale virtual reality session. Therefore another open question is, if the user can remember the visuomotor system adaptation to possible drift in the conditions TOUCHPOINT_FB and HAND_FB and if s/he can transfer this from one touch surface to another touch surface. The position of the touch surface and the relative angle to the user is another factor that needs to be researched.

# References

1. Altenhoff, B., Napieralski, P., Long, L., Bertrand, J., Pagano, C., Babu, S., Davis, T.: Effects of calibration to visual and haptic feedback on near-field depth perception in an immersive virtual environment. In: Proceedings of the ACM Symposium on Applied Perception (SAP 2012), pp. 71–78. ACM, New York, NY, USA (2012)
2. Azmandian, M., Hancock, M., Benko, H., Ofek, E., Wilson, A.: Haptic retargeting: dynamic repurposing of passive haptics for enhanced virtual reality experiences. In: Proceedings of the 2016 CHI Conference on Human Factors in Computing Systems (CHI 2016), pp. 1968–1979. ACM, New York, NY, USA (2016)
3. Bingham, G.: Calibration of distance and size does not calibrate shape information: comparison of dynamic monocular and static and dynamic binocular vision. Ecol. Psychol. **17**(2), 55–74 (2005)
4. Bingham, G., Bradley, A., Bailey, M., Vinner, R.: Accommodation, occlusion, and disparity matching are used to guide reaching: a comparison of actual versus virtual environments. J. Exper. Psychol. Hum. Percept. Perform. **27**(6), 1314–1334 (2001)
5. Bingham, G., Crowell, J., Todd, J.: Distortions of distance and shape are not produced by a single continuous transformation of reach space. Percept. Psychophys. **66**(1), 152–169 (2004)
6. Bingham, G., Zaal, F., Robin, D., Shull, A.: Distortions in definite distance and shape perception as measured by reaching without and with haptic feedback. J. Exper. Psychol. Hum. Percept. Perform. **26**(4), 1436–1460 (2000)
7. Bruder, G., Steinicke, F., Sturzlinger, W.: To touch or not to touch?: Comparing 2D touch and 3D mid-air interaction on stereoscopic tabletop surfaces. In: Proceedings of the 1st Symposium on Spatial User Interaction (SUI 2013), pp. 9–16. ACM, New York, NY, USA (2013)
8. Buschek, D., Alt, F.: Touchml: A machine learning toolkit for modelling spatial touch targeting behaviour. In: Proceedings of the 20th International Conference on Intelligent User Interfaces (IUI 2015). ACM, New York, NY, USA (2015)
9. Cheng, L.P., Ofek, E., Holz, C., Benko, H., Wilson, A.: Sparse haptic proxy: Touch feedback in virtual environments using a general passive prop. In: Proceedings of the 2017 CHI Conference on Human Factors in Computing Systems (CHI '17). pp. 3718–3728 (2017)
10. Creem-Regehr, S., Stefanucci, J., Thompson, W., Nash, N., McCardell, M.: Egocentric distance perception in the oculus rift (dk2). In: Proceedings of the ACM SIGGRAPH Symposium on Applied Perception (SAP 2015), pp. 47–50. ACM, New York, NY, USA (2015)
11. Desai, P., Desai, P., Ajmera, K., Mehta, K.: A review paper on oculus rift-a virtual reality headset. CoRR abs/1408.1173 (2014)
12. Ebrahimi, E., Altenhoff, B., Hartman, L., Jones, A., Babu, S., Pagano, C., Davis, T.: Effects of visual and proprioceptive information in visuo-motor calibration during a closed-loop physical reach task in immersive virtual environments. In: Proceedings of the ACM Symposium on Applied Perception (SAP 2014), pp. 103–110. ACM, New York, NY, USA (2014)
13. Ebrahimi, E., Altenhoff, B., Pagano, C., Babu, S.: Carryover effects of calibration to visual and proprioceptive information on near field distance judgments in 3d user interaction. In: 2015 IEEE Symposium on 3D User Interfaces (3DUI), pp. 97–104 (2015)
14. Harris, C.: Perceptual adaptation to inverted, reversed, and displaced vision. Psychol. Rev. **72**(6), 419–444 (1965)

15. Held, R.: Plasticity in sensory-motor systems. Sci. Am. **213**(5), 84–94 (1965)
16. Jankowski, J., Hachet, M.: Advances in interaction with 3D environments. Comput. Graph. Forum **34**(1), 152–190 (2015)
17. Kelly, J., Hammel, W., Siegel, Z., Sjolund, L.: Recalibration of perceived distance in virtual environments occurs rapidly and transfers asymmetrically across scale. IEEE Trans. Vis. Comput. Graph. **20**(4), 588–595 (2014)
18. Kennedy, R., Lane, N., Berbaum, K., Lilienthal, M.: Simulator sickness questionnaire: an enhanced method for quantifying simulator sickness. Int. J. Aviat. Psychol. **3**(3), 203–220 (1993)
19. Li, J.: The benefit of being physically present. Int. J. Hum Comput Stud. **77**(C), 23–37 (2015)
20. Lillicrap, T., Moreno-Briseno, P., Diaz, R., Tweed, D., Troje, N., Fernandez-Ruiz, J.: Adapting to inversion of the visual field: a new twist on an old problem. Exper. Brain Res. **228**(3), 327–339 (2013)
21. MacKenzie, C., Iberall, T.: The Grasping Hand. In: Advances in Psychology, vol. 104. North-Holland, Amsterdam and New York (1994)
22. Naceri, A., Chellali, R.: Depth perception within peripersonal space using head-mounted display. Presence: Teleoperators Virtual Environ. **20**(3), 254–272 (2011)
23. Napieralski, P., Altenhoff, B., Bertrand, J., Long, L., Babu, S., Pagano, C., Kern, J., Davis, T.: Near-field distance perception in real and virtual environments using both verbal and action responses. ACM Trans. Appl. Percept. **8**(3), 18:1–18:19 (2011)
24. Nilsson, N., Peck, T., Bruder, G., Hodgson, E., Serafin, S., Suma, E., Whitton, M., Steinicke, F.: 15 years of research on redirected walking in immersive virtual environments. IEEE Comput. Graph. Appl. **38**, 44–56 (2018)
25. Pai, Y., Kunze, K.: Armswing: Using arm swings for accessible and immersive navigation in AR/VR spaces. In: Proceedings of the 16th International Conference on Mobile and Ubiquitous Multimedia (MUM 2017), pp. 189–198. ACM, New York, NY, USA (2017)
26. Renner, R., Velichkovsky, B., Helmert, J.: The perception of egocentric distances in virtual environments - a review. ACM Comput. Surv. **46**(2), 1–40 (2013)
27. Simeone, A., Velloso, E., Gellersen, H.: Substitutional reality: Using the physical environment to design virtual reality experiences. In: Proceedings of the 33rd Annual ACM Conference on Human Factors in Computing Systems (CHI 2015), pp. 3307–3316. ACM, New York, NY, USA (2015)
28. Slater, M.: Place illusion and plausibility can lead to realistic behaviour in immersive virtual environments. Philos. Trans. R. Soc. London B: Biol. Sci. **364**(1535), 3549–3557 (2009)
29. Sprague, D., Po, B., Booth, K.: The importance of accurate VR head registration on skilled motor performance. In: Proceedings of Graphics Interface 2006 (GI 2006), pp. 131–137. Canadian Information Processing Society, Toronto, Ont., Canada, Canada (2006)
30. Sra, M., Garrido-Jurado, S., Schmandt, C., Maes, P.: Procedurally generated virtual reality from 3D reconstructed physical space. In: Proceedings of the 22nd ACM Conference on Virtual Reality Software and Technology (VRST 2016), pp. 191–200 (2016)

31. Valkov, D., Giesler, A., Hinrichs, K.: Evaluation of depth perception for touch interaction with stereoscopic rendered objects. In: Proceedings of the 2012 ACM International Conference on Interactive Tabletops and Surfaces (ITS 2012), pp. 21–30. ACM, New York, NY, USA (2012)
32. Valkov, D., Steinicke, F., Bruder, G., Hinrichs, K.: 2d touching of 3d stereoscopic objects. In: Proceedings of the SIGCHI Conference on Human Factors in Computing Systems (CHI 2011), pp. 1353–1362. ACM, New York, NY, USA (2011)

# Interaction on Augmented Reality with Finger Detection and Hand Movement Recognition

Mohammad Fadly Syahputra$^{(\boxtimes)}$, Siti Fatimah$^{(\boxtimes)}$,
and Romi Fadillah Rahmat$^{(\boxtimes)}$

Department of Information Technology, Faculty of Computer Science
and Information Technology, Universitas Sumatera Utara, Medan, Indonesia
{nca.fadly, romi.fadillah}@usu.ac.id,
chitifatimah@students.usu.ac.id

**Abstract.** Indonesia's rare animals are animals whose habitats exist only in Indonesia and are endangered by IUCN (International Union for Conservation of Nature and Natural Resources). In this study, we applied Augmented Reality (AR) technology to represent the endangered species in Indonesia combined with image processing techniques as the interaction between users and the virtual objects of endangered animals. The initial stage is the separation of the desired object from the background with the help of HSV colour method, as well as detecting contour with contour detector. As for the calculation of the number of fingers we are using convex hull and convexity defects. The results of this stage is the number of fingers that will be used as a reference selection of endangered animal. These series of processes generates an augmented reality application where users can view and provide instructions with virtual objects of endangered species of Indonesia. This can provide a different experience for users to learn about Indonesia's endangered species.

**Keywords:** Rare animal in Indonesia · Augmented reality · Image processing
Finger detection

## 1 Introduction

Indonesia's rare animals are one of the proofs of Indonesia's biodiversity. However, the number of Indonesian rare animal populations is decreasing. This is due to the limitation of the animal's habitat [1]. In order to provide knowledge about endangered animal diversity in Indonesia, it is not easy to present them directly to the public due to the diminishing presence of the endangered species. The key solution to this kind of problem is combining it with virtual environment, such as Virtual Reality and Augmented Reality. As we know that augmented reality (AR) technology is a variation of virtual environment that thoroughly reinforces users in an artificial environment [2, 3]. So this technology makes it possible to be utilized as a means of presenting endangered species of Indonesia in its true size without harming the population and its habitat.

In general, the interaction between humans with virtual objects on augmented reality is connected by the input tools such as mouse, keyboard, touch screen and others. The use of such input devices for a long time can trigger the emergence of

© Springer International Publishing AG, part of Springer Nature 2018
L. T. De Paolis and P. Bourdot (Eds.): AVR 2018, LNCS 10851, pp. 702–712, 2018.
https://doi.org/10.1007/978-3-319-95282-6_49

several diseases, such as trigger finger, gorillas arm, and others [4–6]. The use of input tools also makes human interaction with virtual objects less real. Therefore, it takes augmented reality technology that can not only provide good simulation but also must be presented to be able to interact directly with humans without the use of input tools [5–7]. In 2013, Dong Woo Seo and his colleague Jae Yeol Lee conducted research on user interaction with augmented reality objects through fingertips detection [8]. Meanwhile, augmented reality research that also applied the recognition of the palm of the hand is done by Khawla Benabderrahim and his colleague Mohamed Slim Bouhlel. In their study, the palms can be recognized by two methods. Their first method uses subtraction background and the second method is the recognition of the palm of the hand by detecting skin colour [4].

Hand gesture has been implemented for sign language, robotics, virtual reality, games, and so on. In general, the introduction of hand gestures is divided into two types [9]. The other gesture recognition is finger recognition which has been derived from hand gesture recognition [10, 11]. While hand movement recognition which involving contour, convex-hull and convexity defects was conducted before [13, 14] which in practice will involving skin detection [15, 16].

## 2   Methodology

In our proposed method, we will combine image processing techniques to perform hand gesture and finger point recognition to do several action in our Augmented Reality environment. Here we described our proposed method in Fig. 1.

The method used to recognize the number of human fingers through a web camera is used as a human-computer interaction to execute predetermined instructions. This research consists of several steps, as for the steps are: image or image capture through web camera; image resizing; RGB to HSV color conversion; color detection by adjusting the desired HSV range values; fix the image with median blur to eliminate noise and dilation; feature extraction with contour and look for convex-hull from contour that has been captured; calculate convexity defects; count the number of fingers detected. After the step has been done and succeeded it will get the number of human fingers in the form of an instruction or command to 3D objects contained in the application Unity 3D.

### 2.1   Skin Detection

The segmentation process is used to get the object to be identified which in this case is the hand image. So that the hand image of the user will be extracted from the camera and can be identified as a command for the next process. Detection of hand-based objects based on skin color is strongly influenced by the intensity of light on the image and also the quality of the web camera itself and also the background of the object itself. In this study we used HSV color method as image segmentation based on color. The steps to detect human skin color as follows.

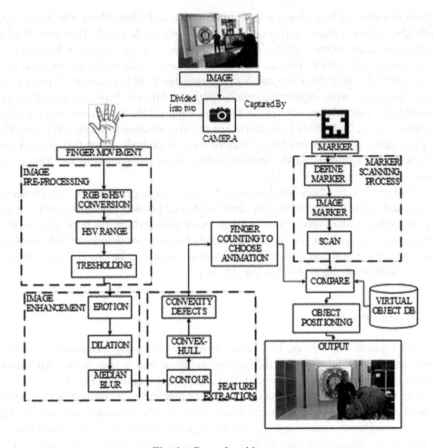

**Fig. 1.** General architecture

### 2.1.1   Convert RGB to HSV

Once the image is captured by the web camera, the image will be converted to the HSV color space. In this process, we get a single channel value (H) that holds the pixel color value and the other two channels (S and V) holding the saturation and pixel level brightness. In this study using the cvtColor () function available in OpenCV. Here is an explanation of the function.

$$cvtColor\,(Mat\,src,\,Mat\,dst,\,Imgproc,\,int\,code);$$

Parameter:

- Src : input rgbaMat
- Dst : output HSVMat
- Code : color conversion COLOR_BGR2HSV

### 2.1.2  Set the HSV Range

Skin color detection is done by determining the range of values of H, S, and V, so that for each pixel in the image, if it is in the range value, it will be regarded as skin color, while those outside the range will be considered as background. To check whether the element is in range in this study used Core.inRange () function available on OpenCV. The following is an explanation of the function.

$$inRange\,(Mat\,src,\,Scalar\,lowerb,\,Scalar\,upperb,\,Mat\,dst);$$

Parameter:

- *src* : input HSVMat
- *dst* : output HSVMat
- *Lowerb* : lower *array*
- *Upperb* : upper *array*

### 2.1.3  Thresholding

For each pixel in the image, if the value of H, S, V is in that range, it will be regarded as skin color and its value will be changed to 255 (white). As for those outside the range, it will be considered as a background and will be changed to 0 (black). With this method, obtained a binary image of skin detection results with white represents the user's hands and black color represents the background.

The result of the segmentation process in the form of black and white image (binary image) that shows the skin of the input image. However, the image of the segmentation results in noise and snippets of some other objects in the image, such as the background image. Therefore, it is necessary to perform several stages of the morphological process to clear the image of the noise and the cut.

### 2.1.4  Erosion

The erosion process removes the pixels from the image or the equivalent white pixels attached to the background area, which will cause the white pixel to decrease in size (shrinking) in order to remove the pixels that have noise in the image. The function used by researchers for the erosion process is.

$$Mat\,element\,=\,getStructuringElement\,(erosion\_type,\,Size\,(2*erosion\_size+1),$$
$$Point\,(erosion\_size,\,erosion\_size));$$
$$Imgproc.erode\,(src,\,dst,\,element);$$

Parameter:

- Src: input image
- Dst: output image

- Element: This is the kernel that will be used to perform operation. If not specified first, then the default is a simple $3 \times 3$ matrix. However, we can determine the shape. For this, we need to use the getStructuringElement function:
- Erosion_type: the shape of the kernel, the form used i.e. MORPH_ELLIPSE in the form of Ellipse
- Erosion_size: linear gap size, size used in this study is 5

### 2.1.5   Dilation

The dilation process will cause the white pixels to increase. The purpose of the dilation process is because when the process of erosion is done on the image, the processed area including the shrinking part that needs to be done a process that returns the area so that the hands will be detected properly.

$$Mat\ element = getStructuringElement(dilation\_type, Size$$
$$(2 * dilation\_size + 1), Point(dilation\_size, dilation\_size));$$
$$Imgproc.dilate(src,\ dst,\ element);$$

Parameter:

- Src: input image
- Dst: output image
- Element: This is the kernel that will be used to perform
- operation. If not specified dahuly, then the default is a simple $3 \times 3$ matrix. However, we can determine the shape. For this, we need to use the getStructuringElement function:
- Dilation_type: the form of the kernel, the form used i.e. MORPH_ELLIPSE in the form of Ellipse
- Dilation_size: linear gap size, size used in this study is 5

### 2.1.6   Median Blur

To eliminate the noise that remains in the image after the dilation process is done Median blur process, so as not to be defined as the object point. The following functions are available in the OpenCV library.

$$medianBlur(InputArray\ src,\ OutputArray\ dst,\ int\ ksize);$$

Parameter:

- src: input image
- ff: Output image
- ksize: linear gap size, usually more than 1, for example: 3, 5, 7.

### 2.1.7   Contour

Contours are drawn around the white dots of the hand found from the thresholding of the input image. The result of the thresholding will form more than one point on the image because of noise from the background image. In this study used findcontours () function that has been available by OpenCV to detect contour points on the image of the previous noise repair results. Here is an explanation of the function.

findContours (src image, contours, hierarcy, mode, method, Point ());

Parameters:

- Image: image input, the image of the image improvement process
- Contours: contour points detected. Each detected contour point will be stored in the vector point list
- hierarchy: the output of an optional vector point. In this parameter we store information from each contour point, such as the previous contour point, the next contour point, the main contour point, etc.
- Mode: how to detect contour spots. This research is done by CV_RE-TR_EXTERNAL, which takes all contour spots and reconstructs the full hierarchy of contoured points connected
- Method: method of contour point approach. This research is done by CV_CHAI-N_APPROX_SIMPLE, which emphasizes on the horizontal, vertical, and diagonal segments and determines the end points on the contours.

After the contour is obtained on the input image, the points obtained will be drawn to form a hand drawing. The function used in this research is drawContours () which has been available in the OpenCV library.

### 2.1.8   Convex-Hull

Convex hull is a method used to detect contours or objects in an image. The points associated with the line that surrounds the contour (the object in the image) into the arrangement of convex hull. After the contour value is obtained, the contour will be searched for the largest contour (the largest hand object) before the convex hull is done. The function used in this research is convexHull (). The explanation of such function is.

convexHull (InputArray points, OutputArray hull);

Parameter:

- Points: contoured points that have been detected and filtered.
- Hull: Convex-hull output.

### 2.1.9   Convexity Defects

After the largest contour and Convex-hull is detected, the next process is Convexity defects. Which is the intersection of the contour and Convex-hull lines. In this study, the convexityDefects () function is available in OpenCV to detect Convexity defects. The following is an explanation of the function.

convexityDefects (contour, convexHull, convexityDefects);

Parameters:
- contour: The largest contour dot is detected
- convexhull: Convex-hull detected
- convexityDefects: Convexity Defects output.

## 3   Result and Discussion

Here are the results of experiments conducted by the author in hand detection on augmented reality application of endangered species of Indonesia.

**Scenario 1:** Trials are conducted on a plain color background and good lighting conditions with a finger distance to the camera 1.5 m with 6 times magnification scale. The test results are shown by Table 1.

**Table 1.** Testing scenario 1

| No. | Number of finger | Number of test (n) | True Positive | False Positive | Accuracy (%) | Error (%) |
|-----|------------------|--------------------|---------------|----------------|--------------|-----------|
| 1   | 1                | 50                 | 45            | 5              | 90           | 10        |
| 2   | 2                | 50                 | 47            | 3              | 94           | 6         |
| 3   | 3                | 50                 | 44            | 6              | 88           | 12        |
| 4   | 4                | 50                 | 50            | 0              | 100          | 0         |
| 5   | 5                | 50                 | 50            | 0              | 100          | 0         |

After several tests, a stable HSV range is detected in H = 70–210, S = 10–190, and V = 25 – 200. The range value is the default range value for the application. Table 1 shows the results of number of finger = 1 in a well-lit room according to scenario 1. In order to execute a command of 3D object based of 1 finger movement, in this case the augmented shows a rhino running is given a silent order, fingers can be recognized by a system with a level high accuracy, i.e. 90% accuracy based on 50 experiments. The errors percentage that may occur in this process because there is a change in the intensity of light which affecting the colour of the skin area of the hand. The skin hand will becomes darker, so that the system cannot recognize as skin colour and fingers are also folded undefined as a finger. If the number of fingers = 2, it can be obtained the result of 94% accuracy based on 50 experiments. From the tests performed in scenario 1 for number of finger from 1 to 5, we obtained the average result of accuracy as follows.

$$A = (90 + 94 + 88 + 100 + 100)/5 = 94.4\%$$

**Scenario 2:** Trials are done on a plain background but poor lighting. The test results are shown by Table 2.

Table 2 above is the result testing for number of finger 1–5 with scenario 2 where the light conditions are dim. The results of testing with number of finger = 1 with augmented movement instruction are in 82% based on 50 experiments. Errors that may

**Table 2.** Test scenario 2

| No. | Number of finger | Number of test (n) | True Positive | False Positive | Accuracy (%) | Error (%) |
|-----|------------------|--------------------|---------------|----------------|--------------|-----------|
| 1 | 1 | 50 | 41 | 9 | 82 | 18 |
| 2 | 2 | 50 | 44 | 6 | 88 | 12 |
| 3 | 3 | 50 | 38 | 12 | 76 | 24 |
| 4 | 4 | 50 | 45 | 5 | 90 | 10 |
| 5 | 5 | 50 | 46 | 4 | 90 | 10 |

occur due to the detection of dark skin color so that the system is difficult to recognize the object of the hand. For number of fingers = 2 on scenario 2 where the light in the room is not bright or dim. The number of fingers that can be recognized by the system is 88% of 50 experiments. For the number of finger 3 results obtained is 76%, while for the number of fingers 4 and 5 by 90%. The average is as follows

$$B = (88 + 82 + 76 + 90 + 90)/5 = 85.2\%$$

Based on two test in Scenario 1 and 2, we can see that the effects of lighting are quite influential by the system in finger recognition. In the bright lights condition, the entire color of the object caught by the webcam will be well defined, otherwise if the lighting in the test chamber is dim, then the system will be difficult to detect the color of the skin due to the color of the object is too dark that cannot be defined as skin color. Here is the calculation of the average accuracy of finger recognition based on light.

$$\text{Average Accuracy} = (94.4 + 85.2)/2 = 89.8\%$$

**Scenario 3:** The test is done over a distance of 2.4 m from the front of the webcam with 6 times magnification scale, with good lighting and plain color background with HSV range settings in scenario 1. The test results are shown by Table 3.

**Table 3.** Scenario test 3

| No. | Number of finger | Number of test (n) | True Positive | False Positive | Accuracy (%) | Error (%) |
|-----|------------------|--------------------|---------------|----------------|--------------|-----------|
| 1 | 1 | 50 | 41 | 8 | 84 | 16 |
| 2 | 2 | 50 | 42 | 5 | 90 | 10 |
| 3 | 3 | 50 | 39 | 11 | 78 | 22 |
| 4 | 4 | 50 | 47 | 3 | 94 | 6 |
| 5 | 5 | 50 | 48 | 2 | 96 | 4 |

Table 3 shows the test results from number of finger 1, with distance of the camera with the finger = 2.4 m with the magnification 6 times gives 84% accuracy from 50 experiments. Errors that occur due to the distance a little distance so that the distance between the fingers look more dense so that the contour area is detected to produce the value of the depth point is too small. The average accuracy for scenario 3 is as follows:

$$C = (84 + 90 + 78 + 94 + 96)/5 = 88.4\%$$

**Scenario 4:** Trial at distance 3.2 m with 6 times magnification from front of webcam, with good lighting and plain color background with HSV range settings above. The test results are shown by Table 4.

**Table 4.** Test scenario 4

| No. | Number of finger | Number of test (n) | True Positive | False Positive | Accuracy (%) | Error (%) |
|-----|------------------|--------------------|---------------|----------------|--------------|-----------|
| 1 | 1 | 50 | 24 | 26 | 48 | 52 |
| 2 | 2 | 50 | 31 | 19 | 62 | 38 |
| 3 | 3 | 50 | 22 | 28 | 44 | 56 |
| 4 | 4 | 50 | 32 | 18 | 64 | 36 |
| 5 | 5 | 50 | 35 | 15 | 70 | 30 |

Table 4 shows the results of testing with the number of fingers 1, and the distance from the camera is 3.2 m shows the accuracy of 48% based on 50 experiments. The result is pretty poor. It can be shown also for number of finger 2, 3, 4, and 5. Distance will create low accuracy. The average accuracy of scenario 4 is as follows.

$$D = (48 + 62 + 44 + 64 + 70)/5 = 57.6\%$$

Based on scenario 3 and 4, we know that the distance to the camera is also quite influential by the system in finger recognition. At a great distance then the contours of the hands are detected will meet and produce the value of the depth point is too small so that cannot be done defects calculation. Here is the calculation of the average accuracy of finger recognition based on light.

$$Average\ Accuracy = (88.4 + 57.6)/2 = 73\%$$

## 4   Conclusions

We can conclude that the application is able to work properly, including marker detection and 3D Object presentation. The finger detection is running well with the best accuracy in 94.4% within the range of 1, 5 m and 6 times magnification scale for the distance between hand and camera. Skin detection is very sensitive to the lightning condition. It is suggested to use good lightning condition. When the distance is farther then 1.5 m, the accuracy will be decreased linearly. The maximum distance is in 3.4 m, if we exceed this limit the system cannot recognize the fingers. This is because of the hand contour is too close in the camera that give small depth point to do convexity defect's calculation. The background is suggested to use non-skin color and non-pattern colour. If we are going to do further with the application, the suggestions are to detect the source of light with real time, and being able to detect and project the shadow that has more than one source of light.

# References

1. Iqbal, M., Kurnia, M.P., Susanti, E.: Tinjauan Yuridis Terhadap Kepemilikan dan Penjualan Satwa Langka Izin di Indonesia. (Analysis of Endangerd Animals and its Selling in Indonesia) Skripsi. Universitas Mulawarman (2014)
2. Brotos, A.: Interactive Augmented Reality Panel Interface for Android. Stanford University (2015)
3. Amin, D., Govilkar, S.: Comprative study of augmented reality SDK's. Int. J. Comput. Sci. Appl. (IJCSA) 5(1), 11–26 (2015)
4. Benabderrahim, K., Bouhlel, M,S.: Detecting and tracking the hand to create an augmented reality system. IOSR J. Comput. Eng. (IOSR-JCE) (2014)
5. Bhatt, R., Fernandes, N., Dhage, A.: Vision based hand gesture recognition for human computer interaction. Int. J. Eng. Sci. Innov. Technol. (IJESIT) 2(3), 110–115 (2013)
6. Bikos, Mario, Itoh, Yuta, Klinker, Gudrun, Monstakas, Konstantinos: An Interactive Augmented Reality Chess Game using Bare-H and Pinch Gestures. University of Patras, Tesis (2014)
7. Dhawan, A., Honrao, V.: Implementation of hand detection based techniques for human computer interaction. Int. J. Comput. Appl. (0975 – 8887) 72(17), 6–13 (2013)
8. Seo, D.W., Lee, J.Y.: Direct Hand Touchable Interactions in Augmented Reality Environments for Natural and Intuitive User Experiences. Chonnam National University, Tesis (2013)
9. Ramjan, M.R., Sandip, R.M., Uttam, P.S., Srimani, W.S.: Dynamic hand gesture recognition and detection for real time using human computer interaction. Int. J. Adv. Res. Comput. Sci. Manag. Stud. (IJARCSMS) 2(3), 425–430 (2014)
10. Syahputra, Mohammad Fadly, Siregar, Ridho K., Rahmat, Romi Fadillah: Finger recognition as interaction media in augmented reality for historical buildings in matsum and kesawan regions of Medan city. In: De Paolis, Lucio Tommaso, Bourdot, Patrick, Mongelli, Antonio (eds.) AVR 2017. LNCS, vol. 10325, pp. 243–250. Springer, Cham (2017). https://doi.org/10.1007/978-3-319-60928-7_21
11. Lee, T., Tobias, H.: Handy AR: Markerless Inspection of Augmented Reality Object Using FingerTip Tracking . Thesis. University of California (2007)
12. Lee, H., Tateyama, Y., Ogi, T.: Hand gesture recognition using blob detection for immersive projection display system. World Academy of Science, Engineering and Technology. Int. J. Computer, Electr. Autom. Control Inf. Eng. 6(2), 260–263 (2012)
13. Yesugade, K.D., Salunke, S., Shinde, K., Gaikwad, S., Shingare, M.: Hand motion recognition. Int. J. Technol. Exploring Eng. (IJITEE) 3(11), 55–61 (2014)
14. Youssef, M.M., Asari, K.V., Tompkins, R.C., Foytik, J.: Hull convexity defects features for human activity recognition. IEEE Applied Imagery Pattern Recognition Workshop (AIPR), pp. 1–7 (2010)

15. Rahmat, R.F., Chairunnisa, T., Gunawan, D., Sitompul, O.S.: Skin color segmentation using multi-color space threshold. In: 3rd International Conference on Computer and Information Sciences (ICCOINS), Kuala Lumpur, pp. 391–396 (2016)
16. Rai, M., Bhootna, V., Yadav, R.K.: Performance based algorithm for the detection and extraction of human skin. First International Conference on Futuristic Trend in Computational Analysis and Knowledge Management (ABLAZE), pp. 127–131 (2015)

# SVM and RGB-D Sensor Based Gesture Recognition for UAV Control

Wilbert G. Aguilar[1,2](✉), Bryan Cobeña[1], Guillermo Rodriguez[1], Vinicio S. Salcedo[1], and Brayan Collaguazo[1]

[1] CICTE Research Center, Universidad de las Fuerzas Armadas ESPE, Sangolquí, Ecuador
wgaguilar@espe.edu.ec
[2] GREC Research Group, Universitat Politècnica de Catalunya, Barcelona, Spain

**Abstract.** This research has the purpose of allowing anyone, with or without experience handling micro aerial vehicles, to operate unmanned aerial vehicles (UAV) in a natural and intuitive way, unlike typical interfaces that need experience and knowledge in piloting to be used. To achieve this, our approach uses gesture recognition, based on machine learning with Support Vector Machine (SVM) for classification and a RGB-D sensor for the feature extraction. Tests for recognition with different Kernel-SVM and for the RGB-D sensor with different levels of light were carried out.

**Keywords:** Machine learning · Support Vector Machine · Gesture recognition
RGB-D sensor · UAV

## 1 Introduction

Unmanned aerial vehicles have shown a significant demand raise in the last few years [1–4], and this will only increase with time [5, 6]. UAVs are used in different applications, such as: object detection [7, 8], surveillance, data collection, fire detection, tracking and planning of trajectories [9].

Despite the amount of UAV applications, many people cannot take advantage of their features because of the lack of experience and understanding of the control interfaces [10, 11], that are often complex and difficult to handle. This research on gesture recognition has being developed in order to allow anyone, even without experience in the operation of multi-rotor aerial micro vehicles, to control UAVs in an intuitive and natural way.

Our gesture recognition approach uses two parts: Feature extraction (front-end) and classification (back-end) [12]. For the front-end, the RGB-D sensor used in this research is a Kinect sensor, because of its high performance in gesture recognition [13, 14]. Support Vector Machine (SVM) is used for classification because of its greater precision in prediction, efficiency in the use of memory and robustness in the face of errors that occur in training [12, 15].

© Springer International Publishing AG, part of Springer Nature 2018
L. T. De Paolis and P. Bourdot (Eds.): AVR 2018, LNCS 10851, pp. 713–719, 2018.
https://doi.org/10.1007/978-3-319-95282-6_50

This paper has the following structure: Sect. 2 presents a description of the working system structure, Sect. 3 presents our approach, Sect. 4 presents experimentation and results and in Sect. 5 conclusions and feature work.

## 2  System Overview

Our approach uses the Bebop mini drone of Parrot, an UAV on the micro scale classification according to [16], and includes flight safety and homecoming, essential features to prevent emerging events and twelve minutes of autonomy in the air.

The feature extraction of human body gestures is performed by the Kinect sensor, because it is a non-invasive and low-cost technology [17]. This RGB-D sensor [18–21] is developed for Microsoft and allows users to control and interact with a system by capturing 3D movements of the body.

The features are obtained from the Kinect sensor, then compared with a prediction model generated by the SVM and finally the signals of the SVM are converted into pre-programmed movements for the control of the bebop drone (Fig. 1). In ROS, we created a topic for each of the gestures needed for the UAV control. These topics publish messages in real time, containing information about the type of gesture being performed.

For the learning stage, based on SVM, the library LibSVM was used [22].

Feature Extraction

Model of prediction with
SVM clasification, signals for
control UAV on ROS

Fig. 1. System structure for gesture recognition for UAV control

## 3  Our Approach

For this research, it is necessary to define gestures that represent the control system input. These gestures have the following classification: iconic, metaphoric, deictic and illustrative [23]. Gestures applied on Human Computer Interaction (HCI) are deictic because they are intuitive and easy to perform [24].

Gestures are classified into three main groups used for controlling the bebop drone during flight. These groups are:

1. Ascending or descending gesture with the left arm.
2. Gestures with the right arm move the bebop drone forward, backward, right and left.
3. Gestures for specific instructions, such as takeoff and landing, are performed with two arms.

We proceed to perform the extraction of features, classification and training with the supervised machine learning based on SVM to obtain the prediction model. This sectioning is done in order to avoid using unnecessary data, which reduces the training time and the complexity of the prediction models.

## 3.1  RGB-D Sensor Based Feature Extraction

Elbows and hands are joints with a high variation when control actions are performed. From these points, we get coordinates on the x, y, z axes respect to the Kinect sensor. The library used for feature extraction is OpenNI tracker.

This algorithm is commonly used in video game platforms using the Kinect sensor [25–27] and based on the division of objects into parts [28, 29]. Using the integrated depth sensor in the Kinect and through decision trees, the algorithm manages to find points of body articulations [13].

The extraction of characteristics was carried out on five users, for each of them the data representing each control action of the bebop drone is collected, and this data is used to perform the classification of the gestures. The characteristics of the users are detailed in Table 1.

**Table 1.**  Users for the extraction of gesture recognition parameters.

| User | Age (years) | Height (m) |
|---|---|---|
| $1^{er}$ User | 23 | 1.72 |
| $2^{o}$ User | 20 | 1.78 |
| $3^{er}$ User | 20 | 1.80 |
| $4^{o}$ User | 21 | 1.82 |
| $5^{o}$ User | 21 | 1.70 |

100 samples were taken for each gesture of each user. This allows redundancy in the data and facilitates the classification by SVM. The samples are divided according to the action they represent and a class identifier is added so that they can be distinguished.

## 3.2  SVM-Based Classification

For SVM based classification, different kernel types can be used, such as: linear, polynomial, function in radial basis (RBF) and sigmoid [30]. All of these kernel types need "C" and gamma cost parameters for their characteristic equation. A summary of the calculations made to obtain optimal classification rate parameters is shown on Table 2.

From the values obtained, the cost represents the soft margin that is added to the training set. A high value means that the data is almost perfectly separable.

For the optimal kernel selection for the classification problem, the number of iterations necessary to perform the classification is taken into account, as well as the number of support vectors needed to find the ideal separation hyperplane, which is the

**Table 2.** Calculated parameters for kernel SVM based kernel classification.

| Gestures | Cost | Gamma | Rate (%) |
|---|---|---|---|
| Left arm | 32 | 0.0078125 | 91.6 |
| | 2048 | 0.5 | 96.3 |
| | 2048 | 2 | 99 |
| | 512 | 2 | 100 |
| | 128 | 2 | 100 |
| Right arm | 32 | 0.0078125 | 95.05 |
| | 32 | 0.5 | 95.05 |
| | 2048 | 0.5 | 99.54 |
| | 128 | 0.2 | 99.92 |
| Both arms | 32 | 0.0078125 | 97.87 |
| | 32 | 0.5 | 99.76 |
| | 2048 | 0.5 | 99.86 |
| | 512 | 0.5 | 100 |

one equidistant from the data set to be classified. The results obtained are shown in Table 3, and we can clearly appreciate that the kernel based on a radial basis is the one that works best in this type of training.

**Table 3.** Kernel selection for gesture classification.

| Gesture | Kernel | Number of iterations | Number of support vectors |
|---|---|---|---|
| Left arm | Polynomial | 211723 | 23 |
| | RBF | 261 | 29 |
| | Sigmoid | 300 | 2000 |
| Right arm | Polynomial | 5940 | 44 |
| | RBF | 206 | 67 |
| | Sigmoid | 250 | 2650 |
| Both arms | Polynomial | 31 | 25 |
| | RBF | 48 | 31 |
| | Sigmoid | 96 | 1270 |

# 4   Experimentation and Results

The gestures recognition tests for UAV control were carried out on six users, of which half of them were not part of the system training. The results obtained are shown in Table 4.

As seen in Table 3, our system manages to correctly identify the corporal gestures of different users, even the ones that were not part of the training. The system works correctly regardless of the user, as long as the features, such as the height of the new users, resemble those of the users who participated in the gesture training stage (Fig. 2).

**Table 4.** System tests with different users.

| User | Part of the training | Flight time (minutes) | Observations |
|------|---------------------|----------------------|--------------|
| 1$^{er}$ User | Yes | 3.23 | All gestures recognized |
| 2$^{o}$ User | Yes | 1.12 | All gestures recognized |
| 3$^{er}$ User | Yes | 2.20 | All gestures recognized |
| 4$^{o}$ User | No | 1.16 | All gestures recognized |
| 5$^{o}$ User | No | 3.15 | All gestures recognized |
| 6$^{o}$ User | No | 4.30 | All gestures recognized |

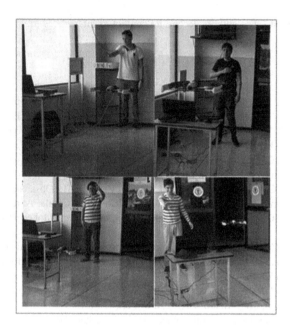

**Fig. 2.** Test with different users.

The Radial Base Function (RBF) kernel offers good performance for corporal gestures classification, as long as a correct calculation of the classification parameters is performed, from which a classification rate as high as possible is achieved. Video results are provided on https://www.youtube.com/watch?v=_7OqrI-Z_DU

## 5  Conclusions and Future Works

This paper presents a gesture recognition system for UAV control, based on SVM and RGB-D sensor. Our system provides good performance, even with users not included in the SVM training stage (as long as they have a similar height).

For the training, we selected kernels suitable for classification based on SVM. The RBF kernel achieves gesture classification with a lower number of iterations and using a smaller number of support vectors.

As future work, we will use models trained with bigger datasets, from users with different characteristics, and tested with several different types of UAVs.

**Acknowledgement.** This work is part of the project "Perception and localization system for autonomous navigation of rotor micro aerial vehicle in gps-denied environments, VisualNav-Drone", 2016-PIC-024, from the Universidad de las Fuerzas Armadas ESPE, directed by Dr. Wilbert G. Aguilar.

**Conflicts of Interest.** The authors declare no conflict of interest.

# References

1. Aguilar, W.G., Salcedo, V.S., Sandoval, D.S., Cobeña, B.: Developing of a video-based model for UAV autonomous navigation. In: Barone, D.A.C., Teles, E.O., Brackmann, C. P. (eds.) LAWCN 2017. CCIS, vol. 720, pp. 94–105. Springer, Cham (2017). https://doi.org/10.1007/978-3-319-71011-2_8
2. Aguilar, W.G., Casaliglla, V.P., Pólit, J.L.: Obstacle avoidance based-visual navigation for micro aerial vehicles. Electronics 6(1), 10 (2017)
3. Aguilar, W.G., Casaliglla, V.P., Pólit, J.L., Abad, V., Ruiz, H.: Obstacle avoidance for flight safety on unmanned aerial vehicles. In: Rojas, I., Joya, G., Catala, A. (eds.) IWANN 2017. LNCS, vol. 10306, pp. 575–584. Springer, Cham (2017). https://doi.org/10.1007/978-3-319-59147-6_49
4. Limnaios, G.: Current usage of unmanned aircraft systems (UAS) and future challenges: a mission oriented simulator for UAS as a tool for design and performance evaluation. J. Comput. Model 4(1), 167–188 (2014)
5. Dickerson, L.: UAV on the rise. In: Aviation Week and Space Technology. Aerospace Source Book, vol. 166. McGraw Hill, New York (2007)
6. Visiongain: The unmanned aerial vehicles (UAV) market 2009–2019. Londres (2009)
7. Aguilar, W.G., Angulo, C.: Real-time model-based video stabilization for microaerial vehicles. Neural Process. Lett. 43(2), 459–477 (2016)
8. Aguilar, W.G., Angulo, C.: Real-time video stabilization without phantom movements for micro aerial vehicles. EURASIP J. Image Video Process 2014, 46 (2014)
9. Chmaj, G., Selvaraj, H.: Distributed processing applications for UAV/drones: a survey. In: Selvaraj, H., Zydek, D., Chmaj, G. (eds.) Progress in Systems Engineering. AISC, vol. 366, pp. 449–454. Springer, Cham (2015). https://doi.org/10.1007/978-3-319-08422-0_66
10. Aguilar, W.G., et al.: Cascade classifiers and saliency maps based people detection. In: De Paolis, L.T., Bourdot, P., Mongelli, A. (eds.) AVR 2017, Part II. LNCS, vol. 10325, pp. 501–510. Springer, Cham (2017). https://doi.org/10.1007/978-3-319-60928-7_42
11. Aguilar, W.G., et al.: Pedestrian detection for UAVs using cascade classifiers and saliency maps. In: Rojas, I., Joya, G., Catala, A. (eds.) IWANN 2017, Part II. LNCS, vol. 10306, pp. 563–574. Springer, Cham (2017). https://doi.org/10.1007/978-3-319-59147-6_48
12. Kurakin, A., Zhang, Z., Liu, Z.: A real time system for dynamic hand gesture recognition with a depth sensor. In: EUSIPCO (2012)

13. Shotton, J., et al.: Real-time human pose recognition in parts from single depth images. In: Cipolla, R., Battiato, S., Farinella, G. (eds.) Machine Learning for Computer Vision. Studies in Computational Intelligence. Springer, Heidelberg (2013). https://doi.org/10.1007/978-3-642-28661-2_5

14. Ren, Z., Yuan, J., Meng, J., Zhang, Z.: Robust part-based hand gesture recognition using kinect sensor. IEEE Trans. Multimed. **15**, 1110–1120 (2013)

15. Kurtulmus, F., Kavdir, I.: Detecting corn tassels using computer vision and support vector machines. Exper. Syst. Appl. **41**, 7390–7397 (2014)

16. Kendoul, F.: Survey of advances in guidance, navigation, and control of unmanned rotorcraft systems. J. Field Robot. **29**(2), 315–378 (2012)

17. Ibañez, R.: Evaluación de técnicas de Machine Learning para el reconocimiento de gestos corporals. In: XLIII Jornadas Argentinas de Informática e Investigación Operativa (2014)

18. Calle, J.L., Balseca, J.M., Medina, R.P.: Test Wisc IV: Una Mirada desde la herramienta kinect. Revista Vínculos **12**, 157–165 (2015)

19. Aguilar, W.G., et al.: Visual SLAM with a RGB-D camera on a quadrotor UAV using on-board processing. In: Rojas, I., Joya, G., Catala, A. (eds.) IWANN 2017, Part II. LNCS, vol. 10306, pp. 596–606. Springer, Cham (2017). https://doi.org/10.1007/978-3-319-59147-6_51

20. Aguilar, W.G., et al.: Real-time 3D modeling with a RGB-D camera and on-board processing. In: De Paolis, L.T., Bourdot, P., Mongelli, A. (eds.) AVR 2017, Part II. LNCS, vol. 10325, pp. 410–419. Springer, Cham (2017). https://doi.org/10.1007/978-3-319-60928-7_35

21. Aguilar, W.G., et al.: On-board visual SLAM on a UGV using a RGB-D camera. In: Huang, Y., Wu, H., Liu, H., Yin, Z. (eds.) ICIRA 2017, Part III. LNCS (LNAI), vol. 10464, pp. 298–308. Springer, Cham (2017). https://doi.org/10.1007/978-3-319-65298-6_28

22. Chang, C.-C., Lin, C.-J.: LIBSVM: Una librería para maquinas de vectores soporte (2017)

23. Mcneill, D.: Hand and Mind: What Gestures Reveal About Thought. The University of Chicago Press, Chicago (1992)

24. Quiroga, F. Reconocimiento de Gestos Dinámicos. Buenos Aires (2014)

25. Microsoft Corp. Redmond WA. Kinect for Xbox 360

26. Aguilar, W.G., Morales, S.G.: 3D environment mapping using the Kinect V2 and path planning based on RRT algorithms. Electronics **5**(4), 70 (2016)

27. Aguilar, W.G., Morales, S., Ruiz, H., Abad, V.: RRT* GL based optimal path planning for real-time navigation of UAVs. In: Rojas, I., Joya, G., Catala, A. (eds.) IWANN 2017, Part II. LNCS, vol. 10306, pp. 585–595. Springer, Cham (2017). https://doi.org/10.1007/978-3-319-59147-6_50

28. Fergus, R., Perona, P., Zisserman, A.: Object class recognition by unsupervised scale-invariant learning. In: Proceedings of CVPR (2003)

29. Winn, J., Shotton, J.: The layout consistent random field for recognizing and segmenting partially occluded objects. In Proceedings of CVPR (2006)

30. Carmona, E.: Tutorial sobre Máquinas de Vectores Soporte (SVM). UNED (2014)

# Author Index

Printed in the United States
By Bookmasters